Poetry Index Annual

1987

Poetry Index Press

Poetry Index Annual
American Poetry Index
Annual Index to Poetry in Periodicals

Poetry Index Annual

1987

A Title, Author, First Line and
Subject Index to Poetry in Anthologies

Prepared by
The Editorial Board, Roth Publishing, Inc.

 Poetry Index Press
Great Neck, New York

International Standard Book Number 0-89609-269-0
International Standard Serial Number 0736-3966

Manufactured in the U.S.A.

Poetry Index Press is a
division of Roth Publishing, Inc.

Contents

Preface   vii

Explanatory Notes   ix

Key to Symbols of Works Indexed   xi

Title, Author, First Line, Translator, and Subject Index   1

Preface

The POETRY INDEX ANNUAL has been developed to provide access to the preponderance of anthologized poetry which is not indexed anywhere.

Standard works, such as Columbia University Press' *Granger's Index*, are selective in scope and do not endeavor to analyze other than the most generally accessible anthologies; they are not cumulative: each new edition adds only some new anthologies and generally eliminates those no longer in print. While the excellence of such references is acknowledged, they do not serve the broader and more specialized needs of many users.

The POETRY INDEX ANNUAL is the first and only work to systematically index *all* poetry anthologies as they are published. Being cumulative, each annual edition is a permanent volume which complements and supplements preceding issues; no superseding editions will be published. Taken together, the annual editions will form an ongoing and comprehensive title, author, and subject index to anthologized verse.

The 1982 edition, covering anthologies published in 1981, was the inaugural volume in the series.

Explanatory Notes

Each anthology indexed is referred to by an alpha-numeric symbol. The complete title of the anthology and other publishing information is contained in the Key to Symbols of Works Indexed section which follows.

Each of the poems collected in each anthology is fully indexed for title, author, first line, translator, and subject. Where it is determined, however, that the full indexing of a work is not appropriate, the anthology is listed in the Key to Symbols with an asterisk, and is printed in the title, author, and subject entries in full capitalization. Collections containing prose are analyzed only for poetry.

Publication Dates. The actual publication date of a book is sometimes difficult to ascertain; copyright dates, announced dates, and other such indicia are not always reliable. In determining the inclusion dates for the POETRY INDEX ANNUAL, the copyright date will be the rule of thumb, although it will not be inflexibly applied. Accordingly, some anthologies copyrighted in 1986 which were not available for this edition are omitted but will be included in the next issue; likewise, earlier anthologies which became available in 1986 are indexed in this volume.

Arrangement. The filing is alphabetical word by word (e.g. "my world" precedes "myself"). Articles at the beginning of titles are retained but disregarded in the alphabetizing (except articles in dialect and foreign articles); otherwise articles have alphabetical value. The alphabetizing is stringently applied: all words are listed as spelled (e.g. "Mr." is filed as such and not as "Mister"). Numbers precede letters, and capital letters precede lower case letters. Punctuation is not disregarded in filing.

Entries. Entries are of five types: title, author, first line, translator, and subject. Each entry is complete in itself and each contains the anthology symbol wherein the poem is located; cross reference is not required. As this is a dictionary index, all entries are filed together in one alphabetical sequence.

1. *Title Entry* This entry contains the title of the poem, its author, and the symbol of the anthology in which it is located. The first word of the title is printed in bold face; the title appears in quotation marks when it is the first line. If only a portion of the poem is contained in the anthology, the abbreviation "sels" follows the title.

2. *Author Entry* Author, title, translator, and anthology symbol are given in this entry. The author's name is printed in bold face. The title is always indented four spaces on the next line; where there is more than one poem by an author, each additional poem begins a new line similarly indented. Where more than one line is required for a poem, any succeeding line is indented an additional two spaces.

There is no author entry for anonymous poems; they are indexed only by title and first line (and translator if any). Where authorship is not certain, the abbreviation "atr." (attributed) is given with the putative author. The name by which a poet is listed generally is the best known writing name, whether a pseudonym, married, or legal name; it is not necessarily the name used in the source anthology or that which appears on the title page of

Explanatory Notes

the poem. This reconciliation of the various forms of an author's name prevents unnecessary duplication and confusion. Cross references from variant forms are made to the main author entry.

Chinese and Japanese poets' names are generally rendered in traditional fashion: family name first, given name second. However, the names of modern Japanese authors writing in English are referred to in the Occidental manner when it is consistent with their own usage. The romanization of Chinese names generally follows that of the source anthology, either Wade-Giles or Pinyan. Exception is made for prominent poets widely known by their Wade-Giles name form, such as Tu Fu (Du Fu in Pinyan). In such cases reconciliation to the Wade-Giles system is undertaken to promote uniformity and to obviate confusion and duplication; cross reference from the Pinyan form to the main entry is provided.

Modern Hebrew-Language poets are indexed by family name in the usual manner. Earlier poets are listed under first name in the style generally utilized by the anthologies, even if the first name is not the family name (e.g. Ephraim Luzzato [1729-92] is indexed under Ephraim). Hebrew names are given in the conventional English spelling in most cases. Readers are advised, however, to check other possible name forms.

3. *First Line Entry* First line access to a poem in addition to the title entry is also provided when the first line is not similar to the title. Title, author, and anthology symbol are included. The first line is always given in quotation marks; the first word is printed in bold face.

4. *Translator Entry* Translated poems are also indexed by a separate translator entry in which title, author, and anthology symbol are provided.

5. *Subject Entry* Title, author, and anthology symbol are also given in this entry. The subject name is printed in bold italics.

While some subjects, such as Love are so universal a theme of poetry as to be excluded from some indexes, they are included here when they are the main theme of a poem.

Users may want to consider the title of a poem in locating subjects, but they should be cautioned that this is often an unreliable methodology.

Key to Symbols of
Works Indexed

P47   An American Christmas. *Jane B. Hill, ed.* (1986)
       Peachtree Publishers, *Ltd.*

P48   The Apocalypse Anthology. *Louise M. Kawada, ed.*
       (1985) Rowan Tree Press

P49   Arrivals: Canadian Poetry in the eighties. *Bruce
       Meyer, ed.* (1986) The Greenfield Review

P50   Best Friends. *Lee Bennett Hopkins, ed.* (1986) Harper &
       Row

P51   The Book of a Thousand Poems. (1986) Peter Bedrick
       Books

P52   Buying Time. *Scott Walker, ed.* (1985) Graywolf Press

P53   Cleaned the Crocodile's Teeth: Nuer Song. *Cerese
       Svoboda, tr.* (1985) The Greenfield Review

P54   Common Ground: poets in a Welsh landscape. *Susan
       Butler, ed.* (1985) Poetry Wales Press

P55   Creatures. *Lee Bennett Hopkins, comp.* (1985) Harcourt
       Brace Jovanovich

P56   Dan River Anthology. *Richard S. Danbury III, ed.*
       (1985) Dan River Press

P57   Despite This Flesh: the disabled in stories and poems.
       Vassar Miller, ed. (1985) The University of Texas Press

P58   Fineline Thunder. (1986). Devil Mountain Books

P59   Four Metaphysical Poets. *Richard Willmott, ed.* (1985)
       Cambridge University Press

P60   Here a Little Child I Stand. *Cynthia Mitchell, comp.*
       (1985) Philomel Books

P61   The Hippopotamus: selected trans'tions. *Charles Guenther, tr.* (1986) BkMk Press

P62   The Homely Touch: folk poetry of Old India. *John T. Roberts, tr.* (1986) Mazda Publishers

P63   Light Year '87. *Robert Wallace, ed.* (1987) Bits Press

P64   Long Island Poets. *Robert Long, ed.* (1986) The Permanent Press

P65   Love Lyrics: Volume I. *Louise Louis, ed.* (1985) Pen Art

P66   A Middle English Anthology. *Ann S. Haskell, ed.* (1985) Wayne State University Press

P67   A Modern Southern Reader. *Ben Forkner and Patrick Samway, S.J., eds.* (1986) Peachtree Publishers, Ltd.

P68   One Score-and-Two Years of Uncommon Fanfare. *John Edward Westburg, ed.* (1986) Westburg Associates

P69   The Poetry of the Sicilian School. *Frede Jensen, ed. & tr.* (1986) Garland Publishing

P70   Poets of Bulgaria. *William Meredith, ed.* (1986) Unicorn Press, Inc.

P71   Poets of Chile: a bilingual anthology. *Steven F. White, ed.* (1986) Unicorn Press

P72   Premier Poets: ninth biennial anthology. *Bohumila Falkowski et. al., eds.* (1986) World Poetry Society International

P73   Rainbow Collection: stories and poetry by young people. *Kathie Janger and* Joan Korenblit, eds. (1985) Young Writer's Contest Foundation

P74   Rainbow Collection: stories and poetry by young people. *Kathie Janger and* Joan Korenblit, eds. (1986) Young Writer's Contest Foundation

P75   Rainy Day: stories and poems. *Caroline Feller Bauer, ed.* (1986) J.B. Lippincott

P76   The Sea Is Calling Me. *Lee Bennett Hopkins, comp.*
       (1986) Harcourt Brace Jovanovich

P77   The Shadows of Light. *Terry Busch, ed.* (1985) Jelm Mt.
       Press

P78   Shaking the Pumpkin: traditional poetry of the Indian
       North Americas. *Jerome Rothenberg, ed.* (1986) Alfred
       van der March Editions

P79   Shenandoah. *James Boatwright, ed.* (1985) Pushcart

P80   Snowy Day: stories and poems. *Caroline Feller Bauer,
       ed.* (1986) J.B. Lippincott

P81   Survey of American Poetry: Volume VI. Twilight
       Interval. (1986) Roth Publishing

P82   Survey of American Poetry: Volume VII. Poetic
       Renaissance. (1986) Roth Publishing

P83   Survey of American Poetry: Volume VIII. Interval
       Between Wars. (1986) Roth Publishing

P84   Survey of American Poetry: Volume IX. World War II &
       Aftermath. (1986) Roth Publishing

P85   Survey of American Poetry: Volume X. Mid Century to
       1984; General Indexes. (1986) Roth Publishing

P86   Tour of Duty. *Cranston Sedrick Knight, ed.* (1986)
       Samisdat

P87   Welsh Verse. *Tony Conran, tr.* (1986) Poetry Wales
       Press

P88   Woman Poet. *Martha Friedberg, ed.* (1985)
       Women-In-Literature, Inc.

P89   The World's Best Poetry for Children. Volume I. (1986)
       Roth Publishing

P90   The World's Best Poetry for Children. Volume II.
       (1986) Roth Publishing

P91   The Worlds of Muslim Imagination. *Alamgir Hashmi, ed.*
       (1986) Gulmohar Islamabad

P92   Writing from the World: II. *Marilyn Chin et.al., eds.*
(1985) University of Iowa Press

"A Dis, a Dis, a Green Grass". Unknown. P51
A-Hunting. Jennie Dunbar. P51
"A-root-toot-toot". School Cheer
        (Progressive Style). Alma Denny. P63
A.W.O.L. James P. Bergman. P86
Aal, Katharyn Machan
        The Beet's Poem. P63
        Office Hours. P63
        Quail. P63
"The aardvark and the armadillo". Alphabet
        Soup. David Cram. P63
"Abandon all hope ye who enter here!.".
        Vietnam P.O.W. Camp. Theodore W.
        Gostas. P86
Abbeys
        Athassel Abbey. Louise Imogen Guiney. P81
Abdul-Sabur, Salah
        The Shadow and the Cross. Issa Bullata
        (tr.). P91
        A Song to God. Issa Bullata (tr.). P91
Abortion
        The Mother, fr. A Street in Bronzeville.
        Gwendolyn Brooks. P84
Abou Ben Adhem. Leigh Hunt. P89
About a Year After He Got Married He Would
        Sit Alone... James Whitehead. P67
About Suffering They Were Never Wrong. Lisel
        Mueller. P88
About the Fairies. Jean Ingelow. P51
About Thirty Jews Were Taken to Chelmno, fr.
        Mass Graves. Charles Reznikoff. P83
"Above our cupped world no tall stack
        opens". The Depression. David Gwenallt
        Jones. P87
"Above the fresh ruffles of the surf".
        Voyages. Hart Crane. P83
"Above the pines the moon was slowly
        drifting". Dickens in Camp. Bret
        Harte. P90
"Above the place where children play". A
        Sussex Legend. Charles Dalmon. P51
Abraham Lincoln Walks at Midnight. Vachel
        Lindsay. P82
Abrahamowicz, Marianna (tr.)
        Ballad for a Solonaut. Joanna Salamon.
        P92
        The Creation of the World. Eva Toth. P92
Acceptance
        A Choice of Weapons. Stanley Kunitz. P83
        The Daily Grind. Fenton Johnson. P82
        In the Desert. Stephen Crane. P81
        The Reader. Fairfield Porter. P64
Accidents
        Auto Wreck. Karl Shapiro. P84
        Helendale. Dick Barnes. P63
        Highway: Michigan. Theodore Roethke. P84
        Views to See Clayton From. Josephine
        Miles. P84
Acevedo, Manuel Silva

Blue Danube. Steven F. White (tr.). P71
Chain Reaction. Steven F. White (tr.).
        P71
A La Apollinaire. Steven F. White (tr.).
        P71
They've Broken the Most Delicate Bone in
        My Ear. Steven F. White (tr.). P71
Wolves and Sheep, sels. Steven F. White
        (tr.). P71
The Achievements of Herrings. Gavin Ewart.
        P63
Achilles
        Achilles' Fatal Flaw. Debbie Dristle. P74
Acker, Peter
        On Hearing of a Man's Death in a Hang
        Glider Accident. P49
The Aconite. A. M. Graham. P51
Acorn, Milton
        The Dolphin-Walk. P49
        A Good Sight of Andromeda. P49
        Gull Passage by Moonlight. P49
The Acorn. Unknown. P51
Acquainted with the Night. Robert Frost. P82
"Across and down". Cross Words. Edmund
        Conti. P63
"Across the pampas relieved only". Iguazu.
        Jules Supervielle. P61
"Across the snow the silver bells". Silver
        Bells. Hamish Hendry. P51
Act of Creation. Peter Stevens. P49
Action Rhyme. E. H. Adams. P51
Adam and Eve
        Hypothesis from the Wilderness. Bonnie
        Squires. P68
Adamkewicz, Joanne
        My Old Journal. P73
Adams, Belle
        To a Mantled Prophet. P68
Adams, Carmen Boitel
        Evening Prayer. P72
Adams, E. H.
        Action Rhyme. P51
        The Paddling Pool. P51
Adams, E. M.
        Haymaking. P51
        The Sea. P51
        Shady Woods. P51
        The Snowman. P51
Adams, H. M.
        Johnny's Farm. P51
Adams, Samantha
        The Horrible Noise. P74
Adcock, Arthur St. John
        Travellers. P51
Addison, Joseph
        Ode, from The Spectator. P89
Adjutor
        Light Talk (I). P72
""Admit that it means something!"". Saint

Cecilia's Day, 1941. Paul Goodman. P84

An **Admonition** Concerning Promptness and Regularity... Edward L. Mayo. P68

Adrian, Vonna
A Plaguey Thing. P63
The Rake's Progress. P63

Adriatc. Charles Tinkham. P56

"**Adrift** upon the summer breeze". Jewels of Freedom. Julia Nelson Walke. P68

Adventure. Benjamin Miller. P73

Adventure and Adventurers
A Fountain, a Bottle, a Donkey's Ears and Some Books. Robert Frost. P82
A Song in the Front Yard, fr. A Street in Bronzeville. Gwendolyn Brooks. P84

Advice
An Admonition Concerning Promptness and Regularity... Edward L. Mayo. P68
Advice Against Being Naive. P. P. Sharma. P72
Advice to a Girl. Thomas Campion. P89
A Farewell, to C. E. G. Charles Kingsley. P51
Parting. Coventry Patmore. P89
Song. Laurence Binyon. P51
To a Young Man. Edwin Markham. P81

Advice Against Being Naive. P. P. Sharma. P72

Advice Against Thumbers. Harold Bond. P63

Advice to a Blue-Bird. Maxwell Bodenheim. P82

Advice to a Girl. Thomas Campion. P89

AEIOU. Jonathan Swift. P51

The **Aeroplane.** Jeannie Kirby. P51

Affair D'Amour. Margaret Deland. P89

Affliction. George Herbert. P59

Affluence. Richard Moore. P63

Affluence. Gary Snyder. P85

"**Afloat**; we move--delicious! Ah". The Gondola. Arthur Hugh Clough. P90

"**Afraid** he's about". Proofreader's Island. Michael Spence. P63

Africa
Africa. Pieter D. Williams. P68
Africa. Claude McKay. P82
They Clapped. Nikki Giovanni. P85

Africa. Pieter D. Williams. P68

"**Africa/Dry**, hot!.". The Children. Abby Crone. P74

After a Hypothetical War. Edwin Muir. P48

After Apple Picking. Robert Frost. P82

After Being Paralyzed from the Neck Down... Ronald Wallace. P57

After Dinner. David Cram. P63

After Experience Taught Me. William DeWitt Snodgrass. P85

After Great Pain. Edward Butscher. P64

After Interrogation. Georgi Djagarov. P70

Aftr Long Grief. Jaye Giammarino. P72

After Stefan George--Mein Kind Kam Heim. Stephen Spender. P79

After Ten Years. Mary Ellen Chihak. P68

"**After** all these years". Reunion. Ulrich Troubetzkoy. P65

"**After** dinner a few drinks then bed". There Is of Course a Legend. Al Purdy. P49

"**After** highschool, she had come down...". The Hand of Emmagene. Peter Taylor. P79

"**After** it snows". Lying on Things. Dennis Lee. P80

"**After** malted, licking his lips, he said". The Ice Cream Parlor Romance. David Ignatow. P84

"**After** our talking about trees". Pulling the Days Together. Graham Everett. P64

"**After** six years this winter has not changed". Freshwater West Revisited. Roland Mathias. P54

After the Face Lift. Lisel Mueller. P88

After the Glory Has Passed Before Us. Karen Kania. P88

After the Revolution for Jesus... Miller Williams. P67

After the Surprising Conversions. Robert Lowell. P84

After the War. Jack Apsche. P86

After Whistler. Lisel Mueller. P88

After Winter. Sterling A. Brown. P89

"**After** the death of memory". Smith's Garage. Robert Minhinnick. P54

"**After** the torchlight red on sweaty faces". What the Thunder Said. Thomas Stearns Eliot. P83

"**After** thirty-five years more". At Home. Edward Willey. P63

Afterglow. Sheila Seiler. P56

Aftermath. Lora Dunetz. P65

Afternoon on a Hill. Edna St. Vincent Millay. P51

The **Afternoon** Will Yet... Antonio Machado. P61

"The **afternoon** turned dark early". During December's Death. Delmore Schwartz. P84

An **Afternoon's** Wandering. Kolyo Sevov. P70

Again. Lyubomir Levchev. P70

"**Again** and again they discovered me". With the Flashes of the Night. Phoebus Delphis. P61

"**Again** last night I dreamed the dream...". The Mad Scene. James Merrill. P85

"**Again** there will be the scent of lilac". Elegy. Georgi Djagarov. P70

Against Time. Louis Untermeyer. P82

Against Waking Early. Bruce Bennett. P63

"**Against** grey walls Picasso...". Penthouse Enigma. James Russell Vaky. P68

"Against the empty sky gulls sweep the
        void". The Stretches of Time and
        Delights. Morgan Hewitt. P68
"Against the wall". Leaving. Jeremy Hooker.
        P54
Agatha. Alfred Austin. P89
"Age forty, Rosetta shudders as she
        gives...". Paolo Dipietro. Joseph
        Maviglia. P49
Age in Prospect. Robinson Jeffers. P83
Age in Youth. Trumbull Stickney. P81
The Age of Wisdom. William Makepeace
        Thackeray. P89
"Age to age rage". Fire. Krishna Srinivas.
        P72
"An age-old idea, the fruits of Coca-Cola".
        Euthanasia. Hans Verhagen. P92
An Aged Rector Named Fiddle. Robert
        Phillips. P63
Agha, Wazir
        Apprehension. C.M. Naim (tr.). P91
        The Calling Mountain. C.M. Naim (tr.).
        P91
        A Night in the War. C.M. Naim (tr.). P91
        A Strange Man. C.M. Naim (tr.). P91
The Agincourt Carol. Unknown. P66
Aging
        After the Face Lift. Lisel Mueller. P88
        Age in Prospect. Robinson Jeffers. P83
        Day and Dark. George Cabot Lodge. P81
        Family Prime. Mark Van Doren. P83
        I Have Seen the Spring. Sara Teasdale.
        P82
        Life. Chrystie Fulmer. P74
        The Men That Once Were, sels. Owen
        Gruffudd. P87
        Montauk Highway. Harvey Shapiro. P64
        My Name Is Man. Alicia Braun. P73
        The 'Old, Old Song'. Charles Kingsley. P89
        Older Is Safer. Robert N. Feinstein. P63
        Our Afterlife. Robert Lowell. P79
        Out from Behind This Mask, from Leaves of
        Grass. Walt Whitman. P90
        Portrait of Mary. Charles Wright. P79
        Reflections. Shawn Ketchum. P73
        The Sun. Alexander Gerov. P70
        Two Views of a Philosopher. Howard
        Nemerov. P79
        The Wood-Pile. Robert Frost. P82
        Youth and Age, from The House of a
        Hundred Lights. (Frederick) Ridgely
        Torrence. P81
An Aging Canvas. Kandy Arnold. P58
"An aging pilgrim on a". On Flower Wreath
        Hill. Kenneth Rexroth. P52
Agnew, Joan
        Freedom. P51
Agnew, John
        Sons of the King. P51

An Agony. As Now. Amiri (LeRoi Jones)
        Baraka. P85
The Agony. George Herbert. P59
"Ah my dear angry Lord". Bitter-Sweet.
        George Herbert. P59
"Ah! I shall kill myself with dreams". The
        Mystic's Vision. Mathilde Blind. P89
"Ah! the morning is grey". Chimney-Tops.
        Unknown. P51
Ah, How Sweet, from Tyrannic love. John
        Dryden. P89
"Ah, cosmos are you conscious?.". The Town
        Tree. Alexander Gerov. P70
"Ah, golden eyes, to win you yet". Golden
        Eyes. Rufinus. P89
"Ah, Jesu Kri". The Chants, sel. Maria
        Sabina. P78
"Ah, little road all whirry in the breeze".
        The Road. Helene Johnson. P90
"Ah, my poems, here you are--.". Envoi. L.
        L. Zieger. P63
Aiken, Conrad
        Bread and Music. P82
        Morning Song from 'Senlin'. P82
        Palimpsest: a Deceitful Portrait. P82
        Time in the Rock or Preludes to
        Definition Selections. P82
Ainsworth, Ruth
        Good Night. P51
Air Raids
        Seekers of Freedom. Walt Jones. P86
Air Travel
        Airport. Perry Brass. P65
        The Obligation. Knute Skinner. P63
Air Travel. See also Travel
Air and Angels. John Donne. P59
"The air is blue enough to scratch".
        October: Sierra. William Howarth. P77
"Air of thin blue shadow. My campfire
        shivers". Night Thoughts, Sierra.
        William Howarth. P77
Airport. Perry Brass. P65
Airport. Elaine Demakas. P58
Airport Phone Booth. Memye Curtis Tucker.
        P63
Aisenberg, Nadya
        'Songs of Apocalypse', sel. P48
Akel, Abdul-Latif
        Self-Portrait. Abdul-Latif Akel (tr.).
        P92
Akenside, Mark
        Song. P89
Akers, Elizabeth
        Rock Me to Sleep. P89
Akers, Tilda S.
        Old Man Winter. P72
Akins, Terese
        October's Wooing. P72
Alar. Virginia M. Hahn. 58

"Alas for our art, scandal". Warning to the
Poets. Sion Tudur. P87
"Alas! As the Ocean of Milk Was Stirred...".
Unknown. P62
Alas, Alas the Wyle, That Ever I Cowde
Daunce. Unknown. P66
"Alas, one more autumn day". An Autumn
Evening. Chris Weideman. P74
Alberts Landing. Hugh Seidman. P64
Alchemy. Alice M. Boughtwood. P68
Aldebaran. Miguel de Unamuno. P48
Aldis, Dorothy
Bursting. P50
Aled, Tudur
The Last Englyn. Tony Conran (tr.). P87
Nobility. Tony Conran (tr.). P87
"Alembics turn to stranger things". Bronze
Trumpets and Sea Water--on Turning
Latin... Elinor Wylie. P82
"Aleta mentions in her tender letters". Wild
May. Claude McKay. P82
Alex. Jason Gruhl. P73
Alexander, F. (tr.)
"All My Boasting Friends," from Mother
Goose... Unknown. P90
"At Me He Winks an Eye," from Mother
Goose... Unknown. P90
"Chin, Chin, Chin," from Mother Goose...
Unknown. P90
"Down the Hill the Waters Cascade," from
Mother... Unknown. P90
"I Do Not Go to the Fields Today," from
Mother... Unknown. P90
"Nana Caliche," from Mother Goose on the
Rio Grande. Unknown. P90
Nature Rhymes. Unknown. P89
"We Are Little Mice," from Mother
Goose... Unknown. P90
"What Day Is Tomorrow?," from Mother
Goose... Unknown. P90
Alexander, Mrs.
The Crow. P51
Alfred Hitchcock U. Geoff Fiorito. P58
Algae
Sea-Weed. David Herbert Lawrence. P76
Ali, Ahmed
I Meet Lee San in the Nether World and
Talk of Home. P91
Alienation
Dante's Angels. Patrick Lane. P49
No One. Gonzalo Millan. P71
On the 401 from Waterloo to Toronto.
Douglas Smith. P49
The Signalled Hour. Juan Cameron. P71
"All Day". Steve Sanfield. P77
All Goats. Elizabeth J. Coatsworth. P89
All Saints' Day
Hallowe'en. Marion Louise Refici. P74
Yarrow. Margaret Drake Elliot. P72

"All along the backwater". Duck's Ditty.
Kenneth Grahame. P51
"All day I have thought of the swans". The
Swans. Grace Schulman. P64
"All day long". The Night Sky. Unknown. P51
"All day long I have been working". Madonna
of the Evening Flowers. Amy Lowell.
P82
"All day subdued, polite". Negro Servant.
Langston Hughes. P83
"All days seem alike". Before the First of
the Next Month. Majeed Amjad. P91
"All endeavor to be beautiful". Primer of
Plato. Jean Garrigue. P84
All in All. C. B. Oppenheimer. P68
All in Red. Eileen Mathias. P51
"All My Boasting Friends," from Mother
Goose... Unknown. P90
All Night Long by Train, All Night Long.
Mauricio Electorat. P71
"All in the April evening". Sheep and Lambs.
Katharine (Hinkson) Tynan. P51
"All in the downs the fleet was moored".
Black-Eyed Susan. John Gay. P89
"All in this pleasant evening...". Old May
Song. Unknown. P51
"All is a kind of toys, all is a kind of
play". Time Passes. Richard Eberhart.
P72
"All mention of the moment". The Moment.
Waldo Williams. P87
"All my problems". Maybe Dats Youwr Pwoblem
Too. Jim Hall. P63
"All nature seems at work...". In
Springtime. Samuel Taylor Coleridge.
P51
"All night autumn winds were howling".
Gathering Leaves. William Crwys
Williams. P87
"All night the boy from Cluny had lain...".
Long Narrow Roadway. Kim Maltman. P49
"All night the rain's soft fists". Letting
Go. Alice Derry. P88
"All night, hip out of joint". Wrestling
with Angels. Walter McDonald. P57
All of Him, the Blue Filigree of the Gaze.
Gonzalo Munoz. P71
All Roads Lead to Rome. Freddie P. Hanson.
P72
All Seasons Shall Be Sweet. Samuel Taylor
Coleridge. P51
All Which Isn't Singing Is Mere Talking.
Edward Estlin Cummings. P83
"All of a sudden the sky turned orange".
Landscape. Omar Lara. P71
"All out-of-doors looked darkly in at him".
An Old Man's Winter Night. Robert
Frost. P82
"All prices, places, means of conveyance".

Follow Your Heart to the Land of
Enchantment. Tom Hawkins. P63
"All responsible winters collect snow".
Melting. Judy Little. P88
"All roads lead to this street...". Street.
Waldo Rojas. P71
"All summer long and all day long he sits".
The Pumpkin Man. Robert Francis. P63
"All the night". Blacksmith. B. K. Pyke. P51
"All the world's a stage". Seven Ages of Man,
from As You Like It. William
Shakespeare. P90
"All the worms are wet again". Variable
Service. Dabney Stuart. P79
"All those buffalos have green horns". A
Song of the Red & Green Buffalo.
Unknown. P78
"All those men who couldn't live without
me". Airport Phone Booth. Memye Curtis
Tucker. P63
"All wrapped up in clouds, the powerful...".
On the Subject of Roses. Abraham
Sutzkever. P48
"All year in the appropriate North his
elves". The Gifts. John N. Morris. P79
All's Well, from The British Fleet. Thomas
Dibdin. P89
"Allah, My Lord". Unknown. P60
Allegories
The Parlement of the Thre Ages. Unknown.
P66
Pearl. Unknown. P66
Allen, Gladys Pearl
Legacy. P72
Allen, Judd
Proud Father with Buried Son. P72
Allen, Marie Louise
First Snow. P80
Allen, Robert F.
Love is Even Lovelier Now. P65
The Peacemakers. P72
The Special Language. P65
Allen, Sarah Van Alstyne
Song for a Surf-Rider. P76
Allen, Shelly A.
"In the Sun Here". P77
"An alley cat is". Haiku. Matthew Woomer.
P74
Allingham, William
The Dirty Old Man. P90
Lovely Mary Donnelly. P89
Wishing. P51
Allison, Helen Thomas
Life in Color. P72
Alma-Tadema, Laurence
Bed-Time. P51
A Blessing for the Blessed, sel. P51
Playgrounds. P51
The Robin. P51

Snowdrops. P51
"Almost a year over here". Support
Troops/Our Brains Are Cooking Bugs.
Robert Schlosser. P86
"Alone at twilight". Dusk. Mary Alice Lipes.
P74
"Alone on Lykaion since man hath been". Mt.
Lykaion. Trumbull Stickney. P81
Alone: Genesis. Karen Kania. P88
Along the Roadside. Edna Jones. P68
"Along the bank of the brook". The Race.
Sylvia Smullin. P74
"Along the pastoral ways I go". A Holiday.
Lizette Woodworth Reese. P81
"Along the shore the tall, thin grass". In
Memory of Colonel Charles Young.
Countee Cullen. P83
Alonso, Damaso
Insects. Charles Guenther (tr.). P61
"Aloof as aged kings". Day's Ending
(Tucson). Sara Teasdale. P82
"Aloof upon the day's immeasured dome". The
Black Vulture. George Sterling. P81
Alpha the Dog. Robert Sward. P49
Alpha/Omega Cycle of Peace. Josette Liliane
Villias. P72
Alphabet Soup. David Cram. P63
An Alphabet. Edward Lear. P90
Alphabets
Hole. Imogene Bolls. P63
"Already they are flying back". Up North.
Lisel Mueller. P88
"Already you are". To One Deaf. Sister Mary
Lucina. P57
Altenburg, Michael
The Battle-Song of Gustavus Adolphus. P90
"Although They Both Exist". Unknown. P62
"Although Water, Because of Fire, Loses".
Guido della Colonne. P69
Alun
Song to the Nightingale. Tony Conran
(tr.). P87
Always Praises You. Nyaruoth Atem. P53
"Always across the distant hills". The Love
of God. William Williams Pantycelyn.
P87
"Always the morning". Amazon. Elisaveta
Bagriana. P70
"Always wanting definitions. Either". Find
the Nerve To Get Excited. Pat Bridges.
P56
Always, from My First Boyhood. John Peale
Bishop. P83
Amadeus. LoVerne Brown. P63
Amarinths
"'Why Don't You Keep Asking the Red
Amarinth'". Unknown. P62
Amaze. Adelaide Crapsey. P81
Amazon. lisaveta Bagriana. P70

"Ambassador Puser the ambassador". Memorial
        Rain. Archibald MacLeish. P83
Ambition
        Drug Store. John V. A. Weaver. P82
Ambush. Phillip Macar. P53
Ameeruddin, Syed
        That...Who. P72
America
        America. Samuel Francis Smith. P90
America. Alfred Kreymborg. P82
America. Samuel Francis Smith. P90
"America, your first two hundred years".
        With Fifty Stars. Francis Brown Price.
        P68
American Body Binding. Elaine Demakas. P58
American Farm, 1934. Genevieve Taggard. P83
American Poetry. Louis Simpson. P85
American Rhapsody. Kenneth Fearing. P83
"The American language explicates...". Home,
        Sweet Home! Gavin Ewart. P63
Amherst Neighbors. Lewis Turco. P63
"Amidst the turmoil that ill blows our
        lives". Magic Reprieve. Walter S. Hay.
        P72
Amjad, Majeed
        Before the First of the Next Month. Faruq
            Hassan (tr.). P91
        The Scream. Faruq Hassan (tr.). P91
        Some Days Ago. Faruq Hassan (tr.). P91
        What Days, Indeed. Faruq Hassan and M.
            Salim-ur-Rahman (tr.). P91
Ammons, Archie Randolph
        Coon Song. P67
        Nelly Myers. P67
        The Yucca Moth. P79
Ammunition
        John Kennedy. Nyagak Pinien. P53
"Among All the Wives of the Village Chief".
        Unknown. P62
Among Shadows. Arthur Davidson Ficke. P82
Among the Nuts. Unknown. P51
"Among the people of earth one has
        poetry...". For W. H. A. John Ronald
        Renel Tolkien. P79
"Among the prescriptions". The Fair Fowl.
        Robert N. Feinstein. P63
"Among thy fancies tell me this". The Kiss.
        Robert Herrick. P89
"Among twenty snowy mountains". Thirteen
        Ways of Looking at a Blackbird.
        Wallace Stevens. P83
"Amongst the princely paragons". A Princely
        Ditty in Praise of the English Rose.
        Thomas Deloney. P51
Amphibian. Walter H. Kerr. P68
Amy Elizabeth Ermyntrude Annie. Queenie
        Scott-Hopper. P51
Anatomy of Melancholy. Ralph Gustafson. P49
The Ancestors: A Suite. Dorothy Livesay. P49

Ancient Convolutions. Elaine Emmons. P77
"Ancient of days, bless the innocent".
        Clams. Stanley Moss. P64
"An ancient story I'll tell you anon". King
        John and the Abbot of Canterbury.
        Unknown. P51
And Back. Rodney Bennett. P51
And Did the Animals?. Mark Van Doren. P83
And For Your Children. Gwyn Thomas. P87
"And after going". Vision. Gonzalo Millan.
        P71
"And behold". Apocalypse. Ernesto Cardenal.
        P48
"And did those feet in ancient time".
        Jerusalem. William Blake. P51
"And especially as the hours". Coma. Liane
        Heller. P49
"And fro that other cost of caldee toward
        the south". Mandeville's Travels,
        sels. Unknown. P66
"And God stepped out on space". The
        Creation. James Weldon Johnson. P83
"And here face down beneath the sun". You,
        Andrew Marvell. Archibald MacLeish.
        P83
"And here on the trunk". Mirror. Salvatore
        Quasimodo. P61
"And his Father made Adam, and he
        placed...". The Myth Revisited: Adam.
        Michael V. McGee. P56
"And how could we sing". In the Willow
        Branches. Salvatore Quasimodo. P61
"And how shall we toil like the crab...".
        Alberts Landing. Hugh Seidman. P64
"And Los & Enitharmon builded Jerusalem...".
        The Four Zoas: 'Night the Ninth, Being
        the Last...'. William Blake. P48
"And now in the dark shell of night".
        Stepping Out with My Big Cats. Naomi
        Lazard. P64
"And now the words". Tsimshian Mourning
        Song. Unknown. P78
"' And now,' said God". At the Briefing for
        Creation Day. Mary Jean Irion. P63
"And O and O". Song of Spring. John Keats.
        P51
"And on the third day I saw the butchers".
        Reincarnation of the Butchers. Oscar
        Hahn. P71
"And phoenix turns to stone". Sleep Work.
        Mohammed Dib. P91
"And see the biped soaring up". On Hearing
        of a Man's Death in a Hang Glider
        Accident. Peter Acker. P49
"' and something that..that is theirs-...".
        The Dispossessed. John Berryman. P84
And the Physician?., from Lost Youth: the
        Last War. Alfred Kreymborg. P82
WAnd the Sins of the Fathers. Stephen Crane.

P81
And the Summer Still Persists. Liliana
    Stefanova. P70
And Then. Prince Redcloud. P80
And Who Am I. Opal Jane O'Neal. P72
And You Love Me?. Stephen Crane. P81
"And the sea". Words or Spoors, fr. Omneros.
    Mohammed Dib. P91
"And the woman coughed up her entrails".
    Love. Sergio Mansilla. P71
"And then I pressed the shell". The Shell.
    James Stephens. P51
"And then went down to the ship". The Cantos,
    sel. Ezra Pound. P82
"And then, worn by the sun, I fell asleep".
    A Tale. Georgi Borisov. P70
"And there they sat, a-popping corn".
    Popping Corn. Unknown. P89
"And there's still the call of the old".
    What Do You Want, Shepherd of Wind?.
    Salvatore Quasimodo. P61
"And this is England! June's undarkened...".
    This Is England. Laurence Binyon. P51
"And this is how I". 'Riffs', sel. Dennis
    Lee. P49
"And Timur again set out for the wars-.".
    Double-Focus. Al Purdy. P49
"And tomorrow". Of the Nameless Birds.
    Teresa Calderon. P71
"And what a day it was!.". Schizophrenic
    Kiss. James Tate. P85
"And what strength have we". Ode to Noise.
    Bozhidar Bozhilov. P70
"And when I flew down to Bangkok". Fear of
    Sky Death. Robert Schlosser. P86
"And when it's over, go with the child".
    Pizarro Teaches the Mentally Retarded
    To Swim. Lee Bassett. P57
"And when she". Syntax. Robert Canzoneri.
    P63
"And when we die at last". Heaven and Hell.
    Nalungiaq. P78
Andersen, Vita
    Costa Del Sol, at Night. Linda Lappin and
    Jannick Storm (tr.). P92
Anderson, John C.
    Sapphics on the Violet. P68
Anderson, Lynne
    Lazy One. P73
Anderson, Mary
    In the April Rain. P51
    Praise. P51
    Thanks to Spring. P51
Anderson, William A.
    Deer Park. P68
"The Andes are nothing for the Cordilleras".
    The Cordilleras of Il Duce. Raul
    Zurita. P71
Andrews, Michael

Body Bags, sel. P86
Anecdote of the Jar. Wallace Stevens.!P83
Aneirin
    The Gododdin, sels. Tony Conran (tr.).
    P87
"An angel came today, and somehow I knew".
    The Angel. William H. Ryder Jr. P86
Angel, Walking. James W. Penha. P56
"An angel, robed in spotless white". Dawn.
    Paul Laurence Dunbar. P89
The Angel. William H. Ryder Jr. P86
Angels
    Angels of Snow. Lorna Crozier. P49
    Expecting an Angel. George Bradley. P79
    The Two Angels. John Greenleaf Whittier.
    P89
    Two or Three Angels. Stephen Crane. P81
The Angels Among Us. Naomi Lazard. P64
Angels of Snow. Lorna Crozier. P49
"The angels you're embroidering". My Mother
    in Paradise. Lyubomir Levchev. P70
"The angels". Heaven's Glowing. Nina Marin.
    P72
The Angelus. Edwin Markham. P81
Anger
    "At the Peak of Bright Sleep". Diane P.
    Lando. P77
    Belinda. Jack H. Palmer. P68
    A God in Wrath. Stephen Crane. P81
    Route Seven. Juan Cameron. P71
    The Sacred Passion of St. Joseph. Jose
    Lacaba. P92
    Trinity. John Knoll. P86
    When Anger Came. Virginia M. Hahn. P58
    Your Anger. Paz Molina. P71
"The angle of the sun, declining, lifts".
    Envoi. John Barton. P49
Angle, Lily D.
    Seedam. P63
"Angry men and furious machines". Dutch
    Graves in Bucks County. Wallace
    Stevens. P83
Anguish. Henry Vaughan. P59
The Anguish. Edna St. Vincent Millay. P82
Animals
    And Did the Animals?. Mark Van Doren. P83
    The Angels Among Us. Naomi Lazard. P64.
    Animals. Aki Raymer. P74
    "As They Fly Around the Shoulders of the
    Ox". Unknown. P62
    At Night in the Wood. Nancy M. Hayes. P51
    The Bells of Heaven. Ralph Hodgson. P51
    "The Buffalo, Tormented by the Heat".
    Unknown. P62
    The Chipmunk Center. Peter Meinke. P63
    The Cock and the Fox. Jean de La
    Fontaine. P90
    Come ino Animal Presence. Denise
    Levertov. P85

Coroner's Inquest. William DeWitt
    Snodgrass. P63
Cow and the Ass. Ann and Jane Taylor. P51
The Crow and the Fox. Jean de La
    Fontaine. P90
"The Crow, Whose Mind Is Given Solely".
    Unknown. P62
"The Crows, Dipping Their Beaks in the
    Stream". Unknown. P62
The Duel. Eugene Field. P90
False Country of the Zoo. Jean Garrigue.
    P84
Familiar Friends. James S. Tippett. P51
A Gift Multiplies. Vivian Moody. P72
Giraffe. C. B. Oppenheimer. P68
The Grasshopper and Cricket. John Keats.
    P51,P89
Grey Brother. U. M. Montgomery. P51
"Having Seen the Tip of a Tooth".
    Unknown. P62
The Housekeeper. Charles Lamb. P89
"In a Grove by the Godavari River, a
    Monkey". Unknown. P62
Kindness to Animals. Unknown. P51
Man Who Loved a Giraffe. Pyke Johnson Jr.
    P63
"The Mate of the Bull Elephant Who Is
    Trampled...". Unknown. P62
"The Monkey Pauses, Shakes the Branch".
    Unknown. P62
The Monkeys. Marianne Moore. P83
The Pangolin. Marianne Moore. P83
Animals. Aki Raymer. P74
"The Rooster Speaks to Thieves". Unknown.
    P62
Sheep and Lambs. Katharine (Hinkson)
    Tynan. P51
The Silent Snake. Unknown. P51
Strange Talk. L. E. Yates. P51
"The Trap-Wary Crow Doesn't Want the Rice
    Ball". Unknown. P62
W. D., Don't Fear That Animal. William
    DeWitt Snodgrass. P63
"When the Pair of Deer Face the Blow".
    Unknown. P62
"When the Solitary Deer, Erect and with
    Longing Ears". Unknown. P62
"Where Has the Disc of the Sun Gone".
    Unknown. P62
The Zookeeper. Jason Goode. P74
Animula. David Wevill. P49
Annabel Lee. Edgar Allen Poe. P89
Annamese Hands. Richard A. Parque. P86
Anne. Lizette Woodworth Reese. P81
Anne Rutledge, from Spoon River Anthology.
    Edgar Lee Masters. P82
"Announced by all the trumpets...". The Snow-
    Storm. Ralph Waldo Emerson. P89
The Annoyer. Nathaniel Parker Willis. P89

Annunciation. Frederika Blankner. P65
Anonymous. John Banister Tabb. P81
Anonymous Biography. Armando Rubio. P71
"Anonymous—nor needs a name". Anonymous.
    John Banister Tabb. P81
Another Fable in Two Languages. Charles W.
    Pratt. P63
Another Side of Me. Beth Hirschfeld. P74
"Another armored animal-scale". The
    Pangolin. Marianne Moore. P83
"Another land, another age, another self".
    Covered Bridge. Robert Penn Warren.
    P67
"Another life I enter". Second-Hand
    Trousers. Taufiq Rafat. P91
"Another season centers on this place". The
    Gourd Dancer. N. Scott Momaday. P85
"Another season come and gone". Cleaning the
    Garage. Edward Butscher. P64
Anoukis and Later Jeanne. Rene Char. P61
Anster, John
    The Fairy Child. P90
Answer to Master Wither's Song. Ben Jonson.
    P89
Answer to Sion Cent, sels. Rhys Goch Eryri.
    P87
Antarctic Regions
    Antarctica. Clement Arthur Phoenix. P68
Ante Mortem. Robinson Jeffers. P83
Anthony, Edward
    I Know an Owl. P75
Anti-Cycle for the New Year. Jane Augustine.
    P64
Antique Harvesters. John Crowe Ransom. P67,
    P83
"Antonius Block played chess with death...".
    Chess. Waldo Rojas. P71
"Antony: O mighty Caesar!...". Mark Antony,
    over the Body of Caesar. William
    Shakespeare. P90
Ants
    The Ants. Mark Thalman. P63
Anxiety
    Naphiri. Edison Mpina. P92
Anyone Lived in a Pretty How Town. Edward
    Estlin Cummings. P83
"Anytime I have nothing to do". My Fantasy.
    Kim Sherry. P73
Apathy. Blossom S. Kirschenbaum. P63
Apocalypse
    The Apocalypse of Our Times, sel. Vasily
    Vasilievich Rosanov. P48
    Blue Danube. Manuel Silva Acevedo. P71
Apocalypse. Ernesto Cardenal. P48
    Darkness. George Gordon, 6th Baron Byron.
    P48
    Epilogue to a Human Drama. Stephen
    Spender. P48
    For a Coming Extinction. William Stanley

Merwin. P48

The Fortunate Traveller. Derek Walcott.
    P48

The Season of Phantasmal Peace. Derek
    Walcott. P48

'Songs of Apocalypse', sel. Nadya
    Aisenberg. P48

The **Apocalypse** of Our Times, sel. Vasily
    Vasilievich Rosanov. P48

Apologies to Verdi. Marlon Fick. P68

Apology for Bad Dreams. Robinson Jeffers.
    P83

Apology of a Genius. Mina Loy. P82

An **Apology**. Diane Wakoski. P85

Apostles

A View Across the Roman Campagna.
    Elizabeth Barrett Browning. P90

Water Walker. Richard Wilbur. P84

An **Apothegm**. Daniel Hoffman. P63

"**Apparent** happiness marks this place".
    Heart's Need. Rajnee Krishnan Kutty.
    P72

"The **apparition** of these faces in the
    crowd". In a Station of the Metro.
    Ezra Pound. P82

Apparitions

The Dutch Patrol. Edmund Clarence
    Stedman. P81

In a Station of the Metro. Ezra Pound.
    P82

Meeting. Arthur Davidson Ficke. P82

Applachian Courtship. Dorothy Williamson
    Worth. P65

Apple Blossoms. Helen Adams Parker. P51

The **Apple** Rhyme. Madeleine Nightingale. P51

Apple Trees

Old Apple Trees. William DeWitt
    Snodgrass. P85

Appleman, Philip

East Hampton: The Structure of Sound. P64

Red Kite. P64

The Tennis Player Waits for What Waits...
    P64

Westhampton Cemetery. P64

Apples

Apples and Leaves. James Richard Hurst.
    P68

Bittern He Took a Bundle. Unknown. P87

Apples and Leaves. James Richard Hurst. P68

Applewhite, James

Drinking Music. P67

My Grandfather's Funeral. P67

Tobacco Men. P67

Appointment in Doctor's Office. Josephine
    Miles. P84

Apprehension. Wazir Agha. P91

The **Approach**. J. D. McClatchy. P79

April

April Rain Song. Langston Hughes. P75

April. Alfred Corn. P79

Leaving Fargo: April. Linda M.
    Hasselstrom. P88

April. Sir William Watson. P51

April Inventory. William DeWitt Snodgrass.
    P85

April Rain. Robert Loveman. P51

April Rain Song. Langston Hughes. P75

"**April** again hotly pursuing March". Home!.
    Lu Cicada. P77

"**April** is the cruellest month, breeding".
    Burial of the Dead, fr. The Waste
    Land. Thomas Stearns Eliot. P83

Apsche, Jack

After the War. P86

Arbeleche and Carolyn Harris, Jorge (tr.)

The Mirror's Place. Jorge Arbeleche. P92

"The **arc** of blue arrows". Blue Angels Sky-
    Dance. Zelma S. Dennis. P72

Archaic Song of Dr. Tom the Shaman. Unknown.
    P78

Archeology

Goat's Hole, Paviland. Nigel Jenkins. P54

Archeology. Virginia M. Hahn. P58

Archibald Higbie, from Spoon River
    Anthology. Edgar Lee Masters. P82

Are the Children at Home? Margaret Elizabeth
    (Munson) Sangster. P89

"' **Are** you awake, Gemelli'.". Star Talk.
    Robert Graves. P90

"**Are** your rocks shelter for ships?.". The
    Shrine. Hilda ("H.D.") Doolittle. P82

Argoed. Thomas Gwynn Jones. P87

Aries Sideshow. Charles Ghigna. P63

Aristophanes

The Cloud Chorus, from The Clouds. Andrew
    Lang (tr.). P89

Women's Chorus. C. W. Collins (tr.). P90

Arithmetic

A Mortifying Mistake. Anna Maria Pratt.
    P89

Arles, 7 p.m. Marge Piercy. P63

Arlington. Edison Mpina. P92

Arlington, Hermit Helene Troy

Everyman's Two Gifts. P68

I Do Not Cry Like People Cry. P68

Arlo Will, from Spoon River Anthology. Edgar
    Lee Masters. P82

Armed Conflict. Pier Munn. P63

Armies

A.W.O.L. James P. Bergman. P86

Storm. Agnes Nemes Nagy. P92

Support Troops/Our Brains Are Cooking
    Bugs. Robert Schlosser. P86

The Toy Band. Henry Newbolt. P51

Transient Barracks. Randall Jarrell. P84

Troop Train. Karl Shapiro. P84

Armour, Richard

The Conscience. P63

Hiding Place. P63
Money. P63
Sequence. P63
To Have and Too Old. P63

Arms
Dagger. Mikhail Lermontov. P90

Armstrong, Martin
Gold. P51

Armstrong, Naomi Young
So Many Moons Ago (Acrostic/Sonnet). P72

Arnold, Kandy
An Aging Canvas. P58
Blind Dates. P58
California Street. P58
Counting the Losses. P58
The Final Battle. P58
Muses. P58
A Romance. P58
Umbrella. P58

Arnold, Matthew
The Forsaken Merman, sel. P51
The Forsaken Merman. P90
Memorial Verses (April 1850). P90

Arnold, Sir Edwin
The Secret of Death. P89

"Around a lemon tree throwing". Paestum.
! James Dickey. P79
"Around a pinch of faith". A Pinch of Faith.
T. Vasudeva Reddy. P72
"Arrayed in snow-white pants and vest". The
Compliment. Eugene Field. P90
Arrival. Vernon Edgar. P72
Arrival. Aristoteles Espana. P71
"Arrive. The ladies from the Ladies'
Betterment". The Lovers of the Poor.
Gwendolyn Brooks. P84
Ars Poetica. Archibald MacLeish. P83
Ars Poetique. Rodrigo Lira. P71

Art and Artists
Annunciation. Frederika Blankner. P65
The Artist. Unknown. P78
The Artist. Arthur Grissom. P90
Breastfeeding at the Art Gallery of
Ontario... Sharon Berg. P49
Child Sketch in Crayon. David Wevill. P49
Colors. Henrietta Liebknecht. P72
Dionysians in a Bad Time. Irving Layton.
P49
The Edge. Ken Norris. P49
F.R. Konecamp. David Gwenallt Jones. P87
From Goethe to Gounod: Concerning a
Mutual Affaire... Patricia Kirby. P68
Harriet Beecher Stowe. Paul Laurence
Dunbar. P90
Hawthorne. Henry Wadsworth Longfellow.
P90
His Matisses, 1938. Julia Keeler. P49
Imitation Is the Sincerest Flattery,
But... Blossom S. Kirschenbaum. P63

In Class We Create Ourselves-Having Been
Told... P. K. Page. P49
In the National Museum. John Tripp. P54
Metropolitan LIfe. John Barton. P49
No Muse Is Good Muse. Rochelle
Distelheim. P63
On a Picture by a Chinese Painter. Henri
Michaux. P61
Painter of Icons. Luchesar Elenkov. P70
Still Life Near Bangalore. Earle Birney.
P49
A Switched Career. X. J. Kennedy. P63
A Tale from the Arabian Nights. Alison
Shepherd. P68
To Whistler, American. Ezra Pound. P82
"Art galleries take in past". Contiguity.
George Georgiev. P72
The **Art** of Poetry. Pierre Emmanuel. P61
"Art thou poor, yet hast thou golden
slumbers". Happy Heart, from Patient
Grissell. Thomas Dekker. P90
Arthur's Passing, sels. Thomas Gwynn Jones.
P87

Arthur, Ruth M.
Snowflakes. P51

Arthurian Legend
Arthur's Passing, sels. Thomas Gwynn
Jones. P87

Artisans
At the Craft Show. Marijane G. Ricketts.
P56
"The **artist** mixes his colors". Colors.
Henrietta Liebknecht. P72
"The **artist**: disciple, abundant...". The
Artist. Unknown. P78
The **Artist**. Arthur Grissom. P90
The **Artist**. Unknown. P78
As a Thousand Years. Jeremy Hooker. P54
As by the Shore At Break of Day. Thomas
Moore. P90
As Helpless as a Dhow on a Still Day. Dhor
Ding Cuol. P53
As I Was Dying at the Steak House... Scott
Bates. P63
"As I Went up the Garden". Unknown. P51
"As deadbeats pass from bar to can". The
Graffiti Fingers of the Theology
Student. James Schevill. P48
"As gunships buzz the canopy". Observation
Post. R. L. Barth. P86
"As he handed over the wallet". Besides.
Mark Irwin. P63
"As he trudged along to school". The Story
of Johnny Head-in-Air. Heinrich
Hoffmann. P90
"As I did the washing one day". Shirt of a
Lad. Unknown. P87
"As I in hoary winter's night stood...". The
Burning Babe. Robert Southwell. P59

"As I lie back". Behind These Lids. R. B.
     Weber. P64
"As I sit looking out of a window of the
     building". The Instruction Manual.
     John Ashbery. P85
"As I stand here beside you". The Ancestors:
     A Suite. Dorothy Livesay. P49
"As I truly remember my life". Bukan. Emha
     Ainunn Nadjib. P92
"As I view the leaf, my theme...". My Own
     House. David Ignatow. P64
"As I wandered in the forest". Wild Flower's
     Song. William Blake. P51
"As I was going to Derby...". The Wonderful
     Derby Ram. Unknown. P51
"As I was walking". Kore. Robert Creeley.
     P85
"As I went down the village green". Ducks.
     Norman Ault. P51
"As I wrap the silk cloth". American Body
     Binding. Elaine Demakas. P58
As if Carbon Is Nothing. Bernice Lever. P49
"As if you'd sketched a fern". Clara
     Schumann at the Piano. Maureen
     Bloomfield. P88
As in the Midst of Battle There Is Room.
     George Santayana. P81
As Joseph Was A-Walking. Unknown. P51
As Sea Birds Sail. Mary Jane Barnes. P68
"As They Fly Around the Shoulders of the
     Ox". Unknown. P62
As You Leave the Room. Wallace Stevens. P83
As You Wish. Mario Luzi. P61
"As in wind the waves are surging". Looking
     Back. Werner Manheim. P72
"As Kandilli flowed through sleep's first
     quarter". Night. Yahya Kemal. P91
"As landscapes richen after rain, the eye".
     Foliage of Vision. James Merrill. P85
"As long as we looked lay the low country".
     The Residual Years. William Everson.
     P84
"As long as you're still alive". Hymn of the
     Lyre Player. Fatthy Said. P91
"As phoenix-self I did as bade". Final
     Migration. Carol Hamilton. P68
"As soon as I'm in bed at night". Mrs.
     Brown. Rose Fyleman. P51
"As sultry as the cruising hum". Muted
     Music. Robert Penn Warren. P67
"As the cat". Poem. William Carlos Williams.
     P82
"As the cool wind blows in". Autumn. Leslie
     Katz. P74
"As the melting park". At the Park Dance.
     William DeWitt Snodgrass. P85
"As the professor speaks". Several Short
     Poems. George Swede. P49
"As the silver mist". Man and Woman. Beryl
     Baigent. P72
"As the sun rises". A Year. Angie You. P73
"As the walrus glides". Dreams. Tom
     Tellesbo. P58
"As virtuous men pass mildly away". A
     Valediction: Forbidding Mourning. John
     Donne. P59
"As we rush, as we rush in the train". In
     the Train. James ("B.V.") Thomson. P51
"As we sat around the campfire". Campfire.
     Marsh Cassady. P56
Asaro, Peter
     December. P73
Ascension Thursday. Saunders Lewis. P87
Ashbery, John
     A Boy. P85
     Endless Variation. P85
     Fear of Death. P85
     The Instruction Manual. P85
     Some Trees. P85
     Some Words. P52
     The Tennis Court Oath. P85
Ashour, Brierly
     Evening Prayer. P68
The Asians Dying. William Stanley Merwin.
     P85
Asiatic Day-Flower. Donald Finkel. P79
Ask No Return. Horace Gregory. P83
Asking a Stallion. Gutun Owain. P87
Asking the Windows. Margo LaGattuta. P88
"Asking what, asking what?--all a boy's
     afternoon". Debate: Question, Quarry,
     Dream. Robert Penn Warren. P83
Aspects of Lilac. Howard Moss. P64
Aspects of Robinson. Weldon Kees. P84
"Asphodel isn't in the". Hohenzollern.
     Barbara Guest. P64
Asquith, Herbert
     The Elephant. P51
     A Ship Sails up to Bideford. P51
Assonance. Barry Callaghan. P49
"Astride the boney jointed ridge". Still
     Life. William Carlos Williams. P79
Astronauts
     Translated to the Seven Astronauts. Mary
     McGowan Slappey. P72
Astronomy and Astronomers
     "I Think That Galileo, Old and Blind".
     Rosemary Davis. P72
     'M 87'. Vernon Payne. P72
     Planetarium. Adrienne Rich. P85
     The Primitive Astronomer. Tom Riley. P63
Asylum, from Your Tired, Your Poor. Lisel
     Mueller. P88
"At Bellevue now you have in a sense
     returned". The Inmate. Margherita
     Faulkner. P68
"At Cedar Point". Midwinter. AllenPlanz.
     P64

"At Christmas time so long ago". The Little
        Fir Tree. Margaret Rose. P51
At a Concert. R. P. Dickey. P63
At Albert's Landing (with my son). Michael
        Heller. P64
At Billings' Bridge Graveyard. Robert
        Billings. P49
At Bosherston Ponds. John Tripp. P54
At Breakfast. Ida M. Mills. P51
"At Daybreak, with Snow Coming". Unknown.
        P62
At Delphi. Abigail S. Bean. P68
At Each Other. Shaheed Quadri. P91
At Home. Edward Willey. P63
At Mass. Vachel Lindsay. P82
"At Me He Winks an Eye," from Mother
        Goose... Unknown. P90
At Melville's Tomb. Hart Crane. P83
At Night. Fairfield Porter. P64
At Night in the Wood. Nancy M. Hayes. P51
At Play in the Field. Edward Butscher. P64
At Sainte-Marguerite. Trumbull Stickney. P81
At Seventy. F. C. Rosenberger. P63
At Sunrise Along the American River...
        William Howarth. P77
At Sunset. Ivy O. Eastwick. P51
"At cocktail parties they serve us".
        Misfortune's Darlings. L. L. Zeiger.
        P63
"At concerts and such". Armed Conflict. Pier
        Munn. P63
"At dawn". The Calling Mountain. Wazir Agha.
        P91
"At dusk the multitude of the dead".
        Wandering Souls. Sergio Mansilla. P71
"At evening when the lamp is lit". The Land
        of Story-Books. Robert Louis
        Stevenson. P89
"At fifteen Jean Calvin made a list".
        Preposterous. Jim Hall. P63
"At first I wondered--.". VNV Rap Group.
        Joseph W. Nugent. P86
"At first the river's very small". The
        Growing River. Rodney Bennett. P51
"At Kandilli, in the ancient garden".
        Evening Music. Yahya Kemal. P91
"At last elected this low place to fill". On
        a Deceased Office-Seeker. Laurence
        Perrine. P63
"At Lourdes everybody drank from the cup".
        Saint Flannery. David Ray. P57
"At midnight in the top". When the Mocking
        Bird Sings. Harriet G. Hunt. P72
"At night". Thunderbird Dynasty. Kevin
        Cline. P58
"At night I make her bed". Lullaby for my
        Mother. Blaga Dimitrova. P70
"At seven, when I go to bed". A Child's
        Thought. Robert Louis Stevenson. P51

"At seventeen (dear) I was strictly
        nowhere". Revival. John Berryman. P79
"At Shelley's birth". To Shelley. John
        Banister Tabb. P81
"At six o'clock this morning". Four Poems in
        One. Anne Porter. P64
"At some point in the pageant there is a
        moment". Endless Variation. John
        Ashbery. P85
"At sundown I reached the top of the ridge".
        On the Watershed. Tibor Tollas. P61
"At table they talk interminably". After
        Dinner. David Cram. P63
"At ten a.m. the young housewife". The Young
        Housewife. William Carlos Williams.
        P82
At the Beach. Sandra Liatsos. P76
At the Briefing for Creation Day. Mary Jean
        Irion. P63
At the Craft Show. Marijane G. Ricketts. P56
At the Florist's. Jacques Prevert. P61
At the Grave of Walker. Joaquin Miller. P81
At the Indian Killer's Grave. Robert Lowell.
        P84
At the Park Dance. William DeWitt Snodgrass.
        P85
"At the Peak of Bright Sleep". Diane P.
        Lando. P77
At the Poetry Reading: 'This Is a Poem About
        That'. Jim Daniels. P63
At the Police Station. Raymond Souster. P49
"At the Round Earth's Imagined...," from
        Divine... John Donne. P59
At the School for the Deaf. Robert
        Pawlowski. P57
At the Shore. Harvey Shapiro. P64
At the Sources. Tomas Segovia. P92
"At the Time of Ploughing". Unknown. P62
At the Used Book Sale. Ken Stone. P56
"At the center of the earth". Song Picture
        No. 17. Unknown. P78
"At the crematorium for my first visit". As
        if Carbon Is Nothing. Bernice Lever.
        P49
"At the door on summer evenings". Hiawatha's
        Childhood, fr. The song of Hiawatha.
        Henry Wadsworth Longfellow. P51
"At the end of a bitter April". East Moors.
        Gillian Clarke. P54
"At the lip of the abstract". Hand Lane:
        Literature. Edward Butscher. P64
"At the marbled institute". Soil. John
        Tripp. P54
"At the Poem Society a black-haired man
        stands...". Fresh Air. Kenneth Koch.
        P85
"At the top of the house...". Moonlit
        Apples. John Drinkwater. P51
"At the very latest hour...". The Vampire

Came. Craig Lawler. P73
"At three o'clock the field is white". Stray
    Dogs. Naomi Lazard. P64
"At Woodlawn I heard the dead cry". The Lost
    Son. Theodore Roethke. P84
Atem, Micen
    The Red Clouds at Sunset. Terese Svoboda
        (tr.). P53
    Who Can Touch Me?. Terese Svoboda (tr.).
        P53
Atem, Nyaruoth
    Always Praises You. Terese Svoboda (tr.).
        P53
Athar, Abbas
    The Plough Is Crooked. C.M. Naim (tr.).
        P91
Athassel Abbey. Louise Imogen Guiney. P81
Atheism
    In Wonderment. Maria E. Boynton. P72
Athena. Alfred Dorn. P65
An Athenian Garden. Trumbull Stickney. P81
Athletes
    The Cyclists. John C. Pine. P77
    From an Athlete Living Old. James Camp.
        P63
    The Front Runner System. Wilma H.
        Clements. P68
    Pole Vaulter. David Allan Evans. P68
Atomic Bomb
    Cassandra with a Tail. Blaga Dimitrova.
        P70
"Atoms as old as stars". The Voice. Sara
    Teasdale. P82
Atop. Prince Redcloud. P50
"Atricoty...And with the star obscure". The
    Star Obscure. Gueni Zaimof. P72
"Attacks while he's on the toilet". The
    Stroke. Christopher Fahy. P57
Attic Dance. Joan Drew Ritchings. P63
Attitudes of Thanksgiving. Jill
    Breckenridge. P88
Attraction. Unknown. P87
Attwood, A. A.
    The Farmyard. P51
Atwood, Margaret
    Cave Series, sel. P49
Atwood, Randy S.
    Vote. P72
Aubade: Lake Erie. Thomas Merton. P84
The Auction. Theodore Roethke. P84
Auden Aetat XX, LX. Stephen Spender. P79
Auden, W. H.
    The Garrison. P79
"Auden, that thou art living at this hour".
    To Wystan Auden in His Birthday. and
    Louise Bogan, Edmund Wilson. P79
Aue, Julia N.
    Yes, Lord. P72
August

August Dusk: Sag Harbor. R. B. Weber. P64
August. Eunice Fallon. P51
August. Dan Murray. P64
    On an August Day. Lee Bennett Hopkins.
        P76
    Poppies. Nesta Wyn Jones. P87
August. Elinor Wylie. P82
August Dusk: Sag Harbor. R. B. Weber. P64
"August ripe-this summer". Pine Night. Wayne
    R. Toensmann. P56
"August Strindberg. Brutal wars with women".
    Dionysians in a Bad Time. Irving
    Layton. P49
"August, in Brittany". Poppies. Nesta Wyn
    Jones. P87
Augustine, Jane
    Anti-Cycle for the New Year. P64
    The Stars. P64
"Augustus was a chubby lad". The Story of
    Augustus Who Would Not Have Any Soup.
    Heinrich Hoffmann. P90
Auld Lang Syne. Robert Burns. P89
Ault, Norman
    Ducks. P51
    The Pig's Tail. P51
Aunt Effie. See Hawkshawe, Ann
"Aunts in orgies of gossip". Moon. Kaiser
    Haq. P91
Aurora. Peter Stevens. P49
Aurora Borealis. Jeane C. Carson. P72
Auroras
    Aurora. Peter Stevens. P49
Austin, Alfred
    Agatha. P89
Authority
    It Was Wrong To Do This. Stephen Crane.
        P81
    "O Son of the Village-Headman". Unknown.
        P62
"The authors are in eternity". Two Dicta of
    William Blake. Robert Duncan. P52
Auto Wreck. Karl Shapiro. P84
Autobiographia Literaria. Frank O'Hara. P85
Autobiographical. Douglas Barbour. P49
Autobiographies
    Autobiographia Literaria. Frank O'Hara.
        P85
    The Triumph of Life: Mary Shelley. Lisel
        Mueller. P88
Automobiles
    Driving. John Newlove. P49
    Plaything of the Gods. Louis J. Cantoni.
        P72
    Vita Longa, Cars Brevis. Mark Stocker.
        P63
Autumn
    Autumn. John Clare. P51
    Autumn. Florence Hoatson. P51
    Autumn. David Ignatow. P64

Autumn. Myron Wahlstrand. P72
Autumn. Leslie Katz. P74
The Autumn Bleat of the Weathervane
    Trombone. Fred Chappell. P67
An Autumn Evening. Chris Weideman. P74
An Autumn Morning. Unknown. P51
The Autumn. Jeremy Yuenger. P74
Autumn. John Clare. P51
Autumn. Georgi Djagarov. P70
    Fall. Karen M. Paik. P74
    Frost Is Coming. Mary Hamilton Neary. P72
    Harvest Song. Ludwig Holty. P89
Autumn. Florence Hoatson. P51
Autumn. David Ignatow. P64
    Immortal Autumn. Archibald MacLeish. P83
Autumn. Leslie Katz. P74
    Late Autumn Afternoons. R. B. Weber. P64
    The Morning Train. Fairfield Porter. P64
    October. S. W. Whitman. P51
    October Afternoon. Sarah Rigg. P74
    October's Party. George Cooper. P51
    Peconic Autumn Day. R. B. Weber. P64
    Quidiron Pro Quo. Paul Sawyer. P63
    Red in Autumn. Elizabeth Gould. P51
    Rich Days. William Henry Davies. P51
    Season of Content. Edna Bacon Morrison.
    P68
    To Autumn. John Keats. P51,P89
    View from Autumn. Jerry Saxton. P72
Autumn. Myron Wahlstrand. P72
    When the Autumn. Ioan Maier. P72
    When the Frost Is on the Punkin. James
    Whitcomb Riley. P89
The Autumn Bleat of the Weathervane
    Trombone. Fred Chappell. P67
Autumn Crocus. Helen Y. Luke. P77
An Autumn Evening. Chris Weideman. P74
Autumn Morning. Adeline White. P51
An Autumn Morning. Unknown. P51
The Autumn Robin. John Clare. P51
The Autumn Sea. Tong-Choon Shin. P72
Autumn Song. Margaret Rose. P51
"Autumn is here". White. Tsutomu Fukuda. P72
"Autumn wind came stealing". The Thief.
    Irene F. Pawsey. P51
"Autumn's strings begin to resound, then".
    The Seasons. Yahya Kemal. P91
The Autumn. Jeremy Yuenger. P74
Ave Caesar. Robinson Jeffers. P83
"Ave Maria! o'er the earth and sea". Evening,
    from Don Juan. George Gordon, 6th
    Baron Byron. P89
Avergun, Arthur
    Saturn the Last Titan. P68
Aviation & Aviators. See also Jet Planes
Aviation and Aviators
    The Aeroplane. Jeannie Kirby. P51
Avison, Margaret
    Goal Far and Near. P49

    Setting for the Portrait. P49
Awad, Joseph
    The Cave. P56
Awaiting Their Return. Katherine Nielsen
    Eckhart. P72
The Awakened Heart. Anne Yannie Corrado. P65
"Awakened before I meant". April. Alfred
    Corn. P79
"Awakened suddenly in dreams...". CIII. Raul
    Zurita. P71
Awakening. Ruth Newton Mattos. P72
Awakening. Margaret Elizabeth (Munson)
    Sangster. P81
Awakening to Music. Fred Chappell. P67
Awakenings (A Sedoka). Linda Hutton. P72
"Away in a manger, no crib for a bed".
    Cradle Hymn. Martin Luther. P51
Awdl. Saunders Lewis. P87
"Axes/After whose stroke the wood rings".
    Words. Sylvia Plath. P85
"The axioms chelated & dedritic". Mecox
    Motel. Anselm Parlatore. P64
"Ay! ay! ay! come out my people". These
    Things Amaze Me. Nyagak Pinien. P53
"Ay, tear her tattered ensign down!.". Old
    Ironsides. Oliver Wendell Holmes. P90
Ayer, Jean
    Everyday Things. P51
Ayoty, Ameen El (tr.)
    A Dialogue. Fatthy Said. P91
    Hymn of the Lyre Player. Fatthy Said. P91
Aytoun, William Edmonstoune
    The Broken Pitcher. P90
Azmi, Khalilur Rahman
    The Distance. C.M. Naim (tr.). P91
Aztec Gods. Rose Rosberg. P56
"Azure blue". The Primal Rain. Erika Schott.
    P72
"An azure sky". Christmas. Mary I. P51

Babicky, Charlotte L.
    Movement, Their Way. P72
Babies
    Baby Beds. Unknown. P51
    Baby May. William Cox Bennett. P89
    The Baby. Kalidasa. P89
    A Blessing for the Blessed, sel. Laurence
    Alma-Tadema. P51
"Babies asleep". Vespers. Hugh McKinley. P68
Baby Beds. Unknown. P51
Baby May. William Cox Bennett. P89
A Baby Verse. Unknown. P51
"Baby loves to play with me". Hide and Seek.
    Phyllis Drayson. P51
Baby-Land. George Cooper. P51
The Baby. Kalidasa. P89

15

Bache, Kaye
    To a Walker of Ridges. P68
Bachelor's Buttons. Maud Morin. P51
Back Country Feminist Landscape. Kay Murphy.
    P88
"Back and forth, back and forth". Fall 1961.
    Robert Lowell. P48
"Back turned to any question". I Never
    Realized. Teresa Calderon. P71
Backstage at the Fillmore. Elaine Demakas.
    P58
"Backward, turn backward, O time...". Rock
    Me to Sleep. Elizabeth Akers. P89
Bad Day. Marci Ridlon. P50
Badgers
    The Badgers. Eden Philpotts. P51
"Baghdad go princess". Mid Eastern. Michael
    Joseph Phillips. P56
Bagliore, Virginia
    The Runner. P72
Bagriana, Elisaveta
    Amazon. Maxine Kumin (tr.). P70
    Descendant. Maxine Kumin (tr.). P70
    The Elements. Maxine Kumin (tr.). P70
Bai, Lakshmi
    Sea Embrace. P72
Baigent, Beryl
    Man and Woman. P72
Bail, Grace Shattuck
    Night Music. P72
Bailey. Knute Skinner. P63
Bailey, Alice Morrey
    If This Be Love. P65
    Nouveau Poor. P65
Bailey, Rebecca
    Time. P73
Baker, Dorothy
    Castles in the Sand. P51
    In the Woods. P51
Baker, Keith
    Patient. P63
Baker, T. M.
    Johnny's Woodpile. P68
Bakers and Baking
    Miller, Miller. Ivy O. Eastwick. P51
Balaban, John (tr.)
    An Afternoon's Wandering. Kolyo Sevov.
    P70
    Cassandra with a Tail. Blaga Dimitrova.
    P70
    Dedication (To Tamara). Luchesar Elenkov.
    P70
    44, Avenue de Maine. Atanas Dalchev. P70
    Hunting Horn. Nikolai Kuntchev. P70
    Jellyfish. Nikolai Kuntchev. P70
    Let Him Be. Georgi Borisov. P70
    A Letter to My Mother in Vidin. Luchesar
    Elenkov. P70
    Lullaby for my Mother. Blaga Dimitrova.
    P70
"'Me, 20-Year-Old Sergeant, Ognyan
    Mihailov'". Luchesar Elenkov. P70
    Mondays. Miriana Basheva. P70
    On Leaving. Atanas Dalchev. P70
    On Their Day Off. Alexander Gerov. P70
    Painter of Icons. Luchesar Elenkov. P70
    Snow 1929. Atanas Dalchev. P70
    Song Between the Sea and Sky. Kolyo
    Sevov. P70
    The Sun. Alexander Gerov. P70
    A Tale. Georgi Borisov. P70
    The Town Tree. Alexander Gerov. P70
    Tree on the Hill. Ivan Tsanev. P70
    A Vision. Kolyo Sevov. P70
    The Water Buffalo (Hanoi, 1972). Blaga
    Dimitrova. P70
    Who Takes Care of the Blind Stork?. Blaga
    Dimitrova. P70
    A Woman Alone on the Road. Blaga
    Dimitrova. P70
"Balasore, on the bank of the river Bura-
    Balam". The Haldighat of New India.
    Kazi Nazrul Islam. P91
Balcom, John J. S. (tr.)
    My Cares. Hsiang Yang. P72
Baldwin, A. W. I.
    Ten Little Dicky-Birds. P51
The Ball Poem. John Berryman. P79
Ball, Jerald
    "Raindrops on Young Leaves". P72
    "Rosemary Blossoms". P72
Ballad for a Solonaut. Joanna Salamon. P92
The Ballad of Chocolate Mabbie, fr. A
    Street in Bronzeville. Gwendolyn
    Brooks. P84
The Ballad of Sue Ellen Westerfield. Robert
    Hayden. P84
Ballad of the Ladder. Lyubomir Levchev. P70
Ballad of the Progress. Jonas Negalha. P72
Ballads
    The Ballad of Chocolate Mabbie, fr. A
    Street in Bronzeville. Gwendolyn
    Brooks. P84
    The Ballad of Sue Ellen Westerfield.
    Robert Hayden. P84
    The Fair Damsel of Avalon. Haywood
    Jackson. P68
"Ballet/Tippy toes...". Dance. Alice E. W.
    Whitmore. P72
The Balloon Man. Rose Fyleman. P51
The Balloon Man. E. Herbert. P51
The Balloon Seller. Elizabeth Fleming. P51
Balloons
    The Balloon Man. Rose Fyleman. P51
    The Balloon Man. E. Herbert. P51
    The Balloon Seller. Elizabeth Fleming.
    P51
    Balloons. Bonnie Squires. P68

Balls
    Song for a Ball-Game. Wilfred Thorley.
        P51
Banani and Jascha Kessler, Amin (tr.)
    Grafts and the Garden. Mehdi Akhavan
        Sales. P91
    A Parched Pitcher. Mehdi Akhavan Sales.
        P91
    Rose. Mehdi Akhavan Sales. P91
' Banbury Fair'. Edith G. Millard. P51
"A Bang". Wind. Krishna Srinivas. P72
Bangkok Sights. Robert Schlosser. P86
Bangs, John Kendrick
    The Little Elf-Man. P51
Banisters
    On the Banisters. Margaret E. Gibbs. P51
Banks, George Linnaeus
    What I Live For. P89
Baptism. Claude McKay. P82
Baraka, Amiri (LeRoi Jones)
    An Agony. As Now. P85
    Beautiful Black Women. P85
    Goodbye! P85
    A Guerrilla Handbook. P85
    In Memory of Radio. P85
    Ka 'Ba. P85
    Political Poem. P85
    Preface to a Twenty Volume Suicide Note.
        P85
Barbara Frietchie. John Greenleaf Whittier.
        P51
Barbers
    Parlez-Vous Francais?. Delmore Schwartz.
        P84
Barbour, Douglas
    Autobiographical. P49
    The Image Repetition. P49
"The Bard of Avon as an eagle flies".
        Shakespeare. Raymond McCarty. P72
Bardis, Panos D.
    Cindy. P72
Barefoot. Robert N. Scott. P68
"Barely a twelvemonth after". The Horses.
        Edwin Muir. P48
"Barely smoking oak embers". On a Yankee
        Hill Morning. Steve LaVine. P77
Bargain Brief (Excerpt). Aline Musyl Marks.
        P65
Barker, Max S.
    Life. P68
Barnes, Dick
    Helendale. P63
Barnes, Mary Jane
    As Sea Birds Sail. P68
    The Chase. P72
    Love in Absentia. P68
    Massasoit. P68
    Through Night's Window. P68
Barnhorst, Colin

    Continental Drift. P68
Barr, Amelia Edith
    The Bottom Drawer. P89
Barra. Robert Lawrence. P49
The Barrel Organ. Alfred Noyes. P51
Barrett and Anita Skeen, Carol
    Interiors. P88
The Barrier (A Manardina). Dorman John
        Grace. P72
Barry, Jan
    In the Footsteps of Ghengis Khan. P86
Bars and Barrooms
    Erin Go Bragh. Jan Glazier. P56
    Tiger at the Bar. Chester G. Rider. P72
Bartee, Darrell H.
    What's Said of Love. P65
Barter. Sara Teasdale. P82
Barth, Louise
    Love's Meaning. P65
Barth, R. L.
    The Lighter That Never Fails. P86
    Observation Post. P86
Barton, Bernard
    Bruce and the Spider. P90
Barton, John
    Envoi. P49
    Metropolitan LIfe. P49
Baseball
    Casey at the Bat. Ernest Lawrence Thayer.
        P90
    Casey's Revenge. James Wilson. P90
    Casey-Twenty Years Later. S. P. McDonald.
        P90
Basheva, Miriana
    Mondays. John Balaban (tr.). P70
"(Bass drum beaten loudly.).". General
        William Booth Enters into Heaven.
        Vachel Lindsay. P82
Bassett, Lee
    Pizarro Teaches the Mentally Retarded To
        Swim. P57
Basty, Nicola
    Colors. P74
The Bat. Robert Hahn. P58
Bates, Arlo
    Death and Love. P81
    Night Song. P81
    There Is Such Power Even in Smallest
        Things. P81
    There Is Such Power, from Sonnets in
        Shadow. P90
Bates, Scott
    As I Was Dying at the Steak House... P63
    Bird Notes on a Beautifiul But Noisy
        April Morning. P63
    Fable of the Curious Crow and the Devious
        Weevil. P63
    Fable of the Terrorist Mouse. P63
    Guide to Paris: Eiffel Tower, Versailles.

P63
"Bathed icons of". Rock Art Prayer. Ron
    Pickup. P77
Baths and Bathing
    Five Women Bathing in Moonlight. Richard
        Wilbur. P84
    The Song of the Bath. Margaret E. Gibbs.
        P51
Bats
    The Bat. Robert Hahn. P58
    To the Bat. Edith King. P51
"Batter My Heart...," from Divine
    Mediations. John Donne. P59
Battle of Argoed Llwyfain. Taliesin. P87
Battle of Tal y Moelfre. Meilir ap
    Gwalchmai. P87
"The battle rent a cobweb diamond-strung".
    Range-Finding. Robert Frost. P82
Battle-Hymn of the Republic. Julia Ward
    Howe. P90
The Battle-Song of Gustavus Adolphus.
    Michael Altenburg. P90
Battlements. Harvey Shapiro. P64
Battles
    Battle of Argoed Llwyfain. Taliesin. P87
    Battle of Tal y Moelfre. Meilir ap
        Gwalchmai. P87
    Camp-Bell. Winthrop Mackworth Praed. P90
    Dutch Graves in Bucks County. Wallace
        Stevens. P83
    The Gododdin, sels. Aneirin. P87
    Incident at Bien Hoa. Herbert M. Kirkham.
        P68
    John Brown of Osawatomie. Edmund Clarence
        Stedman. P81
    Kearny at Seven Pines. Edmund Clarence
        Stedman. P90
    Monterey. Charles Fenno Hoffman. P90
    Okinawa 1945. Ivan McShane. P68
    Recessional. Rudyard Kipling. P90
    The Spooniad, from Spoon River Anthology.
        Edgar Lee Masters. P82
"Bauble-eyed crowd". Dreams-in-Progress.
    Gwendolyn Vincent. P58
Baucom, Margaret
    War or Peace. P72
Baudelaire, Charles
    Cat. Charles Guenther (tr.). P61
Baudin, Paul
    The Spirit of the Wood. P77
Bay Days. Howard Moss. P64
"The bay stretches out". Amphibian. Walter
    H. Kerr. P68
Baylor, Byrd
    Ka-Trum. P75
Bayly, Thomas Haynes
    Oh! Where Do Fairies Hide Their Heads?.
        P90
"' Be Pleased, Oh Beloved!'". Unknown. P62

Be Still. The Hanging Gardens Were a Dream.
    Trumbull Stickney. P81
"Be careful what". Zoo Manners. Eileen
    Mathias. P51
"Be doughty Artours dawes". Sir Launfal.
    Thomas Chestre. P66
"Be natural". The Name. Robert Creeley. P85
"Be not suspicious of the". The Special
    Language. Robert F. Allen. P65
"Be patient, O be patient! Put your ear...".
    Patience, from Poems of Freedom.
    William James Linton. P90
Beach. Juan Cameron. P71
The Beaches of Chile X. Raul Zurita. P71
"The beaches of Chile were nothing more...".
    The Radiant Beaches. Raul Zurita. P71
Bean, Abigail S.
    At Delphi. P68
"A beanfield in blossom smells as sweet".
    The Beanfield. John Clare. P51
The Bear. Galway Kinnell. P85
Bearded Oaks. Robert Penn Warren. P83
The Bearer of Evil Tidings. Robert Frost.
    P82
Bears
    The Bear. Galway Kinnell. P85
    Honey Bear. Elizabeth Lang. P51
"The beast lay". Decompostion. Terry M.
    Paulsgrove. P77
"Beast of Majiok". Kin to the Wolf. Unknown.
    P53
Beasts in Whoredom. Gaston Pelletier. P68
Beautiful Black Women. Amiri (LeRoi Jones)
    Baraka. P85
The Beautiful Changes. Richard Wilbur. P84
"Beautiful Evelyn Hope is dead!.". Evelyn
    Hope. Robert Browning. P89
Beautiful Meals. Thomas Sturge Moore. P51
"The Beautiful Women, in Separation...".
    Unknown. P62
"Beautifully Janet slept". Janet Walking.
    John Crowe Ransom. P83
Beauty
    Barter. Sara Teasdale. P82
    Beauty. Elinor Wylie. P82
    Beauty Competition. Fahmida Riyaz. P91
    A Beauty. Unknown. P87
    Blue Squills. Sara Teasdale. P82
    Euclid Alone Has Looked on Beauty Bare.
        Edna St. Vincent Millay. P82
    Evanescence. Harriet Elizabeth Spofford.
        P81
    I Love All Beauteous Things. Robert
        Bridges. P51
    "Just As the Day, When It Is Early
        Morning". Percivalle Doria. P69
    The Portrait. Thomas Heywood. P89
    Primer of Plato. Jean Garrigue. P84
    Song. Mark Akenside. P89

Thou Art Not Lovelier Than Lilacs,--No. Edna St. Vincent Millay. P82
To a Wind-Flower. Madison Cawein. P81
To a Young Woman. Louis Dudek. P49
Venus Transiens. Amy Lowell. P82
Beauty. Elinor Wylie. P82
Beauty Competition. Fahmida Riyaz. P91
"Beauty calls and gives no warning". Evensong. (Frederick) Ridgely Torrence. P81
A Beauty. Unknown. P87
"Because Her Breasts". Unknown. P62
"Because Love Is Not Invisible". Pier della Vigna. P69
"Because each act of creation is a miracle". Boschka Layton 1921-1984. Irving Layton. P49
"Because he was a butcher and thereby". Reuben Bright. Edward Arlington Robinson. P81
"Because I set no snare". Michael's Song. Wilfred Wilson Gibson. P51
"Because of the Evil Husband I Have". Compagnetto da Prato. P69
Because of You. Cecilia N. Rahl. P72
"Because She Is Overcome at Seeing You". Unknown. P62
"Because the terror they afflict me with...". Tablet IX. Armand Schwerner. P64
"Because there was disquiet in the wind". This Poor Man. William John Gruffydd. P87
"Because they could give it too much ground". In a Bird Sanctuary. Richard Wilbur. P84
Bechhold, Dorothy Mitchell
    Flood of Renaissance. P72
Beck Jr., Chester A.
    Voices from Pompeii. P68
Becker, Therese
    Beergarden Photo. P88
    Geese in Fog. P88
Bed-Time. Laurence Alma-Tadema. P51
Bed-Time. Thomas Hood. P51
Beddoes, Thomas Lovell
    Dream Pedlary. P51
Bedrock. Gary Snyder. P85
The Bedroom. Nino Nikolov. P70
"Bedrooms ease their shingles". East Hampton: The Structure of Sound. Philip Appleman. P64
Beds
    In Bed, sels. Kenneth Koch. P85
Bedtime
    Bed-Time. Laurence Alma-Tadema. P51
    Bed-Time. Thomas Hood. P51
    "Go to Bed Early Wake up with Joy". Unknown. P51

Bedtime Stories. Lilian Moore. P55
The Bee Meeting. Sylvia Plath. P85
"The Bee Which Indeed Wants to Drink the Nectar". Unknown. P62
Beeching, Henry Charles
    Prayers. P51
Been, Margaret Longenecker
    Let Wildness Come. P68
    While Summer Stays. P68
    The World Was No Temptation. P68
The Beer and the Bear. Robert N. Feinstein. P63
Beergarden Photo. Therese Becker. P88
Bees
    The Bee Meeting. Sylvia Plath. P85
    "The Bee Which Indeed Wants to Drink the Nectar". Unknown. P62
    "The Bees Wander Restlessly in the Mango Grove". Unknown. P62
    "The Nectar of the Jasmine Bud". Unknown. P62
    "Oh Bee Desirous of Drinking the Nectar". Unknown. P62
    "Once, Oh Ungrateful Bee". Unknown. P62
    The Queen Bee. Mary K. Robinson. P51
    What Does the Bee Do?. Christina Georgina Rossetti. P51
    "The Young Bees Pursue the Nail-Shredded Mango...". Unknown. P62
"The Bees Wander Restlessly in the Mango Grove". Unknown. P62
The Beet's Poem. Katharyn Machan Aal. P63
Beethoven Pathetique. Mary B. Finn. P68
"Beets: now there's a subject". The Beet's Poem. Katharyn Machan Aal. P63
"Before He Died," from Wolf Songs... Unknown. P78
Before Spring. P. A. Ropes. P51
"Before alighting, the soul sails...". Flight. Yahya Kemal. P91
"Before any contact--a firefight". Reasons Before and After the Fact. John C. Gilmore. P86
"Before I trust my fate to thee". A Woman's Question. Adelaide Anne Procter. P89
Before the First of the Next Month. Majeed Amjad. P91
Before They Made Things Be Alive They Spoke. Lucario Cuevish. P78
"Before the city, where the fields begin". Landscape. Axel Schulze. P92
"Before the ocean-horns of symphony". Memo to My Music Teacher. A. L. Lazarus. P63
"Before the solemn bronze Saint Gaudens made". An Ode in Time of Hesitation. William Vaughn Moody. P81
"Before too old and gaunt and bare". Dutch Elm Disease. George E. Morrissey. P68

The **Beggar** Maid. Lord Tennyson. P51
Beggars
    First Portrait. Sarmad Sehbai. P91
    The Jovial Beggar. Unknown. P51
    Market. Robert Hayden. P84
    The Rag Lady. Nancy McCleery. P88
    Second Portrait. Sarmad Sehbai. P91
Beginning Writer. Bonnie Squires. P72
Beh, Terry P.
    Zebras. P63
Behavior
    Naphiri. Edison Mpina. P92
Behind His Eyes. David Ignatow. P64
Behind These Lids. R. B. Weber. P64
"**Behind** him lay the gray Azores". Columbus.
    Joaquin Miller. P81
"**Behind** King's Chapel what the earth has
    kept". At the Indian Killer's Grave.
    Robert Lowell. P84
"**Behind** the elbow joint". Olecranon. Ernest
    Slyman. P63
"**Behind**, a spectral wake of fume on foam".
    The Approach. J. D. McClatchy. P79
Behn, Harry
    Ghosts. P55
    The Gnome. P55
"**Behold** the genial boy who promised much".
    Two Views of a Philosopher. Howard
    Nemerov. P79
"**Behold** where beauty walks with peace!.". A
    California Christmas. Joaquin Miller.
    P81
Behold, from the Land of the Farther Suns.
    Stephen Crane. P81
Behold, the Grave of a Wicked Man. Stephen
    Crane. P81
Beidog. Jeremy Hooker. P54
Being a Vietnam Veteran. Michael E. Merrill.
    P86
Being Born in the Woods. Bob D'Costa. P72
"**Being** his resting place". A Dog Sleeping on
    My Feet. James Dickey. P67
"**Being** myself so corrupted". Expecting the
    Lord. Ann Griffiths. P87
Belabored Blossom. M. Yvette Hamilton. P56
Belev, Georgi
    Life. Daniel Weissbort (tr.). P70
"**Belgium**, 1944, is another place...". Foot
    Soldier. Rhea Tregebov. P49
Belief
    A Formal Appeal. Kaleem Omar. P91
    The Garrison. W. H. Auden. P79
    Heresy. Gwendolyn Vincent. P58
    A Sword in a Cloud of Light. Kenneth
    Rexroth. P84
    What I Live For. George Linnaeus Banks.
    P89
"**Belief** persists which I cannot ignore".
    After Long Grief. Jaye Giammarino. P72

Belinda. Jack H. Palmer. P68
Belitt, Ben
    Charwoman (Lower Manhattan--6:00 P.M.).
    P57
    Veteran's Hospital. P57
"**Bell** Horses, Bell Horses". Unknown. P51
Bell, Bernard
    Taking a Step. P73
Bell, J. J.
    The Lights. P51
    The Ships. P51
"The **bell-rope** that gathers God at Dawn".
    The Broken Tower. Hart Crane. P83
Belloc, Hilaire
    The Early Morning. P51
    The Elephant. P51
Bells
    The Angelus. Edwin Markham. P81
    The Bells of London. Unknown. P51
    Chimes. Alice Meynell. P51
    Ding-Dong!. Unknown. P51
    Silver Bells. Hamish Hendry. P51
Bells for John Whiteside's Daughter. John
    Crowe Ransom. P67,P83
The **Bells** of Heaven. Ralph Hodgson. P51
The **Bells** of London. Unknown. P51
The **Bells** of Youth. William ("Fiona
    Macleod") Sharp. P51
Belly Dancer. Diane Wakoski. P85
Belsaray, Srinivas
    "Do You Remember Sometimes". P72
Belsen, Day of Liberation. Robert Hayden.
    P84
"**Belshazzar** had a letter,--.". Found
    Wanting. Emily Dickinson. P89
Ben Johnson Entertains a Man from Stratford.
    Edward Arlington Robinson. P81
Benado, Anna Marie
    The Prayer. P72
Bence, Jeff
    Pride of the Farmer. P74
"**Bend** willow, willow bend down deep". Willow
    Bend and Weep. Herbert Clark Johnson.
    P90
Bending the Bow. Robert Duncan. P84
Beneath Each Stone. Walter Hoefler. P71
"**Beneath** my feet the heart of earth".
    Continental Drift. Colin Barnhorst.
    P68
"... **beneath** the rocks the forgotten
    dead...". East, sel. Gonzalo Munoz.
    P71
"**Beneath** the ten gauge fountain". Concrete
    Green. David Schuster. P56
Benedict, Burnette B.
    Loving Lessons (Grandmother). P72
Benediction. Mary Eleanor Cox. P72
Benedictus. Diane Scharper. P68
Benet, Stephen Vincent

Nightmare for Future Reference. P48
Benfras, Dafydd
From Exile. Tony Conran (tr.). P87
"Benn making caskets for fifty-five years".
Making Caskets. Ann Jonas. P56
Bennett, Bruce
Against Waking Early. P63
A Cow's Life. P63
The Dangerous Cliffs. P63
Epitaph for the Lemon Lady. P63
Garza. P63
The Passionate Businessman To His Love.
P63
The Poet Redgrove. P63
The Stones of Florence. P63
Bennett, Rodney
And Back. P51
A Christmas-Tree Song. P51
Easter Praise. P51
Fluttering Leaves. P51
The Growing River. P51
Little Brown Seed. P51
The Little Old Lady. P51
Merry Birds. P51
Mr. Brown. P51
Mrs. Jenny Wren. P51
My Dog, Spot. P51
The Pigeons. P51
Postman's Knock. P51
Robin's Song. P51
Ten Little Christmas Trees. P51
A Thank You for Friends. P51
There--. P51
Three Little Men in a Boat. P51
Wireless. P51
Writing Letters. P51
Bennett, Rowena
Shell Castles. P76
Bennett, William Cox
Baby May. P89
Invocation to Rain in Summer. P89
To a Cricket. P51
"Bent low over the handlebars". The
Cyclists. John C. Pine. P77
Bent, O. M.
The Robin. P51
Benton, Joel
December. P89
Beowulf. Richard Wilbur. P84
Berg, Maryleona
Meeting a Lovely Lady. P68
Berg, Sharon
The Birth Poem. P49
Breastfeeding at the Art Gallery of
Ontario... P49
Berger, Bruce
Bitter Grapes. P63
MSG. P63
One-Up. P63

Bergman, James P.
A.W.O.L. P86
Buffalo Bill Revisited. P86
Vietnam. P86
"Water Buffalo". P86
Berks, Miriam F.
Mary: to Her Completed Child (A Song of
Hope). P72
Berlind, Bruce (tr.)
Four Squares. Agnes Nemes Nagy. P92
The Ghost. Agnes Nemes Nagy. P92
Storm. Agnes Nemes Nagy. P92
Streetcar. Agnes Nemes Nagy. P92
To My Craft. Agnes Nemes Nagy. P92
Bermuda
Bermudas. Andrew Marvell. P59
Bermuda Dream. Katharine Wilson. P72
Bermudas. Andrew Marvell. P59
Bernier, Jack
Flowerings. P56
Berola, Gina
No More. P74
Berry, Wendell
In Rain. P67
The Slip. P67
Where. P67
Work Song. P67
Berryman, John
The Ball Poem. P79
The Dispossessed. P84
The Dream Songs, sels. P84
The Dream Songs, sels. P52
Drunks. P79
Friendless. P79
Homage to Mistress Bradstreet, sels. P84
Monkhood. P79
The Moon and the Night and the Men. P84
The Poet's Final Instructions. P84
Revival. P79
Winter Landscape. P79
The **Berserker**. Blessing Richard A. P68
Berstein, Barbara S.
Conversation in June. P68
"**Beside** a green meadow a stream used to
flow". Cow and the Ass. Ann and Jane
Taylor. P51
Besides. Mark Irwin. P63
Bess, Robert
Domestic Birds. P63
Best of All. J. M. Westrup. P51
The **Best** of All. Margaret G. Rhodes. P51
Bethlehem. William Canton. P51
The **Betrayal** of Violets. Mohammed Ibrahim
Abu Sinnah. P91
Better Refrain. Marian Gleason. P63
"**Better** trust all and be deceived". Faith.
Frances Anne Kemble-Butler. P89
Betts, Gregory
Hearing Heaney Read. P49

Stormwatch: Fogo Island. P49
Betty at the Party. Unknown. P51
"Between me and the rising sun". Cobwebs. E.
      L. M. King. P51
"Between me and the sunset, like a dome".
      The Man Against the Sky. Edward
      Arlington Robinson. P81
"Between my nape and my hand". Fable of
      First Person. Gyorgy Somlyo. P92
"Between night and early day". A Wisconsin
      Dawn. Abby Arthur Johnson. P68
"Between nose and eyes a strange
      contest...". The Nose and the Eyes.
      William Cowper. P90
Between the Anthill and the Heglig Tree.
      Unknown. P53
Beverly Carneiro. Robert Hill Long. P63
"Beware of the ones with red lips". Advice
      Against Thumbers. Harold Bond. P63
Beware the Tides of March. Charles L. Grove.
      P63
Beyond Recall. Robert W. Johnston. P72
Beyond Torture. Aristoteles Espana. P71
Beyond Words. Richard Howard. P79
"Beyond my window in the night". A Town
      Window. John Drinkwater. P51
"Beyond the Isar,-- Reichsdruckmeisterei".
      Siegfriedslage. Lincoln Kirstein. P79
The Bhagavadgita, sel. Unknown. P48
The Bhagawan Buddha. K. K. Moorthy. P72
Bhaskar, Sindhu Ratna Kul
      295. i. P72
"Bi a forest as I gan fare". The Mourning of
      an Hare. Unknown. P66
Bible
      A Biblical Motif. Boris Khristov. P92
      Lines Found in his Bible in the Gate-
      House... Sir Walter Raleigh. P89
      Mary Passed This Morning. Owen Dodson.
      P84
      My Mother's Bible. George Pope Morris.
      P89
      Song of Solomon, Old Testament. Unknown.
      P60
      What Do I Know of the Old Lore?. Robert
      Duncan. P84
A Biblical Motif. Boris Khristov. P92
A Biblical Motif. Boris Kristov. P70
Bicycles
      Bike Flight. Amy Hundley. P74
Big Bang. Jay Meek. P63
The Big Bang. Howard Nemerov. P63
Big Basin Waterfall. Ellis Ovesen. P72
The Big Knot. Nyalual Pal. P53
"Big Rabbit Goes To See His Baby". Unknown.
      P78
Big Wind. Theodore Roethke. P84
"Big bird to paradise". A.W.O.L. James P.
      Bergman. P86

"Big feet". Feet. Irene Thompson. P51
"A big grey elephant". Just Jumbo. Eileen
      Mathias. P51
"Big grown-up parents of iron arms". Do
      Parents Cry, too?. Thad King. P73
Bigamy
      "That Redness of Her Lip". Unknown. P62
Bike Flight. Amy Hundley. P74
Biles, David
      Dragon's Jaw. P86
      Pleiku. P86
"The bilge is a block of ice". Wishing for
      Water in February. Elisavietta
      Ritchie. P56
"Bill the Bachelor lived by himself".
      Bachelor's Buttons. Maud Morin. P51
Billings, Robert
      At Billings' Bridge Graveyard. P49
Billy Boy. Dorothy King. P51
Bingoholic. Shirley Volger Meister. P63
Binyon, Laurence
      The Little Dancers. P51
      Song. P51
      This Is England. P51
Biography
      On Instant Lives. Roy Blount Jr. P63
Bion
      I Dreamt I Saw Great Venus. Leigh Hunt
      (tr.). P89
Birch, Karen
      Glass Walls. P73
The Bird at Dawn. Harold Monro. P51
The Bird Bath. Florence Hoatson. P51
Bird Notes on a Beautifiul But Noisy April
      Morning. Scott Bates. P63
"The bird glides and soars--.". Mystery in
      Flight. Patricia M. Johnson. P72
"A bird springs from the shirt...". Sonnet 1,
      fr. Three Sonnets From 'Deep Within
      the Heart'. Syed Shamsul Haque. P91
Bird's Nests. Millicent Seager. P51
Bird's Nests. Unknown. P51
"A bird's so fine and careless". Rew di
      ranno. Unknown. P87
The Birdie's Breakfast. Unknown. P51
Birds
      Advice to a Blue-Bird. Maxwell Bodenheim.
      P82
      The Autumn Robin. John Clare. P51
      Awaiting Their Return. Katherine Nielsen
      Eckhart. P72
      The Bird at Dawn. Harold Monro. P51
      The Bird Bath. Florence Hoatson. P51
      Bird Notes on a Beautifiul But Noisy
      April Morning. Scott Bates. P63
      Bird's Nests. Millicent Seager. P51
      Bird's Nests. Unknown. P51
      The Birdie's Breakfast. Unknown. P51
      The Birds Have Gone. Omar Lara. P71

The Birds on the School Windowsill.
    Evelyn Dainty. P51
The Birds. Samuel Taylor Coleridge. P51
The Blackbird. Humbert Wolfe. P51
The Blackbird. D. M. Mulock. P51
The Blackbird. Phyllis Drayson. P51
Blue Heron Near the Old Mill Bridge.
    Raymond Souster. P49
The Bobolinks. Christopher Pearse Cranch.
    P89
The Brown Thrush. Lucy Larcom. P51
The Browny Hen. Irene F. Pawsey. P51
Chinese Finches. Katha Pollit. P79
Cocks and Crows. Gavin Ewart. P63
Come Here, Little Robin. Unknown. P51
The Crow. Mrs. Alexander. P51
The Cuckoo. Unknown. P51
Dickey-Birds. Natalie Joan. P51
The Ditances They Keep. Howard Nemerov.
    P79
Domestic Birds. Robert Bess. P63
"The Dove Says Coo". Unknown. P51
Doves. E. J. Falconer. P51
Duck's Ditty. Kenneth Grahame. P51
The Duck. Edith King. P51
Ducks. Norman Ault. P51
Ducks, sel. F. W. Harvey. P51
The Eagle Exterminating Company. James
    Tate. P85
The Eagle. Lord Tennyson. P51
"A Farmer Went Trotting on His Grey
    Mare". Unknown. P51
Field Guide to North American Birds.
    Barbara Crooker. P63
The Fifteen Acres. James Stephens. P51
Fish and Bird. Rosemary Brinckman. P51
Footprints of a Sparrow. N. M. Bodecker.
    P80
For Robin. Stella Browning. P72
Forest. Yaedi Ignatow. P64
Four Scarlet Berries. Mary Vivian. P51
Gay Robin Is Seen No More. Robert
    Bridges. P51
'Good Night', Says the Owl. Lady Erskine
    Crum. P51
The Gosling. Gary Erb. P56
The Green Cornfield. Christina Georgina
    Rossetti. P51
Gull Passage by Moonlight. Milton Acorn.
    P49
Hark! Hark! the Lark. William
    Shakespeare. P51
"Hickety, Pickety". Unknown. P51
"High in the Pine-Tree". Unknown. P51
Hurt Hawks. Robinson Jeffers. P83
In a Bird Sanctuary. Richard Wilbur. P84
Inner Eye. T. A. Shulgin. P58
L'Oiseau Bleu (The Blue Bird). Mary E.
    Coleridge. P51

Lines to the Stormy Petrel. Unknown. P89
A Little Bird's Song. Margaret Rose. P51
Little Birds of the Night. Stephen Crane.
    P81
"A Little Cock Sparrow Sat on a Tree".
    Unknown. P51
Little Friend. David Ignatow. P64
"Little Jenny Wren". Unknown. P51
Little Robin Redbreast. Unknown. P51
"Little Robin Redbreast". Unknown. P51
Little Trotty Wagtail. John Clare. P51
Lonesome Bird. Etty George. P72
Merry Birds. Rodney Bennett. P51
Michael Met a Duck. J. Dupuy. P51
Michael's Song. Wilfred Wilson Gibson.
    P51
Mining in Killdeer Alley. Dabney Stuart.
    P67
The Mocking-Bird. Frank Lebby Stanton.
    P89
Mother Duck. Ann ("Aunt Effie")
    Hawkshawe. P51
Mrs. Jenny Wren. Rodney Bennett. P51
Myths and Texts (Hunting). Gary Snyder.
    P85
Naming the Birds. Jeanne Lohmann. P65
Nicki's Sparrow. Susan Richardson. P56
Night Music. Grace Shattuck Bail. P72
The Nightingale. Katharine (Hinkson)
    Tynan. P51
Nuthatch. Edward Coletti. P63
One Blackbird. Harold Monro. P51
The Oven Bird. Robert Frost. P82
The Owl and the Nightingale, sels.
    Unknown. P66
The Owl. Bryan Waller ("Barry Cornwall")
    Procter. P89
The Owl. Lord Tennyson. P51
The Parrot's Scream. Charles H. Howe. P68
The Peacock. James Merrill. P85
The Pigeon's Story. Jeannie Kirby. P51
The Pigeons. Rodney Bennett. P51
Please Bird. Kazue Mizumura. P80
Purple Grackles. Amy Lowell. P82
Rew di ranno. Unknown. P87
The Rivals. James Stephens. P51
River Roads. Carl Sandburg. P82
"Robin Sang Sweetly". Unknown. P51
Robin's Song. Rodney Bennett. P51
The Robin. O. M. Bent. P51
The Robin. Laurence Alma-Tadema. P51
The Sandpiper. Charlotte Zolotow. P76
Scaring Crows. Unknown. P51
The Scream. Majeed Amjad. P91
The Sea-Gull. Mary Howitt. P51
The Secret. Elizabeth Fleming. P51
The Singers in a Cloud. (Frederick)
    Ridgely Torrence. P81
Song. Samuel Taylor Coleridge. P51

The Song of the Bird. Henry Wadsworth
   Longfellow. P51
Statue and Birds. Louise Bogan. P83
Strange Bird. Stefan Tsanev. P70
Ten Little Dicky-Birds. A. W. I. Baldwin.
   P51
"There Is a Wonder in the Sweep". Mary G.
   Faulconer. P72
Thirteen Ways of Looking at a Blackbird.
   Wallace Stevens. P83
Three Little Birds. Stephen Crane. P81
The Thrush's Nest. John Clare. P51
The Thrush. Dafydd ab [or ab] Gwilym. P87
The Tit. Llywelyn Goch ap Meurig Hen. P87
"To Guide You, He Is". David Kuehnert.
   P77
To the Cuckoo. William Wordsworth. P51,
   P89
Tourists. Josephine Miles. P84
The Town Tree. Alexander Gerov. P70
Two Little Blackbirds. Unknown. P51
Under the Vulture-Tree. David Bottoms.
   P67
Valentine's Day. Charles Kingsley. P51
Vespers. T. E. Brown. P51
"Welcome, Little Robin". Unknown. P51
What the Thrush Says. Queenie Scott-
   Hopper. P51
When the Mocking Bird Sings. Harriet G.
   Hunt. P72
Who Takes Care of the Blind Stork?. Blaga
   Dimitrova. P70
Who?. Florence Hoatson. P51
A Widow Bird. Percy Bysshe Shelley. P51
The Woodpecker. Joyce Sambrook. P51
The **Birds** Have Gone. Omar Lara. P71
"**Birds** and bees and butterflies". Out of
   Doors. E. North. P51
"The **birds** go fluttering in the air". The
   Silent Snake. Unknown. P51
"**Birds** in a whirl, drift to the rooftops".
   Myths and Texts (Hunting). Gary
   Snyder. P85
The **Birds** on the School Windowsill. Evelyn
   Dainty. P51
The **Birds**. Samuel Taylor Coleridge. P51
Birney, Earle
   Rot Below Adam's Peak (Sri Lanka). P49
   Still Life Near Bangalore. P49
Birth
   Being Born in the Woods. Bob D'Costa. P72
   The Birth Poem. Sharon Berg. P49
   First Calving. Nigel Jenkins. P54
   "Intense Physical Pain". Joseph P.
      Butler. P72
   Leaving the Door Open (31), sel. David
      Ignatow. P64
   Love Songs. Mina Loy. P82
   Mary: to Her Completed Child (A Song of

      Hope). Miriam F. Berks. P72
   Poem to Ease Birth. Unknown. P78
   Pregnant Thought. Merry Harris. P63
   The Ring of. Charles Olson. P85
   To Shelley. John Banister Tabb. P81
   Virginia. Lorene Erickson. P88
Birth of the Daisies. Ruth Krauss. P50
The **Birth** Poem. Sharon Berg. P49
"**Birth/Young**, happy". Life. Chrystie Fulmer.
   P74
Birthday Poem. Al Young. P85
A **Birthday** Present. Sylvia Plath. P85
Birthdays
   Birthday Poem. Al Young. P85
   A Birthday Present. Sylvia Plath. P85
   A Giant's Cake. Evelina San Garde. P51
Bishai, Nadia
   Poem. P92
Bishop, Elizabeth
   A Cold Spring. P84
   The Fish. P84
   Florida. P84
   The Imaginary Iceberg. P84
   The Man-Moth. P84
   The Map. P84
   The Monument. P84
   Questions of Travel. P84
Bishop, John Peale
   Always, from My First Boyhood. P83
   In the Dordogne. P83
Bison
   Ka-Trum. Byrd Baylor. P75
   A Song of the Red & Green Buffalo.
      Unknown. P78
   "Water Buffalo". James P. Bergman. P86
Bissett, Bill
   Dew Yu Know. P49
   Looking for th Innr Life in 100 Mile. P49
   Th Lovr Sighs if It All Revolvs Around
      Yu. P49
Biswakesh
   Relics of Love. P72
"**Bit** by bit, as in a picture puzzle". Letter
   to Shadow. Daryl Hine. P79
A **Bit** of Colour. Horace Smith. P51
A **Bit** of Enlightenment. Tom Riley. P63
Bitek, Okot p'
   Song of Lawino, sel. P92
Bithell, Jethro (tr.)
   The Silent Town. Richard Dehmel. P89
Bitter Grapes. Bruce Berger. P63
Bitter-Sweet. George Herbert. P59
Bittern He Took a Bundle. Unknown. P87
Bjornson, Bjornstjerne
   The Boy and the Flute. Sir Edmund Gosse
      (tr.). P89
Black Americans
   Black Majesty. Countee Cullen. P83
   Cultural Exchange. Langston Hughes. P83

Headache. Orhan Veli Kanik. P91
Ka 'Ba. Amiri (LeRoi Jones) Baraka. P85
Theme for English B. Langston Hughes. P83
Black and White. Carolyn Delaney. P74
Black Beloved. Jamini K. Jagadev. P65
Black Lightning. Arthur Sze. P57
Black Mail. Maryann Calendrille. P64
Black Majesty. Countee Cullen. P83
Black Migrants. Pearl Crayton. P68
Black Riders. Stephen Crane. P81
The **Black** Vulture. George Sterling. P81
"**Black** as a chimney is his face". 'Sooeep!'.
      Walter De La Mare. P51
"**Black** cattle anchor". Along the Roadside.
      Edna Jones. P68
"**Black** doe hides". Whitetail, 2:30 a.m.
      Diane P. Lando. P77
"**Black** milk of daybreak we drink...". Death
      Fugue. Paul Celan. P48
"**Black** oil slick eyes". Bright Sunday.
      Elaine Demakas. P58
"**Black** power surges". Dance. Patricia
      Glasgow. P68
"The **black** stealthy shadow runs into the".
      Seekers of Freedom. Walt Jones. P86
Black-Eyed Susan. John Gay. P89
"**Black**-beaked/With blue and yellow wings".
      The Scream. Majeed Amjad. P91
"**Black**/Darkness". Navajo Correspondences
      (Second Set). Unknown. P78
The **Blackbird**. Phyllis Drayson. P51
The **Blackbird**. D. M. Mulock. P51
The **Blackbird**. Humbert Wolfe. P51
Blackout into Sunlight. Yaedi Ignatow. P64
Blacksmith. B. K. Pyke. P51
Blacksmiths and Blacksmithing
      The Blacksmiths. Unknown. P66
      Tubal Cain. Charles Mackay. P90
      The Village Blacksmith. Henry Wadsworth
      Longfellow. P89
The **Blacksmiths**. Unknown. P66
Blackwood, Algernon
      Jack O' the Inkpot. P51
"**Bladud** hafde enne sunne. Leir wes ihaten".
      Brut, sels. Unknown. P66
Blake, James Neal
      My Lady, Lady Jane (Raindrop Tears). P72
Blake, William
      The Divine Image. P51
      The Echoing Green. P51
      The Four Zoas: 'Night the Ninth, Being
      the Last...'. P48
      Jerusalem. P51
      The Lamb. P51
      Laughing Song. P51
      Night. P51
      Opportunity. P90
      The Piper. P51
      The Shepherd. P51

Spring. P51
To Spring. P51
The Tyger. P51
Wild Flower's Song. P51
Blaker, Margaret
      "Hernando DeSoto". P63
"**Blame** this island town for the broken boy".
      The Sentry of Portoferraio. Daniel
      Mark Epstein. P57
Blanchard, Laman
      The Mother's Hope. P89
Bland, Robert (tr.)
      Home. Leonidas. P89
Blank Spaces. Mary Ann Henn. P56
Blankenhorn, Lorraine
      The Road to a Friend's House. P72
Blankenship, F. Anthony
      Taxi Number One-Forty-Nine. P68
Blankner, Frederika
      Annunciation. P65
      Flame of God. P65
      Idyll. P65
      Love Song: Pincio, sels. P65
      Maiden. P65
The **Blanks**. Sheryl L. Nelms. P56
"**Blasted** with sighs, and surrounded with
      tears". Twicknam Garden. John Donne.
      P59
"The **bld**. in my body weighs". Bleeder.
      Hollis Summers. P57
"**Bledsian**, berserker, viking in my veins".
      The Berserker. Blessing Richard A. P68
Bleeder. Hollis Summers. P57
"**Bless** You, Bless You, Bonnie Bee". Unknown.
      P51
"**Blessed** Are the Deaf and Blind". Unknown.
      P62
"**Blessed** Are Those Women". Unknown. P62
Blessed Is the Light. Grace Schulman. P64
Blessing Richard A.
      The Berserker. P68
A **Blessing** for the Blessed, sel. Laurence
      Alma-Tadema. P51
Blessings
      Brother Ass and St. Francis. John
      Banister Tabb. P81
      Christmas Carol. Unknown. P51
      I Am Thankful. Evan Daniels. P74
      Lovely Things. H. M. Sarson. P51
      The Robin's Song. Unknown. P51
      School Creed. Unknown. P51
      The Sisters. John Banister Tabb. P81
Blind Dates. Kandy Arnold. P58
The **Blind** Men and the Elephant. John Godfrey
      Saxe. P90
The **Blind** Men and the Elephant. John Godfrey
      Saxe. P51
Blind William's Song. William Stanley
      Merwin. P85

"A **blind** girl". Black Lightning. Arthur Sze.
    P57
"The **blind** have eyes within". Deductions.
    Teresa Calderon. P71
Blind, Mathilde
    The Mystic's Vision. P89
"The **blindfold** is a slice of darkness". The
    Blindfold. Aristoteles Espana. P71
Blindness
    Black Lightning. Arthur Sze. P57
    Der Blinde Junge. Mina Loy. P82
    The Lace Maker. Barbara Howes. P57
    The Passenger. Kaleem Omar. P91
    Vision. Gonzalo Millan. P71
    Visit to the Institute for the Blind.
        Felix Pollak. P57
Block of Wood. Jauvanta Walker. P68
Block, Alexander
    The Willow-boughs. P51
Bloes, Henry
    Dear Mother. P72
Blomster, Heidi
    Nocturne. P68
Blood and Silence. Ahmad 'Abd Al-Muti
    Hijazi. P91
"The **blood** is sure that courses every vein".
    Love's Meaning. Louise Barth. P65
"**Blood** thins--washing suddenly". Pedestrian.
    Virginia M. Hahn. P58
Blood, Marie
    The Message. P72
Bloomfield, Maureen
    Clara Schumann at the Piano. P88
Blossoms
    Apple Blossoms. Helen Adams Parker. P51
Blount Jr., Roy
    Gutes and Eulas. P63
    On Instant Lives. P63
Blow, Blow, Thou Winter Wind, from As You
    Like It. William Shakespeare. P89
Blue (color)
    God Complex, from Lost Youth: the Last
        War. Alfred Kreymborg. P82
The **Blue** and the Gray. Francis Miles Finch.
    P90
Blue Angels Sky-Dance. Zelma S. Dennis. P72
Blue Danube. Manuel Silva Acevedo. P71
Blue Girls. John Crowe Ransom. P83
Blue Heron Near the Old Mill Bridge. Raymond
    Souster. P49
Blue Island Intersection. Carl Sandburg. P82
Blue Magic. Roberta Goldstein. P72
Blue Poem. Hubert E. Hix. P63
Blue Squills. Sara Teasdale. P82
The **Blue** Symphony. John Gould Fletcher. P82
"**Blue** palm prints of children". The Thousand-
    and-One Nights. Gwendolyn Vincent. P58
"**Blue** wind strains the naked trees". Winter.
    Gary Erb. P56

"**Blue,** brown, blue: sky, sand, sea". XVIII,
    from Irradiations. John Gould
    Fletcher. P82
Bluebells. Olive Enoch. P51
Bluebells. Juliana Horatia Ewing. P51
Bluebells. P. A. Ropes. P51
Blues (music)
    Homesick Blues. Langston Hughes. P83
    The Weary Blues. Langston Hughes. P83
Blunden, Edmund
    The Idlers. P51
    The Midnight Skaters. P89
Blunt, Lynn
    He Was a King. P73
"The **blurred** wooden walls". Near the Screen
    Door. Kevin Cline. P58
Blustering God. Stephen Crane. P81
Blyton, Enid
    Fairy Music. P51
    The Field-Mouse. P51
    What Piggy-Wig Found. P51
    Winter. P51
"A **boat** with a cargo of peanuts passes...".
    For Armando Rubio. Mauricio Electorat.
    P71
"A **boat,** beneath a sunny day". Life, What Is
    It but a Dream?. Charles Lutwidge
    ("Lewis Carroll") Dodgson. P90
The **Boathouse.** Robert Minhinnick. P54
Boats Sail on the Rivers. Christina Rosetti.
    P51
Boats and Boating
    The Gondola. Arthur Hugh Clough. P90
    A Kayak Song. Lucy Diamond. P51
    Lonely Boat. Carla Zeppieri. P74
    River Boats. Grace D. Yerbury. P68
    Stormwatch: Fogo Island. Gregory Betts.
        P49
    Three Little Men in a Boat. Rodney
        Bennett. P51
    Through the Porthole. Marjorie Wilson.
        P51
    Wishing for Water in February.
        Elisavietta Ritchie. P56
"**Bobby** Newly". Portrait. Dick Hayman. P63
The **Bobolinks.** Christopher Pearse Cranch.
    P89
Boccaccio, Giovanni
    Of Three Girls and of Their Talk. Dante
        Gabriel Rossetti (tr.). P90
Bodecker, N. M.
    Footprints of a Sparrow. P80
Bodenheim, Maxwell
    Advice to a Blue-Bird. P82
    Death. P82
    Hill-Side Tree. P82
    Impulsive Dialogue. P82
    Old Age. P82
    The Old Jew. P82

Rear-Porches of an Apartment-Building.
    P82
Songs to a Woman. P82
Bodenstedt, Friedrich Martin von
    Unchanging. P89
Body (human)
    The Body Is Like Roots Stretching Down
        into the Earth. Charles Reznikoff. P83
    Francis Bacon, the Inventor of
        Spectacles... Cynthia MacDonald. P79
    The Garden. Louise Gluck. P85
    The Heavy Bear Who Goes with Me. Delmore
        Schwartz. P84
    Meditations on the Body: Right Hand.
        Maxine Silverman. P88
    Woodknot. Allen Planz. P64
Body Bags, sel. Michael Andrews. P86
The Body Is Like Roots Stretching Down into
    the Earth. Charles Reznikoff. P83
Bogadi, Stephen L.
    Don't Be Afraid To Grow. P72
Bogan, Louise
    Cassandra. P83
    The Dream. P83
    Medusa. P83
    Men Loved Wholly Beyond Wisdom. P83
    Night. P52
    Statue and Birds. P83
    Women. P83
"The Bogus Bride-Night Garment". Unknown.
    P62
Boiles, Charles (tr.)
    Thought-Song One, from Tepehua Thought-
        Songs. Unknown. P78
    Thought-Song Three, from Tepehua Thought-
        Songs. Unknown. P78
    Thought-Song Two, from Tepehua Thought-
        Songs. Unknown. P78
The Boiling Water. Kenneth Koch. P64
Bolay, Karl H.
    Les Saintes-Maries De La Mer. P72
Bolle, Kees W. (tr.)
    The Bhagavadgita, sel. Unknown. P48
Bolls, Imogene
    Hole. P63
Bond, Harold
    Advice Against Thumbers. P63
    The Game. P57
Bone Thoughts on a Dry Day. George Starbuck.
    P85
"Bones I can understand. One after another".
    The South Shore (Aberystwyth). Bobi
    Jones. P87
Bones and Jewels. Paul Monette. P79
The Bones of My Father. Etheridge Knight.
    P52
Boney, Elaine E. (tr.)
    'The Ninth Elegy', from The Duinesian
        Elegies. Rainer Maria Rilke. P48

Bonnard. Christopher Middleton. P79
Bonnette, Jeanne
    Grate Fire. P65
Boobiat. Paul Humphrey. P63
The Book of Chilam Balam: a Chapter..., sel.
    Unknown. P78
"A book of Metaphysics". Piece de
    Resistance. Ann Deagon. P63
Bookends. James W. Proctor. P65
Books. John Higgins. P90
Books and Reading
    The Message. Marie Blood. P72
    My Old Journal. Joanne Adamkewicz. P73
    The Old Bookseller. Gilani Kamran. P91
    Open Sesame. Unknown. P51
    Read the Great Poets. James Tate. P85
    A Shelf Is a Ledge. Gregory Orr. P85
    Song of Lawino, sel. Okot p' Bitek. P92
    Wandering Was Always an Important Theme
        in My Lyric. Tetsuo Nakagami. P92
    What Sparks My Imagination. Kelli Jensen.
        P73
Boots and Shoes
    Boots and Shoes. Lilian McCrea. P51
    The Furry Home. J. M. Westrup. P51
    Jeremy Hobbler. Unknown. P51
Boots and Shoes. Lilian McCrea. P51
    Oh, Dem Olden Slippers!. Alma Denny. P63
    The South Shore (Aberystwyth). Bobi
        Jones. P87
Borba, Jerry F.
    Where God Rested His Head. P72
Boredom
    Rain. Brian Lee. P75
    The Shadow and the Cross. Salah Abdul-
        Sabur. P91
    Tired Tim. Walter De La Mare. P51
Borisov, Georgi
    Let Him Be. John Balaban (tr.). P70
    A Tale. John Balaban (tr.). P70
Born Tying Knots. Samuel Makidemewabe. P78
"Born of the sorrowful of heart". For Paul
    Laurence Dunbar, fr. Four Epitaphs.
    Countee Cullen. P83
Borson, Roo
    City. P49
Boschka Layton 1921-1984. Irving Layton. P49
Bosquet, Alain
    A Good-by. Charles Guenther (tr.). P61
    He Invents a Vertigo. Charles Guenther
        (tr.). P61
    A Nail for Hanging the Soul. Charles
        Guenther (tr.). P61
Boston, Massachusetts
    Communication to the City Fathers of
        Boston. George Starbuck. P85
    Where the Rainbow Ends. Robert Lowell.
        P84
"Both have been weather beat". Man Holding

Cat. Raymond Roseliep. P68
"Both robbed of air, we both lie...". Four
      Epigrams. John Donne. P59
The Bottom Drawer. Amelia Edith Barr. P89
Bottomley, Gordon
      Dawn. P51
Bottoms, David
      Shooting Rats at the Bibb County Dump.
         P67
      Under the Boathouse. P67
      Under the Vulture-Tree. P67
"The boughs do shake and the bells do ring".
      Harvest Song. Unknown. P51
Boughtwood, Alice
      Love. P68
Boughtwood, Alice M.
      Alchemy. P68
      I, Golden Strings. P68
      Let Beauty Shine. P68
      Tiny Grandchild at the Beach. P68
"Bounce ball! bounce ball!". Song for a Ball-
      Game. Wilfred Thorley. P51
"The boundaries of dull straight thinking
      blur". The Primitive Astronomer. Tom
      Riley. P63
Bousono, Carlos
      Three Poems on Death. Charles Guenther
         (tr.). P61
Bovine Town. Mildred Luton. P63
"A Bow, Returning to Its Natural
      Straightness". Unknown. P62
"Bowed by the weight of centuries he leans".
      The Man with the Hoe. Edwin Markham.
      P81
Bowen, Charles
      The Rain It Raineth. P75
Bowen, Euros
      Dylan Thomas. Tony Conran (tr.). P87
      Glint. Tony Conran (tr.). P87
      The Swan. Tony Conran (tr.). P87
      Wild Duck. Tony Conran (tr.). P87
Bowery. David Ignatow. P84
Bowring, Sir John
      From the Recesses of a Lowly Spirit. P89
Boxes
      Sand Scribblings, sel. Carl Sandburg. P76
The Boy and the Deer. Andrew Peynetsa. P78
The Boy and the Flute. Bjornstjerne
      Bjornson. P89
The Boy and the Wolf. Reed Whittemore. P63
The Boy Wants to Leave. Norman H. Russell.
      P68
The Boy Who Killed His Mother. F. Scott
      Fitzgerald. P63
"The boy cried wolf". The Boy and the Wolf.
      Reed Whittemore. P63
"The boy stood on the burning deck".
      Casabianca. Felicia Dorothea Hemans.
      P90

The Boy's Song. Zahid Dar. P91
The Boy's Song. James Hogg. P51
A Boy. John Ashbery. P85
Boydston, Mildred B.
      Space Exploration. P72
Boynton, Maria E.
      In Wonderment. P72
Bozhilov, Bozhidar
      Men. Cornelia Bozhilova (tr.). P70
      Ode to Noise. Cornelia Bozhilova (tr.).
         P70
      Poets. Cornelia Bozhilova (tr.). P70
      Relativity. Cornelia Bozhilova (tr.). P70
Bozhilova, Cornelia (tr.)
      Men. Bozhidar Bozhilov. P70
      Ode to Noise. Bozhidar Bozhilov. P70
      Poets. Bozhidar Bozhilov. P70
      Relativity. Bozhidar Bozhilov. P70
"A brackish reach of shoal off Madaket--".
      The Quaker Graveyard in Nantucket.
      Robert Lowell. P84
Bradley, Ardyth
      Hospital. P88
Bradley, Christine E.
      Skippets, the Bad One. P51
Bradley, George
      Expecting an Angel. P79
      Six of One. P64
      Walking Sag Beach. P64
Bradley, Robert B.
      Reality. P72
Bradshaw, Irene A.
      Octogenarian. P72
Brahma. Ralph Waldo Emerson. P89
Brain
      Brain Wave. Vera Joyce Nelson. P72
Braine, Sheila
      Mr. Scarecrow. P51
Bramble Jam. Irene F. Pawsey. P51
The Branch. Stanley Moss. P64
Brass, Perry
      Airport. P65
      If I Swallowed. P65
      Spun to Life. P65
Bratesch, Verona
      Mysterious Evening. Werner Manheim (tr.).
         P72
Braun, Alicia
      My Name Is Man. P73
Braunecker, Lee Ann
      An Orphan's Wish. P74
The Brave Old Oak. Henry Fothergill Chorley.
      P89
Bravery
      Harmosan. Richard Chenevix Trench. P90
      The Lord of Butrago. John Gibson
         Lockhart. P90
      There Was a Man and a Woman. Stephen
         Crane. P81

Viet Kong. William Trowbridge. P63
Bread. H. E. Wilkinson. P51
Bread and Apples. Lisel Mueller. P88
Bread and Music. Conrad Aiken. P82
"**Bread** is a lovely thing to eat--.". Lovely
       Things. H. M. Sarson. P51
"**Break** forth, break forth, O Sudbury town".
       Lydia. Lizette Woodworth Reese. P81
"**Break** their paws and backs". Two Fool's
       Songs. Emile Verhaeren. P61
Breakfast
       Eggs for Breakfast. Irene F. Pawsey. P51
Breaking Silence. Janice Mirikitani. P85
"**Breaking** the commandments, upholding
       thieves". It Must Someday be Answered.
       Elidir Sais. P87
"The **breaking** waves dashed high". The
       Pilgrim Fathers. Felicia Dorothea
       Hemans. P51
Breastfeeding at the Art Gallery of
       Ontario... Sharon Berg. P49
Breasts
       "Because Her Breasts". Unknown. P62
       The Breasts of Women. David Kirby. P63
"The **breath** of lilies and the hush of
       wings". Annunciation. Frederika
       Blankner. P65
"**Breathe-in** experience, breathe out poetry".
       Poem Out of Childhood. Muriel
       Rukeyser. P84
Breathes There the Man?. Sir Walter Scott.
       P90
Breathing in the Woods. Judith Minty. P88
Breban, Nicolae
       Indian Summer. Malinda Cox (tr.). P92
Brechfa Chapel. Roland Mathias. P54
Breckenridge, Jill
       Attitudes of Thanksgiving. P88
"The **breeze** is on the bluebells". Bluebells.
       Juliana Horatia Ewing. P51
Brennan, Ian
       Untitled #1. P58
       Untitled #2. P58
       Untitled #3. P58
       Untitled #4. P58
Brereton, E. C.
       Three Dogs. P51
Breslin, Kristen
       My Brother. P73
Brewster, Elizabeth
       Is the Pathetic Fallacy True?. P49
The **Bride** of Spring. I. H. Rizvi. P72
A **Bride** of the 80's, Down the Aisle. Blanche
       Farley. P63
"The **Bride's** Beloved's Laughter-Filled
       Eyes". Unknown. P62
"The **bride**, white of hair...". To Have and
       Too Old. Richard Armour. P63
The **Bridge**. Harvey Shapiro. P64

Bridges
       Dragon's Jaw. David Biles. P86
       The Old Bridge at Florence. Henry
              Wadsworth Longfellow. P90
       Proem: To Brooklyn Bridge, fr. The
              Bridge. Hart Crane. P83
Bridges, Pat
       Find the Nerve To Get Excited. P56
       For a Flower Whose Name I Don't Know. P56
Bridges, Robert
       The Cliff-Top. P51
       First Spring Morning. P51
       Gay Robin Is Seen No More. P51
       I Love All Beauteous Things. P51
       I Will Not Let Thee Go. P89
       So Sweet Love Seemed. P89
       Spring Goeth All in White. P51
       The Upper Skies. P51
A **Brief** Resume of the Last 20 Years... Wayne
       Kvam. P68
"The **brief** truce, the night of prey...".
       Hotel De La Gare. Waldo Rojas. P71
"**Brief**, on a flying night". Chimes. Alice
       Meynell. P51
Briggs, David
       Thunderstorms. P73
Bright Sunday. Elaine Demakas. P58
"**Brimming** with emptiness". A Parched
       Pitcher. Mehdi Akhavan Sales. P91
Brinckman, Rosemary
       Fish and Bird. P51
"**Bring** me a letter, postman!.". The Postman.
       Alice Todd. P51
"**Bring** the biggest bath you've seen". The
       Song of the Bath. Margaret E. Gibbs.
       P51
"**Bring** the comb and play upon it!.".
       Marching Song. Robert Louis Stevenson.
       P51
"**Bringing** 'only what is needed--
       essential'.". Veteran's Hospital. Ben
       Belitt. P57
"The **bringing** forth of life". Life. Kathleen
       Chan Wallace. P72
Brisley, Joyce L.
       The Two Families. P51
Britain, Phillip
       Crippled Walls. P72
"The **broad** sun". The Far-Farers. Robert
       Louis Stevenson. P51
"The **broad-bellied** hippopotamus". The
       Hippopotamus. Theophile Gautier. P61
"**Brocks** snuffle from their holt within". The
       Badgers. Eden Philpotts. P51
The **Broken** Home. James Merrill. P85
The **Broken** Pianola. Ralph Gustafson. P49
The **Broken** Pitcher. William Edmonstoune
       Aytoun. P90
Broken Stanza. Jamini K. Jagadev. P65

The **Broken** Sun. Anthony (Tony). Kellman. P68
The **Broken** Tower. Hart Crane. P83
"The **broken** pillar of the wing jags...".
    Hurt Hawks. Robinson Jeffers. P83
Bromeliad. Cathy Matyas. P49
The **Broncho** That Would Not Be Broken. Vachel
    Lindsay. P82
Bronze Trumpets and Sea Water--on Turning
    Latin... Elinor Wylie. P82
Brood Queen (A Vision of Moths). Charles P.
    Martin. P58
The **Brook**. Robert Minhinnick. P54
The **Brook**. Lord Tennyson. P51
Brooks and Streams
    Beidog. Jeremy Hooker. P54
    The Brook. Robert Minhinnick. P54
    The Brook. Lord Tennyson. P51
    Down by the Brook. Tim Henderson. P74
    Stopping by Brook at 18. Genevieve
        Sargent. P72
Brooks, Andrew
    For Barbara. P49
Brooks, Charles Timothy (tr.)
    The Fisher. Johann Wolfgang von Goethe.
        P90
    Harvest Song. Ludwig Holty. P89
    Men and Boys. Karl Theodor Korner. P90
    The Nobleman and the Pensioner. Gottlieb
        Conrad Pfeffel. P90
    Winter. Mathias Claudius. P89
    Winter Song. Ludwig Holty. P89
Brooks, Gwendolyn
    The Ballad of Chocolate Mabbie, fr. A
        Street in Bronzeville. P84
    Cynthia in the Snow. P80
    Hunchback Girl: She Thinks of Heaven, fr.
        A Street... P84
    The Independent Man, fr. A Street in
        Bronzeville. P84
    Kitchenette Building, fr. A Street in
        Bronzeville. P84
    The Lovers of the Poor. P84
    Maurice. P50
    The Mother, fr. A Street in Bronzeville.
        P84
    Negro Hero. P84
    Of De Witt Williams on His Way to Lincoln
        Cemetery, fr. A... P84
    The Preacher: Ruminates Behind the Sermon,
        fr. A Street... P84
    Sadie and Maud, fr. A Street in
        Bronzeville. P84
    A Song in the Front Yard, fr. A Street in
        Bronzeville. P84
    Southeast Corner, fr. A Street in
        Bronzeville. P84
    The Vacant Lot, fr. A Street in
        Bronzeville. P84
Brooks, Maria Gowen

    Song of Egla. P89
The **Brookside**. Richard Monckton Milnes; 1st
    Baron Houghton. P89
Brother Ass and St. Francis. John Banister
    Tabb. P81
Brother Jonathan's Lament for Sister
    Caroline. Oliver Wendell Holmes. P90
"' **Brother** Micha was a good man'.". Last
    Rights. Lu Spurlock. P56
Brothers and Sisters
    Farewell. Cyril Dabydeen. P49
    Five Sisters. Kate Greenaway. P51
    The Horrible Noise. Samantha Adams. P74
    Iqleema. Fahmida Riyaz. P91
    My Brother. Kristen Breslin. P73
    Sadie and Maud, fr. A Street in
        Bronzeville. Gwendolyn Brooks. P84
    The 'Thing' in My House. Heather D.
        Soldato-Subkis. P73
"**Brought** low in Kyoto". How To Survive
    Nuclear War. Maxine Kumin. P48
The **Brown** Frog. Mary K. Robinson. P51
The **Brown** Thrush. Lucy Larcom. P51
"**Brown** and furry". The Catepillar. Christina
    Georgina Rossetti. P51
"**Brown** bunny sits inside his burrow". The
    Rabbit. Edith King. P51
"**Brown** eyes". Polly. William Brighty Rands.
    P89
Brown, John Gracen
    Ice Skaters. P68
Brown, Kate Louise
    The Five-Fingered Maple. P51
    The Lady Moon. P51
    Pine Music. P51
Brown, LoVerne
    Amadeus. P63
Brown, Sterling A.
    After Winter. P89
    Old Lem. P89
Brown, T. E.
    Vespers. P51
Browne, Frances
    O, the Pleasant Days of Old!. P90
Browne, Michael Dennis
    His Toys. P63
Brownell, Henry Howard
    John Brown's Body. P90
Browning, Elizabeth Barrett
    A Musical Instrument. P90
    A View Across the Roman Campagna. P90
Browning, Robert
    Evelyn Hope. P89
    Home Thoughts from Abroad. P51,P89
    How They Brought the Good News from Ghent
        to Aix. P90
    Incident of the French Camp. P90
    The Piped Piper of Hamelin, sel. P51
    Pippa's Song. P51

Youth. P51
Browning, Stella
    For Robin. P72
Brownstone Revisited. Mary B. Finn. P68
Browny Bee. Irene F. Pawsey. P51
The Browny Hen. Irene F. Pawsey. P51
Bruce and the Spider. Bernard Barton. P90
Brugaletta, John J.
    A Lust for the Quaint Old Ways. P63
Bruno, Scott
    Limerick. P73
Brut, sels. Unknown. P66
Bryant, Helen
    Old Woman Doctor. P68
Bryant, Sylvia L.
    A Dream. P72
Bryant, William Cullen
    The Hurricane. P90
    June. P89
    O, Fairest of Rural Maids! P89
Brynbeidog. Jeremy Hooker. P54
Bubbles. L. Nicholson. P51
Buchanan, Robert
    The Little Herd-Boy's Song. P51
Buddha and Buddhism
    The Bhagawan Buddha. K. K. Moorthy. P72
    Buddhist Moon. Prince Chand. P72
    Haein-Sa Temple. Cho Byung-Hwa. P72
    Mahayana, from Paradise. Montri
        Umavijani. P72
"Buddha's Disciples". Sakuzo Takada. P72
Buddhist Moon. Prince Chand. P72
"The budding leaf that welcomes spring".
    Awakening. Ruth Newton Mattos. P72
Buffalo Bill Revisited. James P. Bergman.
    P86
Buffalo Blood. Lance Henson. P78
"The Buffalo, Tormented by the Heat".
    Unknown. P62
Bugs. Carole Oles. P48
"The Bugville team...". Casey-Twenty Years
    Later. S. P. McDonald. P90
Building
    Building for Love. Unknown. P87
    The Tree House. Kaleem Omar. P91
Building for Love. Unknown. P87
"Buildings above the leafless trees".
    Central Park at Dusk. Sara Teasdale.
    P82
"The buildlings are Bradys--.". Reflections
    in the River. James Stephens. P68
Buk Teny Men
    Out of Step. Terese Svoboda (tr.). P53
Buk Teny Women
    He'd Eau Lizards. Terese Svoboda (tr.).
    P53
Bukan. Emha Ainunn Nadjib. P92
Bulgaria. Georgi Djagarov. P70
Bullata, Issa (tr.)

Blood and Silence. Ahmad 'Abd Al-Muti
    Hijazi. P91
The Shadow and the Cross. Salah Abdul-
    Sabur. P91
A Song from Afar. Ahmad 'Abd Al-Muti
    Hijazi. P91
Song of a Dead Pilot. Ahmad 'Abd Al-Muti
    Hijazi. P91
A Song to God. Salah Abdul-Sabur. P91
Bulls
    Crossing the Plains. Joaquin Miller. P81
    No Man's Good Bull. James Seay. P67
"Bumpety, bumpety, bump". Fan, the Filly.
    Wilfred Thorley. P51
"Bums are the spirit of us parked...".
    Bowery. David Ignatow. P84
Bumstead, Eudora S.
    A Summer Lullaby. P51
Bunny Rabbit. Walter De la Mare. P51
Bunse, Lois
    Ox-Eye Daisy. P77
Bunston de Bary, Anna
    Snowdrop. P51
Bunyan, J.
    The Shepherd Boy's Song. P51
Bunyan, John
    The Pilgrim. P51
"Buoyancy/The wind moves". Images of
    Gravity. Grace Schulman. P64
Burch, F. F.
    In a Station of the IRT. P63
"Burdened with diadem, the". Here. Fred
    Chappell. P67
Burdette, Robert Jones
    When My Ship Comes in. P89
Bureaucrat. Lyubomir Levchev. P70
Burgess, Gavin
    The Trust. P72
Burgess, Gelett
    The Purple Cow. P90
Burial. Alice Walker. P67
Burial of Sir John Moore. Charles Wolfe. P90
Burial of the Dead, fr. The Waste Land.
    Thomas Stearns Eliot. P83
Buried Love. Sara Teasdale. P82
A Buried One in Me Sings. Salvatore
    Quasimodo. P61
Buried Treasure
    Ocean Treasures. Constance Andrea
        Keremes. P76
"The burned and dusty garden said:.". An
    Athenian Garden. Trumbull Stickney.
    P81
The Burning Babe. Robert Southwell. P59
Burning Brambles. Roland Mathias. P54
Burning the Christmas Greens. William Carlos
    Williams. P82
Burning the Letters. Randall Jarrell. P84
"Burning upon some hidden shore". The

Lighthouse. Marjorie Wilson. P51

Burnished. Anne Stevenson. P54

Burns (A Poet's Epitaph). Ebenezer Elliot.
      P90

Burns, Allan F. (tr.)
      Conversations in Mayan. Alonzo Gonzales
            Mo. P78
      How Just One Poor Man Lives. Alonzo
            Gonzales Mo. P78
      Things That Happen to You. Alonzo
            Gonzales Mo. P78
      Wizards. Alonzo Gonzales Mo. P78

Burns, Robert
      Auld Lang Syne. P89
      My Heart's in the Highlands. P90

Burns, Robert
      Burns (A Poet's Epitaph). Ebenezer
            Elliot. P90

Burroughs, John
      Waiting. P89

Bursting. Dorothy Aldis. P50

"Bus driver". We Thank You!. L. E. Cox. P51

The Bus. Peter [pseud.]. P51

Busacca, Helle
      Poesia 50 (The Quanta of Anguish). P72

Busch, T.
      Marking Time. P77

A Bushel of Chaff. John Ceiriog Hughes. P87

Business Luncheon. Joel Ferree. P63

"Busy old fool, unruly sun". The Sun Rising.
      John Donne. P59

But I Do Not Need Kindness. Gregory Corso.
      P85

"But a little while ago". Winter and Spring.
      Coventry Patmore. P51

"But chief-surpassing all--a cuckoo
      clock!.". The Cuckoo Clock, from The
      Birthday. Caroline Bowles Southey. P90

"But still after seven years I met you...".
      Eurydice. Hugh Seidman. P64

"But what dream is this on whose shore...".
      We Will Not Hand Over the Night. Waldo
      Rojas. P71

"But you must speak with water...". L'Anne:
      Water in My Hands. Jerry Craven. P65

Butler, Joseph P.
      "Intense Physical Pain". P72

Butscher, Edward
      After Great Pain. P64
      At Play in the Field. P64
      Cleaning the Garage. P64
      Hand Lane: Literature. P64
      Middle Age Summer. P64

A Buttercup. Unknown. P51

Buttercups. Unknown. P51

Buttercups and Daisies. Mary Howitt. P51

"Buttercups golden and gay". Buttercups.
      Unknown. P51

Butterflies

Butterflies. Heather Marshall. P74

The Butterfly. Margaret Rose. P51

Haiku. Laura Davis. P73

Jewels of Freedom. Julia Nelson Walke.
      P68

Butterflies. Heather Marshall. P74
      Roots and Branches. Robert Duncan. P84

"Butterflies fan fragile, filmy wings".
      Twice a Child. Naomi Long Madgett. P88

"A butterfly comes". Haiku. Laura Davis. P73

The Butterfly. Margaret Rose. P51

"' Buy that blouse,' she whispered".
      Christine, on Her Way to China: An
      Earthquake Poem. Judith Minty. P88

Buzzard. Gillian Clarke. P54

"The buzzards over Pondy Woods". Pondy
      Woods. Robert Penn Warren. P83

"By a clear well, within a little field". Of
      Three Girls and of Their Talk.
      Giovanni Boccaccio. P90

"By a quiet little stream on an old mossy
      log". The Frog and the Bird. Vera
      Hessey. P51

"By dark severance the apparition head".
      Painted Head. John Crowe Ransom. P83

"By ear, he sd.". I, Maximus of Gloucester,
      to You. Charles Olson. P85

"By God, you're a fine wood, hillock". To
      the Greyrock Woods. Llywelyn ap y
      Moel. P87

"By such an all-embalming summer day". Near
      Helikon. Trumbull Stickney. P81

By the Pacific Ocean. Joaquin Miller. P81

"By the fall of years I learn...". Work
      Song. Wendell Berry. P67

"By the flow of the inland river". The Blue
      and the Gray. Francis Miles Finch. P90

"By the moon we sport and play". The
      Urchin's Dance. John Lyly. P51

"By the North Gate, the wind blows...".
      Lament of the Frontier Guard. Ezra
      Pound. P82

"By the road to the contagious hospital".
      Spring and All. William Carlos
      Williams. P82

"By the rude bridge that arched the flood".
      Hymn. Ralph Waldo Emerson. P90

"By the turn of the driveway...". Aspects of
      Lilac. Howard Moss. P64

"By the wireless I can hear". Wireless.
      Rodney Bennett. P51

Bychan, y Prydydd
      Elegy for Rhys Gryg. Tony Conran (tr.).
      P87

Byron, George Gordon, 6th Baron
      Darkness. P48
      Evening, from Don Juan. P89
      Farewell to His Wife. P89
      To Thomas Moore. P90

Byung-Hwa, Cho
    Haein-Sa Temple. P72

Cadnum, Michael
    Waiting for the Detective. P63
"Caedmon/Was thought a madman". A Literary
    History of Cheese. Roberta Simone. P63
"Caesar, the amplifier voice, announces".
    Parlez-Vous Francais?. Delmore
    Schwartz. P84
"Cala-Achi! Ha! Aha!...". Rabinal-Achi: Act
    IV. Unknown. P78
Calderon de la Barca, Pedro
    On Living, from Life Is a Dream. Arthur
    Symons (tr.). P90
Calderon, Teresa
    Code of Waters. Steven F. White (tr.).
    P71
    Deductions. Steven F. White (tr.). P71
    Face to Face in Another Time. Steven F.
    White (tr.). P71
    I Never Realized. Steven F. White (tr.).
    P71
    Of the Nameless Birds. Steven F. White
    (tr.). P71
    The Time That Destroys Everything. Steven
    F. White (tr.). P71
Calendar Rhyme. Flora Willis Watson. P51
Calendrille, Maryann
    Black Mail. P64
    In the Big Country Dreams Stay Alive. P64
    New Moon or No?. P64
    See Jane Run. P64
    Tomorrow in a Bubble. P64
Caliban in the Coal Mines. Louis Untermeyer.
    P82
"The Calico fish". Upwardly Mobile Bean
    Curd. Bonnie Jacobson. P63
California
    A California Christmas. Joaquin Miller.
    P81
    One West Coast. Al Young. P85
    Song of Pasadena. Wen-Ying Hsu. P72
A California Christmas. Joaquin Miller. P81
California Street. Kandy Arnold. P58
The Call of the Hills. Laurie Dalziel. P68
"Call the roller of big cigars". The Emperor
    of Ice-Cream. Wallace Stevens. P83
Callaghan, Barry
    Assonance. P49
    Mother and Son. P49
    Snowfall. P49
    So It Was Done. P49
Callimachus
    The Dead Poet-Friend. William Johnson
    Cory (tr.). P89

The Calling Mountain. Wazir Agha. P91
"Calm was the sea to which your course you
    kept". To W.P. George Santayana. P81
Calmer, Gail
    Loveliness. P68
Calmly We Walk Through This April's Day.
    Delmore Schwartz. P84
Calvin. Bayla Winters. P56
The Camel's Complaint [or, Plaint of the
    Camel]. Charles Edward Carryl. P51,90
Cameron, Bella
    Without a Prop. P72
Cameron, Juan
    Beach. Steven F. White (tr.). P71
    Heraclitus. Steven F. White (tr.). P71
    Imperfect Preterite. Steven F. White
    (tr.). P71
    Route Seven. Steven F. White (tr.). P71
    The Signalled Hour. Steven F. White
    (tr.). P71
    Subway. Steven F. White (tr.). P71
    When It's Over. Steven F. White (tr.).
    P71
The Camp at Night, from The Iliad. Homer.
    P89
Camp of the Winds. Pearl Newton Rook. P72
Camp, James
    From an Athlete Living Old. P63
    A Note Toward a Definition of Culture.
    P63
    The Race. P63
    The Rose and the Worm. P63
Camp-Bell. Winthrop Mackworth Praed. P90
Campbell, Jennifer
    Rain on the Island. P74
Campbell, Thomas
    Exile of Erin. P90
    The First Kiss. P89
    Lord Ullin's Daughter. P51,P90
Campbell, Tracy
    Temperature, Temperature. P74
Campfire. Marsh Cassady. P56
Camping and Campers
    The Camp at Night, from The Iliad. Homer.
    P89
    Things to Do Around a Lookout. Gary
    Snyder. P85
"The campion white". The Lamp Flower.
    Margaret Cecilia Furse. P51
Campion, Thomas
    Advice to a Girl. P89
The Campus on the Hill. William DeWitt
    Snodgrass. P85
"Can nobody". Mea Culpa, from Lost Youth:
    the Last War. Alfred Kreymborg. P82
"Can these movements which move themselves".
    Belly Dancer. Diane Wakoski. P85
"Can we poets win the peace?.". Peace in Our
    Time. Minnie Klemme. P72

Canary Morning at the Stop of Darkness. Emma
       Crobaugh. P68
"**Canary-birds** feed on sugar and seed". The
       Camel's Complaint [or, Plaint of the
       Camel]. Charles Edward Carryl. P51,90
Cancion. Denise Levertov. P85
Canciones sin Su Musica. Tomas Segovia. P92
Candle Light. Kum Chan Hwang. P72
Candles
       Tallow. Bruce Kingery. P68
Candy
       Chocolates. Louis Simpson. P85
Candy Stores
       The Pennycandystore Beyond the El.
       Lawrence Ferlinghetti. P85
Cannaday, Mark L.
       Unlikely Path. P68
Cannaday, Mark Lawson
       Peering at the Past. P68
Cannon, Maureen
       Sponge. P63
"The **cannon-smoke** rolling". Rhigos. Robert
       Minhinnick. P54
The **Canonization.** John Donne. P59
Canton, William
       Bethlehem. P51
       A Child's Prayer. P51
Cantoni, Louis J.
       Plaything of the Gods. P72
The **Cantos,** sel. Ezra Pound. P82
Canzoneri, Robert
       Syntax. P63
Capital. John Tripp. P54
"**Capsized,** by some nosing cow". The Ridger.
       Nigel Jenkins. P54
Captain Carpenter. John Crowe Ransom. P83
Captivity
       Crossing the Plains. Joaquin Miller. P81
Captured City. Omar Lara. P71
Caravan. Irene Thompson. P51
The **Caravan.** Madeleine Nightingale. P51
Carden, Lois Roquemore
       "Mariposa Lilies". P72
Cardenal, Ernesto
       Apocalypse. Robert Mill-Pring (tr.). P48
The **Care** and Feeding of a Poet. James
       Laughlin. P63
"**Careful:** my knife drills your soul". The
       Killer. Unknown. P78
Carew, Thomas
       Disdain Returned. P89
       Now That the Winter's Gone. P51
Carey, Henry
       Sally in Our Alley. P89
Carey, Mary P. (Mary Dalles)
       The Cricket. P68
       A Midnight Storm To Turn to. P68
Caribbean
       Letter from the Islands. Diana

       Kwiatkowski. P56
Carl Hamblin, from Spoon River Anthology.
       Edgar Lee Masters. P82
Carleton, Will
       Over the Hill to the Poor-House. P89
Carlson, Mark
       I'm Happy. P73
Carman, Bliss
       Hack and Hew. P90
Carmel by the Sea. Alessandra A. Poles. P72
Carmina LXXII of Catullus. Richard Lovelace.
       P59
Carol. Unknown. P51
The **Carol** Singers. Margaret G. Rhodes. P51
Carols
       The Corpus Christi Carol. Unknown. P66
Carp. M. Rose. P77
Carpe Diem, from The House of a Hundred
       Lights. (Frederick) Ridgely Torrence.
       P81
Carpenter, William
       Origins of the Body. P48
       Running in Winter. P48
Carrieri, Raffaele
       The Green Comb. Charles Guenther (tr.).
       P61
Carroll, Lewis. See Dodgson, Charles L.
Carryl, Charles Edward
       The Camel's Complaint [or, Plaint of the
       Camel]. P51,90
Carson, Jeane C.
       Aurora Borealis. P72
Carter, D.
       Mrs. Indiarubber Duck. P51
Carter, Ellin E.
       Since That Time. P56
Cary, Carl (tr.)
       "I Thought You Were Good". Unknown. P78
       "Now You Love Me". Unknown. P78
       One for Coyote. Unknown. P78
       The Origin of the Skagit Indians... Lucy
       Williams. P78
Casa, Giovanni della
       To Sleep. John Addington Symonds (tr.).
       P89
Casabianca. Felicia Dorothea Hemans. P90
Casey and the Vespula Diabolica. Beverley W.
       Stein. P72
Casey at the Bat. Ernest Lawrence Thayer.
       P90
Casey's Revenge. James Wilson. P90
Casey-Twenty Years Later. S. P. McDonald.
       P90
Casino Royale. Estelle M. Zelner. P72
Cassady, Marsh
       Campfire. P56
Cassandra. Louise Bogan. P83
Cassandra. Faye Kicknosway. P88
Cassandra. Edward Arlington Robinson. P81

Cassandra with a Tail. Blaga Dimitrova. P70
Castell Carreg Cennen. Nigel Jenkins. P54
The Castle by the Sea. Johann Ludwig Uhland.
     P90
Castles
     The Court of Owain Glyndwr at Sycharth.
          Iolo Goch. P87
     The Hall of Ifor Hael. Ieuan Brydydd Hir.
          P87
     Praise of Tenby. Unknown. P87
     Sand Castle. Constance Andrea Keremes.
          P76
Castles in the Sand. Dorothy Baker. P51
Casto, Keith
     Oh, Now I See... P63
     She Don't Bop. P63
Casual Encounter. Edna Bacon Morrison. P68
Cat. Charles Baudelaire. P61
Cat. Josephine Miles. P84
"A Cat Came Fiddling Out of a Barn".
     Unknown. P51
The Cat of Cats. William Brighty Rands. P90
"A cat stretches from one end". Cassandra
     with a Tail. Blaga Dimitrova. P70
The Cat. Julie [pseud.]. P72
Cataract. Theodore Weiss. P84
The Cataract of Lodore. Robert Southey. P90
"Catbirds have inherited the valley".
     Country Music. James Merrill. P79
The Catepillar. Christina Georgina Rossetti.
     P51
The Catholic Martyrs. Waldo Williams. P87
Catina, Ray
     Job Action. P86
     Wise Guys. P86
Cats
     "All Day". Steve Sanfield. P77
     Cassandra with a Tail. Blaga Dimitrova.
          P70
     Cat. Josephine Miles. P84
     Cat. Charles Baudelaire. P61
     The Cat of Cats. William Brighty Rands.
          P90
     The Cat. Julie [pseud.]. P72
     'Four-Paws'. Helen Parry Eden. P51
     Haiku. Matthew Woomer. P74
     Jessie's Cat. Dawn E. Rutter. P72
     The Kitten at Play. William Wordsworth.
          P51
     Kitty. Unknown. P51
     Letting the Cat Die. Gwendolyn Vincent.
          P58
     Milk for the Cat. Harold Monro. P51
     Peace! We Are Saying?. Edna Meudt. P68
     Poem. William Carlos Williams. P82
     "Pussy Cat, Pussy Cat, Where Have You
          Been?". Unknown. P51
     Pussy-Cat and Puppy-Dog. Lilian McCrea.
          P51

     Stepping Out with My Big Cats. Naomi
          Lazard. P64
     Three Little Kittens a Cat's Tale with
          Additions. Eliza Lee Follen. P89
     The Three Little Kittens. Unknown. P51
     Two Little Kittens. Jane Taylor. P51
     What a Fondness!. C. K. Shreedharan. P72
     "Where Are You Going". Unknown. P51
     "'Who's That Ringing at the Front Door
          Bell?'". Unknown. P51
Cattails. Richard Hugo. P79
Caudill, Rebecca
     I Stare. P75
     Summer Storm. P75
     This Year. P75
"Caught in the camera's click of time". The
     Image. Mary B. Finn. P68
"Caught!/But don't stretch your hand".
     Unforgettable Summers. David Winwood.
     P92
Cauquil. Sergio Mansilla. P71
Cause of My Distress. Har Prasad Sharma. P72
Causley, Charles
     Tell Me, Tell Me, Sarah Jane. P76
Caution
     "Go Slowly Over the Stones". Paz Molina.
          P71
     Haste Not! Rest Not!. Johann Wolfgang von
          Goethe. P90
     Homing. Stanley Moss. P64
     My Own Good. Pamela Painter. P88
     The Next Step. W. D. Ehrhart. P86
     Unforgettable Summers. David Winwood. P92
Cave Series, sel. Margaret Atwood. P49
The Cave. Joseph Awad. P56
Caves
     In Front of the Cave. Nikolai Hristozov.
          P70
"' Caw,' said the rook". Bird's Nests.
     Millicent Seager. P51
Cawein, Madison
     Comradery. P81
     Dirge. P81
     The Man Hunt. P81
     To a Wind-Flower. P81
Cedering, Siv
     Fata Morgana. P64
     On Some Such Morning. P64
     On This Shore. P64
     Sea-Drift. P64
Cedifor, Peryf ap
     The Killing of Hywel. Tony Conran (tr.).
          P87
Celan, Paul
     Death Fugue. Michael Hamburger (tr.). P48
The Celestial Passion. Richard Watson
     Gilder. P81
"Celestial choir! enthron'd in realms of
     light". His Excellency General

Washington. Phillis Wheatley. P90
Cells Breathe in the Emptiness. Galway
    Kinnell. P85
Cemeteries
    Arlington. Edison Mpina. P92
    At Melville's Tomb. Hart Crane. P83
    At the Grave of Walker. Joaquin Miller.
        P81
    At the Indian Killer's Grave. Robert
        Lowell. P84
    Buried Love. Sara Teasdale. P82
    Cool Tombs. Carl Sandburg. P82
    Dirge. Madison Cawein. P81
    The Grave of Sophocles. Simmias. P89
    A Grave. Marianne Moore. P83
    Gravepiece. Jean Garrigue. P84
    Hide and Seek. Robert Minhinnick. P54
    Joe Clisby's Song. Donald Davidson. P67
    Ode to the Confederate Dead. Allen Tate.
        P83
    Pitie Three Goode Dere Soules. Vivian
        Trollope-Cagle. P65
    Respected Graves. David Ignatow. P64
    Sandweiler and Hamm, the Military
        Cemeteries... Wayne Kvam. P68
    Southeast Corner, fr. A Street in
        Bronzeville. Gwendolyn Brooks. P84
    The Tilted Tombstone. Vivian Trollope-
        Cagle. P65
    To the Holy Spirit. Yvor Winters. P83
    Westhampton Cemetery. Philip Appleman.
        P64
    Westward Ho!. Joaquin Miller. P81
    The Yewtree. Gruffudd Gryg. P87
"**Cemetery** weather in an unused churchyard".
    Postlude. Edna Meudt. P68
Cent, Sion
    The Lying Muse to Rhys Goch Eryri. Tony
        Conran (tr.). P87
    Repentance. Tony Conran (tr.). P87
Centner, Bernice M.
    Haiku. P72
Central Park at Dusk. Sara Teasdale. P82
"**Centuries** ago". Scalloping Northwest. Allen
    Planz. P64
"A **century** ago the linden tree flourished".
    On the Site of the Convent. Tibor
    Tollas. P61
A **Century** of Miracles. Georgi Djagarov. P70
Ceremony. Richard Wilbur. P84
Ceremony of Sending: a Simultaneity..., sel.
    Unknown. P78
A **Certain** Village. Theodore Weiss. P84
"**Certain** marks one can see, it's a fact".
    Nobility. Tudur Aled. P87
"**Certainly**, If a Man Takes the Initiative".
    Unknown. P62
Cervantes, Lorna Dee
    Poem for the Young White Man Who Asked

Me... P85
"The **Chaffinch** flies fast". Cherry Tree. Ivy
    O. Eastwick. P51
Chain Reaction. Manuel Silva Acevedo. P71
"The **chair** she sat in, like a burnished
    throne". A Game of Chess, fr. The
    Waste Land. Thomas Stearns Eliot. P83
Chakravorty, Juliane
    Day After Day. P72
Challenger Lost. Edwin A. Falkowski. P72
Challenges. Elisavietta Ritchie. P63
Challenges
    Taking a Step. Bernard Bell. P73
Chalmers, Patrick R.
    Hay Harvest. P51
    Puk-Wudjies. P51
    When Mary Goes Walking. P51
Chamberlain, Kent Clair
    To Joya, Despairing. P72
Chances Are. Lisel Mueller. P88
Chandler, Janet Carncross
    First Flight. P77
Change
    Anecdote of the Jar. Wallace Stevens. P83
    Baptism. Claude McKay. P82
    The Beautiful Changes. Richard Wilbur.
        P84
    Bronze Trumpets and Sea Water--on Turning
        Latin... Elinor Wylie. P82
    Change. K. Srilata. P72
    Little Boy Blue. Eugene Field. P81
    Medusa. Louise Bogan. P83
    Mutability. John Gould Fletcher. P82
    "Nests in the Top of the Almond Tree".
        Vachel Lindsay. P82
    Solace. Clarissa Scott Delany. P89
Change. K. Srilata. P72
    Unchanging. Friedrich Martin von
        Bodenstedt. P89
    The Vacant Lot, fr. A Street in
        Bronzeville. Gwendolyn Brooks. P84
    What Happened?. Mary Ann Lowry. P72
    Wolves and Sheep, sels. Manuel Silva
        Acevedo. P71
A **Change** in the Year. William Wordsworth.
    P51
Changelessness
    Neither Out Far nor in Deep. Robert
        Frost. P82
Changing. Mary Ann Hoberman. P50
Changing. Wendi Sloniker. P74
Changing of the Guard. Thomas R. Dame. P68
Changing Times. Vivian M. Singerling. P72
A **Chanted** Calendar. Sydney Dobell. P51
Chants
    The Chants, sel. Maria Sabina. P78
Chaplin, Kathleen M.
    Merry Little Men. P51
Chaplinesque. Hart Crane. P83

Chappell, Fred
    The Autumn Bleat of the Weathervane
        Trombone. P67
    Awakening to Music. P67
    Here. P67
    Humility. P67
Char, Rene
    Anoukis and Later Jeanne. Charles
        Guenther (tr.). P61
    The Inventors. Charles Guenther (tr.).
        P61
    On a Night Without Adornment. Charles
        Guenther (tr.). P61
    Put on Guard. Charles Guenther (tr.). P61
    Sentry of the Silent. Charles Guenther
        (tr.). P61
The Character of a Happy Life. Sir Henry
        Wotton. P90
Charge of the Light Brigade. Lord Tennyson.
        P90
Chariots. Glenna Glee. P68
Charity, Thou Art a Lie. Stephen Crane. P81
Charles XII, from The Vanity of Human
        Wishes. Samuel Johnson. P90
Charwoman (Lower Manhattan--6:00 P.M.). Ben
        Belitt. P57
The Chase. Mary Jane Barnes. P72
The Chatter of a Death Demon. Stephen Crane.
        P81
"Chatter of birds two by two raises a
        night...". Prairie Waters by Night.
        Carl Sandburg. P82
Chaucer, Geoffrey
    The Daisy, from The Legend of Good Women.
        P89
Chaundler, Christine
    A Child's Christmas Carol. P51
    The Tree in the Garden. P51
"Cheeks as soft as July peaches". Baby May.
        William Cox Bennett. P89
Chen and Marilyn Chin, Eunice (tr.)
    The Morning Reading. Wu Cheng. P92
Chen, Aric
    The Earth. P74
Cheney, L. Stanley
    White Morning. P68
Cherry Tree. Ivy O. Eastwick. P51
Cherrylog Road. James Dickey. P67
Cherwinski, Joseph
    Identified Flying Objects. P68
The Cheshire Cat. Juan Luis Martinez. P71
Chess. Waldo Rojas. P71
Chess
    Thunderbird Dynasty. Kevin Cline. P58
Chesterman, Hugh
    Outside. P51
    A Rhyme Sheet of Other Lands. P51
    Sir Nicketty Nox. P51
    Yesterday. P51

Chesterton, F.
    'How Far Is It to Bethlehem?'. P51
Chesterton, Gilbert Keith
    A Christmas Carol. P51
"The chestnut's a fine tree". A Christmas-
        Tree Song. Rodney Bennett. P51
Chestre, Thomas
    Sir Launfal. P66
Chicago. Carl Sandburg. P82
The Chicken Coop. Diego Maquieira. P71
Chickens
    The Clucking Hen. Unknown. P51
    To Let. D. Newey-Johnson. P51
    A Tug-of-War. M. M. Hutchinson. P51
    Wishes. Unknown. P51
"The Chickens grow very fast--.". The Naked
        Eye. Lewis Turco. P63
The Chief Centurions. John Masefield. P89
"A chieftain to the highlands bound". Lord
        Ullin's Daughter. Thomas Campbell. P51
        P90
Chihak, Mary Ellen
    After Ten Years. P68
A Chiild's Grace. Robert Herrick. P51
"A child draws the outline of a body".
        Portrait. Louise Gluck. P85
The Child in Me. LaGrassa Nina. P56
A Child Lost. Sigurdur A. Magnusson. P92
Child Sketch in Crayon. David Wevill. P49
"The child in me". The Loving Thing. Edward
        A. Gloeggler. P65
"Child of sweets and sorrows". Sic Transit
        Vita. Louise Wilkerson Conn. P72
"Child of the pure unclouded brow". The Love-
        Gift of a Fairy-Tale. Charles Lutwidge
        ("Lewis Carroll") Dodgson. P90
A Child's Christmas Carol. Christine
        Chaundler. P51
A Child's Morning Prayer. J. Kirby. P51
A Child's Prayer. William Canton. P51
A Child's Prayer. Siegfried Sassoon. P51
A Child's Prayer. Unknown. P51
Child's Song. Gerald Gould. P51
Child's Song in Spring. E. Nesbit. P51
A Child's Song of Christmas. Marjorie L. C.
        Pickthall. P51
A Child's Thought. Robert Louis Stevenson.
        P51
"Child's eyes to see". The Vision Clear. J.
        M. Westrup. P51
Childhood Memories
    Nelly Myers. Archie Randolph Ammons. P67
Childhood of a Scientist. A. F. Moritz. P49
"Childhood remembrances are always a drag".
        Nikki-Rosa. Nikki Giovanni. P85
Children. Walter Savage Landor. P89
Children and Childhood
    Baby-Land. George Cooper. P51
    The Boy's Song. James Hogg. P51

Bubbles. L. Nicholson. P51
Changing. Mary Ann Hoberman. P50
The Child in Me. LaGrassa Nina. P56
Child's Song. Gerald Gould. P51
Childhood of a Scientist. A. F. Moritz.
    P49
Children. Walter Savage Landor. P89
The City Child. Lord Tennyson. P51
Convalescence. Barbara Dirlam. P68
Day and Night. James Stephens. P51
Dedicatory Entry. Anton Shammas. P92
Dogs Are Shakespearean, Children Are
    Strangers. Delmore Schwartz. P84
Foreign Children. Robert Louis Stevenson.
    P51
Four and Eight. Ffrida Wolfe. P51
Frolic. George William ("A.E.") Russell.
    P51
"Girls and Boys Come Out To Play".
    Unknown. P51
Gorky's Childhood. Lorna Crozier. P49
Half Holiday. Olive Enoch. P51
A Happy Child. Kate Greenaway. P51
"Here a Little Child I Stand". Robert
    Herrick. P60
How Many Days Has My Baby To Play?.
    Unknown. P51
I'd Love To Be a Fairy's Child. Robert
    Graves. P51
III, fr. Irradiations. John Gould
    Fletcher. P82
It Is a Pleasant Day. Unknown. P51
Jen II. Doug Rawlings. P86
Just War. Maria Jacobs. P49
Light and Shadow. Robert Francis. P63
Mother's Milk. Elaine Demakas. P58
My Toys. Lilian McCrea. P51
Nikki-Rosa. Nikki Giovanni. P85
Noises. Aileen Fisher. P50
Old-Time Childhood in Kentucky. Robert
    Penn Warren. P67
The Pirate's Tea-Party. Dorothy Una
    Ratcliffe. P51
Poem Out of Childhood. Muriel Rukeyser.
    P84
Reflections of a Sometime Child. Gaston
    Pelletier. P68
Song of Triumph. Lois Duncan. P50
Speaking in Tongues. Erin Moure. P49
The Story of Fidgety Philip. Heinrich
    Hoffmann. P90
A Sussex Legend. Charles Dalmon. P51
To a Small Voyager Who Shares Her Room.
    Virginia E. Smith. P68
Tricia's Fish. Lee Bennett Hopkins. P50
"Under the Soursop Silver-Leaf Tree". Ian
    McDonald. P60
When Polly Buys a Hat. E. Hill. P51
When We Are Men. E. Stella Mead. P51

Where Knock Is Open Wide. Theodore
    Roethke. P84
"Children are what the mothers are".
    Children. Walter Savage Landor. P89
"Children born of fairy stock". I'd Love To
    Be a Fairy's Child. Robert Graves. P51
"Children dear, was it yesterday". The
    Forsaken Merman, sel. Matthew Arnold.
    P51
Children of the Sun. Fenton Johnson. P82
"The children were shouting together".
    Frolic. George William ("A.E.")
    Russell. P51
The Children's Bells. Eleanor Farjeon. P51
Children's Games
    Hide and Seek. Phyllis Drayson. P51
    I Spy. N. E. Hussey. P51
Children's Stories
    Bedtime Stories. Lilian Moore. P55
"Children/Little children playing--.". And
    For Your Children. Gwyn Thomas. P87
The Children. Abby Crone. P74
Chile
    The Beaches of Chile X. Raul Zurita. P71
    The Radiant Beaches. Raul Zurita. P71
    Subway. Juan Cameron. P71
    The Utopias. Raul Zurita. P71
    VI. Raul Zurita. P71
A Chill. Christina Georgina Rossetti. P51
Chillingham. Mary E. Coleridge. P51
Chimes. Alice Meynell. P51
Chimney-Tops. Unknown. P51
Chin and Jesse Wang, Marilyn (tr.)
    Dog, from My Hometown's Base Creatures.
    Wu Cheng. P92
    A Stone Tablet for Animal Ghosts, from My
    Hometown's... Wu Cheng. P92
Chin and Tae-ch'ul Shin, Marilyn (tr.)
    For the Desert Island, from For the
    Desert Island. Tae-ch'ul Shin. P92
    1974, Not Guilty?., from For the Desert
    Island. Tae-ch'ul Shin. P92
    Waiting for Spring,..., from For the
    Desert Island. Tae-ch'ul Shin. P92
Chin and Tetsuo Nakagami, Marilyn (tr.)
    I'm Lying on the Bed at a Motel and...
    Tetsuo Nakagami. P92
    Wandering Was Always an Important Theme
    in My Lyric. Tetsuo Nakagami. P92
"Chin, Chin, Chin," from Mother Goose...
    Unknown. P90
Chin, Marilyn (tr.)
    Snowy Morning. Ai Qing. P92
China
    Double-Focus. Al Purdy. P49
    Chinese Finches. Katha Pollit. P79
"A Chinese impression--.". Relativity.
    Bozhidar Bozhilov. P70
Chinmoy, Sri

O Bird of Light. P68
"Chipmunk Can't Drag it Along". Unknown. P78
The **Chipmunk** Center. Peter Meinke. P63
"**Chipmunk** was standing". Unknown. P78
"**Chisel**, plane, and hammer". The Sacred
    Passion of St. Joseph. Jose Lacaba.
    P92
Chocolates. Louis Simpson. P85
A **Choice** of Weapons. Stanley Kunitz. P83
Chokecherry Summers. Margot Kriel. P88
Choosing a Name. Mary Lamb. P89
"**Choppers** came in". Johnny Doe. Rick Allen
    House. P73
Chorley, Henry Fothergill
    The Brave Old Oak. P89
Chowdhury, Kabir (tr.)
    Consolation. Al Mahmud. P91
    Wherever I Go. Al Mahmud. P91
Chrastil,Roger A.
    The Dead Wolf. P56
Christ Before Pilate. Robert ab Gwilym Ddu.
    P87
"**Christ**, great generous lord, I ask a
    grace". Elegy for Llywelyn ap Gruffudd,
    the Last Prince. Bleddyn Fardd. P87
"The **Christ-child** lay on Mary's lap". A
    Christmas Carol. Gilbert Keith
    Chesterton. P51
Christian Endeavor, from Lost Youth: the
    Last War. Alfred Kreymborg. P82
Christian, Eddena
    Love. P72
Christine, on Her Way to China: An
    Earthquake Poem. Judith Minty. P88
Christmas
    And Who Am I. Opal Jane O'Neal. P72
    Angel, Walking. James W. Penha. P56
    A Child's Christmas Carol. Christine
        Chaundler. P51
    A Child's Song of Christmas. Marjorie L.
        C. Pickthall. P51
    Christmas. Mary I. P51
    A Christmas Carol. Gilbert Keith
        Chesterton. P51
    Christmas Carols. Henry Wadsworth
        Longfellow. P51
    Christmas Eve. Charlotte Druitt Cole. P51
    Christmas Eve. Edna Kingsley Walla. P51
    The Christmas Party. Adeline White. P51
    A Christmas Song. Unknown. P51
    The Christmas Tree. Isabel de Savitzsky.
        P51
    Christmas-Greetings (From a Fairy to a
        Child). Charles Lutwidge ("Lewis
        Carroll") Dodgson. P90
    "Dame, Get up and Bake Your Pies".
        Unknown. P51
    Feast Days: Christmas. Annie Dillard. P47
    I Am Dreaming of a White Christmas: The

    Natural... Robert Penn Warren. P47
    I Will Keep Christmas. P. A. Ropes. P51
    Letter to a Census Taker. Mario Speracio.
        P65
    The Little Fir Tree. Margaret Rose. P51
    Magic Reprieve. Walter S. Hay. P72
Christmas. Mary I. P51
    An Old Time Christmas, from Marmion. Sir
        Walter Scott. P90
    The Oxen. Thomas Hardy. P89
    A Sword in a Cloud of Light. Kenneth
        Rexroth. P84
    A Visit from St. Nicholas. Clement Clark
        Moore. P89
Christmas Carol. Unknown. P51
A **Christmas** Carol. Gilbert Keith Chesterton.
    P51
Christmas Carols. Henry Wadsworth
    Longfellow. P51
Christmas Eve. Charlotte Druitt Cole. P51
Christmas Eve. Edna Kingsley Walla. P51
"**Christmas** Eve, and the advice columns".
    Silences. David Keller. P57
"**Christmas** Eve, and twelve of the clock".
    The Oxen. Thomas Hardy. P51,P89
Christmas Night. B. E. Milner. P51
The **Christmas** Party. Adeline White. P51
A **Christmas** Song. Unknown. P51
The **Christmas** Tree. Isabel de Savitzsky. P51
Christmas Trees
    Burning the Christmas Greens. William
        Carlos Williams. P82
A **Christmas** Verse. Kay [pseud.]. P51
A **Christmas** Wish. Rose Fyleman. P51
Christmas-Greetings (From a Fairy to a
    Child). Charles Lutwidge ("Lewis
    Carroll") Dodgson. P90
A **Christmas-Tree** Song. Rodney Bennett. P51
Christopherson, Merrill G.
    The Heron. P68
Chrysanthemums. Donald Davie. P79
Chung, Angie
    The Sea. P73
Chung, Tin-wen
    Laughter (I). Nancy Ing (tr.). P72
"The **church** bells break the silence, not
    the". St. George's Harbour. Bruce St.
    John. P68
Churches
    The Broken Tower. Hart Crane. P83
    The Interior Castle. Irene K. Wilson. P72
    Neo Catholicism, from Lost Youth: the
        Last War. Alfred Kreymborg. P82
    The Windows. George Herbert. P59
"The **churches** go on". Neo Catholicism, from
    Lost Youth: the Last War. Alfred
    Kreymborg. P82
The **Churchyard** Dancers of Colbek, fr.
    Handlyng Synne. Robert Mannyng. P66

"Churning counterclockwise". Mere Man.
        Elizabeth Holgate. P56
Ciardi, John
        Rain Sizes. P75
        Read This with Gestures. P80
Cicada, Lu
        Home!. P77
        Last Gift. P77
Cicadas
        Cicadas. Arthur Kushner. P77
CIII. Raul Zurita. P71
Cinderella Spin. Gwendolyn Vincent. P58
"A cindery volcanic soil". Irised Symbols.
        Emma Crobaugh. P68
Cindy. Panos D. Bardis. P72
Cino. Ezra Pound. P82
The Circle Closes Here. Waldo Rojas. P71
Circus
        Francis Bacon, the Inventor of
        Spectacles... Cynthia MacDonald. P79
Cities
        City. Roo Borson. P49
        It Fell in the City. Eve Merriam. P80
        Sonnet. William Wordsworth. P90
        An Urban Convalescence. James Merrill.
        P85
        "Which Is the Way to London Town?".
        Unknown. P51
Citino, David
        The Family in the Suburbs: A Situation
        Comedy. P63
City. Roo Borson. P49
The City Child. Lord Tennyson. P51
City Life
        Acquainted with the Night. Robert Frost.
        P82
        The Ghetto, sel. Lola Ridge. P82
The City Mouse and the Country Mouse. Reed
        Whittemore. P63
The City Mouse and the Garden Mouse.
        Christina Georgina Rossetti. P51
City on Fire. Oscar Hahn. P71
Civil War-American
        Lee in the Mountains 1865-1870. Donald
        Davidson. P67
        Men of the North and West. Richard Henry
        Stoddard. P90
        Ode to the Confederate Dead. Allen Tate.
        P67
Civilization
        New Mexican Mountain. Robinson Jeffers.
        P83
Claire's Braids. Nancy McCleery. P88
Clairemonte, Glenn
        Invitation. P68
Clams. Stanley Moss. P64
"Clapping the door to, in the little light".
        Charwoman (Lower Manhattan--6:00
        P.M.). Ben Belitt. P57

Clara Schumann at the Piano. Maureen
        Bloomfield. P88
"Clarabelle/Clarabelle, regal and proud".
        Jessie's Cat. Dawn E. Rutter. P72
"Clare was cute but crabby, clannish". (914)
        555-4144. Ned Pastor. P63
Clare, John
        Autumn. P51
        The Autumn Robin. P51
        The Beanfield. P51
        Little Maid and Cowslips. P51
        Little Trotty Wagtail. P51
        My Early Home. P51
        Summer Evening. P51
        The Thrush's Nest. P51
Clark, Angel
        Ethiopia. P73
Clark, R. Wallace
        Contest of Wills. P72
Clark, Verna Lee O'Brien
        Why? P56
Clarke, Aidan
        The Journey. P51
Clarke, Gillian
        Buzzard. P54
        East Moors. P54
        Letter from a Far Country. P54
        The Water Diviner. P54
Clarkhandler, Frances
        To George C. Wallace. P72
Claudius, Mathias
        Winter. Charles Timothy Brooks (tr.). P89
"Clean Your Back, Slim-Waisted!.". Unknown.
        P62
"Clean shadows ride across the crescent
        moon". Gull Passage by Moonlight.
        Milton Acorn. P49
Cleaned the Crocodile's Teeth. Nyabuk Col.
        P53
"Cleaning mako shark stoned in firelight".
        Mako. Allen Planz. P64
Cleaning the Garage. Edward Butscher. P64
Cleanliness
        "Clean Your Back, Slim-Waisted!.".
        Unknown. P62
        The Washing-up Song. Elizabeth Gould. P51
Cleanthes
        Hymn to Zeus. P89
"The clear form of your face". The Scream Is
        a Kind of Coffin. Paz Molina. P71
"Clear had the day been from the dawn". A
        Fine Day. Michael Drayton. P51
"Clear smoke". Fire. Robert Creeley. P85
"Clear the brown path...". The Ploughman.
        Oliver Wendell Holmes. P89
"Clearer than limelight now...". A Switched
        Career. X. J. Kennedy. P63
"Clearing in the forest". The Lincoln Child.
        James Oppenheim. P82

"Clearly I'm the swimming animal, the
      light". Tablet XXV. Armand Schwerner.
      P64
Clements, Wilma H.
      The Front Runner System. P68
      Two Daughters Sing an Anniversary Ditty.
      P68
      Weathering. P68
Clean And I. Charles Mackay. P90
Clephane, Elizabeth Cecilia
      The Lost Sheep. P89
Clergy
      Awdl. Saunders Lewis. P87
Clerihew Couples. Roberta Simone. P63
Clerihews. Adrian Vonna. P63
The Clerks. Edward Arlington Robinson. P81
Cleveland, John
      To the Memory of Ben Jonson. P90
The Cliff-Top. Robert Bridges. P51
Clifton, Lucille
      The Poet. P52
      Turning. P52
Climbing Milestone Mountain, August 22,
      1937. Kenneth Rexroth. P84
"Climbing from the lethal dead". Orpheus.
      Yvor Winters. P83
Cline, Charles
      Platinum Rings (11/8/76). P72
Cline, Kevin
      Near the Screen Door. P58
      Partner of the Sea. P58
      Peripheral Vision. P58
      Poorly Run Marionette. P58
      Thunderbird Dynasty. P58
      Untitled #1. P58
"Cling to thy home! if there the
      meanest...". Home. Leonidas. P89
"Clink, clink, clinkety-clink". The Milkman.
      Clive Sansom. P51
"The clipping of scissors snips the air".
      Larks. Saint-Pol-Roux. P61
The Clock. Freya Littledale. P75
Clocks
      Again. Lyubomir Levchev. P70
      The Clock. Freya Littledale. P75
      The Cuckoo Clock, from The Birthday.
      Caroline Bowles Southey. P90
      My Clock. Julia Nelson Walke. P68
      The Old Kitchen Clock. Ann ("Aunt Effie")
      Hawkshawe. P51
      The Speed Track. Peter [pseud.]. P51
Clocks and Locks. Mark Rich. P63
"Clockwise east to west I traverse the
      lake". En Route. Anita H. Rosenau. P68
Clodfelter, Michael D.
      Monsoon. P86
      Piss Tubes. P86
Clorinda and Damon. Andrew Marvell. P59
"Close to the sod". Snowdrop. Anna Bunston

de Bary. P51
Close, Eunice
      Here We Come A-Haying. P51
      The Way to Fairyland. P51
"A closed window looks down". Ka 'Ba. Amiri
      (LeRoi Jones) Baraka. P85
The Closet. Nino Nikolov. P70
Closing of a Day on Earth. B. R. De. P72
The Clothes-Line. Charlotte Druitt Cole. P51
Clothing. Jim Fields. P72
Clothing and Dress
      Joe's Snow Clothes. Karla Kuskin. P80
      Second-Hand Trousers. Taufiq Rafat. P91
      Walking Naked Around the House. R. P.
      Dickey. P63
Cloud. Josephine Miles. P84
The Cloud Chorus, from The Clouds.
      Aristophanes. P89
A Cloud Creates. David Ignatow. P64
"A cloud lay cradled near the setting sun".
      The Evening Cloud. John Wilson. P90
"The cloud looked like Australia". World
      Poets Everywhere. Miriam L. Woolfolk.
      P72
"Cloud water". Navajo Correspondences
      (Fourth Set). Unknown. P78
The Cloud. Percy Bysshe Shelley. P89
Clouds
      Cloud. Josephine Miles. P84
      The Cloud Chorus, from The Clouds.
      Aristophanes. P89
      A Cloud Creates. David Ignatow. P64
      The Cloud. Percy Bysshe Shelley. P89
      Clouds. Stanley Moss. P64
      Clouds. Michael Sandford. P72
      The Evening Cloud. John Wilson. P90
      Mist. Henry David Thoreau. P90
Clouds. Stanley Moss. P64
Clouds. Michael Sandford. P72
      White Sheep. William Henry Davies. P51
Clouds Near the Windmill. Barbara Guest. P64
"The clouds are giants". Thunderstorms.
      David Briggs. P73
Clouds of Evening. Robinson Jeffers. P83
"The clouds unroll us a diorama". November.
      Over the Hills. R. B. Weber. P64
"The clouds were doing unoriginal things".
      Bay Days. Howard Moss. P64
"Clouds, too, can prove that they". Clouds.
      Michael Sandford. P72
Clough, Arthur Hugh
      The Gondola. P90
      Where Lies the Land?. P51
Clover. John Banister Tabb. P81
The Clucking Hen. Unknown. P51
"The coach is at the door at last". Farewell
      to the Farm. Robert Louis Stevenson.
      P51
Coatsworth, Elizabeth J.

All Goats. P89
The Mouse. P51
Song, sel. P55
Witches' Song. P55
The **Cobbler**. Unknown. P51
Cobwebs. E. L. M. King. P51
"**Cock** a Doodle Doo!". Unknown. P51
The **Cock** and the Fox. Jean de La Fontaine.
   P90
"**Cock** Robin Got up Early". Unknown. P51
"The **cock** is crowing". Written in March.
   William Wordsworth. P51
"**Cock-a-doodle-doo** the brass-lined rooster
   says". Dog. John Crowe Ransom. P83
Cocks and Crows. Gavin Ewart. P63
Code of Waters. Teresa Calderon. P71
Coffie, LeRoy
   Love's Not Words. P72
Cohen, Phil
   Melissa's Song. P72
Col and Stephen Ciec Lam, Ret
   Its Shells Pile Before Me. Terese Svoboda
   (tr.). P53
Col, Nyabuk
   Cleaned the Crocodile's Teeth. Terese
   Svoboda (tr.). P53
Cold
   Faces. Lola Ridge. P82
   Night Below Zero. Kenneth Rexroth. P84
   "The Night". Lorenzo. P77
Cold Hangs the Quarter Moon. Frank P.
   Zeidler. P68
A **Cold** Spring. Elizabeth Bishop. P84
"A **cold** and starry darkness moans". Ghosts.
   Harry Behn. P55
"**Cold** heart under a breast of fear--
   grieved". Lament for Llywelyn ap
   Gruffudd, the Last Prince. Gruffudd ab
   yr Ynad Coch. P87
"**Cold** inside and out. The branches...".
   Wednesday's Child. Peggy Kahn. P56
"The **cold** remote islands". Night. Louise
   Bogan. P52
"**Cold** winter's in the wood". In the Wood.
   Eileen Mathias. P51
Cole's Island. Charles Olson. P85
Cole, Charlotte Druitt
   Christmas Eve. P51
   The Clothes-Line. P51
   The Dormouse. P51
   The Green Lady. P51
   Pimpernel. P51
   Pudding Charms. P51
   Sun and Moon. P51
   Three Mice. P51
   The Yellow Fairy. P51
Cole, Eddie-Lou
   Lady with the Torch. P72
Cole, William

Literary River Rhyme. P63
Marriage Couplet. P63
Ribald River Rhyme. P63
What a Friend We Have in Cheeses! P63
Coleridge, Hartley
   She Is Not Fair to Outward View. P89
Coleridge, Mary E.
   Chillingham. P51
   The Deserted House. P51
   L'Oiseau Bleu (The Blue Bird). P51
   Street Lanterns. P51
   The Train. P51
   When Mary Thro' the Garden Went. P51
Coleridge, Samuel Taylor
   All Seasons Shall Be Sweet. P51
   The Birds. P51
   He Prayeth Well. P51
   If I Had But Two Little Wings. P51
   In Springtime. P51
   Rime of the Ancient Mariner. P90
   Song. P51
   Trees. P51
   Up, up! Ye Dames and Lasses Gay. P51
Coles, Abraham (tr.)
   Stabat Mater Dolorosa. Jacopone da Todi
   (Jacobus de Benedictus). P89
Coles, Don
   Photo. P49
Coletti, Edward
   Nuthatch. P63
The **Collar**. George Herbert. P59
College Students
   The Campus on the Hill. William DeWitt
   Snodgrass. P85
   Woman's College. John Frank. P72
The **Collier**. Vernon Watkins. P89
Collins, C. W. (tr.)
   Women's Chorus. Aristophanes. P90
Collins, Mortimer
   Darwin. P90
Colman the Younger, George
   Gluggity Glug, from Myrtle and the Vine.
   P90
"The **colonel** rode by his picket-line". The
   Two Wives. William Dean Howells. P90
Colonne, Guido della
   "Although Water, Because of Fire, Loses".
   Frede Jensen (tr.). P69
   "The Great Pain and the Grievous
   Torment". Frede Jensen (tr.). P69
Colonne, Odo della
   "My Heart, Tormented by Love". Frede
   Jensen (tr.). P69
Color the Day Blue. Helen Lair. P72
"**Color** the same, same hue". Rose. Mehdi
   Akhavan Sales. P91
"**Colored** pictures". The Songs of Maximus.
   Charles Olson. P85
Colors

All in Red. Eileen Mathias. P51
Colors. Nicola Basty. P74
   A Bit of Colour. Horace Smith. P51
   Colors. Nicola Basty. P74
   Colour. Adeline White. P51
Colors. Henrietta Liebknecht. P72
   On a Piece of Tapestry. George Santayana. P81
   A Painter Obsessed by Blue. Fairfield Porter. P64
   Purple. Jennifer Hoyt. P73
   White. Tsutomu Fukuda. P72
"Colors are all around". Colors. Nicola Basty. P74
The Colors of Our Age: Pink and Black. Dave Smith. P67
"The colors of the setting". The Setting Sun. Lawrence V. Jowers. P68
The Colossus. Sylvia Plath. P85
Colour. Unknown. P51
Colour. Adeline White. P51
"Colour is a lovely thing". Colour. Unknown. P51
Colton, Lara
   The Gift. P73
"The Columbine almost became". The Columbine. Elna Forsell Pawson. P72
Columbus. Joaquin Miller. P81
Columbus at Night. Maggie Helwig. P49
Column, Padraic
   The Old Woman of the Roads. P51
Coma. Liane Heller. P49
"The combo of velvet and vanilla proved...". See Jane Run. Maryann Calendrille. P64
Come Here, Little Robin. Unknown. P51
"' Come and see! come and see!'.". What the Thrush Says. Queenie Scott-Hopper. P51
"Come dance with me!.". Spinning Song. M. P. A. Sheaffer. P68
"Come forth poets of the world!.". With Voices Strong. Rosemary Challoner Wilkinson. P72
"Come friends, together let us raise". The Holly. Unknown. P87
"Come from my first, ay come!.". Camp-Bell. Winthrop Mackworth Praed. P90
"Come in the evening, or come in the morning". The Welcome. Thomas Davis. P89
"Come in the garden". The Snowman. E. M. Adams. P51
Come into Animal Presence. Denise Levertov. P85
Come into the Garden, Maud. Lord Tennyson. P89
Come Unto These Yellow Sands. William Shakespeare. P51
"Come let's begin to revel't out". Madrigal. Unknown. P51

"Come live with me and be my love". The Passionate Shepherd to His Love. Christopher Marlowe. P89
"Come live with me and be my love--.". The Passionate Businessman To His Love. Bruce Bennett. P63
"Come my Celia, let us prove". To Celia. Ben Jonson. P59
"Come on, lie to me". Tell Me a Lie. Vladimir Golev. P70
"Come on, sir; here's the place...". Dover Cliff, from King Lear. William Shakespeare. P89
"Come out come out come out". Moon Eclipse Exorcism. Unknown. P78
"Come out of your body among us...". How to Get Grizzly Spirit, from Wolf Songs... Unknown. P78
"Come out, come out, this sunny day". Hay-Time. C. M. Loew. P51
"Come share with me my quiet sanctuary". Memo to a Far Descendant. Ann Shermer. P65
"Come then, my friend! my genius! come along". The Poet's Friend (Lord Bolingbroke). Alexander Pope. P90
"Come you, cartoonists". Halsted Street Car. Carl Sandburg. P82
"Come! Let us both be young again". Idyll. Frederika Blankner. P65
Come, Fill the Cup. Mary V. Traeger. P72
"Come, all you sailors of the southern waters". Phantoms All. Harriet Elizabeth Spofford. P81
"Come, Daniel I will show you where". Snowflower. Tamara Downing. P77
"Come, dear children, let us away". The Forsaken Merman. Matthew Arnold. P90
"Come, follow, follow me". The Fairies. Unknown. P51
"Come, let us go a-roaming!". Travellers. Arthur St. John Adcock. P51
"Come, let us rejoice!.". Tyrant, fr. Three Voices. Faiz Ahmad Faiz. P91
"' Come, little leaves,' said the wind one day". Wind and the Leaves. Unknown. P51
"Come, O thou traveller unknown". Wrestling Jacob. Charles Wesley. P89
"Come, virgin robed in darkness". The Proposal. D. Lyons Gallagher. P65
The Comfort of Darkness. Galway Kinnell. P85
Coming Down from the Mountains. Taufiq Rafat. P91
Coming Home. W. D. Ehrhart. P86
"Coming down on the train from Kandy". Rot Below Adam's Peak (Sri Lanka). Earle Birney. P49
"Coming down the hill we could see the

summer". Returning to De Valera's
    Cottage. Tom McCarthy. P92
The Coming of the Cold. Theodore Roethke.
    P84
"Coming upon you suddenly". Casual
    Encounter. Edna Bacon Morrison. P68
Commencement Day
    Edge of Appalachia. Margielea Stonestreet-
    See. P72
    Semper Paratus: to the Graduating Class.
    Doug Rawlings. P86
Common Land Above Trefenter. Jeremy Hooker.
    P54
Commonplace
    The Red Wheelbarrow. William Carlos
    Williams. P75
Communication
    Envoi. John Barton. P49
    For Barbara. Andrew Brooks. P49
Communication to the City Fathers of Boston.
    George Starbuck. P85
"Companies to Tywyn valley--hosting men".
    Praise of Rhys ap Maredudd. Dafydd
    Nanmor. P87
Compassion
    Doc Hill, from Spoon River Anthology.
    Edgar Lee Masters. P82
    The Fish. Elizabeth Bishop. P84
    "If I Found Pity". Re Enzo. P69
    The Pebble. Elinor Wylie. P82
    Pity. William Mills. P67
    Pity This Busy Monster, Manunkind. Edward
    Estlin Cummings. P83
    Tasting the Earth. James Oppenheim. P82
Compensation, from The House of a Hundred
    Lights. (Frederick) Ridgely Torrence.
    P81
"Complacencies of the peignoir, and late".
    Sunday Morning. Wallace Stevens. P83
The Compliment. Eugene Field. P90
The Computation. John Donne. P59
Computers
    The Mind Machines. Haywood Jackson. P68
Comradery. Madison Cawein. P81
Concentration Camps
    Belsen, Day of Liberation. Robert Hayden.
    P84
Conception
    The Sacred Passion of St. Joseph. Jose
    Lacaba. P92
Concerts
    Summer Concert. Reed Whittemore. P79
The Conclusion of the Whole Matter, from The
    House... (Frederick) Ridgely Torrence.
    P81
Concrete Green. David Schuster. P56
The Congo. Vachel Lindsay. P82
Conn, Louise Wilkerson
    Sic Transit Vita. P72

"The conqueror of Rome behaved". King Alfred
    Explains It. G. N. Gabbard. P63
The Conqueror. Jan Anker Froydarland. P72
Conran, Tony (tr.)
    And For Your Children. Gwyn Thomas. P87
    Answer to Sion Cent, sels. Rhys Goch
    Eryri. P87
    Argoed. Thomas Gwynn Jones. P87
    Arthur's Passing, sels. Thomas Gwynn
    Jones. P87
    Ascension Thursday. Saunders Lewis. P87
    Asking a Stallion. Gutun Owain. P87
    Attraction. Unknown. P87
    Awdl. Saunders Lewis. P87
    Battle of Argoed Llwyfain. Taliesin. P87
    Battle of Tal y Moelfre. Meilir ap
    Gwalchmai. P87
    A Beauty. Unknown. P87
    Bittern He Took a Bundle. Unknown. P87
    Building for Love. Unknown. P87
    A Bushel of Chaff. John Ceiriog Hughes.
    P87
    The Catholic Martyrs. Waldo Williams. P87
    Christ Before Pilate. Robert ab Gwilym
    Ddu. P87
    The Court of Owain Glyndwr at Sycharth.
    Iolo Goch. P87
    Crossing a Shore. Gwyn Thomas. P87
    Cynddylan's Hall, fr. Poetry from Lost
    Sagas. Unknown. P87
    Dartmoor. David Gwenallt Jones. P87
    The Dead. David Gwenallt Jones. P87
    Death in the Channel, fr. From a Travel
    Diary. T.H. Parry-Williams. P87
    Death of Sion y Glyn. Lewis Glyn Cothi.
    P87
    Death Song for Owain ab Urien. Taliesin.
    P87
    Deer. Dafydd ab [or ap] Gwilym. P87
    The Deluge, 1939. Saunders Lewis. P87
    The Depression. David Gwenallt Jones. P87
    Dylan Thomas. Euros Bowen. P87
    The Eagle of Eli, fr. Poetry from Lost
    Sagas. Unknown. P87
    The East Wind. T.H. Parry-Williams. P87
    Eaves. Ellis Jones. P87
    Elegy. Cynddelw Brydydd Mawr. P87
    Elegy for Llywelyn ap Gruffudd, the Last
    Prince. Bleddyn Fardd. P87
    Elegy for Nest, sels. Einion ap
    Gwalchmai. P87
    Elegy for Rhys Gryg. y Prydydd Bychan.
    P87
    Elegy for Syr Owain ap Gwilym. Wiliam
    Llyn. P87
    Epitaph. Dafydd Jones. P87
    Epitaph. Ellis Owen. P87
    Epitaph for Father and Son. John Phillips
    (Tegidon). P87

Exhortation. Dafydd Nanmor. P87
Expecting the Lord. Ann Griffiths. P87
F.R. Konecamp. David Gwenallt Jones. P87
Fair Weather. William Williams
    Pantycelyn. P87
The Flame. Isaac Daniel Hooson. P87
Foam. Roland Jones. P87
For a Girl. Cynddelw Brydydd Mawr. P87
The Fox. Robert Williams Parry. P87
The Free School-house, Llanrwst. Ieuan
    Glan Geirionydd. P87
From Exile. Dafydd Benfras. P87
Full of Wonder. Ann Griffiths. P87
Gathering Leaves. William Crwys Williams.
    P87
The Geese. Robert Williams Parry. P87
A Girls' Hair. Dafydd ab Edmwnd. P87
Glint. Euros Bowen. P87
Gnomic Stanzas. Unknown. P87
God and His Church. Morgan LLwyd. P87
The Gododdin, sels. Aneirin. P87
Goggy. Gwyn Thomas. P87
Going Home. LLawdden. P87
The Grey Friar. Dafydd ab [or ab] Gwilym.
    P87
Gwalchmai's Boat, sels. Meilir ap
    Gwalchmai. P87
Gwen ap Llywarch and his Father, fr.
    Poetry from Lost Sagas . Unknown. P87
The Hall of Ifor Hael. Ieuan Brydydd Hir.
    P87
The Happy Man. Unknown. P87
Heather. Eifion Wyn. P87
The Hirlas of Owain, sels. Owain
    Cyfeiliog. P87
His Affliction. Dafydd ab [or ab] Gwilym.
    P87
The Holly. Unknown. P87
Hope. Robert ab Gwilym Ddu. P87
Horizon. David Emrys James. P87
Hunting the Hare. Unknown. P87
Hywel's Boast of His Country. Hywel ab
    Owain Gwynedd. P87
Hywel's Boast of Women, sels. Hywel ab
    Owain Gwynedd. P87
Hywel's Choice. Hywel ab Owain Gwynedd.
    P87
Idle Robin. Unknown. P87
In His Old Age and Blindness. Guto'r
    Glyn. P87
In Memoriam. R. Williams Parry. P87
In Two Fields. Waldo Williams. P87
Invitation to Morfudd. Robin Ddu. P87
An Invitation. Goronwy Owen. P87
It Must Someday be Answered. Elidir Sais.
    P87
Jerusalem Destroyed, sels. Eben Fardd.
    P87
The Killing of Hywel. Peryf ap Cedifor.

P87
Ladies of Llanbadarn. Dafydd ab [or ab]
    Gwilym. P87
Lament for Gwenhwyfar, sels. Gruffudd ap
    Maredudd. P87
Lament for Llywelyn ap Gruffudd, the Last
    Prince. Gruffudd ab yr Ynad Coch. P87
The Last Englyn. Tudur Aled. P87
Leaf. Gwyn Thomas. P87
A Leave-Taking. William Phylip. P87
Llyn y Gadair. T.H. Parry-Williams. P87
Llywarch the Old, fr. Poetry from Lost
    Sagas. Unknown. P87
Longing for Caernarfon. Sion Gruffudd.
    P87
The Love of God. William Williams
    Pantycelyn. P87
The Lover's Hope. Salbri Powel. P87
The Lying Muse to Rhys Goch Eryri. Sion
    Cent. P87
The Mabinogion. Unknown. P87
Maiden Song, sels. Cynddelw Brydydd Mawr.
    P87
The Men That Once Were, sels. Owen
    Gruffudd. P87
Mercy. Unknown. P87
The Moment. Waldo Williams. P87
Morfudd. Dafydd ab [or ab] Gwilym. P87
My Darling's a Venus. Unknown. P87
My Love. Dewi Havhesp. P87
Never Tell. Unknown. P87
Nightfall. Gwallter Mechain. P87
Nobility. Tudur Aled. P87
The North Star. John Morris-Jones. P87
The Nun. Unknown. P87
O the Jewels. Unknown. P87
Oberammergau. David Gwenallt Jones. P87
Old Age. John Morris-Jones. P87
The Old Boatman. Robert Williams Parry.
    P87
On Deck, fr. From a Travel Diary. T.H.
    Parry-Williams. P87
On His Death Bed. Bleddyn Fardd. P87
On His Death-Bed. Meilyr. P87
An Only Child. Robert ab Gwilym Ddu. P87
Pilgrim. William Williams Pantycelyn. P87
Poem of the Frost and Snow. Lewis Morris.
    P87
The Poet Dies for Love. Unknown. P87
Poppies. Nesta Wyn Jones. P87
A Pothersome Pair. John Ceiriog Hughes.
    P87
Praise of a Girl. Huw Morus. P87
Praise of Rhys ap Maredudd. Dafydd
    Nanmor. P87
Praise of Tenby. Unknown. P87
The Propaganda of the Poet. Robert
    Williams Parry. P87
Repentance. Sion Cent. P87

Rew di ranno. Unknown. P87
Rhydcymerau. David Gwenallt Jones. P87
The Rose and the Heather. Pedrog. P87
Rose of Sharon. Ann Griffiths. P87
The Ruin. Dafydd ab [or ab] Gwilym. P87
The Ruined Hearth of Rheged, fr. Poetry
    from Lost Sagas. Unknown. P87
Sadness in Springtime. Unknown. P87
The Seagull. Dafydd ab [or ab] Gwilym.
    P87
Sheepdog. Thomas Richards. P87
Shirt of a Lad. Unknown. P87
Song to a Child. Unknown. P87
Song to the Nightingale. Alun. P87
The South Shore (Aberystwyth). Bobi
    Jones. P87
The Spoils of Annwn. Unknown. P87
Stanzas for the Harp. Unknown. P87
Stanzas to the Lord Rhys ap Gruffudd,
    Prince of Deheubarth. Cynddelw Brydydd
    Mawr. P87
Star of Bethlehem. Alun Llywelyn-
    Williams. P87
The Storm, sels. William Thomas (Islwyn).
    P87
The Strangeness of Dawn. Robert Williams
    Parry. P87
The Swan. Euros Bowen. P87
There's My Darling. Unknown. P87
This Poor Man. William John Gruffydd. P87
The Thrush. Dafydd ab [or ab] Gwilym. P87
The Tit. Llywelyn Goch ap Meurig Hen. P87
To Hywel ab Ifan Fychan. Guto'r Glyn. P87
To Owain Gwynedd. Meilir ap Gwalchmai.
    P87
To the Greyrock Woods. Llywelyn ap y
    Moel. P87
To the Noble Women of Llanarth Hall. Evan
    Thomas. P87
To the Poetry Clubs of Wales. Bobi Jones.
    P87
Trouble at a Tavern. Dafydd ab [or ab]
    Gwilym. P87
Two-faced. Sion Tudur. P87
Voices. Nesta Wyn Jones. P87
Warning to the Poets. Sion Tudur. P87
Weakness. Unknown. P87
What Passes and Endures. John Ceiriog
    Hughes. P87
A Wife's Epitaph. R. Williams Parry. P87
Wild Duck. Euros Bowen. P87
The Wind's Lament. John Morris-Jones. P87
The Wind. Dafydd ab [or ab] Gwilym. P87
Winter. Unknown. P87
A Wish. Robert Williams Parry. P87
The Wish. Goronwy Owen. P87
The Yewtree. Gruffudd Gryg. P87
Conscience
    The Conscience. Richard Armour. P63

The **Conscientious** Objector. Karl Shapiro.
    P84
Consciousness
    Events Like Palaces. Paz Molina. P71
"**Consider** me again". Song. Robert M. Howell.
    P65
"**Consider** that the thing has died
    before...". The Death of the Loch Ness
    Monster. Gwendolyn Macewen. P49
Consider the Flowers. Marjorie Burney
    Willis. P72
Consolation. Winifred Hamric Farrar. P72
Consolation. Al Mahmud. P91
The **Consolations** of Etymology, with Fanfare.
    John Frederick Nims. P63
Constantly Risking Absurdity. Lawrence
    Ferlinghetti. P85
Constellation/Rorschach. Dan Murray. P64
Content, from Farewell to Follie, 1617.
    Robert Greene. P90
Contentment
    Benediction. Mary Eleanor Cox. P72
    Carpe Diem, from The House of a Hundred
        Lights. (Frederick) Ridgely Torrence.
        P81
    Cleon And I. Charles Mackay. P90
    Content, from Farewell to Follie, 1617.
        Robert Greene. P90
    Contentment ('Man Wants but Little Here
        Below.'). Oliver Wendell Holmes. P90
    Happy Heart, from Patient Grissell.
        Thomas Dekker. P90
    "In the Sun Here". Shelly A. Allen. P77
    Indian Summer. Judith Minty. P88
    Sea Shore Shanty. Bobbi Katz. P76
    Sunday Morning. Wallace Stevens. P83
    There Must Be Something. Orhan Veli
        Kanik. P91
    These Perfect Years. Doanda Putnam
        Wheeler. P72
    To Have You Near. Terri L. Parent. P65
Contentment ('Man Wants but Little Here
    Below.'). Oliver Wendell Holmes. P90
Contest of Wills. R. Wallace Clark. P72
Conti, Edmund
    Cross Words. P63
    Emphasis Mine. P63
    Haiku. P63
    My Son, the Tuba Player. P63
    On First Looking into Chapman's
        Refrigerator. P63
Contiguity. George Georgiev. P72
Continental Drift. Colin Barnhorst. P68
"**Continents**, mountains, oceans". Discovery
    II. Sara DeVaux. P68
Convalescence. Barbara Dirlam. P68
Conversation
    After Dinner. David Cram. P63
    Conversations in Mayan. Alonzo Gonzales

Mo. P78
Effort at Speech Between Two People.
    Muriel Rukeyser. P84
From the Poetry Exchange, Two
    Conversations. Howard Nemerov. P63
Conversation. Rose Fyleman. P51
How Just One Poor Man Lives. Alonzo
    Gonzales Mo. P78
Impulsive Dialogue. Maxwell Bodenheim.
    P82
In a Station of the IRT. F. F. Burch. P63
Spyglass Conversations. Unknown. P78
Things That Happen to You. Alonzo
    Gonzales Mo. P78
A True Account of Talking to the Sun at
    Fire Island. Frank O'Hara. P85
The Witch of Coos. Robert Frost. P82
Conversation in June. Barbara S. Berstein.
    P68
Conversations in Mayan. Alonzo Gonzales Mo.
    P78
Converse, Florence
A Rune of Riches. P51
Conway, Jack
The Gathering. P56
Cook, Eliza
The Mouse and the Cake. P90
The Old Arm-Chair. P89
Try Again. P51
Cooking and Courting (From Tom to Ned).
    Unknown. P89
Cooks and Cooking
Food Processor. L. L. Zeiger. P63
Instant Storm. X. J. Kennedy. P75
Snowflake Souffle. X. J. Kennedy. P80
Some Italian!. Linda Monacelli Johnson.
    P63
The TV Chef. Robert N. Feinstein. P63
Cool Tombs. Carl Sandburg. P82
"Cool is the call of the hills". The Call of
    the Hills. Laurie Dalziel. P68
Cool with Sleeping Rivers. Salvatore
    Quasimodo. P61
Coon Cons Coyote, Coyote Eats Coon...
    Unknown. P78
Coon Song. Archie Randolph Ammons. P67
"A coop was built". A Gift Multiplies.
    Vivian Moody. P72
Cooper, George
Baby-Land. P51
October's Party. P51
Cope, Wendy
The New Regime. P63
Coppola, Salvadore J.
Dream. P72
Cora Punctuated with Strawberries. George
    Starbuck. P85
The Coral Insect. Lydia Huntley Sigourney.
    P89

Coral Stanzas. Michael Heller. P64
The Cordilleras of Il Duce. Raul Zurita. P71
Corn, Alfred
April. P79
Corner. Gonzalo Millan. P71
The Corner of the Eye. Robert Penn Warren.
    P67
Cornford, Frances
Spring Morning. P51
"Cornstalks and arrowheads...". Drinking
    Music. James Applewhite. P67
Cornwall, Barry. See Procter, Bryan Waller
Cornwall, Ursula
Sowing Seeds. P51
Coroner's Inquest. William DeWitt Snodgrass.
    P63
The Coronet. Andrew Marvell. P59
"The corpses are not neatly stacked". The
    Train. Dennis Moore. P86
The Corpus Christi Carol. Unknown. P66
Corrado, Anne Yannie
The Awakened Heart. P65
First Love. P65
Millionfold. P65
Corruption
Shine, Perishing Republic. Robinson
    Jeffers. P83
Corso, Gregory
But I Do Not Need Kindness. P85
Hello. P85
The Mad Yak. P85
Marriage. P85
Uccello. P85
The Vestal Lady on Brattle. P85
Vision of Rotterdam. P85
Waterchew!. P85
Zizi's Lament. P85
Cory, William Johnson (tr.)
The Dead Poet-Friend. Callimachus. P89
Cosmic Resident. Eda Howink. P72
Cosmos
That...Who. Syed Ameeruddin. P72
The Cost of a Sting. X. J. Kennedy. P63
Costa Del Sol, at Night. Vita Andersen. P92
Costello, L. S. (tr.)
Sonnet. Louise Labe. P89
Cot, Moses
You, a Red Man, and I, a Black Man.
    Terese Svoboda (tr.). P53
Cothi, Lewis Glyn
Death of Sion y Glyn. Tony Conran (tr.).
    P87
"Cotton/Motion". Navajo Correspondences
    (Third Set). Unknown. P78
"Could I have what I begged for from
    heaven". The Wish. Goronwy Owen. P87
"Could one tire of a daily sunrise". To the
    Morning. Dawn R. Goodwin. P72
"' Could you tell me the meaning'.". Fable

of the Curious Crow and the Devious
    Weevil. Scott Bates. P63
Counterpoint. Agnes Wathall Tatera. P65
Counting
    Counting. Fenton Johnson. P82
Counting the Losses. Kandy Arnold. P58
"Counting the stars". Stars. Marion Jane
    Richardson. P65
"Counting you one of us". Clouds Near the
    Windmill. Barbara Guest. P64
The Country Child. Irene Thompson. P51
The Country Faith. Norman Gale. P51
Country Life
    The Country Child. Irene Thompson. P51
    Hay Harvest. Patrick R. Chalmers. P51
    Humility. Fred Chappell. P67
    I Must Away. May Sarson. P51
    The Little Herd-Boy's Song. Robert
        Buchanan. P51
    Lonely for the Country. Bronwen Wallace.
        P49
Country Music. James Merrill. P79
Country Road in October. Judith Minty. P88
"Country roads are yellow and brown". Street
    Lanterns. Mary E. Coleridge. P51
Coup de Grace. Mildred Luton. P63
"Couples rummage in their closets". Blind
    Dates. Kandy Arnold. P58
Courage
    Blustering God. Stephen Crane. P81
    Casabianca. Felicia Dorothea Hemans. P90
    Charge of the Light Brigade. Lord
        Tennyson. P90
    Don't Be Afraid To Grow. Stephen L.
        Bogadi. P72
    I Won't Bow My Head for Anyone. Stephen
        Ciec Lam. P53
    Supposing That I Should. Stephen Crane.
        P81
    Symbol of Courage. G. Soosai. P72
    There Were Many Who Went. Stephen Crane.
        P81
"Courage wears her crimson". Life in Color.
    Helen Thomas Allison. P72
"Courage: your tongue has left". Stutterer.
    Alan Dugan. P57
The Court of Owain Glyndwr at Sycharth. Iolo
    Goch. P87
The Court Rests. Robert N. Feinstein. P63
Court, Wesli
    Rondine of the Rare Device. P63
Courtly Love
    "For too Long I Have Thought That I'd
        Conceal". Stefano Protonotaro. P69
    "The Great Pain and the Grievous
        Torment". Guido della Colonne. P69
    The Grey Friar. Dafydd ab [or ab] Gwilym.
        P87
    Hywel's Choice. Hywel ab Owain Gwynedd.

P87
"I Hope to Receive a Reward". Giacomo da
    Lentini. P69
Invitation to Morfudd. Robin Ddu. P87
"Just Like the Butterfly, Which Has Such
    a Nature". Giacomo da Lentini. P69
'The Knight-a Lady's Hero'. Eleanor Otto.
    P65
"Many Lovers Bear Their Illness". Giacomo
    da Lentini. P69
"My lady, I Wish to Tell You". Giacomo da
    Lentini. P69
O the Jewels. Unknown. P87
"Since Mercy Is of No Avail to Me...".
    Giacomo da Lentini. P69
Sir Orfeo. Unknown. P66
Songs to a Woman. Maxwell Bodenheim. P82
"Sweet Beginning:.". Giacomo da Lentini.
    P69
"There Truly First Came to Me Deep
    Sorrow". Giacomo da Lentini. P69
The Tit. Llywelyn Goch ap Meurig Hen. P87
Wild Cherry. Lizette Woodworth Reese. P81
The Wind. Dafydd ab [or ab] Gwilym. P87
"Wonderfully". Giacomo da Lentini. P69
Courtship
    Applachian Courtship. Dorothy Williamson
        Worth. P65
    The Barrier (A Manardina). Dorman John
        Grace. P72
    Come into the Garden, Maud. Lord
        Tennyson. P89
    Cooking and Courting (From Tom to Ned).
        Unknown. P89
    Fishing for Girls with a Rod and Line.
        Kuek Taitai. P53
    The Girl's Hearts Soften. Daniel Cuol
        Long. P53
    How to Ask and Have. Samuel Lover. P89
    Hywel's Boast of Women, sels. Hywel ab
        Owain Gwynedd. P87
    The Lover's Hope. Salbri Powel. P87
    A Match. Algernon Charles Swinburne. P89
    My Darling's a Venus. Unknown. P87
    My Mother's Wedding. Boris Kristov. P70
    The Nun. Unknown. P87
    The Passionate Shepherd to His Love.
        Christopher Marlowe. P89
    Praise of a Girl. Huw Morus. P87
    Sir Lancelot and Queen Guinevere. Lord
        Tennyson. P89
    Somebody's Courting Somebody. Unknown.
        P89
    Vignette from the Past. Mary Frances
        Langford. P65
    The Whistle. Robert Story. P89
    White Girls. Phillip Macar Ruac. P53
Cousin Shamsu, Durzi. Kaiser Haq. P91
Covenant. Merle Price. P65

Covered Bridge. Robert Penn Warren. P67
Covers. Virginia M. Hahn. P58
Cow and the Ass. Ann and Jane Taylor. P51
A Cow's Life. Bruce Bennett. P63
Cowboys
    The Poet Falls in Love with a Cowboy.
        Linda M. Hasselstrom. P88
"Cowhorn-crowned, shockheaded, cornshuck-
        bearded". The Knight, Death, and the
        Devil. Randall Jarrell. P84
Cowper, William
    Light Shining Out of Darkness. P89
    The Nose and the Eyes. P90
    The Snail. P51
    The Woodman's Dog. P51
Cows
    Always Praises You. Nyaruoth Atem. P53
    Awakening to Music. Fred Chappell. P67
    Bovine Town. Mildred Luton. P63
    A Cow's Life. Bruce Bennett. P63
    Dairy Cows. Ron Koertge. P63
    Thank You, Pretty Cow. Jane Taylor. P51
Cox, L. E.
    We Thank You!. P51
Cox, Malinda (tr.)
    Indian Summer. Nicolae Breban. P92
Cox, Mary Eleanor
    Benediction. P72
Coxwell, C. Fillingham (tr.)
    The Peasant and the Sheep. Ivan
        Andreevich Kriloff. P90
Coyotes
    "Sorry". Doc Dachtler. P77
Crabs
    The Dead Crab. Andrew Young. P89
"Crackers, crackers all the way". Deepavali
        (Festival of Lights). A. Padmanaban.
        P72
Cradle Hymn. Martin Luther. P51
Cradle Song. Lord Tennyson. P51
Cradle Song at Bethlehem. E. J. Falconer.
        P51
A Cradle Song. Unknown. P51
Cradle Songs, from Wolf Songs & Others of
        the Tlingit. Unknown. P78
Cradle Songs, from Wolf Songs & Others of
        the Tlingit. Unknown. P78
Cradle Songs, from Wolf Songs & Others of
        the Tlingit. Unknown. P78
Cradle Songs, from Wolf Songs & Others of
        the Tlingit. Unknown. P78
"The craft threads through islands
        without...". The Queen Charlotte
        Islands Meditations. Michael J. Yates.
        P49
Craft, Sheila
    Sanskrit Songs for Modern Dreamers'. P72
Craig, Eugene A.
    I Hypnotize Bugs. P63

Craik, Dinah Maria Mulock
    Now and Afterwards. P89
Cram, David
    After Dinner. P63
    Alphabet Soup. P63
    The Editor Regrets. P63
    Limericks. P63
    Tunnel Vision. P63
Cranch, Christopher Pearse
    The Bobolinks. P89
Crane, Hart
    At Melville's Tomb. P83
    The Broken Tower. P83
    Chaplinesque. P83
    For the Marriage of Faustus and Helen.
        P83
    My Grandmother's Love Letters. P83
    Possessions. P83
    Proem: To Brooklyn Bridge, fr. The
        Bridge. P83
    Voyages. P83
Crane, Stephen
    And the Sins of the Fathers. P81
    And You Love Me?. P81
    Behold, from the Land of the Farther
        Suns. P81
    Behold, the Grave of a Wicked Man. P81
    Black Riders. P81
    Blustering God. P81
    Charity, Thou Art a Lie. P81
    The Chatter of a Death Demon. P81
    Do Not Weep, Maiden. P81
    Fast Rode the Knight. P81
    Friend, Your White Beard Sweeps the
        Ground. P81
    A God Came to Man. P81
    God Fashioned the Ship. P81
    A God in Wrath. P81
    God Lay Dead in Heaven. P81
    I Looked Here. P81
    I Met a Seer. P81
    I Saw a Man. P81
    I Stood Musing in a Black World. P81
    I Stood Upon a High Place. P81
    I Stood Upon a Highway. P81
    I Walked in a Desert. P81
    I Was in the Darkness. P81
    If I Should Cast Off This Tattered Coat.
        P81
    If Love Loves. P81
    If There Is a Witness. P81
    The Impact of a Dollar. P81
    In a Lonely Place. P81,Old Age
    In Heaven. P81
    In the Desert. P81
    In the Night. P81
    It Was Wrong To Do This. P81
    A Learned Man. P81
    Little Birds of the Night. P81

The Livid Lightnings Flashed in the
    Clouds. P81
Love Walked Alone. P81
A Man Adrift on a Slim Spar. P81
A Man Feared. P81
A Man Said to the Universe. P81
A Man Saw a Ball of Gold. P81
A Man Toiled on a Burning Road. P81
A Man Went Before a Strange God. P81
Many Red Devils Ran from My Heart. P81
Many Workmen. P81
Mystic Shadow, Bending Near Me. P81
A Newspaper Is a Collection. P81
The Ocean Said to Me Once. P81
On the Horizon. P81
Once I Knew a Fine Song. P81
Once I Saw Mountains Angry. P81
Once There Was a Man. P81
Once, a Man, Clambering to the House-
    Tops. P81
The Patent of a Lord. P81
Places Among the Stars. P81
The Sage Lectured Brilliantly. P81
Should the Wide World Roll Away. P81
A Slant of Sun. P81
A Spirit Sped. P81
Supposing That I Should. P81
Tell Brave Deeds of War. P81
There Came Whisperings. P81
There Exists the Eternal Fact of
    Conflict. P81
There Was a Crimson Clash of War. P81
There Was a Great Cathedral. P81
There Was a Man and a Woman. P81
There Was a Man Who Lived a Life of Fire.
    P81
There Was One. P81
There Was Set Before Me. P81
There Was, Before Me. P81
There Were Many Who Went. P81
Think as I Think. P81
Three Little Birds. P81
Tradition, Thou Art for Suckling
    Children. P81
The Trees in the Garden. P81
Truth, Said a Traveller. P81
Two or Three Angels. P81
Unwind My Riddle. P81
Upon the Road of My Life. P81
Walking in the Sky. P81
The Wayfarer. P81
Why Do You Strive for Greatness, Fool?
    P81
With Eye and with Gesture. P81
Yes, I Have a Thousand Tongues. P81
You Say You Are Holy. P81
A Youth in Apparel That Glittered. P81
Crapsey, Adelaide
    Amaze. P81

Dirge. P81
The Guarded Wound. P81
The Lonely Death. P81
Moon Shadows. P81
November Night. P81
Song. P81
Susanna and the Elders. P81
Vendor's Song. P81
The Warning. P81
Crapshooters. Carl Sandburg. P82
Crash. Sandra Rasmussen. P72
Crashaw, Richard
    Easter Day. P59
    On Mary Magdalene. P59
Craven, Jerry
    Fire Dream. P65
    L'Anne: Water in My Hands. P65
    New Her Cherokee Face. P65
    The Rain of Time. P65
"Crawford the Ferrywoman...". Triads II.
    James Reaney. P49
Crawford, Julia
    We Parted in Silence. P89
Crawford, Vesta P.
    Passengers in a Time Beyond Orchards. P65
Crayton, Pearl
    Black Migrants. P68
    From Here to Eternity. P68
    Gambler's Wife (Right Diptych, an
        Extract). P68
Creation
    Against Time. Louis Untermeyer. P82
    At the Briefing for Creation Day. Mary
        Jean Irion. P63
    The Creation of the World. Eva Toth. P92
    The Creation. James Weldon Johnson. P83
    A Day in Creation. Helena Parham. P72
    Small Beginnings. Charles Mackay. P89
    A Star Flowed. Yahya Kemal. P91
    Thank You: A Poem in Seventeen Parts.
        Unknown. P78
    The Venetian Blind. Randall Jarrell. P84
    What Days, Indeed. Majeed Amjad. P91
Creation of the World According to Charles
    Slater. Charles Slater. P78
The Creation of the World. Eva Toth. P92
The Creation. James Weldon Johnson. P83
Creativity
    To My Craft. Agnes Nemes Nagy. P92
"Creator of the World". Unknown. P60
"Creator spirit, by whose aid". Veni Creator
    Spiritus. Saint Gregory the Great. P89
"Creature of misproportions and alarms".
    Giraffe. C. B. Oppenheimer. P68
Credo. Edward Arlington Robinson. P81
Credo. William DeWitt Snodgrass. P63
Creeley, Robert
    Fire. P85
    For Fear. P85

For My Mother: Genevieve Jules Creeley.
    P85
For You. P85
A Gift of Great Value. P85
Just Friends. P85
Kore. P85
The Language. P85
Mother's Voice. P52
The Name. P85
The Rescue. P85
Song. P85
Time. P85
The World. P85
Cretaceous Period. A. J. Kealoha Pendzik.
    P74
"**Cricket** in the Whitehouse". First Names.
    Dorothy T. Lewis. P72
"**Cricket** moonlighting". Haiku. Bernice M.
    Centner. P72
The **Cricket**. Mary P. (Mary Dalles) Carey.
    P68
The **Cricket**. Krassin Himmirsky. P70
Crickets
    The Cricket. Mary P. (Mary Dalles) Carey.
        P68
    The Cricket. Krassin Himmirsky. P70
The **Crier**. Philip Kahclamet. P78
Crime and Criminals
    At the Police Station. Raymond Souster.
        P49
    Cattails. Richard Hugo. P79
    Four Sides to a House. Amy Lowell. P82
"**Crimsonflames/Swooped** the rolls". The Red
    Hills '83. Terry M. Paulsgrove. P77
Crippled Walls. Phillip Britain. P72
Cripps, Joy Beaudette
    Let All World Poets Rejoice. P72
"**Crisp** brown leaves tremble at my feet".
    Love's Presence. Alney Norell. P65
Critics and Connoisseurs. Marianne Moore.
    P83
Croasdell, Ann
    The Muffin Man. P51
Crobaugh, Emma
    Canary Morning at the Stop of Darkness.
        P68
    Crystal Rosaries of Long Remembering. P68
    Dawn Climbs over Time. P72
    Easter Hills of Peace. P68
    Irised Symbols. P68
    The Rainbow Dared the Storm. P68
    Winds Curled Incense. P68
The **Crocodile** Scales. Moses Kuac Nyoat. P53
Crocuses. Anna M. Platt. P51
Cromwell, Oliver
    An Horatian Ode upon Cromwell's Return
        from Ireland. Andrew Marvell. P59
Crone, Abby
    The Children. P74

Crooker, Barbara
    Field Guide to North American Birds. P63
Cross Words. Edmund Conti. P63
Cross, Elsa
    Images on the Beach. Eric Walker and Abby
        Wolf (tr.). P92
The **Cross**. Allen Tate. P83
Crossing a Shore. Gwyn Thomas. P87
Crossing over, from Your Tired, Your Poor.
    Lisel Mueller. P88
Crossing the Plains. Joaquin Miller. P81
"**Crossing** the street". The Broken Home.
    James Merrill. P85
The **Crossing**. Salvatore Quasimodo. P61
Crossland, John R.
    Water. P51
Crossword Puzzles
    Love-Deep in Crossword Puzzles. Louis
        Phillips. P63
The **Crow** and the Fox. Jean de La Fontaine.
    P90
"The **Crow**, Whose Mind Is Given Solely".
    Unknown. P62
The **Crow**. Mrs. Alexander. P51
Crows
    Swan Song. R. J. Foster. P68
"**Crows** crowd croaking overehead". Summer
    Evening. John Clare. P51
"**Crows** ravish". Swan Song. R. J. Foster. P68
"The **Crows**, Dipping Their Beaks in the
    Stream". Unknown. P62
Crozier, Lorna
    Angels of Snow. P49
    Gorky's Childhood. P49
Crucifiction. Dan Valenti. P56
Crum, Lady Erskine
    'Good Night', Says the Owl. P51
The **Cry**. Jamie Shepherd. P56
Crying
    Do Parents Cry, too?. Thad King. P73
    I Do Not Cry Like People Cry. Hermit
        Helene Troy Arlington. P68
    Irish Peasant Song. Louise Imogen Guiney.
        P81
    A Tear. Samuel Rogers. P90
    Tears. Danielle Mann. P74
    Tears, Good Little Fellows. William
        Walter De Bolt. P72
    The Thousand-and-One Nights. Gwendolyn
        Vincent. P58
    "Why Do You Cry with Downcast Face".
        Unknown. P62
The **Crystal** Flow. James Richard Hurst. P68
Crystal Rosaries of Long Remembering. Emma
    Crobaugh. P68
"A **crystal** home the rose was given, its
    soft". The Rose and the Heather.
    Pedrog. P87
Cubes. Eleanore-Melissa. P68

The **Cuckoo** Clock, from The Birthday.
        Caroline Bowles Southey. P90
The **Cuckoo**. Unknown. P51
Cuevish, Lucario
        Before They Made Things Be Alive They
                Spoke. Jerome Rothenberg (tr.). P78
        Sioux Metamorphosis. James Koller (tr.).
                P78
Cullen, Countee
        Black Majesty. P83
        For a Lady I Know, fr. Four Epitaphs. P83
        For John Keats, Apostle of Beauty, fr.
                Four Epitaphs. P83
        For My Grandmother, fr. Four Epitaphs.
                P83
        For Paul Laurence Dunbar, fr. Four
                Epitaphs. P83
        Heritage. P83
        In Memory of Colonel Charles Young. P83
        Incident. P83
        Scottsboro, too, Is Worth Its Song. P83
Cultural Exchange. Langston Hughes. P83
Culture
        A Note Toward a Definition of Culture.
                James Camp. P63
        Saffron Pig Pinata. Roger Weingarten. P63
Cummings, Edward Estlin
        All Which Isn't Singing Is Mere Talking.
                P83
        Anyone Lived in a Pretty How Town. P83
        Maggie and Milly and Molly and May. P76
        My Father Moved Through Dooms of Love.
                P83
        Pity This Busy Monster, Manunkind. P83
        Poem ("Everything"). P79
        Poem ("What time"). P79
Cunningham, Allan
        Sea Song. P51
Cunningham, J. V.
        Epigrams. P79
"**Cuol** dances out of step". Out of Step. Buk
        Teny Men. P53
"**Cuol** Jok, how did you take...". Its Shells
        Pile Before Me. Ret Col and Stephen
        Ciec Lam. P53
Cuol, Dhor Ding
        As Helpless as a Dhow on a Still Day.
                Terese Svoboda (tr.). P53
        I Would Give Him a Man. Terese Svoboda
                (tr.). P53
Cupid
        "Love's Arrows Come in Dual Form".
                Unknown. P62
        "Love's Qualities Are Very Frustrating".
                Unknown. P62
        "Oh Cupid, I Will Worship Your Feet".
                Unknown. P62
        "They Torment Us, Yet Give Us Happiness".
                Unknown. P62

Cupid Swallowed. Unknown-Greek. P89
Curfew Summer. Maki Kureishi. P91
"**Curl** your wild and windy arms about me...".
        A Midnight Storm To Turn to. Mary P.
        (Mary Dalles) Carey. P68
"**Curled** in empty dark". Covers. Virginia M.
        Hahn. P58
The **Curliest** Thing. Unknown. P51
Curriculum Change. Ned Pastor. P63
"The **curved** leaves of the little tree are
        shining". A Sunny Day, fr. Five Groups
        of Verse. Charles Reznikoff. P83
"**Cutting** foot holds". Rockbound Pass in
        January. Jon Olander. P77
The **Cyclists**. John C. Pine. P77
Cyfeiliog, Owain
        The Hirlas of Owain, sels. Tony Conran
                (tr.). P87
Cynddylan's Hall, fr. Poetry from Lost
        Sagas. Unknown. P87
Cynthia in the Snow. Gwendolyn Brooks. P80

D'Aleo, Deborah
        My Window, My Wheelchair, and Me. P74
D'Alfonso, Antonio
        Perseverance. P49
d'Amici, Rugieri
        "Often Love Has Made Many Happy". Frede
                Jensen (tr.). P69
d'Aquino, Rinaldo
        "I Shall Never Find Solace". Frede Jensen
                (tr.). P69
        "Into a Grievous Torment". Frede Jensen
                (tr.). P69
        "Thanks to a Perfect Love, I Feel So
                Joyous". Frede Jensen (tr.). P69
D'Arpino, Tony
        The Dull Image. P56
D'Costa, Bob
        Being Born in the Woods. P72
Dabydeen, Cyril
        Farewell. P49
Dacey, Philip
        The Handicapped. P57
Dachtler, Doc
        Firewood (for Steve Sanfield). P77
        Not So Long Gone (for the Maidu). P77
        "Sorry". P77
"**Dad** is never first in, yet". Families at
        the Shore. Graham Everett. P64
Daddy. Sylvia Plath. P85
Daddy Fell Into the Pond. Alfred Noyes. P89
Daffodils
        Daffodils. William Wordsworth. P89
        Daffodils. Lizette Woodworth Reese. P81
Daffodils. P. A. Ropes. P51

Daffodils. William Wordsworth. P89
Dafydd ab Edmwnd
    A Girls' Hair. Tony Conran (tr.). P87
Dafydd ab [or ab] Gwilym
    Deer. Tony Conran (tr.). P87
    The Grey Friar. Tony Conran (tr.). P87
    His Affliction. Tony Conran (tr.). P87
    Ladies of Llanbadarn. Tony Conran (tr.).
      P87
    Morfudd. Tony Conran (tr.). P87
    The Ruin. Tony Conran (tr.). P87
    The Seagull. Tony Conran (tr.). P87
    The Thrush. Tony Conran (tr.). P87
    Trouble at a Tavern. Tony Conran (tr.).
      P87
    The Wind. Tony Conran (tr.). P87
Dagger. Mikhail Lermontov. P90
Daguerreotypie Der Niagara Falls... Herbert
    Morris. P79
Dail-A-Shrink. Ned Pastor. P63
The Daily Grind. Fenton Johnson. P82
Daily Joys. Barbara McCoy. P68
The Daily Planet. Edward Watkins. P63
"Dainty little maiden, whither would
    you...". The City Child. Lord
    Tennyson. P51
Dainty, Evelyn
    The Birds on the School Windowsill. P51
Dairy Cows. Ron Koertge. P63
Daisies and Grasses. Unknown. P51
Daisy Fraser, from Spoon River Anthology.
    Edgar Lee Masters. P82
The Daisy, from The Legend of Good Women.
    Geoffrey Chaucer. P89
The Daisy, sel. James Montgomery. P51
Dalal, Anisa
    I Believe in Me. P73
Dalchev, Atanas
    44, Avenue de Maine. John Balaban (tr.).
      P70
    On Leaving. John Balaban (tr.). P70
    Snow 1929. John Balaban (tr.). P70
Dalles, Mary. See Carey, Mary
Dallman, Elaine
    Late. P65
    The Walled Light. P65
Dalmon, Charles
    A Sussex Legend. P51
Dalziel, Laurie
    The Call of the Hills. P68
"The dam Bellona". Der Blinde Junge. Mina
    Loy. P82
"Dame Trot and Her Cat". Unknown. P51
"Dame, Get up and Bake Your Pies". Unknown.
    P51
Dame, Thomas R.
    Changing of the Guard. P68
"Damn it all! all this our South stinks
    peace". Sestina: Altaforte. Ezra

Pound. P82
"Damon, come drive thy flocks this way".
    Clorinda and Damon. Andrew Marvell.
    P59
"The damp mahogany shade". Hide and Seek.
    Robert Minhinnick. P54
Dance. Patricia Glasgow. P68
Dance. Alice E. W. Whitmore. P72
"A dance of blue-bells in the shady places".
    Sweet Surprises. S. Doudney. P51
Dance of the Rain Gods. Ray Young Bear. P78
Dance of Words. Beth Martin Haas. P72
Dancer. Edgar Degas. P61
Dancing and Dancers
    Alas, Alas the Wyle, That Ever I Cowde
      Daunce. Unknown. P66
    At the Park Dance. William DeWitt
      Snodgrass. P85
    Attic Dance. Joan Drew Ritchings. P63
    The Churchyard Dancers of Colbek, fr.
      Handlyng Synne. Robert Mannyng. P66
    Cinderella Spin. Gwendolyn Vincent. P58
    Dance. Alice E. W. Whitmore. P72
    Dancer. Edgar Degas. P61
    Dancing on the Shore. M. M. Hutchinson.
      P51
    The Deadly Dance. Unknown. P78
    The Gourd Dancer. N. Scott Momaday. P85
    Leapt into the Dance. Nyanpandong. P53
    The Little Dancers. Laurence Binyon. P51
    Lucy Lavender. Ivy O. Eastwick. P51
    My Fantasy. Kim Sherry. P73
    My Papa's Waltz. Theodore Roethke. P84
    Out of Step. Buk Teny Men. P53
    Spinning Song. M. P. A. Sheaffer. P68
    Wandering Off. Unknown. P53
Dancing on the Shore. M. M. Hutchinson. P51
Dancing Waters. Sherry Small Sundick. P72
The Dandelion Puff. Mary K. Robinson. P51
The Dandelions. Unknown. P51
The Dangerous Cliffs. Bruce Bennett. P63
Daniel Webster. Oliver Wendell Holmes. P90
Daniels, Evan
    I Am Thankful. P74
Daniels, Jim
    At the Poetry Reading: 'This Is a Poem
      About That'. P63
    Elegy for Mr. Ed, the Talking Horse. P63
A Danish Cradle Song. Unknown. P51
Danny Murphy. James Stephens. P51
Danse Russe. William Carlos Williams. P82
Dante
    My Lady. Charles Eliot Norton (tr.). P89
Dante's Angels. Patrick Lane. P49
Dar, Zahid
    The Boy's Song. C.M. Naim (tr.). P91
Dark Confusion, from Lost Youth: the Last
    War. Alfred Kreymborg. P82
Dark Friend. Richard M. Mishler. P86

"**Dark** child in your sleeping bag". To a
        Small Voyager Who Shares Her Room.
        Virginia E. Smith. P68
"**Dark** days". Anti-Cycle for the New Year.
        Jane Augustine. P64
"**Dark** is Cynddylan's hall tonight".
        Cynddylan's Hall, fr. Poetry from Lost
        Sagas. Unknown. P87
"The **dark** soft languages are being
        silenced". Cave Series, sel. Margaret
        Atwood. P49
"The **dark**, gloomy, fascinating wave". The
        Sea. Angie Chung. P73
The **Darkening** Garden. Unknown. P51
"**Darkest** Night Has Passed". Unknown. P62
Darkness. George Gordon, 6th Baron Byron.
        P48
Darkness
        Caliban in the Coal Mines. Louis
        Untermeyer. P82
        The Comfort of Darkness. Galway Kinnell.
        P85
        Consolation. Al Mahmud. P91
        I Was in the Darkness. Stephen Crane. P81
The **Darkness** Before. Eleanore-Melissa. P68
"The **darkness** rolls upward". The Blue
        Symphony. John Gould Fletcher. P82
"**Darkness** swept the earth in my dream". The
        Comfort of Darkness. Galway Kinnell.
        P85
"**Darkness**, sunlight and a little holy spit".
        Potato Song. Stanley Moss. P64
Darlene Friendship's Boyfriend. Ron Ikan.
        P63
Darley, George
        The Elfin Pedlar. P51
Dartmoor. David Gwenallt Jones. P87
Darwin. Mortimer Collins. P90
Daughter. Robert Pinsky. P79
Daughter Softly Singing in the Night. Jean
        L. Emerson. P72
Daughters and Sons
        After Stefan George--Mein Kind Kam Heim.
        Stephen Spender. P79
        The Colossus. Sylvia Plath. P85
        Daughter. Robert Pinsky. P79
        Father and Son. Delmore Schwartz. P84
        The Name. Robert Creeley. P85
        Nick and the Candlestick. Sylvia Plath.
        P85
        Port Letter. Mary Trimble. P88
        To Amy from Her Father at Graduation.
        Carl Moorefield. P65
        To My Son. Muriel Ringstad. P72
Davenant, Sir William
        Daybreak. P89
David Hume. Donald Hall. P79
Davidson, Clifford
        Ship, Sea, and Star. P68

Davidson, Donald
        Joe Clisby's Song. P67
        Lee in the Mountains 1865-1870. P67
Davie, Donald
        Chrysanthemums. P79
        The Fountain. P79
        Going to Italy. P79
Davie, Donald (tr.)
        Fable of First Person. Gyorgy Somlyo. P92
Davies, May Carolyn
        The Day Before April. P51
Davies, William Henry
        Leisure. P51,P90
        The Rain. P51
        Rich Days. P51
        White Sheep. P51
Davis Matlock, from Spoon River Anthology.
        Edgar Lee Masters. P82
Davis, Laura
        Haiku. P73
Davis, Rosemary
        "I Think That Galileo, Old and Blind".
        P72
Davis, Thomas
        This Native Land. P51
        The Welcome. P89
Davis, William Virgil
        Houses. P68
        I-35, South of Waco. P63
Dawn. Gordon Bottomley. P51
Dawn. Paul Laurence Dunbar. P89
Dawn Climbs over Time. Emma Crobaugh. P72
"**Dawn** is on the rise". Changing of the
        Guard. Thomas R. Dame. P68
Dawn of Tomorrow. Tomas Segovia. P92
"**Dawn**, Fingerpaints the Sky's". J. Louise
        Pink. P72
"**Dawn**; and the jew's-harp's sawing seesaw
        song". Pilots, Man Your Planes.
        Randall Jarrell. P84
Day. Sir Cecil Spring-Rice. P51
Day After Day. Juliane Chakravorty. P72
"**Day** after day". V. Bogumil Wtorkiewicz. P72
Day and Dark. George Cabot Lodge. P81
Day and Night. Eugenio Montale. P61
Day and Night. James Stephens. P51
A **Day** at the Farm. Unknown. P51
The **Day** Before April. May Carolyn Davies.
        P51
Day Breaking. John E. Moore. P72
"The **day** he shot the lion". Bailey. Knute
        Skinner. P63
A **Day** in Creation. Helena Parham. P72
Day in May. Dominick J. Lepore. P56
Day Into Night. Shane Iliff. P74
"The **Day** Is Done". Elizabeth Madox Roberts.
        P60
Day Is Dying, fr. The Spanish Gypsy. George
        (Mary Ann Cross) Eliot. P89

"The **day** is cold, and dark, and dreary". The Rainy Day. Henry Wadsworth Longfellow. P89

"The **day** is done; the weary day of thought...". Vesper Hymn. Eliza Scudder. P89

"The **day** is waning; in the tired fields". Nocturne. Heidi Blomster. P68

Day of the Dead. Robert Hayden. P84

The **Day** Willis Harder Didn't Kill His Beagle. Hilary Russell. P63

"The **day** the Messiah". Grace. Al Ortolani. P63

"The **day** we opened Mozart's coffin". Amadeus. LoVerne Brown. P63

Day's Ending (Tucson). Sara Teasdale. P82

"**Day,** in melting purple dying". Song of Egla. Maria Gowen Brooks. P89

Day/Night. Graham Everett. P64

Daybreak. Sir William Davenant. P89

Daybreak. Henry Wadsworth Longfellow. P51, P89

Daybreak. Laurene Tibbets. P72

Daybreak in a Garden. Siegfried Sassoon. P51

Days
> Bay Days. Howard Moss. P64
> Before the First of the Next Month. Majeed Amjad. P91
> The Errand Boy's Day Off. Kurt Lipschutz. P63
> Friday. Sir Walter Scott. P51
> On a Beautiful Day. John Sterling. P89
> This Day Is Not Like That Day. Jean Garrigue. P84
> Tuesday. Alma Denny. P63 !
> Wild Day at the Shore. Felice Holman. P76

"The **days** and nights are years away from you". Love in Absentia. Mary Jane Barnes. P68

"**Dazed** lighting". Now and Again. Mary Trimble. P88

Ddu, Robert ab Gwilym
> Christ Before Pilate. Tony Conran (tr.). P87
> Hope. Tony Conran (tr.). P87
> An Only Child. Tony Conran (tr.). P87

Ddu, Robin
> Invitation to Morfudd. Tony Conran (tr.). P87

De Bolt, William Walter
> Ode to Death. P68
> Tears, Good Little Fellows. P72

De Gasztold, Carmen Bernos
> "Dear God". P60

De La Fontaine, Jean. See La Fontaine, Jean de

De la Mare, Walter
> Bunny Rabbit. P51

De La Mare, Walter

> Mrs. MacQueen (or The Lollie-Shop). P51
> Nicholas Nye. P51
> Nod. P51
> Silver. P51
> Someone. P51
> 'Sooeep!'. P51
> Tired Tim. P51

De Vries, Peter
> To His Importunate Mistress. P63

"**De** railroad bridge's". Homesick Blues. Langston Hughes. P83

De, B. R.
> Closing of a Day on Earth. P72

Dead Boy. John Crowe Ransom. P83

Dead Color. Charles Wright. P67

The **Dead** Crab. Andrew Young. P89

Dead Languages. Jay MacPherson. P49

The **Dead** Poet-Friend. Callimachus. P89

The **Dead** Wolf. Roger A. Chrastil. P56

"**Dead** hawk outside my bedrom window". Hawk. Judith Minty. P88

The **Dead.** David Gwenallt Jones. P87

The **Deadly** Dance. Unknown. P78

Deaf-Mute in the Pear Tree. P. K. Page. P49

Deaf-Mutes
> Mutterings Over the Crib of a Deaf Child. James Wright. P57
> They've Broken the Most Delicate Bone in My Ear. Manuel Silva Acevedo. P71
> To One Deaf. Sister Mary Lucina. P57

Deagon, Ann
> E=MCround. P63
> Piece de Resistance. P63

Deahl, James
> The Passing. P49

"**Dear** Father". Unknown. P60

"**Dear** God". Carmen Bernos De Gasztold. P60

Dear Mother. Henry Bloes. P72

"**Dear** boy, you will not hear me speak". Pangloss's Song. Richard Wilbur. P84

"**Dear** cheeks under gay blue eyes, and two brows". My Love. Dewi Havhesp. P87

"**Dear** Jo, Margaret has been taken". Romantic Letter. Josephine Miles. P84

"**Dear** Johnny I love you, I do I do". Letter to Johnny. Bessie Wherry Noe. P65

"**Dear** love, for nothing less than thee". The Dream. John Donne. P59

"**Dear** Mr. Levine". Read to the Animals, or Orpheus at the SPCA. Irving Feldman. P79

"**Dear** Ned, no doubt you'll be surprised". Cooking and Courting (From Tom to Ned). Unknown. P89

"**Dear** one, in that great love...". For One Sweet Sign. Eleanor Gude Ramirez. P72

"**Dear** Sirs: Is it not time we formed a Boston". Communication to the City Fathers of Boston. George Starbuck.

P85
"Dear wife, last midnight, whilst I read".
    Dibdin's Ghost. Eugene Field. P81
"Dear, back wounded heart restore". The
    Divorce. Thomas Stanley. P59
Dearmer, Geoffrey
    Whale. P51
Death
    After the Glory Has Passed Before Us.
        Karen Kania. P88
    Animula. David Wevill. P49
    As if Carbon Is Nothing. Bernice Lever.
        P49
    The Asians Dying. William Stanley Merwin.
        P85
    At the Florist's. Jacques Prevert. P61
    At the Grave of Walker. Joaquin Miller.
        P81
    Bells for John Whiteside's Daughter. John
        Crowe Ransom. P83
    The Betrayal of Violets. Mohammed Ibrahim
        Abu Sinnah. P91
    Beyond Words. Richard Howard. P79
    The Big Knot. Nyalual Pal. P53
    The Blue Symphony. John Gould Fletcher.
        P82
Death. Maxwell Bodenheim. P82
    The Bones of My Father. Etheridge Knight.
        P52
    The Broncho That Would Not Be Broken.
        Vachel Lindsay. P82
    Burial of the Dead, fr. The Waste Land.
        Thomas Stearns Eliot. P83
    Buzzard. Gillian Clarke. P54
    By the Pacific Ocean. Joaquin Miller. P81
    Challenger Lost. Edwin A. Falkowski. P72
    The Chatter of a Death Demon. Stephen
        Crane. P81
    The Chief Centurions. John Masefield. P89
    Cole's Island. Charles Olson. P85
    The Collier. Vernon Watkins. P89
    Consolation. Winifred Hamric Farrar. P72
    Crash. Sandra Rasmussen. P72
    The Crossing. Salvatore Quasimodo. P61
    Dark Friend. Richard M. Mishler. P86
    Day of the Dead. Robert Hayden. P84
    Dead Boy. John Crowe Ransom. P83
    The Dead Poet-Friend. Callimachus. P89
    The Dead. David Gwenallt Jones. P87
    Death. William Carlos Williams. P82
    Death. Maxwell Bodenheim. P82
    Death and Love. Arlo Bates. P81
    "Death Be Not Proud...," from Divine
        Meditations. John Donne. P59
    Death by Water. fr. The Waste Land.
        Thomas Stearns Eliot. P83
    Death Comes Calling. David Mahr. P72
    Death Fugue. Paul Celan. P48
    Death Is Sitting at the Foot of My Bed.

    Oscar Hahn. P71
The Death of the Ball Turret Gunner.
    Randall Jarrell. P84
The Death of the Old Year. Lord Tennyson.
    P90
The Death of the Reference Librarian.
    David Kirby. P63
"Death, Why Have You Waged Such a Fierce
    War on Me". Giacomino Pugliese. P69
"Despite All the Training". Jack Hill.
    P86
Dirge. Madison Cawein. P81
Dirge. Adelaide Crapsey. P81
The Distant Runners. Mark Van Doren. P83
Doctor Meyers, from Spoon River
    Anthology. Edgar Lee Masters. P82
Dutch Graves in Bucks County. Wallace
    Stevens. P83
The Duty of the Prince Is Magnificence.
    Mike Gregory. P56
Dying Is Forever. Michael T. Sargent. P86
The Eagle That Is Forgotten. Vachel
    Lindsay. P82
The Emperor of Ice-Cream. Wallace
    Stevens. P83
An Examination into Life and Death.
    Kenneth Patchen. P84
The Examiner's Death. Peter Meinke. P63
Exodus Unknown. James Marley. P68
Fatal Interview, sel. Edna St. Vincent
    Millay. P82
Fear of Death. John Ashbery. P85
The Final Battle. Kandy Arnold. P58
Final Migration. Carol Hamilton. P68
First Flight. Janet Carncross Chandler.
    P77
For Annie. Edgar Allan Poe. P89
Four Poems in One. Anne Porter. P64
Four Sides to a House. Amy Lowell. P82
The Friendship Only Lasted a Few Seconds.
    Lily Jean Lee-Adams. P86
Funeral Music. Geoffrey Hill. P48
Funeral Song. Patricio Esteve. P92
A Game of Chess, fr. The Waste Land.
    Thomas Stearns Eliot. P83
Gathering the Bones Together. Gregory
    Orr. P85
General William Booth Enters into Heaven.
    Vachel Lindsay. P82
A Gift. Amy Lowell. P82
The Girl Next Door. Knute Skinner. P63
Go Down Death. James Weldon Johnson. P83
God Lay Dead in Heaven. Stephen Crane.
    ´ P81
'Good Night, Willie Lee, I'll See You in
    the Morning'. Alice Walker. P85
Good-Bye. Ralph Waldo Emerson. P89
Grass. Carl Sandburg. P82
Gretel in Darkness. Louise Gluck. P85

The Groundhog. Richard Eberhart. P83
"Having Been Issued". Jack Hill. P86
Here Lies a Lady. John Crowe Ransom. P83
The Hill, from Spoon River Anthology.
     Edgar Lee Masters. P82
The Hollow Men. Thomas Stearns Eliot. P83
How, Like This Spring, Slowly. Susan
     Hauser. P88
Hurt Hawks. Robinson Jeffers. P83
Hymn to God My God, in My Sickness. John
     Donne. P59
I Go to Death. Lewis Moore. P68
I Shall Not Care. Sara Teasdale. P82
'I Wouldn't Be Able To Tell the
     Story...'. Walter Hoefler. P71
If We Must Die. Claude McKay. P82
II, fr. Irradiations. John Gould
     Fletcher. P82
The Image-Maker. Stanley Kunitz. P52
In Memoriam. R. Williams Parry. P87
In the Dordogne. John Peale Bishop. P83
In the Ward: the Sacred Wood. Randall
     Jarrell. P84
Ironica, from Lost Youth: the Last War.
     Alfred Kreymborg. P82
Is There Anyone. Walter Hoefler. P71
Janet Walking. John Crowe Ransom. P83
Johnny Doe. Rick Allen House. P73
King Hayden of Miami Beach. Robert
     Duncan. P84
The Knight, Death, and the Devil. Randall
     Jarrell. P84
Last Gift. Lu Cicada. P77
Last Laugh. M. P. A. Sheaffer. P68
Life. George Herbert. P59
The Lost Love. Fenton Johnson. P82
The Lost Pilot. James Tate. P85
"Loving With a Loyal Heart and With
     Hope". Pier della Vigna. P69
Lullalye-Acidby. Ish Yair. P72
The Mad Yak. Gregory Corso. P85
Many Workmen. Stephen Crane. P81
Memorial Rain. Archibald MacLeish. P83
The Midnight Skaters. Edmund Blunden. P89
Mollie McGee, from Spoon River Anthology.
     Edgar Lee Masters. P82
Moon Shadows. Adelaide Crapsey. P81
Moth Light. Charles P. Martin. P58
Mother and Son. Barry Callaghan. P49
Mother and Son. Allen Tate. P83
Mt. Tamalpais, fr. Andree Rexroth.
     Kenneth Rexroth. P84
My Last Afternoon with Uncle Devereux
     Winslow. Robert Lowell. P84
My Mother. Claude McKay. P82
My Music Teacher. Eric Vio. P72
The Natural Way. Jane S. Spain. P72
Non Omnis Moriar. Teresinka Pereira. P72
O, Breathe Not His Name! (Richard Emmet).

Thomas Moore. P90
Obituary. Kenneth Fearing. P83
Ode for a Master Mariner Ashore. Louise
     Imogen Guiney. P81
Ode to Death. William Walter De Bolt. P68
Old Age. Maxwell Bodenheim. P82
On His Death Bed. Bleddyn Fardd. P87
On His Death-Bed. Meilyr. P87
On the Death of a Metaphysician. George
     Santayana. P81
Only Waiting. Frances Laughton Mace. P89
Open, Time. Louise Imogen Guiney. P81
Origins of the Body. William Carpenter.
     P48
Other Season. Bonnie McConnell. P68
The Pardon. Richard Wilbur. P84
Patterns. Amy Lowell. P82
Pax Pagnanica. Louise Imogen Guiney. P81
Photograph. Oscar Hahn. P71
Pity Ascending with the Fog. James Tate.
     P85
Portrait of an Old Woman. Arthur Davidson
     Ficke. P82
Portrait of Mary. Charles Wright. P79
Post Mortem. Robinson Jeffers. P83
Prelude to Paradise. Dorothea Neale. P72
A Refusal To Mourn the Death, by Fire, of
     a Child... Dylan Thomas. P48
Reincarnation of the Butchers. Oscar
     Hahn. P71
Requiem for Ralph. Sara Lewis Kline. P65
The Science of the Night. Stanley Kunitz.
     P83
The Secret of Death. Sir Edwin Arnold.
     P89
Silent Ship. Yahya Kemal. P91
The Slaughterhouse. Mauricio Electorat.
     P71
Slow but Sure, from Lost Youth: the Last
     War. Alfred Kreymborg. P82
Snows of Aconcagua. Raul Zurita. P71
Song. Richard Hovey. P81
Song of a Dead Pilot. Ahmad 'Abd Al-Muti
     Hijazi. P91
Sonnet. Louise Labe. P89
Southern Gothic. Rodger Kamenetz. P63
The Sower and His Seed. William E. H.
     Lecky. P90
Sphinx Echoes the Sound Left by the Dead.
     Osman Turkay. P72
A Spirit Sped. Stephen Crane. P81
The Stain. Pierre Jean Jouve. P61
The Stars Are Hidden, fr. Five Groups of
     Verse. Charles Reznikoff. P83
Storm. Agnes Nemes Nagy. P92
The Tail of the Buffalo. Nyalual Pal. P53
They Found Him Sitting in a Chair. Horace
     Gregory. P83
They Lived Enamoured of the Lovely Moon.

Trumbull Stickney. P81
Three Poems on Death. Carlos Bousono. P61
To Shelley. John Banister Tabb. P81
Tourist Death. Archibald MacLeish. P83
The Two Mysteries. Mary Mapes Dodge. P89
Uccello. Gregory Corso. P85
The Vampire Came. Craig Lawler. P73
We Needs Must be Divided in the Tomb.
George Santayana. P81
We Parted in Silence. Julia Crawford. P89
When. Sarah Wollsey. P89
When the Green Lies over the Earth.
Angelina Weld Grimke. P89
Whittier. Margaret Elizabeth (Munson)
Sangster. P81
Death. William Carlos Williams. P82
Woe Three. Alice Ryerson. P88
Woman. Sachiko Yoshihara. P92
A Woman Brought Naked Face to Face with
the Sky. Pierre Emmanuel. P61
A Youth in Apparel That Glittered.
Stephen Crane. P81
Death and Love. Arlo Bates. P81
"Death Be Not Proud...," from Divine
Meditations. John Donne. P59
Death by Water, fr. The Waste Land. Thomas
Stearns Eliot. P83
Death Comes Calling. David Mahr. P72
Death Fugue. Paul Celan. P48
Death in the Channel, fr. From a Travel
Diary. T.H. Parry-Williams. P87
Death Is Sitting at the Foot of My Bed.
Oscar Hahn. P71
"Death is an ending and a beginning".
Prelude to Paradise. Dorothea Neale.
P72
Death of a Sunflower. Raymond Souster. P49
Death of Sion y Glyn. Lewis Glyn Cothi. P87
The Death of the Ball Turret Gunner. Randall
Jarrell. P84
The Death of the Loch Ness Monster.
Gwendolyn Macewen. P49
The Death of the Old Year. Lord Tennyson.
P90
The Death of the Reference Librarian. David
Kirby. P63
Death Song for Owain ab Urien. Taliesin. P87
"Death, Why Have You Waged Such a Fierce War
on Me". Giacomino Pugliese. P69
"Death, do not with ambition try". Ode to
Death. William Walter De Bolt. P68

Death-Children
Are the Children at Home? Margaret
Elizabeth (Munson) Sangster. P89
Bells for John Whiteside's Daughter. John
Crowe Ransom. P67
The Bottom Drawer. Amelia Edith Barr. P89
A Child Lost. Sigurdur A. Magnusson. P92
Death of Sion y Glyn. Lewis Glyn Cothi.

P87
The Erl-King. Johann Wolfgang von Goethe.
P90
Evelyn Hope. Robert Browning. P89
The Morning-Glory. Maria White Lowell.
P89
On a Late Schoolboy. Laurence Perrine.
P63
Watching for Papa. Unknown. P89
The Widow's Mite. Frederick Locker-
Lampson. P89
Debate: Question, Quarry, Dream. Robert Penn
Warren. P83

Debauchery
The Presence. William Everson. P84

Decay
Burning Brambles. Roland Mathias. P54
Decompostion. Terry M. Paulsgrove. P77
East Moors. Gillian Clarke. P54
Foliage of Vision. James Merrill. P85
A Game of Chess, fr. The Waste Land.
Thomas Stearns Eliot. P83
The Groundhog. Richard Eberhart. P83
I Play Childish Songs with a Grimace on
My Lips. Gonzalo Millan. P71
Smith's Garage. Robert Minhinnick. P54
Decaying. Jean Pape. P77
December. Peter Asaro. P73
December. Joel Benton. P89

December
December. Peter Asaro. P73
December. Joel Benton. P89
December Leaves. Kaye Starbird. P80
During December's Death. Delmore
Schwartz. P84
December Leaves. Kaye Starbird. P80
"December has the mighty task". December.
Peter Asaro. P73
"December through the high". The Geese.
Robert Williams Parry. P87

Deception
Palimpsest: a Deceitful Portrait. Conrad
Aiken. P82
The Wolf and the Lambs. Ivy O. Eastwick.
P51

Decision Making
The Road Not Taken. Robert Frost. P82
Decompostion. Terry M. Paulsgrove. P77
Decorators Incorporated. Pearl Newton Rook.
P68
Dedication (To Tamara). Luchesar Elenkov.
P70
Dedicatory Entry. Anton Shammas. P92
Deductions. Teresa Calderon. P71
A Deed and a Word. Charles Mackay. P89
Deeds in Orbit. Annie Laurie Leech. P72
"Deep in the desolate". The War. James
Magorian. P68
"Deep in the silence of the forest...". The

Spirit of the Wood. Paul Baudin. P77
"Deep peace, pure white of the moon to you".
    Invocation of Peace, sel. William
    ("Fiona Macleod") Sharp. P51
Deepavali (Festival of Lights). A.
    Padmanaban. P72
Deer. Dafydd ab [or ab] Gwilym. P87
Deer
    Deer in the Open Field. Patricia Hooper.
        P88
    Deer Park. William A. Anderson. P68
    The Deer. Noel M. Valis. P56
    The Girl and Her Fawn. Andrew Marvell.
        P51
    Midwinter. Allen Planz. P64
    Whitetail, 2:30 a.m. Diane P. Lando. P77
"The deer carcass hangs from a rafter".
    Gathering the Bones Together. Gregory
    Orr. P85
Deer in the Open Field. Patricia Hooper. P88
Deer Park. William A. Anderson. P68
"Deer trails". Trails. Tom Tellesbo. P58
The Deer. Noel M. Valis. P56
Defeat
    Victor and Vanquished. Harry Thurston.
        P81
"Defeated/ At the bottom of the stairs".
    Umbrella. Kandy Arnold. P58
The Definition of Love. Andrew Marvell. P59
Deforest, Charlotte B.
    A Lost Snowflake. P80
Degas, Edgar
    Dancer. Charles Guenther (tr.). P61
Degelman, Nan Townsend
    Mother Lode Spring. P77
    Ode to a Nuclear Frieze. P77
Dehmel, Richard
    The Silent Town. Jethro Bithell (tr.).
        P89
    Voice in the Darkness. Margarete A.
        Munsterberg (tr.). P90
Deight in Order, Too. Gary Selden. P63
Deja Vu
    In the Footsteps of Ghengis Khan. Jan
        Barry. P86
Dekker, Thomas
    Happy Heart, from Patient Grissell. P90
Deland, Margaret
    Affair D'Amour. P89
Delaney, Carolyn
    Black and White. P74
Delany, Clarissa Scott
    Interim. P89
    Joy. P90
    Solace. P89
"The Delicate Girl Is Washed". Unknown. P62
"Delicate flowers". Rosemary's French Garden
    Basket. Carolyn O'Harrow Pintye. P72
"Delicate threads weave an intricate

pattern". Inspirations Unlimited.
    Claire Schneider. P72
Delight in Disorder. Robert Herrick. P90
Delight in God. Francis Quarles. P89
The Delight Song of Tsoai-Talee. N. Scott
    Momaday. P85
Deligiorgis, Stavros (tr.)
    Metamorphosis, sel. Argyris Hionis. P92
"Delivers papers to the doors of sleep".
    Herald. Josephine Miles. P84
Deloney, Thomas
    A Princely Ditty in Praise of the English
        Rose. P51
Delphis, Phoebus
    He Lit His Pipe. Charles Guenther (tr.).
        P61
    With the Flashes of the Night. Charles
        Guenther (tr.). P61
The Deluge, 1939. Saunders Lewis. P87
Demakas, Elaine
    Airport. P58
    American Body Binding. P58
    Backstage at the Fillmore. P58
    Bright Sunday. P58
    Lust. P58
    Mother's Milk. P58
    Mr. Computer Science. P58
    Sordid Love. P58
"Deng Duot Nyang's order was heard". Drink
    the Curse. Moses Kuac Nyoat. P53
"Deng's black and white one". Magic That
    Comes at Dawn. Peter Pal Hoth Nyang.
    P53
Denial. George Herbert. P59
Denis, Phillipe
    In the Thickness. Susanna Lang (tr.). P92
Dennis, Zelma S.
    Blue Angels Sky-Dance. P72
Denny, Alma
    I Love Every Hair on Your Head. P63
    Oh, Dem Olden Slippers!. P63
    School Cheer (Progressive Style). P63
    Tuesday. P63
    We and the Weekend. P63
Densmore, Frances (tr.)
    Poems for the Game of Silence. Unknown.
        P78
    The Removal. Unknown. P78
    Spyglass Conversations. Unknown. P78
Departure in Middle Age. Roland Mathias. P54
Dependence
    The Red Wheelbarrow. William Carlos
        Williams. P82
The Depression. David Gwenallt Jones. P87
Der Blinde Junge. Mina Loy. P82
Dereme, Tristan
    The Strawberries. Charles Guenther (tr.).
        P61
DeRoller, Joseph

Poem Found While I Looked for Something
     Else. P63
Derry, Alice
     Letting Go. P88
     These Hills, Mother. P88
Desai, Dhiru
     India. P72
Descendant. Elisaveta Bagriana. P70
Desert Places. Robert Frost. P82
Desert Snow. Vivian L. Martinetz. P72
"The **desert** earth sun-drenched each day".
     Rain Song. Jean Hogan Dudley. P72
"**Desert** spectacular--the sun glories up!.".
     Hallelujah!. Charles Tillman Lockhart.
     P72
The **Deserted** House. Mary E. Coleridge. P51
"**Deserted** by the waning moon". All's Well,
     from The British Fleet. Thomas Dibdin.
     P89
Deserts
     Desert Snow. Vivian L. Martinetz. P72
     To the Immaculate Plains. Raul Zurita.
     P71
Design. Robert Frost. P82
Desire
     About a Year After He Got Married He
     Would Sit Alone... James Whitehead.
     P67
     Answer to Master Wither's Song. Ben
     Jonson. P89
     Asiatic Day-Flower. Donald Finkel. P79
     Chain Reaction. Manuel Silva Acevedo. P71
     The Dream. John Donne. P59
     Elegy 7. John Donne. P59
     The Flea. John Donne. P59
     He Records a Little Song for a Smoking
     Girl. James Whitehead. P67
     Lines to an Indian Air. Percy Bysshe
     Shelley. P89
     "The Sweet Smell of Cedar Sucked Out My
     Breath". Lorenzo. P77
     There Was, Before Me. Stephen Crane. P81
     To His Coy Mistress. Andrew Marvell. P59
Desks Are Places. Glee Knight. P68
Desmond, Walter
     Good Friday. P68
Desnos, Robert
     A Shooting Star. William Kulik (tr.). P48
DeVaux, Sara
     Discovery II. P68
The **Desolate** City. Claude McKay. P82
Despair
     Always, from My First Boyhood. John Peale
     Bishop. P83
     The Anguish. Edna St. Vincent Millay. P82
     As in the Midst of Battle There Is Room.
     George Santayana. P81
     Beach. Juan Cameron. P71
     Cynddylan's Hall, fr. Poetry from Lost

     Sagas. Unknown. P87
     During December's Death. Delmore
     Schwartz. P84
     In the Willow Branches. Salvatore
     Quasimodo. P61
     Letting Go. Alice Derry. P88
     The Lonely Mother. Fenton Johnson. P82
     Mt. Lykaion. Trumbull Stickney. P81
     Over the Hill to the Poor-House. Will
     Carleton. P89
     The Rainy Day. Henry Wadsworth
     Longfellow. P89
     Reasons Before and After the Fact. John
     C. Gilmore. P86
     The Scream. Majeed Amjad. P91
     A Song from Afar. Ahmad 'Abd Al-Muti
     Hijazi. P91
     Victim, fr. Three Voices. Faiz Ahmad
     Faiz. P91
     Why Is Man Born? Georgi Djagarov. P70
     Without Voice, Without Hope. Jozsef
     Tornai. P92
"**Despite** All the Training". Jack Hill. P86
"**Despite** the storm it's dry again".
     Preparing for Winter. Steve Sanfield.
     P77
Destiny
     Everyman's Two Gifts. Hermit Helene Troy
     Arlington. P68
     A Grey Day. William Vaughn Moody. P81
     Luke Havergal. Edward Arlington Robinson.
     P81
     "Through the Ages Man Has Sought HArd to
     Find". Eric-Frederic Wilson. P72
     Unlikely Path. Mark L. Cannaday. P68
     Unmanifest Destiny. Richard Hovey. P81
     Wherever I Go. Al Mahmud. P91
Destruction
     Cora Punctuated with Strawberries. George
     Starbuck. P85
     The Fire Sermon, fr. The Waste Land.
     Thomas Stearns Eliot. P83
     Moss-Gathering. Theodore Roethke. P84
     On the Subject of Roses. Abraham
     Sutzkever. P48
     The Peace of Cities. Richard Wilbur. P84
     Playland at the Beach. Gertrude May Lutz.
     P72
     The Ruin. Dafydd ab [or ab] Gwilym. P87
     The Ruined Hearth of Rheged, fr. Poetry
     from Lost Sagas. Unknown. P87
     Sleep Work. Mohammed Dib. P91
     An Urban Convalescence. James Merrill.
     P85
     The War Against the Trees. Stanley
     Kunitz. P83
     What the Thunder Said. Thomas Stearns
     Eliot. P83
"The **Detective** is late. He called us here".

Waiting for the Detective. Michael
        Cadnum. P63
Deutsch and Avrahm Yarmolinsky, Babette
        (tr.)
        Work. Aleksandr Pushkin. P90
"The **devastation**". No More. Gina Berola. P74
Devil
        The Knight, Death, and the Devil. Randall
        Jarrell. P84
Dew Yu Know. Bill Bissett. P49
"The **dew**, the rain and moonlight". A Net to
        Snare the Moonlight. Vachel Lindsay.
        P82
Dewdney, Christopher
        The Lateshow Diorama. P49
        Winter Central. P49
Di Michele, Mary
        My Hands in Purdah. P49
A **Dialogue** Between the Soul and Body. Andrew
        Marvell. P59
A **Dialogue**. Fatthy Said. P91
Diamond, Lucy
        An Eskimo Baby. P51
        A Greenland Winter. P51
        A Kayak Song. P51
Dib, Mohammed
        Opening Figure. Eric Sellin (tr.). P91
        Sleep Work. Eric Sellin (tr.). P91
        Words or Spoors, fr. Omneros. Eric Sellin
        (tr.). P91
"**Dibbily**, daubily". Imitation Is the
        Sincerest Flattery, But... Blossom S.
        Kirschenbaum. P63
Dibdin's Ghost. Eugene Field. P81
Dibdin, Thomas
        All's Well, from The British Fleet. P89
Dickens in Camp. Bret Harte. P90
Dickey, James
        Cherrylog Road. P67
        A Dog Sleeping on My Feet. P67
        False Youth: Two Seasons (Winter). P67
        Paestum. P79
Dickey, R. P.
        At a Concert. P63
        Materialism. P63
        On a Compliment. P63
        Walking Naked Around the House. P63
Dickey-Birds. Natalie Joan. P51
Dickinson, Emily
        Evening. P51
        Found Wanting. P89
        Heaven. P89
        The Moon. P51
        The World Is Not Conclusion. P48
Dickson, M. (tr.)
        To My Mother. Heinrich Heine. P89
"**Did** the skies". God Complex, from Lost
        Youth: the Last War. Alfred Kreymborg.
        P82

"**Did** you ever hear of Editor Whedon". Daisy
        Fraser, from Spoon River Anthology.
        Edgar Lee Masters. P82
"**Did** you ever see an alligator". Arlo Will,
        from Spoon River Anthology. Edgar Lee
        Masters. P82
"**Did** you hear of the curate...". The Priest
        and the Mulberry Tree. Thomas Love
        Peacock. P51
"**Did** you think all that stuff you gave me".
        Materialism. R. P. Dickey. P63
"**Diddle**, Diddle, Dumpling". Unknown. P51
Different Minds. Richard Chenevix Trench.
        P89
The **Difficult** Poem. Jose Agustin Goytisolo.
        P61
"**difficult** lass is Jennifer Blass". Jennifer
        Blass. Midred Luton. P63
"**Digging** was always my worst work".
        Grandfather in the Garden. Robert
        Minhinnick. P54
Dilemma of the Elm. Genevieve Taggard. P83
Dillard, Annie
        Feast Days: Christmas. P47
"The **dim** boy claps because the others clap".
        The Freaks at Spurgin Road Field.
        Richard Hugo. P57
Dimitrova, Blaga
        Cassandra with a Tail. John Balaban
        (tr.). P70
        Lullaby for my Mother. John Balaban
        (tr.). P70
        Pain. John Updike (tr.). P70
        The Road (Version 1). John Updike (tr.).
        P70
        The Road (Version 2, with echoes of Emily
        Dickinson). John Updike (tr.). P70
        Travelling Alone. John Updike (tr.). P70
        The Water Buffalo (Hanoi, 1972). John
        Balaban (tr.). P70
        Who Takes Care of the Blind Stork?. John
        Balaban (tr.). P70
        A Woman Alone on the Road. John Balaban
        (tr.). P70
Ding-Dong!. Unknown. P51
"**Dinner** depends". The Red-Handled Hatchet.
        Mark Sanders. P63
"**Dinogad's** smock is pied, pied--.". Song to
        a Child. Unknown. P87
Dinosaur Hill. Robert Hahn. P58
Dinosaurs
        Cretaceous Period. A. J. Kealoha Pendzik.
        P74
Dionysians in a Bad Time. Irving Layton. P49
Dirge. Madison Cawein. P81
Dirge. Adelaide Crapsey. P81
Dirlam, Barbara
        Convalescence. P68
The **Dirty** Old Man. William Allingham. P90

Disabilities
    After Being Paralyzed from the Neck
       Down... Ronald Wallace. P57
    Bleeder. Hollis Summers. P57
    The Freaks at Spurgin Road Field. Richard
       Hugo. P57
    The Handicapped. Philip Dacey/ P57
    9:00 a.m. at Broadway and Walnut on Your
       Birthday. Ripley Schemm. P57
    Wrestling with Angels. Walter McDonald.
       P57
The **Disappointed** Shrimper. P. A. Ropes. P51
Disch, Tom
    Riddle with Guesses. P63
    Short-Term Memory Loss. P63
Discontent
    Denial. George Herbert. P59
    Halsted Street Car. Carl Sandburg. P82
    How Now, O, Brightener. Wallace Stevens.
       P79
    A Local Man Doesn't Like the Music. James
       Whitehead. P67
    Miniver Cheevy. Edward Arlington
       Robinson. P81
    Suburbanitis. Grace D. Yerbury. P68
Discount Store. G. N. Gabbard. P63
Discoveries
    The Discovery. Sir John Collings
       ("Solomon Eagle") Squire. P90
    New Sights. Unknown. P51
    To Discover. Janina Zydanowicz. P72
Discovery II. Sara DeVaux. P68
The **Discovery**. Sir John Collings ("Solomon
    Eagle") Squire. P90
Disdain Returned. Thomas Carew. P89
Disfigurement
    Charwoman (Lower Manhattan--6:00 P.M.).
       Ben Belitt. P57
    The Ones That Are Thrown Out. Miller
       Williams. P57
    Stumpfoot on 42nd Street. Louis Simpson.
       P57
    The Subverted Flower. Robert Frost. P82
Disillusion
    The Boy's Song. Zahid Dar. P91
    Disillusionment of Ten O'Clock. Wallace
       Stevens. P83
    Heart's Need. Rajnee Krishnan Kutty. P72
    If I Should Cast Off This Tattered Coat.
       Stephen Crane. P81
    Once and for All. Delmore Schwartz. P84
    Woe Three. Alice Ryerson. P88
Disillusionment of Ten O'Clock. Wallace
    Stevens. P83
Dislocation. Mary Trimble. P88
The **Dispossessed**. John Berryman. P84
A **Dispute** Between Women. Unknown. P78
Distance
    The Road(Version 1). Blaga Dimitrova.

       P70
The **Distance**. Khalilur Rahman Azmi. P91
Distant Exploration. Allan R. Halcrow. P72
The **Distant** Runners. Mark Van Doren. P83
"**Distant** from the centers of the action...".
    She Abandoned Her Body to the Color.
    Gonzalo Munoz. P71
"The **distant** rustling of pine leaves". Dusk.
    N. Krishnan Kutty. P72
Distelheim, Rochelle
    No Muse Is Good Muse. P63
Distractions
    Delight in Disorder. Robert Herrick. P90
Disuse
    Asking the Windows. Margo LaGattuta. P88
The **Ditances** They Keep. Howard Nemerov. P79
The **Diver**. Leslie Nutting. P49
Divertissement. Amy Jo Schoonover. P72
The **Divine** Image. William Blake. P51
Diving and Divers
    The Diver. Leslie Nutting. P49
Diving into the Wreck. Adrienne Rich. P85
Divorce
    Divorce. Maynard G. Teigen. P72
    Divorce. Judy Little. P88
    The Divorce Poem. Janet Beeler Shaw. P88
Divorce. Richard Eberhart. P79
Divorce. Judy Little. P88
    The New Courtship. Richard Moore. P63
Divorce. Maynard G. Teigen. P72
    Untitled #2. Ian Brennan. P58
The **Divorce** Poem. Janet Beeler Shaw. P88
The **Divorce**. Thomas Stanley. P59
Dixie. Albert Pike. P90
Dixon, Mike
    "Splitting Cedar". P77
Djagarov, Georgi
    After Interrogation. Theodore Weiss
     (tr.). P70
    Autumn. Theodore Weiss (tr.). P70
    Bulgaria. William Meredith (tr.). P70
    A Century of Miracles. William Meredith
     (tr.). P70
    Elegy. Richard Wilbur (tr.). P70
    Night. William Meredith (tr.). P70
    Summer Rain. Richard Harteis (tr.). P70
    Why Is Man Born? Reed Whittemore (tr.).
     P70
Do Fairies Like the rain?. Barbara M. Hales.
    P55
"**Do** Not Trust Those Evil Men Who Owe You
    Money". Unknown. P62
Do Not Weep, Maiden. Stephen Crane. P81
Do Parents Cry, too?. Thad King. P73
"**Do** You Remember Sometimes". Srinivas
    Belsaray. P72
Do You Traipse Long-Leggedly Through Murky
    Woodlands. Caroline Knox. P88
"**Do** not name this day". A Hymn for October

15th. Vera Rich. P68

"Do parks get lonely". Snowy Benches. Aileen Fisher. P80

"Do you ask what the birds say?.". The Birds. Samuel Taylor Coleridge. P51

"Do you know pain?.". Cassandra. Faye Kicknosway. P88

"Do you know what I wish?.". An Orphan's Wish. Lee Ann Braunecker. P74

"Do you like marigolds?.". Marigolds. Louise Driscoll. P51

"Do you recall old Mrs. Ay". Amherst Neighbors. Lewis Turco. P63

"Do you think, my boy, when I put my arms...". The Lonely Child. James Oppenheim. P82

Do, Thu-Phuong
    The Loner. P74

Dobell, Sydney
    A Chanted Calendar. P51

Doc Hill, from Spoon River Anthology. Edgar Lee Masters. P82

Doctor Meyers, from Spoon River Anthology. Edgar Lee Masters. P82

"Doctor, you say there are no haloes". Monet Refuses the Operation. Lisel Mueller. P88

The Doctor. David Ignatow. P84

"Doctors who stuck out pence". End Them, If You Can. K. Rathinavelu. P72

Dodge, Mary Mapes
    Snow-Flakes. P89
    The Two Mysteries. P89

Dodgson, Charles Lutwidge ("Lewis Carroll")
    Christmas-Greetings (From a Fairy to a Child). P90
    Jabberwocky, from Through the Looking-Glass. P90
    Life, What Is It but a Dream?. P90
    The Lobster Quadrille. P51
    The Love-Gift of a Fairy-Tale. P90
    The Walrus and the Carpenter, from Alice in Wonderland. P89
    You Are Old, Father William. P90

Dodson, Owen
    I Break the Sky. P84
    Mary Passed This Morning. P84
    Mary Passed This Morning. P84
    Six O'Clock. P84
    Sorrow Is the Only Faithful One. P84

"Does the body rest against his eye, the cool". Bonnard. Christopher Middleton. P79

"Does the road wind up hill all the way?.". Up Hill. Christina Georgina Rossetti. P89

Dog. John Crowe Ransom. P83

Dog Adoption. Claudia Nabors. P72

A Dog Named Ego, the Snowflakes as Kisses. Delmore Schwartz. P84

A Dog Sleeping on My Feet. James Dickey. P67

"The dog stops barking after Robinson has gone". Robinson. Weldon Kees. P84

Dog, from My Hometown's Base Creatures. Wu Cheng. P92

"Dog-tired, suisired, will now my body down". The Poet's Final Instructions. John Berryman. P84

"The Doggies Went to the Mill". Unknown. P51

Dogs
    Alpha the Dog. Robert Sward. P49
    At Breakfast. Ida M. Mills. P51
    Barra. Robert Lawrence. P49
    The Day Willis Harder Didn't Kill His Beagle. Hilary Russell. P63
    Dog. John Crowe Ransom. P83
    Dog Adoption. Claudia Nabors. P72
    A Dog Sleeping on My Feet. James Dickey. P67
    Dog, from My Hometown's Base Creatures. Wu Cheng. P92
    "The Doggies Went to the Mill". Unknown. P51
    Dogs Are Shakespearean, Children Are Strangers. Delmore Schwartz. P84
    English Cocker: Old and Blind. Robert Penn Warren. P67
    My Dog, Spot. Rodney Bennett. P51
    My Doggie. C. Nurton. P51
    My Little Dog. Pearl Forbes MacEwen. P51
    "Old Mother Hubbard". Unknown. P51
    The Pardon. Richard Wilbur. P84
    Puppy and I. A. A. Milne. P51
    Pussy-Cat and Puppy-Dog. Lilian McCrea. P51
    Sheepdog. Thomas Richards. P87
    Stray Dogs. Naomi Lazard. P64
    "There Was a Little Dog, and He Had a Little Tail". Unknown. P51
    Three Dogs. E. C. Brereton. P51
    To a Dog's Memory. Louise Imogen Guiney. P81
    The Woodman's Dog. William Cowper. P51

Dogs Are Shakespearean, Children Are Strangers. Delmore Schwartz. P84

Dolcino to Margaret. Charles Kingsley. P89

Dolls
    Ragged Robin. Elizabeth Godley. P51

The Dolphin-Walk. Milton Acorn. P49

Domain. Constance Studer. P56

Domestic Birds. Robert Bess. P63

Domestic Crisis. X. J. Kennedy. P63

Domestic Violence
    Untitled #1. Ian Brennan. P58

Don't Be Afraid To Grow. Stephen L. Bogadi. P72

Don't Be Discouraged. Phillip Macar. P53

Don't Go, Jo!. Barbara Ireson. P80

"Don't Neglect This One, Saying". Unknown.
    P62
"Don't be a fool, don't go to school". The
    Madness of a Headmistress. Gavin
    Ewart. P63
"Don't believe". Pacifist, from Lost Youth:
    the Last War. Alfred Kreymborg. P82
"Don't forget the crablike". The Hands.
    Denise Levertov. P85
"Don't lie down again". Lying Down, from
    String Games. Unknown. P78
"' Don't send me into an alien'.".
    Question?. E. Manuel Huber. P72
"Don't you know my crime?.". 1974, Not
    Guilty?., from For the Desert Island.
    Tae-ch'ul Shin. P92
Donaldson, Jeffery
    An Old Map of Somewhere. P49
The Donkey. Rose Fyleman. P51
Donkeys
    Nicholas Nye. Walter De La Mare. P51
Donne, John
    Air and Angels. P59
    "At the Round Earth's Imagined...," from
        Divine... P59
    "Batter My Heart...," from Divine
        Mediations. P59
    The Canonization. P59
    The Computation. P59
    "Death Be Not Proud...," from Divine
        Meditations. P59
    The Dream. P59
    The Ecstasy. P59
    Elegy 7. P59
    The Flea. P59
    Four Epigrams. P59
    The Good Morrow. P59
    Hymn to God My God, in My Sickness. P59
    A Hymn to God the Father. P59
    The Legacy. P59
    "Oh My Black Soul!...," from Divine
        Meditations. P59
    The Relic. P59
    Satire 3. P59
    "Since She Whom I Loved...," from Divine
        Meditations. P59
    Song. P59
    The Sun Rising. P59
    The Triple Fool. P59
    Twicknam Garden. P59
    A Valediction: Forbidding Mourning. P59
    Woman's Constancy. P59
Doolittle, Hilda ("H.D.")
    Eurydice. P82
    Heat. P82
    Orchard. P82
    Oread. P82
    Sea Gods. P82
    The Shrine. P82

Doomsday
    Apprehension. Wazir Agha. P91
    The End of the World. Archibald MacLeish.
        P83
    Fire and Ice. Robert Frost. P82
    No More. Gina Berola. P74
"'The door is shut fast'.". Who's In?.
    Elizabeth Fleming. P51
"The door opens with the ease of a page".
    Domain. Constance Studer. P56
"The door was shut, as doors should be".
    Jack Frost. Gabriel Setoun. P51
Doria, Percivalle
    "Just As the Day, When It Is Early
        Morning". Frede Jensen (tr.). P69
"Doris Humphrey's father". Near-Miss Eddy.
    Elizabeth Eddy. P63
The Dormouse. Charlotte Druitt Cole. P51
Dorn, Alfred
    Athena. P65
    From a Marriage Counselor's Notebook. P65
    To a Lady Who Reads Too Much. P65
"Dot a dot dot dot a dot dot". Weather. Eve
    Merriam. P75
"Dotted with streetlights". To Have You
    Near. Terri L. Parent. P65
Double-Face
    "If There Is Someone Above," from Crow
        Versions. William Stanley Merwin
        (tr.). P78
Double-Focus. Al Purdy. P49
Double-Quick. Alice Mackenzie Swaim. P65
Doubt
    Love and Doubt. Harry Thurston. P81
    The World. Frederick William Faber. P89
Doubt and Faith, from In Memoriam. Lord
    Tennyson. P89
"A doubt for rusting the body". A Nail for
    Hanging the Soul. Alain Bosquet. P61
Doudney, S.
    Sweet Surprises. P51
Dougherty, Jay
    Old Women Are Taking Over the World. P63
    A Reply. P63
    Unpleasant Surprise. P63
"The Dove Says Coo". Unknown. P51
Dover Cliff, from King Lear. William
    Shakespeare. P89
Doves. Robert Duncan. P84
Doves. E. J. Falconer. P51
Dowling, Bartholomew
    Revelry of the Dying. P90
Down by the Beach. Dolores Guglielmo. P72
Down by the Brook. Tim Henderson. P74
"Down by the Meadows, Chasing Butterflies".
    Unknown. P51
"Down by the windmill". Not So Long Gone
    (for the Maidu). Doc Dachtler. P77
"Down in the grassy hollow". Merry Little

Men. Kathleen M. Chaplin. P51
"Down in the mission". Erin Go Bragh. Jan
    Glazier. P56
"Down the Hill the Waters Cascade," from
    Mother... Unknown. P90
"Down the road nuclear protestors rally".
    Early May. Graham Everett. P64
"Down the world with Marna!.". The Wander-
    Lovers. Richard Hovey. P81
"Down to the well". Two Steps Forward.
    Jeanine Hathaway. P88
Downes, John A.
    Harmony. P72
Downing, Tamara
    Snowflower. P77
Dowson, Ernest (tr.)
    The Sky Is up Above the Roof. Paul
        Verlaine. P89
The Dracula Vine. Ted Hughes. P55
A Dragon for the Family. Robert Yeo. P92
Dragon's Jaw. David Biles. P86
Dragon-Fly. Hyacinthe Hill. P65
The Dragon. Mary Mullineaux. P51
Drake, John Rodman
    An Elfin Knight. P51
Dramatic Compensation. Francis Brown Price.
    P68
"Draw a Pail of Water". Unknown. P51
Drawbacks. Emily Otis. P63
Drawings
    Bonnard. Christopher Middleton. P79
    Oh, Now I See... Keith Casto. P63
Drayson, Phyllis
    The Blackbird. P51
    Hide and Seek. P51
Drayton, Michael
    A Fine Day. P51
    Pigwiggen. P51
Dream. Salvadore J. Coppola. P72
Dream. Georges Friedenkraft. P72
Dream. Unknown. P78
The Dream Fairy. Thomas Hood. P51
The Dream of Life. Vera La Claustra. P72
Dream of Trains. Paulette Roeske. P88
Dream Pedlary. Thomas Lovell Beddoes. P51
Dream Scars. Kateri Lanthier. P49
The Dream Ship. W. K. Holmes. P51
The Dream Songs, sels. John Berryman. P84
The Dream Songs, sels. John Berryman. P52
A Dream. Sylvia L. Bryant. P72
The Dream. Louise Bogan. P83
The Dream. John Donne. P59
"The dreamer and the dream are never". All
    in All. C. B. Oppenheimer. P68
The Dreamer. Christina Leighty. P74
The Dreamer. Daniel Self. P74
Dreams
    April. Alfred Corn. P79
    Bailey. Knute Skinner. P63

Be Still. The Hanging Gardens Were a
    Dream. Trumbull Stickney. P81
Bermuda Dream. Katharine Wilson. P72
The Big Bang. Howard Nemerov. P63
A Child's Thought. Robert Louis
    Stevenson. P51
CIII. Raul Zurita. P71
Clouds of Evening. Robinson Jeffers. P83
Covers. Virginia M. Hahn. P58
Dream. Georges Friedenkraft. P72
Dream of Trains. Paulette Roeske. P88
Dream Pedlary. Thomas Lovell Beddoes. P51
A Dream. Sylvia L. Bryant. P72
The Dream. Louise Bogan. P83
Dreams. Tom Tellesbo. P58
Dreams-in-Progress. Gwendolyn Vincent.
    P58
The Fairy Sleep and Little Bo-Peep.
    Unknown. P51
Gargoyle. Carl Sandburg. P82
The Ghosts of the Buffaloes. Vachel
    Lindsay. P82
I Dream. Janine A. Parry. P73
I Dream of a Land. Lola E. Hahn. P72
If I Had But Two Little Wings. Samuel
    Taylor Coleridge. P51
In a Lovely Garden Walking. Johann Ludwig
    Uhland. P89
The Instruction Manual. John Ashbery. P85
Jock O' Dreams. Rose Fyleman. P51
Kitchenette Building, fr. A Street in
    Bronzeville. Gwendolyn Brooks. P84
Like Him Whose Spirit. Arthur Davidson
    Ficke. P82
Lunar Baedecker. Mina Loy. P82
The Mad Scene. James Merrill. P85
Meat. Phebe Hanson. P88
Mrs. Brown. Rose Fyleman. P51
Night Visits with the Family. May
    Swenson. P79
"On poetry and geometric truth", fr. The
    prelude. William Wordsworth. P48
A Resolution. Ben Howard. P68
The River of Bees. William Stanley
    Merwin. P85
Saturday Night in the Parthenon. Kenneth
    Patchen. P84
Sunday Morning. Wallace Stevens. P83
Dreams. Tom Tellesbo. P58
Dreams. Thomas Traherne. P59
    "30 Dreams Held in a Hand". Wolfgang D.
        Gugl. P72
    The Tree of the Sound of Silence. Greer
        Newcomb. P72
    'Twas but a Dream. Marjan Lindemans. P73
    Waterchew!. Gregory Corso. P85
    White Symphony. John Gould Fletcher. P82
    The Youth Dreams. Rainer Maria Rilke. P90
"The dreams our son dreams now are

dreams...". Just War. Maria Jacobs.
    P49
Dreams-in-Progress. Gwendolyn Vincent. P58
"Dreary lay the long road...". The Toy Band.
    Henry Newbolt. P51
Driftwood. Trumbull Stickney. P81
Drink the Curse. Moses Kuac Nyoat. P53
Drink to Me Only with Thine Eyes, from The
    Forest. Philostratus. P89
Drinking Music. James Applewhite. P67
Drinks and Drinking
    Drunks. John Berryman. P79
    Dylan Thomas. Euros Bowen. P87
    Food and Drink. Louis Untermeyer. P82
    For a Good Ole Boy. Mary Veazey. P63
    General Self-Satisfied, from Lost Youth:
        the Last War. Alfred Kreymborg. P82
    Gluggity Glug, from Myrtle and the Vine.
        George Colman the Younger. P90
    In Praise of Sobriety. John Frederick
        Nims. P63
    Mr. Flood's Party. Edward Arlington
        Robinson. P81
    To Thomas Moore. George Gordon, 6th Baron
        Byron. P90
    Waiting for the Detective. Michael
        Cadnum. P63
    Wine Coolers. Bern Sharfman. P63
Drinkwater, John
    Moonlit Apples. P51
    Morning Thanksgiving. P51
    "Thank God for sleep in the Long Quiet
        Night". P60
    A Town Window. P51
"Drip. Drip. Drip.". Eskimo Haiku. Robert
    Peters. P63
Driscoll, Louise
    Marigolds. P51
Dristle, Debbie
    Achilles' Fatal Flaw. P74
""Driver, what stream is it?" I asked...".
    The Lordly Hudson. Paul Goodman. P84
Driving. John Newlove. P49
"Droning a drowsy syncopated tune". The
    Weary Blues. Langston Hughes. P83
"Drop down, drop down, white snowflakes!.".
    Winter's Song. Unknown. P51
Drought
    Some Days Ago. Majeed Amjad. P91
Drowning
    A Child Lost. Sigurdur A. Magnusson. P92
    Goal Far and Near. Margaret Avison. P49
    Under the Boathouse. David Bottoms. P67
Drug Addiction
    Lunar Baedecker. Mina Loy. P82
    Melissa's Song. Phil Cohen. P72
    Reasons Before and After the Fact. John
        C. Gilmore. P86
    Variable Service. Dabney Stuart. P79

Drug Store. John V. A. Weaver. P82
The Drunk in the Furnace. William Stanley
    Merwin. P85
The Drunken Fisherman. Robert Lowell. P84
Drunks. John Berryman. P79
Dryden, John
    Ah, How Sweet, from Tyrannic love. P89
    Under the Portrait of John Milton. P90
Dryden, John (tr.)
    Veni Creator Spiritus. Saint Gregory the
        Great. P89
DuBose, Jerri
    Runaway. P74
Duck's Ditty. Kenneth Grahame. P51
The Duck. Edith King. P51
Ducks. Norman Ault. P51
Ducks
    Mrs. Indiarubber Duck. D. Carter. P51
    Sing-Song Rhyme. Unknown. P51
    Wild Duck. Euros Bowen. P87
Ducks, sel. F. W. Harvey. P51
Dudek, Louis
    To a Young Woman. P49
Dudley, Jean Hogan
    Rain Song. P72
The Duel. Eugene Field. P90
Dufferin, Lady. See Sheridan, Helen Selina
"Duffled against a knucklebuster wind".
        Epitaph at Gilfach Goch. John Tripp.
        P54
Dugan, Alan
    Stutterer. P57
Duhameaux, May
    Identity. P72
Duke. Ed Ochester. P63
The Dull Image. Tony D'Arpino. P56
"Dull sounds from the stream". Shinto Tombs.
        Carl Heinz Kurz. P72
"Dumping hot coal ash". January. Graham
        Everett. P64
Dunbar, Jennie
    A-Hunting. P51
Dunbar, Paul Laurence
    Dawn. P89
    Harriet Beecher Stowe. P90
Duncan, Lois
    Song of Triumph. P50
Duncan, Robert
    Bending the Bow. P84
    Doves. P84
    King Hayden of Miami Beach. P84
    Roots and Branches. P84
    Shadows. P84
    Two Dicta of William Blake. P52
    What Do I Know of the Old Lore?. P84
Dunetz, Lora
    Aftermath. P65
Dunlap, Dorothy C.
    Secrets. P72

Dunlap, John Carlisle
    Peace. P72
Duo for Voice & Percussion. E. O. Staley.
    P63
Dupuy, J.
    Michael Met a Duck. P51
Durben, Wolfgang
    Letters. Werner Manheim (tr.). P72
"A duress that much worries me...". Hywel's
    Boast of Women, sels. Hywel ab Owain
    Gwynedd. P87
During December's Death. Delmore Schwartz.
    P84
During the Eichmann Trial, sels. Denise
    Levertov. P85
"During the days of his life". The Poet's
    Days. Omar Lara. P71
Dusk. N. Krishnan Kutty. P72
Dusk. Mary Alice Lipes. P74
Dusk in Changuitad. Sergio Mansilla. P71
"The dusky night rides down the sky". A
    Hunting We Will Go. Henry Fielding.
    P89
Dust
    Dust. P. A. Ropes. P51
The Dust of Delos. Haywood Jackson. P68
The Dustman. Clive Sansom. P51
The Dustman. Unknown. P51
"A dusty road is mine to tread". Pedlar Jim.
    Florence Hoare. P51
A Dutch Courtyard. Richard Wilbur. P84
Dutch Elm Disease. George E. Morrissey. P68
Dutch Graves in Bucks County. Wallace
    Stevens. P83
A Dutch Lullaby. Eugene Field. P89,P81
The Dutch Patrol. Edmund Clarence Stedman.
    P81
The Duty of the Prince Is Magnificence. Mike
    Gregory. P56
"Dweller, are you listening". Dawn of
    Tomorrow. Tomas Segovia. P92
Dwight, J. S. (tr.)
    The Landlady's Daughter. Johann Ludwig
    Uhland. P89
    A Leaf. Johann Ludwig Uhland. P89
"The Dying Chief with Effort Tells His Son".
    Unknown. P62
Dying Is Forever. Michael T. Sargent. P86
Dylan Thomas. Euros Bowen. P87

E Pluribus Ovum. Bob McKenty. P63
E'en as a Lovely Flower. Heinrich Heine. P89
"E'en such is time; that takes in trust".
    Lines Found in his Bible in the Gate-
    House... Sir Walter Raleigh. P89
"E. C. Bentley". David Jacobs. P63

E=MCround. Ann Deagon. P63
Each Age Believed. Terri Brint Joseph. P68
Each Bird Walking. Tess Gallagher. P52
"Each city, each". Postcards. Gerry
    Shikatani. P49
"Each day I ponder this reality". Everyman's
    Two Gifts. Hermit Helene Troy
    Arlington. P68
"Each day, when the glow of sunset". Are the
    Children at Home? Margaret Elizabeth
    (Munson) Sangster. P89
"Each man must bear the scars of battles
    lost". Life, from Thoughts I Caught.
    Frieda Jo Hawes. P72
"Each morning". The Morning Reading. Wu
    Cheng. P92
"Each morning I scan the obituary page". At
    Seventy. F. C. Rosenberger. P63
"Each one showed me his gold medal". Viet
    Kong. William Trowbridge. P63
"Each shift you make in the sunlight
    somewhere". Sunlight Is Imagination.
    Richard Wilbur. P84
"Each year I have a birthday". A Giant's
    Cake. Evelina San Garde. P51
The Eagle Above Us. Unknown. P78
The Eagle Exterminating Company. James Tate.
    P85
The Eagle of Eli, fr. Poetry from Lost
    Sagas. Unknown. P87
The Eagle That Is Forgotten. Vachel Lindsay.
    P82
"Eagle of Eli, loud was its cry tonight--.".
    The Eagle of Eli, fr. Poetry from Lost
    Sagas. Unknown. P87
The Eagle. Lord Tennyson. P51
Eagles
    The Eagle Above Us. Unknown. P78
    The Eagle of Eli, fr. Poetry from Lost
    Sagas. Unknown. P87
Earlene Spratt's Lot. Hilary Russell. P63
Early May. Graham Everett. P64
"Early Morning Sun". Zana. P56
The Early Morning. Hilaire Belloc. P51
The Early Primrose. Henry Kirke White. P89
"Early in the morning". A Watering Rhyme. P.
    A. Ropes. P51
"Early, early, comes the dark". Witches'
    Song. Elizabeth J. Coatsworth. P55
Ears
    Headless. Josephine Miles. P84
Earth
    Continental Drift. Colin Barnhorst. P68
    Earth. Krishna Srinivas. P72
    The Earth. Aric Chen. P74
    God's World. Edna St. Vincent Millay. P82
    Hamlet XX. Stefan Tsanev. P70
    "My Bath Is The Ocean". Madeleine
    L'Engle. P60

Earth. Krishna Srinivas. P72
     Tasting the Earth. James Oppenheim. P82
     Topsyturvey-World. William Brighty Rands.
        P90
     The World. William Brighty Rands. P51,P90
"Earth has borne a little son". The Aconite.
     A. M. Graham. P51
"Earth has not anything to show more fair".
     Sonnet. William Wordsworth. P90
"The earth is billions of years old". Hamlet
     XX. Stefan Tsanev. P70
"Earth is flesh of flames". Earth. Krishna
     Srinivas. P72
"Earth puts her colours by". Envoi. P. H. B.
     Lyon. P51
"The earth was green, the sky was blue". The
     Green Cornfield. Christina Georgina
     Rossetti. P51
"The Earth with Its Palasha Blossoms".
     Unknown. P62
"Earth woman lying flat her feet...". Before
     They Made Things Be Alive They Spoke.
     Lucario Cuevish. P78
"Earth, bind us close, and time...". Theory
     of Flight. Muriel Rukeyser. P84
The Earth. Aric Chen. P74
Earthbound. Bette Warden. P72
"The Earthly life already contains...". The
     Apocalypse of Our Times, sel. Vasily
     Vasilievich Rosanov. P48
Earthquakes
     Christine, on Her Way to China: An
        Earthquake Poem. Judith Minty. P88
East Hampton: The Structure of Sound. Philip
     Appleman. P64
East Moors. Gillian Clarke. P54
The East Wind. T.H. Parry-Williams. P87
East, sel. Gonzalo Munoz. P71
Easter
     Easter. George Herbert. P51
     Easter Eve, 1945. Muriel Rukeyser. P52
     Easter Hills of Peace. Emma Crobaugh. P68
     Easter Praise. Rodney Bennett. P51
     An Egg for Easter. Irene F. Pawsey. P51
     Good Friday. Walter Desmond. P68
Easter. George Herbert. P51
Easter. George Herbert. P59
     Lent in a Year of War. Thomas Merton. P84
     The Willow-boughs. Alexander Block. P51
An Easter Chick. Thirza Wakley. P51
Easter Day. Richard Crashaw. P59
Easter Eve, 1945. Muriel Rukeyser. P52
Easter Hills of Peace. Emma Crobaugh. P68
Easter Praise. Rodney Bennett. P51
Easter Wings. George Herbert. P59
"Easter again, and a small rain falls". The
     Other Side of the River. Charles
     Wright. P52
Eastman, Charles Gamage

A Picture. P89
Eastman, M. (tr.)
     Dagger. Mikhail Lermontov. P90
Eastward the Armies. William Everson. P84
Eastwick, Ivy O.
     At Sunset. P51
     Cherry Tree. P51
     A Feather for My Cap. P51
     Larch Wood Secrets. P51
     Lucy Lavender. P51
     Miller, Miller. P51
     Morning. P51
     Pretty Maid Marion. P51
     The Scarf. P51
     Trouble at the Farm. P51
     The Wolf and the Lambs. P51
Easy As Wind. Grace Schulman. P64
Eat Nothing. Nyapal Kong. P53
"The eaters saddened every heart...". A
     Story of the Eaters. Santiago Mendes
     Zapata. P78
Eating Out. Gene Fehler. P63
Eating. See Food and Eating
Eaves. Ellis Jones. P87
"The ebb slips from the rock, the sunken".
     Night. Robinson Jeffers. P83
Eberhart, Richard
     Divorce. P79
     Flux. P83
     The Fury of Aerial Bombardment. P83
     The Groundhog. P83
     If I Could Only Live at the Pitch That Is
        Near Madness. P83
     Time Passes. P72
Echo and the Lover. Unknown. P90
Echoes. John Zurlo. P56
The Echoing Green. William Blake. P51
Eckhart, Katherine Nielsen
     Awaiting Their Return. P72
Ecology
     Sierra Song. Steve Sanfield. P77
Economics
     Notes for an Unpublished Canto. Ezra
        Pound. P79
The Ecstasy. John Donne. P59
"Ed, Ed". Elegy for Mr. Ed, the Talking
     Horse. Jim Daniels. P63
Eddie's Comet. Barbara Hawkins. P74
Eddy, Elizabeth
     Near-Miss Eddy. P63
Eden, Helen Parry
     'Four-Paws'. P51
Edgar, Vernon
     Arrival. P72
Edge of Appalachia. Margielea Stonestreet-
     See. P72
"The edge of infinity separates". The Light
     at the Edge of the World. Geoffrey
     Parsons. P72

The **Edge**. Ken Norris. P49
The **Editor** Regrets. David Cram. P63
Editor Whedon, from Spoon River Anthology.
    Edgar Lee Masters. P82
Edmonds, Paul
    Little Tommy Tiddler. P51
Edmonson, Munro (tr.)
    The Popol Vuh: Alligator's Struggles...,
    sel. Unknown. P78
    The Popol Vuh: Beginnings, sel. Unknown.
    P78
Edward Curtis Photographs the North American
    Indians. Virginia E. Smith. P68
Edward Lear Finds Paradise (And Loses It).
    J. Patrick Lewis. P63
Edwards, Duane
    No Longer Do I Dwell. P68
Effigy of a Nun. Sara Teasdale. P82
Effort at Speech Between Two People. Muriel
    Rukeyser. P84
An **Egg** for Easter. Irene F. Pawsey. P51
Eggs for Breakfast. Irene F. Pawsey. P51
"The **eggshell** teacup". Autumn. Myron
    Wahlstrand. P72
Eglwys Newydd. John Tripp. P54
Ego at the Wheel. Ernest Kroll. P63
Egypt
    Nile (1). Cathy Matyas. P49
Ehrhart, W. D.
    Coming Home. P86
    The Next Step. P86
    One Night on Guard Duty. P86
Eicher, Margaret Flanagan
    In the Garden of Your Words. P65
Eighth and Broad. Wallace Whatley. P63
Einion ap Gwalchmai
    Elegy for Nest, sels. Tony Conran (tr.).
    P87
Einolf, Doris Eliz
    I Arrive at the Coliseum... P72
"**Either** you will". Prospective Immigrants
    Please Note. Adrienne Rich. P85
Eleanore-Melissa
    Cubes. P68
    The Darkness Before. P68
    One More I'matation. P68
    Reversal. P68
Electorat, Mauricio
    All Night Long by Train, All Night Long.
    Steven F. White (tr.). P71
    For Armando Rubio. Steven F. White (tr.).
    P71
    The Return. Steven F. White (tr.). P71
    Satellite City. Steven F. White (tr.).
    P71
    The Slaughterhouse. Steven F. White
    (tr.). P71
Electrical Storm. Robert Hayden. P84
Elegies

Boschka Layton 1921-1984. Irving Layton.
    P49
Elegy. Cynddelw Brydydd Mawr. P87
Elegy Before Death. Edna St. Vincent
    Millay. P82
Elegy for a Dead Soldier. Karl Shapiro.
    P84
Elegy for Llywelyn ap Gruffudd, the Last
    Prince. Bleddyn Fardd. P87
Elegy for Nest, sels. Einion ap
    Gwalchmai. P87
Elegy for Rhys Gryg. y Prydydd Bychan.
    P87
Elegy for Syr Owain ap Gwilym. Wiliam
    Llyn. P87
Elegy on a Spirit Luster's Polar Site of
    Empyrean... Lee Ver Duft. P68
Elegy on Madam Blaize. Oliver Goldsmith.
    P90
An Elegy To Dispel Gloom. Lawrence
    Ferlinghetti. P85
Epilogue for FDR. David Ignatow. P84
For James Dean. Frank O'Hara. P85
The Gododdin, sels. Aneirin. P87
The Killing of Hywel. Peryf ap Cedifor.
    P87
A Late Elegy for a Baseball Player. Felix
    Stefanile. P57
Nelligan. Laurence Hutchman. P49
Elegies in a City Churchyard. Gloria A.
    Maxson. P63
Elegy. Georgi Djagarov. P70
Elegy. Cynddelw Brydydd Mawr. P87
Elegy 7. John Donne. P59
Elegy Before Death. Edna St. Vincent Millay.
    P82
Elegy for a Dead Soldier. Karl Shapiro. P84
Elegy for Llywelyn ap Gruffudd, the Last
    Prince. Bleddyn Fardd. P87
Elegy for Mr. Ed, the Talking Horse. Jim
    Daniels. P63
Elegy for Nest, sels. Einion ap Gwalchmai.
    P87
Elegy for Rhys Gryg. y Prydydd Bychan. P87
Elegy for Syr Owain ap Gwilym. Wiliam Llyn.
    P87
Elegy for the Other Woman. Elisavietta
    Ritchie. P63
Elegy on a Spirit Luster's Polar Site of
    Empyrean... Lee Ver Duft. P68
Elegy on Madam Blaize. Oliver Goldsmith. P90
An **Elegy** To Dispel Gloom. Lawrence
    Ferlinghetti. P85
The **Elements**. Elisaveta Bagriana. P70
Elenkov, Luchesar
    Dedication (To Tamara). John Balaban
    (tr.). P70
    A Letter to My Mother in Vidin. John
    Balaban (tr.). P70

69

ENDEMANN

"'Me, 20-Year-Old Sergeant, Ognyan
    Mihailov'". John Balaban (tr.). P70
Painter of Icons. John Balaban (tr.). P70
"The **Elephant** is like a wall". The Elephant.
    E. J. Falconer. P51
The **Elephant**. Herbert Asquith. P51
The **Elephant**. Hilaire Belloc. P51
The **Elephant**. E. J. Falconer. P51
Elephants
    The Elephant. Herbert Asquith. P51
    The Elephant. Hilaire Belloc. P51
    The Elephant. E. J. Falconer. P51
    Just Jumbo. Eileen Mathias. P51
"**Eleven** years, the child opened...". Wimmera
    Child's First Waterfall. Joyce Lee.
    P72
The **Elf** and the Dormouse. Oliver Herford.
    P89
An **Elfin** Knight. John Rodman Drake. P51
The **Elfin** Pedlar. George Darley. P51
The **Elfin** People Fill the Tubes. Winifred M.
    Letts. P51
Eliot, George (Mary Ann Cross)
    Day Is Dying, fr. The Spanish Gypsy. P89
    Roses. P51
Eliot, Thomas Stearns
    Burial of the Dead, fr. The Waste Land.
        P83
    Death by Water, fr. The Waste Land. P83
    The Fire Sermon, fr. The Waste Land. P83
    Four Quartets, sels. P83
    A Game of Chess, fr. The Waste Land. P83
    The Hollow Men. P83
    The Love Song of J. Alfred Prufrock. P83
    Rhapsody on a Windy Night. P83
    What the Thunder Said. P83
The **Elixir**. George Herbert. P51,P59
"**Elizabeth** Barrett". Clerihew Couples.
    Roberta Simone. P63
Elliot, Ebenezer
    Burns (A Poet's Epitaph). P90
Elliot, F. Ann
    The Snow. P51
Elliot, Margaret Drake
    Yarrow. P72
Elliot, William Young
    October Morning. P72
Elliott, F. Ann
    Pictures. P51
Ellis, Jaime
    What Could I Be If I Couldn't Be Me?. P74
"The **elongated** corpse of darkness...".
    Sonnet 12, fr. Three Sonnets From
    'Deep Within the Heart'. Syed Shamsul
    Haque. P91
Elsa Wertman, from Spoon River Anthology.
    Edgar Lee Masters. P82
Elwood, Crary
    Spring Freshet. P72

Embrace of Crescents. Daud Kamal. P91
"**Emerging** from scholar's harsh light".
    Woman's College. John Frank. P72
Emerson, Jean L.
    Daughter Softly Singing in the Night. P72
Emerson, Ralph Waldo
    Brahma. P89
    Flower Chorus. P51
    Good-Bye. P89
    Hymn. P90
    Mountain and the Squirrel. P51
    The Mountain and the Squirrel. P51,90
    The Snow-Storm. P89
    Spring Prayer. P51
    The Wind in the Grass. P51
Emigration. See Immigration & Emigration
Emmanuel, Pierre
    The Art of Poetry. Charles Guenther
        (tr.). P61
    London, March 1945. Charles Guenther
        (tr.). P61
    Pledges. Charles Guenther (tr.). P61
    A Woman Brought Naked Face to Face with
        the Sky. Charles Guenther (tr.). P61
Emmons, Elaine
    Ancient Convolutions. P77
    Swimming. P77
Emotions
    Life in Color. Helen Thomas Allison. P72
Emotions Extinction. Patricia Anne Solek-
    Fritsche. P72
Empathy and New Year. James Schuyler. P64
The **Emperor** of Ice-Cream. Wallace Stevens.
    P83
Emphasis Mine. Edmund Conti. P63
Employment
    'Let There Be Translators!'. Grace
        Schulman. P79
    Two Tramps in Mud Time. Robert Frost. P82
"An **empty** ant track, scuffed by delicate
    feet". An Afternoon's Wandering. Kolyo
    Sevov. P70
"An **empty** feeling in your heart". Lonely
    Is... Jeremy Kohburn. P74
En Route. Anita H. Rosenau. P68
"**Enamelled** basins, full". Mangoes. Taufiq
    Rafat. P91
Encounter. Addison Merrick. P56
The **Encyclopedist's** Conundrum. Kirby Olson.
    P63
End of Summer. William Everson. P84
End of the Civil War, from Richard III.
    William Shakespeare. P90
The **End** of the World. Archibald MacLeish.
    P83
End Them, If You Can. K. Rathinavelu. P72
Endemann, Carl T.
    Foot Hills. P56
    The Great Marble Cake. P56

Endless Thought. Ashley Schmidt. P73
Endless Variation. John Ashbery. P85
The Engine Driver. G. S. O. P51
England
> The Best of All. Margaret G. Rhodes. P51
> England. Marianne Moore. P83
> The Gates to England. Marjorie Wilson. P51
> Home Thoughts from Abroad. Robert Browning. P51,P89
> Jerusalem. William Blake. P51
England. Marianne Moore. P83
> O England, Country of My Heart's Desire. E. V. Lucas. P51
> Of England, and of Its Marvels. Fazio degli Uberti. P90
> On First Entering Westminster Abbey. Louise Imogen Guiney. P81
> A Princely Ditty in Praise of the English Rose. Thomas Deloney. P51
> Rule Britannia, from Lost Youth: the Last War. Alfred Kreymborg. P82
> This England. William Shakespeare. P51
> This Is England. Laurence Binyon. P51
> The Union Jack. Jeannie Kirby. P51
"England's done the right thing". Rule Britannia, from Lost Youth: the Last War. Alfred Kreymborg. P82
Engle Jr., John D.
> Financial Note. P63
> Horrorscope. P63
> Mower and Mower. P63
> Smoker's Epitaph. P63
English as a Second Language, from Your Tired... Lisel Mueller. P88
English Cocker: Old and Blind. Robert Penn Warren. P67
English Rats. X. J. Kennedy. P63
Enhanced Embrace. Antonio Giraudier. P65
Ennui. David Ray. P63
Enoch, Olive
> Bluebells. P51
> Half Holiday. P51
> Laughter. P51
"Enormous cloud-mountains that form...". Clouds of Evening. Robinson Jeffers. P83
"Entering his office, he looks at his nurse". The Doctor. David Ignatow. P84
"The entire country is overrun...". Gypsy. Josephine Miles. P84
Envious Satan, from Lost Youth: the Last War. Alfred Kreymborg. P82
Envoi. John Barton. P49
Envoi. P. H. B. Lyon. P51
Envoi. L. L. Zieger. P63
Envoy. Richard Hovey. P81
Envy
> Envy. Naomi F. Faust. P72

> Overhead on a Saltmarsh. Harold Monro. P51
Enzo, Re
> "If I Found Pity". Frede Jensen (tr.). P69
> "There Is a Time for Climbing and for Descending". Frede Jensen (tr.). P69
Epigrams. J. V. Cunningham. P79
Epigrams
> Four Epigrams. John Donne. P59
> Martial's Epigrams, Book X, 47. Sir Richard Fanshawe. P59
Epilogue. Langston Hughes. P83
Epilogue for FDR. David Ignatow. P84
"Epilogue of summer season". October's Wooing. Terese Akins. P72
Epilogue to a Human Drama. Stephen Spender. P48
Epistle To Be Left in the Earth. Archibald MacLeish. P83
Epitaph. Dafydd Jones. P87
Epitaph. Lois Leurgans. P63
Epitaph. Ellis Owen. P87
Epitaph at Gilfach Goch. John Tripp. P54
Epitaph for Father and Son. John Phillips (Tegidon). P87
Epitaph for the Lemon Lady. Bruce Bennett. P63
Epitaph on a Dormouse, Which Some Children... Unknown. P90
Epitaph on a Long Stone. Rudi Holzapfel. P72
Epitaphs
> Ballad for a Solonaut. Joanna Salamon. P92
> Burial of Sir John Moore. Charles Wolfe. P90
> Elegies in a City Churchyard. Gloria A. Maxson. P63
> Elegy. Georgi Djagarov. P70
> Elegy for Mr. Ed, the Talking Horse. Jim Daniels. P63
> Epitaph. Dafydd Jones. P87
> Epitaph. Lois Leurgans. P63
> Epitaph. Ellis Owen. P87
> Epitaph for Father and Son. John Phillips (Tegidon). P87
> Epitaph for the Lemon Lady. Bruce Bennett. P63
> Epitaph on a Dormouse, Which Some Children... Unknown. P90
> Epitaph on a Long Stone. Rudi Holzapfel. P72
> Epitaphs. Orhan Veli Kanik. P91
> Food Director's Testimony. Nancy Simpson. P63
> For a Lady I Know, fr. Four Epitaphs. Countee Cullen. P83
> For Frank (5-70). Bruce Langbien. P86
> For John Keats, Apostle of Beauty, fr.

Four Epitaphs. Countee Cullen. P83
For My Grandmother, fr. Four Epitaphs.
     Countee Cullen. P83
For Paul Laurence Dunbar, fr. Four
     Epitaphs. Countee Cullen. P83
Here Lies a Lady. John Crowe Ransom. P83
In Memory of an English Professor. Reed
     Whittemore. P63
In Memory of Colonel Charles Young.
     Countee Cullen. P83
Epitaphs. Orhan Veli Kanik. P91
Little Elegy. Michael McFee. P63
Mark Antony, over the Body of Caesar.
     William Shakespeare. P90
On a Deceased Office-Seeker. Laurence
     Perrine. P63
Pompous. Paul Ramsey. P63
Posthumous. Jules Supervielle. P61
The Quaker Graveyard in Nantucket. Robert
     Lowell. P84
Smoker's Epitaph. John D. Engle Jr. P63
Streetcar. Agnes Nemes Nagy. P92.
To a Dog's Memory. Louise Imogen Guiney.
     P81
To the Memory of Ben Jonson. John
     Cleveland. P90
To W.P. George Santayana. P81
Two Epitaphs. Louise Imogen Guiney. P81
A Wife's Epitaph. R. Williams Parry. P87
Epoch. Nikola Vaptsarov. P70
Epstein, Daniel Mark
     The Sentry of Portoferraio. P57
Epstein, Mary-Elizabeth
     Retired. P72
"An **equal** radius encloses me". Space.
     Salvatore Quasimodo. P61
Equals. James D. Hartman. P86
Equation. Caroline Perkins. P68
Equations. Yaedi Ignatow. P64
The **Equilibrists.** John Crowe Ransom. P67,P83
Erb, Gary
     The Gosling. P56
     Winter. P56
"**Ere** I freeze, to sing bravely". Poem of the
     Frost and Snow. Lewis Morris. P87
"**Ere** my back was bent, I was ready with
     words:.". Llywarch the Old, fr. Poetry
     from Lost Sagas. Unknown. P87
"The **erect** pole points". Pole Vaulter. David
     Allan Evans. P68
Erickson, Lorene
     The Outing. P88
     Virginia. P88
     You Look. P88
Erin Go Bragh. Jan Glazier. P56
The **Erl-King.** Johann Wolfgang von Goethe.
     P90
Erosion. Miriam Pederson. P88
Erotic Love

Alone: Genesis. Karen Kania. P88
And the Summer Still Persists. Liliana
     Stefanova. P70
Annamese Hands. Richard A. Parque. P86
At Each Other. Shaheed Quadri. P91
Attitudes of Thanksgiving. Jill
     Breckenridge. P88
Beasts in Whoredom. Gaston Pelletier. P68
The Betrayal of Violets. Mohammed Ibrahim
     Abu Sinnah. P91
Boobiat. Paul Humphrey. P63
The Bride of Spring. I. H. Rizvi. P72
Cherrylog Road. James Dickey. P67
Costa Del Sol, at Night. Vita Andersen.
     P92
Decaying. Jean Pape. P77
Deight in Order, Too. Gary Selden. P63
"Do You Remember Sometimes". Srinivas
     Belsaray. P72
"Don't Neglect This One, Saying".
     Unknown. P62
The Equilibrists. John Crowe Ransom. P67,
     P83
The Eventual Music. Liam Rector. P79
Fire Dream. Jerry Craven. P65
Flowerings. Jack Bernier. P56
For Lovers. T. A. Shulgin. P58
Good-bye California. Charles P. Martin.
     P58
Grate Fire. Jeanne Bonnette. P65
Hand Lane: Literature. Edward Butscher.
     P64
Hard to Say. Sheila Seiler. P56
Hieroglyphics. Bernice Fleisher. P65
"His Form Is in My Eyes". Unknown. P62
Hit and Run. Haywood Jackson. P68
Hotel De La Gare. Waldo Rojas. P71
How, Like This Spring, Slowly. Susan
     Hauser. P88
"I Would Like". Lorenzo. P77
"If He Is Not Your Lover". Unknown. P62
If I Swallowed. Perry Brass. P65
Interlude. Miriam Pederson. P56
Interludio Idilico: Coda. Tomas Segovia.
     P92
The Io Moth. Betty Wallace. P68
Landscape. Axel Schulze. P92
Last Dance. Tom Tellesbo. P58
Let Her Be Red. Nyakuoth Macar. P53
Like Swallows. Pearl Newton Rook. P68
Love. Alice Boughtwood. P68
Love in Absentia. Mary Jane Barnes. P68
Love Songs. Mina Loy. P82
Lovers in Wild Grass. Lisa Grenelle. P65
Lust. Elaine Demakas. P58
Meadow's Song. Opie Houston. P65
Methinks the Divine Nectar. Unknown. P62
Mrs. Whitehouse's View of Sexual
     Intercourse. Gavin Ewart. P63

Night in Veracruz. Kathy Strange de
    Olguin. P72
No Longer Do I Dwell. Duane Edwards. P68
Orion. William Everson. P84
Ovid's Elegies, Book I, 13. Christopher
    Marlowe. P59
Paolo's Version. Carl Judson Launius. P63
Poem ("When I am feeling"). Frank O'Hara.
    P85
Pond & Stream. Angela Karszo. P77
Queen-Ann's-Lace. William Carlos
    Williams. P82
Quiet Time. Tom Tellesbo. P58
Rare Stones. John J. Soldo. P65
'Riffs', sel. Dennis Lee. P49
The Scrutiny. Richard Lovelace. P59
Silk Pyjamas. Michael Holstein. P63
Song Between the Sea and Sky. Kolyo
    Sevov. P70
Still Life. William Carlos Williams. P79
Summer Vacation. Kathleen Iddings. P72
"Surely You Dwell in My Heart". Unknown.
    P62
Sweet Sixteen Lines. Al Young. P85
Therese. Harold Leland Johnson. P65
"Thinking to Himself, 'I Will Make Love
    to Her'". Unknown. P62
To a Lady Who Reads Too Much. Alfred
    Dorn. P65
To Celia. Ben Jonson. P59
To the Beloved. Harry Maizel. P72
Tropical Night. John Tworoger. P72
Unfired Pistol. Clive Matson. P65
Up North. Lisel Mueller. P88
Waiting: November 30th. Bruce St. John.
    P68
Waking. T. A. Shulgin. P58
We Say This Prayer. Jozsef Tornai. P92
"With Effort Is a Lover Got". Unknown.
    P62
A Woman Called Maria. Boris Kristov. P70
You Look. Lorene Erickson. P88
Eroticism
    Belly Dancer. Diane Wakoski. P85
    I'm Lying on the Bed at a Motel and...
        Tetsuo Nakagami. P92
    Men. Bozhidar Bozhilov. P70
The **Errand** Boy's Day Off. Kurt Lipschutz.
    P63
Errors
    Faux Pas. William Stafford. P63
Erthe Toc of Erthe. Unknown. P66
Eryri, Rhys Goch
    Answer to Sion Cent, sels. Tony Conran
        (tr.). P87
Esbensen, Barbara Juster
    First Snowfall. P80
The **Escape**. Mark Van Doren. P83
An **Eskimo** Baby. Lucy Diamond. P51

Eskimo Haiku. Robert Peters. P63
Eskimo Sleigh-Ride. Renee Anne Viosca. P72
Eskimos
    An Eskimo Baby. Lucy Diamond. P51
    Eskimo Sleigh-Ride. Renee Anne Viosca.
        P72
Espana, Aristoteles
    Arrival. Steven F. White (tr.). P71
    Beyond Torture. Steven F. White (tr.).
        P71
    The Blindfold. Steven F. White (tr.). P71
    Hell and Solitude. Steven F. White (tr.).
        P71
    Intimate. Steven F. White (tr.). P71
    A Kind of Song. Steven F. White (tr.).
        P71
    Leaving. Steven F. White (tr.). P71
    (No Greater Pain Beneath the Trees).
        Steven F. White (tr.). P71
    Notes. Steven F. White (tr.). P71
    Roads. Steven F. White (tr.). P71
    What Should I Do Now?. Steven F. White
        (tr.). P71
    Wire Meshes. Steven F. White (tr.). P71
Espionage
    P$$$$$T. Felicia Lamport. P63
Essie Parrish in New York. Unknown. P78
Esteve and Linda Lappin, Patricio (tr.)
    Funeral Song. Patricio Esteve. P92
Etchings in Meaning. Grace D. Yerbury. P72
Eternity
    Crossing a Shore. Gwyn Thomas. P87
    L'Echo. Kim Yang-Shik. P72
    Omnia Exeunt in Mysterium. George
        Sterling. P81
    There Was Set Before Me. Stephen Crane.
        P81
    What Are Years?. Marianne Moore. P83
Ethiopia. Angel Clark. P73
Euclid Alone Has Looked on Beauty Bare. Edna
        St. Vincent Millay. P82
Eurydice. Hilda ("H.D.") Doolittle. P82
Eurydice. Hugh Seidman. P64
Euthanasia
    Euthanasia. Hans Verhagen. P92
Evanescence. Harriet Elizabeth Spofford. P81
Evans, David Allan
    The Fence. P68
    Pole Vaulter. P68
Evans, Evelyn
    There Is a Love. P72
Evelyn Hope. Robert Browning. P89
"**Even** Though Everything Gets Burned up ".
        Unknown. P62
"**Even** a flying feather can sketch". Day and
        Night. Eugenio Montale. P61
"**Even** if the highway had been moved...". In
        Traffic. Howard Moss. P64
"**Even** the deepest well". Untitled #4. Ian

Brennan. P58

"Even though we part". Inamorata. Mary
      Margaret Wittner. P72

"Even with the ice & wind". Portrait in
      Veiled Waters. Anselm Parlatore. P64

"Even your name, O Rome...! Why do I love
      you". Love Song: Pincio, sels.
      Frederika Blankner. P65

Evening
      At Sunset. Ivy O. Eastwick. P51
      Closing of a Day on Earth. B. R. De. P72
      Clouds of Evening. Robinson Jeffers. P83
      Day Is Dying, fr. The Spanish Gypsy.
            George (Mary Ann Cross) Eliot. P89

Evening. Emily Dickinson. P51
      Dusk. N. Krishnan Kutty. P72
      Embrace of Crescents. Daud Kamal. P91
      Evening. Emily Dickinson. P51
      Evening Music. Yahya Kemal. P91
      Evening Prayer. Brierly Ashour. P68
      Evening Prayers. Wilma E. McDaniel. P72
      Evening Without Angels. Wallace Stevens.
            P83
      Evening, from Don Juan. George Gordon,
            6th Baron Byron. P89
      Evensong. (Frederick) Ridgely Torrence.
            P81
      Gold. Martin Armstrong. P51
      I See Again. Liliana Stefanova. P70
      Kindred. George Sterling. P81
      A Light in the Doorway. Cary Waterman.
            P88
      Twilight. Heinrich Heine. P90
      Twilight at Sea. Amelia B. Welby. P89

Evening. Unknown. P51
      When on the Marge of Evening. Louise
            Imogen Guiney. P81

The Evening Cloud. John Wilson. P90
Evening Hawk. Robert Penn Warren. P67
Evening Music. Yahya Kemal. P91
Evening Prayer. Carmen Boitel Adams. P72
Evening Prayer. Brierly Ashour. P68
Evening Prayers. Wilma E. McDaniel. P72
Evening Song. Edith King. P51
The Evening Watch. Henry Vaughan. P59
Evening Without Angels. Wallace Stevens. P83
"An evening by the sea". Summer Snow.
      Charlotte Zolotow. P76

"The evening is coming". Bed-Time. Thomas
      Hood. P51

"Evening is tawny on the old". Gold. Martin
      Armstrong. P51

"Evening swallows the gulls". I See Again.
      Liliana Stefanova. P70

Evening, from Don Juan. George Gordon, 6th
      Baron Byron. P89

Evensong. (Frederick) Ridgely Torrence. P81

"The event stands clear of history". Against
      Time. Louis Untermeyer. P82

Events Like Palaces. Paz Molina. P71

"Events can whittle us". Not What We Had in
      Mind. May Richstone. P63

The Eventual Music. Liam Rector. P79

"Ever been kidnapped". Kidnap Poem. Nikki
      Giovanni. P85

"Ever eating, never cloying". Time (An
      Enigma). Jonathan Swift. P90

"Ever since Tuesday the snow has been
      falling". The Snowstorm. Kaye
      Starbird. P80

Everett, Graham
      Day/Night. P64
      Early May. P64
      Families at the Shore. P64
      Here. P64
      January. P64
      Near Thanksgiving. P64
      Pulling the Days Together. P64

Everett, Joann Marie
      A Simple Question. P72

Everson, William
      Eastward the Armies. P84
      End of Summer. P84
      The Illusion. P84
      The Impossible Choices. P84
      In the Dream's Recess. P84
      Orion. P84
      The Presence. P84
      The Residual Years. P84
      Under a Keeping Spring. P84

Every Day. Mary I. Osborn. P51

"Every forgetting is a minor death". For All
      the Violets. Alice Mackenzie Swaim.
      P65

"Every morning at break of day". The Trains.
      Seumas (James Starkey) O'Sullivan. P51

"Every object separated from its noise...".
      The World in Us. Jules Supervielle.
      P61

"Every Sunday she prepared the brown...".
      The Poet of the Mountains. Tom
      McCarthy. P92

"Every Thursday morning". The Dustman. Clive
      Sansom. P51

"Every time I write a letter". Writing
      Letters. Rodney Bennett. P51

Everybody in America Is at the Movies. Louis
      Phillips. P63

"Everybody knows". Cocks and Crows. Gavin
      Ewart. P63

Everyday Things. Jean Ayer. P51

Everyman's Two Gifts. Hermit Helene Troy
      Arlington. P68

Everyman's Walden. Ann Shermer. P65

"Everyone cries". Christian Endeavor, from
      Lost Youth: the Last War. Alfred
      Kreymborg. P82

"Everyone grumbled. The sky was grey". Daddy

Fell Into the Pond. Alfred Noyes. P89

"Everything exCept:". Poem ("Everything").
    Edward Estlin Cummings. P79

"Everything is laughing, singing". It Is a
    Pleasant Day. Unknown. P51

"Everything is sacred, all these mountains".
    The Storm, sels. William Thomas
    (Islwyn). P87

"Everything is so real to me". The Real
    World. Sherry Weakley. P74

"Everything is wearing thin". Erosion.
    Miriam Pederson. P88

"Everything really is a miracle". The Red
    Sea Divides. Peggy Zuleika Lynch. P72

"Everything stops, he said". Hospital.
    Ardyth Bradley. P88

"Everywhere around the world". Within You.
    Jean-Jacques Wilson. P72

"Everywhere the sea, pungent as mustard".
    Sker. Robert Minhinnick. P54

Evil

For You, in the Darkness, Returning.
    Karen Kania. P88

Lord, I Have Seen Too Much. Karl Shapiro.
    P84

On the Eyes of an SS Officer. Richard
    Wilbur. P84

Susanna and the Elders. Adelaide Crapsey.
    P81

To Auden. Fahmida Riyaz. P91

Evolution

Evolution. John Banister Tabb. P81

The Leap. J. M. Girglani. P72

Songs of Our Cells. Grace Schulman. P64

Evolution. John Banister Tabb. P81

Two Steps Forward. Jeanine Hathaway. P88

The Voice. Sara Teasdale. P82

Evolution of Sand. Jean Pape. P77

Ewart, Gavin

The Achievements of Herrings. P63

Cocks and Crows. P63

Home, Sweet Home! P63

Knopf and Dutton. P63

The Living Masters. P63

The Madness of a Headmistress. P63

Mrs. Whitehouse's View of Sexual
    Intercourse. P63

"Scott Joplin". P63

Shakepeare Sonnets Converted into
    Couplets. P63

Ewing, Juliana Horatia

Bluebells. P51

A Friend in the Garden. P51

Little Kings and Queens of the May. P51

Ex Ore Infantium. Francis Thompson. P51

An Examination into Life and Death. Kenneth
    Patchen. P84

The Examiner's Death. Peter Meinke. P63

Excavations

The Dust of Delos. Haywood Jackson. P68

"Except for the half dozen...". Earlene
    Spratt's Lot. Hilary Russell. P63

"Exclamations!.". Haiku. Opie R. Houston.
    P72

The Exclusion Principle. William Mills. P67

Executions

Ballad of the Ladder. Lyubomir Levchev.
    P70

The Lynching. Claude McKay. P82

The Man Hunt. Madison Cawein. P81

The Rowan Tree. Ruth G. Iodice. P68

Rudolph the Headsman, from This Is It.
    Oliver Wendell Holmes. P90

A Song from Afar. Ahmad 'Abd Al-Muti
    Hijazi. P91

The Swimmers. Allen Tate. P67

Exhortation. Dafydd Nanmor. P87

Exile

Asylum, from Your Tired, Your Poor. Lisel
    Mueller. P88

Exile. Yahya Kemal. P91

Exile of Erin. Thomas Campbell. P90

The Exile's Song. Robert Gilfillan. P90

Exile. Yahya Kemal. P91

The Removal. William Stanley Merwin. P85

Under Certain Circumstances. Walter
    Hoefler. P71

When It's Over. Juan Cameron. P71

Exile of Erin. Thomas Campbell. P90

The Exile's Song. Robert Gilfillan. P90

"Exile, what is it, can he know...". Exile.
    Yahya Kemal. P91

Existence

The Closet. Nino Nikolov. P70

The Hippopotamus. Theophile Gautier. P61

A Nail for Hanging the Soul. Alain
    Bosquet. P61

Of Mere Being. Wallace Stevens. P83

The Probable and Improbable Disappearance
    of a Cat... Juan Luis Martinez. P71

Sentry of the Silent. Rene Char. P61

Some Trees. John Ashbery. P85

A Walk in Late Summer. Theodore Roethke.
    P84

"Existing no longer, its loss becomes". The
    Orchard. Robert Minhinnick. P54

Exodus Unknown. James Marley. P68

The Exotic Plant. Mauricia Price. P68

Expecting an Angel. George Bradley. P79

Expecting the Lord. Ann Griffiths. P87

Expediency. Jean Gowan Near. P72

Experience

Critics and Connoisseurs. Marianne Moore.
    P83

"Exploring the cold night...". The Lateshow
    Diorama. Christopher Dewdney. P49

Explosives

Piss Tubes. Michael D. Clodfelter. P86

"An **exterminator**--.". Buffalo Bill
    Revisited. James P. Bergman. P86
The **Eye** (Part II). Richard Wilbur. P57
"An **eye** crashes into the towers of the
    dream". In the Center of the Bedroom.
    Oscar Hahn. P71
"The **eye** tolls as burnished as bell". Wave,
    sel. Barbara Guest. P64
"The **eyelids** glowing, some chill morning".
    Monet: 'Les Nympheas'. William DeWitt
    Snodgrass. P85
Eyes
    The Eye (Part II). Richard Wilbur. P57
    On the Eyes of an SS Officer. Richard
    Wilbur. P84

F.R. Konecamp. David Gwenallt Jones. P87
Faber, Frederick William
    Paradise. P89
    The World. P89
Fable of First Person. Gyorgy Somlyo. P92
Fable of the Curious Crow and the Devious
    Weevil. Scott Bates. P63
Fable of the Terrorist Mouse. Scott Bates.
    P63
Fables
    The Blind Men and the Elephant. John
    Godfrey Saxe. P51
    The Boy and the Deer. Andrew Peynetsa.
    P78
    The Broken Pitcher. William Edmonstoune
    Aytoun. P90
    Coon Cons Coyote, Coyote Eats Coon...
    Unknown. P78
    Fable of the Curious Crow and the Devious
    Weevil. Scott Bates. P63
    Mountain and the Squirrel. Ralph Waldo
    Emerson. P51
    The Mountain and the Squirrel. Ralph
    Waldo Emerson. P51,90
    The Mouse and the Cake. Eliza Cook. P90
    The Popol Vuh: Alligator's Struggles...,
    sel. Unknown. P78
    The Priest and the Mulberry Tree. Thomas
    Love Peacock. P51
    The Table and the Chair. Edward Lear. P90
    The Tale of a Dog and a Bee. Unknown. P51
Face
    Portrait. Dick Hayman. P63
    The Ugly Man. Liliana Stefanova. P70
    What Face?. Ricelda Payne. P72
"A **face** shines, anchored in fog". Things of
    the Blind. Paz Molina. P71
Face to Face in Another Time. Teresa
    Calderon. P71
The **Face**. Jules Supervielle. P61

Faces. Lola Ridge. P82
Facing the Way. Alice Walker. P85
Faded Pictures. William Vaughn Moody. P81
The **Faerie** Fair. Florence Harrison. P51
Fahy, Christopher
    The Stroke. P57
Failure
    Ode to Failure. Allen Ginsberg. P85
The **Fair** Damsel of Avalon. Haywood Jackson.
    P68
The **Fair** Fowl. Robert N. Feinstein. P63
Fair Weather. William Williams Pantycelyn.
    P87
"**Fair** are the flowers and the children...".
    Indirection. Richard Realf. P90
"A **fair** little girl sat under a tree ". Good
    Night and Good Morning. Richard
    Monckton Milnes; 1st Baron Houghton.
    P51
"**Fair** pledges of a fruitful tree". To
    Blossoms. Robert Herrick. P89
Fairies
    About the Fairies. Jean Ingelow. P51
    Do Fairies Like the rain?. Barbara M.
    Hales. P55
    The Dream Fairy. Thomas Hood. P51
    The Elf and the Dormouse. Oliver Herford.
    P89
    An Elfin Knight. John Rodman Drake. P51
    The Elfin Pedlar. George Darley. P51
    The Faerie Fair. Florence Harrison. P51
    Fairies' Song. Thomas Randolph. P90
    The Fairies. Unknown. P51
    The Fairy Child. John Anster. P90
    The Fairy Cobbler. A. Neil Lyons. P51
    A Fairy Dream. Dorothy Gradon. P51
    Fairy Feet. Phyllis L. Garlick. P51
    Fairy Music. Enid Blyton. P51
    The Fairy Ring. Unknown. P51
    The Fairy Shoemaker. Phyllis L. Garlick.
    P51
    A Fairy Song. William Shakespeare. P51
    A Fairy Went A-Marketing. Rose Fyleman.
    P51
    Fairy's Song, from A Midsummer Night's
    Dream. William Shakespeare. P90
    Found in the Woods. Irene F. Pawsey. P51
    The Goblin. Rose Fyleman. P51
    The Green Lady. Charlotte Druitt Cole.
    P51
    Hob the Elf. Norman M. Johnson. P51
    If You See a Fairy Ring. Unknown. P51
    The Light-Hearted Fairy. Unknown. P51
    The Little Elf-Man. John Kendrick Bangs.
    P51
    Little Kings and Queens of the May.
    Juliana Horatia Ewing. P51
    The Little Men. Flora Fearne. P51
    The Mermaid, sel. Lord Tennyson. P51

The Merman, sel. Lord Tennyson. P51
Merry Little Men. Kathleen M. Chaplin.
    P51
Oh! Where Do Fairies Hide Their Heads?.
    Thomas Haynes Bayly. P90
Pudding Charms. Charlotte Druitt Cole.
    P51
Puk-Wudjies. Patrick R. Chalmers. P51
The Rainbow Fairies. Unknown. P51
Rufty and Tufty. Iasbell Hempseed. P51
Sea Fairies. Patricia Hubbell. P55
Sea Fairies. Eileen Mathias. P51
The Seven Ages of Elf-Hood. Rachel
    (Lyman) Field. P55
Slumber in Spring. Elizabeth Gould. P51
The Urchin's Dance. John Lyly. P51
The Way to Fairyland. Eunice Close. P51
Who'll Help a Fairy? Unknown. P51
The Yellow Fairy. Charlotte Druitt Cole.
    P51
"The fairies hold a fair, they say". The
    Faerie Fair. Florence Harrison. P51
Fairies' Song. Thomas Randolph. P90
The Fairies. Unknown. P51
Fairs
    Bittern He Took a Bundle. Unknown. P87
    Caravan. Irene Thompson. P51
The Fairy Child. John Anster. P90
The Fairy Cobbler. A. Neil Lyons. P51
A Fairy Dream. Dorothy Gradon. P51
Fairy Feet. Phyllis L. Garlick. P51
The Fairy Flute. Rose Fyleman. P51
Fairy Music. Enid Blyton. P51
The Fairy Ring. Unknown. P51
The Fairy Shoemaker. Phyllis L. Garlick. P51
The Fairy Sleep and Little Bo-Peep. Unknown.
    P51
A Fairy Song. William Shakespeare. P51
Fairy Tales
    The Love-Gift of a Fairy-Tale. Charles
        Lutwidge ("Lewis Carroll") Dodgson.
        P90
    Pigwiggen. Michael Drayton. P51
Fairy Tales-Satire
    Stalky Jack. William Brighty Rands. P51
A Fairy Went A-Marketing. Rose Fyleman. P51
Fairy's Song, from A Midsummer Night's
    Dream. William Shakespeare. P90
Faith
    After Long Grief. Jaye Giammarino. P72
    An Athenian Garden. Trumbull Stickney.
        P81
    The Catholic Martyrs. Waldo Williams. P87
    Columbus. Joaquin Miller. P81
    The Country Faith. Norman Gale. P51
    A Deed and a Word. Charles Mackay. P89
    Doubt and Faith, from In Memoriam. Lord
        Tennyson. P89
    Fair Weather. William Williams

Pantycelyn. P87
    Faith. George Santayana. P89,P81
    Faith. Alfarata Hansel. P72
    Faith. Frances Anne Kemble-Butler. P89
Faith. Alfarata Hansel. P72
    How Does a Flower Know. James Stearns.
        P68
    I Saw a Man. Stephen Crane. P81
    Judge Not. Adelaide Anne Procter. P89
Faith. Frances Anne Kemble-Butler. P89
    The Moment. Waldo Williams. P87
    The Mystic's Vision. Mathilde Blind. P89
    A Pinch of Faith. T. Vasudeva Reddy. P72
    Polarity. Hirsch Lazaar Silverman. P72
Faith. George Santayana. P89,P81
    The Shadow of Faith. Michael A.
        Hemmingson. P56
    Summer Storm, Highway 37. Gloria Still.
        P88
    This Poor Man. William John Gruffydd. P87
    Ultima Veritas. Washington Gladden. P89
    The Voyage. Caroline Atherton Mason. P89
"Faith and belief are with us". Polarity.
    Hirsch Lazaar Silverman. P72
"Faith is like water". The Shadow of Faith.
    Michael A. Hemmingson. P56
"Faith/Is a candle". Faith. Alfarata Hansel.
    P72
The Faithful Lovers. Unknown. P89
Faiz, Faiz Ahmad
    Tyrant, fr. Three Voices. Daud Kamal
        (tr.). P91
    Victim, fr. Three Voices. Daud Kamal
        (tr.). P91
    Voice from the Unknown, fr. Three Voices.
        Daud Kamal (tr.). P91
Falconer, E. J.
    Cradle Song at Bethlehem. P51
    Doves. P51
    The Elephant. P51
    A Little Finger Game. P51
    Marketing. P51
Falk, Ruth C.
    Out of the Starstream. P72
Falkowski, Bohumila
    Time Is. P72
Falkowski, Edwin A.
    Challenger Lost. P72
Fall. Karen M. Paik. P74
Fall 1961. Robert Lowell. P48
"Fall is when fat, honking Canadian
    geese...". Fall. Karen M. Paik. P74
"The fall moons have been blood streaked".
    Woman of the Late Fall Run. Anselm
    Parlatore. P64
Fallen Angel. Katherine A. Hogan. P65
The Fallen Star. Helen Schleef. P68
"The fallen leaves are cornflakes". December
    Leaves. Kaye Starbird. P80

Falling Water. James Russell Vaky. P68
"Falling into the cracks between the black".
      My Lawn Is Brown and All My Neighbors
      Are Painting... Tom Hansen. P63
Fallon, Eunice
      August. P51
False Country of the Zoo. Jean Garrigue. P84
False Youth: Two Seasons (Winter). James
      Dickey. P67
"False life! a foil and no more, when".
      Quickness. Henry Vaughan. P59
"A false, bad, bold criterion". The Lying
      Muse to Rhys Goch Eryri. Sion Cent.
      P87
Fame
      To George C. Wallace. Frances
      Clarkhandler. P72
Familiar Friends. James S. Tippett. P51
Families at the Shore. Graham Everett. P64
The Family in the Suburbs: A Situation
      Comedy. David Citino. P63
Family Prime. Mark Van Doren. P83
"Family the goal!.". One's Goal. Annie
      Laurie Leech. P72
Fan, the Filly. Wilfred Thorley. P51
Fancy. Mary Agnes White. P72
"The fans move up to the rail". Contest of
      Wills. R. Wallace Clark. P72
Fanshawe, Catharine
      A Riddle. P90
Fanshawe, Sir Richard
      Martial's Epigrams, Book X, 47. P59
Fantasy Voyage. Marjorie Skonnord Martin.
      P72
The Far Field. Theodore Roethke. P84
"Far away from Delhi's power-and-
      politics...". Futile Death Wish.
      Simanchal Patnaik. P72
"Far back when I went zig-zagging". Orion.
      Adrienne Rich. P85
"Far down, down...". Subway Wind. Claude
      McKay. P82
"Far out". The House on the Hill. Rabiul
      Hasan. P56
"Far out at sea". White Horses. Irene F.
      Pawsey. P51
"Far out in the pacific". Encounter. Addison
      Merrick. P56
"Far through the lilac sky the Angelus
      bell". The Angelus. Edwin Markham. P81
"Far up in space, translated by fire".
      Translated to the Seven Astronauts.
      Mary McGowan Slappey. P72
The Far-Farers. Robert Louis Stevenson. P51
Fardd, Bleddyn
      Elegy for Llywelyn ap Gruffudd, the Last
      Prince. Tony Conran (tr.). P87
      On His Death Bed. Tony Conran (tr.). P87
Fardd, Eben

Jerusalem Destroyed, sels. Tony Conran
      (tr.). P87
"Fare thee well! and if forever". Farewell
      to His Wife. George Gordon, 6th Baron
      Byron. P89
Farewell. Cyril Dabydeen. P49
Farewell to His Wife. George Gordon, 6th
      Baron Byron. P89
Farewell to the Farm. Robert Louis
      Stevenson. P51
"' Farewell! farewell!' is often heard".
      Good-Bye. Unknown. P89
"Farewell! I go to sleep; but when". The
      Evening Watch. Henry Vaughan. P59
"Farewell, said I". Autumn. Georgi Djagarov.
      P70
A Farewell, to C. E. G. Charles Kingsley.
      P51
A Farewell. Charles Kingsley. P89
Farid, M.S. (tr.)
      The Betrayal of Violets. Mohammed Ibrahim
      Abu Sinnah. P91
      The Vision of a Martyr. Mohammed Ibrahim
      Abu Sinnah. P91
Farjeon, Eleanor
      The Children's Bells. P51
      The Flower-Seller. P51
      "Morning Has Broken". P60
      The Night Will Never Stay. P51
      There Are Big Waves. P51
      There Isn't Time. P51
Farley, Blanche
      A Bride of the 80's, Down the Aisle. P63
"A Farmer Went Trotting on His Grey Mare".
      Unknown. P51
"The farmer is busy, so busy, to-day".
      Haymaking. E. M. Adams. P51
"A farmer once planted some little brown
      seeds". A Growing Rhyme. J. M.
      Westrup. P51
"The farmer sat in his easy-chair". A
      Picture. Charles Gamage Eastman. P89
"A farmer went trotting upon his grey mare".
      Knee-Bouncing Rhymes. Unknown. P90
"' Farmer, is the harvest ready'.". Bread.
      H. E. Wilkinson. P51
Farming and Farmers
      American Farm, 1934. Genevieve Taggard.
      P83
      As a Thousand Years. Jeremy Hooker. P54
      A Day at the Farm. Unknown. P51
      The Farmyard. A. A. Attwood. P51
      Haymaking. Alfred Perceval Graves. P51
      Haymaking. E. M. Adams. P51
      Here We Come A-Haying. Eunice Close. P51
      Johnny's Farm. H. M. Adams. P51
      Mr. Scarecrow. Sheila Braine. P51
      Off We Go to Market. Gwen A. Smith. P51
      Pride of the Farmer. Jeff Bence. P74

The Ridger. Nigel Jenkins. P54
The Scarecrow. Michael Franklin. P51
Scratch Farmer. John Tripp. P54
Soil. John Tripp. P54
Tobacco Men. James Applewhite. P67
Trouble at the Farm. Ivy O. Eastwick. P51
"Willie Boy, Willie Boy, Where Are You
    Going?". Unknown. P51
Work Song. Wendell Berry. P67
The **Farmyard**. A. A. Attwood. P51
Farquhar, Betty
    Power of Love. P72
Farrar, Winifred Hamric
    Consolation. P72
Farther North. M. Travis Lane. P49
"A **fashion** tour de force". The Zebra. Bob
    McKenty. P63
Fast Rode the Knight. Stephen Crane. P81
"**Faster** than fairies, faster than witches".
    From a Railway Carriage. Robert Louis
    Stevenson. P51
"**Fat** black bucks in a wine-barrel room". The
    Congo. Vachel Lindsay. P82
Fata Morgana. Siv Cedering. P64
Fatal Interview, sel. Edna St. Vincent
    Millay. P82
Fate. Kenneth Koch. P64
Fate and Fatalism
    Futile Death Wish. Simanchal Patnaik. P72
    Introspection. Nikolai Hristozov. P70
    Sisyphus. Albert Tallman. P68
Father. Martha Friedberg. P88
Father and Mother Tongue. Samuel Lover. P90
Father and Son. Stanley Kunitz. P83
Father and Son. Delmore Schwartz. P84
"**Father** don't read Shakespeare". Subway.
    Juan Cameron. P71
"The **father** of my father's father
    brought...". The Man from Leipzig.
    Clemente Riedemann. P71
Father's Bedroom. Robert Lowell. P84
Father's Story. Elizabeth Madox Roberts. P89
"**Father**, I will not ask for wealth or fame".
    The Higher Good. Theodore Parker. P89
"**Father**, we thank Thee for the night". A
    Child's Prayer. Unknown. P51
"**Fathered** by March, the daffodils are here".
    Daffodils. Lizette Woodworth Reese.
    P81
Fathers and Fatherhood
    At Albert's Landing (with my son).
        Michael Heller. P64
    Daddy. Sylvia Plath. P85
    Daddy Fell Into the Pond. Alfred Noyes.
        P89
    Father and Son. Stanley Kunitz. P83
    Father and Son. Delmore Schwartz. P84
    Father's Story. Elizabeth Madox Roberts.
        P89

The Handless Maiden. Janet Beeler Shaw.
    P88
The Lonely Child. James Oppenheim. P82
Lord Ullin's Daughter. Thomas Campbell.
    P51,P90
Meeting My Father at the River. Judith
    Minty. P88
My Father Moved Through Dooms of Love.
    Edward Estlin Cummings. P83
The Soup Jar. Dabney Stuart. P67
Fatigue
    After Apple Picking. Robert Frost. P82
    Job Action. Ray Catina. P86
    Tired. Fenton Johnson. P82
Fau Bauman, Frau Schmidt, and Frau
    Schwartze. Theodore Roethke. P84
Faulconer, Mary G.
    "There Is a Wonder in the Sweep". P72
Faulkner, Margherita
    The Inmate. P68
Faust, Naomi F.
    Envy. P72
Faux Pas. William Stafford. P63
Fear
    Appointment in Doctor's Office. Josephine
        Miles. P84
    "Darkest Night Has Passed". Unknown. P62
    Dover Cliff, from King Lear. William
        Shakespeare. P89
    The Dream. Louise Bogan. P83
    Fear. Lynn Sorlie. P72
    Fear of Death. John Ashbery. P85
    For Fear. Robert Creeley. P85
    Lull. Theodore Roethke. P84
    A Man Feared. Stephen Crane. P81
    Revisiting Detroit. Karen Kania. P88
Fear. Lynn Sorlie. P72
    The Subverted Flower. Robert Frost. P82
    There Was a Great Cathedral. Stephen
        Crane. P81
    Under the Boathouse. David Bottoms. P67
    The Warning. Adelaide Crapsey. P81
"**Fear** not, O little flock! the foe". The
    Battle-Song of Gustavus Adolphus.
    Michael Altenburg. P90
Fear of Death. John Ashbery. P85
Fear of Sky Death. Robert Schlosser. P86
Fearing, Kenneth
    American Rhapsody. P83
    Obituary. P83
    The People vs. The People. P83
Fearne, Flora
    The Little Men. P51
Fearsome Critters. Walter H. Kerr. P68
Feast Days: Christmas. Annie Dillard. P47
A **Feather** for My Cap. Ivy O. Eastwick. P51
"**Feathers** up fast, steeples...". The
    Fountain. Donald Davie. P79
February. Dorothy Una Ratcliffe. P51

Federico II [Frederick II of Hohenstaufen]
    "'My Sweet Lover, You Are Leaving!'".
        Frede Jensen (tr.). P69
"Feeling/The enemy's". Suicide, from Lost
        Youth: the Last War. Alfred Kreymborg.
        P82
A Feeling. Bo Yang. P72
Feelings
    Dislocation. Mary Trimble. P88
    Listen. Dara D. Henderson. P73
    The Signature of Things. Raphael Vargas.
        P92
Feet
    Feet. Irene Thompson. P51
    Five Little Brothers. Ella Wheeler
        Wilcox. P51
Feet. Irene Thompson. P51
Fehler, Gene
    Eating Out. P63
    I'm a Texan Now. P63
Feinstein, Robert N.
    The Beer and the Bear. P63
    The Court Rests. P63
    The Fair Fowl. P63
    Older Is Safer. P63
    The TV Chef. P63
Feldman, Dale Maria Pacileo
    If Only. P72
Feldman, Irving
    Read to the Animals, or Orpheus at the
        SPCA. P79
    (SIC)Transcript Gloria, or The Body
        Politician. P63
Feldman, Oceana
    Wish... P74
Felgenhauer, H. R.
    Star Picker. P68
Fellinger, Margaret L.
    Hands of Gold. P72
Fellman, Stanley A.
    The Manhood of Hebrew Jesus. P72
"A fellow in a market-town". The Razor-
        Seller. John Wolcott. P90
The Fence. David Allan Evans. P68
Fences
    The Last Gate. E. Stella Mead. P51
Fenians All. Brian O'Riordan. P49
Fenner, Cornelius George
    Gulf-Weed. P89
"Ferdinand De Soto lies". The Distant
        Runners. Mark Van Doren. P83
Ferlinghetti, Lawrence
    Constantly Risking Absurdity. P85
    An Elegy To Dispel Gloom. P85
    He. P85
    I Am Waiting. P85
    Monet's Lilies Shuddering. P85
    Night Light. P85
    The Pennycandystore Beyond the El. P85

    Stone Reality Meditation. P85
    The Third World. P85
"The fern was all I wanted there".
        Maidenhair. Nigel Jenkins. P54
Ferree, Joel
    Business Luncheon. P63
Ferries
    The Approach. J. D. McClatchy. P79
"The ferry heaves past the buoys". The
        Immortal. Hugh Seidman. P64
"' Ferry me across the water'.". The
        Ferryman. Christina Georgina Rossetti.
        P51
Festivals
    Deepavali (Festival of Lights). A.
        Padmanaban. P72
    Shared Festivals. Wallace Winchell. P65
"A few dozen tomorrow will die". Osiris'
        Song. Richard Candida Smith. P68
Fick, Marlon
    Apologies to Verdi. P68
Ficke, Arthur Davidson
    Among Shadows. P82
    I Am Weary of Being Bitter. P82
    Like Him Whose Spirit. P82
    Meeting. P82
    Portrait of an Old Woman. P82
Ficke, Arthur Davison
    Loreine: a Horse. P89
"Fiddle-de-dee!.". High June. Catherine A.
        Morin. P51
The Fiddle. Neil Munro. P51
Fidelity. Trumbull Stickney. P81
The Field Daisy. Jane Taylor. P51
Field Guide to North American Birds. Barbara
        Crooker. P63
"The field drifts into darkness". The
        Window. Patricia Hooper. P88
"The field mouse flickers". Where. Wendell
        Berry. P67
Field, Edward (tr.)
    Heaven and Hell. Nalungiaq. P78
    Hunger. Samik. P78
    Magic Words. Unknown. P78
    Magic Wores for Hunting Caribou. Unknown.
        P78
    Magic Words for Hunting Seal. Unknown.
        P78
    Magic Words to Feel Better. Nakasuk. P78
    Orpingalik's Song: In a Time a Sickness.
        Unknown. P78
Field, Eugene
    The Compliment. P90
    Dibdin's Ghost. P81
    The Duel. P90
    A Dutch Lullaby. P89,P81
    Japanese Lullaby. P89
    Little Boy Blue. P81
    Nightfall in Dordrecht. P81

Norse Lullaby. P51
The Rock-a-by Lady. P51
Song. P51
Wynken, Blynken and Nod. P51
Field, Rachel (Lyman)
    Gypsies. P51
    I'd Like To Be a Lighthouse. P76
    The Playhouse Key. P51
    The Seven Ages of Elf-Hood. P55
The Field-Mouse. Enid Blyton. P51
Fielding, Henry
    A Hunting We Will Go. P89
Fields
    Antique Harvesters. John Crowe Ransom.
        P67,P83
    In Two Fields. Waldo Williams. P87
    Poem. Jonaid. P92
Fields, Jim
    Clothing. P72
The Fifteen Acres. James Stephens. P51
The Fifteenth Century. Kaleem Omar. P91
"' Fifty stories more to fall'.". Rhyme of
        Rain. John Holmes. P75
Fighting
    Ambush. Phillip Macar. P53
    As Helpless as a Dhow on a Still Day.
        Dhor Ding Cuol. P53
    Drink the Curse. Moses Kuac Nyoat. P53
    Foreigners with Teeth. Peter Pal Kong.
        P53
    He Will Float in the River Like a
        Waterlily. Kong Tot. P53
    I Would Give Him a Man. Dhor Ding Cuol.
        P53
    Its Eye Ran with Blood. Peter Pal Kong.
        P53
    The Red Clouds at Sunset. Micen Atem. P53
    Who Can Touch Me?. Micen Atem. P53
Fights and Fighting
    Counterpoint. Agnes Wathall Tatera. P65
    In Distrust of Merits. Marianne Moore.
        P83
Filip, Raymond
    Watching Whales Watching Us. P49
The Final Battle. Kandy Arnold. P58
Final Confrontation. Sheila Martindale. P49
The Final Gesture. Gwendolyn Vincent. P58
Final Migration. Carol Hamilton. P68
Finale. Tibor Tollas. P61
Finale, Frank
    Hunting the Snow Owl. P56
    What Trial?. P56
"Finally/they confront me". Final
        Confrontation. Sheila Martindale. P49
Financial Note. John D. Engle Jr. P63
Finch, Donald G.
    On Strawberry Eve. P68
Finch, Francis Miles
    The Blue and the Gray. P90

Finch, Roger (tr.)
    Evening Music. Yahya Kemal. P91
    Exile. Yahya Kemal. P91
    Flight. Yahya Kemal. P91
    Maltepe. Yahya Kemal. P91
    Night. Yahya Kemal. P91
    Pilgrimage. Yahya Kemal. P91
    The Seasons. Yahya Kemal. P91
    Silent Ship. Yahya Kemal. P91
    A Star Flowed. Yahya Kemal. P91
Find the Nerve To Get Excited. Pat Bridges.
        P56
Find Your Love. Nicholas [pseud.]. P72
A Fine Day. Michael Drayton. P51
"The fine air grows among the grass". Dusk
        in Changuitad. Sergio Mansilla. P71
"A fine gull on the tideflow". The Seagull.
        Dafydd ab [or ab] Gwilym. P87
"Fine so we lost paradise because". The
        Signalled Hour. Juan Cameron. P71
"Fine-spun brows, twice-graceful as
        flowers". O the Jewels. Unknown. P87
Finger Folk. H. M. Tharp. P51
Finger Play. Unknown. P51
A Finger Play for a Snowy Day. Unknown. P51
Finkel, Donald
    Asiatic Day-Flower. P79
Finn, Mary B.
    Beethoven Pathetique. P68
    Brownstone Revisited. P68
    The Image. P68
    Lost Poems. P68
    My Dark Kingdom. P68
    Only in a Poem. P68
    The Toads of Spring. P68
Fiorito, Geoff
    Alfred Hitchcock U. P58
    Observe:. P58
    Roads. P58
    The Xenoplile. P58
    Zelda. P58
Fire. Robert Creeley. P85
Fire
    Fire. Krishna Srinivas. P72
    Fires. Elizabeth Fleming. P51
    Here. Graham Everett. P64
    The Lighter That Never Fails. R. L.
        Barth. P86
    Myths and Texts (Burning). Gary Snyder.
        P85
Fire. Krishna Srinivas. P72
Fire and Ice. Robert Frost. P82
"The Fire Burns in the Sacrifice Enclosure".
        Unknown. P62
Fire Dream. Jerry Craven. P65
The Fire Sermon, fr. The Waste Land. Thomas
        Stearns Eliot. P83
"The fire whistles are wailing". Here.
        Graham Everett. P64

"Fire-tongue airs his face...". Poem. Pablo
      Picasso. P61
Fireplaces
      Hearth. Patricia Hampl. P88
Fires. Elizabeth Fleming. P51
Firewood (for Steve Sanfield). Doc Dachtler.
      P77
The First Blue-Bird. James Whitcomb Riley.
      P89
First Calving. Nigel Jenkins. P54
The First Day of Summer. Kathleen Norris.
      P88
The First Draft. Kris Passantino. P74
First Flight. Janet Carncross Chandler. P77
The First Kiss. Thomas Campbell. P89
First Love. Anne Yannie Corrado. P65
First Names. Dorothy T. Lewis. P72
"First came the primrose". A Chanted
      Calendar. Sydney Dobell. P51
"The first day". The Creation of the World.
      Eva Toth. P92
"First having read the book of myths".
      Diving into the Wreck. Adrienne Rich.
      P85
"First I lowered my head". A Woman's Song,
      About Men. Unknown. P78
"First I walked". At the Beach. Sandra
      Liatsos. P76
"First it was the secret place...". The Tire
      Hangs in the Yard. Dave Smith. P67
"First light of day in Mississippi".
      Birthday Poem. Al Young. P85
"The First of April, Some Do Say". Unknown.
      P51
First Portrait. Sarmad Sehbai. P91
First Snow. Marie Louise Allen. P80
First Snowfall. Barbara Juster Esbensen. P80
First Spring Morning. Robert Bridges. P51
First Time. Edwin M. Goldman. P65
"The first salvo is gone before I can turn".
      One Night on Guard Duty. W. D.
      Ehrhart. P86
"First the puss removes his boots--.".
      Letting the Cat Die. Gwendolyn
      Vincent. P58
"First there is time". The Duty of the
      Prince Is Magnificence. Mike Gregory.
      P56
"The first time his grandfather beat him".
      Gorky's Childhood. Lorna Crozier. P49
"First we pass a farm". On the Three-Hour
      Train Ride. Anne Porter. P64
"The first windowpane is a park". Four
      Squares. Agnes Nemes Nagy. P92
"First you bite your fingernails...".
      American Rhapsody. Kenneth Fearing.
      P83
"First, April, she with mellow showers". The
      Four Sweet Months. Robert Herrick. P51

Fischer, Ted
      Time. P72
Fish
      The Achievements of Herrings. Gavin
          Ewart. P63
      Clams. Stanley Moss. P64
      Fish and Bird. Rosemary Brinckman. P51
      The Fish. Marianne Moore. P83
      Precision. Lawrence Herman. P73
      Swimming. Elaine Emmons. P77
      Swish. Christine Stratton. P73
Fish and Bird. Rosemary Brinckman. P51
Fish Poem. Joy Kogawa. P49
The Fish. Elizabeth Bishop. P84
The Fish. Marianne Moore. P83
Fisher, Aileen
      Noises. P50
      Snowball Wind. P80
      Snowy Benches. P80
      Waves of the Sea. P76
Fisher, K.
      Story of the Corn. P51
The Fisher. Johann Wolfgang von Goethe. P90
"Fishermen say fifty years ago...". Watching
      Whales Watching Us. Raymond Filip. P49
Fishing and Fishermen
      Carp. M. Rose. P77
      The Disappointed Shrimper. P. A. Ropes.
          P51
      The Drunken Fisherman. Robert Lowell. P84
      The Fish. Elizabeth Bishop. P84
      The Fisher. Johann Wolfgang von Goethe.
          P90
      Scalloping Northwest. Allen Planz. P64
      The Three Fishers. Charles Kingsley. P90
      Wharf. Myra Cohn Livingston. P76
      "'What's the Matter,' He Says, Tying on
          the". Jon Olander. P77
Fishing for Girls with a Rod and Line. Kuek
      Taitai. P53
Fitzgerald, F. Scott
      The Boy Who Killed His Mother. P63
Fitzpatrick, Winne E.
      Intertwining Love. P72
"The 5th Cavalry had a hell of a good time".
      Body Bags, sel. Michael Andrews. P86
Five Flower World Variations. Unknown. P78
Five Little Brothers. Ella Wheeler Wilcox.
      P51
Five Sisters. Kate Greenaway. P51
Five Women Bathing in Moonlight. Richard
      Wilbur. P84
"Five little sisters walking in a row". Five
      Sisters. Kate Greenaway. P51
The Five-Fingered Maple. Kate Louise Brown.
      P51
"Flagstone steps". Haiku. Alexis Rotella.
      P63
Flame of God. Frederika Blankner. P65

Flame-Heart. Claude McKay. P82
The Flame. Isaac Daniel Hooson. P87
"Flames are shooting". Song Picture No. 86.
     Unknown. P78
"A flaming ruby on the divine forehead".
     Aldebaran. Miguel de Unamuno. P48
Flanders, Jane
     Queen Anne's Legs. P63
Flash Crimson. Carl Sandburg. P82
"The Flash of Lightning Gives a Glimpse of
     the Clouds". Unknown. P62
Flattery
     Portrait of Lady. William Carlos
        Williams. P82
"The flea that bit Caesar's ass when he
     sat". Insects Blind to History. Kirby
     Olson. P63
The Flea. John Donne. P59
"The fleet astronomer can bore". Vanity (1).
     George Herbert. P59
Fleisher, Bernice
     Hieroglyphics. P65
Fleming, Elizabeth
     The Balloon Seller. P51
     Fires. P51
     The Hedgehog and His Coat. P51
     The Hurdy-Gurdy Man. P51
     If I Were a Pig. P51
     In the Mirror. P51
     Old Mrs. Jarvis. P51
     The Patchwork Quilt. P51
     The Secret. P51
     Toadstools. P51
     Who's In?. P51
     The Window Cleaner. P51
Fletcher, John Gould
     The Blue Symphony. P82
     I, fr. Irradiations. P82
     II, fr. Irradiations. P82
     III, fr. Irradiations. P82
     IV, fr. Irradiations. P82
     Mutability. P82
     White Symphony. P82
     XVIII, from Irradiations. P82
Fleysher, Deanna
     White Lie. P73
Flickers. Dwarakanath H. Kabadi. P72
Flight. Yahya Kemal. P91
Flight
     Mystery in Flight. Patricia M. Johnson.
        P72
The Flight of Youth. Richard Henry Stoddard.
     P89
Flint, Roland (tr.)
     A Biblical Motif. Boris Kristov. P70
     Hamlet XX. Stefan Tsanev. P70
     My Mother's Wedding. Boris Kristov. P70
     A Prayer. Boris Kristov. P70
     Strange Bird. Stefan Tsanev. P70

     A Woman Called Maria. Boris Kristov. P70
Flirtations
     "Even Though Everything Gets Burned up ".
        Unknown. P62
     "Grabbing a Handful of Powder in Her
        Hand". Unknown. P62
     "The Laughing Girl is 'liberated'...".
        Unknown. P62
     "On the Pretext of a Rough Descent to the
        River". Unknown. P62
     "The Ploughman Drinks the Bitter-Herb
        Tea". Unknown. P62
     "She Runs in Front of You". Unknown. P62
     "What Was Said by Him, His Eyes
        Blossoming...". Unknown. P62
     "Whatever Part of My Body He Meditates
        On". Unknown. P62
     "When In His View, I Will Stand".
        Unknown. P62
     "Whom Do You Greet, Oh Son". Unknown. P62
"Floating clouds bury the mist's gloomy
     face". My Cares. Hsiang Yang. P72
"A flock of birds swoops over the valley".
     On a Picture by a Chinese Painter.
     Henri Michaux. P61
Flood of Renaissance. Dorothy Mitchell
     Bechhold. P72
"The flood of love, till now expressed".
     Know Knowing. Marian Gleason. P72
The Flooded Valley. Roland Mathias. P54
"The Flop-Eared Dog Is Gone". Unknown. P62
Florida. Elizabeth Bishop. P84
Florida Road Workers. Langston Hughes. P83
"The florist was told, cyclamen or azalea".
     Lines to Accompany Flowers for Eve.
     Carolyn Kizer. P79
Flower Chorus. Ralph Waldo Emerson. P51
A Flower Is Looking Through the Ground.
     Harold Munro. P90
The Flower-Seller. Eleanor Farjeon. P51
"flower-born Blodueda". Song. Richard Hovey.
     P81
"The flower/my heart". Poem To Be Recited
     Every 8 Years While Eating... Unknown.
     P78
The Flower. George Herbert. P59
The Flowering War. Unknown. P78
Flowerings. Jack Bernier. P56
Flowers
     Bachelor's Buttons. Maud Morin. P51
     Before Spring. P. A. Ropes. P51
     Bluebells. P. A. Ropes. P51
     Bluebells. Olive Enoch. P51
     Bluebells. Juliana Horatia Ewing. P51
     A Buttercup. Unknown. P51
     Buttercups. Unknown. P51
     Buttercups and Daisies. Mary Howitt. P51
     A Chanted Calendar. Sydney Dobell. P51
     Chrysanthemums. Donald Davie. P79

The Columbine. Elna Forsell Pawson. P72
Consider the Flowers. Marjorie Burney
    Willis. P72
Crocuses. Anna M. Platt. P51
Daffodils. P. A. Ropes. P51
Daisies and Grasses. Unknown. P51
The Daisy, from The Legend of Good Women.
    Geoffrey Chaucer. P89
The Daisy, sel. James Montgomery. P51
The Dandelion Puff. Mary K. Robinson. P51
The Dandelions. Unknown. P51
Death of a Sunflower. Raymond Souster.
    P49
The Field Daisy. Jane Taylor. P51
Five Flower World Variations. Unknown.
    P78
Five Sisters. Kate Greenaway. P51
Flower Chorus. Ralph Waldo Emerson. P51
For a Flower Whose Name I Don't Know. Pat
    Bridges. P56
The Forget-Me-Not. Unknown. P51
Foxgloves. Mary Webb. P51
Heather. Eifion Wyn. P87
Heigh Ho!. Jean Ingelow. P51
I Wandered Lonely. William Wordsworth.
    P51
I'd Chose To Be a Daisy. Unknown. P51
In My Garden. Unknown. P51
The Lamp Flower. Margaret Cecilia Furse.
    P51
Lilacs. Amy Lowell. P89
Lines to Accompany Flowers for Eve.
    Carolyn Kizer. P79
Little Things. Eileen Mathias. P51
Loosestrife. Elaine Magarrell. P63
Marigolds. Louise Driscoll. P51
"Mariposa Lilies". Lois Roquemore Carden.
    P72
O Dandelion. Unknown. P51
O Wind, Where Have You Been?. Christina
    Georgina Rossetti. P51
Orchids. Theodore Roethke. P84
Ox-Eye Daisy. Lois Bunse. P77
Pale Like Sunshine Music. James Richard
    Hurst. P68
Poppies. Nesta Wyn Jones. P87
Poppies. William E. Morris. P72
Poppies. P. A. Ropes. P51
The Poppies in the Garden. Ffrida Wolfe.
    P51
The Rose and the Heather. Pedrog. P87
The Rose. Johann Wolfgang von Goethe. P89
Rosemary's French Garden Basket. Carolyn
    O'Harrow Pintye. P72
Roses. George (Mary Ann Cross) Eliot. P51
Snowdrop. Anna Bunston de Bary. P51
Snowdrops. Laurence Alma-Tadema. P51
Snowdrops. Mary Vivian. P51
Snowflower. Tamara Downing. P77

Song of Spring. John Keats. P51
The Stately Lady. Flora Sandstrom. P51
Summer Breeze. Unknown. P51
Tall Nettles. Edward Thomas. P51
To a Walker of Ridges. Kaye Bache. P68
To a Wind-Flower. Madison Cawein. P81
The Trees in the Garden. Stephen Crane.
    P81
Violets. Unknown. P51
Violets. John Moultrie. P51
Violets. P. A. Ropes. P51
Waking up. Unknown. P51
The Water-Lily. John Banister Tabb. P89
A Watering Rhyme. P. A. Ropes. P51
What Trial?. Frank Finale. P56
Wild Flower's Song. William Blake. P51
The Wreath. Meleager. P89
"Flowers bloom and trees grow". Spring. Keri
    Walls. P73
"Flowers never fret". Consider the Flowers.
    Marjorie Burney Willis. P72
"The flutter of violets". The Betrayal of
    Violets. Mohammed Ibrahim Abu Sinnah.
    P91
Fluttering Leaves. Rodney Bennett. P51
Flux. Richard Eberhart. P83
The Fly. Karl Shapiro. P84
Flying
    Ballad for a Solonaut. Joanna Salamon.
    P92
    Fear of Sky Death. Robert Schlosser. P86
    Grounded. Alice P. Stein. P63
    Losses. Randall Jarrell. P84
    Theory of Flight. Muriel Rukeyser. P84
Flying. J. M. Westrup. P51
"Flying to moon to breathe the lunar air".
    Taking for Granted. Kim Unsong. P72
Foam. Roland Jones. P87
Fog
    Fog. Carl Sandburg. P82
Fog Horns
    Fog-Horn. William Stanley Merwin. P85
"The fog comes". Fog. Carl Sandburg. P82
Fog-Horn. William Stanley Merwin. P85
"Fog-folded mornings". Vietnam. James P.
    Bergman. P86
"Fog/Leap rolls the sea". White Morning. L.
    Stanley Cheney. P68
Foley, J. W.
    Song of Summer Days. P51
Foliage of Vision. James Merrill. P85
Folklore
    The Blind Men and the Elephant. John
    Godfrey Saxe. P90
Follen, Eliza Lee
    Oh! Look at the Moon. P51
    Three Little Kittens a Cat's Tale with
    Additions. P89
Follow Your Heart to the Land of

Enchantment. Tom Hawkins. P63
"Followed by his lodge, shabby men
        stumbling...". Ghetto Funeral, fr.
        Five Groups of Verse. Charles
        Reznikoff. P83
"Folly and time have fashioned". Athassel
        Abbey. Louise Imogen Guiney. P81
Food and Drink. Louis Untermeyer. P82
Food Director's Testimony. Nancy Simpson.
        P63
Food Processor. L. L. Zeiger. P63
Food and Eating
        Arles, 7 p.m. Marge Piercy. P63
        As I Was Dying at the Steak House...
            Scott Bates. P63
        Beautiful Meals. Thomas Sturge Moore. P51
        Bread. H. E. Wilkinson. P51
        Business Luncheon. Joel Ferree. P63
        Eating Out. Gene Fehler. P63
        English Rats. X. J. Kennedy. P63
        The Fair Fowl. Robert N. Feinstein. P63
        Food and Drink. Louis Untermeyer. P82
        If I Were an Apple. Unknown. P51
        In Her Kitchen. Mark Milotich. P56
        Jennifer Blass. Midred Luton. P63
        Love Portions. Joan Van Poznak. P63
        MSG. Bruce Berger. P63
        The Pancake. Christina Georgina Rossetti.
            P51
        Red Raspberries. Gary Selden. P63
        Three Plum Buns. Christina Georgina
            Rossetti. P51
        Upwardly Mobile Bean Curd. Bonnie
            Jacobson. P63
        What a Friend We Have in Cheeses! William
            Cole. P63
"A fool he wrote". Letters. Wolfgang Durben.
        P72
' Fool!' Said My Muse to Me:. G. N. Gabbard.
        P63
Fool's Fingers. Roland Mathias. P54
The Fool's Prayer. Edward Rowland Sill. P90
Fools
        Upon the Road of My Life. Stephen Crane.
            P81
Foot Hills. Carl T. Endemann. P56
Foot Soldier. Rhea Tregebov. P49
Footprints of a Sparrow. N. M. Bodecker. P80
Footprints on the Glacier. William Stanley
        Merwin. P85
"Footsore miles behind". Traveller's Rest.
        Bernard Hewitt. P72
For a Coming Extinction. William Stanley
        Merwin. P48
For a Comrade. Abraham Sutzkever. P48
For a Flower Whose Name I Don't Know. Pat
        Bridges. P56
For a Girl. Cynddelw Brydydd Mawr. P87
For a Good Ole Boy. Mary Veazey. P63

For a Lady I Know, fr. Four Epitaphs.
        Countee Cullen. P83
For a Lady of Impressions. Richard Parks.
        P68
For All the Violets. Alice Mackenzie Swaim.
        P65
For Annie. Edgar Allan Poe. P89
For Armando Rubio. Mauricio Electorat. P71
For Barbara. Andrew Brooks. P49
For Fear. Robert Creeley. P85
For Frank (5-70). Bruce Langbien. P86
For James Dean. Frank O'Hara. P85
For Jan, in Bar Maria. Carolyn Kizer. P79
For John Keats, Apostle of Beauty, fr. Four
        Epitaphs. Countee Cullen. P83
For Kenneth Patchen. A. D. Williams. P56
For Laura. Myra Cohn Livingston. P50
For Lovers. T. A. Shulgin. P58
For My Birthday, 1939. Paul Goodman. P84
For My Daughter. Weldon Kees. P84
For My Grandmother, fr. Four Epitaphs.
        Countee Cullen. P83
For My Mother: Genevieve Jules Creeley.
        Robert Creeley. P85
For One Sweet Sign. Eleanor Gude Ramirez.
        P72
For Paul Laurence Dunbar, fr. Four Epitaphs.
        Countee Cullen. P83
For Robert Frost. Galway Kinnell. P85
For Robin. Stella Browning. P72
For Sally, with a Piano. Paul Goodman. P84
For Susan, Turning Thirty. Anita Skeen. P88
"For a good decade". The Drunk in the
        Furnace. William Stanley Merwin. P85
"For a long time I've owed you words of
        love". The Incomparable Earth.
        Salvatore Quasimodo. P61
"For a long time now". The Palaces Under the
        Moon. Chems Nadir. P91
"For a moment she was silent, then". Grafts
        and the Garden. Mehdi Akhavan Sales.
        P91
"For a month now, wandering over the
        Sierras". Climbing Milestone Mountain,
        August 22, 1937. Kenneth Rexroth. P84
"For fifteen years I've sent words off...".
        Song Between the Sea and Sky. Kolyo
        Sevov. P70
"For flowers that bloom about our feet".
        Spring Prayer. Ralph Waldo Emerson.
        P51
"For God's sake hold your tongue...". The
        Canonization. John Donne. P59
"For lo, the winter is past". Song of
        Solomon, Old Testament. Unknown. P60
"For many a year I've watched...". The
        Ships. J. J. Bell. P51
"For many years". Minerals from Stone. Joy
        Kogawa. P49

"For mercy, courage, kindness, mirth". Song. Laurence Binyon. P51

"For morn, my dome of blue". A Child's Prayer. Siegfried Sassoon. P51

"For Scotland's and for freedom's right". Bruce and the Spider. Bernard Barton. P90

"For several nights we've heard...". We've Heard the Sea Again. Salvatore Quasimodo. P61

"For ten years the sycamores". Brynbeidog. Jeremy Hooker. P54

For the Candle Light. Angelina Weld Grimke. P89

For the Desert Island, from For the Desert Island. Tae-ch'ul Shin. P92

For the God of Peyote. Unknown. P78

For the Marriage of Faustus and Helen. Hart Crane. P83

"For Those Who Know Their Own Hearts". Unknown. P62

"For the first time in twenty years". After Being Paralyzed from the Neck Down... Ronald Wallace. P57

"For the first twenty years, since yesteday". The Computation. John Donne. P59

"For the sake of the flowing bright wounds of Jesus". The Last Englyn. Tudur Aled. P87

"For three years, out of key with his time". Hugh Selwyn Mauberley (Life and Contacts). Ezra Pound. P82

"For too Long I Have Thought That I'd Conceal". Stefano Protonotaro. P69

For W. H. A. John Ronald Renel Tolkien. P79

For You. Robert Creeley. P85

For You. Orhan Veli Kanik. P91

For You, in the Darkness, Returning. Karen Kania. P88

"For twenty years and more surviving after". Widows, from Spoon River Anthology. Edgar Lee Masters. P82

"For wandering walks". Joe's Snow Clothes. Karla Kuskin. P80

"For why, who writes such histories as these". Books. John Higgins. P90

"For years I drifted in the dark". Love for Poetry, from Wake up, My Heart and Other Poems. John Tworoger. P65

"For years nothing grew". The Marsh. Grace Schulman. P64

Force of Circumstance. Jose Lacaba. P92

Forche, Carolyn
        The Memory of Elena. P52

Ford Maddox Ford. Robert Lowell. P79

"The Ford pickup, painted red but rusted...". I-35, South of Waco. William Virgil Davis. P63

Ford, Ford Madox (Hueffer)
        The Unwritten Song. P51

Foreign Children. Robert Louis Stevenson. P51

Foreign Lands. Robert Louis Stevenson. P51, P89

Foreigners with Teeth. Peter Pal Kong. P53

Forest. Jean Garrigue. P84

Forest. Yaedi Ignatow. P64

Forest. Jules Supervielle. P61

"Forest green pillows covered the floor". Where God Rested His Head. Jerry F. Borba. P72

Forests
        Forest. Jules Supervielle. P61
        Forest. Jean Garrigue. P84
        In the Woods. Dorothy Baker. P51
        My Dream. Scott Gunther. P73
        My Temple. Anne Shaw. P73
        Shady Woods. E. M. Adams. P51
        Sherwood. Alfred Noyes. P51, P90
        The Spirit of the Wood. Paul Baudin. P77
        Stopping by Woods on a Snowy Evening. Robert Frost. P82
        To the Greyrock Woods. Llywelyn ap y Moel. P87
        The Wood of Flowers. James Stephens. P51
        Woods Are Sleeping. Salvatore Quasimodo. P61

The Forget-Me-Not. Unknown. P51

Forgetfulness
        What Lips My Lips Have Kissed, and Where, and Why. Edna St. Vincent Millay. P82

"Forgive my wooden tongue". From a Line by Cyril Dabydeen. Martin Singleton. P49

Forgiveness
        On His Death-Bed. Meilyr. P87
        1974, Not Guilty?., from For the Desert Island. Tae-ch'ul Shin. P92
        Perry Zoll, from Spoon River Anthology. Edgar Lee Masters. P82
        Song. Robert M. Howell. P65

The Forgotten Man. Edwin Markham. P81

"Forlorn and white". White Symphony. John Gould Fletcher. P82

Form All (For Gilda Walker). Hugh McKinley. P72

The Form of Living. Richard Rolle. P66

A Formal Appeal. Kaleem Omar. P91

The Forsaken Merman, sel. Matthew Arnold. P51

The Forsaken Merman. Matthew Arnold. P90

The Fortunate Fall. William Harrold. P68

The Fortunate Traveller. Derek Walcott. P48

44, Avenue de Maine. Atanas Dalchev. P70

"The forward youth that would appear". An Horatian Ode upon Cromwell's Return from Ireland. Andrew Marvell. P59

Foster, R. J.

Swan Song. P68
Foster, Stephen
My Old Kentucky Home. P89
Old Folks at Home. P89
"Found a hole with a light in it...". The
Little Random Creatures. Unknown. P78
Found in the Woods. Irene F. Pawsey. P51
Found Wanting. Emily Dickinson. P89
"Found myself in an island hide-away".
Island Sanctuary (Poetic Rambling).
Cecile C. Metzger. P72
Found--A Poem!. Clarence L. Weaver. P72
Fountain, Helen
Tanka. P72
A Fountain, a Bottle, a Donkey's Ears and
Some Books. Robert Frost. P82
The Fountain. Donald Davie. P79
The Fountain. James Russell Lowell. P51
Fountains
The Palaces Under the Moon. Chems Nadir.
P91
A 4th Stanza for Dr. Johnson, Donald Hall...
X. J. Kennedy. P63
Four and Eight. Ffrida Wolfe. P51
Four Epigrams. John Donne. P59
"Four chubby angels, like adult cheribim".
An Old Map of Somewhere. Jeffery
Donaldson. P49
411 Days and Nights. Doug Rawlings. P86
Four Letter Words. Stella Moss. P63
Four Poems. Ray Young Bear. P78
Four Poems for Robin. Gary Snyder. P85
Four Poems in One. Anne Porter. P64
Four Preludes on Playthings of the Wind.
Carl Sandburg. P82
Four Quartets, sels. Thomas Stearns Eliot.
P83
Four Scarlet Berries. Mary Vivian. P51
Four Sides to a House. Amy Lowell. P82
Four Squares. Agnes Nemes Nagy. P92
The Four Sweet Months. Robert Herrick. P51
The Four Zoas: 'Night the Ninth, Being the
Last...'. William Blake. P48
"Four temples of essential life". Out of
These, the First Love. Wallace William
Winchell. P72
' Four-Paws'. Helen Parry Eden. P51
Foweles in the Frith. Unknown. P66
Fox Terrier Disappears at the
Intersection... Juan Luis Martinez.
P71
The Fox. Robert Williams Parry. P87
Foxes
The Little Random Creatures. Unknown. P78
Three Songs of Mad Coyote. Unknown. P78
"The foxglove bells, with lolling tongue".
Foxgloves. Mary Webb. P51
"The foxglove by the cottage door". Four and
Eight. Ffrida Wolfe. P51

Foxgloves. Mary Webb. P51
"Fragile cupped hand on long slender neck".
Poppies. William E. Morris. P72
Fragments. Perry Walker. P68
"Frail liquid crystal prisms of soft rain".
Prisms. Katherine A. Hogan. P65
Francis Bacon, the Inventor of Spectacles...
Cynthia MacDonald. P79
Francis, Robert
Light and Shadow. P63
The Pumpkin Man. P63
Where to Spend the Winter. P63
Frank. Frona Lane. P72
Frank, John
The Rainbows. P65
Woman's College. P72
"frank, the animal, Fletcher, face peeled".
What's in a Name. Ed Orr. P63
Franklin, Michael
The Scarecrow. P51
Franklin, Richard
Sunsets Be Dear. P65
Fraser, Kathleen
Wrestling. P50
The Freaks at Spurgin Road Field. Richard
Hugo. P57
Frederick II of Hohenstaufen. See Federico
II
Frederick, Audrey
Limited. P72
Free. Esther Uhrman. P72
The Free School-house, Llanrwst. Ieuan Glan
Geirionydd. P87
Free Verse. Joanne Seltzer. P65
"Free-arm to a jigsaw--.". At the Craft
Show. Marijane G. Ricketts. P56
Freedom. Joan Agnew. P51
Freedom
Asylum, from Your Tired, Your Poor. Lisel
Mueller. P88
Dance. Patricia Glasgow. P68
Earthbound. Bette Warden. P72
The Elements. Elisaveta Bagriana. P70
The Escape. Mark Van Doren. P83
Free. Esther Uhrman. P72
Freedom in Dress, from Epicene or The
Silent Woman. Ben Jonson. P90
Freedom in the New Air. Tijan M. Sallah.
P72
Freedom of the Mind. William Lloyd
Garrison. P90
The Funeral of Martin Luther King, Jr.
Nikki Giovanni. P85
Independence. Marion Jane Richardson. P65
The Independent Man, fr. A Street in
Bronzeville. Gwendolyn Brooks. P84
Lesson One. Guanetta Gordon. P72
Let Me Go. Maria Berl Lee. P68
Maybe. Susan Headen Griffith. P72

The New Day. Fenton Johnson. P82

Patience, from Poems of Freedom. William James Linton. P90

The Slave. James Oppenheim. P82

To Althea from Prison. Richard Lovelace. P90

To the Extent That I Haven't a Cat. June Siegel. P63

Freedom in Dress, from Epicene or The Silent Woman. Ben Jonson. P90

Freedom in the New Air. Tijan M. Sallah. P72

Freedom of the Mind. William Lloyd Garrison. P90

Freeman, John
The Tree. P51
The Waits. P51

A **French** Writer Named Sartre. Weldon Kees. P63

Fresh Air. Kenneth Koch. P85

Fresh Horses Should Be Waiting. Caroline Knox. P88

"**Fresh** mown grass". Sanskrit Songs for Modern Dreamers'. Sheila Craft. P72

Fresheners. R. R. Menon. P72

Freshwater West Revisited. Roland Mathias. P54

Freund, Edith
Handling it--. P88
A Woman of Style. P88

Friday. Sir Walter Scott. P51

Friedberg, Martha
Father. P88

Friedenkraft, Georges
Dream. Goh-Chapouthier (tr.). P72

A **Friend** in the Garden. Juliana Horatia Ewing. P51

"**Friend** most of all I value". An Invitation. Goronwy Owen. P87

Friend, Your White Beard Sweeps the Ground. Stephen Crane. P81

Friendless. John Berryman. P79

Friends. Evelyn Sewell Rineer. P65

The **Friends** of the Friends. Caroline Knox. P63

Friendship
Atop. Prince Redcloud. P50
Blow, Blow, Thou Winter Wind, from As You Like It. William Shakespeare. P89
"Certainly, If a Man Takes the Initiative". Unknown. P62
Don't Go, Jo!. Barbara Ireson. P80
The Dream Songs, sels. John Berryman. P52
For Jan, in Bar Maria. Carolyn Kizer. P79
For Susan, Turning Thirty. Anita Skeen. P88
Friends. Evelyn Sewell Rineer. P65
The Friends of the Friends. Caroline Knox. P63
The Friendship Only Lasted a Few Seconds.

Lily Jean Lee-Adams. P86

The Funny House. Margaret Hillert. P50

A Good Play. Robert Louis Stevenson. P89

"However Much It Takes To Create Friendship". Unknown. P62

"In Youth, Oh Daughter, You Are Like a Full River". Unknown. P62

An Invitation. Goronwy Owen. P87

Just Friends. Robert Creeley. P85

"A Man Whose Wife Is the Boss". Unknown. P62

Mary's Melody (To Mary E. Cox). Grace Ridgway Rahamah. P72

Monkhood. John Berryman. P79

"My Dear, Go Down Only the Most Likely Road". Unknown. P62

No Yellow Jackets on the Mountian. Dabney Stuart. P67

"Oh Daughter, If You Enter the House". Unknown. P62

"Oh Friend, Do Not Cry". Unknown. P62

The Oath. Allen Tate. P67

Our Afterlife. Robert Lowell. P79

A Pact. Ezra Pound. P82

The Road to a Friend's House. Lorraine Blankenhorn. P72

"Separation from the One We Love". Unknown. P62

Slumber Party. Carson McCullers. P50

"Surely You Can See That Love Is Proper". Unknown. P62

The Telephone Call. Jack Prelutsky. P50

A Thank You for Friends. Rodney Bennett. P51

To Owain Gwynedd. Meilir ap Gwalchmai. P87

The Unseen Playmate. Robert Louis Stevenson. P89

A Wayfaring Song. Henry Van Dyke. P89

We Have Been Friends Together. Caroline Elizabeth Sarah Norton. P89

The World Is Not a Pleasant Place To Be. Nikki Giovanni. P85

World Poets Everywhere. Miriam L. Woolfolk. P72

Wrestling. Kathleen Fraser. P50

The **Friendship** Only Lasted a Few Seconds. Lily Jean Lee-Adams. P86

"**Friendship** turns. And turns again...". No Yellow Jackets on the Mountian. Dabney Stuart. P67

A **Frisky** Lamb. Christina Georgina Rossetti. P51

The **Frog** and the Bird. Vera Hessey. P51

The **Frog.** Rose Fyleman. P51

Frogs
The Brown Frog. Mary K. Robinson. P51
A Friend in the Garden. Juliana Horatia Ewing. P51

The Frog. Rose Fyleman. P51
The Gathering. Jack Conway. P56
Frolic. George William ("A.E.") Russell. P51
From a Girl in a Mental Institution. Diane Wakoski. P85
From a Line by Cyril Dabydeen. Martin Singleton. P49
From a Marriage Counselor's!Notebook. Alfred Dorn. P65
From a Railway Carriage. Robert Louis Stevenson. P51
From a Walking Song. Charles Williams. P51
From a Watershed. John R. Locke. P68
"From a deserted graveyard". To the Holy Spirit. Yvor Winters. P83
"From a little seed". Little Things. Eileen Mathias. P51
"From a time wound in him like hairspring". After Ten Years. Mary Ellen Chihak. P68
"From a vision red with war...". The New Day. Fenton Johnson. P82
From an Athlete Living Old. James Camp. P63
From Dusk to Dawn: Night Watch II. Ken Stone. P86
From Exile. Dafydd Benfras. P87
"From Ghoulies and Ghosties". Unknown. P60
From Goethe to Gounod: Concerning a Mutual Affaire... Patricia Kirby. P68
From Here to Eternity. Pearl Crayton. P68
"From House to House He Goes". Unknown. P51
From Milton's Translation of Horace's Fifth Ode. Terri B. Joseph. P68
"From blacked-out streets". During the Eichmann Trial, sels. Denise Levertov. P85
"From far she's come, and very old". Age in Youth. Trumbull Stickney. P81
"From ghoulies and ghosties". An Old Cornish Litany, sel. Unknown. P55
"From groves of spice". Hindu Cradle Song. Unknown. P51
"From Merthyr to Dowlais the tramway climbs". The Deluge, 1939. Saunders Lewis. P87
"From my mother's sleep I fell into the state". The Death of the Ball Turret Gunner. Randall Jarrell. P84
"From my mother's sleep I fell...". The Death of the Reference Librarian. David Kirby. P63
"From near the sea, like Whitman...". Ode: Salute to the French Negro Poets. Frank O'Hara. P85
"From nether-heel". Lullalye-Acidby. Ish Yair. P72
"From plane of light to plane...". Evening Hawk. Robert Penn Warren. P67
"From sea and manor and nearby mountain".

The Happy Man. Unknown. P87
"From shelving cliff-darkness...". The Place. Robert Penn Warren. P67
From the Poetry Exchange, Two Conversations. Howard Nemerov. P63
"From the Quiet Stream". Lorenzo. P77
From the Recesses of a Lowly Spirit. Sir John Bowring. P89
From the Train. Marjorie Wilson. P51
From Venice Was That Afternoon. Jean Garrigue. P84
"From the dark emptiness of the heart". To the Beloved. Harry Maizel. P72
"From the greystone tower". The Tower. Gloria H. Procsal. P72
"From the hilltop we could overlook". Westport. Galway Kinnell. P85
"From the map side". Troubles. John Hildebidle. P56
"From the north came ideas". The Tree of the World. Clemente Riedemann. P71
"From the top of this phallus". Guide to Paris: Eiffel Tower, Versailles. Scott Bates. P63
"From unfinished night accidents". Dream Scars. Kateri Lanthier. P49
The Front Runner System. Wilma H. Clements. P68
Frontier and Pioneer Life
The Settler. Alfred Street. P90
Frost
Hard Frost. Cathryn Hankla. P56
Winter Frost. Alison Hoelz. P73
Frost Is Coming. Mary Hamilton Neary. P72
"Frost in the air and music in the air". The Waits. John Freeman. P51
Frost, Robert
Acquainted with the Night. P82
After Apple Picking. P82
The Bearer of Evil Tidings. P82
Desert Places. P82
Design. P82
Fire and Ice. P82
A Fountain, a Bottle, a Donkey's Ears and Some Books. P82
Gathering Leaves. P82
Ghost House. P89
Into My Own. P89
Mowing. P82
Neither Out Far nor in Deep. P82
Nothing Gold Can Stay. P82
An Old Man's Winter Night. P82
The Oven Bird. P82
Range-Finding. P82
The Road Not Taken. P82
Stopping by Woods on a Snowy Evening. P82
The Subverted Flower. P82
The Tuft of Flowers. P82
Two Tramps in Mud Time. P82

The Witch of Coos. P82
The Wood-Pile. P82
Frost, Robert
    For Robert Frost. Galway Kinnell. P85
Froydarland, Jan Anker
    The Conqueror. Kirsten Mason (tr.). P72
"The **frozen** ground is broken". In February.
    P. A. Ropes. P51
Frozen with Time. Sherry Sue McCall. P56
"The **frugal** snail, with forecast of repose".
    The Housekeeper. Charles Lamb. P89
Fruit
    The Apple Rhyme. Madeleine Nightingale.
    P51
    Goblin Market, sel. Christina Georgina
        Rossetti. P51
    Mangoes. Taufiq Rafat. P91
Fugitive. Lisel Mueller. P88
The **Fuhrer** Bunker, sels. William DeWitt
    Snodgrass. P85
Fukuda, Tsutomu
    White. P72
Fukuyama, Betty
    Possession Report. P65
"**Full** Early in the Morning". Unknown. P51
Full Moon. Robert Hayden. P84
Full Moon. Elinor Wylie. P82
"The **Full** Moon Brimming". Jeff Jones. P77
"**Full** knee-deep lies the winter snow". The
    Death of the Old Year. Lord Tennyson.
    P90
"**Full** moonlit night people". The Net of
    Moon: a Pawnee Hand Game Vision.
    Unknown. P78
Full of Wonder. Ann Griffiths. P87
"**Full** of her long white arms and milky
    skin". The Equilibrists. John Crowe
    Ransom. P67,P83
Fulmer, Chrystie
    Life. P74
"The **fundamental** question about revolution".
    Facing the Way. Alice Walker. P85
Funeral Music. Geoffrey Hill. P48
The **Funeral** of Martin Luther King, Jr. Nikki
    Giovanni. P85
Funeral Song. Patricio Esteve. P92
Funeral Song, from Wolf Songs & Others of
    the Tlingit. Unknown. P78
Funerals   !
    After Great Pain. Edward Butscher. P64
    Burial. Alice Walker. P67
    Death in the Channel, fr. From a Travel
        Diary. T.H. Parry-Williams. P87
    Ghetto Funeral, fr. Five Groups of Verse.
        Charles Reznikoff. P83
    The Killer. Unknown. P78
    My Father's Funeral. Karl Shapiro. P84
    Namaste. Katherine E. Landry. P72
    The Ocean Said to Me Once. Stephen Crane.

    P81
    Of De Witt Williams on His Way to Lincoln
        Cemetery, fr. A.... Gwendolyn Brooks.
        P84
    Office for the Dead. Thomas Kinsella. P79
    The Old Boatman. Robert Williams Parry.
        P87
    The Poet's Final Instructions. John
        Berryman. P84
    Postlude. Edna Meudt. P68
    Tract. William Carlos Williams. P82
    Transition. M. Athar Tahir. P91
    Two British Airmen. Thomas Merton. P84
The **Funny** House. Margaret Hillert. P50
"**Fur** in see bi west Spayngne". The Land of
    Cokaygne. Unknown. P66
"A **furlong** from the crest, when the bells'
    cry". The Fox. Robert Williams Parry.
    P87
Furnaces
    The Drunk in the Furnace. William Stanley
        Merwin. P85
Furniture
    Desks Are Places. Glee Knight. P68
The **Furry** Home. J. M. Westrup. P51
"A **furry** coat has the bear to wear". The
    Pig's Tail. Norman Ault. P51
Furse, Margaret Cecilia
    The Lamp Flower. P51
The **Fury** of Aerial Bombardment. Richard
    Eberhart. P83
"A **fury** seethes inside me". Modern Poetry.
    Glenna Glee. P72
Futile Death Wish. Simanchal Patnaik. P72
Future
    The Fifteenth Century. Kaleem Omar. P91
    The Loner. Thu-Phuong Do. P74
    Of the Nameless Birds. Teresa Calderon.
        P71
    Winter Central. Christopher Dewdney. P49
Fyleman, Rose
    The Balloon Man. P51
    A Christmas Wish. P51
    Conversation. P51
    The Donkey. P51
    The Fairy Flute. P51
    A Fairy Went A-Marketing. P51
    The Frog. P51
    The Goblin. P51
    Good Morning. P51
    Jock O' Dreams. P51
    Mice. P51
    Mrs. Brown. P51
    Pretty Lady. P51
    Primrose Hill. P51
    The Weathercock. P51

G. S. O.
 The Engine Driver. P51
Gabbard, G. N.
 Discount Store. P63
 'Fool!' Said My Muse to Me:. P63
 King Alfred Explains It. P63
 To a Fringed Genital. P63
 Witches' Sabbatical. P63
Gabriel, Louise Marsh
 Snow Scene. P72
"The gadget works at top speed". Food
 Processor. L. L. Zeiger. P63
"Gah non wey yo hey". Sound-Poem No. 2.
 Richard Johnny John. P78
The Gain. Dorsha Hayes. P65
Gale, Norman
 The Country Faith. P51
Gallagher, D. Lyons
 The Proposal. P65
Gallagher, Tess
 Each Bird Walking. P52
The Gallant Ship. Sir Walter Scott. P51
"The gallows swayed with laughter". Ballad
 of the Ladder. Lyubomir Levchev. P70
Galsworthy, John
 Prayer for Gentleness to All Creatures.
 P51
Galvao, Linda
 Limericks. P74
Gambler's Wife (Right Diptych, an Extract).
 Pearl Crayton. P68
The Gamblers. Vachel Lindsay. P82
Gambling
 Casino Royale. Estelle M. Zelner. P72
 Crapshooters. Carl Sandburg. P82
 The Gamblers. Vachel Lindsay. P82
 Las Vegas. Ernest Kroll. P63
A Game of Chess, fr. The Waste Land. Thomas
 Stearns Eliot. P83
The Game. Harold Bond. P57
Games
 A Little Finger Game. E. J. Falconer. P51
Garbage
 The Dustman. Clive Sansom. P51
 Goggy. Gwyn Thomas. P87
Garcia, Norma Lopez
 Tell Me. P68
The Garden. Louise Gluck. P85
The Garden. Andrew Marvell. P59
Gardens
 After Winter. Sterling A. Brown. P89
 Grafts and the Garden. Mehdi Akhavan
 Sales. P91
 Grandfather in the Garden. Robert
 Minhinnick. P54
 The Green Man. Kaleem Omar. P91
 A Hex for My Neighbor's Green Thumb.
 Glenna Holloway. P63

My Garden. Norah Hussey. P51
Rondine of the Rare Device. Wesli Court.
 P63
Sowing Seeds. Ursula Cornwall. P51
The Sun is a Globe of Fire. Antonio
 Machado. P61
There Is a Garden in Her Face, from An
 Houre's... Unknown. P89
When Mary Thro' the Garden Went. Mary E.
 Coleridge. P51
Gargoyle. Carl Sandburg. P82
"The Garland-Girl Giving Out Freshly Broken
 Blossoms". Unknown. P62
Garlick, Phyllis L.
 Fairy Feet. P51
 The Fairy Shoemaker. P51
 Lullaby. P51
Garrigue, Jean
 False Country of the Zoo. P84
 Forest. P84
 From Venice Was That Afternoon. P84
 Gravepiece. P84
 Lightly Like Music Running. P84
 The Maimed Grasshopper Speaks Up. P84
 Primer of Plato. P84
 This Day Is Not Like That Day. P84
Garrison, William Lloyd
 Freedom of the Mind. P90
The Garrison. W. H. Auden. P79
Garza. Bruce Bennett. P63
Gas
 Gas Man. Pyke Johnson Jr. P63
 Helium: an Inert Gas. Judson Jerome. P63
Gas Man. Pyke Johnson Jr. P63
"The gates clanged and they walked you into
 jail". The Conscientious Objector.
 Karl Shapiro. P84
The Gates to England. Marjorie Wilson. P51
Gathering Leaves. Robert Frost. P82
Gathering Leaves. William Crwys Williams.
 P87
Gathering the Bones Together. Gregory Orr.
 P85
The Gathering. Jack Conway. P56
"Gauss and Lobatchewsky non-avenues". Non-
 Missing Fox Terrier Does Not
 Reappear... Juan Luis Martinez. P71
"Gauss Avenue is only invisible". Fox
 Terrier Disappears at the
 Intersection... Juan Luis Martinez.
 P71
Gautier, Theophile
 The Hippopotamus. Charles Guenther (tr.).
 P61
Gay Robin Is Seen No More. Robert Bridges.
 P51
"Gay go up and gay go down". The Bells of
 London. Unknown. P51
Gay, Jeremy

Halley's Comet. P74
Gay, John
    Black-Eyed Susan. P89
Geek. David H. Green. P63
Geese
    From a Watershed. John R. Locke. P68
    Geese in Fog. Therese Becker. P88
    The Geese. Robert Williams Parry. P87
Geese in Fog. Therese Becker. P88
The Geese. Robert Williams Parry. P87
Geirionydd, Ieuan Glan
    The Free School-house, Llanrwst. Tony
        Conran (tr.). P87
Gelinas, Jason
    I Am. P73
"Genealogists, geologists, and experts in
    falcony ". Tourists. Josephine Miles.
    P84
General Delivery. Ben L. Hiatt. P77
General Self-Satisfied, from Lost Youth: the
    Last War. Alfred Kreymborg. P82
General Washington. Paul Goodman. P84
General William Booth Enters into Heaven.
    Vachel Lindsay. P82
"The generals ha given up". The Final
    Battle. Kandy Arnold. P58
"Gentle mentor". A Remembered Workshop
    Critic: Louis A. Haselmayer. Herbert
    M. Kirkham. P68
"A gentle rain suddenly showers the island".
    Rain on the Island. Jennifer Campbell.
    P74
Geometry of Love. Anne Marx. P65
"George Washington, your name is on my
    lips". Patriotic Poem. Diane Wakoski.
    P85
George, Etty
    Lonesome Bird. P72
Georgiev, George
    Contiguity. P72
Gerov, Alexander
    On Their Day Off. John Balaban (tr.). P70
    The Sun. John Balaban (tr.). P70
    The Town Tree. John Balaban (tr.). P70
Gertrude and Alice. Joan Van Poznak. P63
"Get up at once, now, Margaret May!.". Eggs
    for Breakfast. Irene F. Pawsey. P51
Getting Berries, from String Games. Unknown.
    P78
Getting Firewood, from String Games.
    Unknown. P78
Getting Up. Lilian McCrea. P51
"Getting off the metro on the way to work".
    Nelligan. Laurence Hutchman. P49
Ghazal. Jonaid. P92
Ghazal. Jonaid. P92
Ghetto Funeral, fr. Five Groups of Verse.
    Charles Reznikoff. P83
The Ghetto, sel. Lola Ridge. P82

Ghigna, Charles
    Aries Sideshow. P63
Ghost & Shaman, from String Games. Unknown.
    P78
Ghost House. Robert Frost. P89
Ghost Sounds. Unknown. P55
Ghost Towns
    The Desolate City. Claude McKay. P82
The Ghost. Agnes Nemes Nagy. P92
Ghosts. Harry Behn. P55
Ghosts
    By the Pacific Ocean. Joaquin Miller. P81
    Dibdin's Ghost. Eugene Field. P81
    Final Confrontation. Sheila Martindale.
        P49
    Ghost Sounds. Unknown. P55
    The Ghost. Agnes Nemes Nagy. P92
    Ghosts. Harry Behn. P55
    Ice. Charles P. Martin. P58
    In the Center of the Bedroom. Oscar Hahn.
        P71
    Little Ghosts. Oscar Hahn. P71
    Little Orphant Annie. James Whitcomb
        Riley. P89
    Non Omnis Moriar. Leilah Wendell. P68
    The Old Wife and the Ghost. James Reeves.
        P55
    A Stone Tablet for Animal Ghosts, from My
        Hometown's... Wu Cheng. P92
    To the Holy Spirit. Yvor Winters. P83
    Villonaud for This Yule. Ezra Pound. P82
    Wandering Souls. Sergio Mansilla. P71
The Ghosts of the Buffaloes. Vachel Lindsay.
    P82
"A gi ya ni a gi yan ni i". A Poem from the
    Sweatbath Poems. Unknown. P78
Giammarino, Jaye
    After Long Grief. P72
A Giant's Cake. Evelina San Garde. P51
Gibbs, Margaret E.
    On the Banisters. P51
    The Song of the Bath. P51
Gibson, Wilfred Wilson
    Michael's Song. P51
A Gift Multiplies. Vivian Moody. P72
A Gift of Great Value. Robert Creeley. P85
A Gift. Amy Lowell. P82
The Gift. Lara Colton. P73
The Gift. Lewis Turco. P63
Gifts. Emma Lazarus. P90
Gifts and Giving
    The Gift. Lewis Turco. P63
    Insult Before Gift-Giving. Unknown. P78
    Lucky Dilemma. Ned Pastor. P63
The Gifts. John N. Morris. P79
Gilbert, Sir William Schwenck
    To the Terrestrial Globe. P90
Gilder, Richard Watson
    The Celestial Passion. P81

Great Nature Is an Army Gay. P89
I Count My Time by Times That I Meet
    Thee. P81
Ode. P81
On the Life-Mask of Lincoln. P81
Sherman. P81
The Sonnet. P90
Gilfillan, Robert
The Exile's Song. P90
Gilgan, Jennifer
Puddles. P73
Gill, David
A Going-Away Poem for Philip Larkin. P72
Gill, David (tr.)
Seashore. Ondra Lysohorsky. P72
Gillespie, Blythe
My Poetic Nature. P73
Gilliam, Elizabeth M.
Meditation. P72
Gilmore, John C.
Reasons Before and After the Fact. P86
"The **gingham** dog and the calico cat". The
    Duel. Eugene Field. P90
Ginsberg, Allen
My Sad Self. P85
Ode to Failure. P85
Plutonian Ode. P52
Wales Visitation. P85
Ginsberg, Allen
He. Lawrence Ferlinghetti. P85
Giovanni, Nikki
The Funeral of Martin Luther King, Jr.
    P85
Kidnap Poem. P85
Knoxville, Tennessee. P85
Nikki-Rosa. P85
Scrapbooks. P85
They Clapped. P85
The World Is Not a Pleasant Place To Be.
    P85
"The **gipsies** lit their fires...". The
    Idlers. Edmund Blunden. P51
Gipsy Jane. William Brighty Rands. P51
Gipsy Man. Dorothy King. P51
Giraffe. C. B. Oppenheimer. P68
Giraudier, Antonio
Enhanced Embrace. P65
"You Stand Like Good Ivory". P72
Girglani, J. M.
The Leap. P72
The **Girl** and Her Fawn. Andrew Marvell. P51
A **Girl** in a Library. Randall Jarrell. P67
The **Girl** Next Door. Knute Skinner. P63
The **Girl** of Rue Joli. Dennis Moore. P86
"A **girl** sits in a black room". Picture of a
    Girl Drawn in Black and White. Diane
    Wakoski. P85
The **Girl's** Hearts Soften. Daniel Cuol Long.
    P53

"**Girls** and Boys Come Out To Play". Unknown.
    P51
A **Girls'** Hair. Dafydd ab Edmwnd. P87
"**Give** a rouse, then, in the Maytime". A
    Stein Song. Richard Hovey. P81
"**Give** place, ye ladies, and begone". The
    Portrait. Thomas Heywood. P89
"**GIve** your hand". Grow. Esther Gress. P72
"**Giving**, while the rain lasts, soft noises".
    Eaves. Ellis Jones. P87
Gladden, Washington
Ultima Veritas. P89
Glasgow, Patricia
Dance. P68
Glass Lady. Virginia M. Hahn. P58
Glass Walls. Karen Birch. P73
Glazier, Jan
Erin Go Bragh. P56
Gleason, Marian
Better Refrain. P63
Know Knowing. P72
Glee, Glenna
Chariots. P68
Modern Poetry. P72
Glickman, Susan
Sassafras. P49
Glint. Euros Bowen. P87
Globes
To the Terrestrial Globe. Sir William
    Schwenck Gilbert. P90
Gloeggler, Edward A.
Idols of Love. P65
Lessons in Love. P65
The Loving Thing. P65
Sleeping Beauty. P65
"**Glory** Be to That God Who Is in the Fire".
    Unknown. P60
"**Glory** and honor and fame and
    everlasting...". Sherman. Richard
    Watson Gilder. P81
Gloucester Moors. William Vaughn Moody. P81
The **Glove** and the Lions. Leigh Hunt. P90
Gloves
My Hands in Purdah. Mary Di Michele. P49
Glow-Worms. P. A. Ropes. P51
Gluck, Louise
The Garden. P85
Gretel in Darkness. P85
Horse. P52
Portrait. P85
World Breaking Apart. P85
Gluggity Glug, from Myrtle and the Vine.
    George Colman the Younger. P90
A **Glutton.** Nyagak Pinien. P53
Gluttony
He'd Eat Lizards. Buk Teny Women. P53
Glyn, Guto'r
In His Old Age and Blindness. Tony Conran
    (tr.). P87

To Hywel ab Ifan Fychan. Tony Conran
     (tr.). P87
"Gnat, have you landed here to look".
     Reading Outdoors. Joan Drew Ritchings.
     P63
The Gnome. Harry Behn. P55
Gnomic Stanzas. Unknown. P87
Go Back. Nirupama Narasimham. P72
Go Down Death. James Weldon Johnson. P83
Go Out. Eileen Mathias. P51
"Go Slowly Over the Stones". Paz Molina. P71
"Go and ask Robin to bring the girls over".
     Vision by Sweetwater. John Crowe
     Ransom. P67
"Go count the stars!.". Counting. Fenton
     Johnson. P82
"Go down to Kew in lilac-time...". The
     Barrel Organ. Alfred Noyes. P51
"Go forth--.". Benediction. Mary Eleanor
     Cox. P72
"Go now, bird, urbane and civil". The Tit.
     Llywelyn Goch ap Meurig Hen. P87
"Go to Bed Early Wake up with Joy". Unknown.
     P51
"Go to Surrey and Wyatt". 'Fool!' Said My
     Muse to Me:. G. N. Gabbard. P63
"Go to the western gate, Luke Havergal".
     Luke Havergal. Edward Arlington
     Robinson. P81
Go, Pretty Child. Robert Herrick. P51
Goal Far and Near. Margaret Avison. P49
Goals
     Foot Hills. Carl T. Endemann. P56
Goat's Hole, Paviland. Nigel Jenkins. P54
Goats
     All Goats. Elizabeth J. Coatsworth. P89
Goblin Market, sel. Christina Georgina
     Rossetti. P51
"A goblin lives in our house, in our
     house...". The Goblin. Rose Fyleman.
     P51
Goch ap Meurig Hen, Llywelyn
     The Tit. Tony Conran (tr.). P87
Goch, Iolo
     The Court of Owain Glyndwr at Sycharth.
     Tony Conran (tr.). P87
God
     Affliction. George Herbert. P59
     The Agony. George Herbert. P59
     Anguish. Henry Vaughan. P59
     Anonymous. John Banister Tabb. P81
     "Batter My Heart...," from Divine
        Mediations. John Donne. P59
     Bitter-Sweet. George Herbert. P59
     Clorinda and Damon. Andrew Marvell. P59
     The Collar. George Herbert. P59
     Delight in God. Francis Quarles. P89
     Easter Wings. George Herbert. P59
     The Elixir. George Herbert. P59

Faded Pictures. William Vaughn Moody. P81
Flame of God. Frederika Blankner. P65
The Flower. George Herbert. P59
The Forgotten Man. Edwin Markham. P81
The Fury of Aerial Bombardment. Richard
     Eberhart. P83
God and His Church. Morgan LLwyd. P87
God Fashioned the Ship. Stephen Crane.
     P81
God Lay Dead in Heaven. Stephen Crane.
     P81
Grandmother God. Jeanine Hathaway. P88
A Guide. Thelma G. Monk. P72
Hack and Hew. Bliss Carman. P90
Hands of Gold. Margaret L. Fellinger. P72
The Happy Man. Unknown. P87
The Holy Spirit. Robert Herrick. P89
I Walked in a Desert. Stephen Crane. P81
Just God. Lewis Turco. P63
Justice (1). George Herbert. P59
'Let There Be Translators!'. Grace
     Schulman. P79
Light Shining Out of Darkness. William
     Cowper. P89
The Livid Lightnings Flashed in the
     Clouds. Stephen Crane. P81
"Lord/When You Bring the Renewing Day".
     Ioan Maier. P72
The Lost Sheep. Elizabeth Cecilia
     Clephane. P89
Love (3). George Herbert. P59
The Love of God. William Williams
     Pantycelyn. P87
The Love of God. Eliza Scudder. P89
A Man Adrift on a Slim Spar. Stephen
     Crane. P81
A Man Went Before a Strange God. Stephen
     Crane. P81
Meditation. Mary K. Mazotti. P72
A Mighty Fortress Is Our God. Martin
     Luther. P89
The New Life. Raul Zurita. P71
Novice in the Woods. L. G. Harvey. P72
O Fire of God, the Comforter. Saint
     Hildegarde. P89
Ode, from The Spectator. Joseph Addison.
     P89
The Old Repair Man. Fenton Johnson. P82
Once, a Man, Clambering to the House-
     Tops. Stephen Crane. P81
Our First Journey. N.M. Rashed. P91
Our God, Our Help in Ages Past. Isaac
     Watts. P89
The Patent of a Lord. Stephen Crane. P81
Peace. Henry Vaughan. P59
Pilgrim. William Williams Pantycelyn. P87
The Preacher: Ruminates Behind the Sermon
     fr. A Street... Gwendolyn Brooks. P84
Psalm 13. Sir Philip Sidney. P59

The Pulley. George Herbert. P59
"Since She Whom I Loved...," from Divine
    Meditations. John Donne. P59
A Song to God. Salah Abdul-Sabur. P91
A Spirit Sped. Stephen Crane. P81
Thee. Louise Louis. P65
To Thy Will, O Lord. Bee Bacherig Long.
    P72
The Trace of God's Hand. Francis O.
    Raniville. P72
The Trust. Gavin Burgess. P72
Unprofitableness. Henry Vaughan. P59
Vanity (1). George Herbert. P59
Veni Creator Spiritus. Saint Gregory the
    Great. P89
Walking in the Sky. Stephen Crane. P81
Where God Rested His Head. Jerry F.
    Borba. P72
Who Is That a-Walking in the Corn?.
    Fenton Johnson. P82
A Wreath. George Herbert. P59
God and His Church. Morgan LLwyd. P87
"God Bless All Those That I Love". Unknown.
    P60
"God Bless the Master of This House".
    Unknown. P60
A God Came to Man. Stephen Crane. P81
God Complex, from Lost Youth: the Last War.
    Alfred Kreymborg. P82
God Fashioned the Ship. Stephen Crane. P81
"God be in my head". The Knight's Prayer.
    Unknown. P51
"God bless the field and bless the furrow".
    The Robin's Song. Unknown. P51
"God bless the master of this house".
    Christmas Carol. Unknown. P51
"God called the nearest angels who
    dwell...". The Two Angels. John
    Greenleaf Whittier. P89
"God came from under the earth...". Creation
    of the World According to Charles
    Slater. Charles Slater. P78
"God gave me". The Trust. Gavin Burgess. P72
A God in Wrath. Stephen Crane. P81
God Lay Dead in Heaven. Stephen Crane. P81
"God is the old repair man". The Old Repair
    Man. Fenton Johnson. P82
"God moves in a mysterious way". Light
    Shining Out of Darkness. William
    Cowper. P89
"God of All Our Cities". Joan Gale Thomas.
    P60
"God of our fathers, known of old,--.".
    Recessional. Rudyard Kipling. P90
"God who created me". Prayers. Henry Charles
    Beeching. P51
God's Rain. Ghulam-Sarwar Yousof. P91
God's World. Edna St. Vincent Millay. P82
"God's angry with the world again".

Electrical Storm. Robert Hayden. P84
"God, consider the soul's need". Death Song
    for Owain ab Urien. Taliesin. P87
"God, though this life is but a wraith".
    Prayer. Louis Untermeyer. P82
"God, we don't like to complain". Caliban in
    the Coal Mines. Louis Untermeyer. P82
"The Godavari River, at Midnight". Unknown.
    P62
The Goddess. Denise Levertov. P85
Godfrey Gordon Gustavus Gore. Unknown. P51
Godley, Elizabeth
    Ragged Robin. P51
The Gododdin, sels. Aneirin. P87
Gods and Goddesses
    Athena. Alfred Dorn. P65
    The Goddess. Denise Levertov. P85
    The Gods of Black Mountain. Lee
        Pennington. P68
    I, Prometheus. Edward L. Meyerson. P68
    In This Age of Hard Trying, Nonchalance
        Is Good And. Marianne Moore. P83
    Laus Veneris (a Picture by Burne-Jones).
        Louise Chandler Moulton. P90
    A Poem to the Mother of the Gods.
        Unknown. P78
    To Diana. Evelyn Sewell Rineer. P65
The Gods of Black Mountain. Lee Pennington.
    P68
Goebbels, Joseph
    The Fuhrer Bunker, sels. William DeWitt
        Snodgrass. P85
"Goethe in Weimar sleeps, and Greece".
    Memorial Verses (April 1850). Matthew
    Arnold. P90
Goethe, Johann Wolfgang von
    The Erl-King. Martin and Aytoun (tr.).
        P90
    The Fisher. Charles Timothy Brooks (tr.).
        P90
    Haste Not! Rest Not!. P90
    The Rose. James Clarence Mangan (tr.).
        P89
    The Shepherd's Lament. Bayard Taylor
        (tr.). P89
Goetz & Sylvanus Morley, Delia (tr.)
    The Popol Vuh: Beginnings, sel. Unknown.
        P78
Goggins, Mary Magog
    Together. P72
Goggy. Gwyn Thomas. P87
Goh-Chapouthier (tr.)
    Dream. Georges Friedenkraft. P72
Going Home. LLawdden. P87
"Going from us at last". The Escape. Mark
    Van Doren. P83
Going to Italy. Donald Davie. P79
Going Under. Paulette Roeske. P88
A Going-Away Poem for Philip Larkin. David

Gill. P72

Gold. Martin Armstrong. P51

"Gold & oil & heroin--.". Trinity. John
        Knoll. P86

Goldberg, Barbara
        Two Women. P63

Golden Eyes. Rufinus. P89

"The golden spider of the sky". Solar Myth.
        Genevieve Taggard. P83

"The golden trees of England". The Jungle
        Trees. Marjorie Wilson. P51

Golden, Virginia
        Moroccan Perfume. P72

Goldenhair. James Joyce. P51

"A goldfinch, at my footstep". Hit and Run.
        Haywood Jackson. P68

Goldman, Edwin M.
        First Time. P65

Goldsmith, Oliver
        Elegy on Madam Blaize. P90

Goldstein, Roberta
        Blue Magic. P72

Golev, Vladimir
        Tell Me a Lie. William Meredith (tr.).
        P70

Golf
        A History of Golf--Sort of. Thomas L.
        Hirsch. P63

The Gondola. Arthur Hugh Clough. P90

"Gone are the robins". Changing Times.
        Vivian M. Singerling. P72

"Gone the three ancient ladies". Fau Bauman,
        Frau Schmidt, and Frau Schwartze.
        Theodore Roethke. P84

"Gone were but the winter". Spring Quiet.
        Christina Georgina Rossetti. P51

Good Friday. Walter Desmond. P68

"A Good Man, Lacking Wealth". Unknown. P62

Good Morning. Rose Fyleman. P51

The Good Morrow. John Donne. P59

Good Night. Ruth Ainsworth. P51

Good Night. Victor Hugo. P51

Good Night and Good Morning. Richard
        Monckton Milnes; 1st Baron Houghton.
        P51

' Good Night', Says the Owl. Lady Erskine
        Crum. P51

' Good Night, Willie Lee, I'll See You in
        the Morning'. Alice Walker. P85

"Good People Are Not Vexed in Misery".
        Unknown. P62

"A Good Person Does Not Get Angry". Unknown.
        P62

A Good Play. Robert Louis Stevenson. P89

A Good Sight of Andromeda. Milton Acorn. P49

The Good Things in Me. Patricia Lounds. P73

"Good morning. This is Koala Capers...".
        Tall Tale Weather. Holly Hester. P74

"Good oars, for Arnold's sake". Pax

Pagnanica. Louise Imogen Guiney. P81

"Good people all, with one accord". Elegy on
        Madam Blaize. Oliver Goldsmith. P90

A Good-by. Alain Bosquet. P61

Good-Bye. Ralph Waldo Emerson. P89

Good-Bye. Unknown. P89

Good-bye California. Charles P. Martin. P58

"Good-bye, little desk at school, good-bye".
        Vacation Time. Frank Hutt. P51

"Good-bye, proud world, I'm going home".
        Good-Bye. Ralph Waldo Emerson. P89

Goodboy. Anton Shammas. P92

Goodbye. Molly Johnson. P73

Goodbye! Amiri (LeRoi Jones) Baraka. P85

Goodbye, Goodbye. Dolores R. Patitz. P68

"Goodbye, the secret of the song...". A
        Leave-Taking. William Phylip. P87

Goode, Jason
        The Zookeeper. P74

Goodier, Sharon
        Unicorn. P49

Goodman, Paul
        For My Birthday, 1939. P84
        For Sally, with a Piano. P84
        General Washington. P84
        The Lordly Hudson. P84
        Reading Adonais. P84
        Saint Cecilia's Day, 1941. P84

Goodwin, Dawn R.
        To the Morning. P72

Gordon, Guanetta
        Lesson One. P72

Gordon, Marilyn
        One Solitary Voice. P72

Gordon, Mark
        The Meeting. P49

Gorky's Childhood. Lorna Crozier. P49

"The gosling breaks the shell off". The
        Gosling. Gary Erb. P56

Gosse, Sir Edmund (tr.)
        The Boy and the Flute. Bjornstjerne
        Bjornson. P89

Gostas, Theodore W.
        Vietnam P.O.W. Camp. P86

"Got all dressed up...". Darlene
        Friendship's Boyfriend. Ron Ikan. P63

"Got up early, waited for the farmer". Dairy
        Cows. Ron Koertge. P63

Gould, E. E.
        The Tadpole. P51

Gould, Elizabeth
        Grace and Thanksgiving. P51
        Midsummer Night. P51
        Mincemeat. P51
        Mistress Comfort. P51
        My New Rabbit. P51
        Red in Autumn. P51
        Shining Things. P51
        Slumber in Spring. P51

Such a Blustery Day!. P51
The Washing-up Song. P51
A Wish. P51
Gould, Gerald
    Child's Song. P51
The Gourd Dancer. N. Scott Momaday. P85
"Government of and". Space Exploration.
    Mildred B. Boydston. P72
Goytisolo, Jose Agustin
    The Difficult Poem. P61
"Grabbing a Handful of Powder in Her Hand".
    Unknown. P62
Grabbling in Yokna Bottom. James Seay. P67
Grace
    Grace. Al Ortolani. P63
Grace and Thanksgiving. Elizabeth Gould. P51
Grace, Dorman John
    The Barrier (A Manardina). P72
"The grackles have come". Purple Grackles.
    Amy Lowell. P82
Gradon, Dorothy
    A Fairy Dream. P51
    The North Wind. P51
    Travelling. P51
    The Wind. P51
    Winter Joys. P51
Graffiti
    The Graffiti Fingers of the Theology
        Student. James Schevill. P48
Graffiti from the Gare Saint-Manque. Marilyn
    Hacker. P79
Grafts and the Garden. Mehdi Akhavan Sales.
    P91
Graham, A. M.
    The Aconite. P51
Graham, Jorie
    History. P48
Graham, Neile
    Map of Vancouver Island. P49
Grahame, Kenneth
    Duck's Ditty. P51
"The grail broken". Shadows. Robert Duncan.
    P84
"The grains of corn were planted". Story of
    the Corn. K. Fisher. P51
"The Grand Old Duke of York". Unknown. P51
"' Grandad was a legislator, he used
    to...'.". Ol' Grandad. Steven C. Levi.
    P56
Grandfather in the Garden. Robert
    Minhinnick. P54
"Grandfather's roof was made of slate".
    Roofs. Lyubomir Levchev. P70
Grandfathers and Grandsons, sels. M.A.
    Nuhman. P91
The Grandfathers. Donald Justice. P67
Grandma's Attic. Camille Marksberry. P74
Grandma-in-Waiting. Betty Jane Simpson. P72
Grandmother God. Jeanine Hathaway. P88

Grandmother's Eyes. Linda McCormick. P56
Grandparents and Grandchildren
    Grandfathers and Grandsons, sels. M.A.
        Nuhman. P91
    The Grandfathers. Donald Justice. P67
    Grandma-in-Waiting. Betty Jane Simpson.
        P72
    Great Chorus (For Gramps). Joseph S.
        Pecorella. P68
    Loving Lessons (Grandmother). Burnette B.
        Benedict. P72
    Maidenhair. Nigel Jenkins. P54
    My Grandfather's Funeral. James
        Applewhite. P67
    Tea Time Remembered. Alma L. Wilson-
        Barry. P72
    Tiny Grandchild at the Beach. Alice M.
        Boughtwood. P68
    A Woman of Style. Edith Freund. P88
    Writing for Nora. Mark Jarman. P85
"Granted a human body, there must be". A
    Problem in Genetics. Vera Rich. P68
The Grape-Vine Swing. William Gilmore Simms.
    P89
Grass. Carl Sandburg. P82
Grass
    The Song of the Grass. Leigh Hunt. P51
The Grasshopper and Cricket. John Keats. P51,
    P89
The Grasshopper and the Cricket. John Keats.
    P51
Grasshopper Green. Unknown. P51
Grate Fire. Jeanne Bonnette. P65
The Grave of Sophocles. Simmias. P89
A Grave. Marianne Moore. P83
Gravepiece. Jean Garrigue. P84
Graves, Alfred Perceval
    Haymaking. P51
Graves, Robert
    I'd Love To Be a Fairy's Child. P51
    Star Talk. P90
"Gray and silver". Snow Scene. Louise Marsh
    Gabriel. P72
"The gray skies before me beckon". Winter.
    Dave Shelton. P74
"The gray tide flows and flounders in the
    rocks". At Sainte-Marguerite. Trumbull
    Stickney. P81
"Gray whale". For a Coming Extinction.
    William Stanley Merwin. P48
"Gray-robed wanderer in sleep...". Meeting.
    Arthur Davidson Ficke. P82
"Great Alexander sailing was from his
    true...". The Speaking Tree. Muriel
    Rukeyser. P84
Great Chorus (For Gramps). Joseph S.
    Pecorella. P68
THe Great Farter. Nakasuk. P78
The Great Marble Cake. Carl T. Endemann. P56

Great Nature Is an Army Gay. Richard Watson
     Gilder. P89
"The Great Pain and the Grievous Torment".
     Guido della Colonne. P69
Great Plains Lit. Mark Sanders. P63
"Great big dog". The Tale of a Dog and a
     Bee. Unknown. P51
"The great blue heron". The Heron. Merrill
     G. Christopherson. P68
"Great is the folly of a feeble brain".
     Virgidemiarum Book I, Satire 7. Joseph
     Hall. P59
"A great sea carried me". City on Fire.
     Oscar Hahn. P71
"great sea-roads to England". The Gates to
     England. Marjorie Wilson. P51
"The Great Sword Bearer only knows just".
     The Conclusion of the Whole Matter,
     from The House... (Frederick) Ridgely
     Torrence. P81
"Great, wide, beautiful, wonderful world".
     The World. William Brighty Rands. P51,
     P90
Greece
     At Delphi. Abigail S. Bean. P68
     Paestum. James Dickey. P79
The Greedy Little Pig. Irene F. Pawsey. P51
"The Greeks invaded Troy...". A Short Epic
     Poem in the English Language... James
     S. Koch. P63
The Green Comb. Raffaele Carrieri. P61
The Green Cornfield. Christina Georgina
     Rossetti. P51
The Green Lady. Charlotte Druitt Cole. P51
The Green Man. Kaleem Omar. P91
Green Mountain, Black Mountain. Anne
     Stevenson. P54
"Green be the turf above thee". Joseph
     Rodman Drake (Died in New York,
     September...). Fitz-Greene Halleck.
     P90
"The green catalpa tree has turned". April
     Inventory. William DeWitt Snodgrass.
     P85
"A green eye--and a red--in the dark". The
     Train. Mary E. Coleridge. P51
"The green grass is blowing". The Wind in
     the Grass. Ralph Waldo Emerson. P51
"Green is a code, saying itself...". Forest.
     Yaedi Ignatow. P64
"Green is the color of everything". One West
     Coast. Al Young. P85
"' Green leaves, what are you doing'.". The
     Five-Fingered Maple. Kate Louise
     Brown. P51
Green, David H.
     Geek. P63
Greenaway, Kate
     Five Sisters. P51

A Happy Child. P51
Greene, Albert G.
     Old Grimes. P90
Greene, Robert
     Content, from Farewell to Follie, 1617.
     P90
Greene, Tatiana (tr.)
     "You Do Know That the Stars". Jean Paul
     Mestas. P72
"The greenest of grass in the long
     meadow...". June. Jane G. Stewart. P51
Greenfield, Marjorie H.
     Things I Like. P51
A Greenland Winter. Lucy Diamond. P51
Greensleeves. Mark Jarman. P85
"Greetings to Thee, Oh Lord of the Day".
     Unknown. P62
Gregory the Great, Saint
     Veni Creator Spiritus. John Dryden (tr.).
     P89
Gregory, Horace
     Ask No Return. P83
     Poems for My Daughter. P83
     They Found Him Sitting in a Chair. P83
Gregory, Mike
     The Duty of the Prince Is Magnificence.
     P56
Grenelle, Lisa
     Lovers in Wild Grass. P65
     Sing Love, Small Frog. P65
     Small Wedding. P65
Gress, Esther
     Grow. Esther Gress (tr.). P72
Gretel in Darkness. Louise Gluck. P85
Grey Brother. U. M. Montgomery. P51
A Grey Day. William Vaughn Moody. P81
The Grey Friar. Dafydd ab [or ab] Gwilym.
     P87
Grey Owl's Poem. Gwendolyn Macewen. P49
"Grey drizzling mists the moorlands drape".
     A Grey Day. William Vaughn Moody. P81
"The grey dust runs on the ground like a
     mouse". Dust. P. A. Ropes. P51
"The grey goat grazed on the hill". Grey
     Brother. U. M. Montgomery. P51
"Grey pussy-willows". Slumber in Spring.
     Elizabeth Gould. P51
"Grey was the morn, all things were grey". A
     Bit of Colour. Horace Smith. P51
"The grief-chewers enter, their shoes...".
     Office for the Dead. Thomas Kinsella.
     P79
Grieve, Christopher M. ("Hugh MacDiarmid")
     The Two Parents. P89
Griffith, Susan Headen
     Maybe. P72
Griffiths, Ann
     Expecting the Lord. Tony Conran (tr.).
     P87

Full of Wonder. Tony Conran (tr.). P87
Rose of Sharon. Tony Conran (tr.). P87
Grimke, Angelina Weld
    For the Candle Light. P89
    When the Green Lies over the Earth. P89
Grissom, Arthur
    The Artist. P90
Grounded. Alice P. Stein. P63
The Groundhog. Richard Eberhart. P83
Grove, Charles L.
    Beware the Tides of March. P63
"The groves are down". Myths and Texts
        (Logging). Gary Snyder. P85
Grow. Esther Gress. P72
A Growing Rhyme. J. M. Westrup. P51
The Growing River. Rodney Bennett. P51
Growing Up
    After Ten Years. Mary Ellen Chihak. P68
    The Ball Poem. John Berryman. P79
    Changing. Wendi Sloniker. P74
    Day's Ending (Tucson). Sara Teasdale. P82
    A Dialogue. Fatthy Said. P91
    Grow. Esther Gress. P72
    The Hurdy-Gurdy Man. Elizabeth Fleming.
        P51
    Papa Says. Libby Stopple. P75
    Still Not Grown Up. Lisa May. P74
Gruffudd ab yr Ynad Coch
    Lament for Llywelyn ap Gruffudd, the Last
        Prince. Tony Conran (tr.). P87
Gruffudd ap Maredudd
    Lament for Gwenhwyfar, sels. Tony Conran
        (tr.). P87
Gruffudd, Owen
    The Men That Once Were, sels. Tony Conran
        (tr.). P87
Gruffudd, Sion
    Longing for Caernarfon. Tony Conran
        (tr.). P87
Gruffydd, William John
    This Poor Man. Tony Conran (tr.). P87
Gruhl, Jason
    Alex. P73
"A Grumpy Old Owl at the Zoo". Laurence
        Perrine. P63
Gryg, Gruffudd
    The Yewtree. Tony Conran (tr.). P87
The Guarded Wound. Adelaide Crapsey. P81
Guenther, Charles (tr.)
    The Afternoon Will Yet... Antonio
        Machado. P61
    Anoukis and Later Jeanne. Rene Char. P61
    The Art of Poetry. Pierre Emmanuel. P61
    As You Wish. Mario Luzi. P61
    At the Florist's. Jacques Prevert. P61
    A Buried One in Me Sings. Salvatore
        Quasimodo. P61
    Cat. Charles Baudelaire. P61
    Cool with Sleeping Rivers. Salvatore

    Quasimodo. P61
    The Crossing. Salvatore Quasimodo. P61
    Dancer. Edgar Degas. P61
    Day and Night. Eugenio Montale. P61
    The Face. Jules Supervielle. P61
    Finale. Tibor Tollas. P61
    Forest. Jules Supervielle. P61
    A Good-by. Alain Bosquet. P61
    The Green Comb. Raffaele Carrieri. P61
    He Invents a Vertigo. Alain Bosquet. P61
    He Lit His Pipe. Phoebus Delphis. P61
    The Hippopotamus. Theophile Gautier. P61
    The Holiday Ended. Pier Paolo Pasolini.
        P61
    The Hunter. Unknown. P61
    I Remember a Season. Maria Luisa
        Spaziani. P61
    Iguazu. Jules Supervielle. P61
    In the Sense of Death. Salvatore
        Quasimodo. P61
    In the Willow Branches. Salvatore
        Quasimodo. P61
    The Incomparable Earth. Salvatore
        Quasimodo. P61
    Insects. Damaso Alonso. P61
    The Inventors. Rene Char. P61
    Larks. Saint-Pol-Roux. P61
    Let's Shield Your Light with Our Hand, My
        Heart. Jules Supervielle. P61
    Light, Light, Somewhat Revolving... Jules
        Romains. P61
    London, March 1945. Pierre Emmanuel. P61
    Make Room. Jules Supervielle. P61
    Memory. Jules Supervielle. P61
    Mirror. Salvatore Quasimodo. P61
    My Whisper. Unknown. P61
    A Nail for Hanging the Soul. Alain
        Bosquet. P61
    Night. Maria Celeste Achille Todde. P61
    Oh, Figures on the Portico... Antonio
        Machado. P61
    On a Night Without Adornment. Rene Char.
        P61
    On a Picture by a Chinese Painter. Henri
        Michaux. P61
    On an Unwritten Letter. Eugenio Montale.
        P61
    On the Site of the Convent. Tibor Tollas.
        P61
    On the Watershed. Tibor Tollas. P61
    Pledges. Pierre Emmanuel. P61
    Poem. Pablo Picasso. P61
    Position. Blas de Otero. P61
    Posthumous. Jules Supervielle. P61
    Put on Guard. Rene Char. P61
    Seascape. Eugenio Montale. P61
    Sentry of the Silent. Rene Char. P61
    The Shade of the Magnolia. Eugenio
        Montale. P61

Space. Salvatore Quasimodo. P61
Springtime. Stephane Mallarme. P61
The Stain. Pierre Jean Jouve. P61
Stone Quarries. Salvatore Quasimodo. P61
The Strawberries. Tristan Dereme. P61
The Sun is a Globe of Fire. Antonio
    Machado. P61
Tavern Guitar Playing a Jota Today...
    Antonio Machado. P61
Tell Me If You Remember, Love. Antonio
    Machado. P61
Three Poems on Death. Carlos Bousono. P61
Time's Horses. Jules Supervielle. P61
Two Fool's Songs. Emile Verhaeren. P61
Visible, Invisible. Salvatore Quasimodo.
    P61
The Waters of Saturday, sel. Maria Luisa
    Spaziani. P61
We've Heard the Sea Again. Salvatore
    Quasimodo. P61
What Do You Want, Shepherd of Wind?.
    Salvatore Quasimodo. P61
Winter. Antal Vizy. P61
With the Flashes of the Night. Phoebus
    Delphis. P61
A Woman Brought Naked Face to Face with
    the Sky. Pierre Emmanuel. P61
Woods Are Sleeping. Salvatore Quasimodo.
    P61
The World in Us. Jules Supervielle. P61
The World Is Full of Voices... Jules
    Supervielle. P61
"The Guernseys lift calm brows...". The
    Autumn Bleat of the Weathervane
    Trombone. Fred Chappell. P67
A Guerrilla Handbook. Amiri (LeRoi Jones)
    Baraka. P85
Guest, Barbara
    Clouds Near the Windmill. P64
    Hohenzollern. P64
    Lawn Bumps. P64
    Sag Harbor, the Tchekov Letters. P64
    Wave, sel. P64
Gugl, Wolfgang D.
    "30 Dreams Held in a Hand". P72
Guglielmo, Dolores
    Down by the Beach. P72
Guide to Paris: Eiffel Tower, Versailles.
    Scott Bates. P63
A Guide. Thelma G. Monk. P72
"Guided by stars, their ship sailed". Ship,
    Sea, and Star. Clifford Davidson. P68
Guilt
    Inquest. William DeWitt Snodgrass. P85
Guiney, Louise Imogen
    Athassel Abbey. P81
    Irish Peasant Song. P81
    Monochrome. P81
    Ode for a Master Mariner Ashore. P81

On First Entering Westminster Abbey. P81
Open, Time. P81
Pax Pagnanica. P81
To a Dog's Memory. P81
Two Epitaphs. P81
When on the Marge of Evening. P81
The Wild Ride. P81
Guitars
    Tavern Guitar Playing a Jota Today...
        Antonio Machado. P61
Gulf-Weed. Cornelius George Fenner. P89
Gull Passage by Moonlight. Milton Acorn. P49
"A gull rides on the ripples of a dream". A
        Walk in Late Summer. Theodore Roethke.
        P84
Gulls
    As Sea Birds Sail. Mary Jane Barnes. P68
    Gulls. William Carlos Williams. P82
    Magic Words to Feel Better. Nakasuk. P78
    Sea Gulls in the Rain. H. Wendy Jones.
        P72
    Summer Snow. Charlotte Zolotow. P76
Gulls. William Carlos Williams. P82
"Gulls over the thickness". Rotterdam. Waldo
        Rojas. P71
The Gun. Karl Shapiro. P84
Guns
    Strutting with My Rifle. Daniel Cuol Lul
        Wur. P53
    To a Military Rifle. Yvor Winters. P83
    Under the Green Ledge. Kenneth Patchen.
        P84
"Guns carried". The Mountain Passes, from
        Lost Youth: the Last War. Alfred
        Kreymborg. P82
Gunther, Scott
    My Dream. P73
Gustafson, Ralph
    Anatomy of Melancholy. P49
    The Broken Pianola. P49
"The gusty morns are here". To a Dog's
        Memory. Louise Imogen Guiney. P81
"Gut is still alive". Why Comtemporary
        American Poets Rarely Write... Louis
        Phillips. P63
Gutes and Eulas. Roy Blount Jr. P63
Guthrie, Lois
    Les Belles Heures. P68
Gwalchmai's Boat, sels. Meilir ap Gwalchmai.
        P87
Gwen ap Llywarch and his Father, fr. Poetry
        from Lost Sagas . Unknown. P87
"Gwynedd's sun, it's a grave, not living--a
        queen". Lament for Gwenhwyfar, sels.
        Gruffudd ap Maredudd. P87
Gymnastics
    Gymnastics. Tim Keegan. P73
Gysies. Rachel (Lyman) Field. P51
Gypsies

Gipsy Man. Dorothy King. P51
Gypsies. Rachel (Lyman) Field. P51
The Idlers. Edmund Blunden. P51
Meg Merrilees. John Keats. P51
The Wraggle Taggle Gipsies. Unknown. P51
Gypsy. Josephine Miles. P84

Haas, Beth Martin
    Dance of Words. P72
Habington, William
    To Castara: the Reward of Innocent Love.
        P59
Hack and Hew. Bliss Carman. P90
Hacker, Marilyn
    Graffiti from the Gare Saint-Manque. P79
"Had we but world enough, and time". To His
        Importunate Mistress. Peter De Vries.
        P63
"Had we two gone down the world together".
        Virgilia. Edwin Markham. P81
"Hadn't seen her". The Blanks. Sheryl L.
        Nelms. P56
Haein-Sa Temple. Cho Byung-Hwa. P72
Hahn, Lola E.
    I Dream of a Land. P72
Hahn, Oscar
    City on Fire. Steven F. White (tr.). P71
    Death Is Sitting at the Foot of My Bed.
        Steven F. White (tr.). P71
    Heartbreak Hotel. Steven F. White (tr.).
        P71
    In the Center of the Bedroom. Steven F.
        White (tr.). P71
    Little Ghosts. Steven F. White (tr.). P71
    Photograph. Steven F. White (tr.). P71
    Reincarnation of the Butchers. Steven F.
        White (tr.). P71
    Vision of Hiroshima. Steven F. White
        (tr.). P71
    Watching T.V. Steven F. White (tr.). P71
Hahn, Robert
    The Bat. P58
    Dinosaur Hill. P58
    October 1st. P58
    Three Morning Scenes. P58
    View of a Comet. P58
Hahn, Virginia M.
    Alar. P58
    Archeology. P58
    Covers. P58
    Glass Lady. P58
    Pedestrian. P58
    Spring Is the Favorite Time for Suicide.
        P58
    Tanker. P58
    When Anger Came. P58

Haiku
    "Buddha's Disciples". Sakuzo Takada. P72
Haiku. Bernice M. Centner. P72
Haiku. Edmund Conti. P63
Haiku. Laura Davis. P73
    Flickers. Dwarakanath H. Kabadi. P72
    Haiku. Matthew Woomer. P74
    Haiku. Jenny Mumzhiu. P73
    Haiku. Bernice M. Centner. P72
    Haiku. Alexis Rotella. P63
    Haiku. Edmund Conti. P63
    Haiku. Laura Davis. P73
    Haiku. Opie R. Houston. P72
Haiku. Jenny Mumzhiu. P73
    "Raindrops on Young Leaves". Jerald Ball.
        P72
    "Rosemary Blossoms". Jerald Ball. P72
Haiku. Alexis Rotella. P63
    Sanskrit Songs for Modern Dreamers'.
        Sheila Craft. P72
    "There's an Old Woman". Sakuzo Takada.
        P72
Haiku. Matthew Woomer. P74
"Hail and beware the dead who will talk
        life...". A Newly Discovered 'Homeric'
        Hymn. Charles Olson. P85
"Hail! Ho!.". A Sea Song from the Shore.
        James Whitcomb Riley. P51
"Hail, holy light, offspring of heaven...".
        Invocation to Light, from Paradise
        Lost. John Milton. P89
Hair
    A Girls' Hair. Dafydd ab Edmwnd. P87
    I Love Every Hair on Your Head. Alma
        Denny. P63
    A Tragic Story. William Makepeace
        Thackeray. P51
Halcrow, Allan R.
    Distant Exploration. P72
The Haldighat of New India. Kazi Nazrul
        Islam. P91
Hales, Barbara M.
    Do Fairies Like the rain?. P55
Half Holiday. Olive Enoch. P51
"Half a league, half a league". Charge of
        the Light Brigade. Lord Tennyson. P90
"Half asleep I float". Bermuda Dream.
        Katharine Wilson. P72
"Half-bridge over nothingness". Northhanger
        Ridge. Charles Wright. P67
"Halfway 'tween grime and grubby". Virus.
        Roberta Mendel. P56
Hall of Fraternity. Justice S. Mohan. P72
The Hall of Ifor Hael. Ieuan Brydydd Hir.
        P87
Hall, Donald
    David Hume. P79
Hall, Jim
    Maybe Dats Youwr Pwoblem Too. P63

Preposterous. P63
Hall, Joseph
Virgidemiarum Book I, Satire 7. P59
Halleck, Fitz-Greene
Joseph Rodman Drake (Died in New York,
September...). P90
Hallelujah!. Charles Tillman Lockhart. P72
Halley's Comet
Eddie's Comet. Barbara Hawkins. P74
Halley's Comet. Jeremy Gay. P74
Halley's Comet. Jaime Quezada. P71
Halley's Comet. Jeremy Gay. P74
Halley's Comet. Jaime Quezada. P71
"Hallo!--what?--where, what can it be". On
Hearing a Little Music-Box. Leigh
Hunt. P90
Hallowe'en. Marion Louise Refici. P74
Halsted Street Car. Carl Sandburg. P82
Hamburger, Michael (tr.)
Death Fugue. Paul Celan. P48
Hamilton Greene, from Spoon River Anthology.
Edgar Lee Masters. P82
Hamilton, Carol
Final Migration. P68
Hamilton, M. Yvette
Belabored Blossom. P56
Hamlet XX. Stefan Tsanev. P70
"Hamm is a permanent dress parade".
Sandweiler and Hamm, the Military
Cemeteries... Wayne Kvam. P60
Hammer, Lillian
Without a Tear. P72
Hampl, Patricia
Hearth. P88
This Is How Memory Works. P88
Hand. Mark McCloskey. P63
Hand Lane: Literature. Edward Butscher. P64
"Hand in hand they dance in a row". The
Clothes-Line. Charlotte Druitt Cole.
P51
"Hand in hand they start across". 9:00 a.m.
at Broadway and Walnut on Your
Birthday. Ripley Schemm. P57
The Hand of Emmagene. Peter Taylor. P79
Handicapped, The
Hunchback Girl: She Thinks of Heaven, fr.
A Street... Gwendolyn Brooks. P84
My Window, My Wheelchair, and Me. Deborah
D'Aleo. P74
The Handicapped. Philip Dacey. P57
The Handless Maiden. Janet Beeler Shaw. P88
Handling it--. Edith Freund. P88
Hands
Amaze. Adelaide Crapsey. P81
Finger Folk. H. M. Tharp. P51
Finger Play. Unknown. P51
Hand. Mark McCloskey. P63
The Hands. Denise Levertov. P85
I Have Seen Black Hands. Richard Wright.

P90
Unfriendly Witness. George Starbuck. P85
Hands of Gold. Margaret L. Fellinger. P72
The Hands. Denise Levertov. P85
Hanf, James A.
Lullaby of Evening. P72
'Sheaves in Winter'. P65
Hankla, Cathryn
Hard Frost. P56
Hansel, Alfarata
Faith. P72
Hansen, Kathryn G.
An Old Fashioned Pipe. P72
Hansen, Tom
My Lawn Is Brown and All My Neighbors Are
Painting... P63
Hanson, Freddie P.
All Roads Lead to Rome. P72
Hanson, Phebe
Meat. P88
Nursing. P88
Happiness
The Character of a Happy Life. Sir Henry
Wotton. P90
Happy Thought. Robert Louis Stevenson.
P51
"I Would Like to Show Openly". Jacopo
Mostacci. P69
I'm Happy. Mark Carlson. P73
Island Sanctuary (Poetic Rambling).
Cecile C. Metzger. P72
Joy. Clarissa Scott Delany. P90
Joys. James Russell Lowell. P51
The Merry Heart. William Shakespeare. P51
My Heart Leaps Up. William Wordsworth.
P89
"Often Love Has Made Many Happy". Rugieri
d'Amici. P69
"Thanks to a Perfect Love, I Feel So
Joyous". Rinaldo d'Aquino. P69
A Happy Child. Kate Greenaway. P51
Happy Heart, from Patient Grissell. Thomas
Dekker. P90
The Happy Man. Unknown. P87
Happy Thought. Robert Louis Stevenson. P51
"Happy people die whole, they are all
dissolved... ". Post Mortem. Robinson
Jeffers. P83
"A happy stone juts north of the bay".
Beach. Juan Cameron. P71
"Happy those early days! when I". The
Retreat.!Henry Vaughan. P59
Haq, Kaiser
Cousin Shamsu, Durzi. P91
Moon. P91
My Village and I. P91
Haq, Kaiser (tr.)
At Each Other. Shaheed Quadri. P91
Haque, Syed Shamsul

Sonnet 1, fr. Three Sonnets From 'Deep
    Within the Heart'. Sonia Khan (tr.).
    P91
Sonnet 12, fr. Three Sonnets From 'Deep
    Within the Heart'. Sonia Khan (tr.).
    P91
Sonnet 25, fr. Three Sonnets From 'Deep
    Within the Heart'. Sonia Khan (tr.).
    P91
Harbors
    St. George's Harbour. Bruce St. John. P68
Hard Frost. Cathryn Hankla. P56
"A hard thing to break". Woodknot. Allen
    Planz. P64
Hard to Say. Sheila Seiler. P56
Hardinge, William M. (tr.)
    The Grave of Sophocles. Simmias. P89
    The Wreath. Meleager. P89
Hardt, Elaine
    I Sing of Spring. P72
Hardy, Thomas
    The Oxen. P51,P89
    Weathers. P51
Hares
    Hunting the Hare. Unknown. P87
Hark! Hark! the Lark. William Shakespeare.
    P51
"Hark! the tiny cowslip bell". Spring Has
    Come. Unknown. P51
Harlem Shadows. Claude McKay. P82
Harmon, William
    The Laxness Monster; or, I Be Singer...
    P63
Harmony. John A. Downes. P72
Harmosan. Richard Chenevix Trench. P90
Harper, Frances E. W.
    Let the Light Enter. P89
Harriet Beecher Stowe. Paul Laurence Dunbar.
    P90
Harris, Merry
    Pregnant Thought. P63
Harrison, Florence
    The Faerie Fair. P51
    A Summer Day. P51
Harrison, Richard
    Verrocchio. P49
Harrold, William
    The Fortunate Fall. P68
Harte, Bret
    Dickens in Camp. P90
Harteis, Richard (tr.)
    Again. Lyubomir Levchev. P70
    The Bedroom. Nino Nikolov. P70
    The Closet. Nino Nikolov. P70
    Summer Rain. Georgi Djagarov. P70
Hartman, James D.
    Equals. P86
    Laundromat Eulogies. P86
Hartwig, Julia

Vigil on a Bay. P92
Harvest
    Harvest. M. M. Hutchinson. P51
    Harvest Song. Unknown. P51
    The Harvest. Alice C. Henderson. P51
Harvest. M. M. Hutchinson. P51
    Story of the Corn. K. Fisher. P51
Harvest Song. Ludwig Holty. P89
Harvest Song. Unknown. P51
The Harvest. Alice C. Henderson. P51
Harvey, F. W.
    Ducks, sel. P51
Harvey, L. G.
    Novice in the Woods. P72
Has Summer Come Without the Rose?. Arthur
    O'Shaughnessy. P89
"Has not altered;--.". Spenser's Ireland.
    Marianne Moore. P83
Hasan, Rabiul
    The House on the Hill. P56
Hashmi, Alamgir
    Poem Which Cannot Be a Letter. P91
    Tomorrow's Forecasts Are All Done. P91
Hasley, Louis
    Tallyho the Fox. P63
Hassan and M. Salim-ur-Rahman, Faruq (tr.)
    What Days, Indeed. Majeed Amjad. P91
Hassan, Faruq (tr.)
    Before the First of the Next Month.
        Majeed Amjad. P91
    The Scream. Majeed Amjad. P91
    Some Days Ago. Majeed Amjad. P91
Hasselstrom, Linda M.
    Leaving Fargo: April. P88
    The Poet Falls in Love with a Cowboy. P88
    Shooting Prairie Dogs. P88
    When My Father Waters His Trees. P88
"' Hast thou seen that lordly castle'.". The
    Castle by the Sea. Johann Ludwig
    Uhland. P90
Haste Not! Rest Not!. Johann Wolfgang von
    Goethe. P90
Hastings, Dick
    Yosemite. P77
Hat Trick. Paul Humphrey. P63
Hate
    And the Sins of the Fathers. Stephen
        Crane. P81
    Archibald Higbie, from Spoon River
        Anthology. Edgar Lee Masters. P82
Hathaway, Jeanine
    Grandmother God. P88
    Two Steps Forward. P88
Hats
    A Feather for My Cap. Ivy O. Eastwick.
        P51
    A 4th Stanza for Dr. Johnson, Donald
        Hall... X. J. Kennedy. P63
    The Saint Wears a Halo. Peter [pseud.].

P51
Haughey, Veronica
    The Net. P72
Hauser, Susan
    How, Like This Spring, Slowly. P88
"Have I really ceased to exist". Bureaucrat.
    Lyubomir Levchev. P70
Have You? I Have Never!. Ned Pastor. P63
"Have you ever heard the rain at night".
    Rain Spirit Passing. Denise Levertov.
    P85
"Have you seen walking through the village".
    Mollie McGee, from Spoon River
    Anthology. Edgar Lee Masters. P82
Havergal, Frances Ridley
    I Gave My Life for Thee. P89
Havhesp, Dewi
    My Love. Tony Conran (tr.). P87
"Having Been Issued". Jack Hill. P86
"Having Seen the Clouds Welling Up".
    Unknown. P62
"Having Seen the Son of the Lord of the
    House". Unknown. P62
"Having Seen the Tip of a Tooth". Unknown.
    P62
"Having been tenant long to a rich Lord".
    Redemption. George Herbert. P59
"Having no father anymore, having got up".
    The Homecoming of Emma Lazarus. Galway
    Kinnell. P85
Hawes, Frieda Jo
    Life, from Thoughts I Caught. P72
Hawk. Judith Minty. P88
Hawkins, Barbara
    Eddie's Comet. P74
Hawkins, Tom
    Follow Your Heart to the Land of
    Enchantment. P63
Hawks
    Evening Hawk. Robert Penn Warren. P67
    Hawk. Judith Minty. P88
    Mortal Limit. Robert Penn Warren. P67
Hawkshawe, Ann ("Aunt Effie")
    Little Rain-Drops. P51
    The Moonlight. P51
    Mother Duck. P51
    The Muffin-Man's Bell. P51
    The Old Kitchen Clock. P51
Hawthorne. Henry Wadsworth Longfellow. P90
Hay Harvest. Patrick R. Chalmers. P51
Hay, John
    Religion and Doctrine. P89
    A Woman's Love. P89
Hay, Walter S.
    Magic Reprieve. P72
Hay-Time. C. M. Loew. P51
Hayden, Robert
    The Ballad of Sue Ellen Westerfield. P84
    Belsen, Day of Liberation. P84

Day of the Dead. P84
    Electrical Storm. P84
    Full Moon. P84
    Market. P84
    Night, Death, Mississippi. P84
    Summertime and the Living... P84
Hayes, Dorsha
    The Gain. P65
    Soul-Search Ode. P65
Hayes, Nancy M.
    At Night in the Wood. P51
    The Shiny Little House. P51
Haymaking. E. M. Adams. P51
Haymaking. Alfred Perceval Graves. P51
Hayman, Carol Bessent
    Poetry Study Group. P72
Hayman, Dick
    Portrait. P63
Hayne, Paul Hamilton
    Patience. P89
Haytime. Irene F. Pawsey. P51
He. Lawrence Ferlinghetti. P85
"He Drinks in the Lovliness of the Young
    Girl's...". Unknown. P62
"He Followed His Own Mind...," from Wolf
    Songs... Unknown. P78
He Invents a Vertigo. Alain Bosquet. P61
"He Is Truly a Friend Who Does What Is To Be
    Done". Unknown. P62
He Lit His Pipe. Phoebus Delphis. P61
He Prayeth Well. Samuel Taylor Coleridge.
    P51
He Records a Little Song for a Smoking Girl.
    James Whitehead. P67
He Was a King. Lynn Blunt. P73
"He Was There," from Crow Versions. Medicine-
    Tail. P78
He Will Float in the River Like a Waterlily.
    Kong Tot. P53
"He always comes on market days". The
    Balloon Man. Rose Fyleman. P51
"He attacked Nhial in Mading's camp". He
    Will Float in the River Like a
    Waterlily. Kong Tot. P53
"He came all so still". Carol. Unknown. P51
"He came down from the hills...". My
    Mother's Wedding. Boris Kristov. P70
"He clasps the crag with crooked hands". The
    Eagle. Lord Tennyson. P51
"He climbs the stair". Waterchew!. Gregory
    Corso. P85
"He comes in the night!.". Santa Claus.
    Unknown. P51
"He didn't know much music". The Mocking-
    Bird. Frank Lebby Stanton. P89
"He fed them generously who were his
    flocks". Mhtis Outis. William DeWitt
    Snodgrass. P85
"He gambols to the shearer's shear". The

Lamb. Bob McKenty. P63

"He got his friends to agree...". Leaving
the Door Open (1), sel. David Ignatow.
P64

"He had harvested the poem's familiar tips".
Dylan Thomas. Euros Bowen. P87

"He had no past and he certainly". Pity
Ascending with the Fog. James Tate.
P85

"He had no royal palace". A Christmas Verse.
Kay [pseud.]. P51

"".

"He had veiled all the mirrors...". The
Mirror's Place. Jorge Arbeleche. P92

"He is not John, the gardener". A Friend in
the Garden. Juliana Horatia Ewing. P51

"He is one of the prophets come back". He.
Lawrence Ferlinghetti. P85

"He killed the noble Mudjokivis". The Modern
Hiawatha. Unknown. P90

"He left. Our love was on the rocks". Love
Portions. Joan Van Poznak. P63

"He lies low in the levelled sand". At the
Grave of Walker. Joaquin Miller. P81

"He lives in the sky". The Eagle Above Us.
Unknown. P78

"He marches in himself to scatter
himself...". He Invents a Vertigo.
Alain Bosquet. P61

"He passed away an ordinary man". A Matter
of Perspective. Ann Shermer. P65

"He picks up the block of wood". Block of
Wood. Jauvanta Walker. P68

"He planted an oak in his father's park".
The Sower and His Seed. William E. H.
Lecky. P90

"He protested all his life long". Mrs.
Meyers, from Spoon River Anthology.
Edgar Lee Masters. P82

"He put his acorn helmet on". An Elfin
Knight. John Rodman Drake. P51

"He puts the hose". When My Father Waters
His Trees. Linda M. Hasselstrom. P88

"He said to love". Aftermath. Lora Dunetz.
P65

"He said, 'Mom,'.". The Friendship Only
Lasted a Few Seconds. Lily Jean Lee-
Adams. P86

"He sat at the dinner table". Just Like a
Man. Unknown. P51

"He snuggles his fingers". After Winter.
Sterling A. Brown. P89

"He spends so much". The Diver. Leslie
Nutting. P49

"He stands by the ocean, in the sand". The
Painter. Peggy Zeaphev Nerl. P72

"He stared at me". Lust. Elaine Demakas. P58

"He stood before the Sanhedrim". Religion
and Doctrine. John Hay. P89

"He stuffs fish out of a paper into his
mouth". The Passenger. Kaleem Omar.
P91

"He that is down needs fear no fall". The
Shepherd Boy's Song. J. Bunyan. P51

"He that loves a rosy cheek". Disdain
Returned. Thomas Carew. P89

"He walks. He talks. He sits to eat". Geek.
David H. Green. P63

"He wants my blood". Poorly Run Marionette.
Kevin Cline. P58

"He was a rat, and she was a rat". What
Became of Them?. Unknown. P51

"He was all back". A Late Elegy for a
Baseball Player. Felix Stefanile. P57

"He was an old wolf, no teeth...". Sioux
Metamorphosis. Lucario Cuevish. P78

"He was as old as old could be". Danny
Murphy. James Stephens. P51

"He was born in Alabama". Of De Witt
Williams on His Way to Lincoln
Cemetery, fr. A.... Gwendolyn Brooks.
P84

"He was soft on Swanson". Silent Lover.
Edward Watkins. P63

"He who bends to himself a joy".
Opportunity. William Blake. P90

"He will flip the brittle disc". The Friends
of the Friends. Caroline Knox. P63

"He woke at five and, unable". Physical
Universe. Louis Simpson. P85

"He wrought with patience long and weary
years". The Artist. Arthur Grissom.
P90

He'd Die for Tobacco. Philip Macar. P53

He'd Eat Lizards. Buk Teny Women. P53

"He's dead". Death. William Carlos Williams.
P82

"He's given up his wickedness for good". On
a Reformed Sinner. Laurence Perrine.
P63

Headache. Orhan Veli Kanik. P91

Headless. Josephine Miles. P84

Healthful Old Age, from As You Like It.
William Shakespeare. P90

"Heap on more wood!--the wind is chill". An
Old Time Christmas, from Marmion. Sir
Walter Scott. P90

"Hear the strings of that guitar". Tropical
Night. John Tworoger. P72

Hearing Heaney Read. Gregory Betts. P49

Heart (human)

I Am to My Own Heart Merely a Serf.
Delmore Schwartz. P84

Heart and Mind. Edith Sitwell. P90

"A heart that longs". Without a Tear.
Lillian Hammer. P72

Heart's Need. Rajnee Krishnan Kutty. P72

Heartbreak Hotel. Oscar Hahn. P71

Heartbreak in Tuktoyaktuk. Louis Phillips.
    P63
Hearth. Patricia Hampl. P88
"The Hearts of Great Men". Unknown. P62
Heat. Hilda ("H.D.") Doolittle. P82
Heather. Eifion Wyn. P87
Heaven
    The Angel. William H. Ryder Jr. P86
    The Celestial Passion. Richard Watson
        Gilder. P81
    Dibdin's Ghost. Eugene Field. P81
Heaven. Emily Dickinson. P89
    General William Booth Enters into Heaven.
        Vachel Lindsay. P82
    Heaven. Emily Dickinson. P89
    Heaven's Glowing. Nina Marin. P72
    Heaven, from A Thai Divine Comedy. Montri
        Umavijani. P92
    I Dream of a Land. Lola E. Hahn. P72
    In Heaven. Stephen Crane. P81
    A Leave-Taking. William Phylip. P87
    Light Talk (I). Adjutor. P72
    The Other World. Harriet Beecher Stowe.
        P89
    Pilgrim. William Williams Pantycelyn. P87
    Post Mortem. Robinson Jeffers. P83
    Song of the Silent Land. Johann Gaudenz
        von Salis-Seewis. P89
    Southeast Corner, fr. A Street in
        Bronzeville. Gwendolyn Brooks. P84
    Tell Me, Ye Winged Winds. Charles Mackay.
        P89
    Up Hill. Christina Georgina Rossetti. P89
    White Symphony. John Gould Fletcher. P82
Heaven and Hell. Nalungiaq. P78
"Heaven is lovelier than the stars".
    Driftwood. Trumbull Stickney. P81
"Heaven is not the earth". Heaven, from A
    Thai Divine Comedy. Montri Umavijani.
    P92
Heaven's Glowing. Nina Marin. P72
Heaven, from A Thai Divine Comedy. Montri
    Umavijani. P92
Heaven, from Paradise. Montri Umavijani. P72
The Heavy Bear Who Goes with Me. Delmore
    Schwartz. P84
"Heavy as the blue thunder I carry the
    book". Edward Curtis Photographs the
    North American Indians. Virginia E.
    Smith. P68
"Heavy to plod snow and ice". Elegy for Syr
    Owain ap Gwilym. Wiliam Llyn. P87
Hebrews. James Oppenheim. P82
Hedge, Frederick Henry (tr.)
    A Mighty Fortress Is Our God. Martin
        Luther. P89
The Hedgehog and His Coat. Elizabeth
    Fleming. P51
The Hedgehog. Edith King. P51

"The hedges are dazed as cock-crow...".
    Departure in Middle Age. Roland
    Mathias. P54
Heide, Florence Parry
    What's That?. P55
Heigh Ho!. Jean Ingelow. P51
Heine, Heinrich
    E'en as a Lovely Flower. K. F. Kroeker
        (tr.). P89
    The Message. K. F. Kroeker (tr.). P89
    The Shepherd Boy. P51
    The Storm. L. Untermeyer (tr.). P90
    To My Mother. M. Dickson (tr.). P89
    Twilight. L. Untermeyer (tr.). P91
Heine-Koehn, Lala
    Letter to an Exile. P49
Helendale. Dick Barnes. P63
Helium: an Inert Gas. Judson Jerome. P63
Hell
    The Cross. Allen Tate. P83
    I Meet Lee San in the Nether World and
        Talk of Home. Ahmed Ali. P91
    In the Dream's Recess. William Everson.
        P84
    The Inn of Earth. Sara Teasdale. P82
Hell and Solitude. Aristoteles Espana. P71
"Hell was real for Molly Gaunt". Molly
    Gaunt. H. Wendell Smith. P63
Heller, Liane
    Coma. P49
Heller, Michael
    At Albert's Landing (with my son). P64
    Coral Stanzas. P64
    On the Beach. P64
    Two Swans in a Meadow by the Sea. P64
Hello. Gregory Corso. P85
Helm, Michele M.
    Trouble. P74
"The helmet no may an hive for bees
    becomes". The Vote. Ralph Knevet. P59
"Help! help!". Trouble at the Farm. Ivy O.
    Eastwick. P51
The Help. James Merrill. P79
Helping Behavior
    Self Help. William Trowbridge. P63
Helwig, Maggie
    Columbus at Night. P49
Hemans, Felicia Dorothea
    Casabianca. P90
    The Pilgrim Fathers. P51
Hemmingson, Michael A.
    The Shadow of Faith. P56
Hemphrey, Malcolm
    Lanes in Summer. P51
Hempseed, Iasbell
    Rufty and Tufty. P51
Henderson, Alice C.
    The Harvest. P51
Henderson, Brian

Nightfall by the River. P49
Henderson, Dara D.
　Listen. P73
Henderson, E. H.
　The March Wind. P51
Henderson, Mary Rebecca
　Never Fall in Love. P74
Henderson, Tim
　Down by the Brook. P74
Hendry, Hamish
　Silver Bells. P51
　The Silver Road. P51
　The Upside-Down World. P51
Henley, William Ernest
　Street Scene. P51
Henn, Mary Ann
　Blank Spaces. P56
　Little Birds Swooping. P63
　No Answers. P56
　You Have No Lasting City Here. P65
"Hens inch in Mustangs, cluck". Las Vegas.
　Ernest Kroll. P63
Henson, Lance
　Buffalo Blood. P78
　Ho Do Vi I. P78
　I Am Singing the Cold Rain. P78
　Ni Hoi Nim Ni Hon. P78
Her Elegy. Unknown. P78
"Her Face in Separation from You". Unknown.
　P62
"Her Face Is Like the Moon--.". Unknown. P62
"Her Lips with Noisy Curses". Unknown. P62
Her Seasons. David Wevill. P49
"Her arms across her breast she laid". The
　Beggar Maid. Lord Tennyson. P51
"Her body is not so white as". Queen-Ann's-
　Lace. William Carlos Williams. P82
"Her eyes be like the violets". Anne.
　Lizette Woodworth Reese. P81
"Her eyes the glow-worm lend thee". On a
　Dark Road. Robert Herrick. P51
"Her eyes' flood licks his feet's fair
　stain". On Mary Magdalene. Richard
　Crashaw. P59
"Her faded cutoffs shrunk tight and frayed".
　Deight in Order, Too. Gary Selden. P63
"Her life was blameless, blameless--.". The
　Examiner's Death. Peter Meinke. P63
"Her parents and her dolls destroyed".
　Belsen, Day of Liberation. Robert
　Hayden. P84
Heraclitus. Juan Cameron. P71
Herald. Josephine Miles. P84
Herbert, E.
　The Balloon Man. P51
Herbert, George
　Affliction. P59
　The Agony. P59
　Bitter-Sweet. P59

The Collar. P59
Denial. P59
Easter. P51
Easter. P59
Easter Wings. P59
The Elixir. P51,P59
The Flower. P59
Hope. P59
Jordan (2). P59
Justice (1). P59
Life. P59
Love (3). P59
Mary Magdalene. P59
Peace. P89
The Pulley. P59
Redemption. P59
Said I Not So?. P89
Time. P59
Vanity (1). P59
Virtue. P59
The Windows. P59
A Wreath. P59
Herbertson, Agnes Grozier
　Little Betty Blue. P51
Here. Fred Chappell. P67
Here. Graham Everett. P64
"Here a Little Child I Stand". Robert
　Herrick. P60
"Here a little child i stand". A Chiild's
　Grace. Robert Herrick. P51
"Here and There in the Bamboo Grove".
　Unknown. P62
Here Lies a Lady. John Crowe Ransom. P83
Here We Come A-Haying. Eunice Close. P51
"Here We Come A-Piping". Unknown. P51
"Here We Go Up, Up, Up". Unknown. P51
"Here comes the elephant". The Elephant.
　Herbert Asquith. P51
"Here from the field's edge we survey".
　Highway: Michigan. Theodore Roethke.
　P84
"Here I am again". Roads. Geoff Fiorito. P58
"Here I am at fourteen with". Photo. Don
　Coles. P49
"Here I come creeping, creeping everywhere".
　The Song of the Grass. Leigh Hunt. P51
"Here in my head, the home that is left...".
　Burning the Letters. Randall Jarrell.
　P84
"Here in the country's heart". The Country
　Faith. Norman Gale. P51
"Here in the foothills". Sierra Song. Steve
　Sanfield. P77
"Here in the upper part of the village".
　Poem. Jonaid. P92
"Here is a house with a pointed door". A
　Little Finger Game. E. J. Falconer.
　P51
"Here is the green lace of spring". The

Music of Spring. Marion Schoeberlein.
    P68
"Here is the long-bided hour...". Work.
    Aleksandr Pushkin. P90
"Here is the train!.". The Holiday Train.
    Irene Thompson. P51
"Here it is so quiet". Summer Rain. Georgi
    Djagarov. P70
"Here lies no light of sun nor stars".
    Taliesin, Selections. Richard Hovey.
    P81
"Here on the lower slopes of Windham
    Mountain". The Chipmunk Center. Peter
    Meinke. P63
"Here room and kingly silence keep". By the
    Pacific Ocean. Joaquin Miller. P81
"Here sparrows build upon the trees". My
    Early Home. John Clare. P51
"Here we bring new water". A New Year Carol.
    Unknown. P51
"Here we go a-walking, so softly...". From a
    Walking Song. Charles Williams. P51
"Here's a guessing story". What Is It?. H.
    E. Wilkinson. P51
"Here's to the Poor Widow from Babylon".
    Unknown. P51
"Here's to Thee". Unknown. P60
"Here, above". The Man-Moth. Elizabeth
    Bishop. P84
"Here, in the withered arbor...". Statue and
    Birds. Louise Bogan. P83
"Here/His gentle speech". At the School for
    the Deaf. Robert Pawlowski. P57
Heresy. Gwendolyn Vincent. P58
Herford, Oliver
    The Elf and the Dormouse. P89
Heritage
    A Brief Resume of the Last 20 Years...
        Wayne Kvam. P68
Heritage. Countee Cullen. P83
    Descendant. Elisaveta Bagriana. P70
    Exhortation. Dafydd Nanmor. P87
    Heritage. Countee Cullen. P83
    The Heritage. James Russell Lowell. P89
    The Idea of Ancestry. Etheridge Knight.
        P67
    Odes. George Santayana. P81
    Rhydcymerau. David Gwenallt Jones. P87
    Tourists. Josephine Miles. P84
The Heritage. James Russell Lowell. P89
Herman, Lawrence
    Precision. P73
"Hermit crabs and cranberry plants". Sea
    Shore Shanty. Bobbi Katz. P76
"Hermit's Cabin". Zana. P56
Hermits
    The World Was No Temptation. Margaret
        Longenecker Been. P68
"Hernando DeSoto". Margaret Blaker. P63

Heroes and Heroines
    Beowulf. Richard Wilbur. P84
    Negro Hero. Gwendolyn Brooks. P84
    Praise of Rhys ap Maredudd. Dafydd
        Nanmor. P87
    Returning to De Valera's Cottage. Tom
        McCarthy. P92
    To Hywel ab Ifan Fychan. Guto'r Glyn. P87
    Walton's Book of Lives, from
        Ecclesiastical Sonnets. William
        Wordsworth. P90
The Heron. Merrill G. Christopherson. P68
Herrick, Robert
    A Chiild's Grace. P51
    Delight in Disorder. P90
    The Four Sweet Months. P51
    Go, Pretty Child. P51
    "Here a Little Child I Stand". P60
    The Holy Spirit. P89
    The Kiss. P89
    'Littles'. P51
    On a Dark Road. P51
    To Blossoms. P89
"Hesitant foot forever poised". Phryne.
    Anita Jepsen. P68
Hesse, Hermann
    Night. L. Lewisohn (tr.). P90
Hessey, Vera
    The Frog and the Bird. P51
Hester, Holly
    Tall Tale Weather. P74
Hewitt, Bernard
    Traveller's Rest. P72
Hewitt, Morgan
    The Stretches of Time and Delights. P68
A Hex for My Neighbor's Green Thumb. Glenna
    Holloway. P63
"Hey Diddle, Dinkety, Poppety Pet". Unknown.
    P51
"Hey let's fight that shaman". Ghost &
    Shaman, from String Games. Unknown.
    P78
"Hey look at that: the Atacama". Like a
    Dream. Raul Zurita. P71
"Hey, Slim-Wasted girl, Clean Off Your
    Back". Unknown. P62
Heywood, Thomas
    Pack, Clouds, Away. P51,P89
    The Portrait. P89
Hiatt, Ben L.
    General Delivery. P77
    "7 a.m. -- Late November". P77
Hiawatha's Brothers. Henry Wadsworth
    Longfellow. P51
Hiawatha's Childhood, fr. The song of
    Hiawatha. Henry Wadsworth Longfellow.
    P51
"Hickety, Pickety". Unknown. P51
Hide and Seek. Phyllis Drayson. P51

Hide and Seek. Robert Minhinnick. P54
Hiding Place. Richard Armour. P63
Hie Away!. Sir Walter Scott. P51
Hieroglyphics. Bernice Fleisher. P65
Higgins, John
     Books. P90
High Holy Days. Jane Shore. P48
"High bare white walls". The Walled Light.
     Elaine Dallman. P65
"High dunes falling away". Two Swans in a
     Meadow by the Sea. Michael Heller. P64
"High in the Pine-Tree". Unknown. P51
High June. Catherine A. Morin. P51
High on a Hill. A. D. Winans. P56
"High on the dove-cot". Doves. E. J.
     Falconer. P51
"High upon a lofty hill". Partial to
     Marshall. Jan M. Stephens. P68
"High upon the hillside...". Skippets, the
     Bad One. Christine E. Bradley. P51
"High walls and huge the body may confine".
     Freedom of the Mind. William Lloyd
     Garrison. P90
A High-Toned Old Christian Woman. Wallace
     Stevens. P83
The Higher Good. Theodore Parker. P89
"The highway's lined with dead black
     drifts". Leaving Fargo: April. Linda
     M. Hasselstrom. P88
Highway: Michigan. Theodore Roethke. P84
Hijazi, Ahmad 'Abd Al-Muti
     Blood and Silence. Issa Bullata (tr.).
        P91
     A Song from Afar. Issa Bullata (tr.). P91
     Song of a Dead Pilot. Issa Bullata (tr.).
        P91
Hildebidle, John
     Troubles. P56
Hildegarde, Saint
     O Fire of God, the Comforter. R. F.
        Littledale (tr.). P89
Hill 190, August '69. Jack Hill. P86
Hill Country Rhythms. Jeremy Hooker. P54
"The hill narrates in flower". Ox-Eye Daisy.
     Lois Bunse. P77
Hill, E.
     When Polly Buys a Hat. P51
Hill, Geoffrey
     Funeral Music. P48
     A Pre-Raphaelite Notebook. P79
Hill, Hyacinthe
     Dragon-Fly. P65
     Love's Miracle. P65
Hill, Jack
     "Despite All the Training". P86
     "Having Been Issued". P86
     Hill 190, August '69. P86
     "In the Morning He Came For Me". P86
Hill, Leslie Pinckney

The Teacher. P90
The Hill, from Spoon River Anthology. Edgar
     Lee Masters. P82
Hill-Side Tree. Maxwell Bodenheim. P82
Hillary, Eileen
     Oedipus in Criminal Court. P68
Hillcrest. Edward Arlington Robinson. P81
Hillert, Margaret
     The Funny House. P50
"The hills speak". From Dusk to Dawn: Night
     Watch II. Ken Stone. P86
Himalayan Balsam. Anne Stevenson. P54
Himmirsky, Krassin
     The Cricket. Denise Levertov (tr.). P70
Hindu Cradle Song. Unknown. P51
Hine, Daryl
     Letter to Shadow. P79
Hionis, Argyris
     Metamorphosis, sel. Stavros Deligiorgis
        (tr.). P92
The Hippopotamus. Theophile Gautier. P61
"The hips undulate, so what?.". Beauty
     Competition. Fahmida Riyaz. P91
Hir, Ieuan Brydydd
     The Hall of Ifor Hael. Tony Conran (tr.).
        P87
"' Hiram, I think the sump is backing up'.".
     Mending Sump. Kenneth Koch. P85
The Hirlas of Owain, sels. Owain Cyfeiliog.
     P87
Hiroshima, Japan
     Vision of Hiroshima. Oscar Hahn. P71
Hirsch, Thomas L.
     A History of Golf--Sort of. P63
Hirschfeld, Beth
     Another Side of Me. P74
His Affliction. Dafydd ab [or ab] Gwilym.
     P87
"His Beauty Remains in My Eyes". Unknown.
     P62
His Excellency General Washington. Phillis
     Wheatley. P90
His Eyes Grew Old. Ethel Squires. P72
"His Form Is in My Eyes". Unknown. P62
His Matisses, 1938. Julia Keeler. P49
His Toys. Michael Dennis Browne. P63
"His brother's wife can't stand Clayton".
     Views to See Clayton From. Josephine
     Miles. P84
"His clumsy body is a golden fruit". Deaf-
     Mute in the Pear Tree. P. K. Page. P49
"His echoing axe the settler swung". The
     Settler. Alfred Street. P90
"His fingers tell water like prayer". The
     Water Diviner. Gillian Clarke. P54
"His fourscore years and five". Whittier.
     Margaret Elizabeth (Munson) Sangster.
     P81
"His head is so white it shines". Cleaned

the Crocodile's Teeth. Nyabuk Col. P53
"His headstone said". The Funeral of Martin
        Luther King, Jr. Nikki Giovanni. P85
"His kiss across my cheek and neck".
        Airport. Perry Brass. P65
"His last month was July, the summerland".
        Beyond Words. Richard Howard. P79
"His smile began with his eyes". His Eyes
        Grew Old. Ethel Squires. P72
"His spirit in smoke ascended to high
        heaven". The Lynching. Claude McKay.
        P82
"His younger brother Coon said to
        Coyote...". Coon Cons Coyote, Coyote
        Eats Coon... Unknown. P78
History
        Bearded Oaks. Robert Penn Warren. P83
History. Jorie Graham. P48
        Heraclitus. Juan Cameron. P71
        History. Jorie Graham. P48
        In the Footsteps of Ghengis Khan. Jan
        Barry. P86
        King Alfred Explains It. G. N. Gabbard.
        P63
        The Negro Speaks of Rivers. Langston
        Hughes. P83
        O Holy Past. Mary Jude Kupper. P72
        Phantoms All. Harriet Elizabeth Spofford.
        P81
        A Short Epic Poem in the English
        Language... James S. Koch. P63
        The Strata: To Llywelyn Sion. Robert
        Minhinnick. P54
"History is a". Tower of Babel. Thomas
        Merton. P84
A History of Golf--Sort of. Thomas L.
        Hirsch. P63
Histrion. Ezra Pound. P82
Hit and Run. Haywood Jackson. P68
Hitchhiking and Hitchhikers
        Advice Against Thumbers. Harold Bond. P63
        Long Narrow Roadway. Kim Maltman. P49
        Sonora Foothill Winter Rainstorm. David
        Kuehnert. P77
"Hither, come hither, ye clouds
        renowned...". The Cloud Chorus, from
        The Clouds. Aristophanes. P89
Hix, Hubert E.
        Blue Poem. P63
Ho Do Vi I. Lance Henson. P78
"Ho! pretty page, with the dimpled chin".
        The Age of Wisdom. William Makepeace
        Thackeray. P89
"Ho-ho-ho-he-he-he". They Went to the Moon
        Mother. Unknown. P78
Hoare, Florence
        Pedlar Jim. P51
Hoatson, Florence
        Autumn. P51

The Bird Bath. P51
        Who?. P51
Hob the Elf. Norman M. Johnson. P51
Hoberman, Mary Ann
        Changing. P50
        Snow. P80
Hochman, Benjamin
        Sons of the Right Hand. P63
Hodgson, Hallie
        Who, Me?. P63
Hodgson, Ralph
        The Bells of Heaven. P51
        Time, You Old Gipsy Man. P51
Hoefler, Walter
        Beneath Each Stone. Steven F. White
        (tr.). P71
        'I Wouldn't Be Able To Tell the
        Story...'. Steven F. White (tr.). P71
        Is There Anyone. Steven F. White (tr.).
        P71
        The Place You Inhabit. Steven F. White
        (tr.). P71
        Survivor. Steven F. White (tr.). P71
        To Write. Steven F. White (tr.). P71
        Under Certain Circumstances. Steven F.
        White (tr.). P71
Hoelz, Alison
        Winter Frost. P73
Hoffman, Charles Fenno
        Monterey. P90
Hoffman, Daniel
        An Apothegm. P63
        Instructions to a Medium To Be
        Transmitted... P79
Hoffmann, Heinrich
        The Story of Augustus Who Would Not Have
        Any Soup. P90
        The Story of Fidgety Philip. P90
        The Story of Johnny Head-in-Air. P90
"Hog butcher for the world". Chicago. Carl
        Sandburg. P82
Hogan, Katherine A.
        Fallen Angel. P65
        Prisms. P65
Hogan, Sheila
        The Ugliest Person. P68
Hogg, James
        The Boy's Song. P51
Hogs
        The Hedgehog and His Coat. Elizabeth
        Fleming. P51
        The Hedgehog. Edith King. P51
Hohenzollern. Barbara Guest. P64
"Hold high the woof, dear friends, that we
        may see ". On a Piece of Tapestry.
        George Santayana. P81
Holder, C. S.
        The King's Wood. P51
Holder, Paul

The Snowflake. P73
"Holding earth the sun". Late Autumn
        Afternoons. R. B. Weber. P64
Hole. Imogene Bolls. P63
Holgate, Elizabeth
    Mere Man. P56
The Holiday Ended. Pier Paolo Pasolini. P61
The Holiday Train. Irene Thompson. P51
A Holiday. Lizette Woodworth Reese. P81
Holidays
    "The First of April, Some Do Say".
        Unknown. P51
    Two Hoorays for Holidays. Ned Pastor. P63
    We and the Weekend. Alma Denny. P63
Holidays, Jewish
    High Holy Days. Jane Shore. P48
Hollander, John
    On the Way to Summer. P79
Holling, Holling C. (tr.)
    "Sleep, Sleep. My Little One!...".
        Unknown. P60
Hollo, Anselm (tr.)
    Dance of the Rain Gods. Ray Young Bear.
        P78
    The Eagle Above Us. Unknown. P78
    Poem To Be Recited Every 8 Years While
        Eating... Unknown. P78
    Poem to Ease Birth. Unknown. P78
    What Happened to a Young Man... Unknown.
        P78
The Hollow Men. Thomas Stearns Eliot. P83
"The hollow winds begin to blow". Signs of
        Rain. Edward Jenner. P89
Holloway, Glenna
    A Hex for My Neighbor's Green Thumb. P63
Holly and Ivy. Unknown. P66
The Holly. Unknown. P87
Hollywood. Joseph W. Nugent. P86
Holman, Felice
    Wild Day at the Shore. P76
Holmes, John
    Rhyme of Rain. P75
Holmes, Oliver Wendell
    Brother Jonathan's Lament for Sister
        Caroline. P90
    Contentment ('Man Wants but Little Here
        Below.'). P90
    Daniel Webster. P90
    The Last Leaf. P89
    Old Ironsides. P90
    The Old Man Dreams. P89
    The Ploughman. P89
    Rudolph the Headsman, from This Is It.
        P90
Holmes, Ruth
    No Thoroughfare. P51
Holmes, W. K.
    The Dream Ship. P51
    The Old Brown Horse. P51

Holocaust
    About Thirty Jews Were Taken to Chelmno,
        fr. Mass Graves. Charles Reznikoff.
        P83
Holstein, Michael
    Silk Pyjamas. P63
Holty, Ludwig
    Harvest Song. Charles Timothy Brooks
        (tr.). P89
    Winter Song. Charles Timothy Brooks
        (tr.). P89
The Holy Spirit. Robert Herrick. P89
"Holy of England! since my light is". On
        First Entering Westminster Abbey.
        Louise Imogen Guiney. P81
"Holy water of spirit". Big Basin Waterfall.
        Ellis Ovesen. P72
Holzapfel, Rudi
    Epitaph on a Long Stone. P72
Homage to Mistress Bradstreet, sels. John
        Berryman. P84
Home. Leonidas. P89
Home. Louise Louis. P65
Home Owner's Lament. Pier Munn. P63
Home Thoughts from Abroad. Robert Browning.
        P51,P89
Home and Family Life
    The Ancestors: A Suite. Dorothy Livesay.
        P49
    Best of All. J. M. Westrup. P51
    The Broken Home. James Merrill. P85
    Brynbeidog. Jeremy Hooker. P54
    California Street. Kandy Arnold. P58
    Domain. Constance Studer. P56
    The Family in the Suburbs: A Situation
        Comedy. David Citino. P63
    Family Prime. Mark Van Doren. P83
    Home. Leonidas. P89
    "The Housewife, Pursuing the Child".
        Unknown. P62
    "The Husband Laughs When His Face".
        Unknown. P62
    Lawn Bumps. Barbara Guest. P64
    Leaving. Jeremy Hooker. P54
    Lucinda Matlock, from Spoon River
        Anthology. Edgar Lee Masters. P82
    Lullaby for Amy. Mark Jarman. P85
    My Early Home. John Clare. P51
    My Father in the Night Commanding No.
        Louis Simpson. P85
    Native Ground. Robert Minhinnick. P54
    "Oh Child, My Own Life Is More Dear to
        Me". Unknown. P62
    "One Nipple Drips, One Is Made Erect".
        Unknown. P62
    One's Goal. Annie Laurie Leech. P72
    An Orphan's Wish. Lee Ann Braunecker. P74
    Physical Universe. Louis Simpson. P85
    A Picture. Charles Gamage Eastman. P89

Song for a Little House. Christopher
    Morley. P51
"'Take a Look at This!' says the wife".
    Unknown. P62
Tales from a Family Album. Donald
    Justice. P67
The Two Families. Joyce L. Brisley. P51
Wednesday's Child. Peggy Kahn. P56
"When Her Son Was Climbing on the Back".
    Unknown. P62
Who's In?. Elizabeth Fleming. P51
Wind Blew Once. Jeremy Hooker. P54
Home!. Lu Cicada. P77
Home, Sweet Home! Gavin Ewart. P63
Home, Sweet Home, fr. Clari. John Howard
    Payne. P89
Homecoming
    Attraction. Unknown. P87
    Going Home. LLawdden. P87
    Home. Louise Louis. P65
    Home, Sweet Home, fr. Clari. John Howard
        Payne. P89
    Homecoming. R. Parthasarathy. P92
    The Homecoming of Emma Lazarus. Galway
        Kinnell. P85
    I Thought They Would Listen. Lily Jean
        Lee-Adams. P86
    A Lust for the Quaint Old Ways. John J.
        Brugaletta. P63
    Lydia. Lizette Woodworth Reese. P81
Homecoming. R. Parthasarathy. P92
    1926. Weldon Kees. P84
    Returning Home. Alice Mann Roney. P72
    These Hills, Mother. Alice Derry. P88
The Homecoming of Emma Lazarus. Galway
    Kinnell. P85
Homeland
    King's Landing. M. Travis Lane. P49
Homer
    The Camp at Night, from The Iliad. P89
"Homer was right: the dawn". Day Breaking.
    John E. Moore. P72
Homesick Blues. Langston Hughes. P83
Homesickness
    A Bushel of Chaff. John Ceiriog Hughes.
        P87
    From Exile. Dafydd Benfras. P87
    Go Back. Nirupama Narasimham. P72
    Home Thoughts from Abroad. Robert
        Browning. P51,P89
    Hywel's Boast of His Country. Hywel ab
        Owain Gwynedd. P87
    Longing for Caernarfon. Sion Gruffudd.
        P87
    Old Folks at Home. Stephen Foster. P89
Homing. Stanley Moss. P64
Homoeroticism
    Graffiti from the Gare Saint-Manque.
        Marilyn Hacker. P79

Honey Bear. Elizabeth Lang. P51
Honeycutt, **April**
    How Lovely. P74
Honeymoon in Rice. Francis J. Smith. P63
"Honeysuckle scented winds". Crystal
    Rosaries of Long Remembering. Emma
    Crobaugh. P68
Honor
    Exhortation. Dafydd Nanmor. P87
    Sherman. Richard Watson Gilder. P81
    To Wystan Auden in His Birthday. and
        Louise Bogan, Edmund Wilson. P79
Hood, **Thomas**
    Bed-Time. P51
    The Dream Fairy. P51
    I Remember, I Remember. P89
    The Little Piggies. P51
    No!. P89
    What Can an Old Man Do But Die?. P89
The Hook. Theodore Weiss. P84
Hooker, **Jeremy**
    As a Thousand Years. P54
    Beidog. P54
    Brynbeidog. P54
    Common Land Above Trefenter. P54
    Hill Country Rhythms. P54
    Leaving. P54
    The Mason's Law. P54
    Shepherd. P54
    Wind Blew Once. P54
Hooper, **Patricia**
    Deer in the Open Field. P88
    The Window. P88
Hooson, **Isaac Daniel**
    The Flame. Tony Conran (tr.). P87
"The hop-poles stand in cones". The Midnight
    Skaters. Edmund Blunden. P89
Hope
    Chances Are. Lisel Mueller. P88
Hope. Robert ab Gwilym Ddu. P87
    A Dragon for the Family. Robert Yeo. P92
    For the Candle Light. Angelina Weld
        Grimke. P89
Hope. George Herbert. P59
    Hope. Robert ab Gwilym Ddu. P87
    Hope. George Herbert. P59
    Interim. Clarissa Scott Delany. P89
    Lines to Accompany Flowers for Eve.
        Carolyn Kizer. P79
    Night Light. Lawrence Ferlinghetti. P85
    Recovery Song. Barry Wallenstein. P57
    The Road (Version 2, with echoes of Emily
        Dickinson). Blaga Dimitrova. P70
    This Poor Man. William John Gruffydd. P87
    When My Ship Comes in. Robert Jones
        Burdette. P89
"Hope is a fat seed pod". Chances Are. Lisel
    Mueller. P88
Hopkins, **Lee Bennett**

In the Pitch of the Night. P55
On an August Day. P76
Tricia's Fish. P50
Hoppin, Ruth
"If We Have Seen What We Are Meant to
See". P72
An Horatian Ode upon Cromwell's Return from
Ireland. Andrew Marvell. P59
Horizon. David Emrys James. P87
"The horns in the harbor booming, vaguely".
The Sin of Hamlet. Delmore Schwartz.
P84
The Horrible Noise. Samantha Adams. P74
Horrorscope. John D. Engle Jr. P63
Horse. Louise Gluck. P52
Horse Racing
Contest of Wills. R. Wallace Clark. P72
Horseback Ride. Siddie Joe Johnson. P50
Horses
Asking a Stallion. Gutun Owain. P87
The Broncho That Would Not Be Broken.
Vachel Lindsay. P82
The Distant Runners. Mark Van Doren. P83
Fan, the Filly. Wilfred Thorley. P51
The Horses. Edwin Muir. P48
How They Brought the Good News from Ghent
to Aix. Robert Browning. P90
"I Had a Little Pony". Unknown. P51
Loreine: a Horse. Arthur Davison Ficke.
P89
October 1st. Robert Hahn. P58
The Old Brown Horse. W. K. Holmes. P51
"Pitty Patty Polt!". Unknown. P51
The Pony. Rachel MacAndrew. P51
The Race. Sylvia Smullin. P74
Song for a Surf-Rider. Sarah Van Alstyne
Allen. P76
"Horses stand in the fall rain...". October
1st. Robert Hahn. P58
"The horses, the pigs". Familiar Friends.
James S. Tippett. P51
The Horses. Edwin Muir. P48
"The horseshoe print on the lawn". Lawn
Bumps. Barbara Guest. P64
Hospital. Ardyth Bradley. P88
Hospitals
In a Country Hospital. Anne Porter. P64
White Death. Tom Tellesbo. P58
Hot Night on Water Street. Louis Simpson.
P85
"Hot-Cross Buns! Hot Cross Buns!". Unknown.
P51
"Hot-headed patriots, many of them bigoted".
General Washington. Paul Goodman. P84
Hotel De La Gare. Waldo Rojas. P71
Hotel Transylvanie. Frank O'Hara. P85
Hotels
Mecox Motel. Anselm Parlatore. P64
Houck, Richard

Platypus. P74
Houghton, Lord. See Milnes, Richard Monckton
"The hour hand and the minute hand...". The
Speed Track. Peter [pseud.]. P51
The House on the Hill. Rabiul Hasan. P56
The House That Jack Built. Unknown. P51
House, Rick Allen
Johnny Doe. P73
Household Employees
Epilogue. Langston Hughes. P83
Negro Servant. Langston Hughes. P83
The Housekeeper. Charles Lamb. P89
Houses
Brownstone Revisited. Mary B. Finn. P68
Houses. William Virgil Davis. P68
The Deserted House. Mary E. Coleridge.
P51
Earlene Spratt's Lot. Hilary Russell. P63
Falling Water. James Russell Vaky. P68
The House on the Hill. Rabiul Hasan. P56
Houses. William Virgil Davis. P68
I Remember, I Remember. Thomas Hood. P89
My Little House. J. M. Westrup. P51
My Own House. David Ignatow. P64
Ocean Beach House. R. B. Weber. P64
Penthouse Enigma. James Russell Vaky. P68
Postcard from Civilization. Charles W.
Pratt. P63
The Rain of Time. Jerry Craven. P65
Roofs. Lyubomir Levchev. P70
The Shiny Little House. Nancy M. Hayes.
P51
"The houses are haunted". Disillusionment of
Ten O'Clock. Wallace Stevens. P83
"The Housewife, Pursuing the Child".
Unknown. P62
Housman, Alfred Edward
Loveliest of Trees. P89
Houssi, Majid El
Ifriqiyad/Alternatives, sels. Eric Sellin
(tr.). P91
Poem, fr. Iris Ifriqiya. Eric Sellin
(tr.). P91
Houston, Opie
Meadow's Song. P65
Houston, Opie R.
Haiku. P72
Hover, Emily
Mr. Beetle. P51
Hovey, Richard
Envoy. P81
The Sea Gypsy. P81
Song. P81
Song, from The Marriage of Guenevere. P81
A Stein Song. P81
Taliesin, Selections. P81
Unmanifest Destiny. P81
The Wander-Lovers. P81
"How Can the One Who Is Somehow the

Sweetheart". Unknown. P62

"How Can There be Unpleasantness from the
      Mouth...". Unknown. P62

How Does a Flower Know. James Stearns. P68

' How Far Is It to Bethlehem?'. F.
      Chesterton. P51

How Her Teeth Were Pulled. Unknown. P78

"How Is It All Gonna Turn Out," from Wolf
      Songs... Unknown. P78

How Just One Poor Man Lives. Alonzo Gonzales
      Mo. P78

"How Like the Black-Spotted Antelope".
      Unknown. P62

How Lovely. April Honeycutt. P74

How Many Days Has My Baby To Play?. Unknown.
      P51

"How Many Miles to Barley Bridge?". Unknown.
      P51

How Now, O, Brightener. Wallace Stevens. P79

How Stump Stood in the Winter. David
      Wagoner. P57

How They Brought the Good News from Ghent to
      Aix. Robert Browning. P90

"How beautiful is the rain!.". Rain in
      Summer. Henry Wadsworth Longfellow.
      P51,P89

"How beautiful it was, that one bright day".
      Hawthorne. Henry Wadsworth Longfellow.
      P90

"How can you do the things you know you'll
      do?--.". The Fuhrer Bunker, sels.
      William DeWitt Snodgrass. P85

"How delicious is the winning". The First
      Kiss. Thomas Campbell. P89

"How did he celebrate". The Manhood of
      Hebrew Jesus. Stanley A. Fellman. P72

"' How does the water'.". The Cataract of
      Lodore. Robert Southey. P90

"How fresh, O Lord, how sweet and clean".
      The Flower. George Herbert. P59

"How funny you are today New York". Steps.
      Frank O'Hara. P85

"How happy is he born and taught". The
      Character of a Happy Life. Sir Henry
      Wotton. P90

"How happy to be a fish". Fish and Bird.
      Rosemary Brinckman. P51

"How he found his life long ago". How Just
      One Poor Man Lives. Alonzo Gonzales
      Mo. P78

"How I want to become transparent!.". Tablet
      XXIII. Armand Schwerner. P64

"How large is a house?.". Interiors. Carol
      Barrett and Anita Skeen. P88

"How long, O Lord, shall I forgotten be?.".
      Psalm 13. Sir Philip Sidney. P59

"How lovely thou art! O green grass".
      Loveliness. Gail Calmer. P68

"How many dawns, chill from this rippling

rest". Proem: To Brooklyn Bridge, fr.
      The Bridge. Hart Crane. P83

"How many million Aprils came". Blue
      Squills. Sara Teasdale. P82

"How many summers, love". The Poet's Song to
      His Wife. Bryan Waller ("Barry
      Cornwall") Procter. P89

"How many thousand of my poorest subjects".
      Sleep, from Henry IV. William
      Shakespeare. P90

"How many times has it been sd. in jest:.".
      Heartbreak in Tuktoyaktuk. Louis
      Phillips. P63

"How many verses have I thrown". Verses Why
      Burnt. Walter Savage Landor. P90

"How many ways can you bring me ten?.".
      Making Tens. M. M. Hutchinson. P51

"How much of joy there is in daily things".
      Daily Joys. Barbara McCoy. P68

"How nice it is to eat!.". Beautiful Meals.
      Thomas Sturge Moore. P51

"How oft have I sat by your bed...". To My
      Son. Muriel Ringstad. P72

"How prone we are to hide and hoard".
      Lavender. Unknown. P89

"How rich, O Lord! how fresh thy visits
      are!". Unprofitableness. Henry
      Vaughan. P59

"How sad when the system". To George C.
      Wallace. Frances Clarkhandler. P72

"How shall I liken Thee?.". Thee. Louise
      Louis. P65

"How shall I speak of doom...". Tales from a
      Family Album. Donald Justice. P67

"How shall we forget your smile". Epilogue
      for FDR. David Ignatow. P84

"How strange that here is nothing as it
      was!.". In a City Garden. Trumbull
      Stickney. P81

"How sweet is the shepherd's sweet lot!.".
      The Shepherd. William Blake. P51

"How sweet she sprawls...A living animal". A
      Good Sight of Andromeda. Milton Acorn.
      P49

"' How sweetly,' said the trembling maid".
      Linda to Hafed, from The Fire-
      Worshippers. Thomas Moore. P89

"How the veins branch around the knuckles".
      Meditations on the Body: Right Hand.
      Maxine Silverman. P88

How to Ask and Have. Samuel Lover. P89

How to Get Grizzly Spirit, from Wolf
      Songs... Unknown. P78

How To Survive Nuclear War. Maxine Kumin.
      P48

"How vainly men themselves amaze". The
      Garden. Andrew Marvell. P59

"How we grow out of them". Houses. William
      Virgil Davis. P68

"How we photographed". Reflections. Miriam
    Waddington. P49
"' How will he hear the bell at school'.".
    Mutterings Over the Crib of a Deaf
    Child. James Wright. P57
"How wonderful is death!.". To Ianthe,
    Sleeping, from Queen Mab. Percy Bysshe
    Shelley. P90
How, Like This Spring, Slowly. Susan Hauser.
    P88
Howard, Ben
    A Resolution. P68
Howard, Richard
    Beyond Words. P79
Howard, Thelma L.
    Tomorrow. P72
Howarth, Ellen Clementine
    'Tis but a Little Faded Flower. P90
Howarth, William
    At Sunrise Along the American River...
    P77
    Night Thoughts, Sierra. P77
    October: Sierra. P77
    Turn To Go. P77
Howe, Charles H.
    The Parrot's Scream. P68
Howe, Julia Ward
    Battle-Hymn of the Republic. P90
Howell, Robert M.
    Song. P65
    To Sing the Song. P65
Howells, William Dean
    The Two Wives. P90
Howes, Barbara
    The Lace Maker. P57
"However Much It Takes To Create
    Friendship". Unknown. P62
"However beautiful the roads". Headache.
    Orhan Veli Kanik. P91
Howink, Eda
    Cosmic Resident. P72
Howitt, Mary
    Buttercups and Daisies. P51
    The Sea-Gull. P51
    September. P51
    The Spider and the Fly. P89
    A Spring Song. P51
    The Squirrel. P51
Howitt, William
    A Summer Noon. P89
"A howling storm is brewing". The Storm.
    Heinrich Heine. P90
Hoyt, Jennifer
    Purple. P73
Hristozov, Nikolai
    In Front of the Cave. William Meredith
    (tr.). P70
    Introspection. William Meredith (tr.).
    P70

Old Age. William Meredith (tr.). P70
Hryciuk, Marshall
    On the Passing of Heidegger. P49
Hsien, Chi
    Spring Steps. P72
Hsu, Wen-Ying
    Song of Pasadena. P72
Hubbell, Patricia
    Sea Fairies. P55
Huber, E. Manuel
    Question?. P72
"Huffy Henry hid the day". The Dream Songs,
    sels. John Berryman. P84
Hugh Selwyn Mauberley (Life and Contacts).
    Ezra Pound. P82
Hughes, John Ceiriog
    A Bushel of Chaff. Tony Conran (tr.). P87
    A Pothersome Pair. Tony Conran (tr.). P87
    What Passes and Endures. Tony Conran
    (tr.). P87
Hughes, Langston
    April Rain Song. P75
    Cultural Exchange. P83
    Epilogue. P83
    Florida Road Workers. P83
    Homesick Blues. P83
    Jazz Band in a Parisian Cabaret. P83
    Negro Servant. P83
    The Negro Speaks of Rivers. P83
    Poem. P50
    Saturday Night. P83
    "Tamborines!". P60
    Theme for English B. P83
    The Weary Blues. P83
Hughes, Ted
    The Dracula Vine. P55
Hugo, Richard
    Cattails. P79
    The Freaks at Spurgin Road Field. P57
Hugo, Victor
    Good Night. P51
"Humankind can indeed bear". Stone Reality
    Meditation. Lawrence Ferlinghetti. P85
The Humble Shell. K. S. Venkataramu. P72
Humility. Fred Chappell. P67
Humor
    Betty at the Party. Unknown. P51
Humorous Verse
    (914) 555-4144. Ned Pastor. P63
    Affluence. Richard Moore. P63
    Against Waking Early. Bruce Bennett. P63
    Amadeus. LoVerne Brown. P63
    Another Fable in Two Languages. Charles
    W. Pratt. P63
    Apathy. Blossom S. Kirschenbaum. P63
    An Apothegm. Daniel Hoffman. P63
    Armed Conflict. Pier Munn. P63
    The Beer and the Bear. Robert N.
    Feinstein. P63

Bingoholic. Shirley Volger Meister. P63
The Compliment. Eugene Field. P90
The Cost of a Sting. X. J. Kennedy. P63
Coup de Grace. Mildred Luton. P63
Cross Words. Edmund Conti. P63
Curriculum Change. Ned Pastor. P63
Discount Store. G. N. Gabbard. P63
Domestic Crisis. X. J. Kennedy. P63
Echo and the Lover. Unknown. P90
Emphasis Mine. Edmund Conti. P63
Ennui. David Ray. P63
Eskimo Haiku. Robert Peters. P63
The Faithful Lovers. Unknown. P89
A Flower Is Looking Through the Ground.
   Harold Munro. P90
Gutes and Eulas. Roy Blount Jr. P63
Hat Trick. Paul Humphrey. P63
Have You? I Have Never!. Ned Pastor. P63
Heartbreak in Tuktoyaktuk. Louis
   Phillips. P63
Hiding Place. Richard Armour. P63
Home Owner's Lament. Pier Munn. P63
I Wish I Were Living in Your Century. A.
   L. Lazarus. P63
Invitation. James Steel Smith. P63
The Laxness Monster; or, I Be Singer...
   William Harmon. P63
A Literary History of Cheese. Roberta
   Simone. P63
Little Birds Swooping. Mary Ann Henn. P63
Living Alone. D. Scott Taylor. P63
The Milkmaid. Jeffreys Taylor. P90
Molly Gaunt. H. Wendell Smith. P63
Mower and Mower. John D. Engle Jr. P63
Mrs. Wilson, Who Never Loved. Virginia
   Long. P63
My Rumi-Nation. Julia Older. P63
My Wife Reads the Paper at Breakfast on
   the Birthday... Miller Williams. P63
The Nose and the Eyes. William Cowper.
   P90
Olecranon. Ernest Slyman. P63
On a Compliment. R. P. Dickey. P63
On First Looking into Chapman's
   Refrigerator. Edmund Conti. P63
One-Up. Bruce Berger. P63
Pisa Visa. Felicia Lamport. P63
Popping Corn. Unknown. P89
Q. E. D. Laurence Perrine. P63
Queen Anne's Legs. Jane Flanders. P63
The Rake's Progress. Vonna Adrian. P63
The Razor-Seller. John Wolcott. P90
Reading Outdoors. Joan Drew Ritchings.
   P63
The Red-Handled Hatchet. Mark Sanders.
   P63
A Reply. Jay Dougherty. P63
Sharper Than a Serpent's Tooth. Paul
   Sawyer. P63

A Short Poem. James S. Koch. P63
Social Zoology: Prep for a Field Trip.
   Gary Pittenger. P63
Sponge. Maureen Cannon. P63
Tallyho the Fox. Louis Hasley. P63
Three. Charles West. P63
To Madame De Sevigne. Mathieu de
   Montreuil. P90
What Did the Midge Say to the Mildew?.
   Bonnie Jacobson. P63
Where Are You Going, My Pretty Maid?.
   Unknown. P89
Worshiper. Gloria A. Maxson. P63
Zebras. Terry P. Beh. P63
Humpbacks. Mary Oliver. P52
Humphrey, Paul
   Boobiat. P63
   Hat Trick. P63
Humphreys, Aletha
   Lipstick Graffito. P68
Hunchback Girl: She Thinks of Heaven, fr. A
   Street... Gwendolyn Brooks. P84
"Hunched over an ancient singer". Cousin
   Shamsu, Durzi. Kaiser Haq. P91
Hundley, Amy
   Bike Flight. P74
"Hundreds of stars in the pretty sky". Our
   Mother. Unknown. P51
Hunger
   For a Comrade. Abraham Sutzkever. P48
   Grabbling in Yokna Bottom. James Seay.
      P67
   Hunger. Samik. P78
   Poem About a Herring. Abraham Sutzkever.
      P48
Hunger. Samik. P78
   The Unappeasable. Cy Patteson. P72
"The hungry come in a dry time". Grabbling
   in Yokna Bottom. James Seay. P67
Hunt, Harriet G.
   When the Mocking Bird Sings. P72
Hunt, Leigh
   Abou Ben Adhem. P89
   The Glove and the Lions. P90
   The Nile. P90
   On Hearing a Little Music-Box. P90
   Sneezing. P90
   The Song of the Grass. P51
Hunt, Leigh (tr.)
   Cupid Swallowed. Unknown-Greek. P89
   I Dreamt I Saw Great Venus. Bion. P89
Hunt, Viola K.
   The Quarrel. P68
The Hunter. Unknown. P61
Hunting Horn. Nikolai Kuntchev. P70
Hunting Song. Sir Walter Scott. P89
Hunting and Hunters
   A-Hunting. Jennie Dunbar. P51
   The Hunter. Unknown. P61

Hunting Horn. Nikolai Kuntchev. P70
Hunting Song. Sir Walter Scott. P89
A Hunting We Will Go. Henry Fielding. P89
Magic Words for Hunting Caribou. Unknown. P78
Magic Words for Hunting Seal. Unknown. P78
The Outlaw. David Ignatow. P84
Song to a Child. Unknown. P87
Under the Green Ledge. Kenneth Patchen. P84
Hunting the Hare. Unknown. P87
Hunting the Snow Owl. Frank Finale. P56
A Hunting We Will Go. Henry Fielding. P89
The Hurdy-Gurdy Man. Elizabeth Fleming. P51
"Hurrah! for a day with the farmer". A Day at the Farm. Unknown. P51
"Hurrah!/Hurray!.". Winter Is Tacked Down. Sister Noemi Weygant. P80
The Hurricane. William Cullen Bryant. P90
Hurricanes
    The Inventors. Rene Char. P61
"' Hurry!' said the leaves.". A Summer Shower. Unknown. P51
Hurst, James Richard
    Apples and Leaves. P68
    The Crystal Flow. P68
    Pale Like Sunshine Music. P68
    Silence. P68
    Time Is Leaving. P68
    Whitened Sand. P68
Hurt Hawks. Robinson Jeffers. P83
"The Husband Laughs When His Face". Unknown. P62
"Husband and wife we loved each other then". The Old Man's Song, About His Wife. Unknown. P78
"Hush, hush. little baby". Evening. Unknown. P51
"Hushed, we hovered between rabbit and dragon". A Dragon for the Family. Robert Yeo. P92
Hussey, N. E.
    I Spy. P51
    Toad the Tailor. P51
Hussey, Norah
    My Garden. P51
Hutchinson, M. M.
    Dancing on the Shore. P51
    Harvest. P51
    Making Tens. P51
    My New Umbrella. P51
    Ten Little Indian Boys. P51
    The Thames. P51
    A Tug-of-War. P51
    Twice. P51
Hutchman, Laurence
    Nelligan. P49
Huts
    My Hut. Eileen Mathias. P51
Hutt, Frank
    Vacation Time. P51
Hutton, Linda
    Awakenings (A Sedoka). P72
Hwang, Kum Chan
    Candle Light. P72
"Hyacinthus bleeds as the violet blooms". Sapphics on the Violet. John C. Anderson. P68
Hymes, Dell (tr.)
    The Crier. Philip Kahclamet. P78
Hymn. Ralph Waldo Emerson. P90
A Hymn for October 15th. Vera Rich. P68
Hymn of the Lyre Player. Fatthy Said. P91
Hymn of the West. Edmund Clarence Stedman. P90
Hymn to God My God, in My Sickness. John Donne. P59
A Hymn to God the Father. John Donne. P59
Hymn to Zeus. Cleanthes. P89
Hymns
    Battle-Hymn of the Republic. Julia Ward Howe. P90
    Harmony. John A. Downes. P72
    Hymn. Ralph Waldo Emerson. P90
    A Hymn for October 15th. Vera Rich. P68
    Hymn of the Lyre Player. Fatthy Said. P91
    A Newly Discovered 'Homeric' Hymn. Charles Olson. P85
    Tanka. Neal Henry Lawrence. P72
Hypocrisy
    Trinity. John Knoll. P86
Hypothesis from the Wilderness. Bonnie Squires. P68
Hywel ab Owain Gwynedd
    Hywel's Boast of His Country. Tony Conran (tr.). P87
    Hywel's Boast of Women, sels. Tony Conran (tr.). P87
    Hywel's Choice. Tony Conran (tr.). P87
Hywel's Boast of His Country. Hywel ab Owain Gwynedd. P87
Hywel's Boast of Women, sels. Hywel ab Owain Gwynedd. P87
Hywel's Choice. Hywel ab Owain Gwynedd. P87

I. Marion Jane Richardson. P65
I Am. Jason Gelinas. P73
"I Am Climbing," from Crow Versions. Unknown. P78
I Am Dreaming of a White Christmas: The Natural... Robert Penn Warren. P47
"I Am Making," from Crow Versions. White-arm. P78
I Am Not Yours. Sara Teasdale. P82

I Am Singing the Cold Rain. Lance Henson. P78

I Am Thankful. Evan Daniels. P74

I Am to My Own Heart Merely a Serf. Delmore Schwartz. P84

I Am Waiting. Lawrence Ferlinghetti. P85

I Am Weary of Being Bitter. Arthur Davidson Ficke. P82

I Arrive at the Coliseum... Doris Eliz Einolf. P72

I Believe in Me. Anisa Dalal. P73

I Blew up the Virgin of My Legs. Diego Maquieira. P71

I Break the Sky. Owen Dodson. P84

I Count My Time by Times That I Meet Thee. Richard Watson Gilder. P81

I Do Not Cry Like People Cry. Hermit Helene Troy Arlington. P68

"I Do Not Go to the Fields Today," from Mother... Unknown. P90

"I Don't Care If You're Married...," from Kiowa... Unknown. P78

"I Don't Know Why You Tell Me I'm Drunk," from Wolf... Unknown. P78

I Dream. Janine A. Parry. P73

I Dream of a Land. Lola E. Hahn. P72

I Dreamt I Saw Great Venus. Bion. P89

I Fear Thy Kisses, Gentle Maiden. Percy Bysshe Shelley. P89

I Gave My Life for Thee. Frances Ridley Havergal. P89

I Go to Death. Lewis Moore. P68

"I Had a Little Hen, the Prettiest Ever Seen". Unknown. P51

"I Had a Little Hobby-Horse". Unknown. P51

"I Had a Little Husband". Unknown. P51

"I Had a Little Nut-Tree, Nothing Would It Bear". Unknown. P51

"I Had a Little Pony". Unknown. P51

"I Have a Little Sister, They Call Her Peep, Peep". Unknown. P51

"I Have No Use for Either the Bad Man or the Good". Unknown. P62

I Have Seen Black Hands. Richard Wright. P90

"I Have Seen the Clear Sky Produce Rain". Giacomo da Lentini. P69

I Have Seen the Spring. Sara Teasdale. P82

"I Have Set My Heart on Serving God". Giacomo da Lentini. P69

"I Heard That Person Say". Unknown. P62

"I Hope to Receive a Reward". Giacomo da Lentini. P69

I Hypnotize Bugs. Eugene A. Craig. P63

"I Keep Dreaming I'm Dead," from Wolf Songs... Unknown. P78

I Know an Owl. Edward Anthony. P75

"I Know How People Get Treated...," from Wolf Songs... Unknown. P78

I Like Summer Rain. Chisachi Suehiro. P75

I Looked Here. Stephen Crane. P81

I Love All Beauteous Things. Robert Bridges. P51

I Love Every Hair on Your Head. Alma Denny. P63

I Meet Lee San in the Nether World and Talk of Home. Ahmed Ali. P91

I Met a Seer. Stephen Crane. P81

I Must Away. May Sarson. P51

I Never Realized. Teresa Calderon. P71

I Play Childish Songs with a Grimace on My Lips. Gonzalo Millan. P71

I Prithee Send Me Back My Heart. Sir John Suckling. P89

I Remember. Gigi Lord. P65

I Remember a Season. Maria Luisa Spaziani. P61

"I Remember Her Mouth Screeching an Oath". Unknown. P62

"I Remember My Beloved Stepping Backwards". Unknown. P62

"I Remember the Joy". Unknown. P62

I Remember, I Remember. Thomas Hood. P89

I Saw a Man. Stephen Crane. P81

I Saw a Ship A-Sailing. Unknown. P51

I See Again. Liliana Stefanova. P70

I See Someone (To My Mother, 'Indira Devi'). Murall Patibandla. P72

"I Shall Never Find Solace". Rinaldo d'Aquino. P69

I Shall Not Care. Sara Teasdale. P82

"I Should Wear Gloves, These White Pages". Simon Perchik. P64

I Sing of Spring. Elaine Hardt. P72

I Spy. N. E. Hussey. P51

I Stare. Rebecca Caudill. P75

I Stood Musing in a Black World. Stephen Crane. P81

I Stood Upon a High Place. Stephen Crane. P81

I Stood Upon a Highway. Stephen Crane. P81

I Syng of a Mayden. Unknown. P66

"I Think About You...," from Wolf Songs & Others... Unknown. P78

I Think I Should Have Loved You Presently. Edna St. Vincent Millay. P82

"I Think That Galileo, Old and Blind". Rosemary Davis. P72

I Thought They Would Listen. Lily Jean Lee-Adams. P86

"I Thought You Were Good". Unknown. P78

I Vow to Thee, My Country. Sir Cecil Spring Rice. P51

I Walked in a Desert. Stephen Crane. P81

I Wandered Lonely. William Wordsworth. P51

I Was as Full of Air as An Old Bullfrog. Pilual Juoc. P53

I Was in the Darkness. Stephen Crane. P81

I Was Mistaken for a Red Dog. Nyakong Makui.

P53

I Will Go into the Ghetto. Charles
     Reznikoff. P83
I Will Keep Christmas. P. A. Ropes. P51
I Will Not Let Thee Go. Robert Bridges. P89
I Wish I Were Living in Your Century. A. L.
     Lazarus. P63
I Won't Bow My Head for Anyone. Stephen Ciec
     Lam. P53
I Wonder. Jeannie Kirby. P51
"I Wonder What the Eagle Did to Him," from
     Wolf... Unknown. P78
I Would Give Him a Man. Dhor Ding Cuol. P53
"I Would Like to Show Openly". Jacopo
     Mostacci. P69
"I Would Like". Lorenzo. P77
' I Wouldn't Be Able To Tell the Story...'.
     Walter Hoefler. P71
"I always like summer". Knoxville,
     Tennessee. Nikki Giovanni. P85
"I am a classic". An Aging Canvas. Kandy
     Arnold. P58
"I am a cosmic resident". Cosmic Resident.
     Eda Howink. P72
"I am a feather on the bright sky". The
     Delight Song of Tsoai-Talee. N. Scott
     Momaday. P85
"I am a fellow". Identity. May Duhameaux.
     P72
"I am a fly". One More I'matation. Eleanore-
     Melissa. P68
"-- I am a gentleman in a dustcoat trying".
     Piazza. John Crowe Ransom. P83
"I am a meter reader". Gas Man. Pyke Johnson
     Jr. P63
"I am a miner. The light burns blue". Nick
     and the Candlestick. Sylvia Plath. P85
"I am a puppet singing cliched songs
     silently". Puppet. John J. Soldo. P65
"I am a star". Out of the Starstream. Ruth
     C. Falk. P72
"' I am always corrected/correcting'.". The
     Lament of the Poet, from Animated
     Film... James Reaney. P49
"I am ashamed before the earth". Therefore I
     Must Tell the Truth. Torlino. P78
"I am black and I have seen black hands...".
     I Have Seen Black Hands. Richard
     Wright. P90
"' I am busy,' said the sea". Day. Sir Cecil
     Spring-Rice. P51
"I am crawling out". Asking the Windows.
     Margo LaGattuta. P88
"I am fevered with the sunset". The Sea
     Gypsy. Richard Hovey. P81
"I am going to market". Marketing. E. J.
     Falconer. P51
"I am here". The Green Man. Kaleem Omar. P91
"I am here according to the logic". Goodboy.

Anton Shammas. P92
"' I am here flying my little star'.". Song
     of a Dead Pilot. Ahmad 'Abd Al-Muti
     Hijazi. P91
"I am ice if I am anything". Ice. Charles P.
     Martin. P58
"I am in love with the laughing sickness".
     Zizi's Lament. Gregory Corso. P85
"I am inside someone". An Agony. As Now.
     Amiri (LeRoi Jones) Baraka. P85
"I am like the fruit". Decaying. Jean Pape.
     P77
"I am living--my exile of cold and fog".
     Poem, fr. Iris Ifriqiya. Majid El
     Houssi. P91
"I am lonesome without you seeing me". For
     Laura. Myra Cohn Livingston. P50
"I am not a painter, I am a poet". Why I Am
     Not a Painter. Frank O'Hara. P85
"I am not cut to the size of these...".
     Suburbanitis. Grace D. Yerbury. P68
"I am not here". Moroccan Perfume. Virginia
     Golden. P72
"I am nothing". Will-O-the-Wisp. Colette
     Verger. P72
"I am one that, by God's will". Longing for
     Caernarfon. Sion Gruffudd. P87
"I am seated on a chair resting...".
     Respected Graves. David Ignatow. P64
"I am somewhere, in a deep forest". My
     Dream. Scott Gunther. P73
"I am staring at the moon". Revisiting
     Detroit. Karen Kania. P88
"I am the 'learning tree'". The Learning
     Tree. Dorothy Lyons. P72
"I am the blue print, the first draft". The
     First Draft. Kris Passantino. P74
"I am the cat of cats. I am". The Cat of
     Cats. William Brighty Rands. P90
"I am the ground". Mary: to Her Completed
     Child (A Song of Hope). Miriam F.
     Berks. P72
"I am the little New Year, ho, ho!.". The
     New Year. Unknown. P51
"I am the spirit of the morning sea". Ode.
     Richard Watson Gilder. P81
"I am thy grass, O Lord!.". Trust. Lizette
     Woodworth Reese. P81
"I am tired of work; I am tired...". Tired.
     Fenton Johnson. P82
"I am two fools, I know". The Triple Fool.
     John Donne. P59
"I am undone: there is no living, none".
     Love's Memory, from All's Well That
     Ends Well. William Shakespeare. P89
"I am watching them churn the last milk".
     The Mad Yak. Gregory Corso. P85
"I am, O pious priest, one ungodly one...".
     Ghazal. Jonaid. P92

"I arise from dreams of thee". Lines to an
      Indian Air. Percy Bysshe Shelley. P89
"I ask for God's favour, saviour of the
      folk". Praise of Tenby. Unknown. P87
"I asked the heaven of stars". Night Song at
      Amalfi. Sara Teasdale. P82
"I axe you sir, this paradox". Xerxes and
      Xanthippe. Caroline Knox. P63
"I beg my bones to be good but". The Poet.
      Lucille Clifton. P52
"I breathe immortal air". Introspection.
      Nikolai Hristozov. P70
"I bring fresh showers for the thirsting
      flowers". The Cloud. Percy Bysshe
      Shelley. P89
"I brought the Nyakuoth's to the Lak dance".
      Fishing for Girls with a Rod and Line.
      Kuek Taitai. P53
"I built a hut in a little wood". My Hut.
      Eileen Mathias. P51
"I call down God's protection--sure your
      gifts". Stanzas to the Lord Rhys ap
      Gruffudd, Prince of Deheubarth.
      Cynddelw Brydydd Mawr. P87
"I called out a cry". The Cry. Jamie
      Shepherd. P56
"I came alone into this life". Beyond
      Recall. Robert W. Johnston. P72
"I came to a choice city". Trouble at a
      Tavern. Dafydd ab [or ab] Gwilym. P87
"I came to meet the". The Autumn Sea. Tong-
      Choon Shin. P72
"I came to the crowded Inn of Earth". The
      Inn of Earth. Sara Teasdale. P82
"I can be myself always in your presence".
      Friends. Evelyn Sewell Rineer. P65
"I can see a picture". Pictures. F. Ann
      Elliott. P51
"I can use it". Song Picture No. 85.
      Unknown. P78
"I can't believe there's not". To John
      Ashbery. Frank O'Hara. P85
"I can't imagine why, or how". A Cow's Life.
      Bruce Bennett. P63
"I can't see into your eyes". On a Gestapo
      Photograph Purported To Be... F. W.
      Watt. P49
"I can't think of anything to write today".
      My Poetic Nature. Blythe Gillespie.
      P73
"I cannot ask you to paint the tops". Asylum,
      from Your Tired, Your Poor. Lisel
      Mueller. P88
"I cannot boast that I am doing a
      service...". On the Eve of Departure
      for Sixth World Congress... Yung-jung
      Lin. P72
"I cannot find my way: there is no star".
      Credo. Edward Arlington Robinson. P81

"I cannot say why". School Yard in Summer.
      T. A. Shulgin. P58
"I cannot skill of these thy ways". Justice
      (1). George Herbert. P59
"I caught a tremendous fish". The Fish.
      Elizabeth Bishop. P84
"I celebrate myself, and sing myself".
      Myself, from The Song of Myself. Walt
      Whitman. P90
"I cling and swing". The Fifteen Acres.
      James Stephens. P51
"I clutched at the coming year". The Rainbow
      Dared the Storm. Emma Crobaugh. P68
"I come from haunts of coot and hern". The
      Brook. Lord Tennyson. P51
"I come from nothing; but from where". The
      Modern Poet (A song of Deriviations).
      Alice Meynell. P90
"I come of a mighty race...". Hebrews. James
      Oppenheim. P82
"I come to thee at close of day". Evening
      Prayer. Carmen Boitel Adams. P72
"I could believe that I am here alone".
      Solipsism. George Santayana. P81
"I could love her with a love so warm". The
      World Is a Mighty Ogre. Fenton
      Johnson. P82
"I count the losses". Counting the Losses.
      Kandy Arnold. P58
"I count the sidewalk slits". Interior
      Dialogue. David Ignatow. P84
"I dance on your paper". Jack O' the Inkpot.
      Algernon Blackwood. P51
"I did not think that I should find them
      here". The Clerks. Edward Arlington
      Robinson. P81
"I didn't know". Blackout into Sunlight.
      Yaedi Ignatow. P64
"I didn't know, I didn't know". Oedipus in
      Criminal Court. Eileen Hillary. P68
"' I dine, I play a game of backgammon'.".
      David Hume. Donald Hall. P79
"I do not say to you, be rich". To a Young
      Man. Edwin Markham. P81
"I do not trust the grey and faithful dove".
      Naming the Birds. Jeanne Lohmann. P65
"I don't apologize for being hard to know".
      Listen. Dara D. Henderson. P73
"I don't forget head down". Awakening to
      Music. Fred Chappell. P67
"I don't have any place to come up through".
      Shaman Song, from Wolf Songs and
      Others of the Tlingit. Unknown. P78
"I don't show my work to anybody...".
      Monkhood. John Berryman. P79
"I don't understand by what perversity". A
      Shelf Is a Ledge. Gregory Orr. P85
"I dream I go out to dinner". Meat. Phebe
      Hanson. P88

"I dream of journeys repeatedly". The Far Field. Theodore Roethke. P84

"I dreamed of a tree". The Tree of the Sound of Silence. Greer Newcomb. P72

"I dreamed of love as only schoolgirls can". Come, Fill the Cup. Mary V. Traeger. P72

"I dreamed of time, that perfect clock". Dream. Salvadore J. Coppola. P72

"I dreamt about you last night". Dream. Unknown. P78

"I dwell in a lonely house I know". Ghost House. Robert Frost. P89

"I ee, children laugh like it's nothing". The Crocodile Scales. Moses Kuac Nyoat. P53

"I ee, I am the big bull, Deng Kuac Jiok". Don't Be Discouraged. Phillip Macar. P53

"I ee, my village, Deng". Foreigners with Teeth. Peter Pal Kong. P53

"I ee, this star was the war star". Its Eye Ran with Blood. Peter Pal Kong. P53

"I exalt the generous descendent of Aeneas". To Owain Gwynedd. Meilir ap Gwalchmai. P87

"I exalt the generous descendent of Rhodri". Battle of Tal y Moelfre. Meilir ap Gwalchmai. P87

"I feel a newer life in every gale". May. J. G. Percival. P51

"I feel that in the days gone by". In Days Gone By. Ida M. Mills. P51

"I fell to his mother's pink bed--.". I Blew up the Virgin of My Legs. Diego Maquieira. P71

"I felt as does the Christmas morning child". The Dust of Delos. Haywood Jackson. P68

"I find you in fortunate landing places". Cool with Sleeping Rivers. Salvatore Quasimodo. P61

"I found a dimpled spider, fat and white". Design. Robert Frost. P82

"I found a little brown purse". Found in the Woods. Irene F. Pawsey. P51

"I found a little fairy flute". Fairy Music. Enid Blyton. P51

"I freed the pampered shoots from plastic...". Middle Age Summer. Edward Butscher. P64

"I gather groups of freshmen...". 'These Students Couldn't Write Their Way...'. Ron Koertge. P63

"I gave to hope a watch of mine: but he". Hope. George Herbert. P59

"I gazed upon the glorious sky". June. William Cullen Bryant. P89

"I get more and more tangled in my fears".

Life. Georgi Belev. P70

"I get terribly annoyed by insects". Insects. Damaso Alonso. P61

"I go in under foliage". In Rain. Wendell Berry. P67

"I got me flowers to strew Thy way". Easter. George Herbert. P51

"I got one good look". Coon Song. Archie Randolph Ammons. P67

"I had a dream, which was not all a dream". Darkness. George Gordon, 6th Baron Byron. P48

"I had come to the house, in a cave of trees". Medusa. Louise Bogan. P83

"I had over-prepared the event". Villanelle: the Psychological Hour. Ezra Pound. P82

"I had to kick their law into their teeth...". Negro Hero. Gwendolyn Brooks. P84

"I have a dog". My Doggie. C. Nurton. P51

"I have a golden ball". A Rune of Riches. Florence Converse. P51

"I have a little house". My Little House. J. M. Westrup. P51

"I have a little shadow...". My Shadow. Robert Louis Stevenson. P89

"I have a neat little scrap of a house". Idle Robin. Unknown. P87

"I have a new umbrella". My New Umbrella. M. M. Hutchinson. P51

"I have a river in my mind". Six O'Clock. Owen Dodson. P84

"I have a secret way of steering". Columbus at Night. Maggie Helwig. P49

"I have a white dog". My Dog, Spot. Rodney Bennett. P51

"I have been here before". Sudden Light. Dante Gabriel Rossetti. P90

"I have been one acquainted with the night". Acquainted with the Night. Robert Frost. P82

"I have been thinking of being a guru". The City Mouse and the Country Mouse. Reed Whittemore. P63

"I have come to bury love". Buried Love. Sara Teasdale. P82

"I have got a new-born sister". Choosing a Name. Mary Lamb. P89

"I have had playmates, I have had companions". The Old Familiar Faces. Charles Lamb. P89

"I have had to learn the simplest things". Maximus, to Himself. Charles Olson. P85

"I have heard a mother bird". Welcome to Spring. Irene Thompson. P51

"I have kissed". Fenians All. Brian O'Riordan. P49

"I have known the silence of the stars...".
    Silence, from Spoon River Anthology.
    Edgar Lee Masters. P82
"I have known the strange nurses of
    kindness". But I Do Not Need Kindness.
    Gregory Corso. P85
"I have never seen him...". The People vs.
    The People. Kenneth Fearing. P83
"I have not been worried about you, I".
    Naphiri. Edison Mpina. P92
"I have seen a gentle, magnanimous girl".
    For a Girl. Cynddelw Brydydd Mawr. P87
"I have set a bread to rise". While Summer
    Stays. Margaret Longenecker Been. P68
"I have three simple eyes". The Maimed
    Grasshopper Speaks Up. Jean Garrigue.
    P84
"I haven't seen your face yet". Spring
    Steps. Chi Hsien. P72
"I hear a sudden cry of pain!.". The Snare.
    James Stephens. P51
"I hear along our street". Christmas Carols.
    Henry Wadsworth Longfellow. P51
"I hear in my heart, I hear in its ominous
    pulses". The Wild Ride. Louise Imogen
    Guiney. P81
"I hear leaves drinking rain". The Rain.
    William Henry Davies. P51
"I hear sheep running on the path...". The
    Sound of the Light. William Stanley
    Merwin. P52
"I hear the halting footsteps...". Harlem
    Shadows. Claude McKay. P82
"I hear the sound of ripening at the core".
    Sound of Ripening. Alice Mackenzie
    Swaim. P65
"I heard a bird at dawn". The Rivals. James
    Stephens. P51
"I heard a mouse". The Mouse. Elizabeth J.
    Coatsworth. P51
"I heard my love tell stories of the sea".
    The Way It All Was. Constance Pultz.
    P65
"I heard one who said: 'Verily". Cassandra.
    Edward Arlington Robinson. P81
"I heard the farm cocks crowing loud".
    Daybreak in a Garden. Siegfried
    Sassoon. P51
"I heard the snowflakes whisper...".
    Snowflakes. Ruth M. Arthur. P51
"I helped a little lame dog". My Little Dog.
    Pearl Forbes MacEwen. P51
"I hereby swear that to uphold your house".
    Sonnet 016, fr. One person. Elinor
    Wylie. P82
"I hope when Tuar's son goes to marry".
    White Girls. Phillip Macar Ruac. P53
"I hoped that he would love me". The Kiss.
    Sara Teasdale. P82

"I hung heedless on the edge". Since That
    Time. Ellin E. Carter. P56
"I implore my king, the hope of grace".
    Elegy. Cynddelw Brydydd Mawr. P87
"I keep running around". Song Picture No.
    56. Unknown. P78
"I knew a boy who took long walks". Stalky
    Jack. William Brighty Rands. P51
"I knew that I would miss you on these
    steps". Autumn Crocus. Helen Y. Luke.
    P77
"I knew the dignity of the words". My
    Grandfather's Funeral. James
    Applewhite. P67
"I knew the sea then, bird friendly...".
    Barefoot. Robert N. Scott. P68
"I knot their praises, for long centuries
    mute". The Catholic Martyrs. Waldo
    Williams. P87
"I know". Amaze. Adelaide Crapsey. P81
"I know a dog called Isaac". Three Dogs. E.
    C. Brereton. P51
"I know a funny little man". Mr. Nobody.
    Unknown. P51
"I know a garden with three strange gates".
    The Last Gate. E. Stella Mead. P51
"I know a little butterfly...". The
    Butterfly. Margaret Rose. P51
"I know a place that holds the sky". The
    Upside-Down World. Hamish Hendry. P51
"' I know a solemn secret...'.". The Elfin
    People Fill the Tubes. Winifred M.
    Letts. P51
"I know the hedge in Briar Lane". I Must
    Away. May Sarson. P51
"I know the ships that pass by day". The
    Lights. J. J. Bell. P51
"I know the sky will fall one day". Child's
    Song. Gerald Gould. P51
"I know thee. My name is Tom". Archaic Song
    of Dr. Tom the Shaman. Unknown. P78
"I know what I am doing here". Snowdrops.
    Nigel Jenkins. P54
"I know what I feel like". Changing. Mary
    Ann Hoberman. P50
"I know, blue modest violets". Violets.
    Unknown. P51
"I leapt until I was exhausted". The Old
    Fashioned Girls. Pilual Juoc. P53
"I left within September's soggy night:.".
    Bookends. James W. Proctor. P65
"I lie down in the short grass". Shooting
    Prairie Dogs. Linda M. Hasselstrom.
    P88
"I lie for a long time on my left side...".
    Dead Color. Charles Wright. P67
"I like blowing bubbles...". Things I Like.
    Marjorie H. Greenfield. P51
"' I like fish,' said the mermaid". Song,

sel. Elizabeth J. Coatsworth. P55
"I like living on a farm". Pride of the
    Farmer. Jeff Bence. P74
"I like the town on rainy nights". Rainy
    Nights. Irene Thompson. P51,P75
"I like to crawl around the house...".
    Cradle Songs, from Wolf Songs & Others
    of the Tlingit. Unknown. P78
"I like to find". Pleasures. Denise
    Levertov. P85
"I like to ride in a tramcar". Travelling.
    Dorothy Gradon. P51
"I like to see a thing I know". New Sights.
    Unknown. P51
"I like to think". Snowdrops. Mary Vivian.
    P51
"I like Tuesday". Tuesday. Alma Denny. P63
"I like Walt Whitman for his doughty beard".
    Position. Blas de Otero. P61
"I like wrestling with Herbie because".
    Wrestling. Kathleen Fraser. P50
"I live among the grasses". The Field-Mouse.
    Enid Blyton. P51
"I live for those who love me". What I Live
    For. George Linnaeus Banks. P89
"I live in a crystal body". The Plough Is
    Crooked. Abbas Athar. P91
"I live in the corner of the world...". A
    Biblical Motif. Boris Khristov. P92
"I live in the town". The Town Child. Irene
    Thompson. P51
"I loathed you, Spoon River...". Archibald
    Higbie, from Spoon River Anthology.
    Edgar Lee Masters. P82
"I look from one face". Love, from A Thai
    Divine Comedy. Montri Umavijani. P92
"I look into the mirror". Reflections. Shawn
    Ketchum. P73
"I look out over the sterile snow". World
    Breaking Apart. Louise Gluck. P85
"I look up from my homework and I see".
    Still Not Grown Up. Lisa May. P74
"I look upon the countryside". Adventure.
    Benjamin Miller. P73
"I looked out the window all night long".
    The Last Quarter of the Night. Gilani
    Kamran. P91
"I love all shining things". Shining Things.
    Elizabeth Gould. P51
"I love it, I love it! and who shall dare".
    The Old Arm-Chair. Eliza Cook. P89
"I love my little son, and yet when he is
    ill". The Two Parents. Christopher M.
    ("Hugh MacDiarmid") Grieve. P89
"I love the fitful gust that shakes".
    Autumn. John Clare. P51
"I love the little winding lanes". Lanes in
    Summer. Malcolm Hemphrey. P51
"I love the way Janie Crawford". Janie

Crawford. Alice Walker. P85
"I love to wander through the woodlands...".
    October. S. W. Whitman. P51
"I love you first because your face is
    fair". V-Letter. Karl Shapiro. P84
"I love you well, my steel-white dagger".
    Dagger. Mikhail Lermontov. P90
"I love you when you're". A La Apollinaire.
    Manuel Silva Acevedo. P71
"I love, and have some cause to love...".
    Delight in God. Francis Quarles. P89
"I loved him in my dawning years--.". A
    Life's Love. Unknown. P90
"I loved my friend". Poem. Langston Hughes.
    P50
"I made a posy, while the day ran by". Life.
    George Herbert. P59
"I made a wish". Wish... Oceana Feldman. P74
"I make a pact with you, Walt Whitman". A
    Pact. Ezra Pound. P82
"I make my shroud, but no one knows--.".
    Song. Adelaide Crapsey. P81
"I met a little elf-man once". The Little
    Elf-Man. John Kendrick Bangs. P51
"I met a man as I went walking". Puppy and
    I. A. A. Milne. P51
"I met a man mowing". Hay Harvest. Patrick
    R. Chalmers. P51
"I met death--he was a sportsman--on
    Cole's". Cole's Island. Charles Olson.
    P85
"I met Galuak at the dance". Strutting with
    My Rifle. Daniel Cuol Lul Wur. P53
"I met her on the dry plains of Samburu".
    Man Who Loved a Giraffe. Pyke Johnson
    Jr. P63
"I met my wife at the marathon". The Race.
    James Camp. P63
"I met you in a retirement home". Meeting a
    Lovely Lady. Maryleona Berg. P68
"I met Zelda Fitzgerald". Zelda. Geoff
    Fiorito. P58
"I must be mad, or very tired". Meeting-
    House Hill. Amy Lowell. P82
"I must have passed the crest a while ago".
    The Long Hill. Sara Teasdale. P82
"I never contemplate a quiet lake".
    Narcissus. Paul Little. P72
"I never feel the slightest guilt". Sponge.
    Maureen Cannon. P63
"I never knew my father". Pleiku. David
    Biles. P86
"I never played the Moor". Unfriendly
    Witness. George Starbuck. P85
"I never saw a moor". Heaven. Emily
    Dickinson. P89
"I never saw a purple cow". The Purple Cow.
    Gelett Burgess. P90
"I never saw her as she was". Old Woman

Doctor. Helen Bryant. P68
"I now think, love is rather deaf...". My
    Picture Left in Scotland. Ben Jonson.
    P59
"I offer you". Untitled. T. M. Raghuram. P72
"I often from America think of Clwb Gwerin
    Cefni". To the Poetry Clubs of Wales.
    Bobi Jones. P87
"I often see in ocean storms great white".
    As Sea Birds Sail. Mary Jane Barnes.
    P68
"I once had a fancy red fish". Swish.
    Christine Stratton. P73
"I only know writing". Writing, from A Thai
    Divine Comedy. Montri Umavijani. P92
"I open cans for lunch--.". Business
    Luncheon. Joel Ferree. P63
"I pick pennies up". Self Employment. Lowell
    E. Sargeant. P63
"I picked fresh mint". My Garden. Norah
    Hussey. P51
"I picked up a leaf". Les Etiquettes Jaunes.
    Frank O'Hara. P85
"I placed a jar in Tennessee". Anecdote of
    the Jar. Wallace Stevens. P83
"I praise a prince, lord of king's country".
    The Spoils of Annwn. Unknown. P87
"I praise, a rarity in these times". A
    Slender Book of Verse and It's
    Purchaser. F. C. Rosenberger. P63
"I promise you these days and an
    understanding". Tourist Death.
    Archibald MacLeish. P83
"I put my hat upon my head". A 4th Stanza
    for Dr. Johnson, Donald Hall... X. J.
    Kennedy. P63
"I recall that California yard...". A Sense
    of Place. Judith Minty. P88
"I remember a long night". Webs. Paul W.
    Tipton. P86
"I remember being born in the woods". Being
    Born in the Woods. Bob D'Costa. P72
"I ride the horse that is the sea". Song for
    a Surf-Rider. Sarah Van Alstyne Allen.
    P76
"I said:.". Scottsboro, too, Is Worth Its
    Song. Countee Cullen. P83
"I sat down upon the rocks". The Mouse.
    Becki Perkins. P74
"I saved my baby's tiny cradle bed". Grandma-
    in-Waiting. Betty Jane Simpson. P72
"I saw a brown squirrel to-day in the wood".
    Mr. Squirrel. V. M. Julian. P51
"I saw a cat on our welcome". Animals. Aki
    Raymer. P74
"I saw a dragon-fly with one wing caught".
    Dragon-Fly. Hyacinthe Hill. P65
"I saw a gnome". The Gnome. Harry Behn. P55
"I saw a mouth jeering...". Gargoyle. Carl

Sandburg. P82
"I saw a ship a-sailing". Romance. Gabriel
    Setoun. P51
"I saw a stately lady". The Stately Lady.
    Flora Sandstrom. P51
"I saw a thick green sheet of oil". The
    Stain. Pierre Jean Jouve. P61
"I saw envy". Envy. Naomi F. Faust. P72
"I saw eternity the other night". The World
    (1). Henry Vaughan. P59
"I saw her plucking cowslips". The Witch.
    Percy H. Ilott. P51
"I saw him dropping the oars crouch". The
    Beaches of Chile X. Raul Zurita. P71
"' I saw him kiss your cheek!...'.". Sly
    Thoughts. Coventry Patmore. P89
"I saw him once before". The Last Leaf.
    Oliver Wendell Holmes. P89
"I saw the farmer plough the field".
    Harvest. M. M. Hutchinson. P51
"I saw the first pear". Orchard. Hilda
    ("H.D."). Doolittle. P82
"I saw the hawk ride updraft in the
    sunset...". Mortal Limit. Robert Penn
    Warren. P67
"I saw the moon". Flying. J. M. Westrup. P51
"I saw the sky descending, black and white".
    Where the Rainbow Ends. Robert Lowell.
    P84
"I saw them kissing in the shade and knew".
    The Young Lovers, from The House of a
    Hundred Lights. (Frederick) Ridgely
    Torrence. P81
"I saw you toss the kites on high". The
    Wind. Robert Louis Stevenson. P51,P89
"I say goodbye to the city". Under Certain
    Circumstances. Walter Hoefler. P71
"' I scheme. You correct'.". Saint Mark,
    from Animated Film... James Reaney.
    P49
"I search everywhere upon this earth". A
    Shade for My Scarred Soul. William
    Zeller. P72
"I search the narrow winding road...". In
    Expectation (To John Paul). Marie G.
    Kent. P72
"I see now through a shrouding mist the
    face". Fallen Angel. Katherine A.
    Hogan. P65
"I see that the black clouds". Fair Weather.
    William Williams Pantycelyn. P87
"I see the horses of a funeral carriage".
    They've Broken the Most Delicate Bone
    in My Ear. Manuel Silva Acevedo. P71
"I see you cruel, you find me less than
    fair". On a Line from Sophocles.
    Carolyn Kizer. P79
"I shall cry God to give me a broken foot".
    Flash Crimson. Carl Sandburg. P82

"I shall discover you in those I love...".
Anoukis and Later Jeanne. Rene Char.
P61

"I shall never get you put together
entirely". The Colossus. Sylvia Plath.
P85

"I shall never know more of stone". Without
Voice, Without Hope. Jozsef Tornai.
P92

"I shall not try again to understand". The
Gain. Dorsha Hayes. P65

"I shall walk down the road". Death. Maxwell
Bodenheim. P82

"I share my kingdom in this golden land".
Massasoit. Mary Jane Barnes. P68

"I should be able to sit down". A Song for
T. S. Cristina Pina. P92

"I should be pleasing myself, you know".
Writing for Nora. Mark Jarman. P85

"I should be vigilant: the Sodomite". Job's
Turkey: a Commentary. Carl Judson
Launius. P63

"I should not forget". Tree on the Hill.
Ivan Tsanev. P70

"I should worry, I should care". I Love
Every Hair on Your Head. Alma Denny.
P63

"I sit here by my window". My Window, My
Wheelchair, and Me. Deborah D'Aleo.
P74

"I sit in my bright and sunny room". I
Dream. Janine A. Parry. P73

"I slept under rhododendron". Four Poems for
Robin. Gary Snyder. P85

"I slipped a thought into my heart".
'Sheaves in Winter'. James A. Hanf.
P65

"I sold good fruit". Epitaph for the Lemon
Lady. Bruce Bennett. P63

"I sometimes think". First Portrait. Sarmad
Sehbai. P91

"I sometimes think I'd like to be". The Best
of All. Margaret G. Rhodes. P51

"I sometimes think of suicide". The Dull
Image. Tony D'Arpino. P56

"I speak this poem now with grave and level
voice". Immortal Autumn. Archibald
MacLeish. P83

"I speak to the unbeautiful of this bird".
The Peacock. James Merrill. P85

"I sprang to the stirrup...". How They
Brought the Good News from Ghent to
Aix. Robert Browning. P90

"I stand here every afernoon". The Balloon
Man. E. Herbert. P51

"I stand on tiptoe to reach....". The
Window. Boris Khristov. P92

"I stand with Thoreau on the wooded shore".
Everyman's Walden. Ann Shermer. P65

"I stayed the night for shelter at a farm".
The Witch of Coos. Robert Frost. P82

"I still have some color and brightness to
my blood". Blood and Silence. Ahmad
'Abd Al-Muti Hijazi. P91

"I stole along through the dark". Night
Song. Arlo Bates. P81

"I stood in your April garden under a
maple". In the Garden of Your Words.
Margaret Flanagan Eicher. P65

"I stroke my frozen ears". Waiting for
Spring,..., from For the Desert
Island. Tae-ch'ul Shin. P92

"I struck the board, and cried, no more".
The Collar. George Herbert. P59

"I studied my tables over and over...". A
Mortifying Mistake. Anna Maria Pratt.
P89

"I stumble barefoot". Color the Day Blue.
Helen Lair. P72

"I switch on the porch light". Evening
Prayers. Wilma E. McDaniel. P72

"I talked to old Lem". Old Lem. Sterling A.
Brown. P89

"I think it must be lonely to be God". The
Preacher: Ruminates Behind the Sermon,
fr. A Street... Gwendolyn Brooks. P84

"I think mice". Mice. Rose Fyleman. P51

"I think of a man my son met". Theory. Dan
Murray. P64

"I think of Amundsen, enormously bit". On
the Eyes of an SS Officer. Richard
Wilbur. P84

"I think of her". Nelly Myers. Archie
Randolph Ammons. P67

"I think of my wife. And I think of Lot".
Marriage Couplet. William Cole. P63

"I thought". Reversal. Eleanore-Melissa. P68

"I thought all it took to cook Italian".
Some Italian!. Linda Monacelli
Johnson. P63

"I thought we knew the earth". 'Songs of
Apocalypse', sel. Nadya Aisenberg. P48

"I thought, once, that your hillshapes...".
Van Gogh. Charles Tomlinson. P48

"I touch you in the night, whose gift was
you". The Science of the Night.
Stanley Kunitz. P83

"I touched his scar, but". The Ugly Man.
Liliana Stefanova. P70

"I try to knead and spin, but my life is
low...". Irish Peasant Song. Louise
Imogen Guiney. P81

"I used to be a romantic animal...". Blue
Danube. Manuel Silva Acevedo. P71

"I used to make fun of you...". Song for the
Richest Woman in Wrangell, from
Wolf... Unknown. P78

"I visioned a planet". Canary Morning at the

Stop of Darkness. Emma Crobaugh. P68

"I wake in a tangle of sheets". June
    @!21/84* a Poem with Mistakes
    Included. Eli Mandel. P49

"I walk down the garden-paths". Patterns.
    Amy Lowell. P82

"I walk the steps". Untitled #2. Ian
    Brennan. P58

"I walking on my birthday met a young". For
    My Birthday, 1939. Paul Goodman. P84

"I wandered by the brookside". The
    Brookside. Richard Monckton Milnes;
    1st Baron Houghton. P89

"I wandered lonely as a cloud". Daffodils.
    William Wordsworth. P89

"I want an egg for Easter". An Egg for
    Easter. Irene F. Pawsey. P51

"I want to be a zookeeper". The Zookeeper.
    Jason Goode. P74

"I want to be liquid, I want". Hard to Say.
    Sheila Seiler. P56

"' I want to be new,' said the duckling".
    The New Duckling. Alfred Noyes. P51

"I want to go aboard my ship...". The Dream
    Ship. W. K. Holmes. P51

"I want to strip my house of walls".
    Earthbound. Bette Warden. P72

"I want to tell you in advance I eat". Two
    Women. Barbara Goldberg. P63

"I wanted". The Birth Poem. Sharon Berg. P49

"I wanted so ably". The World. Robert
    Creeley. P85

"I was a". Number 7. Doug Rawlings. P86

"I was a peasant girl from Germany". Elsa
    Wertman, from Spoon River Anthology.
    Edgar Lee Masters. P82

"I was far forward on the plain, the burning
    swamp ". The Little Girl with Bands on
    her Teeth. Genevieve Taggard. P83

"I was looking for the powerful...". Sixty-
    Six Poems for a Blackfoot Bundle.
    Unknown. P78

"I was mad and I was sad". The Telephone
    Call. Jack Prelutsky. P50

"I was out in my kayak". Spring Fjord.
    Unknown. P78

"I was reading". And Then. Prince Redcloud.
    P80

"I was set adrift". Observe:. Geoff Fiorito.
    P58

"I was the only child of Frances Harris...".
    Hamilton Greene, from Spoon River
    Anthology. Edgar Lee Masters. P82

"I was the sheep who loved to daydream".
    Wolves and Sheep, sels. Manuel Silva
    Acevedo. P71

"I was/I am". 295. i. Sindhu Ratna Kul
    Bhaskar. P72

"I watch the great clock". Again. Lyubomir
Levchev. P70

"I watch the Indians dancing to help the
    young...". New Mexican Mountain.
    Robinson Jeffers. P83

"I went there on Tuesdays". In the National
    Museum. John Tripp. P54

"I went to market and brought me a cat". An
    Old Rhyme. Unknown. P51

"I went to the dances at Chandlerville".
    Lucinda Matlock, from Spoon River
    Anthology. Edgar Lee Masters. P82

"I went to the Wood of Flowers". The Wood of
    Flowers. James Stephens. P51

"I went to turn the grass once after one".
    The Tuft of Flowers. Robert Frost. P82

"I went up and down the streets". Doc Hill,
    from Spoon River Anthology. Edgar Lee
    Masters. P82

"I went up one pair of stairs". Just Like
    me. Unknown. P51

"I will arise and go now, and go to
    Innisfree". The Lake Isle of
    Innisfree. William Butler Yeats. P89

"I will be the gladdest thing". Afternoon on
    a Hill. Edna St. Vincent Millay. P51

"I will do something". Snails in the Grass.
    Nyalual Pal. P53

"I will exist today". Untitled #1. Kevin
    Cline. P58

"I will make you brooches and toys...". The
    Song of a Traveller. Robert Louis
    Stevenson. P51

"I will not abandon you". Alone: Genesis.
    Karen Kania. P88

"I will not let you say a woman's part". A
    Woman's Answer. Adelaide Anne Procter.
    P89

"I will teach you townspeople". Tract.
    William Carlos Williams. P82

"I wish I could cage her". Skunk. Will
    Staple. P77

"I wish I could have been there". An Indian
    Grandaughter's Wish. Molly White. P73

"I wish I had an aeroplane". A Penny Wish.
    Irene Thompson. P51

"I wish I lived in a caravan". The Pedlar's
    Caravan. William Brighty Rands. P51

"I wish I were an Emperor". Wishes. F.
    Rogers. P51

"I wish, how I wish that I had a little
    house". The Shiny Little House. Nancy
    M. Hayes. P51

"I withdraw; the shade". A Buried One in Me
    Sings. Salvatore Quasimodo. P61

""I won't go with you. I want to stay...".".
    My Last Afternoon with Uncle Devereux
    Winslow. Robert Lowell. P84

"I won't see you any more". A Good-by. Alain
    Bosquet. P61

"I wonder by my troth, what thou, and I".
The Good Morrow. John Donne. P59
"I wonder did the violets bloom". Loveliness
Destroyed. Agnes Finch Whitacre. P72
"I wonder now, sitting outside". Belabored
Blossom. M. Yvette Hamilton. P56
"I wonder to whom do atheists plead". In
Wonderment. Maria E. Boynton. P72
"I wonder what my kite can see". The Kite.
Pearl Forbes MacEwen. P51
"I wonder when". What Happened?. Mary Ann
Lowry. P72
"I would have thouhgt". Unpleasant Surprise.
Jay Dougherty. P63
"I would to God I were quenched and fed".
The Anguish. Edna St. Vincent Millay.
P82
I'd Chose To Be a Daisy. Unknown. P51
I'd Like To Be a Lighthouse. Rachel (Lyman)
Field. P76
I'd Love To Be a Fairy's Child. Robert
Graves. P51
"I'd a gem in that son there--.". Death of
Sion y Glyn. Lewis Glyn Cothi. P87
"I'd been away from her for three years...".
The Faithful Lovers. Unknown. P89
"I'd like to knock". Against Waking Early.
Bruce Bennett. P63
"I'd like to live a slower life". The
Weather. John Newlove. P49
"I'd like to peddle toy balloons". The
Balloon Seller. Elizabeth Fleming. P51
"I'd love to give a party". A Wish.
Elizabeth Gould. P51
"I'd run about". Her Elegy. Unknown. P78
"I'd send her sweets to celebrate". Lucky
Dilemma. Ned Pastor. P63
"I'd serve whatever time in hell". Bitter
Grapes. Bruce Berger. P63
"I'd sit inside the abandoned shack...".
About a Year After He Got Married He
Would Sit Alone... James Whitehead.
P67
"I'll do what the raids suggest". A Boy.
John Ashbery. P85
"I'll not break with Morfudd, dear wings of
love". Morfudd. Dafydd ab [or ab]
Gwilym. P87
"I'll shoot a little bird for little
brother". Cradle Songs, from Wolf
Songs & Others of the Tlingit.
Unknown. P78
"I'll sing a little song". My Whisper.
Unknown. P61
"I'll take no tack". Last Laugh. M. P. A.
Sheaffer. P68
"I'll test my power". Song Picture No. 82.
Unknown. P78
I'm a Texan Now. Gene Fehler. P63

"I'm Gonna Die & Won't See You...," from
Wolf Songs... Unknown. P78
I'm Happy. Mark Carlson. P73
I'm Lying on the Bed at a Motel and...
Tetsuo Nakagami. P92
"I'm a dark citizen". Anonymous Biography.
Armando Rubio. P71
"I'm a pretty little thing". The Field
Daisy. Jane Taylor. P51
"I'm a senior citizen and doctor". The Day
Willis Harder Didn't Kill His Beagle.
Hilary Russell. P63
"I'm at Yaddo sheltering myself...". Name-
Dropping. Robert Sward. P49
"I'm but an ailing poet". The Lover's Hope.
Salbri Powel. P87
"I'm coming back, oh dearest mother". Dear
Mother. Henry Bloes. P72
"I'm giving a party to-morrow at three". My
Party. Queenie Scott-Hopper. P51
"I'm glad our house is a little house". Song
for a Little House. Christopher
Morley. P51
"I'm going home like a section line road".
The Poet Falls in Love with a Cowboy.
Linda M. Hasselstrom. P88
"I'm going to bring you something".
Conversations in Mayan. Alonzo
Gonzales Mo. P78
"I'm gonna marry my brother's wife". Cradle
Songs, from Wolf Songs & Others of the
Tlingit. Unknown. P78
"I'm gonna tell you how your great love".
Your Great Love. Diego Maquieira. P71
"I'm hungry, oh so hungry!.". The Birds on
the School Windowsill. Evelyn Dainty.
P51
"I'm living in a cave". Song Picture No. 58.
Unknown. P78
"I'm makin'a road". Florida Road Workers.
Langston Hughes. P83
"I'm more the nomad than the ritualist who".
The Nomad. John Stevens Wade. P68
"I'm music man". Harmony. John A. Downes.
P72
"I'm sitting on the stile, Mary". Lament of
the Irish Emigrant. Helen Selina
Sheridan; Lady Dufferin. P89
"I'm sorry, mom, that I ran away". Runaway.
Jerri DuBose. P74
"I'm the pert little pimpernel". Pimpernel.
Charlotte Druitt Cole. P51
"I'm the virgin of tyranny...". They Dragged
Me Out by My Face. Diego Maquieira.
P71
"I've brought you nuts and hops". October.
Christina Georgina Rossetti. P51
"I've built a castle in the sand". Castles
in the Sand. Dorothy Baker. P51

"I've dug up all my garden". Sowing Seeds. Ursula Cornwall. P51
"I've got a bow and arrow". Robin Hood. Rachel MacAndrew. P51
"I've got a lovely home". Best of All. J. M. Westrup. P51
"I've got a pony". The Pony. Rachel MacAndrew. P51
"I've kept a haughty heart thro' grief...". To My Mother. Heinrich Heine. P89
"I've kissed the blarney stone". Expediency. Jean Gowan Near. P72
"I've known rivers:.". The Negro Speaks of Rivers. Langston Hughes. P83
"I've learned to love between bars". A Kind of Song. Aristoteles Espana. P71
"I've put the deathbed frown behind me". Recovery Song. Barry Wallenstein. P57
"I've questioned myself...". An Only Child. Robert ab Gwilym Ddu. P87
"I've seen a dope addict mother". Melissa's Song. Phil Cohen. P72
"I've seen caravans". Caravan. Irene Thompson. P51
"I've spent my years collecting...". Possession Report. Betty Fukuyama. P65
"I've stayed in the front yard all my life". A Song in the Front Yard, fr. A Street in Bronzeville. Gwendolyn Brooks. P84
"I've yet to see". Nuthatch. Edward Coletti. P63
I, fr. Irradiations. John Gould Fletcher. P82
I, Golden Strings. Alice M. Boughtwood. P68
I, Maximus of Gloucester, to You. Charles Olson. P85
I, Poet. G. Soundararaj. P72
I, Prometheus. Edward L. Meyerson. P68
"I, too, dislike it: there are things that are...". Poetry. Marianne Moore. P83
"I, too, sing America". Epilogue. Langston Hughes. P83
"' I,' said the duck. 'I call it fun'.". Who Likes the Rain?. Unknown. P51
I-35, South of Waco. William Virgil Davis. P63
"I/Am Outside". Outside. Lilian Moore. P75
"I/Laid". Pale Like Sunshine Music. James Richard Hurst. P68
"I/Walked on the whitened sand". Whitened Sand. James Richard Hurst. P68
"I: Van Gogh/Well, he lived among us...". Two Painters. Lyubomir Nikolov. P70
Ice
    Fool's Fingers. Roland Mathias. P54
Ice. Charles P. Martin. P58
    Melting. Judy Little. P88
The Ice Cream Parlor Romance. David Ignatow. P84

Ice Skaters. John Gracen Brown. P68
"Ice had many sons...". How Stump Stood in the Winter. David Wagoner. P57
Icebergs
    The Imaginary Iceberg. Elizabeth Bishop. P84
"Ich wes in one sumer dale". The Owl and the Nightingale, sels. Unknown. P66
Iddings, Kathleen
    Summer Vacation. P72
The Idea of Ancestry. Etheridge Knight. P67
The Idea of Order at Key West. Wallace Stevens. P83
Identified Flying Objects. Joseph Cherwinski. P68
Identities. Al Young. P85
Identity
    After the War. Jack Apsche. P86
    Apology of a Genius. Mina Loy. P82
    Bureaucrat. Lyubomir Levchev. P70
    The Distance. Khalilur Rahman Azmi. P91
Identity. May Duhameaux. P72
    Etchings in Meaning. Grace D. Yerbury. P72
    Fable of First Person. Gyorgy Somlyo. P92
    The Frog and the Bird. Vera Hessey. P51
    Ghazal. Jonaid. P92
    Goodboy. Anton Shammas. P92
    The Hollow Men. Thomas Stearns Eliot. P83
    I Blew up the Virgin of My Legs. Diego Maquieira. P71
    Identities. Al Young. P85
    Identity. May Duhameaux. P72
    Maximus, to Himself. Charles Olson. P85
    The New Duckling. Alfred Noyes. P51
    Ode. Richard Watson Gilder. P81
    Piazza. John Crowe Ransom. P83
    The Plough Is Crooked. Abbas Athar. P91
    Spending the Woodpile Well Into June. Jean Pape. P77
    The Stranger. Adrienne Rich. P85
    Superego Dictatorship. Kenneth Lynn. P72
    295. i. Sindhu Ratna Kul Bhaskar. P72
    The Venetian Blind. Randall Jarrell. P84
"Idiot droplets slide". Glass Lady. Virginia M. Hahn. P58
Idle Robin. Unknown. P87
The Idlers. Edmund Blunden. P51
Idols of Love. Edward A. Gloeggler. P65
Idyll. Frederika Blankner. P65
If. P. A. Ropes. P51
If. Alice Todd. P51
"If All the Seas Were One Sea". Unknown. P51
"If He Is Not Your Lover". Unknown. P62
"If He Is Not Your Lover, Oh Friend". Unknown. P62
"If Her Eyes Are Not Half Shut". Unknown. P62
If I Am Your Daughter. Pearl Newton Rook.

P68
If I Could Control the Weather. Desiree Van
Til. P73
If I Could Only Live at the Pitch That Is
Near Madness. Richard Eberhart. P83
"If I Found Pity". Re Enzo. P69
If I Had But Two Little Wings. Samuel Taylor
Coleridge. P51
If I Should Cast Off This Tattered Coat.
Stephen Crane. P81
If I Swallowed. Perry Brass. P65
If I Were a Pig. Elizabeth Fleming. P51
If I Were an Apple. Unknown. P51
If It Be True That Any Beauteous Thing.
Michelangelo Buonarroti. P89
If Love Loves. Stephen Crane. P81
If Only. Dale Maria Pacileo Feldman. P72
"If People Get Angry, Let Them, If They
Carry On...". Unknown. P62
"If all the world and love were young". The
Nymph's Reply. Sir Walter Raleigh. P89
"If Amoret, that glorious eye". To Amoret,
Walking in a Starry Evening. Henry
Vaughan. P59
"If any have a stone to shy". The Pebble.
Elinor Wylie. P82
"If ever I am old, and all alone". On the
Night of a Friend's Wedding. Edward
Arlington Robinson. P81
"If every man's internal care". Without and
Within. Pietro Metastasio. P90
"If everybody had a horse". The Stones of
Florence. Bruce Bennett. P63
"If I could be a gipsy-boy". The Caravan.
Madeleine Nightingale. P51
"If I could climb the garden wall". There--.
Rodney Bennett. P51
"If I don't take anything to the party...".
Cradle Songs, from Wolf Songs & Others
of the Tlingit. Unknown. P78
"If I had lived in Bethlehem". And Who Am I.
Opal Jane O'Neal. P72
"If I have found a holiness to trust".
Love's Blasphemy. Fran Swarbrick. P65
"If I mention it twice, I'm nagging". Better
Refrain. Marian Gleason. P63
"If I must die". Youth. George Cabot Lodge.
P81
"If I return to your stream". Heraclitus.
Juan Cameron. P71
"If I take an acorn". If. Alice Todd. P51
"If I were". Rain. Brian Winter. P73
"If I were a mouse". The Furry Home. J. M.
Westrup. P51
"If I were in a fairy tale". The Duck. Edith
King. P51
"If I were oh, so very small". If. P. A.
Ropes. P51
"If I were told that I must die to-morrow".

When. Sarah Wollsey. P89
"If I were you I'd just forget it". A
Plaguey Thing. Vonna Adrian. P63
"If in your confusion". Animula. David
Wevill. P49
"If it". The Guarded Wound. Adelaide
Crapsey. P81
"' If it stops raining'.". I'm Lying on the
Bed at a Motel and... Tetsuo Nakagami.
P92
"If Lady Godiva had cut off". Coup de Grace.
Mildred Luton. P63
"If love were not so wicked". Maiden.
Frederika Blankner. P65
"If love were what the rose is". A Match.
Algernon Charles Swinburne. P89
"If market trends can be believed". Yuppies
vs. Nopies. Ned Pastor. P63
"If my head is numb". At the Shore. Harvey
Shapiro. P64
"If nature says to you". The Daily Grind.
Fenton Johnson. P82
"If on the day of Hallowe'en". Yarrow.
Margaret Drake Elliot. P72
"If only love's recall could endure". The
Silver Shadows. Richard Schade. P72
"' If only you bade me farewell at the
airport'.". A Song from Afar. Ahmad
'Abd Al-Muti Hijazi. P91
"If stores of dry and learned lore we gain".
The Memory of the Heart. Daniel
Webster. P89
"If the Traveller Were to Go". Unknown. P62
If There Is a Witness. Stephen Crane. P81
"If There Is Someone Above," from Crow
Versions. Double-Face. P78
If They Come in the Night. Marge Piercy. P52
If This Be Love. Alice Morrey Bailey. P65
"If We Have Seen What We Are Meant to See".
Ruth Hoppin. P72
If We Must Die. Claude McKay. P82
"If You Are Not His Beloved". Unknown. P62
"If You Really Love Me...," from Kiowa '49'
Songs. Unknown. P78
If You See a Fairy Ring. Unknown. P51
If You'd Died, I Would've Cut Off My Hair,
"from Wolf... Unknown. P78
"If the butterfly courted the bee".
Topsyturvey-World. William Brighty
Rands. P90
"If the red slayer think he slays". Brahma.
Ralph Waldo Emerson. P89
"If there comes a time to raise anchor from
time...". Silent Ship. Yahya Kemal.
P91
"If there were dreams to sell". Dream
Pedlary. Thomas Lovell Beddoes. P51
"If they". Semper Paratus: to the Graduating
Class. Doug Rawlings. P86

"If thou dost bid thy friend farewell".
    Parting. Coventry Patmore. P89
"If to be absent were to be". To Lucasta,
    Going Beyond the Seas. Richard
    Lovelace. P59
"If we call". Goodbye! Amiri (LeRoi Jones)
    Baraka. P85
"If when my wife is sleeping". Danse Russe.
    William Carlos Williams. P82
"If you find a paddling pool". The Paddling
    Pool. E. H. Adams. P51
"If you go a-picnicking...". Picnics.
    Unknown. P51
"If you should bid me make a choice". The
    Windmill. E. V. Lucas. P51
"If you should chance to meet a cow". Bovine
    Town. Mildred Luton. P63
"If you smoked a pipe". An Old Fashioned
    Pipe. Kathryn G. Hansen. P51
"If you were an Eskimo baby". An Eskimo
    Baby. Lucy Diamond. P51
"If your arms and legs". Survivor's Manual.
    Doug Rawlings. P86
"If, as they say, you're a fool". A Beauty.
    Unknown. P87
Ifriqiyad/Alternatives, sels. Majid El
    Houssi. P91
Ignatow, David
    Autumn. P64
    Behind His Eyes. P64
    Bowery. P84
    A Cloud Creates. P64
    The Doctor. P84
    Epilogue for FDR. P84
    The Ice Cream Parlor Romance. P84
    Interior Dialogue. P84
    Leaving the Door Open (1), sel. P64
    Leaving the Door Open (31), sel. P64
    Little Friend. P64
    Marriage. P84
    My Own House. P64
    The Outlaw. P84
    The Poet Is a Hospital Clerk. P84
    Respected Graves. P64
Ignatow, Yaedi
    Blackout into Sunlight. P64
    Equations. P64
    Forest. P64
    Limbo. P64
    The Offer. P64
    Praise. P64
Ignorance
    Cassandra. Edward Arlington Robinson. P81
Iguazu. Jules Supervielle. P61
II, fr. Irradiations. John Gould Fletcher.
    P82
III, fr. Irradiations. John Gould Fletcher.
    P82
Ikan, Ron

    Darlene Friendship's Boyfriend. P63
Iliff, Shane
    Day Into Night. P74
Illness
    Coma. Liane Heller. P49
    The Guarded Wound. Adelaide Crapsey. P81
    On the Beach in Puerto Rico. Jones. P49
    Orpingalik's Song: In a Time a Sickness.
        Unknown. P78
    The Stroke. Christopher Fahy. P57
    Temperature, Temperature. Tracy Campbell.
        P74
    Virus. Roberta Mendel. P56
The Illusion II. Jeffrey Adam Sager. P72
The Illusion. William Everson. P84
Illusions
    Behold, from the Land of the Farther
        Suns. Stephen Crane. P81
    Do You Traipse Long-Leggedly Through
        Murky Woodlands. Caroline Knox. P88
    The Dull Image. Tony D'Arpino. P56
    For My Daughter. Weldon Kees. P84
    The Illusion. William Everson. P84
    A Man Saw a Ball of Gold. Stephen Crane.
        P81
    Second Portrait. Sarmad Sehbai. P91
Ilott, Percy H.
    The Witch. P51
The Image Repetition. Douglas Barbour. P49
The Image-Maker. Stanley Kunitz. P52
The Image. Mary B. Finn. P68
Images. Pieter D. Williams. P68
Images of Gravity. Grace Schulman. P64
Images on the Beach. Elsa Cross. P92
The Imaginary Iceberg. Elizabeth Bishop. P84
Imagination
    Always, from My First Boyhood. John Peale
        Bishop. P83
    At the Beach. Sandra Liatsos. P76
    Burnished. Anne Stevenson. P54
    Corner. Gonzalo Millan. P71
    The Dreamer. Christina Leighty. P74
    The Dreamer. Daniel Self. P74
    Endless Thought. Ashley Schmidt. P73
    Grandma's Attic. Camille Marksberry. P74
    I See Someone (To My Mother, 'Indira
        Devi'). Murall Patibandla. P72
    Just Imagine... Geeta Isardas. P74
    The Land of Counterpane. Robert Louis
        Stevenson. P89
    The Land of Story-Books. Robert Louis
        Stevenson. P89
    Making Beasts. Gregory Orr. P85
    Meeting-House Hill. Amy Lowell. P82
    My Fantasy. Kim Sherry. P73
    My Lamp. Elizabeth Osborne. P74
    Perception. Jude Theriot. P74
    "light Drops in Ledge Pools". Jeff
        Jones. P77

IMagination
    Sunlight Is Imagination. Richard Wilbur.
        P84
Imagination
    There Is a Backyard. Haywood Jackson. P68
    What Sparks My Imagination. Amy Rojek.
        P74
"Imagine if the whole world tried". Just
    Imagine... Geeta Isardas. P74
Imitation Is the Sincerest Flattery, But...
    Blossom S. Kirschenbaum. P63
"Immense infant, imperceptibly rocking".
    Tanker. Virginia M. Hahn. P58
Immigration and Emigration
    The Man from Leipzig. Clemente Riedemann.
        P71
    Prospective Immigrants Please Note.
        Adrienne Rich. P85
Immortal Autumn. Archibald MacLeish. P83
The Immortal. Hugh Seidman. P64
Immortality
    Beyond Recall. Robert W. Johnston. P72
    Credo. Edward Arlington Robinson. P81
    Davis Matlock, from Spoon River
        Anthology. Edgar Lee Masters. P82
    Easter Day. Richard Crashaw. P59
    The Evening Watch. Henry Vaughan. P59
    Footprints on the Glacier. William
        Stanley Merwin. P85
    Histrion. Ezra Pound. P82
    'Joy of My Life! While Left Me Here'.
        Henry Vaughan. P59
    The Klondike. Edward Arlington Robinson.
        P81
    A Man Said to the Universe. Stephen
        Crane. P81
    New Moon or No?. Maryann Calendrille. P64
    Phryne. Anita Jepsen. P68
    Quickness. Henry Vaughan. P59
    Red Kite. Philip Appleman. P64
    The Steamboat Bertrand. Gloria A. Martin.
        P68
    'They Are All Gone into the World of
        Light!'. Henry Vaughan. P59
    Time. George Herbert. P59
    To - ("Music, when soft voices"). Percy
        Bysshe Shelley. P90
    The Village Atheist, from Spoon River
        Anthology. Edgar Lee Masters. P82
    Virtue. George Herbert. P59
    The Water-Fall. Henry Vaughan. P59
    Your Leaving Me. Manjushree. P72
The Impact of a Dollar. Stephen Crane. P81
Imperfect Preterite. Juan Cameron. P71
Imperialism
    The Tree of the World. Clemente
        Riedemann. P71
The Impossible Choices. William Everson. P84
Impotence

    To a Fringed Genital. G. N. Gabbard. P63
"Impressed with distortion". The Bat. Robert
    Hahn. P58
"Imprinting hopping beauty". Squirrel. K. V.
    S. Murti. P72
Impulsive Dialogue. Maxwell Bodenheim. P82
"Impulsive look of ordinary lovers". Small
    Wedding. Lisa Grenelle. P65
In a Bird Sanctuary. Richard Wilbur. P84
In a City Garden. Trumbull Stickney. P81
In a Country Hospital. Anne Porter. P64
"In a Forest Region There Might Occur a
    Crooked Tree". Unknown. P62
"In a Grove by the Godavari River, a
    Monkey". Unknown. P62
In a Lonely Place. Stephen Crane. P81,Old
    Age
In a Lovely Garden Walking. Johann Ludwig
    Uhland. P89
In a Stalled Van. Taufiq Rafat. P91
In a Station of the IRT. F. F. Burch. P63
In a Station of the Metro. Ezra Pound. P82
In Ampezzo. Trumbull Stickney. P81
In Bed, sels. Kenneth Koch. P85
In Class We Create Ourselves-Having Been
    Told... P. K. Page. P49
In Days Gone By. Ida M. Mills. P51
In Distrust of Merits. Marianne Moore. P83
In Expectation (To John Paul). Marie G.
    Kent. P72
In February. P. A. Ropes. P51
In Fields of Summer. Galway Kinnell. P85
In Front of the Cave. Nikolai Hristozov. P70
In Heaven. Stephen Crane. P81
In Her Kitchen. Mark Milotich. P56
In His Old Age and Blindness. Guto'r Glyn.
    P87
"In Its Last Hours, the Mind of a Great
    Man". Unknown. P62
In January. James Schuyler. P64
In May. Unknown. P51
In Memoriam. R. Williams Parry. P87
In Memory of an English Professor. Reed
    Whittemore. P63
In Memory of Colonel Charles Young. Countee
    Cullen. P83
In Memory of Radio. Amiri (LeRoi Jones)
    Baraka. P85
In My Garden. Unknown. P51
In November in Mesilla. Peter E. Maas. P56
In Praise of Sobriety. John Frederick Nims.
    P63
In Rain. Wendell Berry. P67
"In Separation, an Unfaithful Woman Is Like
    Poison". Unknown. P62
"In Spring I Look Gay". Unknown. P51
In Springtime. Samuel Taylor Coleridge. P51
In Summer. Trumbull Stickney. P81
"In a box". Archeology. Virginia M. Hahn.

P58

"In a dark hour, tasting the earth". Tasting the Earth. James Oppenheim. P82

"In a dear little home of tarpaulin and boards". No Thoroughfare. Ruth Holmes. P51

"In a dear little vine covered cottage". The Boy Who Killed His Mother. F. Scott Fitzgerald. P63

"In a dirty old house lived a dirty old man". The Dirty Old Man. William Allingham. P90

"In a dream I returned to the river of bees". The River of Bees. William Stanley Merwin. P85

"In a motor boat in dark water". Poets. Bozhidar Bozhilov. P70

"In a room on west tenth street....". Fate. Kenneth Koch. P64

"In a scented wood". The Night. Helen Leuty. P51

"In a small chamber, friendless and unseen". William Lloyd Garrison. James Russell Lowell. P90

"In a somer sesun whon softe was the sonne". Piers Plowman, sels. Unknown. P66

"In a strange, unclamorous host, the dead". In Memoriam. R. Williams Parry. P87

"In a vision". Perception. Jude Theriot. P74

"In all the town of Malibu". Social Zoology: Prep for a Field Trip. Gary Pittenger. P63

"In America, riding to hounds". Tallyho the Fox. Louis Hasley. P63

"In April". The Cuckoo. Unknown. P51

"In autumn". View from Autumn. Jerry Saxton. P72

"In build, the worker bee is weak". The Cost of a Sting. X. J. Kennedy. P63

"In burnt out leaves". A Strange Man. Wazir Agha. P91

"In diamond height on". High on a Hill. A. D. Winans. P56

"In Disneyland, you have to search". The Wonderful World. Robert D. Sutherland. P63

"In Dover too did Kubla Khan". Tunnel Vision. David Cram. P63

"In dreams I hear the songs I cannot hear". Songs of Our Cells. Grace Schulman. P64

"In early days methought that all must last". Unchanging. Friedrich Martin von Bodenstedt. P89

"In emerald green waters". Movement, Their Way. Charlotte L. Babicky. P72

"In England from the train you see". From the Train. Marjorie Wilson. P51

"In fall, we'd hear the peepers call...".

The Gathering. Jack Conway. P56

"In green shadows, leaning". June. Dan Murray. P64

"In halls of sleep you wandered by". Among Shadows. Arthur Davidson Ficke. P82

"In June, amid the golden fields". The Groundhog. Richard Eberhart. P83

"In Kyoto's rooftop". In the Restaurant Polar. John N. Morris. P79

"In Larch Wood". Larch Wood Secrets. Ivy O. Eastwick. P51

"In late winter". The Bear. Galway Kinnell. P85

"In living, as in music". Financial Note. John D. Engle Jr. P63

"In March the gentle zephyrs blow". Beware the Tides of March. Charles L. Grove. P63

"In me is a little painted square". Old Age. Maxwell Bodenheim. P82

"In my father's bedroom". Father's Bedroom. Robert Lowell. P84

"In my garden grows a tree". The Apple Rhyme. Madeleine Nightingale. P51

"In my grandmother's house...". A Story About Chicken Soup. Louis Simpson. P85

"In my grandparent's home the weekly treat". Native Ground. Robert Minhinnick. P54

"In my hometown there is a slaughterhouse", A Stone Tablet for Animal Ghosts, from My Hometown's... Wu Cheng. P92

"In my land there are no distinctions". Poem for the Young White Man Who Asked Me... Lorna Dee Cervantes. P85

"In nineteenfourteen". Twenty Million, from Lost Youth: the Last War. Alfred Kreymborg. P82

"In November it is desolate, and distant". At Bosherston Ponds. John Tripp. P54

"In November, in the days to remember the dead". St. Malachy. Thomas Merton. P84

"In order to face the sky I need a face". The Face. Jules Supervielle. P61

"In ordinary houses". Handling it--. Edith Freund. P88

"In paper case". Epitaph on a Dormouse, Which Some Children... Unknown. P90

"' In quatrains, single rhymes can serve'.". On the Rhyming of Four-Line Verses. J. F. O'Connor. P63

"In Saint Luke's Gospel we are told". The Sifting of Peter. Henry Wadsworth Longfellow. P89

"In small green cup an acorn grew". The Acorn. Unknown. P51

"In southern Chinese". Poem Found While I Looked for Something Else. Joseph DeRoller. P63

"In spheres afar". Void. Krishna Srinivas.

P72

"In summer elms are made for me". Dilemma of the Elm. Genevieve Taggard. P83

"In summer I am very glad". Playgrounds. Laurence Alma-Tadema. P51

"In summer when the woods are green". In the Fair Forest. Unknown. P51

"In temples big and small". Haein-Sa Temple. Cho Byung-Hwa. P72

"In ten years the bitterness". War. Paul W. Tipton. P86

In the April Rain. Mary Anderson. P51

"In the Autumn, the Water of a Great Lake". Unknown. P62

"In the Belly of the Weeping Cloud-Bull". Unknown. P62

In the Big Country Dreams Stay Alive. Maryann Calendrille. P64

In the Center of the Bedroom. Oscar Hahn. P71

In the Desert. Stephen Crane. P81

In the Dordogne. John Peale Bishop. P83

In the Dream's Recess. William Everson. P84

"In the Evening Give Homage". Unknown. P62

In the Fair Forest. Unknown. P51

In the Field, Treasure. Anita Skeen. P88

In the Footsteps of Ghengis Khan. Jan Barry. P86

In the Garden of Your Words. Margaret Flanagan Eicher. P65

In the Midst. Joanne Stevens Sullivan. P72

In the Mirror. Elizabeth Fleming. P51

"In the Month of February". Unknown. P51

"In the Morning He Came For Me". Jack Hill. P86

In the Naked Bed, in Plato's Cave. Delmore Schwartz. P84

In the Name of Progress. William F. Landgraf. P72

In the National Museum. John Tripp. P54

In the Night. Stephen Crane. P81

In the Pitch of the Night. Lee Bennett Hopkins. P55

In the Restaurant Polar. John N. Morris. P79

In the Sense of Death. Salvatore Quasimodo. P61

"In the Sun Here". Shelly A. Allen. P77

In the Thickness. Phillipe Denis. P92

"In the Town Are Many Youths". Unknown. P62

In the Train. James ("B.V.") Thomson. P51

In the Ward: the Sacred Wood. Randall Jarrell. P84

In the Willow Branches. Salvatore Quasimodo. P61

In the Wood. Eileen Mathias. P51

In the Woods. Dorothy Baker. P51

In the Woods in Spring. Raymond Kresensky. P68

In This Age of Hard Trying, Nonchalance Is

Good And. Marianne Moore. P83

"In This Whole Wide Earth". Unknown. P62

In Traffic. Howard Moss. P64

In Two Fields. Waldo Williams. P87

In Wonderment. Maria E. Boynton. P72

"In Youth, Oh Daughter, You Are Like a Full River". Unknown. P62

"In the air the wind is everything". Alar. Virginia M. Hahn. P58

"In the belly of the bus, outside is". Night of Returning. Eddie Silva. P56

"In the best chamber of the house". The Bottom Drawer. Amelia Edith Barr. P89

"In the bitter waves of woe". Ultima Veritas. Washington Gladden. P89

"In the bluebell forest". Bluebells. Olive Enoch. P51

"In the bright hilltop". Marking Time. T. Busch. P77

"In the century of Royal Hospital Road". London, March 1945. Pierre Emmanuel. P61

"In the cold I will rise, I will bathe". The Lonely Death. Adelaide Crapsey. P81

"In the dark swarming the past...". In the Big Country Dreams Stay Alive. Maryann Calendrille. P64

"In the east is the glittering...". A Feeling. Bo Yang. P72

"In the evening". At Sunset. Ivy O. Eastwick. P51

"In the falls, music-woven". Cataract. Theodore Weiss. P84

"In the far corner". The Blackbird. Humbert Wolfe. P51

"In the far west of dreams". Route Seven. Juan Cameron. P71

"In the foyer, this modern temple". Tradition. Helen Winter. P88

"In the gathering twilight". Mist on the Ridge. Mokuo Nagayama. P72

"In the hollow tree, in the ols gray tower". The Owl. Bryan Waller ("Barry Cornwall") Procter. P89

"In the hour of my distress". The Holy Spirit. Robert Herrick. P89

"In the house with the tortoise chair". Poem to Ease Birth. Unknown. P78

"In the hush of the dawn". Daybreak. Laurene Tibbets. P72

"In the middle of the sea". Song Picture No. 54. Unknown. P78

"In the mind's midnight". The Stars. Jane Augustine. P64

"In the monethe of Maye when mirthes bene fele". The Parlement of the Thre Ages. Unknown. P66

"In the morning he steps out". The Crier. Philip Kahclamet. P78

"In the necessary field among the round". Humility. Fred Chappell. P67

"In the night sky". Maps in the Brain. A. J. Wright. P56

"In the old time women's cunts had teeth...". How Her Teeth Were Pulled. Unknown. P78

"In the old time...". A Kalapuya Prophecy. Unknown. P78

"In the other moment of his advance...". All of Him, the Blue Filigree of the Gaze. Gonzalo Munoz. P71

"In the palm". A Guerrilla Handbook. Amiri (LeRoi Jones) Baraka. P85

"In the pavilion of saints...". No One Knows What I'm Talking About. Diego Maquieira. P71

"In the place where I live the worst irritants". Limericks. David Cram. P63

"In the placid summer midnight". Street Scene. William Ernest Henley. P51

"In the prison cell I sit". Tramp, Tramp, Tramp. Unknown. P90

"In the purple light, heavy with redwood...". Apology for Bad Dreams. Robinson Jeffers. P83

"In the quarter of the Negroes". Cultural Exchange. Langston Hughes. P83

"In the room next door". Photograph. Oscar Hahn. P71

"In the rustling shelter of Japanese peach". King Hayden of Miami Beach. Robert Duncan. P84

"In the sedge beyond Chalco". The Flowering War. Unknown. P78

"In the sky I saw Halley's Comet". Halley's Comet. Jeremy Gay. P74

"In the slippery swelter of asphalt". The Tennis Player Waits for What Waits... Philip Appleman. P64

"In the spirit of Ingvar". A Brief Resume of the Last 20 Years... Wayne Kvam. P68

"In the spring, on the trees". Fluttering Leaves. Rodney Bennett. P51

"In the summer of 1910 Halley's Comet". Halley's Comet. Jaime Quezada. P71

"In the sweet pine scent of night". Daughter Softly Singing in the Night. Jean L. Emerson. P72

"In the tale". Bread and Apples. Lisel Mueller. P88

"In the turret's great glass dome...". Siegfried. Randall Jarrell. P84

"In the very earliest time". Magic Words. Unknown. P78

"In the warming sun the dog sleeps...". Eighth and Broad. Wallace Whatley. P63

"In the woods I heard". Tanka. Neal Henry Lawrence. P72

"In these few years". Mother's Voice. Robert Creeley. P52

"In this cold country". Angels of Snow. Lorna Crozier. P49

"In this cold room". The Barrier (A Manardina). Dorman John Grace. P72

"In those early literary days". Not in Vain. Virginia (Jacques). Snyder. P72

"In tomb-dark night". October Is the Cruelest Month. Francis Lehner. P68

"In vain we tried to banish him". The Cricket. Krassin Himmirsky. P70

"In Water Mill the last glacier...". Mecox Nunnery & Saint Dominic. Anselm Parlatore. P64

"In winter-time we go". White Fields. James Stephens. P51

Inamorata. Mary Margaret Wittner. P72

Incest
        The Final Gesture. Gwendolyn Vincent. P58
        Who Plays the Lyre?. Phillip Macar. P53

Incident. Countee Cullen. P83

Incident at Bien Hoa. Herbert M. Kirkham. P68

Incident of the French Camp. Robert Browning. P90

The Incomparable Earth. Salvatore Quasimodo. P61

Independence. Marion Jane Richardson. P65

The Independent Man, fr. A Street in Bronzeville. Gwendolyn Brooks. P84

India. Dhiru Desai. P72

India
        Namaste. Katherine E. Landry. P72

An Indian Grandaughter's Wish. Molly White. P73

"Indian Rice Fields". Maxine Negley. P72

Indian Sky. Alfred Kreymborg. P82

Indian Summer. Nicolae Breban. P92

Indian Summer. Judith Minty. P88

Indians of America
        At Sunrise Along the American River... William Howarth. P77
        Dance of the Rain Gods. Ray Young Bear. P78
        A Dispute Between Women. Unknown. P78
        Edward Curtis Photographs the North American Indians. Virginia E. Smith. P68
        Essie Parrish in New York. Unknown. P78
        For the God of Peyote. Unknown. P78
        Indian Sky. Alfred Kreymborg. P82
        A Kalapuya Prophecy. Unknown. P78
        Legend of Indian Summer. Edna Bacon Morrison. P68
        Navajo Correspondences (First Set). Unknown. P78
        Navajo Correspondences (Fourth Set). Unknown. P78

Navajo Correspondences (Second Set).
  Unknown. P78
Navajo Correspondences (Third Set).
  Unknown. P78
Not So Long Gone (for the Maidu). Doc
  Dachtler. P77
The Origin of the Skagit Indians... Lucy
  Williams. P78
The Removal. Unknown. P78
Sixty-Six Poems for a Blackfoot Bundle.
  Unknown. P78
What Happened to a Young Man... Unknown.
  P78
The Young Indians. Jennie Thorpe. P74
Indians of America—Chile
Wekufe's Dream. Clemente Riedemann. P71
Indians of America—Dances
Three Ghost Songs. Unknown. P78
Indians of America—Folklore
Before They Made Things Be Alive They
  Spoke. Lucario Cuevish. P78
How Her Teeth Were Pulled. Unknown. P78
A Story of the Eaters. Santiago Mendes
  Zapata. P78
Indians of America—Games
Getting Berries, from String Games.
  Unknown. P78
Getting Firewood, from String Games.
  Unknown. P78
Ghost & Shaman, from String Games.
  Unknown. P78
Lying Down, from String Games. Unknown.
  P78
The Net of Moon: a Pawnee Hand Game
  Vision. Unknown. P78
Pieces of Snot, from String Games.
  Unknown. P78
Poems for the Game of Silence. Unknown.
  P78
Indians of America—Legends
Muu's Way or Pictures from the Uterine
  World. Unknown. P78
Indians of America—Poetry
Ceremony of Sending: a Simultaneity...,
  sel. Unknown. P78
Four Poems. Ray Young Bear. P78
A Poem from the Sweatbath Poems. Unknown.
  P78
Poem To Be Recited Every 8 Years While
  Eating... Unknown. P78
Sound-Poem No. 1. Unknown. P78
Sound-Poem No. 2. Richard Johnny John.
  P78
Indians of America—Religion
The Crier. Philip Kahclamet. P78
"He Was There," from Crow Versions.
  Medicine-Tail. P78
Her Elegy. Unknown. P78
"I Am Climbing," from Crow Versions.

Unknown. P78
"I Am Making," from Crow Versions. White-
  arm. P78
"If There Is Someone Above," from Crow
  Versions. Double-Face. P78
They Went to the Moon Mother. Unknown.
  P78
"Your Way," from Crow Versions. Plenty-
  Hawk. P78
Indians of America—Songs & Music
The Flowering War. Unknown. P78
Sioux Metamorphosis. Lucario Cuevish. P78
Song Picture No. 106. Unknown. P78
Song Picture No. 17. Unknown. P78
Song Picture No. 27. Unknown. P78
Song Picture No. 29. Unknown. P78
Song Picture No. 30. Unknown. P78
Song Picture No. 34. Unknown. P78
Song Picture No. 54. Unknown. P78
Song Picture No. 56. Unknown. P78
Song Picture No. 58. Unknown. P78
Song Picture No. 64. Unknown. P78
Song Picture No. 66. Unknown. P78
Song Picture No. 68. Unknown. P78
Song Picture No. 69. Unknown. P78
Song Picture No. 71. Unknown. P78
The 13th Horse Song of Frank Mitchell
  (White). Unknown. P78
Thought-Song One, from Tepehua Thought-
  Songs. Unknown. P78
Thought-Song Three, from Tepehua Thought-
  Songs. Unknown. P78
Thought-Song Two, from Tepehua Thought-
  Songs. Unknown. P78
The 12th Horse Song of Frank Mitchell
  (Blue). Unknown. P78
Indians of America—Songs and Music
Song Picture No. 82. Unknown. P78
Song Picture No. 83. Unknown. P78
Song Picture No. 85. Unknown. P78
Song Picture No. 86. Unknown. P78
Song Picture No. 87. Unknown. P78
Song Picture No. 96. Unknown. P78
Indians of America—Women
New Her Cherokee Face. Jerry Craven. P65
Indians of America—Zuni Language
Zuni Derivations. Unknown. P78
"Indigenous to brass coat trees". Domestic
  Birds. Robert Bess. P63
Indirection. Richard Realf. P90
Individuality
Against Time. Louis Untermeyer. P82
Indolence
Lazy One. Lynne Anderson. P73
"Infamous for eels, bearded, wrist-thick".
  The Brook. Robert Minhinnick. P54
Infidelity
Elsa Wertman, from Spoon River Anthology.
  Edgar Lee Masters. P82

Mrs. Meyers, from Spoon River Anthology. Edgar Lee Masters. P82
"Infinite gentleness, infinite irony". Effigy of a Nun. Sara Teasdale. P82
Ing, Nancy (tr.)
Laughter (I). Tin-wen Chung. P72
Ingelow, Jean
About the Fairies. P51
Heigh Ho!. P51
Injustice
Breaking Silence. Janice Mirikitani. P85
The Inmate. Margherita Faulkner. P68
The Inn of Earth. Sara Teasdale. P82
Inner Eye. T. A. Shulgin. P58
Innocence
If I Could Only Live at the Pitch That Is Near Madness. Richard Eberhart. P83
Innocence-Loss of
A Puritan Lady. Lizette Woodworth Reese. P81
Siegfried. Randall Jarrell. P84
They Failed to Tell Me. James A. Rice. P86
"An innocent walk through the woods". Chain Reaction. Manuel Silva Acevedo. P71
Inquest. William DeWitt Snodgrass. P85
Inquiline. Allen Planz. P64
Insanity
Ante Mortem. Robinson Jeffers. P83
Pinwheels, from Lost Youth: the Last War. Alfred Kreymborg. P82
They Dragged Me Out by My Face. Diego Maquieira. P71
Wild May. Claude McKay. P82
"Inscrutable mystery". The Cat. Julie [pseud.]. P72
Insects. Damaso Alonso. P61
Insects
Brood Queen (A Vision of Moths). Charles P. Martin. P58
Browny Bee. Irene F. Pawsey. P51
Campfire. Marsh Cassady. P56
Casey and the Vespula Diabolica. Beverley W. Stein. P72
The Catepillar. Christina Georgina Rossetti. P51
Cobwebs. E. L. M. King. P51
The Coral Insect. Lydia Huntley Sigourney. P89
Design. Robert Frost. P82
Dragon-Fly. Hyacinthe Hill. P65
First Names. Dorothy T. Lewis. P72
The Fly. Karl Shapiro. P84
Glow-Worms. P. A. Ropes. P51
The Grasshopper and the Cricket. John Keats. P51
Grasshopper Green. Unknown. P51
High June. Catherine A. Morin. P51
I Hypnotize Bugs. Eugene A. Craig. P63

Insects. Damaso Alonso. P61
Insects Blind to History. Kirby Olson. P63
The Maimed Grasshopper Speaks Up. Jean Garrigue. P84
Mr. Beetle. Emily Hover. P51
To a Cricket. William Cox Bennett. P51
To a Mantled Prophet. Belle Adams. P68
The Wasp. William ("Fiona Macleod") Sharp. P51
Water Walker. Richard Wilbur. P84
Where the Bee Sucks. William Shakespeare. P51
Insects Blind to History. Kirby Olson. P63
Inside. Orhan Veli Kanik. P91
"Inside this vast hotel the prairie". Lethbridge, Alberta; Thursday Evening, November... Stephen Scobie. P49
Insomnia
Insomnia. Ardele L. Jessen. P72
Inspirations Unlimited. Claire Schneider. P72
Instant Storm. X. J. Kennedy. P75
Instead. David Lunde. P63
"Instead of leaf-covered branches...". Finale. Tibor Tollas. P61
"Instead of writing this poem". Instead. David Lunde. P63
The Instruction Manual. John Ashbery. P85
Instructions to a Medium To Be Transmitted... Daniel Hoffman. P79
"The instructor said". Theme for English B. Langston Hughes. P83
Instrumental Music
Ode to Strings. Maia Linden. P65
Tuning the Trumpet. Noa Spears. P63
Insult Before Gift-Giving. Unknown. P78
Intellect
In a Lonely Place. Stephen Crane. P81
Mystery of Mind. Mythily. P72
The Net. Veronica Haughey. P72
Six of One. George Bradley. P64
"Intense Physical Pain". Joseph P. Butler. P72
"Intent on teaching me--.". Loving Lessons (Grandmother). Burnette B. Benedict. P72
Interim. Clarissa Scott Delany. P89
The Interior Castle. Irene K. Wilson. P72
Interior Dialogue. David Ignatow. P84
Interiors. Carol Barrett and Anita Skeen. P88
Interlude. Miriam Pederson. P56
Interludio Idilico: Coda. Tomas Segovia. P92
Intertwining Love. Winne E. Fitzpatrick. P72
Intimate. Aristoteles Espana. P71
"Into a Grievous Torment". Rinaldo d'Aquino. P69
Into My Own. Robert Frost. P89

"Into bright sunlight". Journey. Deb
    Plummer. P56
"Into the dance leapt". Leapt into the
    Dance. Nyanpandong. P53
"Into the furnace let me go alone". Baptism.
    Claude McKay. P82
"Into the royal family of Sakya". The
    Bhagawan Buddha. K. K. Moorthy. P72
"Into the silent land!". Song of the Silent
    Land. Johann Gaudenz von Salis-Seewis.
    P89
"Into the street the piper stept". The Piped
    Piper of Hamelin, sel. Robert
    Browning. P51
"Into the sunshine, full of light". The
    Fountain. James Russell Lowell. P51
"Into whose ear the deeds are spoken...".
    History. Jorie Graham. P48
Introspection. Nikolai Hristozov. P70
Inuit-Folklore
    THe Great Farter. Nakasuk. P78
    Heaven and Hell. Nalungiaq. P78
    One for Coyote. Unknown. P78
Invasions
    Coming Down from the Mountains. Taufiq
        Rafat. P91
The **Invention** of White People. Leslie MArmon
    Silko. P78
The **Inventors**. Rene Char. P61
Invitation. Glenn Clairemonte. P68
Invitation. James Steel Smith. P63
Invitation to Morfudd. Robin Ddu. P87
An **Invitation**. Goronwy Owen. P87
Invocation of Peace, sel. William ("Fiona
    Macleod") Sharp. P51
Invocation to Light, from Paradise Lost.
    John Milton. P89
Invocation to Rain in Summer. William Cox
    Bennett. P89
Invocation to the Social Muse. Archibald
    MacLeish. P83
The **Io** Moth. Betty Wallace. P68
Iodice, Ruth G.
    The Rowan Tree. P68
Iqleema. Fahmida Riyaz. P91
Irby, James (tr.)
    At the Sources. Tomas Segovia. P92
    Dawn of Tomorrow. Tomas Segovia. P92
Ireland
    Fenians All. Brian O'Riordan. P49
    Spenser's Ireland. Marianne Moore. P83
Ireson, Barbara
    Don't Go, Jo!. P80
Irion, Mary Jean
    At the Briefing for Creation Day. P63
Irised Symbols. Emma Crobaugh. P68
Irish Peasant Song. Louise Imogen Guiney.
    P81
The **Iron** Wheels of the Tricycle Without

        Tires... Gonzalo Millan. P71
Ironica, from Lost Youth: the Last War.
    Alfred Kreymborg. P82
Irony
    Airport Phone Booth. Memye Curtis Tucker.
        P63
    Cassandra. Edward Arlington Robinson. P81
    Clocks and Locks. Mark Rich. P63
    Firewood (for Steve Sanfield). Doc
        Dachtler. P77
    A Learned Man. Stephen Crane. P81
    A Letter on the Use of Machine Guns at
        Weddings. Kenneth Patchen. P84
    A Little Drama. Paulette Roeske. P88
    Love. Eddena Christian. P72
    Loveliness. Gail Calmer. P68
    A Man Toiled on a Burning Road. Stephen
        Crane. P81
    The Nymph's Reply. Sir Walter Raleigh.
        P89
    O, the Pleasant Days of Old!. Frances
        Browne. P90
    The Rain It Raineth. Charles Bowen. P75
    Rivalry in Love. William Walsh. P89
    When Gods Grow Weary. Steve Kline. P68
    Why?. Thor Thorsen. P72
Irwin, Mark
    Besides. P63
"Is a monstrance". The Moon Is the Number
    18. Charles Olson. P85
"Is a noble task (whatever the...).". The
    Care and Feeding of a Poet. James
    Laughlin. P63
"Is a plastic word". Peace. John Carlisle
    Dunlap. P72
"Is a proverb". An Apothegm. Daniel Hoffman.
    P63
"Is it for tingling sunrises, for a few". On
    an Unwritten Letter. Eugenio Montale.
    P61
"Is it time". Time Is. Bohumila Falkowski.
    P72
"Is it, then, your opinion". The Poet
    Ridiculed by Hysterical Academics.
    William DeWitt Snodgrass. P63
Is the Moon Tired?. Christina Georgina
    Rossetti. P51
Is the Pathetic Fallacy True?. Elizabeth
    Brewster. P49
Is There Anyone. Walter Hoefler. P71
"Is the most horrendous war". A Simple
    Question. Joann Marie Everett. P72
"Is the sea as beautiful as this every
    day?.". There Must Be Something. Orhan
    Veli Kanik. P91
"Is there anything in spring so fair". Apple
    Blossoms. Helen Adams Parker. P51
"Is there, when the winds are singing". The
    Mother's Hope. Laman Blanchard. P89

"Is what you see all that's real". The
        Illusion II. Jeffrey Adam Sager. P72
Isaac and Archibald. Edward Arlington
        Robinson. P81
Isardas, Geeta
        Just Imagine... P74
Islam, Kazi Nazrul
        The Haldighat of New India. Prithwindra
        Mukherjee (tr.). P91
Island Sanctuary (Poetic Rambling). Cecile
        C. Metzger. P72
The Island. Grace Schulman. P64
Islands
        Porth Cwyfan. Roland Mathias. P54
        The Queen Charlotte Islands Meditations.
        Michael J. Yates. P49
        Troubles. John Hildebidle. P56
It All Comes Together Outside the
        Restroom... James Seay. P67
It Fell in the City. Eve Merriam. P80
It Is a Pleasant Day. Unknown. P51
It Must Someday be Answered. Elidir Sais.
        P87
It Was Wrong To Do This. Stephen Crane. P81
"It Would Be Very Pleasant...," from Wolf
        Songs... Unknown. P78
"It ain't like we mean nobody no harm".
        Paolo's Version. Carl Judson Launius.
        P63
"It all begins at the end". So It Was Done.
        Barry Callaghan. P49
"It always comes, and when it comes they
        know". Women in Love. Donald Justice.
        P67
"It began to snow". Snowfall. Barry
        Callaghan. P49
"It blows. Is it snow?.". Desert Snow.
        Vivian L. Martinetz. P72
"It came to pass". Brother Ass and St.
        Francis. John Banister Tabb. P81
"It could have been an arrow". View of a
        Comet. Robert Hahn. P58
"It doesn't matter that you're in there...".
        Writing to Get Through the Night While
        the Baby Cries. Jeanne Murray Walker.
        P63
"It drives me nearly frantic". Tekk Me.
        Beryl Pierce. P72
"It flows through old, hushed Egypt...". The
        Nile. Leigh Hunt. P90
"It hulks". California Street. Kandy Arnold.
        P58
"It is a test you have to pass". Essie
        Parrish in New York. Unknown. P78
"It is an ancient mariner". Rime of the
        Ancient Mariner. Samuel Taylor
        Coleridge. P90
"It is clear to the clergy". Loosestrife.
        Elaine Magarrell. P63

"... It is colder now". Epistle To Be Left
        in the Earth. Archibald MacLeish. P83
"It is disastrous to be a wounded deer".
        Hello. Gregory Corso. P85
"It is from within". Inner Eye. T. A.
        Shulgin. P58
"It is good to be out on the road...".
        Tewkesbury Road. John Masefield. P51
"It is hanging". Poems for the Game of
        Silence. Unknown. P78
"It is late afternoon". A Light in the
        Doorway. Cary Waterman. P88
"It is likely enough that lions and
        scorpions". Ante Mortem. Robinson
        Jeffers. P83
"It is morning and I am kneeling". Nunc
        Dimittis. Patrick Lane. P49
"It is morning, Senlin says...". Morning
        Song from 'Senlin'. Conrad Aiken. P82
"It is not so much trying to keep alive".
        Prisoner at a Desk. May Sarton. P52
"It is portentous, and a thing of state".
        Abraham Lincoln Walks at Midnight.
        Vachel Lindsay. P82
"It is possible that in every feeling". The
        Signature of Things. Raphael Vargas.
        P92
"It is probably innocent, traveling". Snake
        in the Yard. Paulette Roeske. P88
"It is said that if a dog barks at
        midnight". Dog, from My Hometown's
        Base Creatures. Wu Cheng. P92
"It is the custom--.". The Final Gesture.
        Gwendolyn Vincent. P58
"It is the first day of the world". The
        Venetian Blind. Randall Jarrell. P84
"It is the first mild day of March". A
        Change in the Year. William
        Wordsworth. P51
"It is the soft, persistent". Millionfold.
        Anne Yannie Corrado. P65
"It is the soft, sickening squish of your
        boot". Vietnam. Jack Strahan. P86
"It is there where the worm has egress".
        Gravepiece. Jean Garrigue. P84
"It isn't enough that...". Alpha the Dog.
        Robert Sward. P49
"It isn't proper, I guess you know". Read
        This with Gestures. John Ciardi. P80
"It isn't raining rain to me". April Rain.
        Robert Loveman. P51
"It lies around us like a cloud,--.". The
        Other World. Harriet Beecher Stowe.
        P89
"It lies not in our power to love or hate".
        Love, from Hero and Leander.
        Christopher Marlowe. P89
"It looked extremely rocky...". Casey at the
        Bat. Ernest Lawrence Thayer. P90

"It must be the Muse's day off". On Seeing
     Gavin Ewart in Sainsbury's. Joan Van
     Poznak. P63
"It rained some days ago". Some Days Ago.
     Majeed Amjad. P91
"It rains on my bratwurst". Tending a
     Cookout in Pouring Rain... X. J.
     Kennedy. P63
"It seems high time". A Dispute Between
     Women. Unknown. P78
"It seems like a dream". An Autumn Morning.
     Unknown. P51
"It seems the ocean floor comes to meet me".
     A Dream. Sylvia L. Bryant. P72
"It sounds like a phone ringing...". The Way
     Things Are Above and Below. Jaime
     Quezada. P71
"It stops the town we come through...".
     Troop Train. Karl Shapiro. P84
"It sushes". Cynthia in the Snow. Gwendolyn
     Brooks. P80
"It took him years...". Duke. Ed Ochester.
     P63
"It took me some seconds as I drove toward".
     The Meeting. Stanley Moss. P64
"It was a Moorish maiden was sitting by a
     well". The Broken Pitcher. William
     Edmonstoune Aytoun. P90
"It was a privilege, my going to
     Bavaria...". Oberammergau. David
     Gwenallt Jones. P87
"It was a silver sky. Silver". Anatomy of
     Melancholy. Ralph Gustafson. P49
"It was all mouth; only". Francis Bacon, the
     Inventor of Spectacles... Cynthia
     MacDonald. P79
"It was hot. A size too large". High Holy
     Days. Jane Shore. P48
"It was in practice much as you foresaw". A
     Going-Away Poem for Philip Larkin.
     David Gill. P72
"It was in winter. Steeples, spires". The
     Fortunate Traveller. Derek Walcott.
     P48
"It was just". White Lie. Deanna Fleysher.
     P73
"It was Mabbie without the grammar school
     gates". The .Ballad of Chocolate
     Mabbie, fr. A Street in Bronzeville.
     Gwendolyn Brooks. P84
"It was many and many a year ago". Annabel
     Lee. Edgar Allen Poe. P89
"It was near evening, the room was cold".
     The Oath. Allen Tate. P67
"It was not dying: everybody died". Losses.
     Randall Jarrell. P84
"It was not I that crossed...". Arrival.
     Vernon Edgar. P72
"It was nothing but a rose I gave her,--.".

A Sigh. Harriet Elizabeth Spofford.
     P81
"It was six men of Hindostan". The Blind Men
     and the Elephant. John Godfrey Saxe.
     P51
"It was six men of Indostan". The Blind Men
     and the Elephant. John Godfrey Saxe.
     P90
"It was the hole for looking in". It All
     Comes Together Outside the Restroom...
     James Seay. P67
"It was the schooner Hesperus". The Wreck of
     the Hesperus. Henry Wadsworth
     Longfellow. P90
"It was the time". Peripheral Vision. Kevin
     Cline. P58
"It was the west wind caught her up, as".
     The Ring of. Charles Olson. P85
"It was way back". Dragon's Jaw. David
     Biles. P86
"It was, that day". Crossing a Shore. Gwyn
     Thomas. P87
"It would be picturesque to go". Transition.
     M. Athar Tahir. P91
"It's Only Whiskey...," from Wolf Songs...
     Unknown. P78
It's Such a Wonderful Day at Camp. Rana L.
     Landseadel. P73
"It's a risk and a bother". A Woman Alone on
     the Road. Blaga Dimitrova. P70
"It's amazing". Living Alone. D. Scott
     Taylor. P63
"It's autumn in the country I remember".
     Mnemosyne. Trumbull Stickney. P81
"It's been a long time coming". Po Biz.
     Howard Nemerov. P63
"It's bright the icy foam as it flows". From
     Exile. Dafydd Benfras. P87
"It's dangerous to wear one's heart...".
     Advice Against Being Naive. P. P.
     Sharma. P72
"It's evergreen, it blooms in spring".
     Seedam. Lily D. Angle. P63
"It's funny that smells and sounds return".
     Scrapbooks. Nikki Giovanni. P85
"It's growing evening in my soul". In
     Summer. Trumbull Stickney. P81
"It's Hallowe'en". Hallowe'en. Marion Louise
     Refici. P74
"It's holiday night". Riding Westward.
     Harvey Shapiro. P64
"It's late when I try to sleep, resting".
     The Voyages. Gregory Orr. P85
"It's midsummer day". Haytime. Irene F.
     Pawsey. P51
"It's never exactly itself, the beach".
     Walking Sag Beach. George Bradley. P64
"It's never good to give up all for lust--
     .". Shakepeare Sonnets Converted into

Couplets. Gavin Ewart. P63
"It's not a bit windy". Toadstools.
  Elizabeth Fleming. P51
"It's not difficult". Writing in the Dark.
  Denise Levertov. P85
"' It's not forever,' you whisper". Echoes.
  John Zurlo. P56
"It's not that I'm late". Travel Journal,
  sel. Omar Lara. P71
"It's often said that counting sheep". Sheep
  That Pa in the Night. Irene Warsaw.
  P63
"It's only 10:30 and I am in bed". No
  Answers. Mary Ann Henn. P56
"It's raining". Poem 13, from The City.
  Gonzalo Millan. P71
"It's spring, and we are thinking
  daffodils". The Toads of Spring. Mary
  B. Finn. P68
"It's strange to go home". Blank Spaces.
  Mary Ann Henn. P56
"It's the hare that we go hunting". Hunting
  the Hare. Unknown. P87
"It's the same at all these small". General
  Delivery. Ben L. Hiatt. P77
"' It's the same old story'.". Sordid Love.
  Elaine Demakas. P58
"It's true, my philosopher". To Auden.
  Fahmida Riyaz. P91
"It's true--.". Secrets. Dorothy C. Dunlap.
  P72
"It's what I planned. The barber shop
  alone". Cattails. Richard Hugo. P79
"It's/ Mit der Dummheit". Pejorative. Ernest
  Kroll. P63
"Italian Campagna 1309, the open road".
  Cino. Ezra Pound. P82
Italy
  Going to Italy. Donald Davie. P79
  Lodovico Martelli. Trumbull Stickney. P81
  The Stones of Florence. Bruce Bennett.
  P63
Its Eye Ran with Blood. Peter Pal Kong. P53
Its Shells Pile Before Me. Ret Col and
  Stephen Ciec Lam. P53
IV, fr. Irradiations. John Gould Fletcher.
  P82
IX--Royal Favor. Mary F. Lindsley. P72
"Its metal top refused my father's
  twisting". The Soup Jar. Dabney
  Stuart. P67
"Its quick soft silver bell beating,
  beating". Auto Wreck. Karl Shapiro.
  P84
"An ivory magnolia flower, with a full".
  Southern Gothic. Rodger Kamenetz. P63

Jabberwocky, from Through the Looking-Glass.
  Charles Lutwidge ("Lewis Carroll")
  Dodgson. P90
Jack Frost. Cecily E. Pike. P51
Jack Frost. Gabriel Setoun. P51
Jack Frost in the Garden. John P. Smeeton.
  P51
Jack O' the Inkpot. Algernon Blackwood. P51
Jack Tar. Emile Jacot. P51
Jackson, Haywood
  The Dust of Delos. P68
  The Fair Damsel of Avalon. P68
  Hit and Run. P68
  The Mind Machines. P68
  There Is a Backyard. P68
Jacobs, David
  "E. C. Bentley". P63
Jacobs, Maria
  Just War. P49
Jacobsen, Josephine (tr.)
  Whirlpools. Kolyo Sevov. P70
Jacobson, Bonnie
  My Luck. P63
  Things As They Are. P63
  Upwardly Mobile Bean Curd. P63
  What Did the Midge Say to the Mildew?.
  P63
  "'When Windham Lewis'". P63
Jacoby, Russell Powell
  My Love (Her Portrait). P89
Jacopone da Todi (Jacobus de Benedictus)
  Stabat Mater Dolorosa. Abraham Coles
  (tr.). P89
Jacot, Emile
  Jack Tar. P51
  Wandering Jack. P51
  Who's That a-Knocking?. P51
Jagadev, Jamini K.
  Black Beloved. P65
  Broken Stanza. P65
Jagdev, Jaminikanta
  Summer Walks. P72
James, David Emrys
  Horizon. Tony Conran (tr.). P87
Janes, Lola Strong
  Well Bed. P63
Janet Walking. John Crowe Ransom. P83
Janie Crawford. Alice Walker. P85
January. Graham Everett. P64
January
  In January. James Schuyler. P64
  January. Graham Everett. P64
  January. Weldon Kees. P84
  Rockbound Pass in January. Jon Olander.
  P77
"January falls the snow". Calendar Rhyme.
  Flora Willis Watson. P51
Japan

Chrysanthemums. Donald Davie. P79
In the Restaurant Polar. John N. Morris.
    P79
Japanese Lullaby. Eugene Field. P89
"The Japanese have funny things". A Rhyme
    Sheet of Other Lands. Hugh Chesterman.
    P51
Jarman, Mark
    Greensleeves. P85
    Lullaby for Amy. P85
    Writing for Nora. P85
Jarrell, Randall
    Burning the Letters. P84
    The Death of the Ball Turret Gunner. P84
    A Girl in a Library. P67
    In the Ward: the Sacred Wood. P84
    The Knight, Death, and the Devil. P84
    Losses. P84
    Pilots, Man Your Planes. P84
    Siegfried. P84
    Transient Barracks. P84
    The Venetian Blind. P84
"The jaunty traveller that comes to peer".
    Llyn y Gadair. T.H. Parry-Williams.
    P87
Jazz Band in a Parisian Cabaret. Langston
    Hughes. P83
Jealousy
    Anne. Lizette Woodworth Reese. P81
    Challenges. Elisavietta Ritchie. P63
    Elegy for the Other Woman. Elisavietta
        Ritchie. P63
    For a Girl. Cynddelw Brydydd Mawr. P87
    From Milton's Translation of Horace's
        Fifth Ode. Terri B. Joseph. P68
    Maiden Song, sels. Cynddelw Brydydd Mawr.
        P87
    A Woman Called Maria. Boris Kristov. P70
"Jeanie, Come Tie My". Unknown. P51
Jeffers, April
    Raindrops. P74
Jeffers, Robinson
    Age in Prospect. P83
    Ante Mortem. P83
    Apology for Bad Dreams. P83
    Ave Caesar. P83
    Clouds of Evening. P83
    Hurt Hawks. P83
    New Mexican Mountain. P83
    Night. P83
    Post Mortem. P83
    Shine, Perishing Republic. P83
Jellyfish. Nikolai Kuntchev. P70
Jen II. Doug Rawlings. P86
Jenkins, Nigel
    Castell Carreg Cennen. P54
    First Calving. P54
    Goat's Hole, Paviland. P54
    Land of Song. P54
    Maidenhair. P54
    The Ridger. P54
    Snowdrops. P54
Jenner, Edward
    Signs of Rain. P89
Jennifer Blass. Midred Luton. P63
Jenny and Johnny. Dorothy King. P51
"Jenny Wren's got a house". The Secret.
    Elizabeth Fleming. P51
Jensen, Frede (tr.)
    "Although Water, Because of Fire, Loses".
        Guido della Colonne. P69
    "Because Love Is Not Invisible". Pier
        della Vigna. P69
    "Because of the Evil Husband I Have".
        Compagnetto da Prato. P69
    "Death, Why Have You Waged Such a Fierce
        War on Me". Giacomino Pugliese. P69
    "For too Long I Have Thought That I'd
        Conceal". Stefano Protonotaro. P69
    "The Great Pain and the Grievous
        Torment". Guido della Colonne. P69

    "I Have Seen the Clear Sky Produce Rain".
        Giacomo da Lentini. P69
    "I Have Set My Heart on Serving God".
        Giacomo da Lentini. P69
    "I Hope to Receive a Reward". Giacomo da
        Lentini. P69
    "I Shall Never Find Solace". Rinaldo
        d'Aquino. P69
    "I Would Like to Show Openly". Jacopo
        Mostacci. P69
    "If I Found Pity". Re Enzo. P69
    "Into a Grievous Torment". Rinaldo
        d'Aquino. P69
    "Just As the Day, When It Is Early
        Morning". Percivalle Doria. P69
    "Just Like the Butterfly, Which Has Such
        a Nature". Giacomo da Lentini. P69
    "Love Is a Desire Which Comes from the
        Heart". Giacomo da Lentini. P69
    "Love, in Which I Have Placed My Desire
        and My Hope". Pier della Vigna. P69
    "Loving With a Loyal Heart and With
        Hope". Pier della Vigna. P69
    "Many Lovers Bear Their Illness". Giacomo
        da Lentini. P69
    "My Heart, Tormented by Love". Odo della
        Colonne. P69
    "My lady, I Wish to Tell You". Giacomo da
        Lentini. P69
    "'My Sweet Lover, You Are Leaving!'".
        Federico II [Frederick II of
        Hohenstaufen]. P69
    "Often Love Has Made Many Happy". Rugieri
        d'Amici. P69
    "Prodding My Intellect a Little". Jacopo

Mostacci. P69

"Since Mercy Is of No Avail to Me...".
    Giacomo da Lentini. P69

"Six Years Have I Suffered". Mazzeo di
    Ricco. P69

"Sweet Beginning:.". Giacomo da Lentini.
    P69

"The Sweet, Pleasant face". Giacomino
    Pugliese. P69

"Thanks to a Perfect Love, I Feel So
    Joyous". Rinaldo d'Aquino. P69

"There Is a Time for Climbing and for
    Descending". Re Enzo. P69

"There Truly First Came to Me Deep
    Sorrow". Giacomo da Lentini. P69

"To Give Joy to My Heart". Stefano
    Protonotaro. P69

"When I See". Giacomino Pugliese. P69

"Wonderfully". Giacomo da Lentini. P69

Jensen, Kelli
    What Sparks My Imagination. P73

Jepsen, Anita
    Phryne. P68

Jeremy Hobbler. Unknown. P51

Jerome, Judson
    Helium: an Inert Gas. P63

Jerusalem. William Blake. P51

Jerusalem
    Jerusalem Destroyed, sels. Eben Fardd.
        P87

Jessa's Late Assignment. Al Ortolani. P63

Jessen, Ardele L.
    Insomnia. P72

Jessie's Cat. Dawn E. Rutter. P72

"Jest rain and snow! and rain again!.". The
    First Blue-Bird. James Whitcomb Riley.
    P89

Jesus Christ
    And Who Am I. Opal Jane O'Neal. P72
    As Joseph Was A-Walking. Unknown. P51
    Benedictus. Diane Scharper. P68
    Bethlehem. William Canton. P51
    The Burning Babe. Robert Southwell. P59
    Carol. Unknown. P51
    Christ Before Pilate. Robert ab Gwilym
        Ddu. P87
    Christian Endeavor, from Lost Youth: the
        Last War. Alfred Kreymborg. P82
    A Christmas Verse. Kay [pseud.]. P51

Jesus Christ
    Easter. George Herbert. P59
    Ex Ore Infantium. Francis Thompson. P51
    Full of Wonder. Ann Griffiths. P87
    Go, Pretty Child. Robert Herrick. P51
    'How Far Is It to Bethlehem?'. F.
        Chesterton. P51
    Judas Against the World. Edwin Markham.
        P81

The Last Englyn. Tudur Aled. P87

Loveliness Destroyed. Agnes Finch
    Whitacre. P72

The Manhood of Hebrew Jesus. Stanley A.
    Fellman. P72

The Messiah. Wilfred M. Johnson. P72

The Moment. Waldo Williams. P87

On Deck, fr. From a Travel Diary. T.H.
    Parry-Williams. P87

Redemption. George Herbert. P59

Rose of Sharon. Ann Griffiths. P87

Song. Henry Neville Maughan. P51

This Very Hour. Lizette Woodworth Reese.
    P81

The Wreath. Henry Vaughan. P59

Jet Planes
    Blue Angels Sky-Dance. Zelma S. Dennis.
        P72

Jet Planes. See also Aviation...

Jew. Karl Shapiro. P84

"Jewel among nations, set in a circle".
    Switzerland. Edna Bacon Morrison. P68

Jewelry
    Platinum Rings (11/8/76). Charles Cline.
        P72

Jewels of Freedom. Julia Nelson Walke. P68

Jews
    Hebrews. James Oppenheim. P82
    Jew. Karl Shapiro. P84
    Let Other People Come as Streams. Charles
        Reznikoff. P83
    Riding Westward. Harvey Shapiro. P64
    The Synagogue. Karl Shapiro. P84
    To Russia. Joaquin Miller. P81

"Jim says a sailor man". When We Are Men. E.
    Stella Mead. P51

"Jingley, jangley". Apathy. Blossom S.
    Kirschenbaum. P63

"Jiok's hide is as bright as moonlight". The
    Sun's Tongue. Rec Puk. P53

Joan, Natalie
    Dickey-Birds. P51
    The Kind Mouse. P51

Job Action. Ray Catina. P86

Job's Turkey: a Commentary. Carl Judson
    Launius. P63

Jock O' Dreams. Rose Fyleman. P51

Joe. David McCord. P80

Joe Clisby's Song. Donald Davidson. P67

Joe's Snow Clothes. Karla Kuskin. P80

"Jog on, jog on, the footpath way". The
    Merry Heart. William Shakespeare. P51

"John Brown in Kansas settled, like a
    steadfast". John Brown of Osawatomie.
    Edmund Clarence Stedman. P81

John Brown's Body. Henry Howard Brownell.
    P90

John Kennedy. Nyagak Pinien. P53

John and Jerome Rothenberg, Richard Johnny

(tr.)
Thank You: A Poem in Seventeen Parts.
Unknown. P78
John, Richard Johnny
Sound-Poem No. 2. P78
"John, the old bunker fleet at Greenport".
The Bridge. Harvey Shapiro. P64
Johnny Doe. Rick Allen House. P73
"Johnny had a little dove". Johnny's Farm.
H. M. Adams. P51
"Johnny was acting". Bad Day. Marci Ridlon.
P50
Johnny's Farm. H. M. Adams. P51
Johnny's Woodpile. T. M. Baker. P68
Johnson Jr., Pyke
Gas Man. P63
Man Who Loved a Giraffe. P63
Johnson, Abby Arthur
A Wisconsin Dawn. P68
Johnson, Fenton
Children of the Sun. P82
Counting. P82
The Daily Grind. P82
The Lonely Mother. P82
The Lost Love. P82
The New Day. P82
The Old Repair Man. P82
The Scarlet Woman. P82
Tired. P82
Who Is That a-Walking in the Corn?. P82
The World Is a Mighty Ogre. P82
Johnson, Hannah Lyons
That Cheerful Snowman. P80
Johnson, Harold Leland
Therese. P65
Johnson, Helene
The Road. P90
Johnson, Herbert Clark
Willow Bend and Weep. P90
Johnson, James Weldon
The Creation. P83
Go Down Death. P83
O Black and Unknown Bards. P83
Johnson, Linda Monacelli
Some Italian!. P63
Johnson, Molly
Goodbye. P73
Johnson, Norman M.
Hob the Elf. P51
Johnson, Patricia M.
Mystery in Flight. P72
Johnson, Samuel
Charles XII, from The Vanity of Human
Wishes. P90
Shakespeare, from Prologue. P90
Johnson, Siddie Joe
Horseback Ride. P50
Johnson, Wilfred M.
The Messiah. P72

Johnston, Robert W.
Beyond Recall. P72
"A jolly fat friar loved liquor good store".
Gluggity Glug, from Myrtle and the
Vine. George Colman the Younger. P90
"A jolly old sow once lived in a sty". The
Three Little Pigs. Sir Alfred A. Scott-
Gatty. P51
Jonaid
Ghazal. Jonaid and Mary Jane White (tr.).
P92
Ghazal. Mary Jane White and Jonaid (tr.).
P92
Poem. Jonaid (tr.). P92
Jonaid and Mary Jane White (tr.)
Ghazal. Jonaid. P92
Jonas, Ann
Making Caskets. P56
Jones
On the Beach in Puerto Rico. P49
Jones, Bobi
The South Shore (Aberystwyth). Tony
Conran (tr.). P87
To the Poetry Clubs of Wales. Tony Conran
(tr.). P87
Jones, D. G.
Musica Ficta. P49
A Sort of Blues. P49
Jones, Dafydd
Epitaph. Tony Conran (tr.). P87
Jones, David Gwenallt
Dartmoor. Tony Conran (tr.). P87
The Dead. Tony Conran (tr.). P87
The Depression. Tony Conran (tr.). P87
F.R. Konecamp. Tony Conran (tr.). P87
Oberammergau. Tony Conran (tr.). P87
Rhydcymerau. Tony Conran (tr.). P87
Jones, Edna
Along the Roadside. P68
Sound Effect. P68
Jones, Ellis
Eaves. Tony Conran (tr.). P87
Jones, H. Wendy
Sea Gulls in the Rain. P72
Jones, Jeff
"The Full Moon Brimming". P77
"Slight Drops in Ledge Pools". P77
Jones, LeRoi. See Baraka, Amiri
Jones, Nesta Wyn
Poppies. Tony Conran (tr.). P87
Voices. Tony Conran (tr.). P87
Jones, Roland
Foam. Tony Conran (tr.). P87
Jones, Sir William (tr.)
The Baby. Kalidasa. P89
Jones, Thomas Gwynn
Argoed. Tony Conran (tr.). P87
Arthur's Passing, sels. Tony Conran
(tr.). P87

Jones, Walt
  Seekers of Freedom. P86
"Jongbor, Jongbor". Kual Is Left. Unknown.
    P53
"Jonquils and violets smelling sweet".
    Before Spring. P. A. Ropes. P51
Jonson, Ben
  Answer to Master Wither's Song. P89
  Freedom in Dress, from Epicene or The
    Silent Woman. P90
  My Picture Left in Scotland. P59
  On the Portrait of Shakespeare. P90
  To Celia. P59
Jonson, Ben (tr.)
  Drink to Me Only with Thine Eyes, from
    The Forest. Philostratus. P89
Jordan (2). George Herbert. P59
Joseph Rodman Drake (Died in New York,
    September...). Fitz-Greene Halleck.
    P90
Joseph, Terri B.
  From Milton's Translation of Horace's
    Fifth Ode. P68
Joseph, Terri Brint
  Each Age Believed. P68
Journalists
  Carl Hamblin, from Spoon River Anthology.
    Edgar Lee Masters. P82
  Editor Whedon, from Spoon River
    Anthology. Edgar Lee Masters. P82
Journey. Deb Plummer. P56
Journey Back. Delphia Frazier Smith. P72
The Journey. Aidan Clarke. P51
Jouve, Pierre Jean
  The Stain. Charles Guenther (tr.). P61
The Jovial Beggar. Unknown. P51
Jowers, Lawrence V.
  The Setting Sun. P68
Joy. Clarissa Scott Delany. P90
Joy and Sorrow
  Broken Stanza. Jamini K. Jagadev. P65
  Joy of My Life! While Left Me Here'. Henry
    Vaughan. P59
"Joy shakes me like the wind...". Joy.
    Clarissa Scott Delany. P90
Joyce, James
  Goldenhair. P51
Joys. James Russell Lowell. P51
"The joys of their relationship".
    Horrorscope. John D. Engle Jr. P63
Judas Against the World. Edwin Markham. P81
Judge Not. Adelaide Anne Procter. P89
Judgement Day
  I Count My Time by Times That I Meet
    Thee. Richard Watson Gilder. P81
  Voice from the Unknown, fr. Three Voices.
    Faiz Ahmad Faiz. P91
Julia Before the Mirror. Jack H. Palmer. P68
Julian, V. M.&

  Mr. Squirrel. P51
Julie [pseud.]
  The Cat. P72
July. Dan Murray. P64
July. Harvey Shapiro. P64
The Jumblies. Edward Lear. P89
June. William Cullen Bryant. P89
June
  Conversation in June. Barbara S.
    Berstein. P68
  June. Dan Murray. P64
  June. William Cullen Bryant. P89
June. Dan Murray. P64
June. Irene F. Pawsey. P51
June. Jane G. Stewart. P51
June 9. William Carlos Williams. P79
June @!21/84* a Poem with Mistakes Included.
    Eli Mandel. P49
"June, but the morning's cold, the wind".
    Porth Cwyfan. Roland Mathias. P54
Junemann, Virginia
  Tippy-Tap. P72
The Jungle Trees. Marjorie Wilson. P51
"Juniper, Juniper". Unknown. P51
Juoc, Pilual
  I Was as Full of Air as An Old Bullfrog.
    Terese Svoboda (tr.). P53
  The Old Fashioned Girls. Terese Svoboda
    (tr.). P53
  Women Beat the Life Out of Me. Terese
    Svoboda (tr.). P53
Juries
  The People vs. The People. Kenneth
    Fearing. P83
Just Anyone. Nyagak Pinien. P53
"Just As the Day, When It Is Early Morning".
    Percivalle Doria. P69
"Just As the Full Moon, At the Moment of
    Daybreak". Unknown. P62
Just Friends. Robert Creeley. P85
Just God. Lewis Turco. P63
Just Imagine... Geeta Isardas. P74
Just Jumbo. Eileen Mathias. P51
Just Like a Man. Unknown. P51
Just Like me. Unknown. P51
"Just Like the Butterfly, Which Has Such a
    Nature". Giacomo da Lentini. P69
Just Like This. D. A. Olney. P51
"Just Nothingness, Just a Recruiter".
    Unknown. P86
"Just Today He Awoke and Left". Unknown. P62
Just War. Maria Jacobs. P49
"Just now". The Warning. Adelaide Crapsey.
    P81
"Just now and again I catch God watching".
    Novice in the Woods. L. G. Harvey. P72
"'The just right drink for you and me'.".
    Tea Time Remembered. Alma L. Wilson-
    Barry. P72

"Just where the Treasury's marble front".
        Pan in Wall Street. Edmund Clarence
        Stedman. P81
Justice
        Friend, Your White Beard Sweeps the
        Ground. Stephen Crane. P81
        The Garrison. W. H. Auden. P79
        Yussouf. James Russell Lowell. P51
Justice (1). George Herbert. P59
Justice, Donald
        The Grandfathers. P67
        Tales from a Family Album. P67
        Women in Love. P67

Ka 'Ba. Amiri (LeRoi Jones) Baraka. P85
Ka-Trum. Byrd Baylor. P75
Kabadi, Dwarakanath H.
        Flickers. P72
Kachmar, Jessie
        Our Mother the General. P88
Kahclamet, Philip
        The Crier. Dell Hymes (tr.). P78
Kahn, Peggy
        Wednesday's Child. P56
"Kalamazoo toledo springfield springfield".
        The Mocking Bird and the Owl. Reed
        Whittemore. P63
A Kalapuya Prophecy. Unknown. P78
Kalidasa
        The Baby. Sir William Jones (tr.). P89
Kalypso. Trumbull Stickney. P81
Kamal, Daud
        Embrace of Crescents. P91
Kamal, Daud (tr.)
        Mist. Ahmad Nadeem Qasimi. P91
        Thinking of Other Universes. Muneer
        Niazi. P91
        Tyrant, fr. Three Voices. Faiz Ahmad
        Faiz. P91
        Victim, fr. Three Voices. Faiz Ahmad
        Faiz. P91
        Voice from the Unknown, fr. Three Voices.
        Faiz Ahmad Faiz. P91
Kamalan, Ilango
        Poet's Reprieve, from August Presence.
        P72
Kamenetz, Rodger
        Southern Gothic. P63
Kamran, Gilani
        The Last Quarter of the Night. C.M. Naim
        (tr.). P91
        The Old Bookseller. C.M. Naim (tr.). P91
Kania, Karen
        After the Glory Has Passed Before Us. P88
        Alone Genesis. P88
        For You, in the Darkness, Returning. P88

        Revisiting Detroit. P88
Kanik, Orhan Veli
        Epitaphs. Bernard Lewis (tr.). P91
        For You. Bernard Lewis (tr.). P91
        Headache. Bernard Lewis (tr.). P91
        Inside. Bernard Lewis (tr.). P91
        Talk. Bernard Lewis (tr.). P91
        There Must Be Something. Bernard Lewis
        (tr.). P91
Karaangov, Peter
        Winter. John Updike (tr.). P70
"Karolles, wrastlynges, or somour games".
        The Churchyard Dancers of Colbek, fr.
        Handlyng Synne. Robert Mannyng. P66
Karszo, Angela
        Pond & Stream. P77
Katz, Bobbi
        Sea Shore Shanty. P76
Katz, Leslie
        Autumn. P74
Katz, Menke
        Lake Poets. P72
Kaufman, Barry
        Snow. P73
"Kawabata talked about". Snow Country. David
        Wevill. P49
Kay [pseud.]
        A Christmas Verse. P51
A Kayak Song. Lucy Diamond. P51
Kearny at Seven Pines. Edmund Clarence
        Stedman. P90
Keats, John
        The Grasshopper and the Cricket. P51
        The Grasshopper and Cricket. P51,P89
        Meg Merrilees. P51
        A Song About Myself, sel. P51
        Song of Spring. P51
        To Autumn. P51,P89
Keegan, Tim
        Gymnastics. P73
Keeler, Julia
        His Matisses, 1938. P49
"Keep quiet undress close your eyes".
        Interludio Idilico: Coda. Tomas
        Segovia. P92
"Keep your eyes peeled for the numerous...".
        Vision of Hiroshima. Oscar Hahn. P71
Kees, Weldon
        Aspects of Robinson. P84
        For My Daughter. P84
        A French Writer Named Sartre. P63
        January. P84
        Mitzi. P63
        1926. P84
        Robinson. P84
Kej, Tor
        Who Will Bury Me? Terese Svoboda (tr.).
        P53
Keller, David

Silences. P57
Kellman, Anthony (Tony).
    The Broken Sun. P68
Kemal, Yahya
    Evening Music. Roger Finch (tr.). P91
    Exile. Roger Finch (tr.). P91
    Flight. Roger Finch (tr.). P91
    Maltepe. Roger Finch (tr.). P91
    Night. Roger Finch (tr.). P91
    Pilgrimage. Roger Finch (tr.). P91
    The Seasons. Roger Finch (tr.). P91
    Silent Ship. Roger Finch (tr.). P91
    A Star Flowed. Roger Finch (tr.). P91
Kemble-Butler, Frances Anne
    Faith. P89
Kennedy, X. J.
    The Cost of a Sting. P63
    Domestic Crisis. P63
    English Rats. P63
    A 4th Stanza for Dr. Johnson, Donald
        Hall... P63
    Instant Storm. P75
    Moonwalk. P80
    Snowflake Souffle. P80
    A Switched Career. P63
    Tending a Cookout in Pouring Rain... P63
Kent, Marie G.
    In Expectation (To John Paul). P72
"Kentucky water, clear springs: a boy
        fleeing". The Swimmers. Allen Tate.
        P67
Keremes, Constance Andrea
    Ocean Treasures. P76
    Sand Castle. P76
Kerr, Walter H.
    Amphibian. P68
    Fearsome Critters. P68
Ketchum, Shawn
    Reflections. P73
Key, Francis Scott
    The Star-Spangled Banner. P90
Khan, Sonia (tr.)
    Sonnet 1, fr. Three Sonnets From 'Deep
        Within the Heart'. Syed Shamsul Haque.
        P91
    Sonnet 12, fr. Three Sonnets From 'Deep
        Within the Heart'. Syed Shamsul Haque.
        P91
    Sonnet 25, fr. Three Sonnets From 'Deep
        Within the Heart'. Syed Shamsul Haque.
        P91
Khristov, Boris
    A Biblical Motif. Vladimir Phillipov
        (tr.). P92
    The Window. Vladimir Phillipov (tr.). P92
Kicknosway, Faye
    Cassandra. P88
    Today, There Is Love. P88
Kidnap Poem. Nikki Giovanni. P85

The Killer. Unknown. P78
The Killing of Hywel. Peryf ap Cedifor. P87
Kilpatrick and A. G. Kilpatrick, J. K. (tr.)
    Magic Words, from Run Towards the
        Nightland. Unknown. P78
Kin to the Wolf. Unknown. P53
Kind Deeds. Isaac Watts. P51
The Kind Mouse. Natalie Joan. P51
A Kind of Song. Aristoteles Espana. P71
"Kind pity chokes my spleen; brave
        scorn...". Satire 3. John Donne. P59
"A kind voice calls,'Come, little ones'.".
        Crocuses. Anna M. Platt. P51
"The Kindly Speech of a Great Man". Unknown.
        P62
Kindness
    But I Do Not Need Kindness. Gregory
        Corso. P85
    Kind Deeds. Isaac Watts. P51
Kindness to Animals. Unknown. P51
Kindred. George Sterling. P81
King Alfred Explains It. G. N. Gabbard. P63
"King Bruce of Scotland flung himself down".
        Try Again. Eliza Cook. P51
"King Francis was a hearty king...". The
        Glove and the Lions. Leigh Hunt. P90
King Hayden of Miami Beach. Robert Duncan.
        P84
King John and the Abbot of Canterbury.
        Unknown. P51
"The King is out a-hunting". The King's
        Wood. C. S. Holder. P51
"King Lear's canon of sins, in sooth".
        Sharper Than a Serpent's Tooth. Paul
        Sawyer. P63
"King Winter sat in his hall one day".
        Outside. Hugh Chesterman. P51
The King of China's Daughter. Edith Sitwell.
        P51
King's Landing. M. Travis Lane. P49
King's Orders. Jose Lacaba. P92
The King's Wood. C. S. Holder. P51
King, Dorothy
    Billy Boy. P51
    Gipsy Man. P51
    Jenny and Johnny. P51
King, E. L. M.
    Cobwebs. P51
King, Edith
    The Duck. P51
    Evening Song. P51
    The Hedgehog. P51
    Pebbles. P51
    The Rabbit. P51
    To the Bat. P51
King, H. (tr.)
    A Transformation, from The Metamorphoses.
        Ovid. P90
King, Helen Carter

Let Us Forego Life's Puppet Show. P72
King, Thad
Do Parents Cry, too?. P73
Kingery, Bruce
Tallow. P68
Kingfishers
The Kingfishers. Charles Olson. P85
Kings River Canyon, fr. Andree Rexroth.
Kenneth Rexroth. P84
Kings and Rulers
The Agincourt Carol. Unknown. P66
Brut, sels. Unknown. P66
Charles XII, from The Vanity of Human
Wishes. Samuel Johnson. P90
He Was a King. Lynn Blunt. P73
King John and the Abbot of Canterbury.
Unknown. P51
Le Morte Darthur, sels. Sir Thomas
Malory. P66
Sleep, from Henry IV. William
Shakespeare. P90
Sons of the King. John Agnew. P51
Try Again. Eliza Cook. P51
"Kings' armies thundered". The Messiah.
Wilfred M. Johnson. P72
Kingsley, Charles
Dolcino to Margaret. P89
A Farewell, to C. E. G. P51
A Farewell. P89
The'Old, Old Song'. P89
The Sands O' Dee. P90
The Three Fishers. P90
Valentine's Day. P51
When All the World Is Young. P51
Kinnell, Galway
The Bear. P85
Cells Breathe in the Emptiness. P85
The Comfort of Darkness. P85
For Robert Frost. P85
The Homecoming of Emma Lazarus. P85
In Fields of Summer. P85
The Seekonk Woods. P52
Vapor Trail Reflected in the Frog Pond.
P85
Westport. P85
Kinsella, Thomas
Office for the Dead. P79
Kintner, Donald J.
Three Threnodies. P68
Trees. P68
Kipling, Rudyard
Land of Our Birth. P51
Limerick. P90
Recessional. P90
Kirby, David
The Breasts of Women. P63
The Death of the Reference Librarian. P63
Kirby, J.
A Child's Mrning Prayer. P51

Kirby, Jeannie
The Aeroplane. P51
I Wonder. P51
The Pigeon's Story. P51
Proud Little Spruce Fir. P51
Timid Bunnies. P51
The Union Jack. P51
Kirby, Patricia
From Goethe to Gounod: Concerning a
Mutual Affaire... P68
Kirby, Patricia P.
Sonnet to a Seagull. P68
Kirkham, Herbert M.
Incident at Bien Hoa. P68
A Remembered Workshop Critic: Louis A.
Haselmayer. P68
Kirschenbaum, Blossom S.
Apathy. P63
Imitation Is the Sincerest Flattery,
But... P63
Kirstein, Lincoln
Siegfriedslage. P79
"Kiss me!..This is the first day of love".
The Vision of a Martyr. Mohammed
Ibrahim Abu Sinnah. P91
The Kiss. Robert Herrick. P89
The Kiss. Sara Teasdale. P82
Kissam, Edward (tr.)
The Deadly Dance. Unknown. P78
A Poem to the Mother of the Gods.
Unknown. P78
Kisses
The Kiss. Sara Teasdale. P82
The Kiss. Robert Herrick. P89
Kisses. William Strode. P89
Maiden. Frederika Blankner. P65
Sly Thoughts. Coventry Patmore. P89
Song of the Milkmaid, from Queen Mary.
Lord Tennyson. P89
Kisses. William Strode. P89
"The kitchen fire that wakes so soon".
Fires. Elizabeth Fleming. P51
Kitchenette Building, fr. A Street in
Bronzeville. Gwendolyn Brooks. P84
The Kite. Pearl Forbes MacEwen. P51
Kites
Alar. Virginia M. Hahn. P58
The Kite. Pearl Forbes MacEwen. P51
The Kitten at Play. William Wordsworth. P51
"A kitten can". Where Knock Is Open Wide.
Theodore Roethke. P84
Kitty. Unknown. P51
Kizer, Carolyn
For Jan, in Bar Maria. P79
Lines to Accompany Flowers for Eve. P79
On a Line from Sophocles. P79
Klemme, Minnie
Peace in Our Time. P72
Kline, Sara Lewis

Requiem for Ralph. P65
Kline, Steve
    When Gods Grow Weary. P68
The Klondike. Edward Arlington Robinson. P81
Knee-Bouncing Rhymes. Unknown. P90
Knevet, Ralph
    The Vote. P59
"A Knight and a Lady". Unknown. P51
The Knight's Prayer. Unknown. P51
The Knight, Death, and the Devil. Randall
    Jarrell. P84
Knight, Etheridge
    The Bones of My Father. P52
    The Idea of Ancestry. P67
Knight, Glee
    Desks Are Places. P68
'The Knight-a Lady's Hero'. Eleanor Otto.
    P65
Knighthood and Knights
    The Conqueror. Jan Anker Froydarland. P72
    Fast Rode the Knight. Stephen Crane. P81
    The Glove and the Lions. Leigh Hunt. P90
    Gwalchmai's Boat, sels. Meilir ap
        Gwalchmai. P87
    The Hirlas of Owain, sels. Owain
        Cyfeiliog. P87
    Sir Gawayn and the Grene Knyght. Unknown.
        P66
    Sir Launfal. Thomas Chestre. P66
    The Spoils of Annwn. Unknown. P87
Knitted Things. Karla Kuskin. P55
Knitting
    The Scarf. Ivy O. Eastwick. P51
Knitting-Sitting Song. James Steel Smith.
    P63
Knives
    Wound and Knife. Gyorgy Somlyo. P92
"Knives/May still aid". Pinwheels, from Lost
    Youth: the Last War. Alfred Kreymborg.
    P82
Knoll, John
    Trinity. P86
Knopf and Dutton. Gavin Ewart. P63
"The knots". Knitting-Sitting Song. James
    Steel Smith. P63
Know Knowing. Marian Gleason. P72
"Know what I'll promise you?.". Song Picture
    No. 64. Unknown. P78
"Knowing that the music knows". Thought-Song
    One, from Tepehua Thought-Songs.
    Unknown. P78
Knowledge
    Critics and Connoisseurs. Marianne Moore.
        P83
    Deductions. Teresa Calderon. P71
    Endless Variation. John Ashbery. P85
    Epistle To Be Left in the Earth.
        Archibald MacLeish. P83
    I Never Realized. Teresa Calderon. P71

I Wonder. Jeannie Kirby. P51
Old Manuscript. Alfred Kreymborg. P82
The Sail of Ulysses. Wallace Stevens. P83
Seth Compton, from Spoon River Anthology.
    Edgar Lee Masters. P82
Shakespearean Sonnet. Leah Wroten. P73
So It Was Done. Barry Callaghan. P49
Speech to a Crowd. Archibald MacLeish.
    P83
The Water Diviner. Gillian Clarke. P54
"Knows Rama". Maya. C. Ramamohan Rao. P72
Knox, Caroline
    Do You Traipse Long-Leggedly Through
        Murky Woodlands. P88
    Fresh Horses Should Be Waiting. P88
    The Friends of the Friends. P63
    Religion Poem. P63
    Xerxes and Xanthippe. P63
Knoxville, Tennessee. Nikki Giovanni. P85
Knupfer, Anne (tr.)
    A Song for T. S. Cristina Pina. P92
Koch, James S.
    A Short Epic Poem in the English
        Language... P63
    A Short Poem. P63
Koch, Kenneth
    The Boiling Water. P64
    Fate. P64
    Fresh Air. P85
    In Bed, sels. P85
    Mending Sump. P85
    You Were Wearing. P85
Kocis, Kevin
    Poetry I. P72
Koertge, Ron
    Dairy Cows. P63
    'These Students Couldn't Write Their
        Way...'. P63
Kogawa, Joy
    Fish Poem. P49
    Minerals from Stone. P49
Kohburn, Jeremy
    Lonely Is... P74
Koller, James (tr.)
    "Before He Died," from Wolf Songs...
        Unknown. P78
    Cradle Songs, from Wolf Songs & Others of
        the Tlingit. Unknown. P78
    Cradle Songs, from Womf Songs & Others of
        the Tlingit. Unknown. P78
    Cradle Songs, from Wolf Songs & Others of
        the Tlingit. Unknown. P78
    Cradle Songs, from Wolf Songs & Others of
        the Tlingit. Unknown. P78
    Funeral Song, from Wolf Songs & Others of
        the Tlingit. Unknown. P78
    "He Followed His Own Mind...," from Wolf
        Songs... Unknown. P78
    "How Is It All Gonna Turn Out," from Wolf

Songs... Unknown. P78

How to Get Grizzly Spirit, from Wolf
Songs... Unknown. P78

"I Don't Know Why You Tell Me I'm Drunk,"
from Wolf... Unknown. P78

"I Keep Dreaming I'm Dead," from Wolf
Songs... Unknown. P78

"I Know How People Get Treated...," from
Wolf Songs... Unknown. P78

"I Think About You...," from Wolf Songs &
Others... Unknown. P78

"I Wonder What the Eagle Did to Him,"
from Wolf... Unknown. P78

"I'm Gonna Die & Won't See You...," from
Wolf Songs... Unknown. P78

If You'd Died, I Would've Cut Off My Hair,
"from Wolf... Unknown. P78

"It Would Be Very Pleasant...," from Wolf
Songs... Unknown. P78

"It's Only Whiskey...," from Wolf
Songs... Unknown. P78

"My Wife Went Away, Left Me," from Wolf
Songs... Unknown. P78

Shaman Song, from Wolf Songs and Others
of the Tlingit. Unknown. P78

Sioux Metamorphosis. Lucario Cuevish. P78

Song for the Richest Woman in Wrangell,
from Wolf... Unknown. P78

Song on the Way to Jail, from Wolf
Songs... Unknown. P78

"That's a Rich Man Coming," from Wolf
Songs... Unknown. P78

"Throw Him Into the River," from Wolf
Songs... Unknown. P78

"We've All Been Invited up to Killisnoo,"
from Wolf... Unknown. P78

"You Surprise Me, Crow," from Wolf
Songs... Unknown. P78

Kong, Nyapal
Eat Nothing. Terese Svoboda (tr.). P53

Kong, Peter Pal
Foreigners with Teeth. Terese Svoboda
(tr.). P53
Its Eye Ran with Blood. Terese Svoboda
(tr.). P53

Kore. Robert Creeley. P85

Korner, Karl Theodor
Men and Boys. Charles Timothy Brooks
(tr.). P90

Korosy and William Jay Smith, Maria (tr.)
Wound and Knife. Gyorgy Somlyo. P92

Koteliansky, S. S. (tr.)
The Apocalypse of Our Times, sel. Vasily
Vasilievich Rosanov. P48

Kotowicz, Caroline
L'Envoi. P72

Kounrouri, Eleftheria
Report 'Present'. Amy Mims (tr.). P72

Krasnopresnenskaya Station. N. Scott

Momaday. P85

Krauss, Ruth
Birth of the Daisies. P50

Kreis, Michael
Summer. P74

Kresensky, Raymond
In the Woods in Spring. P68

Kreymborg, Alfred
America. P82
And the Physician?., from Lost Youth: the
Last War. P82
Christian Endeavor, from Lost Youth: the
Last War. P82
Dark Confusion, from Lost Youth: the Last
War. P82
Envious Satan, from Lost Youth: the Last
War. P82
General Self-Satisfied, from Lost Youth:
the Last War. P82
God Complex, from Lost Youth: the Last
War. P82
Indian Sky. P82
Ironica, from Lost Youth: the Last War.
P82
Martial Ditty, from Lost Youth: the Last
War. P82
Mea Culpa, from Lost Youth: the Last War.
P82
The Mountain Passes, from Lost Youth: the
Last War. P82
Neo Catholicism, from Lost Youth: the
Last War. P82
Old Manuscript. P82
Pacifist, from Lost Youth: the Last War.
P82
Pinwheels, from Lost Youth: the Last War.
P82
Rule Britannia, from Lost Youth: the Last
War. P82
Sarajevo, from Lost Youth: the Last War.
P82
Slow but Sure, from Lost Youth: the Last
War. P82
Suicide, from Lost Youth: the Last War.
P82
Twenty Million, from Lost Youth: the Last
War. P82
Vanishing Patriot, from Lost Youth: the
Last War. P82

Kriel, Margot
Chokecherry Summers. P88

Kriloff, Ivan Andreevich
The Peasant and the Sheep. C. Fillingham
Coxwell (tr.). P90

Kristov, Boris
A Biblical Motif. Roland Flint (tr.). P70
My Mother's Wedding. Roland Flint (tr.).
P70
A Prayer. Roland Flint (tr.). P70

A Woman Called Maria. Roland Flint (tr.).
    P70
Kroeker, K. F. (tr.)
    E'en as a Lovely Flower. Heinrich Heine.
    P89
    The Message. Heinrich Heine. P89
Kroll, Ernest
    Ego at the Wheel. P63
    Las Vegas. P63
    Pejorative. P63
    The Vaunting Song of Louis L'Amour. P63
Kual Is Left. Unknown. P53
Kuehnert, David
    Sonora Foothill Winter Rainstorm. P77
    "To Guide You, He Is". P77
Kukubaiska, Maria
    Sunny Eye. Maria Kukubaiska (tr.). P72
Kulik, William (tr.)
    A Shooting Star. Robert Desnos. P48
Kulkarni, Hemant
    Rose of God. P72
Kumin, Maxine
    How To Survive Nuclear War. P48
    Sunset Blues. P76
Kumin, Maxine (tr.)
    Amazon. Elisaveta Bagriana. P70
    Descendant. Elisaveta Bagriana. P70
    The Elements. Elisaveta Bagriana. P70
Kunitz, Stanley
    A Choice of Weapons. P83
    Father and Son. P83
    The Image-Maker. P52
    The Science of the Night. P83
    The War Against the Trees. P83
Kuntchev, Nikolai
    Hunting Horn. John Balaban (tr.). P70
    Jellyfish. John Balaban (tr.). P70
Kupper, Mary Jude
    O Holy Past. P72
Kureishi, Maki
    Curfew Summer. P91
Kurz, Carl Heinz
    Shinto Tombs. Werner Manheim (tr.). P72
Kushner, Arthur
    Cicadas. P77
Kuskin, Karla
    Joe's Snow Clothes. P80
    Knitted Things. P55
    Sitting in the Sand. P76
    Snow. P80
    When I Went Out. P75
Kusserow, Todd
    The Ocean's Treasure. P74
Kutty, N. Krishnan
    Dusk. P72
Kutty, Rajnee Krishnan
    Heart's Need. P72
Kvam, Wayne
    A Brief Resume of the Last 20 Years...

    P68
    Sandweiler and Hamm, the Military
        Cemeteries... P68
    South Dakota Scenery. P68
Kwabenya. Okai. P92
Kwiatkowski, Diana
    Letter from the Islands. P56

L'Anne: Water in My Hands. Jerry Craven. P65
L'Echo. Kim Yang-Shik. P72
L'Engle, Madeleine
    "My Bath Is The Ocean". P60
L'Envoi. Caroline Kotowicz. P72
L'Oiseau Bleu (The Blue Bird). Mary E.
    Coleridge. P51
A La Apollinaire. Manuel Silva Acevedo. P71
La Claustra, Vera
    The Dream of Life. P72
La Fontaine, Jean de
    The Cock and the Fox. E. Wright (tr.).
        P90
    The Crow and the Fox. Sir Edward Marsh
        (tr.). P90
"La carence or damn slimness". Notes for an
    Unpublished Canto. Ezra Pound. P79
"La traviata! La traviata!.". Apologies to
    Verdi. Marlon Fick. P68
Labe, Louise
    Sonnet. L. S. Costello (tr.). P89
Labor and Laborers
    Antique Harvesters. John Crowe Ransom.
        P67,P83
    Blacksmith. B. K. Pyke. P51
    Florida Road Workers. Langston Hughes.
        P83
    The Flower-Seller. Eleanor Farjeon. P51
    The .Late Snow and Lumber Strike of the
        Summer of Fifty-Four. Gary Snyder. P85
    Making Caskets. Ann Jonas. P56
    The Milkman. Clive Sansom. P51
    Moviestars. Daniel Cuol Long. P53
    Mr. Coggs. E. V. Lucas. P51
Labor and laborers
    Postman's Knock. Rodney Bennett. P51
Labor and Laborers
    The Postman. Alice Todd. P51
    The Scissor-Man. Madeleine Nightingale.
        P51
    The Sower. Edwin Markham. P81
    The Watchmaker's Shop. Unknown. P51
    The Window Cleaner. Elizabeth Fleming.
        P51
Lacaba, Jose
    Force of Circumstance. Jose Lacaba (tr.).
        P92
    King's Orders. Jose Lacaba (tr.). P92

The Sacred Passion of St. Joseph. Jose
    Lacaba (tr.). P92
Lacaba, Jose (tr.)
    Force of Circumstance. Jose Lacaba. P92
    King's Orders. Jose Lacaba. P92
    The Sacred Passion of St. Joseph. Jose
        Lacaba. P92
The Lace Maker. Barbara Howes. P57
The Lace Peddler. Catherine A. Morin. P51
Lacey, Florence
    Promise. P51
LaGattuta, Margo
    Asking the Windows. P88
LaGrassa Nina
    The Child in Me. P56
"Ladd Y the daunce a myssomur day". Alas,
    Alas the Wyle, That Ever I Cowde
    Daunce. Unknown. P66
Ladies of Llanbadarn. Dafydd ab [or ab]
    Gwilym. P87
"Lads and lasses gathering". The Willow-
    boughs. Alexander Block. P51
Lady Moon. Richard Monckton Milnes; 1st
    Baron Houghton. P51
The Lady Moon. Kate Louise Brown. P51
"Lady and gentlemen fays, come buy!.". The
    Elfin Pedlar. George Darley. P51
"Lady dear, if fairies may". Christmas-
    Greetings (From a Fairy to a Child).
    Charles Lutwidge ("Lewis Carroll")
    Dodgson. P90
"Lady in the leopard skin". Cat. Josephine
    Miles. P84
"The lady put off her fur, it was so
    warm...". Appointment in Doctor's
    Office. Josephine Miles. P84
Lady with the Torch. Eddie-Lou Cole. P72
Lair, Helen
    Color the Day Blue. P72
The Lake Isle of Innisfree. William Butler
    Yeats. P89
Lake Poets. Menke Katz. P72
"The lake blue below the hill". L'Oiseau
    Bleu (The Blue Bird). Mary E.
    Coleridge. P51
Lakes
    Aubade: Lake Erie. Thomas Merton. P84
    Llyn y Gadair. T.H. Parry-Williams. P87
    To Seneca Lake. J. G. Percival. P51
Lakeward. Trumbull Stickney. P81
Lam, Stephen Ciec
    I Won't Bow My Head for Anyone. Terese
        Svoboda (tr.). P53
Lamb, Charles
    The Housekeeper. P89
    The Old Familiar Faces. P89
Lamb, Mary
    Choosing a Name. P89
The Lamb. William Blake. P51

The Lamb. Bob McKenty. P63
Lambs
    Lambs at Play. Christina Georgina
        Rossetti. P51
Lament. Charles P. Martin. P58
Lament for Gwenhwyfar, sels. Gruffudd ap
    Maredudd. P87
Lament for Llywelyn ap Gruffudd, the Last
    Prince. Gruffudd ab yr Ynad Coch. P87
Lament of the Frontier Guard. Ezra Pound.
    P82
Lament of the Irish Emigrant. Helen Selina
    Sheridan; Lady Dufferin. P89
The Lament of the Poet, from Animated
    Film... James Reaney. P49
A Lament. Percy Bysshe Shelley. P89
Laments
    Buried Love. Sara Teasdale. P82
    Good-Bye. Unknown. P89
    Lament for Gwenhwyfar, sels. Gruffudd ap
        Maredudd. P87
    Lament for Llywelyn ap Gruffudd, the Last
        Prince. Gruffudd ab yr Ynad Coch. P87
    Lament of the Frontier Guard. Ezra Pound.
        P82
    Lament of the Irish Emigrant. Helen
        Selina Sheridan; Lady Dufferin. P89
    A Lament. Percy Bysshe Shelley. P89
    Maud Muller. John Greenleaf Whittier. P89
    The Mourning of an Hare. Unknown. P66
    The Nevermore. Dante Gabriel Rossetti.
        P89
    Samson on His Blindness, from Samson
        Agonistes. John Milton. P89
    She Is Not Fair to Outward View. Hartley
        Coleridge. P89
    The Shepherd's Lament. Johann Wolfgang
        von Goethe. P89
    Songs of Autumn. Paul Verlaine. P89
    Three Threnodies. Donald J. Kintner. P68
    When in the Chronicle of Wasted Time
        (Sonnet CVI). William Shakespeare. P89
    The Widow's Lament in Springtime. William
        Carlos Williams. P82
    Zizi's Lament. Gregory Corso. P85
The Lamp Flower. Margaret Cecilia Furse. P51
Lamport, Felicia
    P$$$$$T. P63
    Pisa Visa. P63
"Lana Turner has collapsed!.". Poem ("Lana
    Turner"). Frank O'Hara. P85
"Land lies in water; it is shadowed green".
    The Map. Elizabeth Bishop. P84
The Land of Cokaygne. Unknown. P66
The Land of Counterpane. Robert Louis
    Stevenson. P89
Land of Our Birth. Rudyard Kipling. P51
Land of Song. Nigel Jenkins. P54
The Land of Story-Books. Robert Louis

Stevenson. P89
"Land scanned by water". The Place You
    Inhabit. Walter Hoefler. P71
"The land was overmuch with scenery".
    Beowulf. Richard Wilbur. P84
"A land--a human palm". Bulgaria. Georgi
    Djagarov. P70
Landfall. T. A. Shulgin. P58
Landgraf, William F.
    In the Name of Progress. P72
The Landlady's Daughter. Johann Ludwig
    Uhland. P89
Lando, Diane P.
    "At the Peak of Bright Sleep". P77
    Whitetail, 2:30 a.m. P77
Landor, W. D.
    Winter. P51
Landor, Walter Savage
    Children. P89
    Verses Why Burnt. P90
Landry, Katherine E.
    Namaste. P72
Landscape
    Apology for Bad Dreams. Robinson Jeffers.
        P83
    Back Country Feminist Landscape. Kay
        Murphy. P88
    Canary Morning at the Stop of Darkness.
        Emma Crobaugh. P68
    Country Road in October. Judith Minty.
        P88
    Dartmoor. David Gwenallt Jones. P87
    Florida. Elizabeth Bishop. P84
Landscape. Omar Lara. P71
Landscape. Axel Schulze. P92
    44, Avenue de Maine. Atanas Dalchev. P70
    Four Squares. Agnes Nemes Nagy. P92
    Hallelujah!. Charles Tillman Lockhart.
        P72
    Here. Fred Chappell. P67
    Horizon. David Emrys James. P87
    In Ampezzo. Trumbull Stickney. P81
    "Indian Rice Fields". Maxine Negley. P72
    Lakeward. Trumbull Stickney. P81
    Landfall. T. A. Shulgin. P58
    Landscape. Axel Schulze. P92
    Let Wildness Come. Margaret Longenecker
        Been. P68
    A Mendocino Memory. Edwin Markham. P81
    Mist. Ahmad Nadeem Qasimi. P91
    Northhanger Ridge. Charles Wright. P67
    Paestum. James Dickey. P79
    The Red Hills '83. Terry M. Paulsgrove.
        P77
    Spring and All. William Carlos Williams.
        P82
    Tomorrow's Forecasts Are All Done.
        Alamgir Hashmi. P91
    Visitors. Kathleen Norris. P88

The Vital Brine. Lois Wilson Parker. P68
Where. Wendell Berry. P67
Winter Landscape. John Berryman. P79
A Wisconsin Dawn. Abby Arthur Johnson.
    P68
You, Andrew Marvell. Archibald MacLeish.
    P83
Landscape Gardening
    Make Room. Jules Supervielle. P61
Landseadel, Rana L.
    It's Such a Wonderful Day at Camp. P73
Lane, Frona
    Frank. P72
Lane, M. Travis
    Farther North. P49
    King's Landing. P49
Lane, Patrick
    Dante's Angels. P49
    Nunc Dimittis. P49
Lanes in Summer. Malcolm Hemphrey. P51
Lang, Andrew (tr.)
    The Cloud Chorus, from The Clouds.
        Aristophanes. P89
    Golden Eyes. Rufinus. P89
    The Rose. Pierre de Ronsard. P90
    Spring. Meleager. P89
Lang, Elizabeth
    Honey Bear. P51
Lang, Susanna (tr.)
    In the Thickness. Phillipe Denis. P92
Langbien, Bruce
    For Frank (5-70). P86
Langford, Mary Frances
    Vignette from the Past. P65
Language
    At the School for the Deaf. Robert
        Pawlowski. P57
    Bronze Trumpets and Sea Water--on Turning
        Latin... Elinor Wylie. P82
    Cave Series, sel. Margaret Atwood. P49
    E Pluribus Ovum. Bob McKenty. P63
    English as a Second Language, from Your
        Tired... Lisel Mueller. P88
    Home, Sweet Home! Gavin Ewart. P63
    Knopf and Dutton. Gavin Ewart. P63
    Land of Song. Nigel Jenkins. P54
    Languages. Carl Sandburg. P82
    "My Apparition There Is No". Gonzalo
        Munoz. P71
    Pejorative. Ernest Kroll. P63
    A Plaguey Thing. Vonna Adrian. P63
    Poem ("Everything"). Edward Estlin
        Cummings. P79
    Poem Found While I Looked for Something
        Else. Joseph DeRoller. P63
    Poem, fr. Iris Ifriqiya. Majid El Houssi.
        P91
    The Romance Language. James Merrill. P79
    Silences. David Keller. P57

The Special Language. Robert F. Allen.
    P65
Stutterer. Alan Dugan. P57
Tekk Me. Beryl Pierce. P72
What Passes and Endures. John Ceiriog
    Hughes. P87
The Language. Robert Creeley. P85
Languages. Carl Sandburg. P82
Lanthier, Kateri
    Dream Scars. P49
Lappin and Jannick Storm, Linda (tr.)
    Costa Del Sol, at Night. Vita Andersen.
    P92
Lara, Omar
    The Birds Have Gone. Steven F. White
        (tr.). P71
    Captured City. Steven F. White (tr.). P71
    Landscape. Steven F. White (tr.). P71
    Photograph. Steven F. White (tr.). P71
    The Poet's Days. Steven F. White (tr.).
        P71
    Siege. Steven F. White (tr.). P71
    Travel Journal, sel. Steven F. White
        (tr.). P71
    Wishing. Steven F. White (tr.). P71
Larbes, R. J.
    Summer Sonnet. P68
Larch Wood Secrets. Ivy O. Eastwick. P51
Larcom, Lucy
    The Brown Thrush. P51
Larios, Luis (tr.)
    Non Omnis Moriar. Teresinka Pereira. P72
"The lark now leaves his watery nest".
    Daybreak. Sir William Davenant. P89
"The lark sings for joy in her own loved
    land". Lines to the Stormy Petrel.
    Unknown. P89
Larks
    Larks. Saint-Pol-Roux. P61
Lart, K. C.
    A Walk in Spring. P51
Las Vegas. Ernest Kroll. P63
Last Dance. Tom Tellesbo. P58
The Last Days. George Sterling. P81
The Last Englyn. Tudur Aled. P87
The Last Gate. E. Stella Mead. P51
Last Gift. Lu Cicada. P77
Last Laugh. M. P. A. Sheaffer. P68
The Last Leaf. Oliver Wendell Holmes. P89
Last Night. Unknown-Swedish. P89
The Last Quarter of the Night. Gilani
    Kamran. P91
Last Rights. Lu Spurlock. P56
Last Will & Testament No. 1. Robyn Martin.
    P77
Last Words. James Merrill. P85
"The last double scotch is consumed...". The
    Obligation. Knute Skinner. P63
"Last night at black midnight I woke...".

The Ghosts of the Buffaloes. Vachel
    Lindsay. P82
"Last night I asked the stars to stop...".
    Turning Once To Look Back. Ross
    Leckie. P49
"Last night I heard him in the woods". The
    Woodpecker. Joyce Sambrook. P51
"Last night I saw a horse above". Letter to
    an Exile. Lala Heine-Koehn. P49
"Last night I saw a silver road". The Silver
    Road. Hamish Hendry. P51
"Last night the carol-singers came". The
    Carol Singers. Margaret G. Rhodes. P51
"Last night the gypsies came--.". Gypsies.
    Rachel (Lyman) Field. P51
"Last night, within my dreaming". Pine
    Music. Kate Louise Brown. P51
"Last winter, everything iced over".
    Attitudes of Thanksgiving. Jill
    Breckenridge. P88
Late. Elaine Dallman. P65
Late Autumn Afternoons. R. B. Weber. P64
A Late Elegy for a Baseball Player. Felix
    Stefanile. P57
The . Late Snow and Lumber Strike of the
    Summer of Fifty-Four. Gary Snyder. P85
"Late fall finishes the season for
    marketing". Tobacco Men. James
    Applewhite. P67
"Late in autumn every year". Old Man Winter.
    Tilda S. Akers. P72
"The late peach yields a subtle musk". The
    Coming of the Cold. Theodore Roethke.
    P84
"A late snow beats". Faces. Lola Ridge. P82
"Lately he went away some place". Report
    'Present'. Eleftheria Kounrouri. P72
"Lately, I've become accustomed to the way".
    Preface to a Twenty Volume Suicide
    Note. Amiri (LeRoi Jones) Baraka. P85
The Lateshow Diorama. Christopher Dewdney.
    P49
Latin America
    Market. Robert Hayden. P84
The Latin American Solidarity Committee
    Fundraising... Ed Ochester. P63
Latin Night. Noel Peattie. P56
"The Laughing Girl is 'liberated'...".
    Unknown. P62
Laughing Song. William Blake. P51
Laughlin, James
    The Care and Feeding of a Poet. P63
Laughter
    Bursting. Dorothy Aldis. P50
Laughter. Olive Enoch. P51
    Laughing Song. William Blake. P51
    Laughter (I). Tin-wen Chung. P72
Laundromat Eulogies. James D. Hartman. P86
Laundry and Laundering

Wash‡Day. Lilian McCrea. P51
Launius, Carl Judson
    Job's Turkey: a Commentary. P63
    Paolo's Version. P63
LaVine, Steve
    Micro/Macro. P77
    On a Yankee Hill Morning. P77
Laus Veneris (a Picture by Burne-Jones).
    Louise Chandler Moulton. P90
Lavatories
    The Wonderful World. Robert D.
        Sutherland. P63
Lavender. Unknown. P89
"Lavender/Jasmine-scented nights". Night
    Brushes. Kitty Yeager. P72
Lawler, Craig
    The Vampire Came. P73
Lawn Bumps. Barbara Guest. P64
"The lawn-mower had only three wheels". At
    Play in the Field. Edward Butscher.
    P64
Lawrence, Arline Beryl
    Mendocino Meadow. P72
Lawrence, David Herbert
    Sea-Weed. P76
Lawrence, Neal Henry
    Tanka. P72
Lawrence, Robert
    Barra. P49
Laws of Drifting. Alane Rollings. P88
The Laxness Monster; or, I Be Singer...
    William Harmon. P63
"Lay down these words". Riprap. Gary Snyder.
    P85
Layton, Irving
    Boschka Layton 1921-1984. P49
    Dionysians in a Bad Time. P49
Lazard, Naomi
    The Angels Among Us. P64
    Stepping Out with My Big Cats. P64
    Stray Dogs. P64
    Walking with Lulu in the Wood. P64
Lazarus, A. L.
    I Wish I Were Living in Your Century. P63
    Memo to My Music Teacher. P63
Lazarus, Emma
    Gifts. P90
    The New Colossus. P90
Lazarus, Emma
    The Homecoming of Emma Lazarus. Galway
        Kinnell. P85
Lazy One. Lynne Anderson. P73
"Lazy sheep, pray tell me why". The Sheep.
    Ann Taylor. P51
Le Morte Darthur, sels. Sir Thomas Malory.
    P66
Lea, John
    The Silver House. P51
The Leaden-Eyed. Vachel Lindsay. P82

Leaf. Gwyn Thomas. P87
"A leaf falls soflty at my feet". A Leaf.
    Johann Ludwig Uhland. P89
"The leaf from the tree is shed". Leaf. Gwyn
    Thomas. P87
"A leaf lies shaking". Autumn. David
    Ignatow. P64
The Leaf-Picking. Frederic Mistral. P89
A Leaf. Johann Ludwig Uhland. P89
"Lean out of the window". Goldenhair. James
    Joyce. P51
The Leap. J. M. Girglani. P72
Leapt into the Dance. Nyanpandong. P53
Lear, Edward
    An Alphabet. P90
    The Jumblies. P89
    The Owl and the Pussycat. P51,P89
    The Table and the Chair. P90
    "There Was a Young Lady of Wales". P90
    "There Was an Old Lady of France". P90
    "There Was an Old Man of Moldavia". P90
    "There Was an Old Man Who Supposed". P90
    "There Was an Old Man, Who When Little".
        P90
    "There Was an Old Person of Hurst". P90
    "There Was an Old Person Whose Habits".
        P90
Lear, Edward
    Edward Lear Finds Paradise (And Loses
        It). J. Patrick Lewis. P63
    Old Foss, (The Cat) Recalls His Life...
        J. Patrick Lewis. P63
    The Queen Takes Drawing Lessons from King
        Lear. J. Patrick Lewis. P63
A Learned Man. Stephen Crane. P81
Learning
    April Inventory. William DeWitt
        Snodgrass. P85
    "Despite All the Training". Jack Hill.
        P86
    The Morning Reading. Wu Cheng. P92
    These Strewn Thoughts by the Mountain
        Pathway Sprung. George Santayana. P81
    The Train. Dennis Moore. P86
    Trying to Remember. Judith Minty. P88
The Learning Tree. Dorothy Lyons. P72
A Leave-Taking. William Phylip. P87
Leaves
    December Leaves. Kaye Starbird. P80
    Fluttering Leaves. Rodney Bennett. P51
    Gathering Leaves. Robert Frost. P82
    Leaf. Gwyn Thomas. P87
    Leaves. Katharine (Hinkson) Tynan. P51
    The Leaves. Unknown. P51
    Les Etiquettes Jaunes. Frank O'Hara. P85
Leaves. Katharine (Hinkson) Tynan. P51
"The leaves floated down, crisp, brown". His
    Matisses, 1938. Julia Keeler. P49
"The leaves had a wonderful frolic". The

Leaves. Unknown. P51
"Leaves infused with chromates". Water
       Color. T. A. Shulgin. P58
The Leaves. Unknown. P51
Leavetaking. Anne Porter. P64
Leaving. Aristoteles Espana. P71
Leaving. Jeremy Hooker. P54
Leaving. Sergio Mansilla. P71
Leaving Fargo: April. Linda M. Hasselstrom.
       P88
Leaving the Door Open (1), sel. David
       Ignatow. P64
Leaving the Door Open (31), sel. David
       Ignatow. P64
Leckie, Ross
       Turning Once To Look Back. P49
Lecky, William E. H.
       The Sower and His Seed. P90
Lee in the Mountains 1865-1870. Donald
       Davidson. P67
Lee, B. J.
       Troll Trick. P55
Lee, Brian
       Rain. P75
Lee, Dennis
       Lying on Things. P80
       'Riffs', sel. P49
Lee, Joyce
       Wimmera Child's First Waterfall. P72
Lee, Maria Berl
       Let Me Go. P68
Lee-Adams, Lily Jean
       The Friendship Only Lasted a Few Seconds.
       P86
       I Thought They Would Listen. P86
Leech, Annie Laurie
       Deeds in Orbit. P72
       One's Goal. P72
Legacy. Gladys Pearl Allen. P72
The Legacy. John Donne. P59
Legend of Indian Summer. Edna Bacon
       Morrison. P68
Legends
       The Berserker. Blessing Richard A. P68
       Hiawatha's Brothers. Henry Wadsworth
       Longfellow. P51
       Hiawatha's Childhood, fr. The song of
       Hiawatha. Henry Wadsworth Longfellow.
       P51
       The Invention of White People. Leslie
       MArmon Silko. P78
       The Myth Revisited: Adam. Michael V.
       McGee. P56
       Sir Orfeo. Unknown. P66
       The Song of Hiawatha Selections. Henry
       Wadsworth Longfellow. P90
       Telling About Coyote. Simon Ortiz. P78
       A Transformation, from The Metamorphoses.
       Ovid. P90

Lehman, David
       Wystan Hugh Auden: a Villanelle. P63
Lehner, Francis
       October Is the Cruelest Month. P68
Leighty, Christina
       The Dreamer. P74
Leisure
       Afternoon on a Hill. Edna St. Vincent
       Millay. P51
Leisure. William Henry Davies. P51,P90
       The Echoing Green. William Blake. P51
       Freedom. Joan Agnew. P51
       On Their Day Off. Alexander Gerov. P70
       Under the Greenwood Tree. William
       Shakespeare. P51
Lemuel's Blessing. William Stanley Merwin.
       P85
Lenski, Lois
       "Sing a Song of People". P60
Lent in a Year of War. Thomas Merton. P84
Lentini, Giacomo da
       "I Have Set My Heart on Serving God".
       Frede Jensen (tr.). P69
       "I Have Seen the Clear Sky Produce Rain".
       Frede Jensen (tr.). P69
       "I Hope to Receive a Reward". Frede
       Jensen (tr.). P69
       "Just Like the Butterfly, Which Has Such
       a Nature". Frede Jensen (tr.). P69
       "Love Is a Desire Which Comes from the
       Heart". Frede Jensen (tr.). P69
       "Many Lovers Bear Their Illness". Frede
       Jensen (tr.). P69
       "My lady, I Wish to Tell You". Frede
       Jensen (tr.). P69
       "Since Mercy Is of No Avail to Me...".
       Frede Jensen (tr.). P69
       "Sweet Beginning:.". Frede Jensen (tr.).
       P69
       "There Truly First Came to Me Deep
       Sorrow". Frede Jensen (tr.). P69
       "Wonderfully". Frede Jensen (tr.). P69
"Leonardo's angel". Verrocchio. Richard
       Harrison. P49
Leonidas
       Home. Robert Bland (tr.). P89
Lepore, Dominick J.
       Day in May. P56
Lermontov, Mikhail
       Dagger. M. Eastman (tr.). P90
       A Sail. P90
Les Belles Heures. Lois Guthrie. P68
Les Etiquettes Jaunes. Frank O'Hara. P85
Les Saintes-Maries De La Mer. Karl H. Bolay.
       P72
Lesson One. Guanetta Gordon. P72
Lessons in Love. Edward A. Gloeggler. P65
"Lest the sharp tongue become a sword". My
       Prayer. Bessie Wherry Noe. P72

Let All World Poets Rejoice. Joy Beaudette
    Cripps. P72
Let Beauty Shine. Alice M. Boughtwood. P68
Let Her Be Red. Nyakuoth Macar. P53
Let Him Be. Georgi Borisov. P70
Let Me Go. Maria Berl Lee. P68
Let No Charitable Hope. Elinor Wylie. P82
Let Other People Come as Streams. Charles
    Reznikoff. P83
"Let from no earth-engendered thing...". In
    the Dream's Recess. William Everson.
    P84
"Let me be your servant". Healthful Old Age,
    from As You Like It. William
    Shakespeare. P90
"Let me but do my work from day to day".
    Work. Henry Van Dyke. P90
"Let me mention". Feast Days: Christmas.
    Annie Dillard. P47
"' Let me see if Philip can'.". The Story of
    Fidgety Philip. Heinrich Hoffmann. P90
"Let not soft slumber close my eyes". Self-
    Inquiry. Isaac Watts. P89
"Let not young souls be smothered out
    before". The Leaden-Eyed. Vachel
    Lindsay. P82
"Let poetry be like a skeleton key". Ars
    Poetique. Rodrigo Lira. P71
Let the Light Enter. Frances E. W. Harper.
    P89
' Let There Be Translators!'. Grace
    Schulman. P79
Let Us Forego Life's Puppet Show. Helen
    Carter King. P72
Let Wildness Come. Margaret Longenecker
    Been. P68
"Let the crows go by hawking their caw and
    caw". River Roads. Carl Sandburg. P82
"Let the crumbs of our flesh be strewn...".
    A Song to God. Salah Abdul-Sabur. P91
"Let the gentle be at rest...". A Wife's
    Epitaph. R. Williams Parry. P87
"Let the man be who had nothing to tell
    you". Let Him Be. Georgi Borisov. P70
"Let the rain kiss you". April Rain Song.
    Langston Hughes. P75
"Let the typewriter be my lover". Beginning
    Writer. Bonnie Squires. P72
"' Let there be light,' God said...". Light,
    from Paradise Lost. John Milton. P89
"Let us dance and let us sing". The Fairy
    Ring. Unknown. P51
"Let us gather all the rifles, all". Medals.
    Richard M. Mishler. P86
"Let us go then, you and I". The Love Song
    of J. Alfred Prufrock. Thomas Stearns
    Eliot. P83
"Let us no more turn and run". Terror to
    Unborn Children. Tonya McCulley. P74

"Let us not sit upon the ground". An Elegy
    To Dispel Gloom. Lawrence
    Ferlinghetti. P85
"Let us walk in the white snow". Velvet
    Shoes. Elinor Wylie. P89
Let's Shield Your Light with Our Hand, My
    Heart. Jules Supervielle. P61
"Let's allow the infinity of the
    Atacama...". To the Immaculate Plains.
    Raul Zurita. P71
"Let's get mad, fellow losers, fellow
    flops". Self Help. William Trowbridge.
    P63
Lethbridge, Alberta; Thursday Evening,
    November... Stephen Scobie. P49
Letter from a Far Country. Gillian Clarke.
    P54
A Letter from Gwyther Street. Roland
    Mathias. P54
Letter from the Islands. Diana Kwiatkowski.
    P56
"The letter of the sunny eye". Sunny Eye.
    Maria Kukubaiska. P72
A Letter on the Use of Machine Guns at
    Weddings. Kenneth Patchen. P84
Letter to a Census Taker. Mario Speracio.
    P65
Letter to an Exile. Lala Heine-Koehn. P49
Letter to Johnny. Bessie Wherry Noe. P65
A Letter to My Mother in Vidin. Luchesar
    Elenkov. P70
Letter to My Parents. F. W. Watt. P49
Letter to Shadow. Daryl Hine. P79
The Letter. Amy Lowell. P82
Letters. Wolfgang Durben. P72
Letters and Letter Writing
    Epistle To Be Left in the Earth.
        Archibald MacLeish. P83
    Found Wanting. Emily Dickinson. P89
    Letter to Johnny. Bessie Wherry Noe. P65
    A Letter to My Mother in Vidin. Luchesar
        Elenkov. P70
    The Letter. Amy Lowell. P82
    Letters. Wolfgang Durben. P72
    Mary Passed This Morning. Owen Dodson.
        P84
    My Grandmother's Love Letters. Hart
        Crane. P83
    On an Unwritten Letter. Eugenio Montale.
        P61
    Read to the Animals, or Orpheus at the
        SPCA. Irving Feldman. P79
    V-Letter. Karl Shapiro. P84
Letting Go. Alice Derry. P88
Letting Him Go. James Tate. P85
Letting the Cat Die. Gwendolyn Vincent. P58
Letts, Winifred M.
    The Elfin People Fill the Tubes. P51
    Pensioners. P51

Spring, the Travelling Man. P51

Leurgans, Lois
Epitaph. P63

Leuty, Helen
The Night. P51
Poplars. P51

Levchev, Lyubomir
Again. Richard Harteis (tr.). P70
Ballad of the Ladder. William Meredith
(tr.). P70
Bureaucrat. William Meredith (tr.). P70
My Mother in Paradise. May Swenson (tr.).
P70
P. S. Instead of a Beginning. William
Meredith (tr.). P70
Roofs. William Meredith (tr.). P70

Lever, Bernice
As if Carbon Is Nothing. P49

Levertov, Denise
Cancion. P85
Come into Animal Presence. P85
During the Eichmann Trial, sels. P85
The Goddess. P85
The Hands. P85
The Old Adam. P85
Pleasures. P85
Rain Spirit Passing. P85
Scenes from the Life of the Peppertrees.
P85
Wedding-Ring. P85
Writing in the Dark. P85

Levertov, Denise (tr.)
The Artist. Unknown. P78
The Cricket. Krassin Himmirsky. P70
The Ugly Man. Liliana Stefanova. P70

Levi, Steven C.
Ol' Grandad. P56

Leviathan. William Stanley Merwin. P85

Levin and Emha Ainunn Nadjib, Harriet (tr.)
Bukan. Emha Ainunn Nadjib. P92

Levine, Philip
New Season. P52

Lewis, Bernard (tr.)
Epitaphs. Orhan Veli Kanik. P91
For You. Orhan Veli Kanik. P91
Headache. Orhan Veli Kanik. P91
Inside. Orhan Veli Kanik. P91
Talk. Orhan Veli Kanik. P91
There Must Be Something. Orhan Veli
Kanik. P91

Lewis, Dorothy T.
First Names. P72

Lewis, J. Patrick
Edward Lear Finds Paradise (And Loses
It). P63
Old Foss, (The Cat) Recalls His Life...
P63
The Queen Takes Drawing Lessons from King
Lear. P63

Lewis, Saunders
Ascension Thursday. Tony Conran (tr.).
P87
Awdl. Tony Conran (tr.). P87
The Deluge, 1939. Tony Conran (tr.). P87

Lewisohn, L. (tr.)
Night. Hermann Hesse. P90
The Youth Dreams. Rainer Maria Rilke. P90

Liatsos, Sandra
At the Beach. P76
Seashell. P76

"The lie shone in your face before you
spoke". Nike. James Merrill. P79

Liebknecht, Henrietta
Colors. P72

Lies and Lying
Charity, Thou Art a Lie. Stephen Crane.
P81
Life. Georgi Belev. P70
Tell Me. Norma Lopez Garcia. P68
Tell Me a Lie. Vladimir Golev. P70
Two-faced. Sion Tudur. P87
White Lie. Deanna Fleysher. P73
With Eye and with Gesture. Stephen Crane.
P81
Yes, I Have a Thousand Tongues. Stephen
Crane. P81

Life
After the Revolution for Jesus... Miller
Williams. P67
Alberts Landing. Hugh Seidman. P64
Assonance. Barry Callaghan. P49
At a Concert. R. P. Dickey. P63
At Sainte-Marguerite. Trumbull Stickney.
P81

Life. Max S. Barker. P68
Barter. Sara Teasdale. P82

Life. Georgi Belev. P70
Beneath Each Stone. Walter Hoefler. P71
A Biblical Motif. Boris Khristov. P92
The Corner of the Eye. Robert Penn
Warren. P67
Davis Matlock, from Spoon River
Anthology. Edgar Lee Masters. P82
Dawn Climbs over Time. Emma Crobaugh. P72
Day After Day. Juliane Chakravorty. P72
Dead Color. Charles Wright. P67
The Dream of Life. Vera La Claustra. P72
The Dream Songs, sels. John Berryman. P84
Driftwood. Trumbull Stickney. P81
Epoch. Nikola Vaptsarov. P70
Equation. Caroline Perkins. P68
An Examination into Life and Death.
Kenneth Patchen. P84
A Feeling. Bo Yang. P72
Finale. Tibor Tollas. P61
Fish Poem. Joy Kogawa. P49
The Form of Living. Richard Rolle. P66
Fugitive. Lisel Mueller. P88

Life. Chrystie Fulmer. P74
    Gnomic Stanzas. Unknown. P87
    A God Came to Man. Stephen Crane. P81
    Handling it--. Edith Freund. P88
Life. George Herbert. P59
    If There Is a Witness. Stephen Crane. P81
    "In the Sun Here". Shelly A. Allen. P77
    Is the Pathetic Fallacy True?. Elizabeth
        Brewster. P49
    It All Comes Together Outside the
        Restroom... James Seay. P67
    Jellyfish. Nikolai Kuntchev. P70
    Laundromat Eulogics. James D. Hartman.
        P86
    Leisure. William Henry Davies. P90
    Les Saintes-Maries De La Mer. Karl H.
        Bolay. P72
Life. Kathleen Chan Wallace. P72
Life. Richard Henry Wilde. P90
Life. Sergio Mansilla. P71
Life. Max S. Barker. P68
Life. Bryan Waller ("Barry Cornwall")
        Procter. P89
    Life, from Thoughts I Caught. Frieda Jo
        Hawes. P72
    Life, What Is It but a Dream?. Charles
        Lutwidge ("Lewis Carroll") Dodgson.
        P90
    Limbo. Yaedi Ignatow. P64
    Lucinda Matlock, from Spoon River
        Anthology. Edgar Lee Masters. P82
Life. Sergio Mansilla. P71
    Maya. C. Ramamohan Rao. P72
    The Naked Eye. Lewis Turco. P63
    Notes from the Castle. Howard Moss. P64
    On Living, from Life Is a Dream. Pedro
        Calderon de la Barca. P90
    On the Beach. Michael Heller. P64
    A Parched Pitcher. Mehdi Akhavan Sales.
        P91
Life. Bryan Waller ("Barry Cornwall")
        Procter. P89
    A Psalm of Life. Henry Wadsworth
        Longfellow. P89
    The Quality of Life. Steve Sanfield. P77
    Reversal. Eleanore-Melissa. P68
    Right Now and Here. Barbara Kitterman
        Shepherd. P68
    Seven Ages of Man, from As You Like It.
        William Shakespeare. P90
    Sic Transit Vita. Louise Wilkerson Conn.
        P72
    The Sky Eats up the Trees. James
        Schuyler. P64
    A Slant of Sun. Stephen Crane. P81
    Survivor. Walter Hoefler. P71
    Tears. Lizette Woodworth Reese. P81
    There Was a Man Who Lived a Life of Fire.
        Stephen Crane. P81

    Things As They Are. Bonnie Jacobson. P63
    Three Darknesses. Robert Penn Warren. P67
    Vapor Trail Reflected in the Frog Pond.
        Galway Kinnell. P85
Life. Kathleen Chan Wallace. P72
    When All the World Is Young. Charles
        Kingsley. P51
    Whirlpools. Kolyo Sevov. P70
Life. Richard Henry Wilde. P90
    "With a Sieve". Tilly Boesche Zacharow.
        P72
    Woe One. Alice Ryerson. P88
"**Life** doesn't offer much better". Silk
        Pyjamas. Michael Holstein. P63
"**Life** feeds on life". The Unappeasable. Cy
        Patteson. P72
"**Life** has loveliness to sell". Barter. Sara
        Teasdale. P82
Life in Color. Helen Thomas Allison. P72
"**Life** is not at all what you might
        think...". Some Words. John Ashbery.
        P52
A **Life's** Love. Unknown. P90
"**Life's** a jail where men have common lot".
        The Gamblers. Vachel Lindsay. P82
Life, from Thoughts I Caught. Frieda Jo
        Hawes. P72
Life, What Is It but a Dream?. Charles
        Lutwidge ("Lewis Carroll") Dodgson.
        P90
Life-Brevity of
    Heart and Mind. Edith Sitwell. P90
    Hymn of the Lyre Player. Fatthy Said. P91
    The Leaden-Eyed. Vachel Lindsay. P82
    Trust. Lizette Woodworth Reese. P81
Life-Conduct of
    "Although They Both Exist". Unknown. P62
    American Rhapsody. Kenneth Fearing. P83
    Anyone Lived in a Pretty How Town. Edward
        Estlin Cummings. P83
    "Blessed Are the Deaf and Blind".
        Unknown. P62
    "A Bow, Returning to Its Natural
        Straightness". Unknown. P62
    "Do Not Trust Those Evil Men Who Owe You
        Money". Unknown. P62
    "The Dying Chief with Effort Tells His
        Son". Unknown. P62
    Find the Nerve To Get Excited. Pat
        Bridges. P56
    "The Fire Burns in the Sacrifice
        Enclosure". Unknown. P62
    Flux. Richard Eberhart. P83
    "For Those Who Know Their Own Hearts".
        Unknown. P62
    If They Come in the Night. Marge Piercy.
        P52
    "Just As the Full Moon, At the Moment of
        Daybreak". Unknown. P62

King Hayden of Miami Beach. Robert
    Duncan. P84
"Oh Clever Poverty, You Are Enamoured".
    Unknown. P62
"Oh Heart, Unafraid of Your Own
    Judgement". Unknown. P62
"Overcoming Untimely Anger". Unknown. P62
"People Who Do Not Even Know the
    Alphabet". Unknown. P62
The Seekonk Woods. Galway Kinnell. P52
Some Words. John Ashbery. P52
A Sunny Day, fr. Five Groups of Verse.
    Charles Reznikoff. P83
"There Are Some Especially Who Stretch
    Their Mouths". Unknown. P62
"We Think Less of Women When Out of Our
    Vision". Unknown. P62
"Who Does Not Gain Wisdom". Unknown. P62
"Who Uses Goods Made by the Base?.".
    Unknown. P62
"Whoever Is Fat Was Born Like That".
    Unknown. P62

Life-Nature of
Chess. Waldo Rojas. P71
Portrait. Louise Gluck. P85
Stone Reality Meditation. Lawrence
    Ferlinghetti. P85

Life-Unlived
The Old Adam. Denise Levertov. P85
"... Life/Is harbor and magnetized orbit".
    When You Realize That... Virginia
    Rodas. P72

Light
Invocation to Light, from Paradise Lost.
    John Milton. P89
Light. Elizabeth Simpson Todd. P72
Light, from Paradise Lost. John Milton.
    P89
Light, Light, Somewhat Revolving... Jules
    Romains. P61
Seer. Josephine Miles. P84
Light. Elizabeth Simpson Todd. P72
Light and Shadow. Robert Francis. P63
The Light at the Edge of the World. Geoffrey
    Parsons. P72
A Light in the Doorway. Cary Waterman. P88
Light Shining Out of Darkness. William
    Cowper. P89
Light Talk (I). Adjutor. P72
"Light is my canopy". Light. Elizabeth
    Simpson Todd. P72
"' Light! more light! the shadows deepen'.".
    Let the Light Enter. Frances E. W.
    Harper. P89
Light, from Paradise Lost. John Milton. P89
Light, Light, Somewhat Revolving... Jules
    Romains. P61
The Light-Hearted Fairy. Unknown. P51
"The lighted candle moves". Night. Maria

Celeste Achille Todde. P61
The Lighter That Never Fails. R. L. Barth.
    P86
The Lighthouse. Marjorie Wilson. P51
Lighthouses
I'd Like To Be a Lighthouse. Rachel
    (Lyman) Field. P76
"Lighting cavern zero". Summer Storm,
    Highway 37. Gloria Still. P88
Lightly Like Music Running. Jean Garrigue.
    P84
"The lights are all on...". Rain. Brian Lee.
    P75
The Lights. J. J. Bell. P51
Like a Dream. Raul Zurita. P71
"Like a Warden at the Evening Meal". Simon
    Perchik. P64
Like Him Whose Spirit. Arthur Davidson
    Ficke. P82
Like Swallows. Pearl Newton Rook. P68
"Like a drowsy, rain-browned saint". Hill-
    Side Tree. Maxwell Bodenheim. P82
"Like a lily, gleaming maid". The Poet Dies
    for Love. Unknown. P87
"Like a magnet". Aries Sideshow. Charles
    Ghigna. P63
"Like a witch with one foot". The Rag Lady.
    Nancy McCleery. P88
"Like battered old millhands, they
    stand...". Old Apple Trees. William
    DeWitt Snodgrass. P85
"Like brambles twisted in a thicket, six".
    The Lighter That Never Fails. R. L.
    Barth. P86
"Like crumbled tissue paper, road map
    lines". Octogenarian. Irene A.
    Bradshaw. P72
"Like Jonson's son, I am of the right hand".
    Sons of the Right Hand. Benjamin
    Hochman. P63
"Like Sal Paradise, a mouse gets wet...".
    Wandering Was Always an Important
    Theme in My Lyric. Tetsuo Nakagami.
    P92
"Like souls that balance joy and pain". Sir
    Lancelot and Queen Guinevere. Lord
    Tennyson. P89
"Like still thoughts they sit". Geese in
    Fog. Therese Becker. P88
"Like survivors on an isle of alyssum".
    Summer Vacation. Kathleen Iddings. P72
"Like the brilliance of an eye in darkness".
    Your Anger. Paz Molina. P71
"Like the soldier, like the sailor...". A
    Letter on the Use of Machine Guns at
    Weddings. Kenneth Patchen. P84
"Like watching rings extend in water". For
    You. Robert Creeley. P85
"Like wisteria brushing us...". Shared

Festivals. Wallace Winchell. P65
Lilacs. Amy Lowell. P89
"Lilacs along the strap iron fence". At
    Billings' Bridge Graveyard. Robert
    Billings. P49
"Lilacs/False blue". Lilacs. Amy Lowell. P89
Lilies
    The Water-Lily. John Banister Tabb. P81
"Lilies Are White". Unknown. P51
Limbo. Yaedi Ignatow. P64
Limerick. Scott Bruno. P73
Limerick. Rudyard Kipling. P90
Limerick. Justin Petosa. P73
Limericks
    An Aged Rector Named Fiddle. Robert
        Phillips. P63
    Bitter Grapes. Bruce Berger. P63
    Clerihew Couples. Roberta Simone. P63
    Clerihews. Adrian Vonna. P63
Limericks. David Cram. P63
    Drawbacks. Emily Otis. P63
    "E. C. Bentley". David Jacobs. P63
    E=MCround. Ann Deagon. P63
    A French Writer Named Sartre. Weldon
        Kees. P63
Limericks. Linda Galvao. P74
    "A Grumpy Old Owl at the Zoo". Laurence
        Perrine. P63
    "Hernando DeSoto". Margaret Blaker. P63
    The Lamb. Bob McKenty. P63
    Limerick. Rudyard Kipling. P90
    Limerick. Justin Petosa. P73
    Limerick. Scott Bruno. P73
    Limericks. David Cram. P63
    Limericks. Linda Galvao. P74
    Limericks. Unknown. P90
    Literary River Rhyme. William Cole. P63
    "Margaret Sanger". Tom Riley. P63
    Mitzi. Weldon Kees. P63
    Not What We Had in Mind. May Richstone.
        P63
    Office Hours. Katharyn Machan Aal. P63
    The Passionate Businessman To His Love.
        Bruce Bennett. P63
    Quail. Katharyn Machan Aal. P63
    Ribald Siver Rhyme. William Cole. P63
    "Scott Joplin". Gavin Ewart. P63
    Seedam. Lily D. Angle. P63
    She Don't Bop. Keith Casto. P63
    "Shirley Temple". Paul Curry Steele. P63
    Swish. Christine Stratton. P73
    "There Was a Young Lady of Wales". Edward
        Lear. P90
    "There Was an Old Lady of France". Edward
        Lear. P90
    "There Was an Old Man of Moldavia".
        Edward Lear. P90
    "There Was an Old Man Who Supposed".
        Edward Lear. P90

    "There Was an Old Man, Who When Little".
        Edward Lear. P90
    "There Was an Old Person of Hurst".
        Edward Lear. P90
    "There Was an Old Person Whose Habits".
        Edward Lear. P90
Limericks. Unknown. P90
    "Walter Savage Landor". James Steel
        Smith. P63
    Well Bed. Lola Strong Janes. P63
    "'When Windham Lewis'". Bonnie Jacobson.
        P63
    The Zebra. Bob McKenty. P63
Limited. Audrey Frederick. P72
Limping Boat. J. Bapu Reddy. P72
Lin, Yung-jung
    On the Eve of Departure for Sixth World
        Congress... P72
The Lincoln Child. James Oppenheim. P82
Lincoln, Abraham
    Abraham Lincoln Walks at Midnight. Vachel
        Lindsay. P82
    The Lincoln Child. James Oppenheim. P82
    Lincoln, the Man of the People. Edwin
        Markham. P81
    On the Life-Mask of Lincoln. Richard
        Watson Gilder. P81
    Three Hundred Thousand More. Unknown. P90
Lincoln, the Man of the People. Edwin
    Markham. P81
Linda to Hafed, from The Fire-Worshippers.
    Thomas Moore. P89
Lindemans, Marjan
    'Twas but a Dream. P73
Linden, Maia
    Ode to Strings. P65
Lindsay, Vachel
    Abraham Lincoln Walks at Midnight. P82
    At Mass. P82
    The Broncho That Would Not Be Broken. P82
    The Congo. P82
    The Eagle That Is Forgotten. P82
    The Gamblers. P82
    General William Booth Enters into Heaven.
        P82
    The Ghosts of the Buffaloes. P82
    The Leaden-Eyed. P82
    "Nests in the Top of the Almond Tree".
        P82
    A Net to Snare the Moonlight. P82
    The Spider and the Ghost of the Fly. P82
Lindsley, Mary F.
    IX--Royal Favor. P72
"A line of poplars, joining hands". Trees.
    Donald J. Kintner. P68
Lines Found in his Bible in the Gate-
    House... Sir Walter Raleigh. P89
"The lines of love would not be hard to
    draw". Geometry of Love. Anne Marx.

P65
Lines to Accompany Flowers for Eve. Carolyn
    Kizer. P79
Lines to an Indian Air. Percy Bysshe
    Shelley. P89
Lines to the Stormy Petrel. Unknown. P89
Linton, William James
    Patience, from Poems of Freedom. P90
"The Lion and the Unicorn". Unknown. P51
Lipes, Mary Alice
    Dusk. P74
"Lips that touch liquor...". In Praise of
    Sobriety. John Frederick Nims. P63
Lipschutz, Kurt
    The Errand Boy's Day Off. P63
Lipstick Graffito. Aletha Humphreys. P68
"Liquid, water". Zuni Derivations. Unknown.
    P78
Lira, Rodrigo
    Ars Poetique. Steven F. White (tr.). P71
"List' to me". Nature. Nicholas [pseud.].
    P68
Listen. Dara D. Henderson. P73
"Listen old man listen". Sweat-House Ritual
    No.1. Unknown. P78
"Listen to leaf fall". Hard Frost. Cathryn
    Hankla. P56
"Listen to the kitchen clock". The Old
    Kitchen Clock. Ann ("Aunt Effie")
    Hawkshawe. P51
"Listen to the song". Wandering Jack. Emile
    Jacot. P51
"Listen! In the April rain". In the April
    Rain. Mary Anderson. P51
"Listen, my children, and you shall hear".
    Paul Revere's Ride. Henry Wadsworth
    Longfellow. P90
"Listen, my clansmen". Song of Lawino, sel.
    Okot p' Bitek. P92
"Listen, my colleague traduced...". Dead
    Languages. Jay MacPherson. P49
"Listen./It is by this". On This Shore. Siv
    Cedering. P64
"Listen/With faint dry sound". November
    Night. Adelaide Crapsey. P81
"Lit/At either end". Tallow. Bruce Kingery.
    P68
A Literary History of Cheese. Roberta
    Simone. P63
Literary River Rhyme. William Cole. P63
Literature
    Great Plains Lit. Mark Sanders. P63
"Lithe and long as the serpent train". The
    Grape-Vine Swing. William Gilmore
    Simms. P89
Little Betty Blue. Agnes Grozier Herbertson.
    P51
Little Billee. William Makepeace Thackeray.
    P90

A Little Bird's Song. Margaret Rose. P51
Little Birds of the Night. Stephen Crane.
    P81
Little Birds Swooping. Mary Ann Henn. P63
Little Blue Apron. Unknown. P51
Little Boy Blue. Eugene Field. P81
"Little Boy Blue, Come, Blow up Your Horn".
    Unknown. P51
Little Brown Seed. Rodney Bennett. P51
Little Clotilda. Unknown. P51
"A Little Cock Sparrow Sat on a Tree".
    Unknown. P51
Little Dame Crump. Unknown. P51
The Little Dancers. Laurence Binyon. P51
A Little Drama. Paulette Roeske. P88
Little Elegy. Michael McFee. P63
The Little Elf-Man. John Kendrick Bangs. P51
A Little Finger Game. E. J. Falconer. P51
The Little Fir Tree. Margaret Rose. P51
Little Friend. David Ignatow. P64
Little Ghosts. Oscar Hahn. P71
The Little Girl with Bands on her Teeth.
    Genevieve Taggard. P83
'"Little Girl, Little Girl'.". Unknown. P51
The Little Herd-Boy's Song. Robert Buchanan.
    P51
"Little Jenny Wren". Unknown. P51
Little Kings and Queens of the May. Juliana
    Horatia Ewing. P51
Little Lucy Lester. M. Steel. P51
Little Maid and Cowslips. John Clare. P51
The Little Men. Flora Fearne. P51
The Little Moon. Henry Wadsworth Longfellow.
    P51
The Little Old Lady. Rodney Bennett. P51
Little Orphant Annie. James Whitcomb Riley.
    P89
The Little Piggies. Thomas Hood. P51
Little Rain-Drops. Ann ("Aunt Effie")
    Hawkshawe. P51
The Little Random Creatures. Unknown. P78
Little Robin Redbreast. Unknown. P51
"Little Robin Redbreast". Unknown. P51
Little Seashell. Celia Uhrman. P72
Little Things. Eileen Mathias. P51
The Little Things That Happen. Marjorie
    Wilson. P51
Little Tommy Tiddler. Paul Edmonds. P51
Little Trotty Wagtail. John Clare. P51
"Little bat, little bat". To the Bat. Edith
    King. P51
"A little bit of blowing". Thoughts for a
    Cold Day. Unknown. P51
"Little Bo-Peep". The Fairy Sleep and Little
    Bo-Peep. Unknown. P51
"Little children, never give". Kindness to
    Animals. Unknown. P51
"A little colt-broncho, loaned to the farm".
    The Broncho That Would Not Be Broken.

Vachel Lindsay. P82

"The **little** cousin is dead, by foul subtraction". Dead Boy. John Crowe Ransom. P83

"**Little** cramped words scrawling all over...". The Letter. Amy Lowell. P82

"**Little** drops of water". Kind Deeds. Isaac Watts. P51

"A **little** fairy comes at night". The Dream Fairy. Thomas Hood. P51

"A **little** green frog lived under a log". Strange Talk. L. E. Yates. P51

"A **little** green frog once lived in a pool". The Frog. Rose Fyleman. P51

"**Little** I ask, my wants are few". Contentment ('Man Wants but Little Here Below.'). Oliver Wendell Holmes. P90

"**Little** Indian, Sioux, or Crow". Foreign Children. Robert Louis Stevenson. P51

"**Little** Jesus wast Thou shy". Ex Ore Infantium. Francis Thompson. P51

"**Little** ladies, white and green". Snowdrops. Laurence Alma-Tadema. P51

"**Little** lamb, who made thee?.". The Lamb. William Blake. P51

"**Little** lambs, little lambs". Baby Beds. Unknown. P51

"**Little** Lucy Lavender". Lucy Lavender. Ivy O. Eastwick. P51

"**Little** masters, hat in hand". Clover. John Banister Tabb. P81

"**Little** mistress comfort". Mistress Comfort. Elizabeth Gould. P51

"**Little** Mr. Browny Bee". Browny Bee. Irene F. Pawsey. P51

"A **little** old woman". Bramble Jam. Irene F. Pawsey. P51

"A **little** pig lived in a sty". The Greedy Little Pig. Irene F. Pawsey. P51

"A **little** prince of long ago". Sons of the King. John Agnew. P51

"The **little** red lark". Morning. Ivy O. Eastwick. P51

"A **little** saint best fits a little shrine". 'Littles'. Robert Herrick. P51

""**little** soul, little flirting".". Prothalamion. Delmore Schwartz. P84

"A **little** stream had lost its way". A Deed and a Word. Charles Mackay. P89

"The **little** toy dog is covered with dust". Little Boy Blue. Eugene Field. P81

"A **little** yellow buttercup". A Buttercup. Unknown. P51

"**Little** young lambs, oh! why do you stay". The Wolf and the Lambs. Ivy O. Eastwick. P51

Little, Judy
Divorce. P88

Melting. P88
Television News. P88

Little, Paul
Narcissus. P72

Littledale, Freya
The Clock. P75

Littledale, R. F. (tr.)
O Fire of God, the Comforter. Saint Hildegarde. P89

' **Littles**'. Robert Herrick. P51

Livesay, Dorothy
The Ancestors: A Suite. P49

The **Livid** Lightnings Flashed in the Clouds. Stephen Crane. P81

Living Alone. D. Scott Taylor. P63

The **Living** Masters. Gavin Ewart. P63

Livingston, Myra Cohn
For Laura. P50
Rain-Walking. P75
Wharf. P76
Winter. P80

LLawdden
Going Home. Tony Conran (tr.). P87

LLwyd, Morgan
God and His Church. Tony Conran (tr.). P87

Llyn y Gadair. T.H. Parry-Williams. P87

Llyn, Wiliam
Elegy for Syr Owain ap Gwilym. Tony Conran (tr.). P87

Llywarch the Old, fr. Poetry from Lost Sagas. Unknown. P87

Llywelyn ap y Moel
To the Greyrock Woods. Tony Conran (tr.). P87

"**Llywelyn**, jackhammers ring in unison". The Strata: To Llywelyn Sion. Robert Minhinnick. P54

Llywelyn-Williams, Alun
Star of Bethlehem. Tony Conran (tr.). P87

"**Loacated** on the room's mantelpiece". The Probable and Improbable Disappearance of a Cat... Juan Luis Martinez. P71

"A **load** of apples going out". The Quality of Life. Steve Sanfield. P77

"**Loaded** on beer and whiskey, we ride". Shooting Rats at the Bibb County Dump. David Bottoms. P67

"The **lobbed** ball plops, then dribbles...". Ford Maddox Ford. Robert Lowell. P79

Lobster
The Lobster Quadrille. Charles Lutwidge ("Lewis Carroll") Dodgson. P51

A **Local** Man Doesn't Like the Music. James Whitehead. P67

"**Locate** I". The Language. Robert Creeley. P85

Lochinvar. Sir Walter Scott. P51

Locke, John R.

From a Watershed. P68
"Locked at last in our last embrace". The
          New Courtship. Richard Moore. P63
Locker-Lampson, Frederick
     The Widow's Mite. P89
Lockhart, Charles Tillman
     Hallelujah!. P72
Lockhart, John Gibson
     The Lord of Butrago. P90
Lodge, George Cabot
     Day and Dark. P81
     A Song of the Wave. P81
     Youth. P81
Lodovico Martelli. Trumbull Stickney. P81
Loew, C. M.
     Hay-Time. P51
Logging and Loggers
     Affluence. Gary Snyder. P85
     Myths and Texts (Logging). Gary Snyder.
          P85
Logic and 'the Magic Flute'. Marianne Moore.
          P79
Lohmann, Jeanne
     Naming the Birds. P65
London Rain. Nancy Byrd Turner. P75
London Trees. Beryl Netherclift. P51
London, England
     London Rain. Nancy Byrd Turner. P75
     London, March 1945. Pierre Emmanuel. P61
Loneliness
     The Afternoon Will Yet... Antonio
          Machado. P61
     Alex. Jason Gruhl. P73
     Bread and Music. Conrad Aiken. P82
     Danse Russe. William Carlos Williams. P82
     Desert Places. Robert Frost. P82
     "The Flash of Lightning Gives a Glimpse
          of the Clouds". Unknown. P62
     For Laura. Myra Cohn Livingston. P50
     For the Desert Island, from For the
          Desert Island. Tae-ch'ul Shin. P92
     Friendless. John Berryman. P79
     Ghost House. Robert Frost. P89
     Glass Walls. Karen Birch. P73
     Loneliness. Trumbull Stickney. P81
     Lonely Is... Jeremy Kohburn. P74
     The Loner. Thu-Phuong Do. P74
     Missing You. Charlotte Zolotow. P50
     Mnemosyne. Trumbull Stickney. P81
     "The Mother-in-Law, with singleness of
          Purpose". Unknown. P62
     Mr. Flood's Party. Edward Arlington
          Robinson. P81
     My Window, My Wheelchair, and Me. Deborah
          D'Aleo. P74
     On the Night of a Friend's Wedding.
          Edward Arlington Robinson. P81
     Since Hanna Moved Away. Judith Viorst.
          P50

     Song of the Lonely. Kelly Morris. P73
     Spring Night. Sara Teasdale. P82
Loneliness. Trumbull Stickney. P81
     "To Grandfather". Lorenzo. P77
     "The Traveller's Wife with Continually
          Flowing Tears". Unknown. P62
     V. Bogumil Wtorkiewicz. P72
     Waiting. T. A. Shulgin. P58
     Water Color. T. A. Shulgin. P58
     The Way Things Are Above and Below. Jaime
          Quezada. P71
     What Lips My Lips Have Kissed, and Where,
          and Why. Edna St. Vincent Millay. P82
     Woe Two. Alice Ryerson. P88
     "The Woman, with the Palm of Her Hand".
          Unknown. P62
Lonely Boat. Carla Zeppieri. P74
The Lonely Child. James Oppenheim. P82
The Lonely Death. Adelaide Crapsey. P81
"The lonely blood". For Barbara. Andrew
          Brooks. P49
Lonely for the Country. Bronwen Wallace. P49
Lonely Is... Jeremy Kohburn. P74
The Lonely Mother. Fenton Johnson. P82
"Lonely, save for a few faint stars, the
          sky". The Little Dancers. Laurence
          Binyon. P51
"The loner off". Ego at the Wheel. Ernest
          Kroll. P63
The Loner. Thu-Phuong Do. P74
Lonesome Bird. Etty George. P72
The Long Hill. Sara Teasdale. P82
The Long Island Night. Howard Moss. P64
Long Narrow Roadway. Kim Maltman. P49
"Long ago her mother". What the Informant
          Said to Franz Boas in 1920. Unknown.
          P78
"Long ago on a night of danger and vigil".
          If They Come in the Night. Marge
          Piercy. P52
"Long ago there was a church". The Interior
          Castle. Irene K. Wilson. P72
"Long buried, ancient men-at-arms". Two
          British Airmen. Thomas Merton. P84
"Long I've loved a tall young maid".
          Building for Love. Unknown. P87
"Long past the age for speaking". Childhood
          of a Scientist. A. F. Moritz. P49
Long, Bee Bacherig
     To Thy Will, O Lord. P72
Long, Daniel Cuol
     The Girl's Hearts Soften. Terese Svoboda
          (tr.). P53
     Moviestars. Terese Svoboda (tr.). P53
Long, Howard O.
     Sho Chiku Bai. P72
Long, Robert Hill
     Beverly Carneiro. P63
     The Official Frisbee-Chasing Champion of

Colorado. P63

Long, Virginia
Mrs. Wilson, Who Never Loved. P63

"Long/Brown hair". Quiet Time. Tom Tellesbo.
P58

"The longer he grew, for once he knew". The
Leap. J. M. Girglani. P72

"The longest road". Untitled #3. Ian
Brennan. P58

Longfellow, Henry Wadsworth
Christmas Carols. P51
Daybreak. P51,P89
Hawthorne. P90
Hiawatha's Brothers. P51
Hiawatha's Childhood, fr. The song of
Hiawatha. P51
The Little Moon. P51
The Old Bridge at Florence. P90
Paul Revere's Ride. P90
A Psalm of Life. P89
Rain in Summer. P51,P89
The Rainy Day. P89
Santa Filomena (Florence Nightingale).
P89
Serenade, from The Spanish Student. P89
The Sifting of Peter. P89
Snow. P51
The Song of the Bird. P51
The Song of Hiawatha Selections. P90
Sunset. P51
The Village Blacksmith. P89
The Wreck of the Hesperus. P90

Longfellow, Henry Wadsworth (tr.)
The Castle by the Sea. Johann Ludwig
Uhland. P90
Song of the Silent Land. Johann Gaudenz
von Salis-Seewis. P89

Longing
"Love, in Which I Have Placed My Desire
and My Hope". Pier della Vigna. P69
Night Song. Arlo Bates. P81
The River-Merchant's Wife: a Letter. Ezra
Pound. P82
The Science of the Night. Stanley Kunitz.
P83
Song, from The Marriage of Guenevere.
Richard Hovey. P81
Terminal. Geoff Peterson. P86
Tomorrow. Thelma L. Howard. P72
Will You Be There?. Shelly Repine. P74
The World Is a Mighty Ogre. Fenton
Johnson. P82
Your Face, a Better Indian Rose!. S.
Yesupatham. P72

Longing for Caernarfon. Sion Gruffudd. P87

Look Evening's Black Feet Are. Carol Pearce.
P68

"Look at me standing". Saffron Pig Pinata.
Roger Weingarten. P63

"**Look** at the aeroplane". The Aeroplane.
Jeannie Kirby. P51

"**Look** at the little sandpiper". The
Sandpiper. Charlotte Zolotow. P76

"**Look** at the night beaten to death...". On a
Night Without Adornment. Rene Char.
P61

"**Look** at yourself". Old Women Are Taking
Over the World. Jay Dougherty. P63

"**Look** down on me, a little one". A Child's
Morning Prayer. J. Kirby. P51

"**Look** for me in the depths of the sea".
Life. Max S. Barker. P68

"**Look** in my face; my name is Might-have-
been;". The Nevermore. Dante Gabriel
Rossetti. P89

"**Look** in the caves at the edge of the sea".
Sea Fairies. Patricia Hubbell. P55

"**Look** out! look out!.". Jack Frost. Cecily
E. Pike. P51

"**Look**! a Bow-Shaped Line". Unknown. P62

"**Look**! a Newly Dyed Flag Put on the Roof".
Unknown. P62

"**Look**! At the Gate of the Little Village
Temple". Unknown. P62

"**Look**! Coming Out of the Hollow Tree".
Unknown. P62

"**Look**! Coming Out of the Ripe Mango Seed".
Unknown. P62

"**Look**! In the Middle of the Cow-Pen".
Unknown. P62

"**Look**! Motionless and Still on a Lotus-
Leaf". Unknown. P62

"**Look**! Oh Slender One. The White Clouds in
the Fall". Unknown. P62

"**Look**! Suspended Upside-Down on His Web".
Unknown. P62

"**Look**! The Anger Held by This Strong-Minded
Girl". Unknown. P62

"**Look**! look! the spring is come". First
Spring Morning. Robert Bridges. P51

"**Look**! the Buffalo Cows, Being Led Away...".
Unknown. P62

"**Look**! The Cloud, Not Strong Enough".
Unknown. P62

"**Look**! the Forest Elephant Vainly Tries".
Unknown. P62

"**Look**! the Traveller Smells, Touches,
Kisses". Unknown. P62

"**Look**! There Descends from the Plane of the
Heavens". Unknown. P62

"**Look**! There Is a Sobbing from the Laundry".
Unknown. P62

"**Look**, Oh Traveller, Even That Shadow of
Yours". Unknown. P62

"**Look**, a mirage, like a round rim, a
strange". Horizon. David Emrys James.
P87

"**Look**, between the myrtles standing". Rose

of Sharon. Ann Griffiths. P87
Looking Back. Werner Manheim. P72
"**Looking** as I've looked before...". The
        Stranger. Adrienne Rich. P85
"**Looking** down into my father's". 'Good Night,
        Willie Lee, I'll See You in the
        Morning'. Alice Walker. P85
Looking for th Innr Life in 100 Mile. Bill
        Bissett. P49
"**Looking** into my daughter's eyes I read".
        For My Daughter. Weldon Kees. P84
Loosestrife. Elaine Magarrell. P63
Loot. Taufiq Rafat. P91
"**Loquacious** angel". Seen in Wawa. Michael
        Joseph Phillips. P56
The **Lord** of Butrago. John Gibson Lockhart.
        P90
"**Lord** of Sea and Earth and Air". Cecil
        Roberts. P60
Lord Ullin's Daughter. Thomas Campbell. P51,
        P90
"**Lord** of the morning". Yes, Lord. Julia N.
        Aue. P72
"**Lord** of the winds! I feel thee nigh". The
        Hurricane. William Cullen Bryant. P90
Lord, Gigi
        I Remember. P65
        Pleasure. P65
Lord, I Have Seen Too Much. Karl Shapiro.
        P84
"**Lord,** how can man preach thy eternal
        word?.". The Windows. George Herbert.
        P59
"**Lord,** who am I to teach the way". The
        Teacher. Leslie Pinckney Hill. P90
"**Lord,** who createdst man in wealth and
        store". Easter Wings. George Herbert.
        P59
"**Lord/When** You Bring the Renewing Day". Ioan
        Maier. P72
The **Lordly** Hudson. Paul Goodman. P84
Loreine: a Horse. Arthur Davison Ficke. P89
Lorenzo
        "From the Quiet Stream". P77
        "I Would Like". P77
        "The Night". P77
        "The Sweet Smell of Cedar Sucked Out My
        Breath". P77
        "To Grandfather". P77
Loss
        Autumn Crocus. Helen Y. Luke. P77
        The Ball Poem. John Berryman. P79
        Bookends. James W. Proctor. P65
        Bread and Music. Conrad Aiken. P82
        A Certain Village. Theodore Weiss. P84
        Crippled Walls. Phillip Britain. P72
        Crucifiction. Dan Valenti. P56
        Cynddylan's Hall, fr. Poetry from Lost
        Sagas. Unknown. P87

Dawn of Tomorrow. Tomas Segovia. P92
Departure in Middle Age. Roland Mathias.
        P54
Fallen Angel. Katherine A. Hogan. P65
The Flight of Youth. Richard Henry
        Stoddard. P89
The Gain. Dorsha Hayes. P65
Has Summer Come Without the Rose?. Arthur
        O'Shaughnessy. P89
The Iron Wheels of the Tricycle Without
        Tires... Gonzalo Millan. P71
Lament. Charles P. Martin. P58
A Leaf. Johann Ludwig Uhland. P89
Letting Him Go. James Tate. P85
Maurice. Gwendolyn Brooks. P50
"The Mirror a Convict Holds Out". Simon
        Perchik. P64
"'My Sweet Lover, You Are Leaving!'".
        Federico II [Frederick II of
        Hohenstaufen]. P69
Mysterious. Rosemary Witty. P72
The Old Familiar Faces. Charles Lamb. P89
An Only Child. Robert ab Gwilym Ddu. P87
Pain. Blaga Dimitrova. P70
Poem. Langston Hughes. P50
Puppet. John J. Soldo. P65
Reading. M. P. A. Sheaffer. P56
The River-Merchant's Wife: a Letter. Ezra
        Pound. P82
The Scream Is a Kind of Coffin. Paz
        Molina. P71
See Jane Run. Maryann Calendrille. P64
So Sweet Love Seemed. Robert Bridges. P89
To a Portrait. Arthur Symons. P89
Walking with Lulu in the Wood. Naomi
        Lazard. P64
You Have No Lasting City Here. Mary Ann
        Henn. P65
Losses. Randall Jarrell. P84
The **Lost** Love. Fenton Johnson. P82
The **Lost** Pilot. James Tate. P85
Lost Poems. Mary B. Finn. P68
The **Lost** Sheep. Elizabeth Cecilia Clephane.
        P89
A **Lost** Snowflake. Charlotte B. Deforest. P80
The **Lost** Son. Theodore Roethke. P84
Louis, Louise
        Home. P65
        Song of the Fleece. P65
        Thee. P65
"**Louise** Leroy, gentleman's gentleman". The
        Help. James Merrill. P79
Lounds, Patricia
        The Good Things in Me. P73
Love
        Afterglow. Sheila Seiler. P56
        Aftermath. Lora Dunetz. P65
        Ah, How Sweet, from Tyrannic love. John
        Dryden. P89

165   LOVE

Air and Angels. John Donne. P59
"Although Water, Because of Fire, Loses".
    Guido della Colonne. P69
"Among All the Wives of the Village
    Chief". Unknown. P62
And You Love Me?. Stephen Crane. P81
Ask No Return. Horace Gregory. P83
At the Sources. Tomas Segovia. P92
The Awakened Heart. Anne Yannie Corrado.
    P65
"'Be Pleased, Oh Beloved!'". Unknown. P62
Because of You. Cecilia N. Rahl. P72
The Beggar Maid. Lord Tennyson. P51
Behold, the Grave of a Wicked Man.
    Stephen Crane. P81
Birth of the Daisies. Ruth Krauss. P50
Love. Alice Boughtwood. P68
"The Bride's Beloved's Laughter-Filled
    Eyes". Unknown. P62
Bright Sunday. Elaine Demakas. P58
The Broken Sun. Anthony (Tony). Kellman.
    P68
The Brookside. Richard Monckton Milnes;
    1st Baron Houghton. P89
The Canonization. John Donne. P59
Carmina LXXII of Catullus. Richard
    Lovelace. P59
Cause of My Distress. Har Prasad Sharma.
    P72
Love. Eddena Christian. P72
City on Fire. Oscar Hahn. P71
Clara Schumann at the Piano. Maureen
    Bloomfield. P88
Compensation, from The House of a Hundred
    Lights. (Frederick) Ridgely Torrence.
    P81
The Computation. John Donne. P59
Cupid Swallowed. Unknown-Greek. P89
The Darkness Before. Eleanore-Melissa.
    P68
Dawn of Tomorrow. Tomas Segovia. P92
Deaf-Mute in the Pear Tree. P. K. Page.
    P49
Death and Love. Arlo Bates. P81
The Definition of Love. Andrew Marvell.
    P59
Disdain Returned. Thomas Carew. P89
Divertissement. Amy Jo Schoonover. P72
The Divorce. Thomas Stanley. P59
Drink to Me Only with Thine Eyes, from
    The Forest. Philostratus. P89
E'en as a Lovely Flower. Heinrich Heine.
    P89
The Ecstasy. John Donne. P59
Effort at Speech Between Two People.
    Muriel Rukeyser. P84
Emotions Extinction. Patricia Anne Solek-
    Fritsche. P72
Enhanced Embrace. Antonio Giraudier. P65

Evolution of Sand. Jean Pape. P77
Expediency. Jean Gowan Near. P72
Face to Face in Another Time. Teresa
    Calderon. P71
Fatal Interview, sel. Edna St. Vincent
    Millay. P82
Fidelity. Trumbull Stickney. P81
Find Your Love. Nicholas [pseud.]. P72
The First Kiss. Thomas Campbell. P89
First Love. Anne Yannie Corrado. P65
For One Sweet Sign. Eleanor Gude Ramirez.
    P72
For the Marriage of Faustus and Helen.
    Hart Crane. P83
The Fortunate Fall. William Harrold. P68
"The Godavari River, at Midnight".
    Unknown. P62
Golden Eyes. Rufinus. P89
The Good Morrow. John Donne. P59
A Good Sight of Andromeda. Milton Acorn.
    P49
Goodbye! Amiri (LeRoi Jones) Baraka. P85
Goodbye, Goodbye. Dolores R. Patitz. P68
Gwalchmai's Boat, sels. Meilir ap
    Gwalchmai. P87
"Having Seen the Son of the Lord of the
    House". Unknown. P62
"He Drinks in the Lovliness of the Young
    Girl's...". Unknown. P62
"Here and There in the Bamboo Grove".
    Unknown. P62
"Hey, Slim-Wasted girl, Clean Off Your
    Back". Unknown. P62
Himalayan Balsam. Anne Stevenson. P54
Holly and Ivy. Unknown. P66
Honeymoon in Rice. Francis J. Smith. P63
Hotel Transylvanie. Frank O'Hara. P85
I Am Not Yours. Sara Teasdale. P82
I Dreamt I Saw Great Venus. Bion. P89
I Fear Thy Kisses, Gentle Maiden. Percy
    Bysshe Shelley. P89

Love

"I Have Seen the Clear Sky Produce Rain".
    Giacomo da Lentini. P69
"I Have Set My Heart on Serving God".
    Giacomo da Lentini. P69
I Looked Here. Stephen Crane. P81
I Prithee Send Me Back My Heart. Sir John
    Suckling. P89
I Think I Should Have Loved You
    Presently. Edna St. Vincent Millay.
    P82
Idols of Love. Edward A. Gloeggler. P65
"If He Is Not Your Lover, Oh Friend".
    Unknown. P62
"If Her Eyes Are Not Half Shut". Unknown.
    P62
If It Be True That Any Beauteous Thing.

Michelangelo Buonarroti. P89
If Love Loves. Stephen Crane. P81
"If People Get Angry, Let Them, If They
  Carry On...". Unknown. P62
If This Be Love. Alice Morrey Bailey. P65
"If You Are Not His Beloved". Unknown.
  P62
The Immortal. Hugh Seidman. P64
In the Midst. Joanne Stevens Sullivan.
  P72
Inamorata. Mary Margaret Wittner. P72
The Incomparable Earth. Salvatore
  Quasimodo. P61
Inspirations Unlimited. Claire Schneider.
  P72
"Into a Grievous Torment". Rinaldo
  d'Aquino. P69
Invitation. Glenn Clairemonte. P68
June 9. William Carlos Williams. P79
Kings River Canyon, fr. Andree Rexroth.
  Kenneth Rexroth. P84
The Kiss. Sara Teasdale. P82
Know Knowing. Marian Gleason. P72
Kore. Robert Creeley. P85
L'Anne: Water in My Hands. Jerry Craven.
  P65
A La Apollinaire. Manuel Silva Acevedo.
  P71
The Legacy. John Donne. P59
Lessons in Love. Edward A. Gloeggler. P65
"Lilies Are White". Unknown. P51
Lochinvar. Sir Walter Scott. P51
The Lonely Child. James Oppenheim. P82
"Look! The Anger Held by This Strong-
  Minded Girl". Unknown. P62
Love. Sergio Mansilla. P71
Love and Doubt. Harry Thurston. P81
Love in Labrador. Carl Sandburg. P82
Love Me -- I Love You. Christina Georgina
  Rossetti. P51
Love Me--I Love You. Christine Rosetti.
  P51
Love Not Me for Comely Grace. Unknown.
  P89
Love Song for Today. Alice MacKenzie
  Swaim. P65
The Love Song of J. Alfred Prufrock.
  Thomas Stearns Eliot. P83
Love Theme. Dorothea Neale. P65
Love Walked Alone. Stephen Crane. P81
Love's Logic. Unknown. P89
Love's Miracle. Hyacinthe Hill. P65
Love's Not Words. LeRoy Coffie. P72
Love's Presence. Alney Norell. P65
Love, from A Thai Divine Comedy. Montri
  Umavijani. P92
Love, from Hero and Leander. Christopher
  Marlowe. P89
Love, from The Merchant of Venice.

William Shakespeare. P89
Lovely Mary Donnelly. William Allingham.
  P89
Loving You Less Than Life, a Little Less.
  Edna St. Vincent Millay. P82
Madonna of the Evening Flowers. Amy
  Lowell. P82

Men Loved Wholly Beyond Wisdom. Louise
  Bogan. P83
The Message. Heinrich Heine. P89
Miscalculation. Kathleen W. Vander Meide.
  P68
The Mower to the Glow-Worms. Andrew
  Marvell. P59
The Mower's Song. Andrew Marvell. P59
"My Boy, She Takes Notice of Other
  Youths". Unknown. P62
"My Friends, Why Do You Tell Me".
  Unknown. P62
"My Heart, Tormented by Love". Odo della
  Colonne. P69
My Lady. Dante. P89
My Love (Her Portrait). Russell Powell
  Jacoby. P89
My Love (Liliaceae). Kim Young Sam. P72
"My Old Friends Are Gone". Unknown. P62
My Picture Left in Scotland. Ben Jonson.
  P59
My True-Love Hath My Heart. Sir Philip
  Sidney. P89
Not in a Silver Casket Cool with Pearls.
  Edna St. Vincent Millay. P82
"Oh Auntie, Just as Thirst Is Not
  Quenched". Unknown. P62
"Oh Beloved with Eyes Closed in Feigned
  Sleep--.". Unknown. P62
"Oh Heart, If You Must Depart, Then
  Leave". Unknown. P62
"Oh Madhuka Flower in the Great Glade".
  Unknown. P62
'Oh Mother, Today I am Pained". Unknown.
  P62
"Oh Thou Shameless and Ungrateful!.".
  Unknown. P62
"Often Love Has Made Many Happy". Rugieri
  d'Amici. P69
On Strawberry Eve. Donald G. Finch. P68

"The Ones Who Know Not How". Unknown. P62

Only in a Poem. Mary B. Finn. P68
Pack, Clouds, Away. Thomas Heywood. P51,
  P89
Pangloss's Song. Richard Wilbur. P84
Partial to Marshall. Jan M. Stephens. P68
Patterns. Amy Lowell. P82
Perseverance. Antonio D'Alfonso. P49
Phillis Is My Only Joy. Sir Charles

Sedley. P89
Poems for My Daughter. Horace Gregory.
 P83
Power of Love. Betty Farquhar. P72
Primer of Plato. Jean Garrigue. P84
Re-cognition. Don Mager. P65
The Reconciliation. Archibald MacLeish.
 P83
"The Redness of Her Lower Lip". Unknown.
 P62
The Relic. John Donne. P59
"Remembering the Angry Words in the
 Meeting with Her". Unknown. P62
"Remembering, with Full Throat Uplifted".
 Unknown. P62
A Romance. Kandy Arnold. P58
Seated Nude. Richard Ronan. P57
"She Who in Love-Making Gave Hundreds of
 Orders". Unknown. P62
A Shooting Star. Robert Desnos. P48
Should the Wide World Roll Away. Stephen
 Crane. P81
The Silver Shadows. Richard Schade. P72
"The Slender Girl". Unknown. P62
Song. John Donne. P59
Song of the Fleece. Louise Louis. P65
Space. Salvatore Quasimodo. P61
The Spinning-Wheel Song. John Francis
 Waller. P89
Spun to Life. Perry Brass. P65
The Sun Rising. John Donne. P59
Sunsets Be Dear. Richard Franklin. P65
"The Sweet, Pleasant face". Giacomino
 Pugliese. P69
"Tell Me, Oh Subhaga, Which One Of Your
 Mistakes". Unknown. P62
Terminal. Geoff Peterson. P86
Th Lovr Sighs if It All Revolvs Around
 Yu. Bill Bissett. P49
The Third Poem of Leave-Taking. Hamid
 Skif. P91
"Thoughtless!.". Unknown. P62
To Amoret, of the Difference 'Twixt
 Him... Henry Vaughan. P59
To Amoret, Walking in a Starry Evening.
 Henry Vaughan. P59
To Castara: the Reward of Innocent Love.
 William Habington. P59
"To Give Joy to My Heart". Stefano
 Protonotaro. P69
To Lucasta, Going Beyond the Seas.
 Richard Lovelace. P59
Tomorrow in a Bubble. Maryann
 Calendrille. P64
The Tower. Gloria H. Procsal. P72
The Triple Fool. John Donne. P59
True Love. Wade Newman. P63
Trying to Remember. Judith Minty. P88
Twicknam Garden. John Donne. P59

Two Ways. John V. A. Weaver. P82
The Two Wives. William Dean Howells. P90
The Ugly Man. Liliana Stefanova. P70
Untitled. T. M. Raghuram. P72
V-Letter. Karl Shapiro. P84
A Valediction: Forbidding Mourning. John
 Donne. P59
Virgidemiarum Book I, Satire 7. Joseph
 Hall. P59
"Virtuous Women, Still Undressed and
 Bashful". Unknown. P62
We Love But Few. Unknown. P89
The Welcome. Thomas Davis. P89
"What Does the Beautiful One". Unknown.
 P62
"Whatever Tune My Lover Plays I Dance
 to". Unknown. P62
"When I See". Giacomino Pugliese. P69
"When the Noble Girl Looks at Her New
 Nail Wounds". Unknown. P62
"Who Is Stronger Than a Couple Angered by
 Love". Unknown. P62
"Why Is It, Even as I Lie on My Half of
 the Bed". Unknown. P62
"With Lamp Blown Out, Breath Held".
 Unknown. P62
A Woman's Answer. Adelaide Anne Procter.
 P89
Woman's Constancy. John Donne. P59
"You Stand Like Good Ivory". Antonio
 Giraudier. P72
The Young Lovers, from The House of a
 Hundred Lights. (Frederick) Ridgely
 Torrence. P81
Love (3). George Herbert. P59
Love and Doubt. Harry Thurston. P81
Love Dissembled, from As You Like It.
 William Shakespeare. P89
"Love and words grow weak". Survivor. Walter
 Hoefler. P71
"Love bade me welcome: yet my soul drew
 back". Love (3). George Herbert. P59
"Love carries her burdens". Power of Love.
 Betty Farquhar. P72
"Love come often". Idols of Love. Edward A.
 Gloeggler. P65
"Love cried in". Divorce. Maynard G. Teigen.
 P72
Love for Poetry, from Wake up, My Heart and
 Other Poems. John Tworoger. P65
Love in Absentia. Mary Jane Barnes. P68
Love in Labrador. Carl Sandburg. P82
"Love Is a Desire Which Comes from the
 Heart". Giacomo da Lentini. P69
Love is Even Lovelier Now. Robert F. Allen.
 P65
' Love Is Life That Lasts Ay'. Richard
 Rolle. P66
Love Me -- I Love You. Christina Georgina

Rossetti. P51

Love Me--I Love You. Christine Rosetti. P51

Love Not Me for Comely Grace. Unknown. P89

"Love is like a ship at sea". Find Your
    Love. Nicholas [pseud.]. P72

"Love is loneliness redeemed". Enhanced
    Embrace. Antonio Giraudier. P65

"Love is the kiss". Sleeping Beauty. Edward
    A. Gloeggler. P65

"Love knoweth every form of air". The
    Annoyer. Nathaniel Parker Willis. P89

The Love of God. William Williams
    Pantycelyn. P87

The Love of God. Eliza Scudder. P89

Love Portions. Joan Van Poznak. P63

Love Song for Today. Alice MacKenzie Swaim.
    P65

The Love Song of J. Alfred Prufrock. Thomas
    Stearns Eliot. P83

Love Song: Pincio, sels. Frederika Blankner.
    P65

Love Songs. Mina Loy. P82

Love Theme. Dorothea Neale. P65

Love Walked Alone. Stephen Crane. P81

"Love's Arrows Come in Dual Form". Unknown.
    P62

Love's Blasphemy. Fran Swarbrick. P65

Love's Logic. Unknown. P89

Love's Meaning. Louise Barth. P65

Love's Memory, from All's Well That Ends
    Well. William Shakespeare. P89

Love's Miracle. Hyacinthe Hill. P65

Love's Not Words. LeRoy Coffie. P72

Love's Presence. Alney Norell. P65

"Love's Qualities Are Very Frustrating".
    Unknown. P62

Love's Songs. Vivian Trollope-Cagle. P65

Love, from A Thai Divine Comedy. Montri
    Umavijani. P92

Love, from Hero and Leander. Christopher
    Marlowe. P89

Love, from The Merchant of Venice. William
    Shakespeare. P89

"Love, in Which I Have Placed My Desire and
    My Hope". Pier della Vigna. P69

Love-Deep in Crossword Puzzles. Louis
    Phillips. P63

The Love-Gift of a Fairy-Tale. Charles
    Lutwidge ("Lewis Carroll") Dodgson.
    P90

Love-Nature of
    "Because Love Is Not Invisible". Pier
        della Vigna. P69
    Geometry of Love. Anne Marx. P65
    In the Sense of Death. Salvatore
        Quasimodo. P61
    "Love Is a Desire Which Comes from the
        Heart". Giacomo da Lentini. P69
    Love is Even Lovelier Now. Robert F.

Allen. P65

'Love Is Life That Lasts Ay'. Richard
    Rolle. P66

Love's Blasphemy. Fran Swarbrick. P65

Love's Meaning. Louise Barth. P65

The Loving Thing. Edward A. Gloeggler.
    P65

"Prodding My Intellect a Little". Jacopo
    Mostacci. P69

Testament of Love. Dorothea Neale. P65

Today, There Is Love. Faye Kicknosway.
    P88

The Way It All Was. Constance Pultz. P65

What's Said of Love. Darrell H. Bartee.
    P65

Love-Plaints and Protests
    Annabel Lee. Edgar Allen Poe. P89
    The Annoyer. Nathaniel Parker Willis. P89
    Ladies of Llanbadarn. Dafydd ab [or ab]
        Gwilym. P87
    The Landlady's Daughter. Johann Ludwig
        Uhland. P89
    Last Night. Unknown-Swedish. P89
    Linda to Hafed, from The Fire-
        Worshippers. Thomas Moore. P89
    Love's Memory, from All's Well That Ends
        Well. William Shakespeare. P89
    Never Fall in Love. Mary Rebecca
        Henderson. P74
    Never May the Fruit Be Plucked. Edna St.
        Vincent Millay. P82
    "Six Years Have I Suffered". Mazzeo di
        Ricco. P69
    The Spider and the Ghost of the Fly.
        Vachel Lindsay. P82
    Trouble at a Tavern. Dafydd ab [or ab]
        Gwilym. P87
    Unrequited Love, from Twelfth Night.
        William Shakespeare. P89
    A Woman's Love. John Hay. P89

Love-Unrequited
    Grafts and the Garden. Mehdi Akhavan
        Sales. P91
    His Affliction. Dafydd ab [or ab] Gwilym.
        P87
    The Poet Dies for Love. Unknown. P87

Lovelace, Richard
    Carmina LXXII of Catullus. P59
    The Scrutiny. P59
    To Althea from Prison. P90
    To Lucasta, Going Beyond the Seas. P59

Loveliest of Trees. Alfred Edward Housman.
    P89

Loveliness. Gail Calmer. P68

Loveliness Destroyed. Agnes Finch Whitacre.
    P72

Lovely Mary Donnelly. William Allingham. P89

Lovely Things. H. M. Sarson. P51

"A lovely green lady". The Green Lady.

Charlotte Druitt Cole. P51

Loveman, Robert
April Rain. P51

The **Lover's** Hope. Salbri Powel. P87

Lover, Samuel
Father and Mother Tongue. P90
How to Ask and Have. P89

"The **lovers** came on strawberry eve". On
Strawberry Eve. Donald G. Finch. P68

Lovers in Wild Grass. Lisa Grenelle. P65

The **Lovers** of the Poor. Gwendolyn Brooks.
P84

Loving Lessons (Grandmother). Burnette B.
Benedict. P72

The **Loving** Thing. Edward A. Gloeggler. P65

"**Loving** With a Loyal Heart and With Hope".
Pier della Vigna. P69

Loving You Less Than Life, a Little Less.
Edna St. Vincent Millay. P82

"**Low** spake the knight to the peasant-girl".
The Rose and the Gauntlet. John
Sterling. P90

"The **low** wind talks on the boards of the
house". The Illusion. William Everson.
P84

"**Low-anchored** cloud". Mist. Henry David
Thoreau. P90

Lowell, Amy
Four Sides to a House. P82
A Gift. P82
The Letter. P82
Lilacs. P89
Madonna of the Evening Flowers. P82
Meeting-House Hill. P82
Patterns. P82
Purple Grackles. P82
Sea Shell. P51
Venus Transiens. P82

Lowell, James Russell
The Fountain. P51
The Heritage. P89
Joys. P51
William Lloyd Garrison. P90
Yussouf. P51

Lowell, Maria White
The Morning-Glory. P89

Lowell, Robert
After the Surprising Conversions. P84
At the Indian Killer's Grave. P84
The Drunken Fisherman. P84
Fall 1961. P48
Father's Bedroom. P84
Ford Maddox Ford. P79
My Last Afternoon with Uncle Devereux
Winslow. P84
Our Afterlife. P79
The Quaker Graveyard in Nantucket. P84
To Delmore Schwartz. P84
Where the Rainbow Ends. P84

Lowell, Robert T. S.
The Relief of Lucknow (September 25,
1857). P90

Lowenstein, Tom (tr.)
A Dispute Between Women. Unknown. P78

Lower the Standard. Karl Shapiro. P84

Lowery, Vance
Music. P73

"The **Lowest** in my book:.". Four Letter
Words. Stella Moss. P63

Lowry, Mary Ann
What Happened?. P72

Loy, Mina
Apology of a Genius. P82
Der Blinde Junge. P82
Love Songs. P82
Lunar Baedecker. P82

Loyalty
Expecting the Lord. Ann Griffiths. P87
Morfudd. Dafydd ab [or ab] Gwilym. P87
Shirt of a Lad. Unknown. P87

Lual, Nyalang Pinien
The One-Eyed. Terese Svoboda (tr.). P53

Lucas, E. V.
Mr. Coggs. P51
O England, Country of My Heart's Desire.
P51
The Windmill. P51

"**Lucid/Iris-dawn**". The Crystal Flow. James
Richard Hurst. P68

Lucifer Alone. Josephine Miles. P84

Lucina, Sister Mary
To One Deaf. P57

Lucinda Matlock, from Spoon River Anthology.
Edgar Lee Masters. P82

Lucky Dilemma. Ned Pastor. P63

Lucy Lavender. Ivy O. Eastwick. P51

"**Luf** es lyf that lastes ay...". 'Love Is
Life That Lasts Ay'. Richard Rolle.
P66

Luke Havergal. Edward Arlington Robinson.
P81

Luke, Helen Y.
Autumn Crocus. P77

Lul, John Gatwec
The Radio, with its Breath Like a Trapped
Bee. Terese Svoboda (tr.). P53

Lull. Theodore Roethke. P84

Lull, Janis
The Seducer Steps Out, Just at Dusk. P88

Lullabies
Cradle Hymn. Martin Luther. P51
Cradle Song. Lord Tennyson. P51
Cradle Song at Bethlehem. E. J. Falconer.
P51
A Cradle Song. Unknown. P51
A Danish Cradle Song. Unknown. P51
A Dutch Lullaby. Eugene Field. P89,P81
Evening. Unknown. P51

Hindu Cradle Song. Unknown. P51
Japanese Lullaby. Eugene Field. P89
Lullaby. William Brighty Rands. P51
Lullaby. Phyllis L. Garlick. P51
Lullaby for my Mother. Blaga Dimitrova.
        P70
Lullaby of Evening. James A. Hanf. P72
Lullaby, from The Princess. Lord
        Tennyson. P89
Norse Lullaby. Eugene Field. P51
Rock Me to Sleep. Elizabeth Akers. P89
The Rock-a-by Lady. Eugene Field. P51
Sleep Baby Sleep. J. Pembroke Waller. P68
A Summer Lullaby. Eudora S. Bumstead. P51
Sweet and Low. Lord Tennyson. P51
You Spotted Snakes. William Shakespeare.
        P51
Lullaby. Phyllis L. Garlick. P51
Lullaby. William Brighty Rands. P51
Lullaby for Amy. Mark Jarman. P85
Lullaby for my Mother. Blaga Dimitrova. P70
Lullaby of Evening. James A. Hanf. P72
Lullaby, from The Princess. Lord Tennyson.
        P89
"Lullaby, sweet baby mine!.". A Danish
        Cradle Song. Unknown. P51
Lullalye-Acidby. Ish Yair. P72
"Lully, lulley, lully, lulley". The Corpus
        Christi Carol. Unknown. P66
Lunar Baedecker. Mina Loy. P82
Lunde, David
        Instead. P63
"Lurching from gloomy limousines we slip".
        My Father's Funeral. Karl Shapiro. P84
Lust. Elaine Demakas. P58
Lust
        Possessions. Hart Crane. P83
        The Window. Boris Khristov. P92
A Lust for the Quaint Old Ways. John J.
        Brugaletta. P63
"Lusty and passionate steed, it's jealous I
        am". Maiden Song, sels. Cynddelw
        Brydydd Mawr. P87
Luther, Martin
        Cradle Hymn. P51
        A Mighty Fortress Is Our God. Frederick
        Henry Hedge (tr.). P89
Luton, Midred
        Jennifer Blass. P63
Luton, Mildred
        Bovine Town. P63
        Coup de Grace. P63
Lutz, Gertrude May
        Playland at the Beach. P72
Luxuries
        Political Poem. Amiri (LeRoi Jones)
        Baraka. P85
Luzi, Mario
        As You Wish. Charles Guenther (tr.). P61

Lydia. Lizette Woodworth Reese. P81
Lying Down, from String Games. Unknown. P78
The Lying Muse to Rhys Goch Eryri. Sion
        Cent. P87
"Lying atop". Atop. Prince Redcloud. P50
"Lying in bed". The Errand Boy's Day Off.
        Kurt Lipschutz. P63
Lying on Things. Dennis Lee. P80
Lyly, John
        The Urchin's Dance. P51
Lynch, Peggy Zuleika
        The Red Sea Divides. P72
The Lynching. Claude McKay. P82
Lynn, Kenneth
        Superego Dictatorship. P72
Lyon, P. H. B.
        Envoi. P51
Lyons, A. Neil
        The Fairy Cobbler. P51
Lyons, Dorothy
        The Learning Tree. P72
Lysohorsky, Ondra
        Poetry. Hugh McKinley (tr.). P68
        Seashore. David Gill (tr.). P72

' M 87'. Vernon Payne. P72
Maas, Peter E.
        In November in Mesilla. P56
The Mabinogion. Unknown. P87
MacDonald, G. (tr.)
        In a Lovely Garden Walking. Johann Ludwig
        Uhland. P89
McCall, Sherry Sue
        Frozen with Time. P56
MacAndrew, Rachel
        The Pony. P51
        Robin Hood. P51
McDaniel, Wilma E.
        Evening Prayers. P72
Macar, Nyakuoth
        Let Her Be Red. Terese Svoboda (tr.). P53
Macar, Philip
        He'd Die for Tobacco. Terese Svoboda
        (tr.). P53
Macar, Phillip
        Ambush. Terese Svoboda (tr.). P53
        Don't Be Discouraged. Terese Svoboda
        (tr.). P53
        Who Plays the Lyre?. Terese Svoboda
        (tr.). P53
McCarthy, Tom
        The Poet of the Mountains. P92
        Returning to De Valera's Cottage. P92
McCarty, Raymond
        Shakespeare. P72
McKay, Claude

Africa. P82
Baptism. P82
The Desolate City. P82
Flame-Heart. P82
Harlem Shadows. P82
If We Must Die. P82
The Lynching. P82
My Mother. P82
Spring in New Hampshire. P82
Subway Wind. P82
To the White Fiends. P82
Wild May. P82
MacDiarmid, Hugh. See Grieve, Christopher M.
MacDonald, Cynthia
    Francis Bacon, the Inventor of
        Spectacles... P79
Mace, Frances Laughton
    Only Waiting. P89
McFee, Michael
    Little Elegy. P63
McGee, Michael V.
    The Myth Revisited: Adam. P56
McKenty, Bob
    E Pluribus Ovum. P63
    The Lamb. P63
    The Zebra. P63
Macewen, Gwendolyn
    The Death of the Loch Ness Monster. P49
    Grey Owl's Poem. P49
    The Names. P49
MacEwen, Pearl Forbes
    The Kite. P51
    My Little Dog. P51
Machado, Antonio
    The Afternoon Will Yet... Charles
        Guenther (tr.). P61
    Oh, Figures on the Portico... Charles
        Guenther (tr.). P61
    The Sun is a Globe of Fire. Charles
        Guenther (tr.). P61
    Tavern Guitar Playing a Jota Today...
        Charles Guenther (tr.). P61
    Tell Me If You Remember, Love. Charles
        Guenther (tr.). P61
McShane, Ivan
    The Oaks. P68
    Okinawa 1945. P68
Machinery
    Tanker. Virginia M. Hahn. P58
"Machines, steel, machines". Epoch. Nikola
    Vaptsarov. P70
McKinley, Hugh
    Form All (For Gilda Walker). P72
    Vespers. P68
Mackay, Charles
    Cleon And I. P90
    A Deed and a Word. P89
    Small Beginnings. P89
    Tell Me, Ye Winged Winds. P89

Tubal Cain. P90
McClatchy, J. D.
    The Approach. P79
McCleery, Nancy
    Claire's Braids. P88
    The Rag Lady. P88
MacLeish, Archibald
    Ars Poetica. P83
    The End of the World. P83
    Epistle To Be Left in the Earth. P83
    Immortal Autumn. P83
    Invocation to the Social Muse. P83
    Memorial Rain. P83
    The Reconciliation. P83
    Speech to a Crowd. P83
    Tourist Death. P83
    You, Andrew Marvell. P83
Macleod, Fiona. See Sharp, William
MacLeod, Iris Jean
    Solitude. P72
McCloskey, Mark
    Hand. P63
McDonald, Ian
    "Under the Soursop Silver-Leaf Tree". P60
McDonald, S. P.
    Casey-Twenty Years Later. P90
McDonald, Walter
    Wrestling with Angels. P57
McConnell, Bonnie
    Other Season. P68
McCord, David
    Joe. P80
McCormick, Linda
    Grandmother's Eyes. P56
McDowell, Leonorv (I am Cree).
    Windsong. P72
McCoy, Barbara
    Daily Joys. P68
MacPherson, Jay
    Dead Languages. P49
McCrea, Lilian
    Boots and Shoes. P51
    Getting Up. P51
    My Toys. P51
    Noises in the Night. P51
    Pussy-Cat and Puppy-Dog. P51
    Rain. P51
    Wash-Day. P51
McArthur, Mary J.
    Mssrs. Mice And Co. P63
McCullers, Carson
    Slumber Party. P50
McCulley, Tonya
    Terror to Unborn Children. P74
McCullough, Sally T.
    With the Dawn. P68
The Mad Scene. James Merrill. P85
The Mad Yak. Gregory Corso. P85
Madgett, Naomi Long

Twice a Child. P88
Madhav, Harshdev
  Solitude. P72
The Madness of a Headmistress. Gavin Ewart.
  P63
Madonna of the Evening Flowers. Amy Lowell.
  P82
Madrigal. Unknown. P51
Madrigal. Unknown. P51
Magarrell, Elaine
  Loosestrife. P63
Magdalene, Mary
  On Mary Magdalene. Richard Crashaw. P59
Mager, Don
  Re-cognition. P65
Maggie and Milly and Molly and May. Edward
  Estlin Cummings. P76
Magic
  Magic That Comes at Dawn. Peter Pal Hoth
    Nyang. P53
  Magic Words. Unknown. P78
  Magic Words, from Run Towards the
    Nightland. Unknown. P78
  Sonnet 1, fr. Three Sonnets From 'Deep
    Within the Heart'. Syed Shamsul Haque.
    P91
The Magic Piper. E. L. Marsh. P51
Magic Reprieve. Walter S. Hay. P72
Magic That Comes at Dawn. Peter Pal Hoth
  Nyang. P53
The Magic Whistle. Margaret Rose. P51
Magic Words. Unknown. P78
Magic Words for Hunting Caribou. Unknown.
  P78
Magic Words for Hunting Seal. Unknown. P78
Magic Words to Feel Better. Nakasuk. P78
Magic Words, from Run Towards the Nightland.
  Unknown. P78
"Magic wand, I do not need you now". My Dark
  Kingdom. Mary B. Finn. P68
Magnusson, Sigurdur A.
  A Child Lost. Sigurdur A. Magnusson
    (tr.). P92
Magorian, James
  The War. P68
Mahayana, from Paradise. Montri Umavijani.
  P72
Mahmud, Al
  Consolation. Kabir Chowdhury (tr.). P91
  Wherever I Go. Kabir Chowdhury (tr.). P91
Mahr, David
  Death Comes Calling. P72
"The maid will do if you are not ambitious--
  .". Rondine of the Rare Device. Wesli
  Court. P63
Maiden. Frederika Blankner. P65
Maiden Song, sels. Cynddelw Brydydd Mawr.
  P87
Maidenhair. Nigel Jenkins. P54

Maier, Ioan
  "Lord/When You Bring the Renewing Day".
    P72
  When the Autumn. P72
The Maimed Grasshopper Speaks Up. Jean
  Garrigue. P84
Maizel, Harry
  To the Beloved. P72
Majewski, A.
  Marianne's Shalimar. P72
Make Room. Jules Supervielle. P61
"Make my poems as simple as". South Dakota
  Scenery. Wayne Kvam. P68
Makidemewabe, Samuel
  Born Tying Knots. Howard Norman (tr.).
    P78
  Saw the Cloud Lynx. Howard Norman (tr.).
    P78
  Tree Old Woman. Howard Norman (tr.). P78
Making Beasts. Gregory Orr. P85
Making Caskets. Ann Jonas. P56
Making Tens. M. M. Hutchinson. P51
Mako. Allen Planz. P64
Makui, Nyakong
  I Was Mistaken for a Red Dog. Terese
    Svoboda (tr.). P53
"The male sea horse". Pregnant Thought.
  Merry Harris. P63
Mallarme, Stephane
  Springtime. Charles Guenther (tr.). P61
Malory, Sir Thomas
  Le Morte Darthur, sels. P66
Maltepe. Yahya Kemal. P91
Maltman, Kim
  Long Narrow Roadway. P49
"Malual, their people make up stories". I
  Was Mistaken for a Red Dog. Nyakong
  Makui. P53
Mammen, P. M.
  The Political Asses. P72
Man. Henry Vaughan. P59
A Man Adrift on a Slim Spar. Stephen Crane.
  P81
The Man Against the Sky. Edward Arlington
  Robinson. P81
Man and Woman. Beryl Baigent. P72
A Man Feared. Stephen Crane. P81
"Man can't create a butterfly". Limited.
  Audrey Frederick. P72
"Man desires to find". Mystery of Mind.
  Mythily. P72
"A man enters a florist's". At the
  Florist's. Jacques Prevert. P61
The Man from Leipzig. Clemente Riedemann.
  P71
Man Holding Cat. Raymond Roseliep. P68
The Man Hunt. Madison Cawein. P81
"A man has been tied to a tree and
  thinks...". Behind His Eyes. David

Ignatow. P64
"Man in might, youth in years". The Gododdin,
        sels. Aneirin. P87
"The Man in the Wilderness Asked of Me".
        Unknown. P51
"A Man Is Not Angered by an Event". Unknown.
        P62
A Man Said to the Universe. Stephen Crane.
        P81
A Man Saw a Ball of Gold. Stephen Crane. P81
A Man Toiled on a Burning Road. Stephen
        Crane. P81
"A Man Went A-Hunting at Reigate". Unknown.
        P51
A Man Went Before a Strange God. Stephen
        Crane. P81
Man Who Loved a Giraffe. Pyke Johnson Jr.
        P63
The Man Who Made up Roses, from Animated
        Film... James Reaney. P49
"A Man Whose Wife Is the Boss". Unknown. P62
"Man is a sacred city...". The Chief
        Centurions. John Masefield. P89
"Man learned to fly". Ballad of the
        Progress. Jonas Negalha. P72
"Man looking into the sea". A Grave.
        Marianne Moore. P83
"The man sits in a timelessness". The
        Rescue. Robert Creeley. P85
"A man went out". The Hunter. Unknown. P61
"The man who sold his lawn to standard oil".
        The War Against the Trees. Stanley
        Kunitz. P83
"The man with no ears". Headless. Josephine
        Miles. P84
The Man with the Hoe. Edwin Markham. P81
The Man with the Nitroglycerine Tears.
        Robert Priest. P49
"Man you". Insult Before Gift-Giving.
        Unknown. P78
A Man's Song About His Daughter. Unknown.
        P78
The Man-Moth. Elizabeth Bishop. P84
"Man-like". Eskimo Sleigh-Ride. Renee Anne
        Viosca. P72
Mandel, Eli
        June @!21/84* a Poem with Mistakes
        Included. P49
Mandeville's Travels, sels. Unknown. P66
Mangan, James Clarence (tr.)
        The Rose. Johann Wolfgang von Goethe. P89
Mangoes. Taufiq Rafat. P91
Manheim, Werner
        Looking Back. P72
Manheim, Werner (tr.)
        Heaven's Glowing. Nina Marin. P72
        Letters. Wolfgang Durben. P72
        Mysterious Evening. Verona Bratesch. P72
        Shinto Tombs. Carl Heinz Kurz. P72

"With a Sieve". Tilly Boesche Zacharow.
        P72
The Manhood of Hebrew Jesus. Stanley A.
        Fellman. P72
Manjushree
        Your Leaving Me. P72
Mankind
        Ballad of the Progress. Jonas Negalha.
        P72
        The Black Vulture. George Sterling. P81
        The Clerks. Edward Arlington Robinson.
        P81
        From Here to Eternity. Pearl Crayton. P68
        Funeral Song. Patricio Esteve. P92
        The Fury of Aerial Bombardment. Richard
        Eberhart. P83
        Geek. David H. Green. P63
        Gloucester Moors. William Vaughn Moody.
        P81
        Hall of Fraternity. Justice S. Mohan. P72
        Let Him Be. Georgi Borisov. P70
        Man. Henry Vaughan. P59
        The Man with the Hoe. Edwin Markham. P81
        Mere Man. Elizabeth Holgate. P56
        A Net to Snare the Moonlight. Vachel
        Lindsay. P82
        Peering at the Past. Mark Lawson
        Cannaday. P68
        Peripheral Vision. Kevin Cline. P58
        Pity This Busy Monster, Manunkind. Edward
        Estlin Cummings. P83
        Soul. Eleanor Otto. P72
        Space Exploration. Mildred B. Boydston.
        P72
        There Will Come Soft Rains. Sara
        Teasdale. P82
        View of a Comet. Robert Hahn. P58
Mann, Danielle
        Tears. P74
Mannyng, Robert
        The Churchyard Dancers of Colbek, fr.
        Handlyng Synne. P66
Mansilla, Sergio
        Cauquil. Steven F. White (tr.). P71
        Dusk in Changuitad. Steven F. White
        (tr.). P71
        Leaving. Steven F. White (tr.). P71
        Life. Steven F. White (tr.). P71
        Love. Steven F. White (tr.). P71
        Time. Steven F. White (tr.). P71
        Wandering Souls. Steven F. White (tr.).
        P71
"Many Lovers Bear Their Illness". Giacomo da
        Lentini. P69
Many Red Devils Ran from My Heart. Stephen
        Crane. P81
Many Workmen. Stephen Crane. P81
"Many a tear flow on its way". Elegy for
        Rhys Gryg. y Prydydd Bychan. P87

"Many prophets have failed, their voices
      silent". Ode to Failure. Allen
      Ginsberg. P85
Map of Vancouver Island. Neile Graham. P49
The Map. Elizabeth Bishop. P84
Maps
      Map of Vancouver Island. Neile Graham.
      P49
      The Map. Elizabeth Bishop. P84
      An Old Map of Somewhere. Jeffery
      Donaldson. P49
      The Xenoplile. Geoff Fiorito. P58
Maps in the Brain. A. J. Wright. P56
Maquieira, Diego
      The Chicken Coop. Steven F. White (tr.).
      P71
      I Blew up the Virgin of My Legs. Steven
      F. White (tr.). P71
      No One Knows What I'm Talking About.
      Steven F. White (tr.). P71
      They Dragged Me Out by My Face. Steven F.
      White (tr.). P71
      Your Great Love. Steven F. White (tr.).
      P71
      Your Little Friends Were a Bunch of Dogs.
      Steven F. White (tr.). P71
March
      Beware the Tides of March. Charles L.
      Grove. P63
      March. William Morris. P89
The March Wind. E. H. Henderson. P51
Marching Song. Robert Louis Stevenson. P51
"Margaret Sanger". Tom Riley. P63
Marianne's Shalimar. A. Majewski. P72
Marie. Lola Ridge. P82
Marigolds. Louise Driscoll. P51
Marin, Nina
      Heaven's Glowing. Werner Manheim!(tr.).
      P72
"Mariposa Lilies". Lois Roquemore Carden.
      P72
"A maritime history less blissful...". Sag
      Harbor, the Tchekov Letters. Barbara
      Guest. P64
Mark Antony, over the Body of Caesar.
      William Shakespeare. P90
"Mark but this flea, and mark in this". The
      Flea. John Donne. P59
Mark, Rickman
      Snow in Town. P51
"Mark, when the evening's cooler wings". To
      Amoret, of the Difference 'Twixt
      Him... Henry Vaughan. P59
Market. Robert Hayden. P84
Marketing. E. J. Falconer. P51
Markham, Edwin
      The Angelus. P81
      The Forgotten Man. P81
      Judas Against the World. P81

Lincoln, the Man of the People. P81
      The Man with the Hoe. P81
      A Mendocino Memory. P81
      Our Israfel. P81
      A Prayer. P51
      The Sower. P81
      To a Young Man. P81
      Virgilia. P81
      Walt Whitman. P81
Marking Time. T. Busch. P77
Marks, Aline Musyl
      Bargain Brief (Excerpt). P65
Marksberry, Camille
      Grandma's Attic. P74
Marley, James
      Exodus Unknown. P68
Marlowe, Christopher
      Love, from Hero and Leander. P89
      Ovid's Elegies, Book I, 13. P59
      The Passionate Shepherd to His Love. P89
Marriage
      "At the Time of Ploughing". Unknown. P62
      "The Bogus Bride-Night Garment". Unknown.
      P62
      A Bride of the 80's, Down the Aisle.
      Blanche Farley. P63
Marriage. Gregory Corso. P85
      Dolcino to Margaret. Charles Kingsley.
      P89
      Double-Quick. Alice Mackenzie Swaim. P65
      Epigrams. J. V. Cunningham. P79
      For the Marriage of Faustus and Helen.
      Hart Crane. P83
      From a Marriage Counselor's Notebook.
      Alfred Dorn. P65
      "How Can the One Who Is Somehow the
      Sweetheart". Unknown. P62
      "If the Traveller Were to Go". Unknown.
      P62
Marriage. David Ignatow. P84
      "In the Town Are Many Youths". Unknown.
      P62
      Intertwining Love. Winne E. Fitzpatrick.
      P72
      "Just Today He Awoke and Left". Unknown.
      P62
      A Letter on the Use of Machine Guns at
      Weddings. Kenneth Patchen. P84
      Loot. Taufiq Rafat. P91
      Marriage. David Ignatow. P84
      Marriage. Gregory Corso. P85
      Marriage Couplet. William Cole. P63
      The Marsh. Grace Schulman. P64
      Nocturne. John V. A. Weaver. P82
      "Oh God, Make an Affair with Another
      Woman...". Unknown. P62
      Poem Which Cannot Be a Letter. Alamgir
      Hashmi. P91
      The Poet's Song to His Wife. Bryan Waller

("Barry Cornwall") Procter. P89

A Pothersome Pair. John Ceiriog Hughes. P87

The Proposal. D. Lyons Gallagher. P65

Prothalamion. Delmore Schwartz. P84

"Quickly Embracing the Neck of Her Husband". Unknown. P62

The Race. James Camp. P63

"Seeing Her Beloved with a Swollen Lip". Unknown. P62

Sequence. Richard Armour. P63

Small Wedding. Lisa Grenelle. P65

"Smiling Without Showing Her Teeth". Unknown. P62

Stanzas for the Harp. Unknown. P87

The Tests of Marriage (A Mason Sonnet Sequence). Anne Marx. P65

"Those Who Know the Good and Bad". Unknown. P62

To Have and Too Old. Richard Armour. P63

"Today with My Remembrance of Pleasures". Unknown. P62

Two Daughters Sing an Anniversary Ditty. Wilma H. Clements. P68

Two in August. John Crowe Ransom. P67,P83

"The Unfaithful Wife Gathers Together, Crying". Unknown. P62

"When Her Husband's Brother Is of Improper Mind". Unknown. P62

"Wherever the Brother-in-Law Whirls". Unknown. P62

"While Her Husband Is Asleep". Unknown. P62

"Your Wife Is Faithful, but Mine Is Unfaithful". Unknown. P62

Marriage Couplet. William Cole. P63

"Marsh grasses, tip-high above drowning". Mendocino Meadow. Arline Beryl Lawrence. P72

Marsh, E. L.
    The Magic Piper. P51

Marsh, Sir Edward (tr.)
    The Crow and the Fox. Jean de La Fontaine. P90

The Marsh. Grace Schulman. P64

Marshall, Heather
    Butterflies. P74

"Martha/Mary passed this morning". Mary Passed This Morning. Owen Dodson. P84

"Martha/Mary passed thisa morning". Mary Passed This Morning. Owen Dodson. P84

Martial Ditty, from Lost Youth: the Last War. Alfred Kreymborg. P82

Martial's Epigrams, Book X, 47. Sir Richard Fanshawe. P59

Martin and Aytoun (tr.)
    The Erl-King. Johann Wolfgang von Goethe. P90

Martin, Charles P.

Brood Queen (A Vision of Moths). P58

Good-bye California. P58

Ice. P58

Lament. P58

Moth Light. P58

Northwest Passage. P58

Martin, Gloria A.
    The Steamboat Bertrand. P68

Martin, Marjorie Skonnord
    Fantasy Voyage. P72

Martin, Robyn
    Last Will & Testament No. 1. P77

Martindale, Sheila
    Final Confrontation. P49

Martinetz, Vivian L.
    Desert Snow. P72

Martinez, Juan Luis
    The Cheshire Cat. Steven F. White (tr.). P71

    Fox Terrier Disappears at the Intersection... Steven F. White (tr.). P71

    Non-Missing Fox Terrier Does Not Reappear... Steven F. White (tr.). P71

    The Probable and Improbable Disappearance of a Cat... Steven F. White (tr.). P71

"Martini-time: time to draw the curtains and". The Garrison. W. H. Auden. P79

Martins, Julio Monteiro
    The Position. P92

Martyrs
    Mrs. Alfred Uruguay. Wallace Stevens. P83

    No One Knows What I'm Talking About. Diego Maquieira. P71

    The Sentry of Portoferraio. Daniel Mark Epstein. P57

    The Vision of a Martyr. Mohammed Ibrahim Abu Sinnah. P91

Marvell, Andrew
    Bermudas. P59

    Clorinda and Damon. P59

    The Coronet. P59

    The Definition of Love. P59

    A Dialogue Between the Soul and Body. P59

    The Garden. P59

    The Girl and Her Fawn. P51

    An Horatian Ode upon Cromwell's Return from Ireland. P59

    Mourning. P59

    The Mower to the Glow-Worms. P59

    The Mower's Song. P59

    On a Drop of Dew. P59

    The Picture of Little T. C. in a Prospect of Flowers. P59

    To His Coy Mistress. P59

Marx, Anne
    Geometry of Love. P65

    The Tests of Marriage (A Mason Sonnet Sequence). P65

Mary I.
    Christmas. P51
Mary Magdalene. George Herbert. P59
Mary Passed This Morning. Owen Dodson. P84
Mary Passed This Morning. Owen Dodson. P84
Mary's Melody (To Mary E. Cox). Grace
    Ridgway Rahamah. P72
Mary, Virgin
    A Problem in Genetics. Vera Rich. P68
    Stabat Mater Dolorosa. Jacopone da Todi
        (Jacobus de Benedictus). P89
"Mary, your twenty-odd years now threaten
    you". Portrait of Mary. Charles
    Wright. P79
Mary: to Her Completed Child (A Song of
    Hope). Miriam F. Berks. P72
Marzials, T. (tr.)
    Last Night. Unknown-Swedish. P89
Masefield, John
    The Chief Centurions. P89
    Roadways. P51
    Tewkesbury Road. P51
Masks
    Two Masks Unearthed in Bulgaria. William
    Meredith. P70
The Mason's Law. Jeremy Hooker. P54
Mason, Caroline Atherton
    The Voyage. P89
Mason, Kirsten (tr.)
    The Conqueror. Jan Anker Froydarland. P72
Masonry and Masons
    The Mason's Law. Jeremy Hooker. P54
Massasoit. Mary Jane Barnes. P68
"Master! Within you". The Bhagavadgita, sel.
    Unknown. P48
"Master, this very hour". This Very Hour.
    Lizette Woodworth Reese. P81
"Masterly wind of the sky". The Wind. Dafydd
    ab [or ab] Gwilym. P87
"MAud went to college". Sadie and Maud, fr.
    A Street in Bronzeville. Gwendolyn
    Brooks. P84
Masters, Edgar Lee
    Anne Rutledge, from Spoon River
    Anthology. P82
    Archibald Higbie, from Spoon River
    Anthology. P82
    Arlo Will, from Spoon River Anthology.
    P82
    Carl Hamblin, from Spoon River Anthology.
    P82
    Daisy Fraser, from Spoon River Anthology.
    P82
    Davis Matlock, from Spoon River
    Anthology. P82
    Doc Hill, from Spoon River Anthology. P82
    Doctor Meyers, from Spoon River
    Anthology. P82
    Editor Whedon, from Spoon River

    Anthology. P82
    Elsa Wertman, from Spoon River Anthology.
    P82
    Hamilton Greene, from Spoon River
    Anthology. P82
    The Hill, from Spoon River Anthology. P82
    Lucinda Matlock, from Spoon River
    Anthology. P82
    Mollie McGee, from Spoon River Anthology.
    P82
    Mrs. Meyers, from Spoon River Anthology.
    P82
    Perry Zoll, from Spoon River Anthology.
    P82
    Petit, the Poet, from Spoon River
    Anthology. P82
    Rutherford McDowell, from Spoon River
    Anthology. P82
    Seth Compton, from Spoon River Anthology.
    P82
    Silence, from Spoon River Anthology. P82
    The Spooniad, from Spoon River Anthology.
    P82
    The Village Atheist, from Spoon River
    Anthology. P82
    Widows, from Spoon River Anthology. P82
A Match. Algernon Charles Swinburne. P89
"The Mate of the Bull Elephant Who Is
    Trampled...". Unknown. P62
Materialism. R. P. Dickey. P63
Mathias, Eileen
    All in Red. P51
    Go Out. P51
    In the Wood. P51
    Just Jumbo. P51
    Little Things. P51
    My Hut. P51
    Sea Fairies. P51
    Tall Trees. P51
    Zoo Manners. P51
Mathias, Roland
    Brechfa Chapel. P54
    Burning Brambles. P54
    Departure in Middle Age. P54
    The Flooded Valley. P54
    Fool's Fingers. P54
    Freshwater West Revisited. P54
    A Letter from Gwyther Street. P54
    Porth Cwyfan. P54
    They Have Not Survived. P54
Matson, Clive
    Unfired Pistol. P65
A Matter of Perspective. Ann Shermer. P65
Matthews, Washington (tr.)
    Therefore I Must Tell the Truth. Torlino.
    P78
Mattos, Ruth Newton
    Awakening. P72
Matyas, Cathy

Bromeliad. P49
Nile (1). P49
Maud Muller. John Greenleaf Whittier. P89
Maughan, Henry Neville
    Song. P51
Maunders, Ruth O.
    Window Seat. P72
Maunula, Allan
    No Anger in a Fallen Tree. P72
Maurice. Gwendolyn Brooks. P50
Maviglia, Joseph
    Paolo Dipietro. P49
Mawr, Cynddelw Brydydd
    Elegy. Tony Conran (tr.). P87
    For a Girl. Tony Conran (tr.). P87
    Maiden Song, sels. Tony Conran (tr.). P87
    Stanzas to the Lord Rhys ap Gruffudd,
        Prince of Deheubarth. Tony Conran
        (tr.). P87
Maximus, to Himself. Charles Olson. P85
Maxson, Gloria A.
    Elegies in a City Churchyard. P63
    Worshiper. P63
May
    The Green Comb. Raffaele Carrieri. P61
May. J. G. Percival. P51
"May her plane explode". Elegy for the Other
    Woman. Elisavietta Ritchie. P63
"May I be forever delivered". Love. Eddena
    Christian. P72
"May I, for my own self, song's truth
    reckon". The Seafarer. Ezra Pound. P82
"May the dreamer's favorite color". A
    Resolution. Ben Howard. P68
"May your shovel break, may your
    fertilizer...". A Hex for My
    Neighbor's Green Thumb. Glenna
    Holloway. P63
May, Lisa
    Still Not Grown Up. P74
"May, and the day's long, time to give
    freely". Elegy for Nest, sels. Einion
    ap Gwalchmai. P87
May-Time. Unknown. P51
"May-day, the day of might, day of
    possibility". On the Way to Summer.
    John Hollander. P79
Maya. C. Ramamohan Rao. P72
Maya Indians
    The Book of Chilam Balam: a Chapter...,
        sel. Unknown. P78
    Rabinal-Achi: Act IV. Unknown. P78
Maybe. Susan Headen Griffith. P72
Maybe Dats Youwr Pwoblem Too. Jim Hall. P63
"Maybe you should". 411 Days and Nights.
    Doug Rawlings. P86
Mayne, Seymour (tr.)
    For a Comrade. Abraham Sutzkever. P48
    On the Subject of Roses. Abraham

Sutzkever. P48
    Poem About a Herring. Abraham Sutzkever.
        P48
Mayo, Edward L.
    An Admonition Concerning Promptness and
        Regularity... P68
"The mayor of Avalon". The Fair Damsel of
    Avalon. Haywood Jackson. P68
"The mayor was certain". Percussion Grenade
    Democracy. C. J. Roner. P72
Mazotti, Mary K.
    Meditation. P72
McKinley, Hugh (tr.)
    Poetry. Ondra Lysohorsky. P68
Me Wants a Minks. E. W. Sneed. P63
"' Me, 20-Year-Old Sergeant, Ognyan
    Mihailov'". Luchesar Elenkov. P70
Mea Culpa, from Lost Youth: the Last War.
    Alfred Kreymborg. P82
Mead, E. Stella
    The Last Gate. P51
    When We Are Men. P51
Meadow's Song. Opie Houston. P65
The Meadows. Ann and Jane Taylor. P51
Meat. Phebe Hanson. P88
Mechain, Gwallter
    Nightfall. Tony Conran (tr.). P87
Mecox Motel. Anselm Parlatore. P64
Mecox Nunnery & Saint Dominic. Anselm
    Parlatore. P64
Medals
    Medals. Richard M. Mishler. P86
Medicine-Tail
    "He Was There," from Crow Versions.
        William Stanley Merwin (tr.). P78
Meditation. Elizabeth M. Gilliam. P72
Meditation. Mary K. Mazotti. P72
Meditation
    Meditation. Elizabeth M. Gilliam. P72
    The Strawberries. Tristan Dereme. P61
Meditations on the Body: Right Hand. Maxine
    Silverman. P88
Medusa. Louise Bogan. P83
"Mee-ow, Mee-ow". Pussy-Cat and Puppy-Dog.
    Lilian McCrea. P51
Meek, Jay
    Big Bang. P63
Meeting. Arthur Davidson Ficke. P82
Meeting. Vassilis A. Papantoniou. P72
Meeting a Lovely Lady. Maryleona Berg. P68
Meeting My Father at the River. Judith
    Minty. P88
"Meeting with time, slack thing, said I".
    Time. George Herbert. P59
Meeting-House Hill. Amy Lowell. P82
The Meeting. Mark Gordon. P49
The Meeting. Stanley Moss. P64
Meg Merrilees. John Keats. P51
Meide, Kathleen W. Vander

Miscalculation. P68
Meilir ap Gwalchmai
Battle of Tal y Moelfre. Tony Conran
(tr.). P87
Gwalchmai's Boat, sels. Tony Conran
(tr.). P87
To Owain Gwynedd. Tony Conran (tr.). P87
Meilyr
On His Death-Bed. Tony Conran (tr.). P87
Meinke, Peter
The Chipmunk Center. P63
The Examiner's Death. P63
Meister, Shirley Volger
Bingoholic. P63
Melancholy
Anatomy of Melancholy. Ralph Gustafson.
P49
At Bosherston Ponds. John Tripp. P54
Meleager
Spring. Andrew Lang (tr.). P89
The Wreath. William M. Hardinge (tr.).
P89
Melissa's Song. Phil Cohen. P72
"**Mellifluous** as bees, these brittle men". On
First Looking in on Blogett's Keats's
'Chapman's Homer'. . George Starbuck.
P85
"**Mellow** the moonlight to shine...". The
Spinning-Wheel Song. John Francis
Waller. P89
Melting. Judy Little. P88
Memo to a Far Descendant. Ann Shermer. P65
Memo to My Music Teacher. A. L. Lazarus. P63
Memorial Rain. Archibald MacLeish. P83
Memorial Verses (April 1850). Matthew
Arnold. P90
Memories
Among Shadows. Arthur Davidson Ficke. P82
Archeology. Virginia M. Hahn. P58
Auld Lang Syne. Robert Burns. P89
Autobiographical. Douglas Barbour. P49
Bargain Brief (Excerpt). Aline Musyl
Marks. P65
The Boathouse. Robert Minhinnick. P54
The Bridge. Harvey Shapiro. P64
Burial of the Dead, fr. The Waste Land.
Thomas Stearns Eliot. P83
Calmly We Walk Through This April's Day.
Delmore Schwartz. P84
Chokecherry Summers. Margot Kriel. P88
The Colors of Our Age: Pink and Black.
Dave Smith. P67
Crystal Rosaries of Long Remembering.
Emma Crobaugh. P68
Day in May. Dominick J. Lepore. P56
Dedication (To Tamara). Luchesar Elenkov.
P70
Fate. Kenneth Koch. P64
Fau Bauman, Frau Schmidt, and Frau

Schwartze. Theodore Roethke. P84
The Fence. David Allan Evans. P68
Flame-Heart. Claude McKay. P82
For All the Violets. Alice Mackenzie
Swaim. P65
The Free School-house, Llanrwst. Ieuan
Glan Geirionydd. P87
Fresheners. R. R. Menon. P72
Green Mountain, Black Mountain. Anne
Stevenson. P54
Greensleeves. Mark Jarman. P85
"Her Lips with Noisy Curses". Unknown.
P62
Homecoming. R. Parthasarathy. P92
I Remember. Gigi Lord. P65
In a City Garden. Trumbull Stickney. P81
In Days Gone By. Ida M. Mills. P51
Incident. Countee Cullen. P83
Late. Elaine Dallman. P65
Lavender. Unknown. P89
Letter to an Exile. Lala Heine-Koehn. P49
Like Him Whose Spirit. Arthur Davidson
Ficke. P82
The Little Things That Happen. Marjorie
Wilson. P51
Looking Back. Werner Manheim. P72
Loving You Less Than Life, a Little Less.
Edna St. Vincent Millay. P82
Marianne's Shalimar. A. Majewski. P72
Meeting My Father at the River. Judith
Minty. P88
Memories. Bobi Shields. P74
Memories. K. V. Venkataramana. P72
Memories for Storage. Barbara Stevens.
P72
Memory. John J. Soldo. P65
The Memory of the Heart. Daniel Webster.
P89
The Milking-Maid. Christina Georgina
Rossetti. P89
Mirage of Memory. Alice Mackenzie Swaim.
P68
Mnemosyne. Trumbull Stickney. P81
Muse. Tobin F. Rockey. P68
Music in the Night. Harriet Elizabeth
Spofford. P81
Muted Music. Robert Penn Warren. P67
My Grandmother's Love Letters. Hart
Crane. P83
My Last Afternoon with Uncle Devereux
Winslow. Robert Lowell. P84
My Old Kentucky Home. Stephen Foster. P89
"Nests in the Top of the Almond Tree".
Vachel Lindsay. P82
Nouveau Poor. Alice Morrey Bailey. P65
Now and Again. Mary Trimble. P88
Oft in the Stilly Night. Thomas Moore.
P90
The Old Arm-Chair. Eliza Cook. P89

Memories. Bobi Shields. P74
Memories. K. V. Venkataramana. P72
    1926. Weldon Kees. P84
    The Other Side of the River. Charles
       Wright. P52
    Penarth. John Tripp. P54
    Photo. Don Coles. P49
    Poems for My Daughter. Horace Gregory.
       P83
    Poets. Bozhidar Bozhilov. P70
    Prisms. Katherine A. Hogan. P65
    The Rainbows. John Frank. P65
    Reunion. Ulrich Troubetzkoy. P65
    Schizophrenic Kiss. James Tate. P85
    Scrapbooks. Nikki Giovanni. P85
    A Sigh. Harriet Elizabeth Spofford. P81
    Snowy Morning. Ai Qing. P92
    The Storm, sels. William Thomas (Islwyn).
       P87
    Sudden Light. Dante Gabriel Rossetti. P90
    Tell Me If You Remember, Love. Antonio
       Machado. P61
    The Tennis Player Waits for What Waits...
       Philip Appleman. P64
    There Is Such Power Even in Smallest
       Things. Arlo Bates. P81
    There Is Such Power, from Sonnets in
       Shadow. Arlo Bates. P90
    Thinking of Other Universes. Muneer
       Niazi. P91
    This Is How Memory Works. Patricia Hampl.
       P88
    The Tin Shop. Colleen Thibaudeau. P49
    The Tire Hangs in the Yard. Dave Smith.
       P67
    'Tis but a Little Faded Flower. Ellen
       Clementine Howarth. P90
    Tropical Night. John Tworoger. P72
    Turning Once To Look Back. Ross Leckie.
       P49
    Virgilia. Edwin Markham. P81
    With the Dawn. Sally T. McCullough. P68
    You Were Wearing. Kenneth Koch. P85
"Memories are like". Memories. K. V.
    Venkataramana. P72
"Memories are real rainbows". The Rainbows.
    John Frank. P65
Memories for Storage. Barbara Stevens. P72
"Memories surround me". Memories. Bobi
    Shields. P74
Memory
    Bread and Apples. Lisel Mueller. P88
    "I Remember Her Mouth Screeching an
       Oath". Unknown. P62
    "I Remember My Beloved Stepping
       Backwards". Unknown. P62
    "I Remember the Joy". Unknown. P62
    Memory. Jules Supervielle. P61
    The Memory of Elena. Carolyn Forche. P52

Short-Term Memory Loss. Tom Disch. P63
Memory. John J. Soldo. P65
Memory. Jules Supervielle. P61
    We've Heard the Sea Again. Salvatore
       Quasimodo. P61
    "With Deep Regret for My Anger". Unknown.
       P62
"Memory is a cool autumn evening". Memory.
    John J. Soldo. P65
"Memory is fiction". Autobiographical.
    Douglas Barbour. P49
The Memory of Elena. Carolyn Forche. P52
The Memory of the Heart. Daniel Webster. P89
"Memory's the freshener of life when we
    find". Fresheners. R. R. Menon. P72
Men. Bozhidar Bozhilov. P70
Men
    Danny Murphy. James Stephens. P51
    "A Good Man, Lacking Wealth". Unknown.
       P62
    "Good People Are Not Vexed in Misery".
       Unknown. P62
    "A Good Person Does Not Get Angry".
       Unknown. P62
    "He Is Truly a Friend Who Does What Is To
       Be Done". Unknown. P62
    "The Hearts of Great Men". Unknown. P62
    "How Can There be Unpleasantness from the
       Mouth...". Unknown. P62
    "I Have No Use for Either the Bad Man or
       the Good". Unknown. P62
    "In a Forest Region There Might Occur a
       Crooked Tree". Unknown. P62
    "In Its Last Hours, the Mind of a Great
       Man". Unknown. P62
    "In the Autumn, the Water of a Great
       Lake". Unknown. P62
    Just Like a Man. Unknown. P51
    "The Kindly Speech of a Great Man".
       Unknown. P62
    "A Man Is Not Angered by an Event".
       Unknown. P62
    Men and Boys. Karl Theodor Korner. P90
    "The Necklace of a Young Women". Unknown.
       P62
    An Old Man's Winter Night. Robert Frost.
       P82
    "The Secrets of a Good Man". Unknown. P62
    'Sooeep!'. Walter De La Mare. P51
    "A Thing of True Value Is That Which Is
       Handy". Unknown. P62
    Windy Nights. Robert Louis Stevenson. P51
Men and Boys. Karl Theodor Korner. P90
Men Loved Wholly Beyond Wisdom. Louise
    Bogan. P83
"The Men of Ceylon, Oh Son". Unknown. P62
Men of the North and West. Richard Henry
    Stoddard. P90
The Men That Once Were, sels Owen Gruffudd.

P87

"The **men** relax within the bar". On Their Day
    Off. Alexander Gerov. P70
"**Men** stand alone by the river". Men.
    Bozhidar Bozhilov. P70
"The **men** the". Slow but Sure, from Lost
    Youth: the Last War. Alfred Kreymborg.
    P82
"**Men** with picked voices chant the names".
    Overture to a Dance of Locomotives.
    William Carlos Williams. P82
Men-Black
    The Help. James Merrill. P79
    Old Lem. Sterling A. Brown. P89
Mendel, Roberta
    Virus. P56
"The **Mendicant** Watches the Circle of Her
    Navel". Unknown. P62
Mending Sump. Kenneth Koch. P85
Mendocino Meadow. Arline Beryl Lawrence. P72
A **Mendocino** Memory. Edwin Markham. P81
Menon, R. R.
    Fresheners. P72
Mental Disorders
    From a Girl in a Mental Institution.
        Diane Wakoski. P85
    The Inmate. Margherita Faulkner. P68
    The Shape of the Fire. Theodore Roethke.
        P84
Mercy. Unknown. P87
Mere Man. Elizabeth Holgate. P56
Meredith, William
    An Old Photograph of Strangers. P79
    Two Masks Unearthed in Bulgaria. P70
Meredith, William (tr.)
    And the Summer Still Persists. Liliana
        Stefanova. P70
    Ballad of the Ladder. Lyubomir Levchev.
        P70
    Bulgaria. Georgi Djagarov. P70
    Bureaucrat. Lyubomir Levchev. P70
    A Century of Miracles. Georgi Djagarov.
        P70
    Epoch. Nikola Vaptsarov. P70
    I See Again. Liliana Stefanova. P70
    In Front of the Cave. Nikolai Hristozov.
        P70
    Introspection. Nikolai Hristozov. P70
    Night. Georgi Djagarov. P70
    Old Age. Nikolai Hristozov. P70
    P. S. Instead of a Beginning. Lyubomir
        Levchev. P70
    Roofs. Lyubomir Levchev. P70
    Song. Nikola Vaptsarov. P70
    Tell Me a Lie. Vladimir Golev. P70
The **Mermaid**, sel. Lord Tennyson. P51,P55
Mermaids and Mermen
    The Forsaken Merman. Matthew Arnold. P90
    The Mermaid, sel. Lord Tennyson. P55

Song, sel. Elizabeth J. Coatsworth. P55
The **Merman**, sel. Lord Tennyson. P51
Merriam, Eve
    It Fell in the City. P80
    Subway Seasoning. P63
    Summer Rain. P75
    Weather. P75
Merrick, Addison
    Encounter. P56
Merrill, James
    The Broken Home. P85
    Country Music. P79
    Foliage of Vision. P85
    The Help. P79
    Last Words. P85
    The Mad Scene. P85
    Nike. P79
    The Octopus. P85
    The Parnassians. P85
    The Peacock. P85
    The Romance Language. P79
    An Urban Convalescence. P85
Merrill, Michael E.
    Being a Vietnam Veteran. P86
"**Merrily**, merrily". Merry Birds. Rodney
    Bennett. P51
The **Merry** Heart. William Shakespeare. P51
Merry Little Men. Kathleen M. Chaplin. P51
"**Merry** have we met". A Party Song. Unknown.
    P51
"The **merry** March wind is a boisterous
    fellow". The March Wind. E. H.
    Henderson. P51
"A **merry** wind danced over the hill". Such a
    Blustery Day!. Elizabeth Gould. P51
Merton, Thomas
    Aubade: Lake Erie. P84
    Lent in a Year of War. P84
    A Psalm. P84
    St. Malachy. P84
    The Strife Between the Poet and Ambition.
        P84
    There Has to be a Jail for Ladies. P84
    Tower of Babel. P84
    Two British Airmen. P84
Merwin, William Stanley
    The Asians Dying. P85
    Blind William's Song. P85
    The Drunk in the Furnace. P85
    Fog-Horn. P85
    Footprints on the Glacier. P85
    For a Coming Extinction. P48
    Lemuel's Blessing. P85
    Leviathan. P85
    The Removal. P85
    The River of Bees. P85
    The Sound of the Light. P52
Merwin, William Stanley (tr.)
    "He Was There," from Crow Versions.

Medicine-Tail. P78
"I Am Climbing," from Crow Versions.
    Unknown. P78
"I Am Making," from Crow Versions. White-
    arm. P78
"If There Is Someone Above," from Crow
    Versions. Double-Face. P78
A Story of the Eaters. Santiago Mendes
    Zapata. P78
"Your Way," from Crow Versions. Plenty-
    Hawk. P78
The **Message**. Marie Blood. P72
The **Message**. Heinrich Heine. P89
The **Messiah**. Wilfred M. Johnson. P73
"Messier/By night and day". 'M 87'. Vernon
    Payne. P72
Mestas, Jean Paul
    "You Do Know That the Stars"/ Tatiana
        Greene (tr.). P72
"A **metal** monster". Precision. Lawrence
    Herman. P73
Metamorphosis, sel. Argyris Hionis. P92
THe **Metaphor's** Shine. K. Sree Ramachandra
    Murthi. P72
Metaphors and Similes
    Metaphors of a Magnifico. Wallace
        Stevens. P83
    Piece of Resistance. Ann Deagon. P63
Metaphors of a Magnifico. Wallace Stevens.
    P83
Metastasio, Pietro
    Without and Within. P90
Methinks the Divine Nectar. Unknown. P62
Metropolitan LIfe. John Barton. P49
Metzger, Cecile C.
    Island Sanctuary (Poetic Rambling). P72
Meudt, Edna
    On the Hazards of Writing Gloomy Verse.
        P68
    Peace! We Are Saying?. P68
    Plain Chant for a Tree. P68
    Postlude. P68
Meyerson, Edward L.
    I, Prometheus. P68
Meynell, Alice
    Chimes. P51
    The Modern Poet (A song of Deriviations).
        P90
Mhtis Outis. William DeWitt Snodgrass. P85
Mice
    The City Mouse and the Country Mouse.
        Reed Whittemore. P63
    The City Mouse and the Garden Mouse.
        Christina Georgina Rossetti. P51
    Conversation. Rose Fyleman. P51
    The Dormouse. Charlotte Druitt Cole. P51
    Fable of the Terrorist Mouse. Scott
        Bates. P63
    The Field-Mouse. Enid Blyton. P51

Mice. Rose Fyleman. P51
    The Kind Mouse. Natalie Joan. P51
    Mice. Rose Fyleman. P51
    The Mouse. Thirza Wakley. P51
    The Mouse. Becki Perkins. P74
    The Mouse. Elizabeth J. Coatsworth. P51
MIce
    Mssrs. Mice And Co. Mary J. McArthur. P63
Mice
    Three Mice. Charlotte Druitt Cole. P51
Michael Met a Duck. J. Dupuy. P51
"Michael brought the ornament...". Angel,
    Walking. James W. Penha. P56
Michael's Song. Wilfred Wilson Gibson. P51
Michaux, Henri
    On a Picture by a Chinese Painter.
        Charles Guenther (tr.). P61
Michelangelo Buonarroti
    If It Be True That Any Beauteous Thing.
        J. E. Taylor (tr.). P89
    To the Supreme Being. William Wordsworth
        (tr.). P89
Micro/Macro. Steve LaVine. P77
Mid Eastern. Michael Joseph Phillips. P56
"Mid pleasures and palaces though we may
    roam". Home, Sweet Home, fr. Clari.
    John Howard Payne. P89
Middle Age
    The Age of Wisdom. William Makepeace
        Thackeray. P89
    Through Night's Window. Mary Jane Barnes.
        P68
Middle Age Summer. Edward Butscher. P64
Middle East
    Mid Eastern. Michael Joseph Phillips. P56
Middleton, Christopher
    Bonnard. P79
Midnight. Lisel Mueller. P88
The **Midnight** Skaters. Edmund Blunden. P89
A **Midnight** Storm To Turn to. Mary P. (Mary
    Dalles) Carey. P68
Midsummer Moon. E.M.G. R. P51
Midsummer Night. Elizabeth Gould. P51
Midwinter. Allen Planz. P64
"Might have known it--.". Song Picture No.
    96. Unknown. P78
A **Mighty** Fortress Is Our God. Martin Luther.
    P89
Migrant Workers
    Black Migrants. Pearl Crayton. P68
"Mild offspring of a dark and sullen sire".
    The Early Primrose. Henry Kirke White.
    P89
"A **mile** behind is Gloucester town".
    Gloucester Moors. William Vaughn
    Moody. P81
Miles, Josephine
    Appointment in Doctor's Office. P84
    Cat. P84

Cloud. P84
Gypsy. P84
Headless. P84
Herald. P84
Lucifer Alone. P84
Personification. P84
Romantic Letter. P84
Seer. P84
Ten Dreamers in a Motel. P84
Tourists. P84
Views to See Clayton From. P84
Vigils. P79
Milk for the Cat. Harold Monro. P51
The **Milking-Maid**. Christina Georgina
      Rossetti. P89
"A **milkmaid**, who poised a full pail...". The
      Milkmaid. Jeffreys Taylor. P90
The **Milkman**. Clive Sansom. P51
"The **mill** goes toiling slowly around".
      Nightfall in Dordrecht. Eugene Field.
      P81
Mill-Pring, Robert (tr.)
      Apocalypse. Ernesto Cardenal. P48
Millan, Gonzalo
      Corner. Steven F. White (tr.). P71
      I Play Childish Songs with a Grimace on
        My Lips. Steven F. White (tr.). P71
      The Iron Wheels of the Tricycle Without
        Tires... Steven F. White (tr.). P71
      No One. Steven F. White (tr.). P71
      Poem 13, from The City. Steven F. White
        (tr.). P71
      Poem 20, from The City. Steven F. White
        (tr.). P71
      Poem 48, from The City. Steven F. White
        (tr.). P71
      Poem 60, from The City. Steven F. White
        (tr.). P71
      Vision. Steven F. White (tr.). P71
Millard, Edith G.
      'Banbury Fair'. P51
Millay, Edna St. Vincent
      Afternoon on a Hill. P51
      The Anguish. P82
      Elegy Before Death. P82
      Euclid Alone Has Looked on Beauty Bare.
        P82
      Fatal Interview, sel. P82
      God's World. P82
      I Think I Should Have Loved You
        Presently. P82
      Loving You Less Than Life, a Little Less.
        P82
      Never May the Fruit Be Plucked. P82
      Not in a Silver Casket Cool with Pearls.
        P82
      Recuerdo. P82
      Thou Art Not Lovelier Than Lilacs,--No.
        P82

      What Lips My Lips Have Kissed, and Where,
        and Why. P82
Miller, Benjamin
      Adventure. P73
Miller, Cincinnatus. See Miller, "Joaquin"
Miller, Heather
      Necessities. P73
Miller, Joaquin
      At the Grave of Walker. P81
      By the Pacific Ocean. P81
      A California Christmas. P81
      Columbus. P81
      Crossing the Plains. P81
      To Russia. P81
      Westward Ho!. P81
Miller, Miller. Ivy O. Eastwick. P51
Miller, William
      Willie Winkie. P89
"A **million** summers before Los Angeles came".
      Turn To Go. William Howarth. P77
"**Millionares**, presidents--even kings".
      Everyday Things. Jean Ayer. P51
Millionfold. Anne Yannie Corrado. P65
Mills and Millers
      The Windmill. E. V. Lucas. P51
Mills, Ida M.
      At Breakfast. P51
      In Days Gone By. P51
Mills, William
      The Exclusion Principle. P67
      Pity. P67
      Southern Vortex. P67
Milne, A. A.
      Puppy and I. P51
Milner, B. E.
      Christmas Night. P51
Milnes; 1st Baron Houghton, Richard Monckton
      The Brookside. P89
      Good Night and Good Morning. P51
      Lady Moon. P51
Milotich, Mark
      In Her Kitchen. P56
Milton by Firelight. Gary Snyder. P85
Milton, John
      Invocation to Light, from Paradise Lost.
        P89
      Light, from Paradise Lost. P89
      Samson on His Blindness, from Samson
        Agonistes. P89
Milton, John
      Milton by Firelight. Gary Snyder. P85
      Under the Portrait of John Milton. John
        Dryden. P90
"The **Milwaukee** road dissects the town".
      Dream of Trains. Paulette Roeske. P88
Mims, Amy (tr.)
      Report 'Present'. Eleftheria Kounrouri.
        P72
Mincemeat. Elizabeth Gould. P51

The **Mind** Machines. Haywood Jackson. P68
Mind and Body
    Painted Head. John Crowe Ransom. P83
"The **mind** has shown itself at times". For
      the Marriage of Faustus and Helen.
      Hart Crane. P83
"The **mind** is a short of seine". The Net.
      Veronica Haughey. P72
"**Mine** be a cot beside a hill". A Wish.
      Samuel Rogers. P51
"**Mine** eyes have seen the glory...". Battle-
      Hymn of the Republic. Julia Ward Howe.
      P90
Minerals from Stone. Joy Kogawa. P49
Mines and Miners
    Caliban in the Coal Mines. Louis
      Untermeyer. P82
    Epitaph at Gilfach Goch. John Tripp. P54
    Mining the American. Jon Olander. P77
    They Have Not Survived. Roland Mathias.
      P54
Minhinnick, Robert
    The Boathouse. P54
    The Brook. P54
    Grandfather in the Garden. P54
    Hide and Seek. P54
    Native Ground. P54
    The Orchard. P54
    Rhigos. P54
    Sker. P54
    Smith's Garage. P54
    The Strata: To Llywelyn Sion. P54
Mining in Killdeer Alley. Dabney Stuart. P67
Mining the American. Jon Olander. P77
Miniver Cheevy. Edward Arlington Robinson.
    P81
Minnie and Mattie. Christina Georgina
    Rosetti. P51
Minty, Judith
    Breathing in the Woods. P88
    Christine, on Her Way to China: An
      Earthquake Poem. P88
    Country Road in October. P88
    Hawk. P88
    Indian Summer. P88
    Meeting My Father at the River. P88
    A Sense of Place. P88
    Six Poems for Nine Crows. P88
    Trying to Remember. P88
    Walking. P88
Miracles
    The Red Sea Divides. Peggy Zuleika Lynch.
      P72
Mirage of Memory. Alice Mackenzie Swaim. P68
Mirikitani, Janice
    Breaking Silence. P85
    Sing with Your Body. P85
Mirror. Salvatore Quasimodo. P61
"The **Mirror** a Convict Holds Out". Simon

    Perchik. P64
The **Mirror's** Place. Jorge Arbeleche. P92
Mirrors
    In the Mirror. Elizabeth Fleming. P51
    Mirror. Salvatore Quasimodo. P61
    The Mirror's Place. Jorge Arbeleche. P92
Miscalculation. Kathleen W. Vander Meide.
    P68
Misconception. Mildred Offerle. P72
Misfortune's Darlings. L. L. Zeiger. P63
Misfortunes
    Doctor Meyers, from Spoon River
      Anthology. Edgar Lee Masters. P82
    Flux. Richard Eberhart. P83
    Gambler's Wife (Right Diptych, an
      Extract). Pearl Crayton. P68
    It's Such a Wonderful Day at Camp. Rana
      L. Landseadel. P73
    Misfortune's Darlings. L. L. Zeiger. P63
    My Cares. Hsiang Yang. P72
    Trouble at a Tavern. Dafydd ab [or ab]
      Gwilym. P87
Mishler, Richard M.
    Dark Friend. P86
    Medals. P86
Missing You. Charlotte Zolotow. P50
"The **missing** legs". The Handicapped. Philip
    Dacey. P57
Mission of No Ends. P. K. Padhy. P72
Mist. Ahmad Nadeem Qasimi. P91
Mist. Henry David Thoreau. P90
Mist on the Ridge. Mokuo Nagayama. P72
"**Mist-enshrouded**". Mist. Ahmad Nadeem
    Qasimi. P91
Mistral, Frederic
    The Leaf-Picking. Harriet Waters Preston
      (tr.). P89
Mistress Comfort. Elizabeth Gould. P51
"**Mists** of Autumn". Frost Is Coming. Mary
    Hamilton Neary. P72
Mitzi. Weldon Kees. P63
"**Mix** a pancake". The Pancake. Christina
    Georgina Rossetti. P51
Mizumura, Kazue
    Please Bird. P80
Mnemosyne. Trumbull Stickney. P81
Mo, Alonzo Gonzales
    Conversations in Mayan. Allan F. Burns
      (tr.). P78
    How Just One Poor Man Lives. Allan F.
      Burns (tr.). P78
    Things That Happen to You. Allan F. Burns
      (tr.). P78
    Wizards. Allan F. Burns (tr.). P78
The **Mocking** Bird and the Owl. Reed
    Whittemore. P63
The **Mocking-Bird.** Frank Lebby Stanton. P89
The **Modern** Hiawatha. Unknown. P90
The **Modern** Poet (A song of Deriviations).

Alice Meynell. P90
Modern Poetry. Glenna Glee. P72
"Modestly we violets cower". Violets. P. A.
    Ropes. P51
Mohan, Justice S.
    Hall of Fraternity. P72
"A molded juniper bends...". The Cricket.
    Mary P. (Mary Dalles) Carey. P68
"Mole Makes His Pole Redhot". Unknown. P78
Molina, Paz
    Events Like Palaces. Steven F. White
        (tr.). P71
    "Go Slowly Over the Stones". Steven F.
        White (tr.). P71
    The Scream Is a Kind of Coffin. Steven F.
        White (tr.). P71
    Things of the Blind. Steven F. White
        (tr.). P71
    Your Anger. Steven F. White (tr.). P71
Mollie McGee, from Spoon River Anthology.
    Edgar Lee Masters. P82
Molly Gaunt. H. Wendell Smith. P63
Momaday, N. Scott
    The Delight Song of Tsoai-Talee. P85
    The Gourd Dancer. P85
    Krasnopresnenskaya Station. P85
"Moment to". Time. Robert Creeley. P85
The Moment. Waldo Williams. P87
"Momma said I sure looked thin". Hill 190,
    August '69. Jack Hill. P86
"Monday's Child Is Fair of Face". Unknown.
    P51
Mondays. Miriana Basheva. P70
Monet Refuses the Operation. Lisel Mueller.
    P88
"Monet never knew". Monet's Lilies
    Shuddering. Lawrence Ferlinghetti. P85
Monet: 'Les Nympheas'. William DeWitt
    Snodgrass. P85
Monette, Paul
    Bones and Jewels. P79
Money. Richard Armour. P63
Money
    Daisy Fraser, from Spoon River Anthology.
        Edgar Lee Masters. P82
    Financial Note. John D. Engle Jr. P63
    The Impact of a Dollar. Stephen Crane.
        P81
    Loot. Taufiq Rafat. P91
    Money. Richard Armour. P63
    The Offer. Yaedi Ignatow. P64
"Money and fame break in the room". The
    Strife Between the Poet and Ambition.
    Thomas Merton. P84
Monk, Thelma G.
    A Guide. P72
"The Monkey Pauses, Shakes the Branch".
    Unknown. P62
The Monkeys. Marianne Moore. P83

Monkhood. John Berryman. P79
Monochrome. Louise Imogen Guiney. P81
Monro, Harold
    The Bird at Dawn. P51
    Milk for the Cat. P51
    One Blackbird. P51
    Overhead on a Saltmarsh. P51
Monsoon. Michael D. Clodfelter. P86
Monsters
    The Death of the Loch Ness Monster.
        Gwendolyn Macewen. P49
    The Dracula Vine. Ted Hughes. P55
    The Dragon. Mary Mullineaux. P51
    Kual Is Left. Unknown. P53
    The Man-Moth. Elizabeth Bishop. P84
    An Old Cornish Litany, sel. Unknown. P55
    What's That?. Florence Parry Heide. P55
Montale, Eugenio
    Day and Night. Charles Guenther (tr.).
        P61
    On an Unwritten Letter. Charles Guenther
        (tr.). P61
    Seascape. Charles Guenther (tr.). P61
    The Shade of the Magnolia. Charles
        Guenther (tr.). P61
Montauk Highway. Harvey Shapiro. P64
Monterey. Charles Fenno Hoffman. P90
Montgomery, James
    The Daisy, sel. P51
    What Is Prayer?. P89
Montgomery, U. M.
    Grey Brother. P51
"Month of leaves". June. Irene F. Pawsey.
    P51
"Month of May, loveliest season". Sadness in
    Springtime. Unknown. P87
Months
    April. Sir William Watson. P51
    A Change in the Year. William Wordsworth.
        P51
    February. Dorothy Una Ratcliffe. P51
    The Four Sweet Months. Robert Herrick.
        P51
    In May. Unknown. P51
    June. Irene F. Pawsey. P51
    June. Jane G. Stewart. P51
    May. J. G. Percival. P51
    May-Time. Unknown. P51
    November. Margaret Rose. P51
    October. Christina Georgina Rossetti. P51
    Old May Song. Unknown. P51
    September. Mary Howitt. P51
    Wild Peaches. Elinor Wylie. P82
Montreuil, Mathieu de
    To Madame De Sevigne. P90
The Monument. Elizabeth Bishop. P84
Moody, Vivian
    A Gift Multiplies. P72
Moody, William Vaughn

Faded Pictures. P81
Gloucester Moors. P81
A Grey Day. P81
An Ode in Time of Hesitation. P81
Moon
Flying. J. M. Westrup. P51
"From the Quiet Stream". Lorenzo. P77
Full Moon. Elinor Wylie. P82
Full Moon. Robert Hayden. P84
Moon. Kaiser Haq. P91
Is the Moon Tired?. Christina Georgina
Rossetti. P51
Lady Moon. Richard Monckton Milnes; 1st
Baron Houghton. P51
The Lady Moon. Kate Louise Brown. P51
The Little Moon. Henry Wadsworth
Longfellow. P51
Moon. Kaiser Haq. P91
Moon Eclipse Exorcism. Unknown. P78
The Moon Is the Number 18. Charles Olson.
P85
Moon Shadows. Adelaide Crapsey. P81
The Moon. Emily Dickinson. P51
The Moonlight. Ann ("Aunt Effie")
Hawkshawe. P51
Moonwalk. X. J. Kennedy. P80
Note on Moonlight. Wallace Stevens. P79
Oh! Look at the Moon. Eliza Lee Follen.
P51
Poem. Nadia Bishai. P92
Silver. Walter De La Mare. P51
The Silver House. John Lea. P51
The Silver Road. Hamish Hendry. P51
Sun and Moon. Charlotte Druitt Cole. P51
TAJ. T. G. Prabha Shankar. P72
The Moon and the Night and the Men. John
Berryman. P84
Moon Eclipse Exorcism. Unknown. P78
The Moon Is the Number 18. Charles Olson.
P85
Moon Shadows. Adelaide Crapsey. P81
"The Moon Shines Bright". Unknown. P60
"The moon is like a lamp". The Weathercock.
Rose Fyleman. P51
"The moon is shining". Poem. Nadia Bishai.
P92
"The moon on the one hand...". The Early
Morning. Hilaire Belloc. P51
"Moon shine on Mars". Fancy. Mary Agnes
White. P72
"The moon shines clear as silver". Sun and
Moon. Charlotte Druitt Cole. P51
"The Moon was but a chin of gold". The Moon.
Emily Dickinson. P51
"The moon waxes and then". Buddhist Moon.
Prince Chand. P72
"Moon, boat, lilies, long ago, when Li Po".
The Meeting. Mark Gordon. P49
"The Moon-Beams, Set in Motion". Unknown.

P62
The Moon. Emily Dickinson. P51
Mooney, James (tr.)
Three Ghost Songs. Unknown. P78
The Moonlight. Ann ("Aunt Effie") Hawkshawe.
P51
Moonlit Apples. John Drinkwater. P51
Moonwalk. X. J. Kennedy. P80
Moore, Clement Clark
A Visit from St. Nicholas. P89
Moore, Dennis
The Girl of Rue Joli. P86
Somewhere Near the Mekong River, 1966.
P86
The Train. P86
Moore, Frances Adams
This Humanity. P72
Moore, John E.
Day Breaking. P72
Moore, Lewis
I Go to Death. P68
Moore, Lilian
Bedtime Stories. P55
Outside. P75
Snowy Morning. P80
Until I Saw the Sea. P76
Moore, Marianne
Critics and Connoisseurs. P83
England. P83
The Fish. P83
A Grave. P83
In Distrust of Merits. P83
In This Age of Hard Trying, Nonchalance
Is Good And. P83
Logic and 'the Magic Flute'. P79
The Monkeys. P83
No Swan So Fine. P83
The Pangolin. P83
Poetry. P83
Spenser's Ireland. P83
What Are Years?. P83
Moore, Richard
Affluence. P63
The New Courtship. P63
Moore, Thomas
As by the Shore At Break of Day. P90
Linda to Hafed, from The Fire-
Worshippers. P89
O, Breathe Not His Name! (Richard Emmet).
P90
Oft in the Stilly Night. P90
'Tis the Last Rose of Summer, from Irish
Melodies. P89
Moore, Thomas Sturge
Beautiful Meals. P51
Moorefield, Carl
To Amy from Her Father at Graduation. P65
Moorthy, K. K.
The Bhagawan Buddha. P72

Morales, Goldie
    Mutiny. P72
"More beautiful than Gaudelupe's". In
        November in Mesilla. Peter E. Maas.
        P56
"The more intolerant I get". Consolation. Al
        Mahmud. P91
Morfudd. Dafydd ab [or ab] Gwilym. P87
Morgan, Lewis Henry (tr.)
    Song of the Bald Eagle. Unknown. P78
Morin, Catherine A.
    High June. P51
    The Lace Peddler. P51
Morin, Maud
    Bachelor's Buttons. P51
    Shower and Sunshine. P51
Moritz, A. F.
    Childhood of a Scientist. P49
Morley, Christopher
    Song for a Little House. P51
Morning
    Autumn Morning. Adeline White. P51
    The Calling Mountain. Wazir Agha. P91
    Canciones sin Su Musica. Tomas Segovia.
        P92
    Changing of the Guard. Thomas R. Dame.
        P68
    Dawn. Gordon Bottomley. P51
    Dawn. Paul Laurence Dunbar. P89
    "Dawn, Fingerpaints the Sky's". J. Louise
        Pink. P72
    Day Breaking. John E. Moore. P72
    Day/Night. Graham Everett. P64
    Daybreak. Laurene Tibbets. P72
    Daybreak. Henry Wadsworth Longfellow. P51,
        P89
    Daybreak. Sir William Davenant. P89
    Daybreak in a Garden. Siegfried Sassoon.
        P51
    The Early Morning. Hilaire Belloc. P51
    East Hampton: The Structure of Sound.
        Philip Appleman. P64
Morning. Ivy O. Eastwick. P51
    In November in Mesilla. Peter E. Maas.
        P56
    In the Naked Bed, in Plato's Cave.
        Delmore Schwartz. P84
    The Light at the Edge of the World.
        Geoffrey Parsons. P72
    Maltepe. Yahya Kemal. P91
    Man and Woman. Beryl Baigent. P72
    "Morning Has Broken". Eleanor Farjeon.
        P60
    Morning Song from 'Senlin'. Conrad Aiken.
        P82
    Morning Stillness. Violet Wilcox. P72
    "Now Another Day Is Breaking". Ogden
        Nash. P60
    On a Yankee Hill Morning. Steve LaVine.

    P77
    On Some Such Morning. Siv Cedering. P64
    Snowy Morning. Lilian Moore. P80
    The Strangeness of Dawn. Robert Williams
        Parry. P87
    Three Morning Scenes. Robert Hahn. P58
    To the Morning. Dawn R. Goodwin. P72
    Waking Up. Jaime Quezada. P71
    White Morning. L. Stanley Cheney. P68
    Window Seat. Ruth O. Maunders. P72
"Morning Has Broken". Eleanor Farjeon. P60
The Morning Reading. Wu Cheng. P92
Morning Song from 'Senlin'. Conrad Aiken.
    P82
Morning Stillness. Violet Wilcox. P72
Morning Thanksgiving. John Drinkwater. P51
The Morning Train. Fairfield Porter. P64
"Morning and evening". Goblin Market, sel.
    Christina Georgina Rossetti. P51
"The morning is clean and blue...". IV, fr.
    Irradiations. John Gould Fletcher. P82
"The morning wakes me as a broken door
    vibrating...". From a Girl in a Mental
    Institution. Diane Wakoski. P85
Morning, Noon and Night in Pacifica. Marrie
    Nunn. P72
The Morning-Glory. Maria White Lowell. P89
The Morning-Watch. Henry Vaughan. P59
"Morning: blue, cold, and still". January.
    Weldon Kees. P84
"Mornings in bed". In Bed, sels. Kenneth
    Koch. P85
Moroccan Perfume. Virginia Golden. P72
Morris, George Pope
    My Mother's Bible. P89
    Woodman, Spare That Tree. P89
Morris, Herbert
    Daguerreotypie Der Niagara Falls... P79
Morris, John N.
    The Gifts. P79
    In the Restaurant Polar. P79
Morris, Kelly
    Song of the Lonely. P73
Morris, Lewis
    Poem of the Frost and Snow. Tony Conran
        (tr.). P87
Morris, William
    March. P89
Morris, William E.
    Poppies. P72
Morris-Jones, John
    The North Star. Tony Conran (tr.). P87
    Old Age. Tony Conran (tr.). P87
    The Wind's Lament. Tony Conran (tr.). P87
Morrison, Edna Bacon
    Casual Encounter. P68
    Legend of Indian Summer. P68
    Season of Content. P68
    Switzerland. P68

Morrison, Lillian
    Sailing, Sailing. P63
Morrissey, George E.
    Dutch Elm Disease. P68
Mortal Limit. Robert Penn Warren. P67
Mortality
    The Conclusion of the Whole Matter, from
        The House... (Frederick) Ridgely
        Torrence. P81
    'The Ninth Elegy', from The Duinesian
        Elegies. Rainer Maria Rilke. P48
    On Hearing of a Man's Death in a Hang
        Glider Accident. Peter Acker. P49
    Paolo Dipietro. Joseph Maviglia. P49
    Snowdrops. Nigel Jenkins. P54
A Mortifying Mistake. Anna Maria Pratt. P89
Morton, R. Meir
    Music. P72
Morus, Huw
    Praise of a Girl. Tony Conran (tr.). P87
Moses, LaNita
    Stay. P72
"Mosquitoes tickle with their feet".
    Drawbacks. Emily Otis. P63
Moss, Howard
    Aspects of Lilac. P64
    Bay Days. P64
    In Traffic. P64
    The Long Island Night. P64
    Notes from the Castle. P64
Moss, Stanley
    The Branch. P64
    Clams. P64
    Clouds. P64
    Homing. P64
    The Meeting. P64
    Potato Song. P64
    The Seagull. P64
Moss, Stella
    Four Letter Words. P63
Moss-Gathering. Theodore Roethke. P84
"Most glorious of all the undying...". Hymn
    to Zeus. Cleanthes. P89
"Most of the time my brother is good". My
    Brother. Kristen Breslin. P73
"Most poetry is of the longer sort". A Short
    Poem. James S. Koch. P63
Mostacci, Jacopo
    "I Would Like to Show Openly". Frede
        Jensen (tr.). P69
    "Prodding My Intellect a Little". Frede
        Jensen (tr.). P69
Moth Light. Charles P. Martin. P58
Mother and Son. Barry Callaghan. P49
Mother and Son. Allen Tate. P83
Mother Duck. Ann ("Aunt Effie") Hawkshawe.
    P51
Mother Lode Spring. Nan Townsend Degelman.
    P77

"The **mother** of Judas Iscariot". Judas
    Against the World. Edwin Markham. P81
"**Mother** of mouthings". Doves. Robert Duncan.
    P84
"' **Mother**! father! hurry, hurry!'.".
    Domestic Crisis. X. J. Kennedy. P63
The **Mother's** Hope. Laman Blanchard. P89
Mother's Milk. Elaine Demakas. P58
Mother's Voice. Robert Creeley. P52
The **Mother**, fr. A Street in Bronzeville.
    Gwendolyn Brooks. P84
"**Mother**, teach me". If I Am Your Daughter.
    Pearl Newton Rook. P68
"The **Mother-in-Law**, with singleness of
    Purpose". Unknown. P62
Mothers and Motherhood
    Daughter Softly Singing in the Night.
        Jean L. Emerson. P72
    Dear Mother. Henry Bloes. P72
    Each Bird Walking. Tess Gallagher. P52
    The Face. Jules Supervielle. P61
    For My Mother: Genevieve Jules Creeley.
        Robert Creeley. P85
    A Gift of Great Value. Robert Creeley.
        P85
    If I Am Your Daughter. Pearl Newton Rook.
        P68
    The Image. Mary B. Finn. P68
    Lipstick Graffito. Aletha Humphreys. P68
    The Mother's Hope. Laman Blanchard. P89
    Mother's Voice. Robert Creeley. P52
    Our Mother. Unknown. P51
    Tell Me, Tell Me, Sarah Jane. Charles
        Causley. P76
    To My Mother. Heinrich Heine. P89
Moths
    The Yucca Moth. Archie Randolph Ammons.
        P79
Motion Pictures
    Duke. Ed Ochester. P63
    Everybody in America Is at the Movies.
        Louis Phillips. P63
    Hollywood. Joseph W. Nugent. P86
    Silent Lover. Edward Watkins. P63
Moulton, Louise Chandler
    Laus Veneris (a Picture by Burne-Jones).
        P90
Moultrie, John
    Violets. P51
Mountain Climbing
    The Long Hill. Sara Teasdale. P82
Mountain and the Squirrel. Ralph Waldo
    Emerson. P51
The **Mountain** and the Squirrel. Ralph Waldo
    Emerson. P51,90
The **Mountain** Passes, from Lost Youth: the
    Last War. Alfred Kreymborg. P82
A **Mountain** Place. Ruby Phillipy. P72
"The **mountain** is not high". A Guide. Thelma

G. Monk. P72

"**Mountain** snow, everywhere white". Gnomic
Stanzas. Unknown. P87

Mountains
The Call of the Hills. Laurie Dalziel.
P68
The Cordilleras of Il Duce. Raul Zurita.
P71
In the Night. Stephen Crane. P81
Mist on the Ridge. Mokuo Nagayama. P72
A Mountain Place. Ruby Phillipy. P72
Mt. Tamalpais, fr. Andree Rexroth.
Kenneth Rexroth. P84
Nui Ba Den (Black Virgin Mountain).
Michael Petrini. P86
On a Mountain Road. Kaleem Omar. P91
On the Horizon. Stephen Crane. P81
Once I Saw Mountains Angry. Stephen
Crane. P81
Turn To Go. William Howarth. P77

Moure, Erin
Speaking in Tongues. P49

Mourning. Andrew Marvell. P59

The **Mourning** of an Hare. Unknown. P66

The **Mouse** and the Cake. Eliza Cook. P90

The **Mouse,** the Frog and the Little Red Hen.
Unknown. P51

The **Mouse.** Elizabeth J. Coatsworth. P51

The **Mouse.** Becki Perkins. P74

The **Mouse.** Thirza Wakley. P51

"**Mousie,** mousie". Conversation. Rose
Fyleman. P51

"**Mouth** cupped violent spring". The Fallen
Star. Helen Schleef. P68

"**Move** over, ham". Hiding Place. Richard
Armour. P63

Movement, Their Way. Charlotte L. Babicky.
P72

"**Movement,** and the yellow sea undulates".
Julia Before the Mirror. Jack H.
Palmer. P68

Movements on a Theme. Maxine Silverman. P88

"**Movies** show the warrior falling".
Hollywood. Joseph W. Nugent. P86

Moviestars. Daniel Cuol Long. P53

"**Moving** into the slow". Fish Poem. Joy
Kogawa. P49

Mower and Mower. John D. Engle Jr. P63

The **Mower** to the Glow-Worms. Andrew Marvell.
P59

The **Mower's** Song. Andrew Marvell. P59

Mowing. Robert Frost. P82

Mpina, Edison
Arlington. P92
Naphiri. P92

Mr. Beetle. Emily Hover. P51

Mr. Brown. Rodney Bennett. P51

Mr. Coggs. E. V. Lucas. P51

Mr. Computer Science. Elaine Demakas. P58

Mr. Flood's Party. Edward Arlington
Robinson. P81

"**Mr.** Lear had widely traveled". Edward Lear
Finds Paradise (And Loses It). J.
Patrick Lewis. P63

Mr. Nobody. Unknown. P51

Mr. Pennycomequick. P. M. Stone. P51

Mr. Pope. Allen Tate. P83

Mr. Scarecrow. Sheila Braine. P51

Mr. Squirrel. V. M. Julian. P51

Mrs. Alfred Uruguay. Wallace Stevens. P83

Mrs. Brown. Rose Fyleman. P51

"**Mrs.** Coley's three-flat brick". The Vacant
Lot, fr. A Street in Bronzeville.
Gwendolyn Brooks. P84

Mrs. Indiarubber Duck. D. Carter. P51

Mrs. Jenny Wren. Rodney Bennett. P51

Mrs. MacQueen (or The Lollie-Shop). Walter
De La Mare. P51

Mrs. Meyers, from Spoon River Anthology.
Edgar Lee Masters. P82

Mrs. Whitehouse's View of Sexual
Intercourse. Gavin Ewart. P63

Mrs. Wilson, Who Never Loved. Virginia Long.
P63

MSG. Bruce Berger. P63

Mssrs. Mice And Co. Mary J. McArthur. P63

Mt. Lykaion. Trumbull Stickney. P81

Mt. Tamalpais, fr. Andree Rexroth. Kenneth
Rexroth. P84

"**Much** can hinge on memory". The Fence. David
Allan Evans. P68

Mueller, Lisel
About Suffering They Were Never Wrong.
P88
After the Face Lift. P88
After Whistler. P88
Asylum, from Your Tired, Your Poor. P88
Bread and Apples. P88
Chances Are. P88
Crossing over, from Your Tired, Your
Poor. P88
English as a Second Language, from Your
Tired... P88
Fugitive. P88
Midnight. P88
Monet Refuses the Operation. P88
The Triumph of Life: Mary Shelley. P88
Up North. P88
Voyager. P88
Widow. P88

The **Muffin** Man. Ann Croasdell. P51

The **Muffin-Man's** Bell. Ann ("Aunt Effie")
Hawkshawe. P51

Muir, Edwin
After a Hypothetical War. P48
The Horses. P48

Mukherjee, Prithwindra (tr.)
The Haldighat of New India. Kazi Nazrul

Islam. P91

Mullineaux, Mary
The Dragon. P51

Mulock, D. M.
The Blackbird. P51

Mumzhiu, Jenny
Haiku. P73

Munn, Henry (tr.)
The Chants, sel. Maria Sabina. P78

Munn, Pier
Armed Conflict. P63
Home Owner's Lament. P63

Munoz, Gonzalo
All of Him, the Blue Filigree of the
Gaze. Steven F. White (tr.). P71
East, sel. Steven F. White (tr.). P71
"My Apparition There Is No". Steven F.
White (tr.). P71
She Abandoned Her Body to the Color.
Steven F. White (tr.). P71
The Stains Slid from Top to Bottom in
Silence. Steven F. White (tr.). P71

Munro, Harold
A Flower Is Looking Through the Ground.
P90

Munro, Neil
The Fiddle. P51

Munsterberg, Margarete A. (tr.)
Voice in the Darkness. Richard Dehmel.
P90

Murder
And For Your Children. Gwyn Thomas. P87
The Boy Who Killed His Mother. F. Scott
Fitzgerald. P63
The Fuhrer Bunker, sels. William DeWitt
Snodgrass. P85
Night, Death, Mississippi. Robert Hayden.
P84
The Outing. Lorene Erickson. P88
Pondy Woods. Robert Penn Warren. P83
The Position. Julio Monteiro Martins. P92
Rot Below Adam's Peak (Sri Lanka). Earle
Birney. P49
Webs. Paul W. Tipton. P86

"**Murdered** comrade". For a Comrade. Abraham
Sutzkever. P48

"**Murderous** middle age is my engine". Montauk
Highway. Harvey Shapiro. P64

Murphy, Kay
Back Country Feminist Landscape. P88

Murphy, P. D.
Window. P56

Murray, Dan
August. P64
Constellation/Rorschach. P64
July. P64
June. P64
Passamaquoddy Sunrise. P64
Theory. P64

Murthi, K. Sree Ramachandra
THe Metaphor's Shine. P72

Murti, K. V. S.
Squirrel. P72

Muse. Tobin F. Rockey. P68

"The **Muse's** fairest light in no dark time".
To the Memory of Ben Jonson. John
Cleveland. P90

The **Muse.** Bhanushanker O. Vyas. P72

Muses. Kandy Arnold. P58

Museums
Contiguity. George Georgiev. P72

Music. Vance Lowery. P73

Music. R. Meir Morton. P72

"**Music** I heard with you was more than
music". Bread and Music. Conrad Aiken.
P82

Music and Musicians
Apologies to Verdi. Marlon Fick. P68
Beethoven Pathetique. Mary B. Finn. P68
Bending the Bow. Robert Duncan. P84
Beyond Words. Richard Howard. P79
The Boy and the Flute. Bjornstjerne
Bjornson. P89
Clara Schumann at the Piano. Maureen
Bloomfield. P88
Dramatic Compensation. Francis Brown
Price. P68
The Fiddle. Neil Munro. P51
Heartbreak Hotel. Oscar Hahn. P71
The Horrible Noise. Samantha Adams. P74
I Am Weary of Being Bitter. Arthur
Davidson Ficke. P82
I, Golden Strings. Alice M. Boughtwood.
P68
Jazz Band in a Parisian Cabaret. Langston
Hughes. P83
Logic and 'the Magic Flute'. Marianne
Moore. P79
Madrigal. Unknown. P51
Memo to My Music Teacher. A. L. Lazarus.
P63
Movements on a Theme. Maxine Silverman.
P88
Music. Vance Lowery. P73
Music. R. Meir Morton. P72
A Musical Instrument. Elizabeth Barrett
Browning. P90
My Dark Kingdom. Mary B. Finn. P68
My Lawn Is Brown and All My Neighbors Are
Painting... Tom Hansen. P63
Old Morgan. G. D. Roberts. P51
On Hearing a Little Music-Box. Leigh
Hunt. P90
The Piper. Seumas (James Starkey)
O'Sullivan. P51
Response to Music. Dorothea Neale. P65
Saint Cecilia's Day, 1941. PaulGoodman.
P84

The Seasons. Yahya Kemal. P91
Tippy-Tap. Virginia Junemann. P72
Untuned Lute. Chems Nadir. P91
The Weary Blues. Langston Hughes. P83
Music in the Night. Harriet Elizabeth
    Spofford. P81
"Music is like the rising sea". Response to
    Music. Dorothea Neale. P65
"Music is my heart and soul". Music. Vance
    Lowery. P73
The Music of Spring. Marion Schoeberlein.
    P68
"Music of a thrush clearbright". The Thrush.
    Dafydd ab [or ab] Gwilym. P87
"Music, swaddling us". Music. R. Meir
    Morton. P72
"Music, when soft voices die". To - ("Music,
    when soft voices"). Percy Bysshe
    Shelley. P90
Musica Ficta. D. G. Jones. P49
A Musical Instrument. Elizabeth Barrett
    Browning. P90
Musical Instruments
    The Fairy Flute. Rose Fyleman. P51
"Musing, between the sunset and the dark".
    Kindred. George Sterling. P81
"Must we unbuild or find another cave?.".
    The Rain of Time. Jerry Craven. P65
Mutability. John Gould Fletcher. P82
Muted Music. Robert Penn Warren. P67
Mutiny. Goldie Morales. P72
Mutterings Over the Crib of a Deaf Child.
    James Wright. P57
Muu's Way or Pictures from the Uterine
    World. Unknown. P78
"My Apparition There Is No". Gonzalo Munoz.
    P71
"My Bath Is The Ocean". Madeleine L'Engle.
    P60
"' My Boy, Just As an Old Cow Pours Forth
    Milk'". Unknown. P62
"My Boy, She Takes Notice of Other Youths".
    Unknown. P62
My Brother. Kristen Breslin. P73
My Cares. Hsiang Yang. P72
My Clock. Julia Nelson Walke. P68
My Dark Kingdom. Mary B. Finn. P68
My Darling's a Venus. Unknown. P87
"My Dear, Go Down Only the Most Likely
    Road". Unknown. P62
My Dog, Spot. Rodney Bennett. P51
My Doggie. C. Nurton. P51
My Dream. Scott Gunther. P73
My Early Home. John Clare. P51
My Everlasting Vision. William Zeller. P65
My Fantasy. Kim Sherry. P73
My Father in the Night Commanding No. Louis
    Simpson. P85
y Father Moved Through Dooms of Love.

Edward Estlin Cummings. P83
My Father Paints the Summer. Richard Wilbur.
    P84
My Father's Funeral. Karl Shapiro. P84
"My Friends, Why Do You Tell Me". Unknown.
    P62
My Garden. Norah Hussey. P51
My Grandfather's Funeral. James Applewhite.
    P67
My Grandmother's Love Letters. Hart Crane.
    P83
My Hands in Purdah. Mary Di Michele. P49
My Heart Leaps Up. William Wordsworth. P89
My Heart's in the Highlands. Robert Burns.
    P90
"My Heart, Tormented by Love". Odo della
    Colonne. P69
My Hut. Eileen Mathias. P51
My Lady. Dante. P89
My Lady Spring. Unknown. P51
"My aircraft lingers at its gate". Grounded.
    Alice P. Stein. P63
"My arm shot upward". Star Picker. H. R.
    Felgenhauer. P68
"My bands of silk and miniver". Full Moon.
    Elinor Wylie. P82
"My bed isn't made: sheets on the floor".
    Death Is Sitting at the Foot of My
    Bed. Oscar Hahn. P71
"My beloved chauffer for bards". Chariots.
    Glenna Glee. P68
"My biggest worry is this:.". Orpingalik's
    Song: In a Time a Sickness. Unknown.
    P78
"My boarder's new girl, a zippy brunette".
    Challenges. Elisavietta Ritchie. P63
"My boat is on the shore". To Thomas Moore.
    George Gordon, 6th Baron Byron. P90
"My boy came home". After Stefan George--
    Mein Kind Kam Heim. Stephen Spender.
    P79
"My brother has a little flute". The Fairy
    Flute. Rose Fyleman. P51
"My brown ox has grown old like Wunbiel's
    ox". I Won't Bow My Head for Anyone.
    Stephen Ciec Lam. P53
"My child laughs; his laughter". Laughter
    (I). Tin-wen Chung. P72
"My children". Three Ghost Songs. Unknown.
    P78
"My choosing, a lovely girl, graceful and
    slender". Hywel's Choice. Hywel ab
    Owain Gwynedd. P87
"My counterpane is soft as silk". A Child's
    Song of Christmas. Marjorie L. C.
    Pickthall. P51
"My country of reeds, of willows". King's
    Landing. M. Travis Lane. P49
"My country, 'tis of thee". America. Samuel

Francis Smith. P90

"My craft, bewitching one". To My Craft.
    Agnes Nemes Nagy. P92

"My dance line wanders off". Wandering Off.
    Unknown. P53

"My day went wrong: dark as a noose".
    Whirlpools. Kolyo Sevov. P70

"' My dear, be sensible!...'.". Love's
    Logic. Unknown. P89

"My dear, we are getting old". Together.
    Mary Magog Goggins. P72

"My doctor tells me:.". On the Beach.
    Michael Heller. P64

"My dog lay dead five days without a grave".
    The Pardon. Richard Wilbur. P84

"My donkey has a bridle". The Donkey. Rose
    Fyleman. P51

"My dresses can no longer hide". The
    Quickening. Miriam Pederson. P88

"My ego, like a pink balloon". Helium: an
    Inert Gas. Judson Jerome. P63

"My fairest child, I have no song to give
    you". A Farewell. Charles Kingsley.
    P89

"My fairest child, I have no song to sing
    thee". A Farewell, to C. E. G. Charles
    Kingsley. P51

"My father died in the summer, and the
    barrier". Dedicatory Entry. Anton
    Shammas. P92

"My father left me three acres of land".
    Sing Ivy. Unknown. P51

"My father lost his job today". Necessities.
    Heather Miller. P73

"My father taught me to think". The Triumph
    of Life: Mary Shelley. Lisel Mueller.
    P88

"My Father, it is surely a blue place".
    Hunchback Girl: She Thinks of Heaven,
    fr. A Street... Gwendolyn Brooks. P84

"My father, the drunk". Three. Charles West.
    P63

"My favorite spot of all is home". A Lust
    for the Quaint Old Ways. John J.
    Brugaletta. P63

"My feet romance the ground". The Runner.
    Virginia Bagliore. P72

"My first shot president". Television News.
    Judy Little. P88

"My friend Pedro died upside down...". The
    Position. Julio Monteiro Martins. P92

"My God and king! to thee". Anguish. Henry
    Vaughan. P59

"My God is hunger". The New Life. Raul
    Zurita. P71

"My God, keep in Thy sight me, Owen--on a
    poor". Mercy. Unknown. P87

"' My god, kiss my lips with thine". God and
    His Church. Morgan LLwyd. P87

"My hat leaps up when I behold". W. D.,
    Don't Fear That Animal. William DeWitt
    Snodgrass. P63

"My heart everyday". Praise of a Girl. Huw
    Morus. P87

"My heart is a song and the theme is you".
    Love Theme. Dorothea Neale. P65

"My heart sings of spring". I Sing of
    Spring. Elaine Hardt. P72

"My home is a house". The Country Child.
    Irene Thompson. P51

"My house is empty but for a pair of boots".
    The Flooded Valley. Roland Mathias.
    P54

"My house is red--a little house". A Happy
    Child. Kate Greenaway. P51

"My lady, I Wish to Tell You". Giacomo da
    Lentini. P69

My Lady, Lady Jane (Raindrop Tears). James
    Neal Blake. P72

My Lamp. Elizabeth Osborne. P74

My Last Afternoon with Uncle Devereux
    Winslow. Robert Lowell. P84

My Lawn Is Brown and All My Neighbors Are
    Painting... Tom Hansen. P63

My Little Dog. Pearl Forbes MacEwen. P51

My Little House. J. M. Westrup. P51

My Love. Dewi Havhesp. P87

My Love (Her Portrait). Russell Powell
    Jacoby. P89

My Love (Liliaceae). Kim Young Sam. P72

My Luck. Bonnie Jacobson. P63

My Mother. Claude McKay. P82

My Mother in Paradise. Lyubomir Levchev. P70

"My Mother Said That I Never Should".
    Unknown. P51

My Mother's Bible. George Pope Morris. P89

My Mother's Wedding. Boris Kristov. P70

My Music Teacher. Eric Vio. P72

My Name Is Man. Alicia Braun. P73

My New Rabbit. Elizabeth Gould. P51

My New Umbrella. M. M. Hutchinson. P51

"My Old Friends Are Gone". Unknown. P62

My Old Journal. Joanne Adamkewicz. P73

My Old Kentucky Home. Stephen Foster. P89

My Own Good. Pamela Painter. P88

My Own House. David Ignatow. P64

My Papa's Waltz. Theodore Roethke. P84

My Party. Queenie Scott-Hopper. P51

My Picture Left in Scotland. Ben Jonson. P59

My Playmate. Mary I. Osborn. P51

My Poetic Nature. Blythe Gillespie. P73

My Prayer. Bessie Wherry Noe. P72

My Rumi-Nation. Julia Older. P63

My Sad Self. Allen Ginsberg. P85

My Shadow. Robert Louis Stevenson. P89

My Son, the Tuba Player. Edmund Conti. P63

"' My Sweet Lover, You Are Leaving!'".
    Federico II [Frederick II of

Hohenstaufen]. P69

My Temple. Anne Shaw. P73

My Toys. Lilian McCrea. P51

My True-Love Hath My Heart. Sir Philip Sidney. P89

My Village and I. Kaiser Haq. P91

My Whisper. Unknown. P61

My Wife Reads the Paper at Breakfast on the Birthday... Miller Williams. P63

"My Wife Went Away, Left Me," from Wolf Songs... Unknown. P78

My Window, My Wheelchair, and Me. Deborah D'Aleo. P74

"My left door won't open". Equations. Yaedi Ignatow. P64

"My life is like the summer rose". Life. Richard Henry Wilde. P90

"My life is running away with me". Fugitive. Lisel Mueller. P88

"My life, your light green eyes". Last Words. James Merrill. P85

"My lives with you are awkward". Dante's Angels. Patrick Lane. P49

"My long two-pointed ladder's sticking...". After Apple Picking. Robert Frost. P82

"My longing makes a jumble of". All Roads Lead to Rome. Freddie P. Hanson. P72

"My love". The Third Poem of Leave-Taking. Hamid Skif. P91

"My love and I for kisses played". Kisses. William Strode. P89

"My love is called John, Kuac Reu". John Kennedy. Nyagak Pinien. P53

"My love is of a birth as rare". The Definition of Love. Andrew Marvell. P59

"My love, the blood trickles away". Intimate. Aristoteles Espana. P71

"My lover's good eye's dark pupil". Perseverance. Antonio D'Alfonso. P49

"My mind was once the true survey". The Mower's Song. Andrew Marvell. P59

"My mother writes". Poem Which Cannot Be a Letter. Alamgir Hashmi. P91

"My name's immaterial". My Village and I. Kaiser Haq. P91

"my neighbor bought a newer mower". Mower and Mower. John D. Engle Jr. P63

"My net". The Disappointed Shrimper. P. A. Ropes. P51

"My old friend the cucumber's soul". Another Fable in Two Languages. Charles W. Pratt. P63

"My oxen are scattered like grain on a skin". I Was as Full of Air as An Old Bullfrog. Pilual Juoc. P53

"My pensioners who daily". Pensioners. Winifred M. Letts. P51

"My people talk to the winds...". Windsong.

Leonorv (I am Cree). McDowell. P72

"My reading program has increased". Patient. Keith Baker. P63

"My red engine goes chuff-chuff-choo...". My Toys. Lilian McCrea. P51

"My reflection". Four Poems. Ray Young Bear. P78

"My roses are orange". Marianne's Shalimar. A. Majewski. P72

"My sister had a slumber party". Slumber Party. Carson McCullers. P50

"My son and I go walking in the garden". New Season. Philip Levine. P52

"My son tears the daffodils from someone's". What Trial?. Frank Finale. P56

"My son's not keen on music". Curriculum Change. Ned Pastor. P63

"My songs to sell, good sir!.". Vendor's Song. Adelaide Crapsey. P81

"My sorrow is so wide". Kings River Canyon, fr. Andree Rexroth. Kenneth Rexroth. P84

"My soul, there is a country". Peace. Henry Vaughan. P59

"My spirit is a pestilential city". The Desolate City. Claude McKay. P82

"My thanks, friends...". Perry Zoll, from Spoon River Anthology. Edgar Lee Masters. P82

"My thoughts come back to you...". Letter to My Parents. F. W. Watt. P49

"My three fingers". Writing, from A Thai Divine Comedy. Montri Umavijani. P92

"My tongue in English chains". Homecoming. R. Parthasarathy. P92

"My townspeople, beyond in the great world". Gulls. William Carlos Williams. P82

"My wedding-ring lies in a basket". Wedding-Ring. Denise Levertov. P85

"My Wellington boots go". Boots and Shoes. Lilian McCrea. P51

"My window opens out into the trees". Solace. Clarissa Scott Delany. P89

"My windows open onto Wall Street". Everybody in America Is at the Movies. Louis Phillips. P63

"Myriads and myriads plumed...". Leaves. Katharine (Hinkson) Tynan. P51

"Myriads of Buddhas sit". Mahayana, from Paradise. Montri Umavijani. P72

Myself, from The Song of Myself. Walt Whitman. P90

Mysterious. Rosemary Witty. P72

Mysterious Evening. Verona Bratesch. P72

"Mysterious as that distant star". Mysterious. Rosemary Witty. P72

Mystery in Flight. Patricia M. Johnson. P72

Mystery of Mind. Mythily. P72

Mystic Shadow, Bending Near Me. Stephen

Crane. P81
The Mystic's Vision. Mathilde Blind. P89
"Mysticism, but let us have no words". Time
        in the Rock or Preludes to Definition
        Selections. Conrad Aiken. P82
A Myth of the Human Universe. Unknown. P78
The Myth Revisited: Adam. Michael V. McGee.
        P56
Mythily
        Mystery of Mind. P72
Mythology
        The Mabinogion. Unknown. P87
        Solar Myth. Genevieve Taggard. P83
Mythology-Egyptian
        Osiris' Song. Richard Candida Smith. P68
Mythology-Greek
        Eurydice. Hilda ("H.D.") Doolittle. P82
        Oedipus in Criminal Court. Eileen
        Hillary. P68
        Pan in Wall Street. Edmund Clarence
        Stedman. P81
Mythology-Indians of America
        A Myth of the Human Universe. Unknown.
        P78
Myths and Texts (Burning). Gary Snyder. P85
Myths and Texts (Hunting). Gary Snyder. P85
Myths and Texts (Logging). Gary Snyder. P85

Nabors, Claudia
        Dog Adoption. P72
Nadir, Chems
        The Palaces Under the Moon. Eric Sellin
        (tr.). P91
        Untuned Lute. Eric Sellin (tr.). P91
Nadjib, Emha Ainunn
        Bukan. Harriet Levin and Emha Ainunn
        Nadjib (tr.). P92
Nagayama, Mokuo
        Mist on the Ridge. P72
Nagy, Agnes Nemes
        Four Squares. Bruce Berlind (tr.). P92
        The Ghost. Bruce Berlind (tr.). P92
        Storm. Bruce Berlind (tr.). P92
        Streetcar. Bruce Berlind (tr.). P92
        To My Craft. Bruce Berlind (tr.). P92
A Nail for Hanging the Soul. Alain Bosquet.
        P61
Naim, C.M. (tr.)
        Apprehension. Wazir Agha. P91
        Beauty Competition. Fahmida Riyaz. P91
        The Boy's Song. Zahid Dar. P91
        The Calling Mountain. Wazir Agha. P91
        The Distance. Khalilur Rahman Azmi. P91
        Iqleema. Fahmida Riyaz. P91
        The Last Quarter of the Night. Gilani
        Kamran. P91

A Night in the War. Wazir Agha. P91
The Old Bookseller. Gilani Kamran. P91
Our First Journey. N.M. Rashed. P91
The Plough Is Crooked. Abbas Athar. P91
A Strange Man. Wazir Agha. P91
To Auden. Fahmida Riyaz. P91
Nakagami, Tetsuo
        I'm Lying on the Bed at a Motel and...
        Marilyn Chin and Tetsuo Nakagami
        (tr.). P92
        Wandering Was Always an Important Theme
        in My Lyric. Marilyn Chin and Tetsuo
        Nakagami (tr.). P92
Nakasuk
        THe Great Farter. Jerome Rothenberg
        (tr.). P78
        Magic Words to Feel Better. Edward Field
        (tr.). P78
The Naked Eye. Lewis Turco. P63
Nalungiaq
        Heaven and Hell. Edward Field (tr.). P78
Namaste. Katherine E. Landry. P72
"The name is immortal but only the name...".
        Jew. Karl Shapiro. P84
Name-Dropping. Robert Sward. P49
The Name. Robert Creeley. P85
Names
        Alphabet Soup. David Cram. P63
        Anonymous. John Banister Tabb. P81
        Born Tying Knots. Samuel Makidemewabe.
        P78
        Choosing a Name. Mary Lamb. P89
        Cindy. Panos D. Bardis. P72
        The Consolations of Etymology, with
        Fanfare. John Frederick Nims. P63
        Near-Miss Eddy. Elizabeth Eddy. P63
        Saw the Cloud Lynx. Samuel Makidemewabe.
        P78
        Sons of the Right Hand. Benjamin Hochman.
        P63
        Tree Old Woman. Samuel Makidemewabe. P78
        What's in a Name. Ed Orr. P63
The Names. Gwendolyn Macewen. P49
Naming the Birds. Jeanne Lohmann. P65
"Nana Caliche," from Mother Goose on the Rio
        Grande. Unknown. P90
Nanmor, Dafydd
        Exhortation. Tony Conran (tr.). P87
        Praise of Rhys ap Maredudd. Tony Conran
        (tr.). P87
Naphiri. Edison Mpina. P92
Napoleon
        Incident of the French Camp. Robert
        Browning. P90
Narasimham, Nirupama
        Go Back. P72
Narcissus. Paul Little. P72
Narratives
        Argoed. Thomas Gwynn Jones. P87

The Bearer of Evil Tidings. Robert Frost.
    P82
Ben Johnson Entertains a Man from
    Stratford. Edward Arlington Robinson.
    P81
The Cantos, sel. Ezra Pound. P82
Captain Carpenter. John Crowe Ransom. P83
Creation of the World According to
    Charles Slater. Charles Slater. P78
The Creation. James Weldon Johnson. P83
The Dirty Old Man. William Allingham. P90
Go Down Death. James Weldon Johnson. P83
The Hand of Emmagene. Peter Taylor. P79
Homage to Mistress Bradstreet, sels. John
    Berryman. P84
Isaac and Archibald. Edward Arlington
    Robinson. P81
John Brown of Osawatomie. Edmund Clarence
    Stedman. P81
Judas Against the World. Edwin Markham.
    P81
Kalypso. Trumbull Stickney. P81
Lodovico Martelli. Trumbull Stickney. P81
Lord Ullin's Daughter. Thomas Campbell.
    P51,P90
Marie. Lola Ridge. P82
The Nobleman and the Pensioner. Gottlieb
    Conrad Pfeffel. P90
Pan in Wall Street. Edmund Clarence
    Stedman. P81
Pondy Woods. Robert Penn Warren. P83
The Popol Vuh: Beginnings, sel. Unknown.
    P78

NArratives
The Popol Vuh: Beginnings, sel. Unknown.
    P78

Narratives
Rachel Plummer's Dream Winter 1836.
    Eleanor Ross Taylor. P79
The Relief of Lucknow (September 25,
    1857). Robert T. S. Lowell. P90
Rime of the Ancient Mariner. Samuel
    Taylor Coleridge. P90
Rizpah 17--. Lord Tennyson. P90
The Rose and the Gauntlet. John Sterling.
    P90
The Sands O' Dee. Charles Kingsley. P90
Sir Gawaine and the Green Knight. Yvor
    Winters. P83

Nash, Ogden
"Now Another Day Is Breaking". P60
Winter Morning. P80

National Songs
The Star-Spangled Banner. Francis Scott
    Key. P90

Native Ground. Robert Minhinnick. P54
The **Natural** Way. Jane S. Spain. P72

Nature
Aspects of Lilac. Howard Moss. P64

At Billings' Bridge Graveyard. Robert
    Billings. P49
Bedrock. Gary Snyder. P85
Blessed Is the Light. Grace Schulman. P64
Boats Sail on the Rivers. Christina
    Rosetti. P51
Brechfa Chapel. Roland Mathias. P54
Cells Breathe in the Emptiness. Galway
    Kinnell. P85
Chillingham. Mary E. Coleridge. P51
Colour. Unknown. P51
Day. Sir Cecil Spring-Rice. P51
Divorce. Richard Eberhart. P79
"The Earth with Its Palasha Blossoms".
    Unknown. P62
The Far Field. Theodore Roethke. P84
Foweles in the Frith. Unknown. P66
Great Nature Is an Army Gay. Richard
    Watson Gilder. P89
Grey Owl's Poem. Gwendolyn Macewen. P49
Hie Away!. Sir Walter Scott. P51
Hill Country Rhythms. Jeremy Hooker. P54
A Holiday. Lizette Woodworth Reese. P81
Images of Gravity. Grace Schulman. P64
"In the Belly of the Weeping Cloud-Bull".
    Unknown. P62
The Learning Tree. Dorothy Lyons. P72
Limited. Audrey Frederick. P72
"Look! a Bow-Shaped Line". Unknown. P62
"Look! a Newly Dyed Flag Put on the
    Roof". Unknown. P62
"Look! At the Gate of the Little Village
    Temple". Unknown. P62
"Look! Coming Out of the Hollow Tree".
    Unknown. P62
"Look! Coming Out of the Ripe Mango
    Seed". Unknown. P62
"Look! In the Middle of the Cow-Pen".
    Unknown. P62
"Look! Motionless and Still on a Lotus-
    Leaf". Unknown. P62
"Look! Oh Slender One. The White Clouds
    in the Fall". Unknown. P62
"Look! Suspended Upside-Down on His Web".
    Unknown. P62
"Look! the Buffalo Cows, Being Led
    Away...". Unknown. P62
"Look! The Cloud, Not Strong Enough".
    Unknown. P62
"Look! the Forest Elephant Vainly Tries".
    Unknown. P62
"Look! There Descends from the Plane of
    the Heavens". Unknown. P62
"Look! There Is a Sobbing from the
    Laundry". Unknown. P62
"Look, Oh Traveller, Even That Shadow of
    Yours". Unknown. P62
The Meadows. Ann and Jane Taylor. P51
"The Men of Ceylon, Oh Son". Unknown. P62

Mowing. Robert Frost. P82
Nature. Nicholas [pseud.]. P68
Nature Rhymes. Unknown. P89
"The New-Moon Sliver in the Sky".
    Unknown. P62
Nature. Nicholas [pseud.]. P68
    Nothing Gold Can Stay. Robert Frost. P82
    "Oh Friend, Whoever Stretched and
      Dappled". Unknown. P62
    Out of Doors. E. North. P51
    Petit, the Poet, from Spoon River
      Anthology. Edgar Lee Masters. P82
    The Place You Inhabit. Walter Hoefler.
      P71
    Poesia 50 (The Quanta of Anguish). Helle
      Busacca. P72
    Prairie Waters by Night. Carl Sandburg.
      P82
    "The Pulinda Tribesmen Standing on the
      Mountain Peak". Unknown. P62
    Range-Finding. Robert Frost. P82
    "The Row of Bees, Delighted by the
      Nectar". Unknown. P62
    A Rune of Riches. Florence Converse. P51
    Secret Places. Irene Thompson. P51
    The Shape of the Fire. Theodore Roethke.
      P84
    Six Poems for Nine Crows. Judith Minty.
      P88
    Sweet Surprises. S. Doudney. P51
    The Tables Turned. William Wordsworth.
      P89
    "Truly, Mother, Winter Has Made".
      Unknown. P62
    Try Tropic. Genevieve Taggard. P83
    Walking Early by the Wye. Anne Stevenson.
      P54
    Without a Prop. Bella Cameron. P72
Nature Rhymes. Unknown. P89
"Nature's first green is gold". Nothing Gold
    Can Stay. Robert Frost. P82
"Nature's lay idiot, I taught thee to love".
    Elegy 7. John Donne. P59
Navajo Correspondences (First Set). Unknown.
    P78
Navajo Correspondences (Fourth Set).
    Unknown. P78
Navajo Correspondences (Second Set).
    Unknown. P78
Navajo Correspondences (Third Set). Unknown.
    P78
"The Navajo word for unleaded was not". The
    Official Frisbee-Chasing Champion of
    Colorado. Robert Hill Long. P63
"Nay, Ivy, nay, hyt shal not be, iwys".
    Holly and Ivy. Unknown. P66
Neale, Dorothea
    Love Theme. P65
    Prelude to Paradise. P72

Response to Music. P65
Testament of Love. P65
Near Helikon. Trumbull Stickney. P81
Near Thanksgiving. Graham Everett. P64
"Near dawn, still crouched...". Painter of
    Icons. Luchesar Elenkov. P70
"Near Rhydcymerau". Rhydcymerau. David
    Gwenallt Jones. P87
Near the Screen Door. Kevin Cline. P58
"Near the wall of the abbey". The Yewtree.
    Gruffudd Gryg. P87
Near, Jean Gowan
    Expediency. P72
Near-Miss Eddy. Elizabeth Eddy. P63
"Nearing the start of that mysterious...".
    Leavetaking. Anne Porter. P64
Neary, Mary Hamilton
    Frost Is Coming. P72
Necessities
    Everyday Things. Jean Ayer. P51
Necessities. Heather Miller. P73
"The Necklace of a Young Women". Unknown.
    P62
"The Nectar of the Jasmine Bud". Unknown.
    P62
"The needle convinces me". Going Under.
    Paulette Roeske. P88
"Needle, needle open up". The Lace Maker.
    Barbara Howes. P57
Neely, Andy
    Raccoon. P74
Negalha, Jonas
    Ballad of the Progress. P72
Negley, Maxine
    "Indian Rice Fields". P72
Negro Hero. Gwendolyn Brooks. P84
Negro Servant. Langston Hughes. P83
The Negro Speaks of Rivers. Langston Hughes.
    P83
"A Negro sprouts from the pavement...".
    Stumpfoot on 42nd Street. Louis
    Simpson. P57
Negroes
    The Congo. Vachel Lindsay. P82
Negroes. See also Men-...& Women-Blacks
Neighbors
    Amherst Neighbors. Lewis Turco. P63
    Eighth and Broad. Wallace Whatley. P63
Neither Out Far nor in Deep. Robert Frost.
    P82
"Neither love, the subtlety of refinement".
    The Presence. William Everson. P84
"Neither on horseback nor seated". Walt
    Whitman at Bear Mountain. Louis
    Simpson. P85
Nelligan. Laurence Hutchman. P49
Nelly Myers. Archie Randolph Ammons. P67
Nelms, Sheryl L.
    The Blanks. P56

Nelson, Vera Joyce
    Brain Wave. P72
Nemerov, Howard
    The Big Bang. P63
    The Ditances They Keep. P79
    From the Poetry Exchange, Two
        Conversations. P63
    Night Operations, Coastal Command RAF.
        P63
    Po Biz. P63
    Two Views of a Philosopher. P79
Neo Catholicism, from Lost Youth: the Last
    War. Alfred Kreymborg. P82
Nerl, Peggy Zeaphev
    The Painter. P72
"A nervous young woman named Trudy". She
    Don't Bop. Keith Casto. P63
Nesbit, E.
    Child's Song in Spring. P51
"Nests in the Top of the Almond Tree".
    Vachel Lindsay. P82
"Nests well hidden". Secret Places. Irene
    Thompson. P51
The Net of Moon: a Pawnee Hand Game Vision.
    Unknown. P78
A Net to Snare the Moonlight. Vachel
    Lindsay. P82
The Net. Veronica Haughey. P72
Netherclift, Beryl
    London Trees. P51
Never Fall in Love. Mary Rebecca Henderson.
    P74
Never May the Fruit Be Plucked. Edna St.
    Vincent Millay. P82
Never Tell. Unknown. P87
"Never for more than a year stay in
    England". Attraction. Unknown. P87
"Never love unless you can". Advice to a
    Girl. Thomas Campion. P89
"Never mind the day we left, or the day...".
    The Klondike. Edward Arlington
    Robinson. P81
"Never the nightingale". Dirge. Adelaide
    Crapsey. P81
"Never thought I could do it". Stage Fright.
    Jennie H. Sandbank. P72
"Never until the mankind making". A Refusal
    To Mourn the Death, by Fire, of a
    Child... Dylan Thomas. P48
"Never yet was a springtime". Awakening.
    Margaret Elizabeth (Munson) Sangster.
    P81
The Nevermore. Dante Gabriel Rossetti. P89
The New Colossus. Emma Lazarus. P90
The New Courtship. Richard Moore. P63
The New Day. Fenton Johnson. P82
The New Duckling. Alfred Noyes. P51
New England
    Our State. John Greenleaf Whittier. P90

New England Village. Lou Orfanella. P72
New Her Cherokee Face. Jerry Craven. P65
The New Life. Raul Zurita. P71
New Mexican Mountain. Robinson Jeffers. P83
New Moon or No?. Maryann Calendrille. P64
The New Regime. Wendy Cope. P63
New Season. Philip Levine. P52
New Sights. Unknown. P51
New Year
    A New Year Carol. Unknown. P51
    New Year's Days. Celia Standish. P51
    The New Year, from In Memoriam. Lord
        Tennyson. P89
    The New Year. Unknown. P51
    The New Year. Unknown. P51
A New Year Carol. Unknown. P51
New Year's Days. Celia Standish. P51
The New Year, from In Memoriam. Lord
    Tennyson. P89
The New Year. Unknown. P51
The New Year. Unknown. P51
New York City
    Steps. Frank O'Hara. P85
"New snow, and I follow". Breathing in the
    Woods. Judith Minty. P88
"The New-Moon Sliver in the Sky". Unknown.
    P62
Newbolt, Henry
    The Toy Band. P51
Newcomb, Greer
    The Tree of the Sound of Silence. P72
Newey-Johnson, D.
    To Let. P51
Newlove, John
    Driving. P49
    The Weather. P49
A Newly Discovered 'Homeric' Hymn. Charles
    Olson. P85
Newman, Wade
    True Love. P63
"News from a foreign country came". On News.
    Thomas Traherne. P59
A Newspaper Is a Collection. Stephen Crane.
    P81
"The newspaper comes. It". The Sky Eats up
    the Trees. James Schuyler. P64
Newspapers
    Herald. Josephine Miles. P84
    A Newspaper Is a Collection. Stephen
        Crane. P81
The Next Step. W. D. Ehrhart. P86
"The next time you leave me". Goodbye,
    Goodbye. Dolores R. Patitz. P68
Ni Hoi Nim Ni Hon. Lance Henson. P78
Niazi, Muneer
    Thinking of Other Universes. Daud Kamal
        (tr.). P91
Nibenegenesabe, Jacob
    The Wishing Bone Cycle, sel. Howard

Norman (tr.). P78

Nicaragua
    Proud Father with Buried Son. Judd Allen.
       P72

Nicholas Nye. Walter De La Mare. P51

Nicholas [pseud.]
    Find Your Love. P72
    Nature. P68

Nicholson, L.
    Bubbles. P51

Nick and the Candlestick. Sylvia Plath. P85

"Nicki holds a sparrow in her teeth".
    Nicki's Sparrow. Susan Richardson. P56

Night
    Acquainted with the Night. Robert Frost.
       P82
    At Night. Fairfield Porter. P64
    Aurora Borealis. Jeane C. Carson. P72

Night. William Blake. P51

Night. Louise Bogan. P52
    Christmas Night. B. E. Milner. P51
    "The Day Is Done". Elizabeth Madox
       Roberts. P60

Night. Georgi Djagarov. P70
    The Dustman. Unknown. P51
    Envoi. P. H. B. Lyon. P51
    From Dusk to Dawn: Night Watch II. Ken
       Stone. P86
    Good Night. Victor Hugo. P51
    Good Night. Ruth Ainsworth. P51

Night. Hermann Hesse. P90
    High on a Hill. A. D. Winans. P56
    The Holiday Ended. Pier Paolo Pasolini.
       P61
    Hot Night on Water Street. Louis Simpson.
       P85
    In the Pitch of the Night. Lee Bennett
       Hopkins. P55

Night. Robinson Jeffers. P83

Night. Yahya Kemal. P91
    The Last Quarter of the Night. Gilani
       Kamran. P91
    The Lateshow Diorama. Christopher
       Dewdney. P49
    Latin Night. Noel Peattie. P56
    The Long Island Night. Howard Moss. P64
    Maps in the Brain. A. J. Wright. P56
    Midsummer Moon. E.M.G. R. P51
    Midsummer Night. Elizabeth Gould. P51
    Moonlit Apples. John Drinkwater. P51
    Music in the Night. Harriet Elizabeth
       Spofford. P81
    Night. Maria Celeste Achille Todde. P61
    Night. Unknown. P51
    Night. Hermann Hesse. P90
    Night. Robinson Jeffers. P83
    Night. Yahya Kemal. P91
    Night. William Blake. P51
    Night. Louise Bogan. P52

Night. Georgi Djagarov. P70
Night Brushes. Kitty Yeager. P72
Night Has Been as Beautiful as Virginia.
    Kenneth Patchen. P84
A Night in June. William Wordsworth. P51
Night of Spring. Thomas Westwood. P51
The Night Sky. Unknown. P51
The Night Will Never Stay. Eleanor
    Farjeon. P51
Night, Death, Mississippi. Robert Hayden.
    P84
The Night. James Stephens. P51
The Night. Helen Leuty. P51
The Night. Nellie Parodi. P72
Nightfall. Gwallter Mechain. P87
Nightfall in Dordrecht. Eugene Field. P81
Nocturne. Heidi Blomster. P68
Noises in the Night. Lilian McCrea. P51
On a Dark Road. Robert Herrick. P51
On a Night Without Adornment. Rene Char.
    P61
One Night on Guard Duty. W. D. Ehrhart.
    P86
Pine Night. Wayne R. Toensmann. P56
Rainy Nights. Irene Thompson. P75
Rhapsody on a Windy Night. Thomas Stearns
    Eliot. P83
Sonnet 12, fr. Three Sonnets From 'Deep
    Within the Heart'. Syed Shamsul Haque.
    P91
A Sort of Blues. D. G. Jones. P49
Street Scene. William Ernest Henley. P51
To Night. Percy Bysshe Shelley. P89

Night. Maria Celeste Achille Todde. P61

Night. Unknown. P51
    The Window. Patricia Hooper. P88
    With the Flashes of the Night. Phoebus
       Delphis. P61
    "You Do Know That the Stars". Jean Paul
       Mestas. P72
    You, Andrew Marvell. Archibald MacLeish.
       P83

Night Below Zero. Kenneth Rexroth. P84

Night Brushes. Kitty Yeager. P72

Night Has Been as Beautiful as Virginia.
    Kenneth Patchen. P84

"Night has begun its long slide west". Three
    Morning Scenes. Robert Hahn. P58

A **Night** in June. William Wordsworth. P51

A **Night** in the War. Wazir Agha. P91

Night in Veracruz. Kathy Strange de Olguin.
    P72

Night Light. Lawrence Ferlinghetti. P85

Night Music. Grace Shattuck Bail. P72

"The night is awake". God's Rain. Ghulam-
    Sarwar Yousof. P91

"The night is come, but not too soon". The
    Little Moon. Henry Wadsworth
    Lonfellow. P51

"Night is the harbinger of pain". Victim,
  fr. Three Voices. Faiz Ahmad Faiz. P91
Night of Returning. Eo'ie Silva. P56
Night of Spring. Thomas Westwood. P51
Night Operations, Coastal Command RAF.
  Howard Nemerov. P63
The Night Sky. Unknown. P51
Night Song. Arlo Bates. P81
Night Song at Amalfi. Sara Teasdale. P82
Night Thoughts, Sierra. William Howarth. P77
Night Visits with the Family. May Swenson.
  P79
The Night Will Never Stay. Eleanor Farjeon.
  P51
"The night sweeps, sweeps the sooty air".
  Aurora Borealis. Jeane C. Carson. P72
"The night was made for rest and sleep".
  Interim. Clarissa Scott Delany. P89
"A night wreck out on the highway".
  Helendale. Dick Barnes. P63
"The Night". Lorenzo. P77
Night, Death, Mississippi. Robert Hayden.
  P84
"Night, night". Night Light. Lawrence
  Ferlinghetti. P85
The Night. Helen Leuty. P51
The Night. Nellie Parodi. P72
The Night. James Stephens. P51
"Night? Then it's right". Latin Night. Noel
  Peattie. P56
Nightfall. Gwallter Mechain. P87
Nightfall by the River. Brian Henderson. P49
Nightfall in Dordrecht. Eugene Field. P81
"A nightingale once lost his voice from".
  Youth and Age, from The House of a
  Hundred Lights. (Frederick) Ridgely
  Torrence. P81
Nightingale, Madeleine
  The Apple Rhyme. P51
  The Caravan. P51
  The Scissor-Man. P51
The Nightingale. Katharine (Hinkson) Tynan.
  P51
Nightingales
  Song to the Nightingale. Alun. P87
Nightmare for Future Reference. Stephen
  Vincent Benet. P48
Nijmeijer, Peter (tr.)
  Euthanasia. Hans Verhagen. P92
Nike. James Merrill. P79
Nikki-Rosa. Nikki Giovanni. P85
Nikolov, Lyubomir
  Two Painters. May Swenson (tr.). P70
Nikolov, Nino
  The Bedroom. Richard Harteis (tr.). P70
  The Closet. Richard Harteis (tr.). P70
  The Room. May Swenson (tr.). P70
Nile (1). Cathy Matyas. P49
The Nile. Leigh Hunt. P90

Nims, John Frederick
  The Consolations of Etymology, with
   Fanfare. P63
  In Praise of Sobriety. P63
9:00 a.m. at Broadway and Walnut on Your
  Birthday. Ripley Schemm. P57
(914) 555-4144. Ned Pastor. P63
'The Ninth Elegy', from The Duinesian
  Elegies. Rainer Maria Rilke. P48
No Anger in a Fallen Tree. Allan Maunula.
  P72
No Answers. Mary Ann Henn. P56
(No Greater Pain Beneath the Trees).
  Aristoteles Espana. P71
No Longer Do I Dwell. Duane Edwards. P68
No Man's Good Bull. James Seay. P67
No More. Gina Berola. P74
No Muse Is Good Muse. Rochelle Distelheim.
  P63
No One. Gonzalo Millan. P71
No One Knows What I'm Talking About. Diego
  Maquieira. P71
No Swan So Fine. Marianne Moore. P83
No Thoroughfare. Ruth Holmes. P51
No Yellow Jackets on the Mountian. Dabney
  Stuart. P67
"No bitterness: our ancestors did it". Ave
  Caesar. Robinson Jeffers. P83
"No color isolates itself like blue". A
  Painter Obsessed by Blue. Fairfield
  Porter. P64
"No cork to eye, no sniff, no snip". Wine
  Coolers. Bern Sharfman. P63
"No doubt to-morrow I will hide". At Mass.
  Vachel Lindsay. P82
"No fawn-tinged hospital pajamas...". The
  Old Jew. Maxwell Bodenheim. P82
"No gorilla heart in me!.". The Natural Way.
  Jane S. Spain. P72
"No longer throne of a goddess to whom we
  pray". Full Moon. Robert Hayden. P84
"No man hath dared to write this thing as
  yet". Histrion. Ezra Pound. P82
"No matter they are down-at-heel". Oh, Dem
  Olden Slippers!. Alma Denny. P63
"No more work and no more play". Good Night.
  Ruth Ainsworth. P51
"' No mouse is an Iland'.". Fable of the
  Terrorist Mouse. Scott Bates. P63
"No one has he". Elegies in a City
  Churchyard. Gloria A. Maxson. P63
"No one in the garden". Laughter. Olive
  Enoch. P51
"No one says that May is here". The Green
  Comb. Raffaele Carrieri. P61
"No one's body could be that light".
  Voyager. Lisel Mueller. P88
"No other man, unless it was Doc Hill".
  Doctor Meyers, from Spoon River

Anthology. Edgar Lee Masters. P82
"No place for elegies, in these stern".
	Westhampton Cemetery. Philip Appleman.
	P64
"No prodigal but has turned". Home. Louise
	Louis. P65
"No rule nor ruler: only water and day".
	After a Hypothetical War. Edwin Muir.
	P48
"No sleep for twelve days". What Happened to
	a Young Man... Unknown. P78
"No sound of any storm that shakes".
	Hillcrest. Edward Arlington Robinson.
	P81
"No sun--no moon!.". No!. Thomas Hood. P89
"No sutures in the steep brow". Buzzard.
	Gillian Clarke. P54
"No thunder. No earthquakes". Good Friday.
	Walter Desmond. P68
""No water so still as the ".". No Swan So
	Fine. Marianne Moore. P83
No!. Thomas Hood. P89
"No, not ever, in no time". The Impossible
	Choices. William Everson. P84
"No, not that door--.". I Am Dreaming of a
	White Christmas: The Natural... Robert
	Penn Warren. P47
Noah
	And Did the Animals?. Mark Van Doren. P83
	Still, Citizen Sparrow. Richard Wilbur.
	P84
Nobility. Tudur Aled. P87
Noble, Virginia
	Sonnet to a Road Runner. P72
The Nobleman and the Pensioner. Gottlieb
	Conrad Pfeffel. P90
"Nobody lives in the cottage now". Fairy
	Feet. Phyllis L. Garlick. P51
"Nobody planted roses, he recalls".
	Summertime and the Living... Robert
	Hayden. P84
"' Nobody's perfect,' she said". Q. E. D.
	Laurence Perrine. P63
"The nocturnal life". Sequence. Richard
	Armour. P63
Nocturne. Heidi Blomster. P68
Nocturne. John V. A. Weaver. P82
Nod. Walter De La Mare. P51
Noe, Bessie Wherry
	Letter to Johnny. P65
	My Prayer. P72
	To an Optimist. P65
Noise
	Ode to Noise. Bozhidar Bozhilov. P70
Noises. Aileen Fisher. P50
Noises in the Night. Lilian McCrea. P51
The Oomad. John Stevens Wade. P68
Non Omnis Moriar. Teresinka Pereira. P72
Non Omnis Moriar. Leila Wendell. P68

Non-Missing Fox Terrier Does Not Reappear...
	Juan Luis Martinez. P71
"None of my ancestors...". Descendant.
	Elisaveta Bagriana. P70
Nonsense
	"All My Boasting Friends," from Mother
		Goose... Unknown. P90
	"At Me He Winks an Eye," from Mother
		Goose... Unknown. P90
	The Boy and the Wolf. Reed Whittemore.
		P63
	"Chin, Chin, Chin," from Mother Goose...
		Unknown. P90
	"Down the Hill the Waters Cascade," from
		Mother... Unknown. P90
	Fearsome Critters. Walter H. Kerr. P68
	"I Do Not Go to the Fields Today," from
		Mother... Unknown. P90
	Jabberwocky, from Through the Looking-
		Glass. Charles Lutwidge ("Lewis
		Carroll") Dodgson. P90
	Knitting-Sitting Song. James Steel Smith.
		P63
	Little Billee. William Makepeace
		Thackeray. P90
	The Mocking Bird and the Owl. Reed
		Whittemore. P63
	The Modern Hiawatha. Unknown. P90
	Mr. Nobody. Unknown. P51
	"Nana Caliche," from Mother Goose on the
		Rio Grande. Unknown. P90
	The Owl and the Pussycat. Edward Lear.
		P51
	The Peasant and the Sheep. Ivan
		Andreevich Kriloff. P90
	The Purple Cow. Gelett Burgess. P90
	Tall Tale Weather. Holly Hester. P74
	Topsy-Turvy Land. Phyllis M. Stone. P51
	Topsy-Turvy Land. H. E. Wilkinson. P51
	Unpleasant Surprise. Jay Dougherty. P63
	The Upside-Down World. Hamish Hendry. P51
	The Vaunting Song of Louis L'Amour.
		Ernest Kroll. P63
	"We Are Little Mice," from Mother
		Goose... Unknown. P90
	Weather. Eve Merriam. P75
	"What Day Is Tomorrow?," from Mother
		Goose... Unknown. P90
	Wystan Hugh Auden: a Villanelle. David
		Lehman. P63
	Xerxes and Xanthippe. Caroline Knox. P63
Norell, Alney
	Love's Presence. P65
Norman, Howard (tr.)
	Born Tying Knots. Samuel Makidemewabe.
		P78
	Saw the Cloud Lynx. Samuel Makidemewabe.
		P78
	Tree Old Woman. Samuel Makidemewabe. P78

The Wishing Bone Cycle, sel. Jacob
    Nibenegenesabe. P78
Norris, Kathleen
    The First Day of Summer. P88
    On the Northwest Hiawatha. P88
    Visitors. P88
Norris, Ken
    The Edge. P49
Norse Lullaby. Eugene Field. P51
The North Star. John Morris-Jones. P87
The North Wind. Dorothy Gradon. P51
The North Wind. Unknown. P51
"The north wind cracks the clay". As You
    Wish. Mario Luzi. P61
North, E.
    Out of Doors. P51
Northeast. Martin Singleton. P49
Northhanger Ridge. Charles Wright. P67
Northwest Passage. Charles P. Martin. P58
"Northwind whittles the last acorns...".
    Near Thanksgiving. Graham Everett. P64
Norton, Caroline Elizabeth Sarah
    We Have Been Friends Together. P89
Norton, Charles Eliot (tr.)
    My Lady. Dante. P89
The Nose and the Eyes. William Cowper. P90
"Not a drum was heard, not a funeral note".
    Burial of Sir John Moore. Charles
    Wolfe. P90
"Not a shank of the long lane upwards".
    Brechfa Chapel. Roland Mathias. P54
"Not a soul, only". As a Thousand Years.
    Jeremy Hooker. P54
"Not awake yet, the sun begins".
    Passamaquoddy Sunrise. Dan Murray. P64
"Not by the city bells that chime the
    hours". A Summer Day. Florence
    Harrison. P51
"Not everything is named, either". Fool's
    Fingers. Roland Mathias. P54
Not in a Silver Casket Cool with Pearls.
    Edna St. Vincent Millay. P82
Not in Vain. Virginia (Jacques). Snyder. P72
Not Overlooked. James Oppenheim. P82
Not So Long Gone (for the Maidu). Doc
    Dachtler. P77
Not What We Had in Mind. May Richstone. P63
"Not in the touch of hands". Grate Fire.
    Jeanne Bonnette. P65
"Not like the brazen giant of Greek fame".
    The New Colossus. Emma Lazarus. P90
"Not long ago I moved to Texas". I'm a Texan
    Now. Gene Fehler. P63
"Not long ago the proud". Death of a
    Sunflower. Raymond Souster. P49
"Not lost or won but above all endeavor".
    Fidelity. Trumbull Stickney. P81
"Not much happened today". Ennui. David Ray.
    P63

"Not noisily, but solemnly and pale". III,
    fr. Irradiations. John Gould Fletcher.
    P82
"Not on our golden fortunes builded high--
    .". The Forgotten Man. Edwin Markham.
    P81
"Not that the appearance would alter us".
    Expecting an Angel. George Bradley.
    P79
"Not while, but long after he had told me".
    Each Bird Walking. Tess Gallagher. P52
"Not writ in a water nor in mist". For John
    Keats, Apostle of Beauty, fr. Four
    Epitaphs. Countee Cullen. P83
A Note from Plwmp. John Tripp. P54
"A note from my friend on this morning...".
    Trying to Remember. Judith Minty. P88
Note on Moonlight. Wallace Stevens. P79
A Note Toward a Definition of Culture. James
    Camp. P63
Notes. Aristoteles Espana. P71
Notes for an Unpublished Canto. Ezra Pound.
    P79
Notes from the Castle. Howard Moss. P64
"' Nothin' or everythin' it's got to be'.".
    Nocturne. John V. A. Weaver. P82
Nothing Gold Can Stay. Robert Frost. P82
"Nothing as miserable has happened before".
    The Long Island Night. Howard Moss.
    P64
"Nothing is new; I have seen the spring...".
    I Have Seen the Spring. Sara Teasdale.
    P82
"Nothing is quite so quiet and clean". Snow
    in Town. Rickman Mark. P51
"Nothing made him suffer in this world".
    Epitaphs. Orhan Veli Kanik. P91
"Nothing surpasses". Brain Wave. Vera Joyce
    Nelson. P72
Nothingness
    Bukan. Emha Ainunn Nadjib. P92
    The Shadow and the Cross. Salah Abdul-
    Sabur. P91
Nou Goth Sonne Under Wod. Unknown. P66
"Nou sprinkes the sprai". Now Springs the
    Spray. Unknown. P66
Nouveau Poor. Alice Morrey Bailey. P65
November
    The Last Days. George Sterling. P81
    No!. Thomas Hood. P89
    November Night. Adelaide Crapsey. P81
    November. Over the Hills. R. B. Weber.
    P64
November. Margaret Rose. P51
    Scorpion Summer. Terry M. Paulsgrove. P77
    "7 a.m. -- Late November". Ben L. Hiatt.
    P77
November 25, 1970. Brian O'Riordan. P49
November Night. Adelaide Crapsey. P81

"**November** is a spinner". November. Margaret
    Rose. P51
"**November** winds returning bite with beaks".
    Passengers in a Time Beyond Orchards.
    Vesta P. Crawford. P65
November. Over the Hills. R. B. Weber. P64
Novice in the Woods. L. G. Harvey. P72
"**Now** after school the children come". In the
    Woods in Spring. Raymond Kresensky.
    P68
"**Now** all day long the man who is not dead".
    Mother and Son. Allen Tate. P83
Now and Afterwards. Dinah Maria Mulock
    Craik. P89
Now and Again. Mary Trimble. P88
"**Now** Another Day Is Breaking". Ogden Nash.
    P60
Now Springs the Spray. Unknown. P66
Now That the Book Is Finished. Alice Walker.
    P85
Now That the Winter's Gone. Thomas Carew.
    P51
"**Now** You Love Me". Unknown. P78
"**Now** autumn tints your orchard's leaves". A
    Letter to My Mother in Vidin. Luchesar
    Elenkov. P70
"**Now** can you see the monument? It is of
    wood". The Monument. Elizabeth Bishop.
    P84
"**Now** dead but never quick, he lagged...". On
    a Late Schoolboy. Laurence Perrine.
    P63
"**Now** finally, I have the time". The Bedroom.
    Nino Nikolov. P70
"**Now** he's older and less virile". The Rake's
    Progress. Vonna Adrian. P63
"**Now** I am slow and placid, fond of sun".
    With Child. Genevieve Taggard. P83
"**Now** I mostly remember". Nursing. Phebe
    Hanson. P88
"**Now** I turn my thoughts to prayer".
    Repentance. Sion Cent. P87
"**Now** in the suburbs and the falling light".
    Father and Son. Stanley Kunitz. P83
"**Now** is the winter of our discontent". End
    of the Civil War, from Richard III.
    William Shakespeare. P90
"**Now** let no charitable hope". Let No
    Charitable Hope. Elinor Wylie. P82
"**Now** o'er the sea from her old love comes
    she". Ovid's Elegies, Book I, 13.
    Christopher Marlowe. P59
"**Now** so high". The Swing. Mary I. Osborn.
    P51
"**Now** so many people that are in this place".
    Thank You: A Poem in Seventeen Parts.
    Unknown. P78
"**Now** the bright crocus flames, and now".
    Spring. Meleager. P89

"**Now** the daisies pied, and violets blue".
    Spring. William Shakespeare. P51
"**Now** the day moves out". Old Age. Nikolai
    Hristozov. P70
"**Now** the golden fields of sunset rose on
    rose...". Day and Dark. George Cabot
    Lodge. P81
"**Now** the moisty wood discloses". Spring
    Morning. Frances Cornford. P51
"**Now** the thinkers our old ones remember".
    Dance of the Rain Gods. Ray Young
    Bear. P78
"**Now** the third and fatal conflict...".
    Harmosan. Richard Chenevix Trench. P90
"**Now** these were songs to her:.". Love's
    Songs. Vivian Trollope-Cagle. P65
"**Now** thou hast loved me one whole day".
    Woman's Constancy. John Donne. P59
"**Now** to Great Britain we must make our way".
    Of England, and of Its Marvels. Fazio
    degli Uberti. P90
"**Now** where's a song for our small dear". The
    Unwritten Song. Ford Madox (Hueffer)
    Ford. P51
"**Now** who could take you off to tiny life".
    The Independent Man, fr. A Street in
    Bronzeville. Gwendolyn Brooks. P84
"**Now** will I weave white violets...". The
    Wreath. Meleager. P89
"**Now!** the red tobacco has come to
    strike...". Magic Words, from Run
    Towards the Nightland. Unknown. P78
"**Now,** even at the solstice, darkest week".
    Running in Winter. William Carpenter.
    P48
"' **Now,** John, go brush your Sunday suit'.".
    Edge of Appalachia. Margielea
    Stonestreet-See. P72
"**Now,** lifting I my hand to shield my sight".
    Sonnet to a Seagull. Patricia P.
    Kirby. P68
"**Now,** rocking horse! rocking horse!...".
    Through Nurseryland. Unknown. P51
"**Now/Here** in the kitchen". Praise. Yaedi
    Ignatow. P64
Noyes, Alfred
    The Barrel Organ. P51
    Daddy Fell Into the Pond. P89
    The New Duckling. P51
    Sherwood. P51,P90
Nuclear War
    Apocalypse. Ernesto Cardenal. P48
    Fall 1961. Robert Lowell. P48
    How To Survive Nuclear War. Maxine Kumin.
        P48
    The Return. Mauricio Electorat. P71
Nugent, Joseph W.
    Hollywood. P86
    VNV Rap Group. P86

Nuhman, M.A.
     Grandfathers and Grandsons, sels. S.
          Pathmanathan (tr.). P91
Nui Ba Den (Black Virgin Mountain). Michael
     Petrini. P86
"Number 1: Stasis". Images. Pieter D.
     Williams. P68
Number 7. Doug Rawlings. P86
Numbers
     Ten Little Christmas Trees. Rodney
          Bennett. P51
"A nun went past, and her girdle swung". On
     Deck, fr. From a Travel Diary. T.H.
     Parry-Williams. P87
The Nun. Unknown. P87
Nunc Dimittis. Patrick Lane. P49
Nunn, Marrie
     Morning, Noon and Night in Pacifica. P72
Nuns
     Effigy of a Nun. Sara Teasdale. P82
     Mecox Nunnery & Saint Dominic. Anselm
          Parlatore. P64
Nursery Rhymes
     "A Dis, a Dis, a Green Grass". Unknown.
          P51
     AEIOU. Jonathan Swift. P51
     Amy Elizabeth Ermyntrude Annie. Queenie
          Scott-Hopper. P51
     "As I Went up the Garden". Unknown. P51
     A Baby Verse. Unknown. P51
     'Banbury Fair'. Edith G. Millard. P51
     The Barrel Organ. Alfred Noyes. P51
     "Bell Horses, Bell Horses". Unknown. P51
     Billy Boy. Dorothy King. P51
     "Bless You, Bless You, Bonnie Bee".
          Unknown. P51
     The Bus. Peter [pseud.]. P51
     "A Cat Came Fiddling Out of a Barn".
          Unknown. P51
     The Children's Bells. Eleanor Farjeon.
          P51
     The Clothes-Line. Charlotte Druitt Cole.
          P51
     "Cock a Doodle Doo!". Unknown. P51
     "Diddle, Diddle, Dumpling". Unknown. P51
     "Down by the Meadows, Chasing
          Butterflies". Unknown. P51
     "Draw a Pail of Water". Unknown. P51
     The Ferryman. Christina Georgina
          Rossetti. P51
     A Frisky Lamb. Christina Georgina
          Rossetti. P51
     "From House to House He Goes". Unknown.
          P51
     Good Morning. Rose Fyleman. P51
     "The Grand Old Duke of York". Unknown.
          P51
     A Growing Rhyme. J. M. Westrup. P51
     "Here We Go Up, Up, Up". Unknown. P51

     "Here's to the Poor Widow from Babylon".
          Unknown. P51
     "Hey Diddle, Dinkety, Poppety Pet".
          Unknown. P51
     "Hot-Cross Buns! Hot Cross Buns!".
          Unknown. P51
     The House That Jack Built. Unknown. P51
     "How Many Miles to Barley Bridge?".
          Unknown. P51
     "I Had a Little Hen, the Prettiest Ever
          Seen". Unknown. P51
     "I Had a Little Hobby-Horse". Unknown.
          P51
     "I Had a Little Husband". Unknown. P51
     "I Had a Little Nut-Tree, Nothing Would
          It Bear". Unknown. P51
     "I Have a Little Sister, They Call Her
          Peep, Peep". Unknown. P51
     I Saw a Ship A-Sailing. Unknown. P51
     If. P. A. Ropes. P51
     "If All the Seas Were One Sea". Unknown.
          P51
     "In Spring I Look Gay". Unknown. P51
     Jack Tar. Emile Jacot. P51
     "Jeanie, Come Tie My". Unknown. P51
     Jenny and Johnny. Dorothy King. P51
     Just Like me. Unknown. P51
     Just Like This. D. A. Olney. P51
     The King of China's Daughter. Edith
          Sitwell. P51
     Knee-Bouncing Rhymes. Unknown. P90
     "A Knight and a Lady". Unknown. P51
     "The Lion and the Unicorn". Unknown. P51
     Little Betty Blue. Agnes Grozier
          Herbertson. P51
     Little Blue Apron. Unknown. P51
     "Little Boy Blue, Come, Blow up Your
          Horn". Unknown. P51
     Little Clotilda. Unknown. P51
     '"Little Girl, Little Girl'.". Unknown.
          P51
     Little Lucy Lester. M. Steel. P51
     Little Maid and Cowslips. John Clare. P51
     Little Tommy Tiddler. Paul Edmonds. P51
     'Littles'. Robert Herrick. P51
     Making Tens. M. M. Hutchinson. P51
     "The Man in the Wilderness Asked of Me".
          Unknown. P51
     "A Man Went A-Hunting at Reigate".
          Unknown. P51
     Minnie and Mattie. Christina Georgina
          Rosetti. P51
     Mistress Comfort. Elizabeth Gould. P51
     "Monday's Child Is Fair of Face".
          Unknown. P51
     Mr. Brown. Rodney Bennett. P51
     Mr. Pennycomequick. P. M. Stone. P51
     Mrs. MacQueen (or The Lollie-Shop).
          Walter De La Mare. P51

The Muffin Man. Ann Croasdell. P51
The Muffin-Man's Bell. Ann ("Aunt Effie")
    Hawkshawe. P51
"My Mother Said That I Never Should".
    Unknown. P51
Old Mother Goose. Unknown. P51
An Old Rhyme. Unknown. P51
"Once There Lived a Little Man". Unknown.
    P51
"One Misty Moisty Morning". Unknown. P51
"One, Two". Unknown. P51
A Party Song. Unknown. P51
"Peter and Paul Were Two Little Menikin".
    Unknown. P51
"Poor Old Robinson Crusoe!". Unknown. P51
Pretty Maid Marion. Ivy O. Eastwick. P51
A Rhyme for Washing Hands. Unknown. P51
"Ride a-Cock Horse to Banbury Cross".
    Unknown. P51
"Robin and Richard". Unknown. P51
Robin Hood. Rachel MacAndrew. P51
"Robin Hood, Robin Hood". Unknown. P51
"Rock-a-bye, Baby, thy Cradle Is Green".
    Unknown. P51
"Round About in a Fair Ring-a". Unknown.
    P51
"Said a Frog on a Log". Unknown. P51
Shining Things. Elizabeth Gould. P51
Shower and Sunshine. Maud Morin. P51
"Simple Simon". Unknown. P51
Sing Ivy. Unknown. P51
"Six Little Mice Sat Down To Spin".
    Unknown. P51
Someone. Walter De La Mare. P51
Ten Little Indian Boys. M. M. Hutchinson.
    P51
"There Was a Crooked Man, and He Went a
    Crooked Mile". Unknown. P51
Things I Like. Marjorie H. Greenfield.
    P51
"This Is the Key of the Kingdom".
    Unknown. P51
Through Nurseryland. Unknown. P51
"To Market, to Market, To Buy a Fat Pig".
    Unknown. P51
Toad the Tailor. N. E. Hussey. P51
Toadstools. Elizabeth Fleming. P51
Twice. M. M. Hutchinson. P51
Wandering Jack. Emile Jacot. P51
What Piggy-Wig Found. Enid Blyton. P51
What the Weather Does. Unknown. P51
"When Good King Arthur Ruled This Land".
    Unknown. P51
"When I Was a Little Boy". Unknown. P51
"When the Wind Is in the East". Unknown.
    P51
"Whether the Weather Be Fine...".
    Unknown. P51
"'Which Is the Way to London Town'".

    Unknown. P51
    Who's That a-Knocking?. Emile Jacot. P51
Nurses
    The Doctor. David Ignatow. P84
    Santa Filomena (Florence Nightingale).
        Henry Wadsworth Longfellow. P89
Nursing. Phebe Hanson. P88
Nursing Homes
    Meeting a Lovely Lady. Maryleona Berg.
        P68
NUts
    The Acorn. Unknown. P51
Nurton, C.
    My Doggie. P51
Nuthatch. Edward Coletti. P63
Nuts
    Among the Nuts. Unknown. P51
    Pink Almond. Katharine (Hinkson) Tynan.
        P51
Nutting, Leslie
    The Diver. P49
"Nyalang's boy craves someone". He'd Die for
    Tobacco. Philip Macar. P53
Nyang, Peter Pal Hoth
    Magic That Comes at Dawn. Terese Svoboda
        (tr.). P53
    Paddlewheel Under a Boat. Terese Svoboda
        (tr.). P53
Nyanpandong
    Leapt into the Dance. Terese Svoboda
        (tr.). P53
The Nymph's Reply. Sir Walter Raleigh. P89
"Nymph, nymph, what are your beads?.".
    Overhead on a Saltmarsh. Harold Monro.
    P51
Nyoat, Moses Kuac
    The Crocodile Scales. Terese Svoboda
        (tr.). P53
    Drink the Curse. Terese Svoboda (tr.).
        P53

"Oh Auntie, Just as Thirst Is Not Quenched".
    Unknown. P62
"Oh Bee Desirous of Drinking the Nectar".
    Unknown. P62
"Oh Beloved with Eyes Closed in Feigned
    Sleep--.". Unknown. P62
O Bird of Light. Sri Chinmoy. P68
O Black and Unknown Bards. James Weldon
    Johnson. P83
O Captain! My Captain!. Walt Whitman. P90
"Oh Child, My Own Life Is More Dear to Me".
    Unknown. P62
"Oh Clever Poverty, You Are Enamoured".
    Unknown. P62
"Oh Cupid, I Will Worship Your Feet".

Unknown. P62

O Dandelion. Unknown. P51

"Oh Daughter, If You Enter the House".
    Unknown. P62

O England, Country of My Heart's Desire. E.
    V. Lucas. P51

O Fire of God, the Comforter. Saint
    Hildegarde. P89

"Oh Friend, Do Not Cry". Unknown. P62

"Oh Friend, Whoever Stretched and Dappled".
    Unknown. P62

"Oh God, Make an Affair with Another
    Woman...". Unknown. P62

"Oh Heart, at the End of the Third Day".
    Unknown. P62

"Oh Heart, If You Must Depart, Then Leave".
    Unknown. P62

"Oh Heart, Unafraid of Your Own Judgement".
    Unknown. P62

O Holy Past. Mary Jude Kupper. P72

"Oh Madhuka Flower in the Great Glade".
    Unknown. P62

"Oh Mendicant, Go Your Way". Unknown. P62

"Oh Moon, Full of Nectar, Diadem of the
    Heavens". Unknown. P62

' Oh Mother, Today I am Pained". Unknown.
    P62

"Oh My Black Soul!...," from Divine
    Meditations. John Donne. P59

"O Our Mother the Earth, O Our Father the
    Sky". Unknown. P60

O Sailor, Come Ashore. Christina Georgina
    Rossetti. P51

"Oh Slave-Girl Longing for the Sound...".
    Unknown. P62

"O Son of the Village-Headman". Unknown. P62

"O all you little blackey tops". Scaring
    Crows. Unknown. P51

"O black-maned, horse-haired, unworthy one".
    To the Noble Women of Llanarth Hall.
    Evan Thomas. P87

"O blackbird, what a boy you are!.".
    Vespers. T. E. Brown. P51

"Oh blind musician, the caresses of your
    fingers". Untuned Lute. Chems Nadir.
    P91

"O blithe new-comer, I have heard". To the
    Cuckoo. William Wordsworth. P51,P89

"O city, o white filagree...". Coral
    Stanzas. Michael Heller. P64

"Oh daughter of mine". To Amy from Her
    Father at Graduation. Carl Moorefield.
    P65

"Oh dragonfly, come to rest on my sleeve".
    Indian Summer. Judith Minty. P88

"O flower fawn". Five Flower World
    Variations. Unknown. P78

"O foolish dream of life...". The Dream of
    Life. Vera La Claustra. P72

"O for one hour of youthful joy!.". The Old
    Man Dreams. Oliver Wendell Holmes. P89

"O Gaddi, ope the casement, open wide".
    Lodovico Martelli. Trumbull Stickney.
    P81

"O gentle, gentle summer rain". Invocation
    to Rain in Summer. William Cox
    Bennett. P89

"O God! methinks, it were a happy life". The
    Shepherd's Life, from Henry VI.
    William Shakespeare. P89

"O God, in the dream the terrible horse
    began". The Dream. Louise Bogan. P83

"' O hell, what do mine eyes'.". Milton by
    Firelight. Gary Snyder. P85

"O hideous little bat, the size of snot".
    The Fly. Karl Shapiro. P84

"O Johnny O". Little Elegy. Michael McFee.
    P63

"O joys! Infinite sweetness...". The Morning-
    Watch. Henry Vaughan. P59

"O little light". Flame of God. Frederika
    Blankner. P65

"O loss of sight, of thee I must
    complain!.". Samson on His Blindness,
    from Samson Agonistes. John Milton.
    P89

"O lovely Mary Donnelly...". Lovely Mary
    Donnelly. William Allingham. P89

"O lucky me!.". My Lamp. Elizabeth Osborne.
    P74

"O Martians, if you read the Times". The
    Daily Planet. Edward Watkins. P63

"' O Mary, go and call the cattle home'.".
    The Sands O' Dee. Charles Kingsley.
    P90

"O often wonder how it is". My Playmate.
    Mary I. Osborn. P51

"O paradise, O paradise". Paradise.
    Frederick William Faber. P89

"O sea goddess Nuliajuk". Magic Words for
    Hunting Seal. Unknown. P78

"O seeded grass, you army of little men". II,
    fr. Irradiations. John Gould
    Fletcher. P82

"O sentinel, magnet, north". O Tree. Hugh
    Seidman. P64

"O shaggy god of the ground, barbaric
    Pan!.". Walt Whitman. Edwin Markham.
    P81

"O sleep, O tranquil son of noiseless
    night". To Sleep. Giovanni della Casa.
    P89

"O such a commotion under the ground".
    Flower Chorus. Ralph Waldo Emerson.
    P51

"Oh that horse I see so high". A Gift of
    Great Value. Robert Creeley. P85

"O that she who in a glade". The Grey Friar.

Dafydd ab [or ab] Gwilym. P87
"O that the chemist's magic art". A Tear.
     Samuel Rogers. P90
O the Jewels. Unknown. P87
"Oh Thou Shameless and Ungrateful!.".
     Unknown. P62
O Tree. Hugh Seidman. P64
O Wind, Where Have You Been?. Christina
     Georgina Rossetti. P51
"O they hanged your love on the rowan tree".
     The Rowan Tree. Ruth G. Iodice. P68
"O thou, whose glorious orbs on high". Hymn
     of the West. Edmund Clarence Stedman.
     P90
"O thou, with dewy locks who lookest down".
     To Spring. William Blake. P51
"O unseen Spirit! now a calm divine". On a
     Beautiful Day. John Sterling. P89
"Oh what a joy it is to see thee bow".
     Boobiat. Paul Humphrey. P63
"Oh what is so merry, so merry, heigh ho!".
     The Light-Hearted Fairy. Unknown. P51
"Oh where have you been all day". In the
     Woods. Dorothy Baker. P51
"O white and midnight sky! O starry bath!.".
     The Celestial Passion. Richard Watson
     Gilder. P81
"O who will walk a mile with me". A
     Wayfaring Song. Henry Van Dyke. P89
"O wind, rend open the heat". Heat. Hilda
     ("H.D.") Doolittle. P82
"O Winter's a beautiful time of the year".
     Winter. Enid Blyton. P51
"O woman, I". Assonance. Barry Callaghan.
     P49
"O world! O life! O time!.". A Lament. Percy
     Bysshe Shelley. P89
"O world, I cannot hold thee close
     enough!.". God's World. Edna St.
     Vincent Millay. P82
"O world, thou choosest not the better
     part!.". Faith. George Santayana. P89,
     P81
"' O World-God, give me wealth!'...". Gifts.
     Emma Lazarus. P90
"O Year, grow slowly, exquisite, Holy". Slow
     Spring. Katharine (Hinkson) Tynan. P51
O'Connor, J. F.
     On the Rhyming of Four-Line Verses. P63
O'Hara, Frank
     Autobiographia Literaria. P85
     For James Dean. P85
     Hotel Transylvanie. P85
     Les Etiquettes Jaunes. P85
     Ode: Salute to the French Negro Poets.
        P85
     Poem ("Lana Turner"). P85
     Poem ("When I am feeling"). P85
     Steps. P85

To John Ashbery. P85
A True Account of Talking to the Sun at
     Fire Island. P85
Why I Am Not a Painter. P85
O'Neal, Opal Jane
     And Who Am I. P72
O'Riordan, Brian
     Fenians All. P49
     November 25, 1970. P49
O'Shaughnessy, Arthur
     Has Summer Come Without the Rose?. P89
O'Sullivan, Seumas (James Starkey)
     The Piper. P51
     The Trains. P51
O, Breathe Not His Name! (Richard Emmet).
     Thomas Moore. P90
O, Fairest of Rural Maids! William Cullen
     Bryant. P89
"O, espionage looked starry...". P$$$$$T.
     Felicia Lamport. P63
"O, say, can you see by the dawn's early
     light". The Star-Spangled Banner.
     Francis Scott Key. P90
"O, that last day in Lucknow fort!.". The
     Relief of Lucknow (September 25,
     1857). Robert T. S. Lowell. P90
O, the Pleasant Days of Old!. Frances
     Browne. P90
"O, to have a little house!.". The Old Woman
     of the Roads. Padraic Column. P51
"O, who shall from this dungeon raise". A
     Dialogue Between the Soul and Body.
     Andrew Marvell. P59
"O, young Lochinvar is come out of the
     west". Lochinvar. Sir Walter Scott.
     P51
"Oak grows between lake and lake". The
     Mabinogion. Unknown. P87
"The oak is called the king of trees".
     Trees. Samuel Taylor Coleridge. P51
"The oaks are casting off". Spending the
     Woodpile Well Into June. Jean Pape.
     P77
"The oaks, how subtle and marine". Bearded
     Oaks. Robert Penn Warren. P83
The Oaks. Ivan McShane. P68
The Oath. Allen Tate. P67
Oberammergau. David Gwenallt Jones. P87
Obituary. Kenneth Fearing. P83
"An object among dreams, you sit here...". A
     Girl in a Library. Randall Jarrell.
     P67
The Obligation. Knute Skinner. P63
"' Oblivion, great day, come, oh swallow
     me'.". Saturn the Last Titan. Arthur
     Avergun. P68
Observation Post. R. L. Barth. P86
Observe:. Geoff Fiorito. P58
Ocean Beach House. R. B. Weber. P64

The **Ocean** Said to Me Once. Stephen Crane.
P81
Ocean Treasures. Constance Andrea Keremes.
P76
"**Ocean** waves rush in". On an August Day. Lee
Bennett Hopkins. P76
The **Ocean's** Treasure. Todd Kusserow. P74
Ochester, Ed
Duke. P63
The Latin American Solidarity Committee
Fundraising... P63
October
Country Road in October. Judith Minty.
P88
October Among the Hills. Wallace
Winchell. P65
October Is the Cruelest Month. Francis
Lehner. P68
October Morning. William Young Elliot.
P72
October's Wooing. Terese Akins. P72
October: Sierra. William Howarth. P77
October. Christina Georgina Rossetti. P51
October. S. W. Whitman. P51
October 1st. Robert Hahn. P58
October Afternoon. Sarah Rigg. P74
October Among the Hills. Wallace Winchell.
P65
October Is the Cruelest Month. Francis
Lehner. P68
October Morning. William Young Elliot. P72
"**October** gave a party". October's Party.
George Cooper. P51
"**October** is a piper". Autumn Song. Margaret
Rose. P51
October's Party. George Cooper. P51
October's Wooing. Terese Akins. P72
"**October's** moon is here so crisp and gay".
Awaiting Their Return. Katherine
Nielsen Eckhart. P72
October: Sierra. William Howarth. P77
Octogenarian. Irene A. Bradshaw. P72
The **Octopus**. James Merrill. P85
"**Odd**, how from the hum of restaurant noise".
Eating Out. Gene Fehler. P63
Ode. Richard Watson Gilder. P81
Ode for a Master Mariner Ashore. Louise
Imogen Guiney. P81
An **Ode** in Time of Hesitation. William Vaughn
Moody. P81
Ode to a Nuclear Frieze. Nan Townsend
Degelman. P77
Ode to Death. William Walter De Bolt. P68
Ode to Failure. Allen Ginsberg. P85
Ode to Noise. Bozhidar Bozhilov. P70
Ode to Strings. Maia Linden. P65
Ode to the Confederate Dead. Allen Tate. P67,
P83
Ode, from The Spectator. Joseph Addison. P89

Ode: Salute to the French Negro Poets. Frank
O'Hara. P85
Odes. George Santayana. P81
Oedipus in Criminal Court. Eileen Hillary.
P68
Of a Contented Spirit. Thomas, 2nd Baron
Vaux. P90
Of a Rose, a Lovely Rose. Unknown. P66
Of De Witt Williams on His Way to Lincoln
Cemetery, fr. A.... Gwendolyn Brooks.
P84
Of England, and of Its Marvels. Fazio degli
Uberti. P90
Of Late. George Starbuck. P85
Of Mere Being. Wallace Stevens. P83
Of Modern Poetry. Wallace Stevens. P83
"**Of** all the floures in the mede". The Daisy,
from The Legend of Good Women.
Geoffrey Chaucer. P89
"**Of** all the girls that are so smart". Sally
in Our Alley. Henry Carey. P89
"**Of** all the torments, all the cares".
Rivalry in Love. William Walsh. P89
"**Of** course, it may well be that the
mind...". Six of One. George Bradley.
P64
"**Of** John Cabanis' wrath and of the strife".
The Spooniad, from Spoon River
Anthology. Edgar Lee Masters. P82
Of the Nameless Birds. Teresa Calderon. P71
Of Three Girls and of Their Talk. Giovanni
Boccaccio. P90
"**Off** Highway 106.". Cherrylog Road. James
Dickey. P67
Off We Go to Market. Gwen A. Smith. P51
The **Offer**. Yaedi Ignatow. P64
Offerle, Mildred
Misconception. P72
Office for the Dead. Thomas Kinsella. P79
Office Hours. Katharyn Machan Aal. P63
The **Official** Frisbee-Chasing Champion of
Colorado. Robert Hill Long. P63
"**Oft** a solitary bird comes to the green
tree". Lonesome Bird. Etty George. P72
Oft in the Stilly Night. Thomas Moore. P90
"**Often** Love Has Made Many Happy". Rugieri
d'Amici. P69
"**Often** beneath the wave, wide from this
ledge". At Melville's Tomb. Hart
Crane. P83
"**Often** she wears bon bon colors". Food
Director's Testimony. Nancy Simpson.
P63
"**Often** they speak at night". River Boats.
Grace D. Yerbury. P68
"**Often** this thought wakens me unawares".
Night. Hermann Hesse. P90
"**Oggy!** oggy! oggy!". Land of Song. Nigel
Jenkins. P54

Oh! Look at the Moon. Eliza Lee Follen. P51
Oh! Where Do Fairies Hide Their Heads?.
        Thomas Haynes Bayly. P90
"Oh! hush Thee, oh! hush Thee, my baby...".
        Cradle Song at Bethlehem. E. J.
        Falconer. P51
"Oh! I wish I were a tiny brown bird...".
        Valentine's Day. Charles Kingsley. P51
"Oh! I'm the New Year". The New Year.
        Unknown. P51
"Oh! is it bale-fire in thy brazen hand--.".
        To the Goddess of Liberty. George
        Sterling. P81
"' Oh! what shall I do?' sobbed a tiny
        mole". Who'll Help a Fairy? Unknown.
        P51
"Oh! why left I my home?.". The Exile's
        Song. Robert Gilfillan. P90
"' Oh, 'tis time I should talk...'.". How to
        Ask and Have. Samuel Lover. P89
Oh, Dem Olden Slippers!. Alma Denny. P63
Oh, Figures on the Portico... Antonio
        Machado. P61
Oh, Now I See... Keith Casto. P63
"Oh, a girl loves us, the Tuitui". The
        Girl's Hearts Soften. Daniel Cuol
        Long. P53
"Oh, darling of caprice and wine". Okinawa
        1945. Ivan McShane. P68
"Oh, for a book and a shady nook". Open
        Sesame. Unknown. P51
"Oh, golden flower opened up". A Poem to the
        Mother of the Gods. Unknown. P78
"Oh, how lucky, harried brethren!.". Dail-A-
        Shrink. Ned Pastor. P63
"Oh, I shall never set out". Hunting Horn.
        Nikolai Kuntchev. P70
"Oh, I should love to be like one of those".
        The Youth Dreams. Rainer Maria Rilke.
        P90
"Oh, like a tree". The Tree. John Freeman.
        P51
"Oh, my mother's moaning by the river". The
        Lonely Mother. Fenton Johnson. P82
"Oh, ten-tassled one, people like to
        blame...". Paddlewheel Under a Boat.
        Peter Pal Hoth Nyang. P53
"Oh, the stars were out in the pale
        moonlight". Eddie's Comet. Barbara
        Hawkins. P74
"Oh, the white sea-gull, the wild sea-gull".
        The Sea-Gull. Mary Howitt. P51
"Oh, the wild joy of living...". Youth.
        Robert Browning. P51
"Oh, to be in England now that April's
        there". Home Thoughts from Abroad.
        Robert Browning. P51,P89
"Oh, to walk naturally". Without a Prop.
        Bella Cameron. P72

"Oh, where do you come from". Little Rain-
        Drops. Ann ("Aunt Effie") Hawkshawe.
        P51
"Oh, where has my honey gone?.". The Lost
        Love. Fenton Johnson. P82
"Oh, yes, we mean all kind words that we
        say". We Love But Few. Unknown. P89
"Ohohoho hehehe heya heya". Sound-Poem No.
        1. Unknown. P78
Okai
        Kwabenya. P92
Okinawa 1945. Ivan McShane. P68
Ol' Grandad. Steven C. Levi. P56
Olander, Jon
        Mining the American. P77
        Rockbound Pass in January. P77
        "'What's the Matter,' He Says, Tying on
        the". P77
The Old Adam. Denise Levertov. P85
Old Age
        Age in Youth. Trumbull Stickney. P81
        At Seventy. F. C. Rosenberger. P63
Old Age. Maxwell Bodenheim. P82
        The Drunken Fisherman. Robert Lowell. P84
        Farther North. M. Travis Lane. P49
        Healthful Old Age, from As You Like It.
        William Shakespeare. P90
Old Age. Nikolai Hristozov. P70
        In His Old Age and Blindness. Guto'r
        Glyn. P87
        In Summer. Trumbull Stickney. P81
        The Last Leaf. Oliver Wendell Holmes. P89
        Lazy One. Lynne Anderson. P73
        Llywarch the Old, fr. Poetry from Lost
        Sagas. Unknown. P87
Old Age. John Morris-Jones. P87
        Octogenarian. Irene A. Bradshaw. P72
        Old Age. Nikolai Hristozov. P70
        Old Age. John Morris-Jones. P87
        Old Age. Maxwell Bodenheim. P82
        Old Grimes. Albert G. Greene. P90
        The Old Man Dreams. Oliver Wendell
        Holmes. P89
        The Old Man's Comforts and How He Gained
        Them. Robert Southey. P90
        An Old Man's Winter Night. Robert Frost.
        P82
        Old Mother. Betty Jane Sachara. P72
        Portrait of an Old Woman. Arthur Davidson
        Ficke. P82
        Sir Nicketty Nox. Hugh Chesterman. P51
        To Waken an Old Lady. William Carlos
        Williams. P82
        Together. Mary Magog Goggins. P72
        Twice a Child. Naomi Long Madgett. P88
        Weakness. Unknown. P87
        What Can an Old Man Do But Die?. Thomas
        Hood. P89
        When You Are Old. William Butler Yeats.

P90
Whittier. Margaret Elizabeth (Munson) Sangster. P81
You Are Old, Father William. Charles Lutwidge ("Lewis Carroll") Dodgson. P90
Old Apple Trees. William DeWitt Snodgrass. P85
The Old Arm-Chair. Eliza Cook. P89
The Old Boatman. Robert Williams Parry. P87
The Old Bookseller. Gilani Kamran. P91
The Old Bridge at Florence. Henry Wadsworth Longfellow. P90
The Old Brown Horse. W. K. Holmes. P51
An Old Cornish Litany, sel. Unknown. P55
The Old Familiar Faces. Charles Lamb. P89
The Old Fashioned Girls. Pilual Juoc. P53
An Old Fashioned Pipe. Kathryn G. Hansen. P72
Old Folks at Home. Stephen Foster. P89
Old Foss, (The Cat) Recalls His Life... J. Patrick Lewis. P63
Old Grimes. Albert G. Greene. P90
Old Ironsides. Oliver Wendell Holmes. P90
The Old Jew. Maxwell Bodenheim. P82
The Old Kitchen Clock. Ann ("Aunt Effie") Hawkshawe. P51
Old Lem. Sterling A. Brown. P89
The Old Man Dreams. Oliver Wendell Holmes. P89
Old Man Winter. Tilda S. Akers. P72
The Old Man's Comforts and How He Gained Them. Robert Southey. P90
The Old Man's Song, About His Wife. Unknown. P78
An Old Man's Winter Night. Robert Frost. P82
Old Manuscript. Alfred Kreymborg. P82
An Old Map of Somewhere. Jeffery Donaldson. P49
Old May Song. Unknown. P51
Old Morgan. G. D. Roberts. P51
Old Mother. Betty Jane Sachara. P72
Old Mother Goose. Unknown. P51
"Old Mother Hubbard". Unknown. P51
Old Mrs. Jarvis. Elizabeth Fleming. P51
An Old Photograph of Strangers. William Meredith. P79
Old Photograph of the Future. Robert Penn Warren. P67
The Old Repair Man. Fenton Johnson. P82
An Old Rhyme. Unknown. P51
An Old Time Christmas, from Marmion. Sir Walter Scott. P90
The Old Wife and the Ghost. James Reeves. P55
Old Woman Doctor. Helen Bryant. P68
The Old Woman of the Roads. Padraic Column. P51
Old Women Are Taking Over the World. Jay

Dougherty. P63
"Old age has taken my quality, my top grown grey". Weakness. Unknown. P87
"Old age is". To Waken an Old Lady. William Carlos Williams. P82
"' Old age never comes alone'--it brings sighs". Old Age. John Morris-Jones. P87
"The old clock sits on the desk in the den". My Clock. Julia Nelson Walke. P68
"Old coyote". Telling About Coyote. Simon Ortiz. P78
"Old crow, upon the tall tree-top". The Crow. Mrs. Alexander. P51
"Old Davis owned a solid mica mountain". A Fountain, a Bottle, a Donkey's Ears and Some Books. Robert Frost. P82
"Old Eben Flood, climbing alone one night". Mr. Flood's Party. Edward Arlington Robinson. P81
"An old elephant". Woe Two. Alice Ryerson. P88
"The old man ate more than a hyena". He'd Eat Lizards. Buk Teny Women. P53
"The old man looks at himself in the mirror". Poem 60, from The City. Gonzalo Millan. P71
"The old man shook his head...". The Invention of White People. Leslie MArmon Silko. P78
"' Old man, God bless you...'.". The Nobleman and the Pensioner. Gottlieb Conrad Pfeffel. P90
"Old Meg she was a gipsy". Meg Merrilees. John Keats. P51
"Old mother duck has hatched a brood". Mother Duck. Ann ("Aunt Effie") Hawkshawe. P51
"Old Mrs. Tressider". The Scarf. Ivy O. Eastwick. P51
"Old Nellie is so very high". Horseback Ride. Siddie Joe Johnson. P50
"The old Penobscot Indian". Flux. Richard Eberhart. P83
"An old roll of tickets". Corner. Gonzalo Millan. P71
"Old Sodos no longer makes saddles". The Ghetto, sel. Lola Ridge. P82
"The old squaw". Indian Sky. Alfred Kreymborg. P82
"Old Tubal Cain was a man of might". Tubal Cain. Charles Mackay. P90
"The old watch: their". Vapor Trail Reflected in the Frog Pond. Galway Kinnell. P85
"Old winter is the man for me--.". Winter. Mathias Claudius. P89
The' Old, Old Song'. Charles Kingsley. P89
"Old, old". The Men That Once Were, sels.

Owen Gruffudd. P87
Old-Time Childhood in Kentucky. Robert Penn
    Warren. P67
Older Is Safer. Robert N. Feinstein. P63
Older, Julia
    My Rumi-Nation. P63
Olecranon. Ernest Slyman. P63
Oles, Carole
    Bugs. P48
Olguin, Kathy Strange de
    Night in Veracruz. P72
Oliver, Mary
    Humpbacks. P52
Olney, D. A.
    Just Like This. P51
Olson, Charles
    Cole's Island. P85
    I, Maximus of Gloucester, to You. P85
    The Kingfishers. P85
    Maximus, to Himself. P85
    The Moon Is the Number 18. P85
    A Newly Discovered 'Homeric' Hymn. P85
    The Ring of. P85
    The Songs of Maximus. P85
Olson, Charles (tr.)
    A Myth of the Human Universe. Unknown.
    P78
Olson, Kirby
    The Encyclopedist's Conundrum. P63
    Insects Blind to History. P63
Omar, Kaleem
    The Fifteenth Century. P91
    A Formal Appeal. P91
    The Green Man. P91
    On a Mountain Road. P91
    The Passenger. P91
    The Tree House. P91
Omens
    End of Summer. William Everson. P84
Omnia Exeunt in Mysterium. George Sterling.
    P81
On a Beautiful Day. John Sterling. P89
On a Compliment. R. P. Dickey. P63
On a Dark Road. Robert Herrick. P51
On a Deceased Office-Seeker. Laurence
    Perrine. P63
On a Drop of Dew. Andrew Marvell. P59
On a Gestapo Photograph Purported To Be...
    F. W. Watt. P49
On a Late Schoolboy. Laurence Perrine. P63
On a Line from Sophocles. Carolyn Kizer. P79
On a Mountain Road. Kaleem Omar. P91
On a Night Without Adornment. Rene Char. P61
On a Picture by a Chinese Painter. Henri
    Michaux. P61
On a Piece of Tapestry. George Santayana.
    P81
On a Reformed Sinner. Laurence Perrine. P63
On a Yankee Hill Morning. Steve LaVine. P77

"On a bright winter morning". Homing.
    Stanley Moss. P64
"On a cold winter day the snow came down".
    Proud Little Spruce Fir. Jeannie
    Kirby. P51
"On a gravesite is a flame, flipping in".
    Arlington. Edison Mpina. P92
"On a last late Sunday in October". Ode to a
    Nuclear Frieze. Nan Townsend Degelman.
    P77
On an August Day. Lee Bennett Hopkins. P76
On an Unwritten Letter. Eugenio Montale. P61
On Deck, fr. From a Travel Diary. T.H. Parry-
    Williams. P87
On First Entering Westminster Abbey. Louise
    Imogen Guiney. P81
On First Looking in on Blogett's Keats's
    'Chapman's Homer'. . George Starbuck.
    P85
On First Looking into Chapman's
    Refrigerator. Edmund Conti. P63
On Flower Wreath Hill. Kenneth Rexroth. P52
On Hearing a Little Music-Box. Leigh Hunt.
    P90
On Hearing of a Man's Death in a Hang Glider
    Accident. Peter Acker. P49
On His Death Bed. Bleddyn Fardd. P87
On His Death-Bed. Meilyr. P87
On Instant Lives. Roy Blount Jr. P63
On Leaving. Atanas Dalchev. P70
On Living, from Life Is a Dream. Pedro
    Calderon de la Barca. P90
On Mary Magdalene. Richard Crashaw. P59
"On Monday We Dance". Unknown. P51
"On' On My Hands and Feet'". Unknown. P62
On News. Thomas Traherne. P59
"On blue horizons". Hunting the Snow Owl.
    Frank Finale. P56
"On Christmas Eve my mother read". Christmas
    Eve. Edna Kingsley Walla. P51
"On Christmas Eve the little stars".
    Christmas Eve. Charlotte Druitt Cole.
    P51
"On early winter's path". For Robin. Stella
    Browning. P72
"On holidays, like weekends". Two Hoorays
    for Holidays. Ned Pastor. P63
"On my little magic whistle I will play...".
    The Magic Whistle. Margaret Rose. P51
"On our temperate side we have a series...".
    Put on Guard. Rene Char. P61
"On parents' knees, a naked, new-born
    child". The Baby. Kalidasa. P89
"On Primrose Hill in the early spring".
    Primrose Hill. Rose Fyleman. P51
"On Scotland's rolling highlands in". A
    History of Golf--Sort of. Thomas L.
    Hirsch. P63
"On poetry and geometric truth", fr. The

prelude. William Wordsworth. P48

On Seeing Gavin Ewart in Sainsbury's. Joan Van Poznak. P63

On Some Shells Found Inland. Trumbull Stickney. P81

On Some Such Morning. Siv Cedering. P64

On Strawberry Eve. Donald G. Finch. P68

On the 401 from Waterloo to Toronto. Douglas Smith. P49

On the Banisters. Margaret E. Gibbs. P51

On the Beach. Michael Heller. P64

On the Beach in Puerto Rico. Jones. P49

On the Concert. Trumbull Stickney. P81

On the Death of a Metaphysician. George Santayana. P81

On the Eve of Departure for Sixth World Congress... Yung-jung Lin. P72

On the Eyes of an SS Officer. Richard Wilbur. P84

On the Hazards of Writing Gloomy Verse. Edna Meudt. P68

On the Horizon. Stephen Crane. P81

On the Life-Mask of Lincoln. Richard Watson Gilder. P81

On the Night of a Friend's Wedding. Edward Arlington Robinson. P81

On the Northwest Hiawatha. Kathleen Norris. P88

On the Passing of Heidegger. Marshall Hryciuk. P49

On the Portrait of Shakespeare. Ben Jonson. P90

"On the Pretext of a Rough Descent to the River". Unknown. P62

On the Rhyming of Four-Line Verses. J. F. O'Connor. P63

On the Site of the Convent. Tibor Tollas. P61

On the Subject of Roses. Abraham Sutzkever. P48

On the Three-Hour Train Ride. Anne Porter. P64

On the Watershed. Tibor Tollas. P61

On the Way to Summer. John Hollander. P79

On Their Day Off. Alexander Gerov. P70

On This Shore. Siv Cedering. P64

"On the big staircase in this picture". An Old Photograph of Strangers. William Meredith. P79

"On the borderline between sea and earth". Les Saintes-Maries De La Mer. Karl H. Bolay. P72

"On the corner the three pieced mayor...". New England Village. Lou Orfanella. P72

"On the docks". Adriatc. Charles Tinkham. P56

"On the eighteenth day I got it". On the Beach in Puerto Rico. Jones. P49

"On the final bleak day of February". Subway Seasoning. Eve Merriam. P63

"On the first warm day". Sea-Drift. Siv Cedering. P64

"On the grassy banks". Lambs at Play. Christina Georgina Rossetti. P51

"On the high hill pastures". Wild Thyme. Joyce Sambrook. P51

"On the last day". After the Glory Has Passed Before Us. Karen Kania. P88

"On the nape of the rock, he". To Hywel ab Ifan Fychan. Guto'r Glyn. P87

"On the night of the Belgian surrender...". The Moon and the Night and the Men. John Berryman. P84

"On the potter's wheel". To Sing the Song. Robert M. Howell. P65

"On the row behind her mother". A Bride of the 80's, Down the Aisle. Blanche Farley. P63

"On the Rue St. Honore". Pleasure. Gigi Lord. P65

"On these occasions, the feelings surprise". Father and Son. Delmore Schwartz. P84

"On this evening path from camp". Meeting My Father at the River. Judith Minty. P88

"On thy fair bosom, silver lake". To Seneca Lake. J. G. Percival. P51

"On unhurrying moccasins". October Among the Hills. Wallace Winchell. P65

"On what foundations...". Charles XII, from The Vanity of Human Wishes. Samuel Johnson. P90

"On winter afternoons we gather...". Poetry Study Group. Carol Bessent Hayman. P72

"Once a boy beheld a bright". The Rose. Johann Wolfgang von Goethe. P89

"Once a mouse, a frog and a little red hen". The Mouse, the Frog and the Little Red Hen. Unknown. P51

"Once a sleepy wife there was". A Pothersome Pair. John Ceiriog Hughes. P87

"Once again looking between iron bars". Dartmoor. David Gwenallt Jones. P87

Once and for All. Delmore Schwartz. P84

Once I Knew a Fine Song. Stephen Crane. P81

Once I Saw Mountains Angry. Stephen Crane. P81

"Once There Lived a Little Man". Unknown. P51

Once There Was a Man. Stephen Crane. P81

"Once death in malice cruel sought to slay". Death and Love. Arlo Bates. P81

"Once he was a little boy". Plaything of the Gods. Louis J. Cantoni. P72

"Once I loved a spider". The Spider and the Ghost of the Fly. Vachel Lindsay. P82

"Once I was ood like the Virgin Mary...". The Scarlet Woman. Fenton Johnson. P82

"Once in late summer". A Certain Village. Theodore Weiss. P84

"Once in my lonely, eager youth I rode". A Mendocino Memory. Edwin Markham. P81

"Once my exiled brothers and sisters...". Freedom in the New Air. Tijan M. Sallah. P72

"Once nobody on earth...". Birth of the Daisies. Ruth Krauss. P50

"Once on a summer day". An Admonition Concerning Promptness and Regularity... Edward L. Mayo. P68

"Once on returning home, purse-proud and hale". The Auction. Theodore Roethke. P84

"Once riding in old Baltimore". Incident. Countee Cullen. P83

"Once some people were visiting Chekhov". Chocolates. Louis Simpson. P85

"Once there was a little kitty". Kitty. Unknown. P51

"Once we laughed together". Missing You. Charlotte Zolotow. P50

Once, a Man, Clambering to the House-Tops. Stephen Crane. P81

"Once, Oh Ungrateful Bee". Unknown. P62

"Once, when I was a boy". Once and for All. Delmore Schwartz. P84

"Oncet in the museum". Two Ways. John V. A. Weaver. P82

"1. Who is your favorite poet?.". From the Poetry Exchange, Two Conversations. Howard Nemerov. P63

"One Arc Ends Where the Next Begins". Judy Palen. P72

One Blackbird. Harold Monro. P51

"One arch of the sky". Love in Labrador. Carl Sandburg. P82

"One black horse standing by the gate". The Farmyard. A. A. Attwood. P51

"One blue eye beside the path". Asiatic Day-Flower. Donald Finkel. P79

"One day in Thrift-Rite Supermart". Instant Storm. X. J. Kennedy. P75

"One day when coyote". One for Coyote. Unknown. P78

"One feels that these". On Instant Lives. Roy Blount Jr. P63

One for Coyote. Unknown. P78

"One Misty Moisty Morning". Unknown. P51

One More I'matation. Eleanore-Melissa. P68

One Night on Guard Duty. W. D. Ehrhart. P86

"One Nipple Drips, One Is Made Erect". Unknown. P62

One Solitary Voice. Marilyn Gordon. P72

"One has flippers. This one is like a seal". The Ones That Are Thrown Out. Miller Williams. P57

"One has to die a martyr these days...".
F.R. Konecamp. David Gwenallt Jones. P87

"One listless day I confused Handel". Whistling in the Air. Jaime Quezada. P71

"One little dickey-bird". Ten Little Dicky-Birds. A. W. I. Baldwin. P51

"One little Indian boy making a canoe". Ten Little Indian Boys. M. M. Hutchinson. P51

"One lovely summer evening a shooting star...". A Shooting Star. Robert Desnos. P48

"One man goes north to ski". Where to Spend the Winter. Robert Francis. P63

"The one moonlight, in the simple-colored...". Note on Moonlight. Wallace Stevens. P79

"One morning in St. Thomas, when I tried". The Eye (Part II). Richard Wilbur. P57

"One night in Albany". Drunks. John Berryman. P79

"One of Erins' sons has". Intertwining Love. Winne E. Fitzpatrick. P72

"One of my wishes is that those dark trees". Into My Own. Robert Frost. P89

"One of you is a major, made of cord and catskin". Lent in a Year of War. Thomas Merton. P84

"One of your flowers, Lord?.". Tiny Grandchild at the Beach. Alice M. Boughtwood. P68

"The one on the right, crouching down...". Photograph. Omar Lara. P71

"One pale Novmber day". Affair D'Amour. Margaret Deland. P89

"One rat across the floor and quick...". Lucifer Alone. Josephine Miles. P84

"One road leads to London". Roadways. John Masefield. P51

"One silent night before Easter". A Woman of Style. Edith Freund. P88

"One small mountain rounding out of waves". Barra. Robert Lawrence. P49

"One sound. Then the hiss and whir". The Garden. Louise Gluck. P85

"One summer I stayed". The Two Families. Joyce L. Brisley. P51

"One thought, one tune, one resonance--.". O Bird of Light. Sri Chinmoy. P68

1974, Not Guilty?., from For the Desert Island. Tae-ch'ul Shin. P92

"1931, when this town's ribs". Belinda. Jack H. Palmer. P68

1926. Weldon Kees. P84

One West Coast. Al Young. P85

"One time I wanted two moons". The Wishing Bone Cycle, sel. Jacob Nibenegenesabe. P78

"One time we had an acre and a cow". Nouveau
        Poor. Alice Morrey Bailey. P65
"One wading a fall meadow finds on all
        sides". The Beautiful Changes. Richard
        Wilbur. P84
"One! two! three!.". Sing-Song Rhyme.
        Unknown. P51
One's Goal. Annie Laurie Leech. P72
"One, Two". Unknown. P51
"One, and then another, they settled...".
        Mining in Killdeer Alley. Dabney
        Stuart. P67
"One, round the candytuft". I Spy. N. E.
        Hussey. P51
The One-Eyed. Nyalang Pinien Lual. P53
One-Up. Bruce Berger. P63
"A one-armed man conveyed the flowers". The
        Gift. Lewis Turco. P63
"One-letter alphabet". Hole. Imogene Bolls.
        P63
The Ones That Are Thrown Out. Miller
        Williams. P57
"The Ones Who Know Not How". Unknown. P62
An Only Child. Robert ab Gwilym Ddu. P87
"Only auburn gold could grace the head". To
        Diana. Evelyn Sewell Rineer. P65
Only in a Poem. Mary B. Finn. P68
Only Waiting. Frances Laughton Mace. P89
"Only When Women's Eyes". Unknown. P62
"Only once more and not again--the larches".
        In Ampezzo. Trumbull Stickney. P81
"Only the deep well". I Break the Sky. Owen
        Dodson. P84
"Only the imagination is real! You
        declared...". Sassafras. Susan
        Glickman. P49
"Only two patient eyes to stare". Faded
        Pictures. William Vaughn Moody. P81
"Onto that long snowing of sand". Red Kite.
        Philip Appleman. P64
"Onward flies the rushing train". The Engine
        Driver. G. S. O. P51
Open Sesame. Unknown. P51
"An open solitude, sea of blue". Antarctica.
        Clement Arthur Phoenix. P68
Open, Time. Louise Imogen Guiney. P81
Opening Figure. Mohammed Dib. P91
Oppenheim, James
        Hebrews. P82
        The Lincoln Child. P82
        The Lonely Child. P82
        Not Overlooked. P82
        The Slave. P82
        Tasting the Earth. P82
Oppenheimer, C. B.
        All in All. P68
        Giraffe. P68
Opportunity. William Blake. P90
Oppression

Captured City. Omar Lara. P71
King's Orders. Jose Lacaba. P92
The Old Jew. Maxwell Bodenheim. P82
We Will Not Hand Over the Night. Waldo
        Rojas. P71
Optimism
        To an Optimist. Bessie Wherry Noe. P65
Orchard. Hilda ("H.D.") Doolittle. P82
The Orchard. Robert Minhinnick. P54
Orchards
        Orchard. Hilda ("H.D.") Doolittle. P82
        The Orchard. Robert Minhinnick. P54
"Orchid-lipped, loose-jointed...". Himalayan
        Balsam. Anne Stevenson. P54
Orchids. Theodore Roethke. P84
Oread. Hilda ("H.D.") Doolittle. P82
Orfanella, Lou
        New England Village. P72
"Orfeo was a king". Sir Orfeo. Unknown. P66
The Origin of the Skagit Indians... Lucy
        Williams. P78
Origins of the Body. William Carpenter. P48
Orion. William Everson. P84
Orion. Adrienne Rich. P85
An Orphan's Wish. Lee Ann Braunecker. P74
Orpheus
        Orpheus. Yvor Winters. P83
Orpingalik's Song: In a Time a Sickness.
        Unknown. P78
Orr, Ed
        What's in a Name. P63
Orr, Gregory
        Gathering the Bones Together. P85
        Making Beasts. P85
        A Shelf Is a Ledge. P85
        The Voyages. P85
Ortiz, Simon
        Telling About Coyote. P78
Ortolani, Al
        Grace. P63
        Jessa's Late Assignment. P63
Osborn, Mary I.
        Every Day. P51
        My Playmate. P51
        The Swing. P51
Osborne, Elizabeth
        My Lamp. P74
Osiris' Song. Richard Candida Smith. P68
"Ostracized as we are with God--.". Apology
        of a Genius. Mina Loy. P82
Otero, Blas de
        Position. Charles Guenther (tr.). P61
Other Season. Bonnie McConnell. P68
The Other Side of the River. Charles Wright.
        P52
The Other World. Harriet Beecher Stowe. P89
"The others endured the cold". The Dead
        olf. Roger A. Chrastil. P56
"Others have died or left". Shepherd. Jeremy

Hooker. P54

Otis, Emily
Drawbacks. P63

Otto, Eleanor
'The Knight-a Lady's Hero'. P65
Soul. P72

Our Afterlife. Robert Lowell. P79
Our First Journey. N.M. Rashed. P91
Our God, Our Help in Ages Past. Isaac Watts. P89
Our Israfel. Edwin Markham. P81
Our Mother. Unknown. P51
Our Mother the General. Jessie Kachmar. P88
Our Parents. Vicki Schneider. P72
Our State. John Greenleaf Whittier. P90
"Our blood no longer". Farewell. Cyril Dabydeen. P49
"Our children, my love". Little Ghosts. Oscar Hahn. P71
"Our Christmas pudding was made in November". Pudding Charms. Charlotte Druitt Cole. P51
"Our dear soul". In Memory of an English Professor. Reed Whittemore. P63
"Our father land! and wouldst thou know". Father and Mother Tongue. Samuel Lover. P90
"Our garden's very near the trains". Trains. Hope Shepherd. P51
"Our God is one". You, a Red Man, and I, a Black Man. Moses Cot. P53
"Our golden age was then, when lamp and rug". Family Prime. Mark Van Doren. P83
"Our grandpa had". Grandfathers and Grandsons, sels. M.A. Nuhman. P91
"Our heaven was a ribbon-store". Bargain Brief (Excerpt). Aline Musyl Marks. P65
"Our mothers are, at seventy". The Sun. Alexander Gerov. P70
"Our tomcat, Boo, tail and hindquarters...". Peace! We Are Saying?. Edna Meudt. P68
"Our words but touch the surface of a sea". Mutiny. Goldie Morales. P72
"Out for a walk, after a week in bed". An Urban Convalescence. James Merrill. P85
Out from Behind This Mask, from Leaves of Grass. Walt Whitman. P90
"Out in the garden". The Pigeons. Rodney Bennett. P51
"Out in the garden, sunny and still". Freedom. Joan Agnew. P51
Out of Doors. E. North. P51
Out of Step. Buk Teny Men. P53
"Out of me unworthy and unknown". Anne Rutledge, from Spoon River Anthology. Edgar Lee Masters. P82

"Out of my clothes, I ran past the boathouse". Under the Boathouse. David Bottoms. P67
"Out of perfection beauty shines". Let Beauty Shine. Alice M. Boughtwood. P68
"Out of the". Independence. Marion Jane Richardson. P65
Out of the Starstream. Ruth C. Falk. P72
Out of These, the First Love. Wallace William Winchell. P72
"Out of the bosom of the air". Snow. Henry Wadsworth Longfellow. P51
"Out of the dusk a shadow". Evolution. John Banister Tabb. P81
"Out of the grey". First Snowfall. Barbara Juster Esbensen. P80
"Out of the mud two strangers came". Two Tramps in Mud Time. Robert Frost. P82
"Out of the rumbling dark". At Night. Fairfield Porter. P64
"Out of the table endlessly rocking". Just Friends. Robert Creeley. P85
"Out walking in the frozen swamp...". The Wood-Pile. Robert Frost. P82
Outbreak of Spring. George Starbuck. P85
"An outburst of morning light appears". Shakespearean Sonnet. Leah Wroten. P73
The Outing. Lorene Erickson. P88
The Outlaw. David Ignatow. P84
Outside. Hugh Chesterman. P51
Outside. Lilian Moore. P75
"Outside of space and matter". Beyond Torture. Aristoteles Espana. P71
"Outside the vineyard is a caravan". Graffiti from the Gare Saint-Manque. Marilyn Hacker. P79
"Outside the window the night burned". The Angels Among Us. Naomi Lazard. P64
"The oval of heaven opened and I joyfully". Invitation. Glenn Clairemonte. P68
The Oven Bird. Robert Frost. P82
"Over hill, over dale". A Fairy Song. William Shakespeare. P51
"Over my heart the shield's worn thin". Gwen ap Llywarch and his Father, fr. Poetry from Lost Sagas . Unknown. P87
Over the Fields. Adeline White. P51
Over the Hill to the Poor-House. Will Carleton. P89
"Over the dark water". A Kayak Song. Lucy Diamond. P51
"Over the dunb campagna-sea". A View Across the Roman Campagna. Elizabeth Barrett Browning. P90
"Over the forest". Song. Nikola Vaptsarov. P70
"Over the gray glazed ice". Ice Skaters. John Gracen Brown. P68
"Over the roof-tops race the shadows of

clouds". I, fr. Irradiations. John
        Gould Fletcher. P82
"Over the western ridge". Landfall. T. A.
        Shulgin. P58
"Over this prairie stretched to bursting".
        Season of Content. Edna Bacon
        Morrison. P68
"Overcoming Untimely Anger". Unknown. P62
"Overhead at sunset all heard the choir".
        The Singers in a Cloud. (Frederick)
        Ridgely Torrence. P81
Overhead on a Saltmarsh. Harold Monro. P51
"Overnight/we rush pell-mell". Bromeliad.
        Cathy Matyas. P49
Overture to a Dance of Locomotives. William
        Carlos Williams. P82
Ovesen, Ellis
        Big Basin Waterfall. P72
Ovid
        A Transformation, from The Metamorphoses.
        H. King (tr.). P90
Ovid's Elegies, Book I, 13. Christopher
        Marlowe. P59
Owain, Gutun
        Asking a Stallion. Tony Conran (tr.). P87
Owen, Ellis
        Epitaph. Tony Conran (tr.). P87
Owen, Goronwy
        An Invitation. Tony Conran (tr.). P87
        The Wish. Tony Conran (tr.). P87
The Owl and the Nightingale, sels. Unknown.
        P66
The Owl and the Pussycat. Edward Lear. P51,
        P89
The Owl. Bryan Waller ("Barry Cornwall")
        Procter. P89
The Owl. Lord Tennyson. P51
Owls
        I Know an Owl. Edward Anthony. P75
        The Owl and the Pussycat. Edward Lear.
        P89
"The owls have feathers lined with down".
        The Hedgehog and His Coat. Elizabeth
        Fleming. P51
"Owre kynge went forth to Normandy". The
        Agincourt Carol. Unknown. P66
Ox-Eye Daisy. Lois Bunse. P77
Oxen
        The Oxen. Thomas Hardy. P51
        The Radio, with its Breath Like a Trapped
        Bee. John Gatwec Lul. P53
        The Sun's Tongue. Rec Puk. P53
The Oxen. Thomas Hardy. P51,P89
Oysters
        The Walrus and the Carpenter, from Alice
        in Wonderland. Charles Lutwidge
        ("Lewis Carroll") Dodgson. P89

PSSSSST. Felicia Lamport. P63
P. S. Instead of a Beginning. Lyubomir
        Levchev. P70
Pacifist, from Lost Youth: the Last War.
        Alfred Kreymborg. P82
Pack, Clouds, Away. Thomas Heywood. P51,P89
A Pact. Ezra Pound. P82
Paddlewheel Under a Boat. Peter Pal Hoth
        Nyang. P53
The Paddling Pool. E. H. Adams. P51
Padhy, P. K.
        Mission of No Ends. P72
Padmanaban, A.
        Deepavali (Festival of Lights). P72
Paestum. James Dickey. P79
Page, P. K.
        Deaf-Mute in the Pear Tree. P49
        In Class We Create Ourselves-Having Been
        Told... P49
"Pages coming together piping voice". Let
        All World Poets Rejoice. Joy Beaudette
        Cripps. P72
Paik, Karen M.
        Fall. P74
Pain
        The Broken Pianola. Ralph Gustafson. P49
Pain. Blaga Dimitrova. P70
        Dream Scars. Kateri Lanthier. P49
        The Last Englyn. Tudur Aled. P87
        The Man with the Nitroglycerine Tears.
        Robert Priest. P49
        Nunc Dimittis. Patrick Lane. P49
        Revisiting Detroit. Karen Kania. P88
        Wound and Knife. Gyorgy Somlyo. P92
Painted Head. John Crowe Ransom. P83
A Painter Obsessed by Blue. Fairfield
        Porter. P64
Painter of Icons. Luchesar Elenkov. P70
"The painter quiets all but his busy brush".
        Still Life Near Bangalore. Earle
        Birney. P49
Painter, Pamela
        My Own Good. P88
The Painter. Peggy Zeaphev Nerl. P72
Paintings and Painters
        A Dutch Courtyard. Richard Wilbur. P84
        Monet Refuses the Operation. Lisel
        Mueller. P88
        Monet: 'Les Nympheas'. William DeWitt
        Snodgrass. P85
        My Father Paints the Summer. Richard
        Wilbur. P84
        On the Concert. Trumbull Stickney. P81
        The Painter. Peggy Zeaphev Nerl. P72
        A Pre-Raphaelite Notebook. Geoffrey Hill.
        P79
        The Stains Slid from Top to Bottom in

Silence. Gonzalo Munoz. P71
There Is of Course a Legend. Al Purdy.
P49
Two Painters. Lyubomir Nikolov. P70
Verrocchio. Richard Harrison. P49
Pal, Nyalual
The Big Knot. Terese Svoboda (tr.). P53
Snails in the Grass. Terese Svoboda
(tr.). P53
The Tail of the Buffalo. Terese Svoboda
(tr.). P53
The **Palaces** Under the Moon. Chems Nadir. P91
Pale Like Sunshine Music. James Richard
Hurst. P68
"The **Pale** Stone Under My Rib". Simon
Perchik. P64
Palen, Judy
"One Arc Ends Where the Next Begins". P72
Palimpsest: a Deceitful Portrait. Conrad
Aiken. P82
"**Pallid** with too much longing". Laus Veneris
(a Picture by Burne-Jones). Louise
Chandler Moulton. P90
"The **palm** at the end of the mind". Of Mere
Being. Wallace Stevens. P83
Palmer, Jack H.
Belinda. P68
Julia Before the Mirror. P68
Pan in Wall Street. Edmund Clarence Stedman.
P81
The **Pancake.** Christina Georgina Rossetti.
P51
Pangloss's Song. Richard Wilbur. P84
The **Pangolin.** Marianne Moore. P83
Pantycelyn, William Williams
Fair Weather. Tony Conran (tr.). P87
The Love of God. Tony Conran (tr.). P87
Pilgrim. Tony Conran (tr.). P87
Paolo Dipietro. Joseph Maviglia. P49
Paolo's Version. Carl Judson Launius. P63
Papa Says. Libby Stopple. P75
Papantoniou, Vassilis A.
Meeting. P72
Pape, Jean
Decaying. P77
Evolution of Sand. P77
Spending the Woodpile Well Into June. P77
"**Parabola** of light". Embrace of Crescents.
Daud Kamal. P91
Parades
Marching Song. Robert Louis Stevenson.
P51
The Train. Dennis Moore. P86
Paradise
Arlo Will, from Spoon River Anthology.
Edgar Lee Masters. P82
A California Christmas. Joaquin Miller.
P81
Paradise. Frederick illiam Faber. P89

Heaven, from Paradise. Montri Umavijani.
P72
My Mother in Paradise. Lyubomir Levchev.
P70
Paradise. Frederick William Faber. P89
The Stupas, from Paradise. Montri
Umavijani. P72
There Is a Love. Evelyn Evans. P72
A **Parched** Pitcher. Mehdi Akhavan Sales. P91
"**Pardon** me, lady, but I wanta ast you". Drug
Store. John V. A. Weaver. P82
The **Pardon.** Richard Wilbur. P84
Parent, Terri L.
To Have You Near. P65
Parents and Parenthood
Dedicatory Entry. Anton Shammas. P92
Father. Martha Friedberg. P88
Letter to My Parents. F. W. Watt. P49
My Papa's Waltz. Theodore Roethke. P84
Our Parents. Vicki Schneider. P72
A Poem for Emily. Miller Williams. P67
The Two Parents. Christopher M. ("Hugh
MacDiarmid") Grieve. P89
Voyager. Lisel Mueller. P88
Where Knock Is Open Wide. Theodore
Roethke. P84
Yuppies vs. Nopies. Ned Pastor. P63
"**Parents** are a splendid thing". Our Parents.
Vicki Schneider. P72
Parham, Helena
A Day in Creation. P72
Paris, France
Guide to Paris: Eiffel Tower, Versailles.
Scott Bates. P63
"The **park** is filled with night and fog".
Spring Night. Sara Teasdale. P82
Parker, Helen Adams
Apple Blossoms. P51
Parker, Jason
War. P74
Parker, Lois Wilson
The Vital Brine. P68
Parker, Theodore
The Higher Good. P89
Parks
Snowy Benches. Aileen Fisher. P80
Parks, Richard
For a Lady of Impressions. P68
Parlatore, Anselm
Mecox Motel. P64
Mecox Nunnery & Saint Dominic. P64
Portrait in Veiled Waters. P64
Woman of the Late Fall Run. P64
The **Parlement** of the Thre Ages. Unknown. P66
Parlez-Vous Francais?. Delmore Schwartz. P84
The **Parnassians.** James Merrill. P85
Parodi, Nellie
The Night. P72
Parodies

Job's Turkey: a Commentary. Carl Judson Launius. P63

To His Importunate Mistress. Peter De Vries. P63

Triolet, After Titian. Sylvester Pollet. P63

Tunnel Vision. David Cram. P63

Parque, Richard A.
Annamese Hands. P86

The **Parrot's** Scream. Charles H. Howe. P68

Parry, Janine A.
I Dream. P73

Parry, R. Williams
In Memoriam. Tony Conran (tr.). P87
A Wife's Epitaph. Tony Conran (tr.). P87

Parry, Robert Williams
The Fox. Tony Conran (tr.). P87
The Geese. Tony Conran (tr.). P87
The Old Boatman. Tony Conran (tr.). P87
The Propaganda of the Poet. Tony Conran (tr.). P87
The Strangeness of Dawn. Tony Conran (tr.). P87
A Wish. Tony Conran (tr.). P87

Parry-Williams, T.H.
Death in the Channel, fr. From a Travel Diary. Tony Conran (tr.). P87
The East Wind. Tony Conran (tr.). P87
Llyn y Gadair. Tony Conran (tr.). P87
On Deck, fr. From a Travel Diary. Tony Conran (tr.). P87

"Parsley, sage, rosemary, thyme". MSG. Bruce Berger. P63

Parsons, Geoffrey
The Light at the Edge of the World. P72

Parthasarathy, R.
Homecoming. P92

Partial to Marshall. Jan M. Stephens. P68

Parties
My Party. Queenie Scott-Hopper. P51
Saturday Night. Langston Hughes. P83
A Social Engagement. Knute Skinner. P63

Parting. Coventry Patmore. P89

"Partly cloudy in the east". Weathering. Wilma H. Clements. P68

Partner of the Sea. Kevin Cline. P58

A **Party** Song. Unknown. P51

"Pasadena, Pasadena". Song of Pasadena. Wen-Ying Hsu. P72

Pasolini, Pier Paolo
The Holiday Ended. Charles Guenther (tr.). P61

Passamaquoddy Sunrise. Dan Murray. P64

Passantino, Kris
The First Draft. P74

The **Passenger.** Kaleem Omar. P91

Passengers in a Time Beyond Orchards. Vesta P. Crawford. P65

"Passing through the castles of anger". Woe

Three. Alice Ryerson. P88

The **Passing.** James Deahl. P49

The **Passionate** Businessman To His Love. Bruce Bennett. P63

The **Passionate** Shepherd to His Love. Christopher Marlowe. P89

Past
Bearded Oaks. Robert Penn Warren. P83
Four Preludes on Playthings of the Wind. Carl Sandburg. P82
An Ode in Time of Hesitation. William Vaughn Moody. P81
Poem 48, from The City. Gonzalo Millan. P71

"Past exchanges have left orbits of rain...". An Apology. Diane Wakoski. P85

"The past seems to shred to smithereens". Etchings in Meaning. Grace D. Yerbury. P72

"Past turbulence of our initial fears". The Tests of Marriage (A Mason Sonnet Sequence). Anne Marx. P65

Pastor, Ned
Curriculum Change. P63
Dail-A-Shrink. P63
Have You? I Have Never!. P63
Lucky Dilemma. P63
(914) 555-4144. P63
Two Hoorays for Holidays. P63
What's All This Fuss About Tax Reform?. P63
Yuppies vs. Nopies. P63

Patchen, Kenneth
An Examination into Life and Death. P84
A Letter on the Use of Machine Guns at Weddings. P84
Night Has Been as Beautiful as Virginia. P84
Saturday Night in the Parthenon. P84
Under the Green Ledge. P84

The **Patchwork** Quilt. Elizabeth Fleming. P51

The **Patent** of a Lord. Stephen Crane. P81

"The path dividing the old cemetery". After Great Pain. Edward Butscher. P64

"The path winds. You are around a bend". At Albert's Landing (with my son). Michael Heller. P64

Pathmanathan, S. (tr.)
Grandfathers and Grandsons, sels. M.A. Nuhman. P91

Patibandla, Murall
I See Someone (To My Mother, 'Indira Devi'). P72

Patience. Paul Hamilton Hayne. P89

Patience, from Poems of Freedom. William James Linton. P90

Patient. Keith Baker. P63

Patitz, Dolores R.

Goodbye, Goodbye. P68

Patmore, Coventry
    Parting. P89
    Sly Thoughts. P89
    Winter and Spring. P51

Patnaik, Simanchal
    Futile Death Wish. P72

Patriotic Poem. Diane Wakoski. P85

Patriotism
    Barbara Frietchie. John Greenleaf
      Whittier. P51
    The Battle-Song of Gustavus Adolphus.
      Michael Altenburg. P90
    Blood and Silence. Ahmad 'Abd Al-Muti
      Hijazi. P91
    Breathes There the Man?. Sir Walter
      Scott. P90
    Bulgaria. Georgi Djagarov. P70
    A Century of Miracles. Georgi Djagarov.
      P70
    Crossing over, from Your Tired, Your
      Poor. Lisel Mueller. P88
    Father and Mother Tongue. Samuel Lover.
      P90
    I Vow to Thee, My Country. Sir Cecil
      Spring Rice. P51
    Land of Our Birth. Rudyard Kipling. P51
    My Heart's in the Highlands. Robert
      Burns. P90
    O Captain! My Captain!. Walt Whitman. P90
    An Ode in Time of Hesitation. William
      Vaughn Moody. P81
    Peace. John Carlisle Dunlap. P72
    The Peacemakers. Robert F. Allen. P72
    Sherman. Richard Watson Gilder. P81
    There Exists the Eternal Fact of
      Conflict. Stephen Crane. P81
    This Native Land. Thomas Davis. P51
    War or Peace. Margaret Baucom. P72

Patterns. Amy Lowell. P82

Patteson, Cy
    The Unappeasable. P72

Paul Revere's Ride. Henry Wadsworth
    Longfellow. P90

Paulsgrove, Terry M.
    Decompostion. P77
    The Red Hills '83. P77
    Scorpion Summer. P77

Pawlowski, Robert
    At the School for the Deaf. P57

Pawsey, Irene F.
    Bramble Jam. P51
    Browny Bee. P51
    The Browny Hen. P51
    An Egg for Easter. P51
    Eggs for Breakfast. P51
    Found in the Woods. P51
    The Greedy Little Pig. P51
    Haytime. P51

    June. P51
    The Thief. P51
    White Horses. P51

Pawson, Elna Forsell
    The Columbine. P72

Pax Pagnanica. Louise Imogen Guiney. P81

Payne, John Howard
    Home, Sweet Home, fr. Clari. P89

Payne, Ricelda
    What Face?. P72

Payne, Vernon
    'M 87'. P72

Peace
    Alpha/Omega Cycle of Peace. Josette
      Liliane Villias. P72
    Peace. John Carlisle Dunlap. P72
    Peace. George Herbert. P89
    I Shall Not Care. Sara Teasdale. P82
    Invocation of Peace, sel. William ("Fiona
      Macleod") Sharp. P51
    Peace. George Herbert. P89
    Peace in Our Time. Minnie Klemme. P72
    Peace Is a Green Bough. Arwin G. Sexauer.
      P72
    Peace. Henry Vaughan. P59
    The Vote. Ralph Knevet. P59
    Peace in Our Time. Minnie Klemme. P72
    Peace Is a Green Bough. Arwin G. Sexauer.
      P72

"Peace lay upon her features white as wax".
    My Music Teacher. Eric Vio. P72

The Peace of Cities. Richard Wilbur. P84

Peace! We Are Saying?. Edna Meudt. P68

"The peaceful mind". The Trace of God's
    Hand. Francis O. Raniville. P72

"The peacemakers are meeting". The
    Peacemakers. Robert F. Allen. P72

Peacock, Thomas Love
    The Priest and the Mulberry Tree. P51

The Peacock. James Merrill. P85

"The Peaks of the Vinhya Mountains".
    Unknown. P62

Pearce, Carol
    Look Evening's Black Feet Are. P68

Pearl. Unknown. P66

"The pearl grey dusk, its cloud,
    knitting...". Nightfall by the River.
    Brian Henderson. P49

"The pearl-shell in the poet's hand". The
    Humble Shell. K. S. Venkataramu. P72

The Peasant and the Sheep. Ivan Andreevich
    Kriloff. P90

Peattie, Noel
    Latin Night. P56

The Pebble. Elinor Wylie. P82

Pebbles. Edith King. P51

Pebbles on a Lonely Beach. H. Olav Wang. P68

Peconic Autumn Day. R. B. Weber P64

Pecorella, Joseph S.

Great Chorus (For Gramps). P68
Peddlers and Peddling
      The Lace Peddler. Catherine A. Morin. P51
Pederson, Miriam
      Erosion. P88
      Interlude. P56
      The Quickening. P88
Pedestrian. Virginia M. Hahn. P58
Pedlar Jim. Florence Hoare. P51
The Pedlar's Caravan. William Brighty Rands.
      P51
Pedrog
      The Rose and the Heather. Tony Conran
      (tr.). P87
Peering at the Past. Mark Lawson Cannaday.
      P68
Pejorative. Ernest Kroll. P63
Pelletier, Gaston
      Beasts in Whoredom. P68
      Reflections of a Sometime Child. P68
Penarth. John Tripp. P54
Pendzik, A. J. Kealoha
      Cretaceous Period. P74
Penha, James W.
      Angel, Walking. P56
Pennington, Lee
      The Gods of Black Mountain. P68
      The Water and your Eyes. P72
A Penny Wish. Irene Thompson. P51
The Pennycandystore Beyond the El. Lawrence
      Ferlinghetti. P85
Pensioners. Winifred M. Letts. P51
"A pensive photograph". To a Portrait.
      Arthur Symons. P89
Penthouse Enigma. James Russell Vaky. P68
People
      Airport. Elaine Demakas. P58
      Alfred Hitchcock U. Geoff Fiorito. P58
      Ave Caesar. Robinson Jeffers. P83
      Different Minds. Richard Chenevix Trench.
      P89
      The People Will Live On. Carl Sandburg.
      P82
      The Ploughman. Oliver Wendell Holmes. P89
      "Sing a Song of People". Lois Lenski. P60
"The people along the sand". Neither Out Far
      nor in Deep. Robert Frost. P82
"People on the moon love a pet". The Dracula
      Vine. Ted Hughes. P55
The People vs. The People. Kenneth Fearing.
      P83
"People Who Do Not Even Know the Alphabet".
      Unknown. P62
The People Will Live On. Carl Sandburg. P82
"The people walk upon their heads". Topsy-
      Turvy Land. H. E. Wilkinson. P51
Pepper Trees
      Scenes from the Life of the Peppertrees.
      Denise Levertov. P85

Perception. Jude Theriot. P74
"Perched on a chimney upon one leg". Who
      Takes Care of the Blind Stork?. Blaga
      Dimitrova. P70
"Perched/On an old earthen vessel". Limping
      Boat. J. Bapu Reddy. P72
Perchik, Simon
      "I Should Wear Gloves, These White
      Pages". P64
      "Like a Warden at the Evening Meal". P64
      "The Mirror a Convict Holds Out". P64
      "The Pale Stone Under My Rib". P64
Percival, J. G.
      May. P51
      To Seneca Lake. P51
Percussion Grenade Democracy. C. J. Roner.
      P72
Pereira, Teresinka
      Non Omnis Moriar. Luis Larios (tr.). P72
Performance. Phyllis Webb. P49
"Perhaps it is wrong to dream of you". Moth
      Light. Charles P. Martin. P58
"Perhaps piano notes are best". Therese.
      Harold Leland Johnson. P65
"Perhaps they will read you...". A Social
      Engagement. Knute Skinner. P63
"Perhaps you've heard them passing...". From
      a Watershed. John R. Locke. P68
"Perhaps, if you". Hob the Elf. Norman M.
      Johnson. P51
Peripheral Vision. Kevin Cline. P58
"A periphrastic insult, not a banal".
      Epigrams. J. V. Cunningham. P79
Perkins, Becki
      The Mouse. P74
Perkins, Caroline
      Equation. P68
"Perle, plesaunte to prynces paye". Pearl.
      Unknown. P66
Permanence
      Block of Wood. Jauvanta Walker. P68
      Building for Love. Unknown. P87
      Stay. LaNita Moses. P72
      Tradition, Thou Art for Suckling
      Children. Stephen Crane. P81
Perrine, Laurence
      "A Grumpy Old Owl at the Zoo". P63
      On a Deceased Office-Seeker. P63
      On a Late Schoolboy. P63
      On a Reformed Sinner. P63
      Q. E. D. P63
Perry Zoll, from Spoon River Anthology.
      Edgar Lee Masters. P82
Perseverance
      Bruce and the Spider. Bernard Barton. P90
Perseverance. Antonio D'Alfonso. P49
      The People Will Live On. Carl Sandburg.
      P82
      Try Again. Unknown. P89

Personification. Josephine Miles. P84
Perspective
    A Matter of Perspective. Ann Shermer. P65
"The petals". Lessons in Love. Edward A.
        Gloeggler. P65
Peter [pseud.]
    The Bus. P51
    The Saint Wears a Halo. P51
    The Speed Track. P51
"Peter and Paul Were Two Little Menikin".
    Unknown. P51
"Peter, Peter, along the ground". Four Sides
    to a House. Amy Lowell. P82
Peters, Robert
    Eskimo Haiku. P63
Peterson, Geoff
    Terminal. P86
Petit, the Poet, from Spoon River Anthology.
    Edgar Lee Masters. P82
Petosa, Justin
    Limerick. P73
Petrarch, Francesco
    Summer Is Gone. Henry Howard, Earl of
        Surrey (tr.). P89
Petrini, Michael
    Nui Ba Den (Black Virgin Mountain). P86
Pets
    Man Holding Cat. Raymond Roseliep. P68
Peynetsa, Andrew
    The Boy and the Deer. Dennis Tedlock
        (tr.). P78
Pfeffel, Gottlieb Conrad
    The Nobleman and the Pensioner. Charles
        Timothy Brooks (tr.). P90
Phantoms All. Harriet Elizabeth Spofford.
    P81
"Phildelphia was fascinated by New Orleans".
    Laws of Drifting. Alane Rollings. P88
Phillipov, Vladimir (tr.)
    A Biblical Motif. Boris Khristov. P92
    The Window. Boris Khristov. P92
Phillips (Tegidon), John
    Epitaph for Father and Son. Tony Conran
        (tr.). P87
Phillips, Louis
    Everybody in America Is at the Movies.
        P63
    Heartbreak in Tuktoyaktuk. P63
    Love-Deep in Crossword Puzzles. P63
    Why Comtemporary American Poets Rarely
        Write... P63
Phillips, Michael Joseph
    Mid Eastern. P56
    Seen in Wawa. P56
Phillips, Robert
    An Aged Rector Named Fiddle. P63
Phillipy, Ruby
    A Mountain Place. P72
Phillis Is My Only Joy. Sir Charles Sedley.

    P89
"Philosophers have measured mountains". The
    Agony. George Herbert. P59
Philosophy and Philosophers
    On the Passing of Heidegger. Marshall
        Hryciuk. P49
Philostratus
    Drink to Me Only with Thine Eyes, from
        The Forest. Ben Jonson (tr.). P89
Philpotts, Eden
    The Badgers. P51
"Phlebas the Phoenician, a fortnight dead".
    Death by Water, fr. The Waste Land.
    Thomas Stearns Eliot. P83
Phoenix, Clement Arthur
    Antarctica. P68
Photo. Don Coles. P49
"A photo of someone else's childhood". The
    Old Adam. Denise Levertov. P85
Photograph. Oscar Hahn. P71
Photograph. Omar Lara. P71
Photographs and Photographers
    Beergarden Photo. Therese Becker. P88
    Calvin. Bayla Winters. P56
    Daguerreotypie Der Niagara Falls...
        Herbert Morris. P79
    Hill 190, August '69. Jack Hill. P86
    An Old Photograph of Strangers. William
        Meredith. P79
    On a Gestapo Photograph Purported To
        Be... F. W. Watt. P49
    Picture of a Girl Drawn in Black and
        White. Diane Wakoski. P85
    Rutherford McDowell, from Spoon River
        Anthology. Edgar Lee Masters. P82
    Visitors. David Wevill. P49
Phryne. Anita Jepsen. P68
Phylip, William
    A Leave-Taking. Tony Conran (tr.). P87
Physical Universe. Louis Simpson. P85
Physicians
    Appointment in Doctor's Office. Josephine
        Miles. P84
    Archaic Song of Dr. Tom the Shaman.
        Unknown. P78
    The Doctor. David Ignatow. P84
    Old Woman Doctor. Helen Bryant. P68
Pianos
    Black and White. Carolyn Delaney. P74
    For Sally, with a Piano. Paul Goodman.
        P84
Piazza. John Crowe Ransom. P83
Picasso, Pablo
    Poem. Charles Guenther (tr.). P61
"Picking up drops from under one of my
    apples". Porcupine Sonnet. Charles W.
    Pratt. P63
Pickthall, Marjorie L. C.
    A Child's Song of Christmas. P51

Pickup, Ron
    Rock Art Prayer. P77
Picnics
    Picnics. Unknown. P51
Picture of a Girl Drawn in Black and White.
    Diane Wakoski. P85
The Picture of Little T. C. in a Prospect of
    Flowers. Andrew Marvell. P59
A Picture. Charles Gamage Eastman. P89
Pictures. F. Ann Elliott. P51
Piece de Resistance. Ann Deagon. P63
Pieces of Snot, from String Games. Unknown.
    P78
Pierce, Beryl
    Tekk Me. P72
Piercy, Marge
    Arles, 7 p.m. P63
    If They Come in the Night. P52
Piers Plowman, sels. Unknown. P66
The Pig's Tail. Norman Ault. P51
The Pigeon's Story. Jeannie Kirby. P51
The Pigeons. Rodney Bennett. P51
"Piggy-wig found he had four little feet".
    What Piggy-Wig Found. Enid Blyton. P51
Pigs
    The Greedy Little Pig. Irene F. Pawsey.
        P51
    If I Were a Pig. Elizabeth Fleming. P51
    Little Dame Crump. Unknown. P51
    The Little Piggies. Thomas Hood. P51
    The Pig's Tail. Norman Ault. P51
    Seven Little Pigs. Unknown. P51
    The Three Little Pigs. Sir Alfred A.
        Scott-Gatty. P51
Pigwiggen. Michael Drayton. P51
Pike, Albert
    Dixie. P90
Pike, Cecily E.
    Jack Frost. P51
"Pile the bodies high at Austerlitz...".
    Grass. Carl Sandburg. P82
Pilgrim. William Williams Pantycelyn. P87
The Pilgrim Fathers. Felicia Dorothea
    Hemans. P51
"Pilgrim I am in a desert land". Pilgrim.
    William Williams Pantycelyn. P87
The Pilgrim. John Bunyan. P51
Pilgrimage. Yahya Kemal. P91
Pilgrimages and Pilgrims
    The Pilgrim Fathers. Felicia Dorothea
        Hemans. P51
    The Pilgrim. John Bunyan. P51
    Pilgrimage. Yahya Kemal. P91
Pilots, Man Your Planes. Randall Jarrell.
    P84
Pimpernel. Charlotte Druitt Cole. P51
Pina, Cristina
    A Song for T. S. Anne Knupfer (tr.). P92
A Pinch of Faith. T. Vasudeva Reddy. P72

Pine Music. Kate Louise Brown. P51
Pine Night. Wayne R. Toensmann. P56
Pine, John C.
    The Cyclists. P77
"Pine, bamboo and plum". Sho Chiku Bai.
    Howard O. Long. P72
Pinien, Nyagak
    A Glutton. Terese Svoboda (tr.). P53
    John Kennedy. Terese Svoboda (tr.). P53
    Just Anyone. Terese Svoboda (tr.). P53
    Road to the Congo. Terese Svoboda (tr.).
        P53
    These Things Amaze Me. Terese Svoboda
        (tr.). P53
"Pinionjay Shits Pebbles". Unknown. P78
Pink Almond. Katharine (Hinkson) Tynan. P51
Pink, J. Louise
    "Dawn, Fingerpaints the Sky's". P72
"Pinky wiggled, 'End, begin--'.". Hand. Mark
    McCloskey. P63
Pinsky, Robert
    Daughter. P79
Pintye, Carolyn O'Harrow
    Rosemary's French Garden Basket. P72
Pinwheels, from Lost Youth: the Last War.
    Alfred Kreymborg. P82
"A pious, dark-eyed maiden". The Nun.
    Unknown. P87
The Piped Piper of Hamelin, sel. Robert
    Browning. P51
"A piper in the streets to-day". The Piper.
    Seumas (James Starkey) O'Sullivan. P51
The Piper. William Blake. P51
The Piper. Seumas (James Starkey)
    O'Sullivan. P51
Pipes and Piping
    The Piped Piper of Hamelin, sel. Robert
        Browning. P51
    "Piping down the valleys wild". The Piper.
        William Blake. P51
Pippa's Song. Robert Browning. P51
The Pirate's Tea-Party. Dorothy Una
    Ratcliffe. P51
Pisa Visa. Felicia Lamport. P63
Piss Tubes. Michael D. Clodfelter. P86
Pitie Three Goode Dere Soules. Vivian
    Trollope-Cagle. P65
Pittenger, Gary
    Social Zoology: Prep for a Field Trip.
        P63
"Pitter-patter, hear it raining?.". Rain.
    Lilian McCrea. P51
"Pitty Patty Polt!". Unknown. P51
Pity. William Mills. P67
Pity Ascending with the Fog. James Tate. P85
Pity This Busy Monster, Manunkind. Edward
    Estlin Cummings. P83
Pizarro Teaches the Mentally Retarded To
    Swim. Lee Bassett. 57

The **Place** You Inhabit. Walter Hoefler. P71
"The **place** was dark and sordid as a tomb".
    Beasts in Whoredom. Gaston Pelletier.
    P68
The **Place**. Robert Penn Warren. P67
Places Among the Stars. Stephen Crane. P81
"**Plague** take the women here--.". Ladies of
    Llanbadarn. Dafydd ab [or ab] Gwilym.
    P87
A **Plaguey** Thing. Vonna Adrian. P63
Plain Chant for a Tree. Edna Meudt. P68
Planetarium. Adrienne Rich. P85
Planets
    Saturn the Last Titan. Arthur Avergun.
    P68
Plantos, Ted
    Twain's Comet. P49
Plants and Planting
    The Aconite. A. M. Graham. P51
    Clover. John Banister Tabb. P81
    The Exotic Plant. Mauricia Price. P68
    Gulf-Weed. Cornelius George Fenner. P89
    Middle Age Summer. Edward Butscher. P64
    Pimpernel. Charlotte Druitt Cole. P51
    Transplanting. Theodore Roethke. P84
Planz, Allen
    Inquiline. P64
    Mako. P64
    Midwinter. P64
    Scalloping Northwest. P64
    Woodknot. P64
"The **plate** shatters". Untitled #1. Ian
    Brennan. P58
Plath, Sylvia
    The Bee Meeting. P85
    A Birthday Present. P85
    The Colossus. P85
    Daddy. P85
    Nick and the Candlestick. P85
    Words. P85
Platinum Rings (11/8/76). Charles Cline. P72
Platt, Anna M.
    Crocuses. P51
Platypus. Richard Houck. P74
Play
    Lying on Things. Dennis Lee. P80
    My Playmate. Mary I. Osborn. P51
    Playgrounds. Laurence Alma-Tadema. P51
    Snow. Karla Kuskin. P80
"**Play** it once". Saturday Night. Langston
    Hughes. P83
"The **play** she's in has no central
    character". Woe One. Alice Ryerson.
    P88
"**Play** that thing". Jazz Band in a Parisian
    Cabaret. Langston Hughes. P83
Playgrounds. Laurence Alma-Tadema. P51
Playgrounds
    School Yard in Summer. T. A. hulgin. P58

The **Playhouse** Key. Rachel (Lyman) Field. P51
Playland at the Beach. Gertrude May Lutz.
    P72
Plays and Playwriting
    The Dispossessed. John Berryman. P84
    Woe One. Alice Ryerson. P88
Plaything of the Gods. Louis J. Cantoni. P72
Playtpus
    Platypus. Richard Houck. P74
Please Bird. Kazue Mizumura. P80
"**Please/Start** speaking". To Discover. Janina
    Zydanowicz. P72
Pleasure. Gigi Lord. P65
Pleasure
    Pleasures. Denise Levertov. P85
Pledges. Pierre Emmanuel. P61
Pleiku. David Biles. P86
Plenty-Hawk
    "Your Way," from Crow Versions. William
    Stanley Merwin (tr.). P78
The **Plough** Is Crooked. Abbas Athar. P91
"The **Ploughman** Drinks the Bitter-Herb Tea".
    Unknown. P62
The **Ploughman**. Oliver Wendell Holmes. P89
Plummer, Deb
    Journey. P56
Plutonian Ode. Allen Ginsberg. P52
Po Biz. Howard Nemerov. P63
Poe, Edgar Allan
    For Annie. P89
Poe, Edgar Allen
    Annabel Lee. P89
Poem. Nadia Bishai. P92
Poem. Langston Hughes. P50
Poem. Jonaid. P92
Poem. Pablo Picasso. P61
Poem. James Schuyler. P64
Poem. William Carlos Williams. P82
Poem ("Everything"). Edward Estlin Cummings.
    P79
Poem ("Lana Turner"). Frank O'Hara. P85
Poem ("What time"). Edward Estlin Cummings.
    P79
Poem ("When I am feeling"). Frank O'Hara.
    P85
Poem 13, from The City. Gonzalo Millan. P71
Poem 20, from The City. Gonzalo Millan. P71
Poem 48, from The City. Gonzalo Millan. P71
Poem 60, from The City. Gonzalo Millan. P71
Poem About a Herring. Abraham Sutzkever. P48
"The **poem** considers any hypothesis". Bugs.
    Carole Oles. P48
A **Poem** for Emily. Miller Williams. P67
Poem for the Young White Man Who Asked Me...
    Lorna Dee Cervantes. P85
Poem Found While I Looked for Something
    Else. Joseph DeRoller. P63
A **Poem** from the Sweatbath Poems. Unknown.
    P78

"The **poem** is inside". The Difficult Poem.
        Jose Agustin Goytisolo. P61
"The **poem** is just beyond te corner of the
        eye". The Corner of the Eye. Robert
        Penn Warren. P67
Poem of the Forgotten Things. Jaime Quezada.
        P71
Poem of the Frost and Snow. Lewis Morris.
        P87
Poem Out of Childhood. Muriel Rukeyser. P84
Poem To Be Recited Every 8 Years While
        Eating... Unknown. P78
"The **poem** of the mind in the act of
        finding". Of Modern Poetry. Wallace
        Stevens. P83
"A **poem** should be palpable and mute". Ars
        Poetica. Archibald MacLeish. P83
Poem to Ease Birth. Unknown. P78
A **Poem** to the Mother of the Gods. Unknown.
        P78
Poem Which Cannot Be a Letter. Alamgir
        Hashmi. P91
Poem, fr. Iris Ifriqiya. Majid El Houssi.
        P91
"**Poems** are 1 lighthouses". Re Ezra Pound.
        Wilfred Watson. P49
Poems for My Daughter. Horace Gregory. P83
Poems for the Game of Silence. Unknown. P78
Poesia 50 (The Quanta of Anguish). Helle
        Busacca. P72
The **Poet** Dies for Love. Unknown. P87
The **Poet** Falls in Love with a Cowboy. Linda
        M. Hasselstrom. P88
The **Poet** Is a Hospital Clerk. David Ignatow.
        P84
"**Poet** burns to be honored, the headline
        said". My Wife Reads the Paper at
        Breakfast on the Birthday... Miller
        Williams. P63
"A **poet** in black tie?...". Form All (For
        Gilda Walker). Hugh McKinley. P72
The **Poet** of the Mountains. Tom McCarthy. P92
The **Poet** Redgrove. Bruce Bennett. P63
The **Poet** Ridiculed by Hysterical Academics.
        William DeWitt Snodgrass. P63
The **Poet's** Days. Omar Lara. P71
The **Poet's** Final Instructions. John
        Berryman. P84
The **Poet's** Friend (Lord Bolingbroke).
        Alexander Pope. P90
Poet's Reprieve, from August Presence.
        Ilango Kamalan. P72
The **Poet's** Song to His Wife. Bryan Waller
        ("Barry Cornwall") Procter. P89
A **Poet**, from A Thai Divine Comedy. Montri
        Umavijani. P92
"**Poet**. Will you, like other men". Impulsive
        Dialogue. Maxwell Bodenheim. P82
The **Poet**. ucille Clifton. P52

Poetry. Ondra Lysohorsky. P68
Poetry. Marianne Moore. P83
Poetry. Becky Taylor. P74
Poetry I. Kevin Kocis. P72
Poetry Study Group. Carol Bessent Hayman.
        P72
Poetry and Poets
        Alchemy. Alice M. Boughtwood. P68
        American Poetry. Louis Simpson. P85
        Anoukis and Later Jeanne. Rene Char. P61
        Answer to Sion Cent, sels. Rhys Goch
            Eryri. P87
        Ars Poetica. Archibald MacLeish. P83
        Ars Poetique. Rodrigo Lira. P71
        The Art of Poetry. Pierre Emmanuel. P61
        At the Poetry Reading: 'This Is a Poem
            About That'. Jim Daniels. P63
        Auden Aetat XX, LX. Stephen Spender. P79
        Blue Poem. Hubert E. Hix. P63
        Buffalo Blood. Lance Henson. P78
        The Care and Feeding of a Poet. James
            Laughlin. P63
        Chariots. Glenna Glee. P68
        A Choice of Weapons. Stanley Kunitz. P83
        Comradery. Madison Cawein. P81
        Constantly Risking Absurdity. Lawrence
            Ferlinghetti. P85
        The Coronet. Andrew Marvell. P59
        Dance of Words. Beth Martin Haas. P72
        Dead Languages. Jay MacPherson. P49
        Dew Yu Know. Bill Bissett. P49
        The Difficult Poem. Jose Agustin
            Goytisolo. P61
        The Editor Regrets. David Cram. P63
        Envoi. L. L. Zieger. P63
        For Kenneth Patchen. A. D. Williams. P56
        For W. H. A. John Ronald Renel Tolkien.
            P79
        For You. Robert Creeley. P85
        Form All (For Gilda Walker). Hugh
            McKinley. P72
        Found--A Poem!. Clarence L. Weaver. P72
        Free Verse. Joanne Seltzer. P65
        Fresh Air. Kenneth Koch. P85
        A Going-Away Poem for Philip Larkin.
            David Gill. P72
        Hearing Heaney Read. Gregory Betts. P49
        A High-Toned Old Christian Woman. Wallace
            Stevens. P83
        Ho Do Vi I. Lance Henson. P78
        Hugh Selwyn Mauberley (Life and
            Contacts). Ezra Pound. P82
        I. Marion Jane Richardson. P65
        I Am Singing the Cold Rain. Lance Henson.
            P78
        I, Poet. G. Soundararaj. P72
        Invocation to the Social Muse. Archibald
            MacLeish. P83
        Jordan (2). George Herbert. P59

Kidnap Poem. Nikki Giovanni. P85
L'Envoi. Caroline Kotowicz. P72
Lake Poets. Menke Katz. P72
The Latin American Solidarity Committee
    Fundraising... Ed Ochester. P63
Let All World Poets Rejoice. Joy
    Beaudette Cripps. P72
Let Beauty Shine. Alice M. Boughtwood.
    P68
The Living Masters. Gavin Ewart. P63
Lost Poems. Mary B. Finn. P68
Love for Poetry, from Wake up, My Heart
    and Other Poems. John Tworoger. P65
The Lying Muse to Rhys Goch Eryri. Sion
    Cent. P87
The Meeting. Mark Gordon. P49
Memorial Verses (April 1850). Matthew
    Arnold. P90
THe Metaphor's Shine. K. Sree Ramachandra
    Murthi. P72
The Modern Poet (A song of Deriviations).
    Alice Meynell. P90
Modern Poetry. Glenna Glee. P72
Moroccan Perfume. Virginia Golden. P72
Mr. Pope. Allen Tate. P83
Ni Hoi Nim Ni Hon. Lance Henson. P78
Ode: Salute to the French Negro Poets.
    Frank O'Hara. P85
Of Modern Poetry. Wallace Stevens. P83
On Seeing Gavin Ewart in Sainsbury's.
    Joan Van Poznak. P63
On the Eve of Departure for Sixth World
    Congress... Yung-jung Lin. P72
Our Israfel. Edwin Markham. P81
The Parnassians. James Merrill. P85
Performance. Phyllis Webb. P49
Petit, the Poet, from Spoon River
    Anthology. Edgar Lee Masters. P82
Plutonian Ode. Allen Ginsberg. P52
Po Biz. Howard Nemerov. P63
Poem. Pablo Picasso. P61
Poem ("Lana Turner"). Frank O'Hara. P85
The Poet Redgrove. Bruce Bennett. P63
The Poet Ridiculed by Hysterical
    Academics. William DeWitt Snodgrass.
    P63
The Poet's Days. Omar Lara. P71
The Poet's Friend (Lord Bolingbroke).
    Alexander Pope. P90
A Poet, from A Thai Divine Comedy. Montri
    Umavijani. P92
The Poet. Lucille Clifton. P52
Poetry. Becky Taylor. P74
Poetry. Ondra Lysohorsky. P68
Poetry. Marianne Moore. P83
Poetry I. Kevin Kocis. P72
Poetry Study Group. Carol Bessent Hayman.
    P72
Position. Blas de Otero. P61

Praise of Tenby. Unknown. P87
Preface. Theodore Weiss. P84
The Propaganda of the Poet. Robert
    Williams Parry. P87
Put on Guard. Rene Char. P61
Randall Jarrell. Karl Shapiro. P84
Re Ezra Pound. Wilfred Watson. P49
Reading Adonais. Paul Goodman. P84
Relativity. Bozhidar Bozhilov. P70
A Remembered Workshop Critic: Louis A.
    Haselmayer. Herbert M. Kirkham. P68
The Rose and the Worm. James Camp. P63
Sassafras. Susan Glickman. P49
Scottsboro, too, Is Worth Its Song.
    Countee Cullen. P83
Seen in Wawa. Michael Joseph Phillips.
    P56
Several Short Poems. George Swede. P49
Since That Time. Ellin E. Carter. P56
A Slender Book of Verse and It's
    Purchaser. F. C. Rosenberger. P63
A Song About Myself, sel. John Keats. P51
A Song for T. S. Cristina Pina. P92
South Dakota Scenery. Wayne Kvam. P68
Stanzas to the Lord Rhys ap Gruffudd,
    Prince of Deheubarth. Cynddelw Brydydd
    Mawr. P87
Stray Animals. James Tate. P85
The Strife Between the Poet and Ambition.
    Thomas Merton. P84
Tablet IX. Armand Schwerner. P64
Tablet XXIII. Armand Schwerner. P64
Tablet XXV. Armand Schwerner. P64
Ten Definitions of Poetry. Carl Sandburg.
    P82
To Hywel ab Ifan Fychan. Guto'r Glyn. P87
To John Ashbery. Frank O'Hara. P85
To Owain Gwynedd. Meilir ap Gwalchmai.
    P87
To the Poetry Clubs of Wales. Bobi Jones.
    P87
Two Dicta of William Blake. Robert
    Duncan. P52
Two Fool's Songs. Emile Verhaeren. P61
Vigils. Josephine Miles. P79
Walking. Judith Minty. P88
Warning to the Poets. Sion Tudur. P87
When You Realize That... Virginia Rodas.
    P72
Why Comtemporary American Poets Rarely
    Write... Louis Phillips. P63
Why I Am Not a Painter. Frank O'Hara. P85
Why? Verna Lee O'Brien Clark. P56
With Voices Strong. Rosemary Challoner
    Wilkinson. P72
A Young Poet, from A Thai Divine Comedy.
    Montri Umavijani. P92

Poetry and Poets—Parody
Mending Sump. Kenneth Koch. P85

Poetry and Poets-Satire
On First Looking in on Blogett's Keats's 'Chapman's Homer'. . George Starbuck. P85
"Poetry is a fountain". Poetry. Ondra Lysohorsky. P68
"Poetry is a projection across silence...". Ten Definitions of Poetry. Carl Sandburg. P82
"Poetry is a signature of". Poetry. Becky Taylor. P74
"Poetry is but a melody". Poetry I. Kevin Kocis. P72
"Poetry is the supreme fiction, madame". A High-Toned Old Christian Woman. Wallace Stevens. P83
"The poetry of earth is never dead". The Grasshopper and the Cricket. John Keats. P51
Poets. Bozhidar Bozhilov. P70
"Poets make pets of pretty, docile words". Pretty Words. Elinor Wylie. P82
Polarity. Hirsch Lazaar Silverman. P72
Pole Vaulter. David Allan Evans. P68
Poles, Alessandra A.
Carmel by the Sea. P72
Police
Action Rhyme. E. H. Adams. P51
The Political Asses. P. M. Mammen. P72
Political Poem. Amiri (LeRoi Jones) Baraka. P85
Politics and Politicians
Ol' Grandad. Steven C. Levi. P56
The Political Asses. P. M. Mammen. P72
(SIC)Transcript Gloria, or The Body Politician. Irving Feldman. P63
The Spooniad, from Spoon River Anthology. Edgar Lee Masters. P82
Vote. Randy S. Atwood. P72
Pollak, Felix
Visit to the Institute for the Blind. P57
Pollet, Sylvester
Triolet, After Titian. P63
Pollit, Katha
Chinese Finches. P79
Pollution
Cloud. Josephine Miles. P84
Each Age Believed. Terri Brint Joseph. P68
Polly. William Brighty Rands. P89
Polonaise. David Wevill. P49
Pompeii
Voices from Pompeii. Chester A. Beck Jr. P68
Pompous. Paul Ramsey. P63
Pond & Stream. Angela Karszo. P77
Pondy Woods. Robert Penn Warren. P83
The Pony. Rachel MacAndrew. P51
Pools

The Paddling Pool. E. H. Adams. P51
"Poor I am now: if any should call me home". Epitaph. Dafydd Jones. P87
"The Poor Man in the Wintertime". Unknown. P62
"Poor Old Robinson Crusoe!". Unknown. P51
The Poor Snail. J. M. Westrup. P51
"Poor little raccoon". Raccoon. Andy Neely. P74
"A poor sight the hall of Ifor Hael-- mounds". The Hall of Ifor Hael. Ieuan Brydydd Hir. P87
"Poor tired Tim! It's sad for him". Tired Tim. Walter De La Mare. P51
Poorly Run Marionette. Kevin Cline. P58
Pope, Alexander
The Poet's Friend (Lord Bolingbroke). P90
Poplars. Helen Leuty. P51
The Popol Vuh: Alligator's Struggles..., sel. Unknown. P78
The Popol Vuh: Beginnings, sel. Unknown. P78
The Popol Vuh: Beginnings, sel. Unknown. P78
Poppies. Nesta Wyn Jones. P87
Poppies. William E. Morris. P72
Poppies. P. A. Ropes. P51
The Poppies in the Garden. Ffrida Wolfe. P51
Popping Corn. Unknown. P89
"The porchlight coming on again". 1926. Weldon Kees. P84
Porcupine Sonnet. Charles W. Pratt. P63
Port Letter. Mary Trimble. P88
Porter, Anne
Four Poems in One. P64
In a Country Hospital. P64
Leavetaking. P64
On the Three-Hour Train Ride. P64
Porter, Fairfield
At Night. P64
The Morning Train. P64
A Painter Obsessed by Blue. P64
The Reader. P64
September. P64
Porth Cwyfan. Roland Mathias. P54
Portrait. Louise Gluck. P85
Portrait. Dick Hayman. P63
Portrait d'une Femme. Ezra Pound. P82
Portrait in Veiled Waters. Anselm Parlatore. P64
Portrait of an Old Woman. Arthur Davidson Ficke. P82
Portrait of Lady. William Carlos Williams. P82
Portrait of Mary. Charles Wright. P79
The Portrait. Thomas Heywood. P89
Portraits of Men
Aspects of Robinson. Weldon Kees. P84
Epilogue for FDR. David Ignatow. P84
Self-Portrait. Abdul-Latif Akel. P92
A Strange Man. Wazir Agha. P91

Portraits of Women
    Cousin Shamsu, Durzi. Kaiser Haq. P91
    Faded Pictures. William Vaughn Moody. P81
    First Portrait. Sarmad Sehbai. P91
    For a Lady of Impressions. Richard Parks.
      P68
    Glint. Euros Bowen. P87
    Julia Before the Mirror. Jack H. Palmer.
      P68
    My Love. Dewi Havhesp. P87
Position. Blas de Otero. P61
The Position. Julio Monteiro Martins. P92
Possession Report. Betty Fukuyama. P65
Possessions. Hart Crane. P83
Possessive Love
    Talk. Orhan Veli Kanik. P91
Post Mortem. Robinson Jeffers. P83
Postal Service
    The Postman. Clive Sansom. P51
Postcard from Civilization. Charles W.
    Pratt. P63
Postcards
    Postcards. Gerry Shikatani. P49
Posthumous. Jules Supervielle. P61
Postlude. Edna Meudt. P68
Postman's Knock. Rodney Bennett. P51
The Postman. Clive Sansom. P51
The Postman. Alice Todd. P51
Potato Song. Stanley Moss. P64
A Pothersome Pair. John Ceiriog Hughes. P87
Pound, Ezra
    The Cantos, sel. P82
    Cino. P82
    Histrion. P82
    Hugh Selwyn Mauberley (Life and
      Contacts). P82
    In a Station of the Metro. P82
    Lament of the Frontier Guard. P82
    Notes for an Unpublished Canto. P79
    A Pact. P82
    Portrait d'une Femme. P82
    The River-Merchant's Wife: a Letter. P82
    The Seafarer. P82
    Sestina: Altaforte. P82
    To Whistler, American. P82
    Villanelle: the Psychological Hour. P82
    Villonaud for This Yule. P82
Poverty
    Common Land Above Trefenter. Jeremy
      Hooker. P54
    Harlem Shadows. Claude McKay. P82
    Poem 20, from The City. Gonzalo Millan.
      P71
    "The Poor Man in the Wintertime".
      Unknown. P62
    Rear-Porches of an Apartment-Building.
      Maxwell Bodenheim. P82
    To Elsie. William Carlos Williams. P82
"Poverty is not a curse". Symbol of Courage.

    G. Soosai. P72
Powel, Salbri
    The Lover's Hope. Tony Conran (tr.). P87
Power
    The Game. Harold Bond. P57
Power of Love. Betty Farquhar. P72
"The Power of Snow". Steve Sanfield. P77
Praed, Winthrop Mackworth
    Camp-Bell. P90
Prairie Waters by Night. Carl Sandburg. P82
Prairies
    Westport. Galway Kinnell. P85
Praise. Mary Anderson. P51
Praise. Yaedi Ignatow. P64
Praise of a Girl. Huw Morus. P87
Praise of Rhys ap Maredudd. Dafydd Nanmor.
    P87
Praise of Tenby. Unknown. P87
"Praise Pasupati's Evening Libation".
    Unknown. P62
"Praise the Lord for all the seasons".
    Praise. Mary Anderson. P51
"Praise youth's hot blood if you will...".
    Age in Prospect. Robinson Jeffers. P83
Prato, Compagnetto da
    "Because of the Evil Husband I Have".
      Frede Jensen (tr.). P69
Pratt, Anna Maria
    A Mortifying Mistake. P89
Pratt, Charles W.
    Another Fable in Two Languages. P63
    Porcupine Sonnet. P63
    Postcard from Civilization. P63
"Pray richly from this book of hours". Les
    Belles Heures. Lois Guthrie. P68
"Pray, where are the little bluebells gone".
    About the Fairies. Jean Ingelow. P51
Prayer
    "Allah, My Lord". Unknown. P60
    The Angelus. Edwin Markham. P81
    A Chiild's Grace. Robert Herrick. P51
    A Child's Morning Prayer. J. Kirby. P51
    A Child's Prayer. William Canton. P51
    A Child's Prayer. Siegfried Sassoon. P51
    A Child's Prayer. Unknown. P51
    "Creator of the World". Unknown. P60
    "Dear Father". Unknown. P60
    "Dear God". Carmen Bernos De Gasztold.
      P60
    The Divine Image. William Blake. P51
    A Dragon for the Family. Robert Yeo. P92
    The Elixir. George Herbert. P51
    Evening Prayer. Carmen Boitel Adams. P72
    Evening Song. Edith King. P51
    The Fool's Prayer. Edward Rowland Sill.
      P90
    "From Ghoulies and Ghosties". Unknown.
      P60
    From the Recesses of a Lowly Spirit. Sir

John Bowring. P89

Gifts. Emma Lazarus. P90

"Glory Be to That God Who Is in the Fire". Unknown. P60

"God Bless All Those That I Love". Unknown. P60

"God Bless the Master of This House". Unknown. P60

"God of All Our Cities". Joan Gale Thomas. P60

Grace and Thanksgiving. Elizabeth Gould. P51

"Greetings to Thee, Oh Lord of the Day". Unknown. P62

The Higher Good. Theodore Parker. P89

Hymn to Zeus. Cleanthes. P89

If Only. Dale Maria Pacileo Feldman. P72

"If We Have Seen What We Are Meant to See". Ruth Hoppin. P72

"In the Evening Give Homage". Unknown. P62

The Knight's Prayer. Unknown. P51

The Last Quarter of the Night. Gilani Kamran. P91

Lemuel's Blessing. William Stanley Merwin. P85

Les Belles Heures. Lois Guthrie. P68

Let the Light Enter. Frances E. W. Harper. P89

"Lord of Sea and Earth and Air". Cecil Roberts. P60

Mercy. Unknown. P87

"The Moon Shines Bright". Unknown. P60

My Prayer. Bessie Wherry Noe. P72

Now and Afterwards. Dinah Maria Mulock Craik. P89

"O Our Mother the Earth, O Our Father the Sky". Unknown. P60

"Praise Pasupati's Evening Libation". Unknown. P62

Prayer. Louis Untermeyer. P82

Prayer After World War. Carl Sandburg. P82

Prayer for Gentleness to All Creatures. John Galsworthy. P51

A Prayer. Boris Kristov. P70

A Prayer. Edwin Markham. P51

The Prayer. Anna Marie Benado. P72

Prayers. Henry Charles Beeching. P51

The Rainbow Dared the Storm. Emma Crobaugh. P68

Reality. Robert B. Bradley. P72

Rebecca's Hymn, from Ivanhoe. Sir Walter Scott. P89

Religion Poem. Caroline Knox. P63

Rock Art Prayer. Ron Pickup. P77

"Sleep, Sleep. My Little One!...". Unknown. P60

"Thank God for sleep in the Long Quiet Night". John Drinkwater. P60

To the Supreme Being. Michelangelo Buonarroti. P89

Prayer. Louis Untermeyer. P82

Vesper Hymn. Eliza Scudder. P89

Vespers. Hugh McKinley. P68

The Vision Clear. J. M. Westrup. P51

We Say This Prayer. Jozsef Tornai. P92

What Is Prayer?. James Montgomery. P89

"When I'm Out of the House in the Open, I Feel Joy". Unknown. P60

Wrestling Jacob. Charles Wesley. P89

Yes, Lord. Julia N. Aue. P72

Prayer After World War. Carl Sandburg. P82

Prayer for Gentleness to All Creatures. John Galsworthy. P51

"Prayer is the soul's sincere desire". What Is Prayer?. James Montgomery. P89

A Prayer. Boris Kristov. P70

A Prayer. Edwin Markham. P51

The Prayer. Anna Marie Benado. P72

Prayers. Henry Charles Beeching. P51

"The prayers I make will then be sweet indeed". To the Supreme Being. Michelangelo Buonarroti. P89

A Pre-Raphaelite Notebook. Geoffrey Hill. P79

The Preacher: Ruminates Behind the Sermon, fr. A Street... Gwendolyn Brooks. P84

Precision. Lawrence Herman. P73

Preface. Theodore Weiss. P84

Preface to a Twenty Volume Suicide Note. Amiri (LeRoi Jones) Baraka. P85

Pregnancy

Elsa Wertman, from Spoon River Anthology. Edgar Lee Masters. P82

The Quickening. Miriam Pederson. P88

With Child. Genevieve Taggard. P83

Pregnancy. See also Conception

The Voyages. Gregory Orr. P85

Pregnant Thought. Merry Harris. P63

Prelude to Paradise. Dorothea Neale. P72

Prelutsky, Jack

The Telephone Call. P50

Preparing for Winter. Steve Sanfield. P77

Preposterous. Jim Hall. P63

The Presence. William Everson. P84

"The press of the Spoon River Clarion...". Carl Hamblin, from Spoon River Anthology. Edgar Lee Masters. P82

"Pressure of sun on the rockslide". Water. Gary Snyder. P85

Preston, Harriet Waters (tr.)

The Leaf-Picking. Frederic Mistral. P89

Pretense

Do You Traipse Long-Leggedly Through Murky Woodlands. Caroline Knox. P88

Villanelle: the Psychological Hour. Ezra Pound. P82

"The **prettiest** lady that ever I've seen".
    Pretty Lady. Rose Fyleman. P51
Pretty Maid Marion. Ivy O. Eastwick. P51
Pretty Words. Elinor Wylie. P82
"**Pretty** little crocus, in your cosy bed".
    Waking up. Unknown. P51
"The **pretty** red squirrel lives up in a
    tree". The Squirrel. Mary Howitt. P51
Prevert, Jacques
    At the Florist's. Charles Guenther (tr.).
    P61
Price, Francis Brown
    Dramatic Compensation. P68
    White Ink on Sky Parchment. P68
    With Fifty Stars. P68
Price, Mauricia
    The Exotic Plant. P68
Price, Merle
    Covenant. P65
Pride and Vanity
    Black Majesty. Countee Cullen. P83
    If We Must Die. Claude McKay. P82
    Stage Fright. Jennie H. Sandbank. P72
    Why Do You Strive for Greatness, Fool?
        Stephen Crane. P81
Pride of the Farmer. Jeff Bence. P74
The **Priest** and the Mulberry Tree. Thomas
    Love Peacock. P51
Priest, Robert
    The Man with the Nitroglycerine Tears.
    P49
The **Primal** Rain. Erika Schott. P72
Primer of Plato. Jean Garrigue. P84
Primeval Method. Selma Youngdahl. P72
The **Primitive** Astronomer. Tom Riley. P63
Primrose Hill. Rose Fyleman. P51
"**Primroses**; salutations; the miry skull". A
    Pre-Raphaelite Notebook. Geoffrey
    Hill. P79
Prince Chand
    Buddhist Moon. P72
A **Princely** Ditty in Praise of the English
    Rose. Thomas Deloney. P51
Prisms. Katherine A. Hogan. P65
Prisoner at a Desk. May Sarton. P52
Prisoners of War
    Vietnam P.O.W. Camp. Theodore W. Gostas.
    P86
Prisons and Prisoners
    After Interrogation. Georgi Djagarov. P70
    Arrival. Aristoteles Espana. P71
    Beyond Torture. Aristoteles Espana. P71
    Climbing Milestone Mountain, August 22,
        1937. Kenneth Rexroth. P84
    Hell and Solitude. Aristoteles Espana.
    P71
    In the Dordogne. John Peale Bishop. P83
    Intimate. Aristoteles Espana. P71
    A Kind of Song. Aristoteles Espana. P71

    Leaving. Aristoteles Espana. P71
    On the Site of the Convent. Tibor Tollas.
    P61
    Read to the Animals, or Orpheus at the
        SPCA. Irving Feldman. P79
    Roads. Aristoteles Espana. P71
    Somewhere Near the Mekong River, 1966.
        Dennis Moore. P86
    There Has to be a Jail for Ladies. Thomas
        Merton. P84
    Tramp, Tramp, Tramp. Unknown. P90
    What Should I Do Now?. Aristoteles
        Espana. P71
    Wire Meshes. Aristoteles Espana. P71
The **Probable** and Improbable Disappearance of
    a Cat... Juan Luis Martinez. P71
"**Probably** it will always escape them". A
    Century of Miracles. Georgi Djagarov.
    P70
Problem Solving
    Maybe Dats Youwr Pwoblem Too. Jim Hall.
    P63
A **Problem** in Genetics. Vera Rich. P68
"The **procession**". The Removal. William
    Stanley Merwin. P85
"**Processionals** in the exemplary cave".
    Funeral Music. Geoffrey Hill. P48
Procsal, Gloria H.
    The Tower. P72
Procter, Adelaide Anne
    Judge Not. P89
    A Woman's Answer. P89
    A Woman's Question. P89
Procter, Bryan Waller ("Barry Cornwall")
    Life. P89
    The Owl. P89
    The Poet's Song to His Wife. P89
    The Sea. P89
    Sit Down, Sad Soul. P89
Proctor, James W.
    Bookends. P65
"**Prodding** My Intellect a Little". Jacopo
    Mostacci. P69
Proem: To Brooklyn Bridge, fr. The Bridge.
    Hart Crane. P83
Progress
    In the Name of Progress. William F.
        Landgraf. P72
    Irised Symbols. Emma Crobaugh. P68
    Westward Ho!. Joaquin Miller. P81
Promise. Florence Lacey. P51
"**Promise** me the world". Vote. Randy S.
    Atwood. P72
Promises
    Covenant. Merle Price. P65
    Misconception. Mildred Offerle. P72
    Mondays. Miriana Basheva. P70
    Pledges. Pierre Emmanuel. P61
    Villanelle: the Psychological Hour. Ezra

Pound. P82
"Proof/There is beauty in sorrow". Equation.
    Caroline Perkins. P68
Proofreader's Island. Michael Spence. P63
The Propaganda of the Poet. Robert Williams
    Parry. P87
Property
    Gypsy. Josephine Miles. P84
    Possession Report. Betty Fukuyama. P65
"Prophet, you appeared suddenly". To a
    Mantled Prophet. Belle Adams. P68
Prophets and Prophecy
    Cassandra. Faye Kicknosway. P88
    With Trembling Hands. Rex Quartey. P72
The Proposal. D. Lyons Gallagher. P65
Prospective Immigrants Please Note. Adrienne
    Rich. P85
Prostitution and Prostitutes
    The Girl of Rue Joli. Dennis Moore. P86
    Laws of Drifting. Alane Rollings. P88
    Metamorphosis, sel. Argyris Hionis. P92
    The Scarlet Woman. Fenton Johnson. P82
    Wild May. Claude McKay. P82
Protests
    Ode to a Nuclear Frieze. Nan Townsend
        Degelman. P77
    Of Late. George Starbuck. P85
    Sierra Song. Steve Sanfield. P77
Prothalamion. Delmore Schwartz. P84
Protonotaro, Stefano
    "For too Long I Have Thought That I'd
        Conceal". Frede Jensen (tr.). P69
    "To Give Joy to My Heart". Frede Jensen
        (tr.). P69
Proud Father with Buried Son. Judd Allen.
    P72
Proud Little Spruce Fir. Jeannie Kirby. P51
"Przemek changed into a bird". Ballad for a
    Solonaut. Joanna Salamon. P92
Psalm 13. Sir Philip Sidney. P59
A Psalm of Life. Henry Wadsworth Longfellow.
    P89
A Psalm. Thomas Merton. P84
"The psychic metaphysician sat tight in the
    white". Seer. Josephine Miles. P84
Psychotherapy
    Dail-A-Shrink. Ned Pastor. P63
Pudding Charms. Charlotte Druitt Cole. P51
Puddles. Jennifer Gilgan. P73
Pugliese, Giacomino
    "Death, Why Have You Waged Such a Fierce
        War on Me". Frede Jensen (tr.). P69
    "The Sweet, Pleasant face". Frede Jensen
        (tr.). P69
    "When I See". Frede Jensen (tr.). P69
Puk, Rec
    The Sun's Tongue. Terese Svoboda (tr.).
        P53
Puk-Wudjies. Patrick R. Chalmers. P51

"The Pulinda Tribesmen Standing on the
    Mountain Peak". Unknown. P62
The Pulley. George Herbert. P59
Pulling the Days Together. Graham Everett.
    P64
Pultz, Constance
    The Way It All Was. P65
The Pumpkin Man. Robert Francis. P63
"' Punctured, broken hut, laid low ". The
    Ruin. Dafydd ab [or ab] Gwilym. P87
Punishment
    Brother Ass and St. Francis. John
        Banister Tabb. P81
Puppet. John J. Soldo. P65
Puppy and I. A. A. Milne. P51
Purdy, Al
    Double-Focus. P49
    There Is of Course a Legend. P49
"The pure products of America". To Elsie.
    William Carlos Williams. P82
A Puritan Lady. Lizette Woodworth Reese. P81
Purple. Jennifer Hoyt. P73
The Purple Cow. Gelett Burgess. P90
Purple Grackles. Amy Lowell. P82
"Purple echo". L'Echo. Kim Yang-Shik. P72
"Purple is the sharp sound of ripe grapes".
    Purple. Jennifer Hoyt. P73
Pushkin, Aleksandr
    Work. Babette Deutsch and Avrahm
        Yarmolinsky (tr.). P90
"Pussy Cat, Pussy Cat, Where Have You
    Been?". Unknown. P51
Pussy-Cat and Puppy-Dog. Lilian McCrea. P51
Put on Guard. Rene Char. P61
Puzzles
    The Vowels: an Enigma. Jonathan Swift.
        P90
Pyke, B. K.
    Blacksmith. P51

Q. E. D. Laurence Perrine. P63
Qasimi, Ahmad Nadeem
    Mist. Daud Kamal (tr.). P91
Qing, Ai
    Snowy Morning. Marilyn Chin (tr.). P92
Quadri, Shaheed
    At Each Other. Kaiser Haq (tr.). P91
Quail. Katharyn Machan Aal. P63
"The quail go hyperspace". Micro/Macro.
    Steve LaVine. P77
The Quaker Graveyard in Nantucket. Robert
    Lowell. P84
"Quaker lady dressed in gray". Vignette from
    the Past. Mary Frances Langford. P65
The Quality of Life. Steve Sanfield. P77
Quarles, Francis

Delight in God. P89

The **Quarrel**. Viola K. Hunt. P68

Quartey, Rex
With Trembling Hands. P72

Quasha, George (tr.)
Essie Parrish in New York. Unknown. P78

Quasimodo, Salvatore
A Buried One in Me Sings. Charles
Guenther (tr.). P61
Cool with Sleeping Rivers. Charles
Guenther (tr.). P61
The Crossing. Charles Guenther (tr.). P61
In the Sense of Death. Charles Guenther
(tr.). P61
In the Willow Branches. Charles Guenther
(tr.). P61
The Incomparable Earth. Charles Guenther
(tr.). P61
Mirror. Charles Guenther (tr.). P61
Space. Charles Guenther (tr.). P61
Stone Quarries. Charles Guenther (tr.).
P61
Visible, Invisible. Charles Guenther
(tr.). P61
We've Heard the Sea Again. Charles
Guenther (tr.). P61
What Do You Want, Shepherd of Wind?.
Charles Guenther (tr.). P61
Woods Are Sleeping. Charles Guenther
(tr.). P61

"A **quavering** cry. Screech-owl?.". Night,
Death, Mississippi. Robert Hayden. P84

Queen Anne's Legs. Jane Flanders. P63

The **Queen** Bee. Mary K. Robinson. P51

The **Queen** Charlotte Islands Meditations.
Michael J. Yates. P49

The **Queen** Takes Drawing Lessons from King
Lear. J. Patrick Lewis. P63

"The **queen** is gone a-hunting in the royal
wood". A-Hunting. Jennie Dunbar. P51

"The **Queen** of England drew but one". The
Queen Takes Drawing Lessons from King
Lear. J. Patrick Lewis. P63

Queen-Ann's-Lace. William Carlos Williams.
P82

Question?. E. Manuel Huber. P72

Questions and Answers
Debate: Question, Quarry, Dream. Robert
Penn Warren. P83
Interiors. Carol Barrett and Anita Skeen.
P88
Mea Culpa, from Lost Youth: the Last War.
Alfred Kreymborg. P82

Questions of Travel. Elizabeth Bishop. P84

"**Questions** of falters pain". Emotions
Extinction. Patricia Anne Solek-
Fritsche. P72

Quezada, Jaime
Halley's Comet. Steven F. White (tr.).

P71
Poem of the Forgotten Things. Steven F.
White (tr.). P71
Waking Up. Steven F. White (tr.). P71
The Way Things Are Above and Below.
Steven F. White (tr.). P71
Whistling in the Air. Steven F. White
(tr.). P71

"**Quick**! hit the dirt! take cover! down!".
The Poet Redgrove. Bruce Bennett. P63

The **Quickening**. Miriam Pederson. P88

"**Quickly** Embracing the Neck of Her Husband".
Unknown. P62

Quickness. Henry Vaughan. P59

Quidiron Pro Quo. Paul Sawyer. P63

Quiet Time. Tom Tellesbo. P58

"**Quiet** at noon--a few seagull cries".
Seashore. Ondra Lysohorsky. P72

"**Quiet** in the woods". Haiku. Jenny Mumzhiu.
P73

"**Quiet** the breeze, side of long slope". The
Ruined Hearth of Rheged, fr. Poetry
from Lost Sagas. Unknown. P87

Quilts
The Patchwork Quilt. Elizabeth Fleming.
P51

"**Quite** unexpectedly as Vasserot". The End of
the World. Archibald MacLeish. P83

"**Quo** vadis, O centurion?.". Africa. Pieter
D. Williams. P68

R.,E.M.G.
Midsummer Moon. P51

The **Rabbit**. Edith King. P51

Rabbits
Bunny Rabbit. Walter De la Mare. P51
My New Rabbit. Elizabeth Gould. P51
The Rabbit. Edith King. P51
Skippets, the Bad One. Christine E.
Bradley. P51
The Snare. James Stephens. P51
"There Was a Little Rabbit Sprig".
Unknown. P51
Timid Bunnies. Jeannie Kirby. P51

Rabinal-Achi: Act IV. Unknown. P78

Raccoon. Andy Neely. P74

The **Race**. James Camp. P63

The **Race**. Sylvia Smullin. P74

Races, Human
The Great Marble Cake. Carl T. Endemann.
P56

Rachel Plummer's Dream Winter 1836. Eleanor
Ross Taylor. P79

"**Racing** quickly under the sun". Lonely Boat.
Carla Zeppieri. P74

Racism

Poem for the Young White Man Who Asked
    Me... Lorna Dee Cervantes. P85
Racoons
    Coon Song. Archie Randolph Ammons. P67
The **Radiant** Beaches. Raul Zurita. P71
Radio
    In Memory of Radio. Amiri (LeRoi Jones)
        Baraka. P85
    Wireless. Rodney Bennett. P51
The **Radio,** with its Breath Like a Trapped
        Bee. John Gatwec Lul. P53
Rafat, Taufiq
    Coming Down from the Mountains. P91
    In a Stalled Van. P91
    Loot. P91
    Mangoes. P91
    Second-Hand Trousers. P91
Rafat, Taufiq (tr.)
    First Portrait. Sarmad Sehbai. P91
    Second Portrait. Sarmad Sehbai. P91
The **Rag** Lady. Nancy McCleery. P88
Ragged Robin. Elizabeth Godley. P51
"**Ragged** boys". Market. Robert Hayden. P84
Raghuram, T. M.
    Untitled. P72
"**Rags** and tatters". Ragged Robin. Elizabeth
        Godley. P51
Rahamah, Grace Ridgway
    Mary's Melody (To Mary E. Cox). P72
Rahl, Cecilia N.
    Because of You. P72
Railroads
    All Night Long by Train, All Night Long.
        Mauricio Electorat. P71
    The Engine Driver. G. S. O. P51
    44, Avenue de Maine. Atanas Dalchev. P70
    From a Railway Carriage. Robert Louis
        Stevenson. P51
    From the Train. Marjorie Wilson. P51
    The Holiday Train. Irene Thompson. P51
    In the Train. James ("B.V.") Thomson. P51
    On the Northwest Hiawatha. Kathleen
        Norris. P88
    On the Three-Hour Train Ride. Anne
        Porter. P64
    Overture to a Dance of Locomotives.
        William Carlos Williams. P82
    The Song of the Engine. H. Worsley-
        Benison. P51
    The Train. Mary E. Coleridge. P51
    Trains. Hope Shepherd. P51
    The Trains. Seumas (James Starkey)
        O'Sullivan. P51
    Troop Train. Karl Shapiro. P84
Rain
    April Rain. Robert Loveman. P51
    A Boy. John Ashbery. P85
    Code of Waters. Teresa Calderon. P71
    Glass Lady. Virginia M. Hahn. P58

God's Rain. Ghulam-Sarwar Yousof. P91
I Like Summer Rain. Chisachi Suehiro. P75
I Stare. Rebecca Caudill. P75
In a Stalled Van. Taufiq Rafat. P91
In Rain. Wendell Berry. P67
In the April Rain. Mary Anderson. P51
Invocation to Rain in Summer. William Cox
    Bennett. P89
Rain. Brian Lee. P75
Little Rain-Drops. Ann ("Aunt Effie")
    Hawkshawe. P51
Rain. Lilian McCrea. P51
Memorial Rain. Archibald MacLeish. P83
Millionfold. Anne Yannie Corrado. P65
Monsoon. Michael D. Clodfelter. P86
My Lady, Lady Jane (Raindrop Tears).
    James Neal Blake. P72
My New Umbrella. M. M. Hutchinson. P51
Outside. Lilian Moore. P75
Pedestrian. Virginia M. Hahn. P58
Poem 13, from The City. Gonzalo Millan.
    P71
The Primal Rain. Erika Schott. P72
Rain. Brian Winter. P73
Rain. Lilian McCrea. P51
Rain in Summer. Henry Wadsworth
    Longfellow. P51,P89
Rain on the Island. Jennifer Campbell.
    P74
Rain Sizes. John Ciardi. P75
Rain Song. Jean Hogan Dudley. P72
Rain Spirit Passing. Denise Levertov. P85
Rain-Walking. Myra Cohn Livingston. P75
The Rain. William Henry Davies. P51
The Rain. Unknown. P51
Raindrops. April Jeffers. P74
Rainy Nights. Irene Thompson. P51
Rhyme of Rain. John Holmes. P75
Signs of Rain. Edward Jenner. P89
Summer Rain. Eve Merriam. P75
A Summer Shower. Unknown. P51
Tending a Cookout in Pouring Rain... X.
    J. Kennedy. P63
"War Is as Natural as the Rain". James
    Webb. P86
Who Likes the Rain?. Unknown. P51
Rain. Brian Winter. P73
Writing, from A Thai Divine Comedy.
    Montri Umavijani. P92
Written in March. William Wordsworth. P51
"The **rain** arrives to contemplate the plaza".
    Imperfect Preterite. Juan Cameron. P71
"**Rain** comes in various sizes". Rain Sizes.
    John Ciardi. P75
"The **rain** drizzled and shifted". The Water
    Buffalo (Hanoi, 1972). Blaga
    Dimitrova. P70
"**Rain** dropping heavily".Sonora Foothill
    Winter Rainstorm. David Kuehnert. P77

Rain in Summer. Henry Wadsworth Longfellow.
    P51,P89
The **Rain** It Raineth. Charles Bowen. P75
The **Rain** of Time. Jerry Craven. P65
"**Rain** on the Green Grass". The Rain.
    Unknown. P51
Rain on the Island. Jennifer Campbell. P74
Rain Sizes. John Ciardi. P75
Rain Song. Jean Hogan Dudley. P72
Rain Spirit Passing. Denise Levertov. P85
"The **rain** overtook us in the dusky wood". In
    Front of the Cave. Nikolai Hristozov.
    P70
Rain-Walking. Myra Cohn Livingston. P75
"The **rain**". Code of Waters. Teresa Calderon.
    P71
The **Rain**. William Henry Davies. P51
The **Rain**. Unknown. P51
The **Rainbow** Dared the Storm. Emma Crobaugh.
    P68
The **Rainbow** Fairies. Unknown. P51
The **Rainbows**. John Frank. P65
Raindrops. April Jeffers. P74
"**Raindrops** on Young Leaves". Jerald Ball.
    P72
The **Rainy** Day. Henry Wadsworth Longfellow.
    P89
Rainy Nights. Irene Thompson. P51,P75
The **Rake's** Progress. Vonna Adrian. P63
Raleigh, Sir Walter
    Lines Found in his Bible in the Gate-
    House... P89
    The Nymph's Reply. P89
Ramirez, Eleanor Gude
    For One Sweet Sign. P72
Ramsey, Jarold (tr.)
    How Her Teeth Were Pulled. Unknown. P78
    A Kalapuya Prophecy. Unknown. P78
Ramsey, Paul
    Pompous. P63
Randall Jarrell. Karl Shapiro. P84
Randolph, Thomas
    Fairies' Song. P90
Rands, William Brighty
    The Cat of Cats. P90
    Gipsy Jane. P51
    Lullaby. P51
    The Pedlar's Caravan. P51
    Polly. P89
    Stalky Jack. P51
    Topsyturvey-World. P90
    The World. P51,P90
Range-Finding. Robert Frost. P82
"**Ranged** in the trees". The Old Bookseller.
    Gilani Kamran. P91
Raniville, Francis O.
    The Trace of God's Hand. P72
Ransom, John Crowe
    Antique Harvesters. P67,P83

Bells for John Whiteside's Daughter. P67,
    P83
Blue Girls. P83
Captain Carpenter. P83
Dead Boy. P83
Dog. P83
The Equilibrists. P67,P83
Here Lies a Lady. P83
Janet Walking. P83
Painted Head. P83
Piazza. P83
Two in August. P67,P83,P83
Vision by Sweetwater. P67
Rao, C. Ramamohan
    Maya. P72
Rape
    Force of Circumstance. Jose Lacaba. P92
Rare Stones. John J. Soldo. P65
"**Rarely** does the artist transcend his". From
    Goethe to Gounod: Concerning a Mutual
    Affaire... Patricia Kirby. P68
Rashed, N.M.
    Our First Journey. C.M. Naim (tr.). P91
Rasmussen, Sandra
    Crash. P72
"The **rasped** edge of the poet's voice".
    Hearing Heaney Read. Gregory Betts.
    P49
"**Rat**-a-tat-tat, rat-a-tat-tat". The Postman.
    Clive Sansom. P51
Ratcliffe, Dorothy Una
    February. P51
    The Pirate's Tea-Party. P51
Rathinavelu, K.
    End Them, If You Can. P72
Rats
    Dark Confusion, from Lost Youth: the Last
    War. Alfred Kreymborg. P82
    Shooting Rats at the Bibb County Dump.
    David Bottoms. P67
    What Became of Them?. Unknown. P51
"**Rats**/Running over". Dark Confusion, from
    Lost Youth: the Last War. Alfred
    Kreymborg. P82
"**Rattat!** rattat!.". Postman's Knock. Rodney
    Bennett. P51
"**Ravages** of time have left no mark". Hall of
    Fraternity. Justice S. Mohan. P72
"**Ravening** coyote comes". Three Songs of Mad
    Coyote. Unknown. P78
Rawlings, Doug
    411 Days and Nights. P86
    Jen II. P86
    Number 7. P86
    Semper Paratus: to the Graduating Class.
    P86
    Survivor's Manual. P86
Ray, David
    Ennui. P63

Saint Flannery. P57
Raymer, Aki
Animals. P74
The **Razor-Seller**. John Wolcott. P90
Re Ezra Pound. Wilfred Watson. P49
Re-cognition. Don Mager. P65
Read the Great Poets. James Tate. P85
Read This with Gestures. John Ciardi. P80
Read to the Animals, or Orpheus at the SPCA.
Irving Feldman. P79
The **Reader**. Fairfield Porter. P64
Reading
Patient. Keith Baker. P63
Reading. M. P. A. Sheaffer. P56
Reading Adonais. Paul Goodman. P84
Reading Outdoors. Joan Drew Ritchings. P63
The **Real** World. Sherry Weakley. P74
Realf, Richard
Indirection. P90
Reality. Robert B. Bradley. P72
Reality
Fata Morgana. Siv Cedering. P64
He Lit His Pipe. Phoebus Delphis. P61
The Illusion II. Jeffrey Adam Sager. P72
In the Thickness. Phillipe Denis. P92
Photograph. Omar Lara. P71
The Real World. Sherry Weakley. P74
Song of the Bald Eagle. Unknown. P78
Speech to a Crowd. Archibald MacLeish.
P83
""**Really**, it is not the ".". In This Age of
Hard Trying, Nonchalance Is Good And.
Marianne Moore. P83
Reaney, James
The Lament of the Poet, from Animated
Film... P49
The Man Who Made up Roses, from Animated
Film... P49
Saint Mark, from Animated Film... P49
Triads II. P49
Rear-Porches of an Apartment-Building.
Maxwell Bodenheim. P82
Reasons Before and After the Fact. John C.
Gilmore. P86
Rebecca's Hymn, from Ivanhoe. Sir Walter
Scott. P89
Rebellion
Lower the Standard. Karl Shapiro. P84
The Old Jew. Maxwell Bodenheim. P82
Once There Was a Man. Stephen Crane. P81
"**Receive** me, my King, master of
Christendom". On His Death Bed.
Bleddyn Fardd. P87
Recessional. Rudyard Kipling. P90
Reckoning. Harry B. Sheftel. P72
The **Reconciliation**. Archibald MacLeish. P83
Recovery Song. Barry Wallenstein. P57
Rector, Liam
The Eventual Music. P79

Recuerdo. Edna St. Vincent Millay. P82
The **Red** Clouds at Sunset. Micen Atem. P53
The **Red** Hills '83. Terry M. Paulsgrove. P77
"A **red** caravan, a greyhound bitch". The
Flame. Isaac Daniel Hooson. P87
"**Red** clay and flood". The Vital Brine. Lois
Wilson Parker. P68
"**Red** for Santa's fur-lined cloak". All in
Red. Eileen Mathias. P51
Red in Autumn. Elizabeth Gould. P51
Red Kite. Philip Appleman. P64
Red Raspberries. Gary Selden. P63
The **Red** Sea Divides. Peggy Zuleika Lynch.
P72
The **Red** Wheelbarrow. William Carlos
Williams. P75,P82
"**Red** willow". Navajo Correspondences (First
Set). Unknown. P78
"The **red** young men under the ground". A Song,
from Red Ant Way. Unknown. P78
The **Red-Handled** Hatchet. Mark Sanders. P63
Redcloud, Prince
And Then. P80
Atop. P50
Reddy, J. Bapu
Limping Boat. P72
Reddy, T. Vasudeva
A Pinch of Faith. P72
Redemption. George Herbert. P59
"The **Redness** of Her Lower Lip". Unknown. P62
Reese, Lizette Woodworth
Anne. P81
Daffodils. P81
A Holiday. P81
Lydia. P81
A Puritan Lady. P81
Tears. P81
This Very Hour. P81
Trust. P81
Wild Cherry. P81
Reeves, James
The Old Wife and the Ghost. P55
Refici, Marion Louise
Hallowe'en. P74
"**Reflected** in the kindness of your eyes".
Love's Miracle. Hyacinthe Hill. P65
Reflections. Shawn Ketchum. P73
Reflections. Miriam Waddington. P49
Reflections in the River. James Stephens.
P68
Reflections of a Sometime Child. Gaston
Pelletier. P68
A **Refusal** To Mourn the Death, by Fire, of a
Child... Dylan Thomas. P48
"**Reg** wished me to go with him to the field".
My Mother. Claude McKay. P82
Regeneration. Henry Vaughan. P59
Reincanation of the Butchers. Oscar Hahn.
P71

"The **relationship** between knife and wound".
    Wound and Knife. Gyorgy Somlyo. P92
Relationships, Human
    At Home. Edward Willey. P63
    At Play in the Field. Edward Butscher.
        P64
    At the Shore. Harvey Shapiro. P64
    At the Used Book Sale. Ken Stone. P56
    Backstage at the Fillmore. Elaine
        Demakas. P58
    Better Refrain. Marian Gleason. P63
    The Blanks. Sheryl L. Nelms. P56
    Blind Dates. Kandy Arnold. P58
    Counting the Losses. Kandy Arnold. P58
    The Dangerous Cliffs. Bruce Bennett. P63
    Echoes. John Zurlo. P56
    Eurydice. Hugh Seidman. P64
    Firewood (for Steve Sanfield). Doc
        Dachtler. P77
    Four Poems for Robin. Gary Snyder. P85
    Horrorscope. John D. Engle Jr. P63
    Horse. Louise Gluck. P52
    In the Big Country Dreams Stay Alive.
        Maryann Calendrille. P64
    Inquiline. Allen Planz. P64
    Interior Dialogue. David Ignatow. P84
    Krasnopresnenskaya Station. N. Scott
        Momaday. P85
    Mr. Computer Science. Elaine Demakas. P58
    The New Regime. Wendy Cope. P63
    Polonaise. David Wevill. P49
    The Seducer Steps Out, Just at Dusk.
        Janis Lull. P88
    Song. Robert Creeley. P85
    Sordid Love. Elaine Demakas. P58
    Triads II. James Reaney. P49
    Two in August. John Crowe Ransom. P83
    Untitled #4. Ian Brennan. P58
    Viola D'Amore. Joan Van Poznak. P63
    Weathers. R. B. Weber. P64
    "Wherever I Look". Unknown. P62
    Who, Me?. Hallie Hodgson. P63
    Wife, Children and Friends. William
        Robert Spencer. P89
    Winter. Peter Karaangov. P70
    The World. Robert Creeley. P85
Relativity. Bozhidar Bozhilov. P70
The **Relic.** John Donne. P59
Relics of Love. Biswakesh. P72
The **Relief** of Lucknow (September 25, 1857).
    Robert T. S. Lowell. P90
Religion
    Brahma. Ralph Waldo Emerson. P89
    I Gave My Life for Thee. Frances Ridley
        Havergal. P89
    Question?. E. Manuel Huber. P72
    Religion and Doctrine. John Hay. P89
    Saint Flannery. David Ray. P57
    Satire 3. John Donne. P59

    Tradition. Helen Winter. P88
    The Wosld (1). Henry Vaughan. P59
Religion and Doctrine. John Hay. P89
Religion Poem. Caroline Knox. P63
Religion, Primitive
    I Stood Upon a Highway. Stephen Crane.
        P81
Religious Poetry
    The Bhagavadgita, sel. Unknown. P48
Remedies
    And the Physician?., from Lost Youth: the
        Last War. Alfred Kreymborg. P82
    Try Tropic. Genevieve Taggard. P83
"**Remember,** friend, the little town". In the
    Name of Progress. William F. Landgraf.
    P72
A **Remembered** Workshop Critic: Louis A.
    Haselmayer. Herbert M. Kirkham. P68
"**Remembering** that war, I'd near believe".
    Night Operations, Coastal Command RAF.
    Howard Nemerov. P63
"**Remembering** the Angry Words in the Meeting
    with Her". Unknown. P62
"**Remembering,** with Full Throat Uplifted".
    Unknown. P62
"**Remote** and beyond, lonely farms...". Orion.
    William Everson. P84
The **Removal.** William Stanley Merwin. P85
The **Removal.** Unknown. P78
Rendall, Elizabeth
    The Wind. P51
Renewal
    The Celestial Passion. Richard Watson
        Gilder. P81
    Evolution. John Banister Tabb. P81
    I Will Go into the Ghetto. Charles
        Reznikoff. P83
    Out of These, the First Love. Wallace
        William Winchell. P72
    Spring Freshet. Crary Elwood. P72
    Trust. Lizette Woodworth Reese. P81
"**Repeated** dawn climbs over time". Dawn
    Climbs over Time. Emma Crobaugh. P72
Repentance. Sion Cent. P87
Repine, Shelly
    Will You Be There?. P74
A **Reply.** Jay Dougherty. P63
Report 'Present'. Eleftheria Kounrouri. P72
"**Reptilian** green the wrinkled throat". Sir
    Gawaine and the Green Knight. Yvor
    Winters. P83
"**Repute** and dishonour confused, and, like
    enough". Two-faced. Sion Tudur. P87
Requiem for Ralph. Sara Lewis Kline. P65
The **Rescue.** Robert Creeley. P85
The **Residual** Years. William Everson. P84
A **Resolution.** Ben Howard. P68
Respected Graves. David Ignatow. P64
Response to Music. Dorothea Neale. P65

Responsibilities
    Stopping by Woods on a Snowy Evening.
      Robert Frost. P82
Retired. Mary-Elizabeth Epstein. P72
The **Retreat**. Henry Vaughan. P59
"A **retrospective**". Breastfeeding at the Art
    Gallery of Ontario... Sharon Berg. P49
The **Return**. Mauricio Electorat. P71
Returning Home. Alice Mann Roney. P72
Returning to De Valera's Cottage. Tom
    McCarthy. P92
Reuben Bright. Edward Arlington Robinson.
    P81
Reunion. Ulrich Troubetzkoy. P65
Reunions
    Frank. Frona Lane. P72
    I Remember a Season. Maria Luisa
      Spaziani. P61
    Midnight. Lisel Mueller. P88
    The Reconciliation. Archibald MacLeish.
      P83
    Song of Egla. Maria Gowen Brooks. P89
    Spring Freshet. Crary Elwood. P72
Revelry of the Dying. Bartholomew Dowling.
    P90
Revenge
    End Them, If You Can. K. Rathinavelu. P72
    Siege. Omar Lara. P71
    To the White Fiends. Claude McKay. P82
Revere, Paul
    Paul Revere's Ride. Henry Wadsworth
      Longfellow. P90
Reversal. Eleanore-Melissa. P68
"**Reviewing** me without undue elation". A
    Choice of Weapons. Stanley Kunitz. P83
Revisiting Detroit. Karen Kania. P88
Revival. John Berryman. P79
Revolutions and Revolutionaries
    Facing the Way. Alice Walker. P85
    A Guerrilla Handbook. Amiri (LeRoi Jones)
      Baraka. P85
Rew di ranno. Unknown. P87
Rewards
    It Must Someday be Answered. Elidir Sais.
      P87
"**Rex** regum, prince, easy of eulogy". On His
    Death-Bed. Meilyr. P87
Rexroth, Kenneth
    Climbing Milestone Mountain, August 22,
      1937. P84
    Kings River Canyon, fr. Andree Rexroth.
      P84
    Mt. Tamalpais, fr. Andree Rexroth. P84
    Night Below Zero. P84
    On Flower Wreath Hill. P52
    A Sword in a Cloud of Light. P84
Reznikoff, Charles
    About Thirty Jews Were Taken to Chelmno,
      fr. Mass Graves. P83

    The Body Is Like Roots Stretching Down
      into the Earth. P83
    Ghetto Funeral, fr. Five Groups of Verse.
      P83
    I Will Go into the Ghetto. P83
    Let Other People Come as Streams. P83
    The Stars Are Hidden, fr. Five Groups of
      Verse. P83
    A Sunny Day, fr. Five Groups of Verse.
      P83
Rhapsody on a Windy Night. Thomas Stearns
    Eliot. P83
Rhigos. Robert Minhinnick. P54
Rhodes, Margaret G.
    The Best of All. P51
    The Carol Singers. P51
Rhydcymerau. David Gwenallt Jones. P87
Rhyme
    On the Rhyming of Four-Line Verses. J. F.
      O'Connor. P63
A **Rhyme** for Washing Hands. Unknown. P51
Rhyme of Rain. John Holmes. P75
A **Rhyme** Sheet of Other Lands. Hugh
    Chesterman. P51
"**Rhys**, rose of the summer moor".
    Exhortation. Dafydd Nanmor. P87
Ribald River Rhyme. William Cole. P63
Ricco, Mazzeo di
    "Six Years Have I Suffered". Frede Jensen
      (tr.). P69
Rice, James A.
    They Failed to Tell Me. P86
Rice, Sir Cecil Spring
    I Vow to Thee, My Country. P51
Rich Days. William Henry Davies. P51
"The **rich** man's son inherits lands". The
    Heritage. James Russell Lowell. P89
Rich, Adrienne
    Diving into the Wreck. P85
    Orion. P85
    Planetarium. P85
    Prospective Immigrants Please Note. P85
    Snapshots of a Daughter-in-Law. P85
    The Stranger. P85
Rich, Mark
    Clocks and Locks. P63
Rich, Vera
    A Hymn for October 15th. P68
    A Problem in Genetics. P68
"**Richard** & Randall, & one who never did".
    The Dream Songs, sels. John Berryman.
    P52
Richard Cory. Edward Arlington Robinson. P89,
    P81
Richards, Thomas
    Sheepdog. Tony Conran (tr.). P87
Richardson, Marion Jane
    I. P65
    Independence. P65

Stars. P65
Richardson, Susan
    Nicki's Sparrow. P56
Richstone, May
    Not What We Had in Mind. P63
Ricketts, Marijane G.
    At the Craft Show. P56
Riddle with Guesses. Tom Disch. P63
A Riddle. Catharine Fanshawe. P90
Riddles
    The Encyclopedist's Conundrum. Kirby
        Olson. P63
    Riddle with Guesses. Tom Disch. P63
    A Riddle. Catharine Fanshawe. P90
    Unwind My Riddle. Stephen Crane. P81
    What Is It?. H. E. Wilkinson. P51
"Ride a-Cock Horse to Banbury Cross".
    Unknown. P51
Rider, Chester G.
    Tiger at the Bar. P72
Rides and Riding-Horses
    Fresh Horses Should Be Waiting. Caroline
        Knox. P88
    The Wild Ride. Louise Imogen Guiney. P81
Ridge, Lola
    Faces. P82
    The Ghetto, sel. P82
    Marie. P82
The Ridger. Nigel Jenkins. P54
"Ridiculous dreamer:.". Events Like Palaces.
    Paz Molina. P71
Riding Westward. Harvey Shapiro. P64
Ridlon, Marci
    Bad Day. P50
Riedemann, Clemente
    The Man from Leipzig. Steven F. White
        (tr.). P71
    The Tree of the World. Steven F. White
        (tr.). P71
    Wekufe's Dream. Steven F. White (tr.).
        P71
' Riffs', sel. Dennis Lee. P49
Rigg, Sarah
    October Afternoon. P74
Right Now and Here. Barbara Kitterman
    Shepherd. P68
"Right at the open limepit". Poem About a
    Herring. Abraham Sutzkever. P48
Riley, James Whitcomb
    The First Blue-Bird. P89
    Little Orphant Annie. P89
    A Sea Song from the Shore. P51
    When the Frost Is on the Punkin. P89
Riley, Tom
    A Bit of Enlightenment. P63
    "Margaret Sanger". P63
    The Primitive Astronomer. P63
Rilke, Rainer Maria
    'The Ninth Elegy', from The Duinesian

Elegies. Elaine E. Boney (tr.). P48
    The Youth Dreams. L. Lewisohn (tr.). P90
Rime of the Ancient Mariner. Samuel Taylor
    Coleridge. P90
Rineer, Evelyn Sewell
    Friends. P65
    To Diana. P65
The Ring of. Charles Olson. P85
"Ring out, wild bells, to the wild sky". The
    New Year, from In Memoriam. Lord
    Tennyson. P89
"Ring-ting! I wish I were a primrose".
    Wishing. William Allingham. P51
Rings (jewelry)
    Wedding-Ring. Denise Levertov. P85
Ringstad, Muriel
    To My Son. P72
Riprap. Gary Snyder. P85
"Rise heart; thy Lord is risen...". Easter.
    George Herbert. P59
"Rise, heir of fresh eternity". Easter Day.
    Richard Crashaw. P59
Ritchie, Elisavietta
    Challenges. P63
    Elegy for the Other Woman. P63
    Wishing for Water in February. P56
Ritchings, Joan Drew
    Attic Dance. P63
    Reading Outdoors. P63
Rites and Ceremonies
    Ascension Thursday. Saunders Lewis. P87
    Ceremony. Richard Wilbur. P84
    Oberammergau. David Gwenallt Jones. P87
    Paddlewheel Under a Boat. Peter Pal Hoth
        Nyang. P53
    Sweat-House Ritual No.1. Unknown. P78
"Ritual around purple toilet bowl:.".
    Bangkok Sights. Robert Schlosser. P86
Rivalry in Love. William Walsh. P89
The Rivals. James Stephens. P51
River Boats. Grace D. Yerbury. P68
"A river is born". Water. Krishna Srinivas.
    P72
The River of Bees. William Stanley Merwin.
    P85
River Roads. Carl Sandburg. P82
"The river reverses its flow". Poem 48, from
    The City. Gonzalo Millan. P71
"The river takes the land, and leaves
    nothing". The Slip. Wendell Berry. P67
"The river's tent is broken...". The Fire
    Sermon, fr. The Waste Land. Thomas
    Stearns Eliot. P83
The River-Merchant's Wife: a Letter. Ezra
    Pound. P82
Rivers
    The Cataract of Lodore. Robert Southey.
        P90
    Cool with Sleeping Rivers. Salvatore

Quasimodo. P61

The Growing River. Rodney Bennett. P51

Home!. Lu Cicada. P77

The Klondike. Edward Arlington Robinson. P81

The Lordly Hudson. Paul Goodman. P84

The Negro Speaks of Rivers. Langston Hughes. P83

The Nile. Leigh Hunt. P90

Reflections in the River. James Stephens. P68

The Thames. M. M. Hutchinson. P51

"'The rivers rush into the sea'.". The Song of the Bird. Henry Wadsworth Longfellow. P51

Riyaz, Fahmida
Beauty Competition. C.M. Naim (tr.). P91
Iqleema. C.M. Naim (tr.). P91
To Auden. C.M. Naim (tr.). P91

Rizpah 17--. Lord Tennyson. P90

Rizvi, I. H.
The Bride of Spring. P72

The **Road** (Version 1). Blaga Dimitrova. P70

The **Road** (Version 2, with echoes of Emily Dickinson). Blaga Dimitrova. P70

The **Road** Not Taken. Robert Frost. P82

The **Road** to a Friend's House. Lorraine Blankenhorn. P72

Road to the Congo. Nyagak Pinien. P53

The **Road** to Town. H. M. Sarson. P51

The **Road**. Helene Johnson. P90

Roads. Aristoteles Espana. P71

Roads. Geoff Fiorito. P58

Roads and Trails
Florida Road Workers. Langston Hughes. P83
The Poet Falls in Love with a Cowboy. Linda M. Hasselstrom. P88
The Road to Town. H. M. Sarson. P51
The Road. Helene Johnson. P90
Roads. Geoff Fiorito. P58
Roadways. John Masefield. P51
Street. Waldo Rojas. P71
Tewkesbury Road. John Masefield. P51

Roadways. John Masefield. P51

Roberts, Cecil
"Lord of Sea and Earth and Air". P60

Roberts, Elizabeth Madox
"The Day Is Done". P60
Father's Story. P89

Roberts, G. D.
Old Morgan. P51

Roberts, John T. (tr.)
"Alas! As the Ocean of Milk Was Stirred...". Unknown. P62
"Although They Both Exist". Unknown. P62
"Among All the Wives of the Village Chief". Unknown. P62
"As They Fly Around the Shoulders of the Ox". Unknown. P62
"At Daybreak, with Snow Coming". Unknown. P62
"At the Time of Ploughing". Unknown. P62
"'Be Pleased, Oh Beloved!'". Unknown. P62
"The Beautiful Women, in Separation...". Unknown. P62
"Because Her Breasts". Unknown. P62
"Because She Is Overcome at Seeing You". Unknown. P62
"The Bee Which Indeed Wants to Drink the Nectar". Unknown. P62
"The Bees Wander Restlessly in the Mango Grove". Unknown. P62
"Blessed Are the Deaf and Blind". Unknown. P62
"Blessed Are Those Women". Unknown. P62
"The Bogus Bride-Night Garment". Unknown. P62
"A Bow, Returning to Its Natural Straightness". Unknown. P62
"The Bride's Beloved's Laughter-Filled Eyes". Unknown. P62
"The Buffalo, Tormented by the Heat". Unknown. P62
"Certainly, If a Man Takes the Initiative". Unknown. P62
"Clean Your Back, Slim-Waisted!.". Unknown. P62
"The Crow, Whose Mind Is Given Solely". Unknown. P62
"The Crows, Dipping Their Beaks in the Stream". Unknown. P62
"Darkest Night Has Passed". Unknown. P62
"The Delicate Girl Is Washed". Unknown. P62
"Do Not Trust Those Evil Men Who Owe You Money". Unknown. P62
"Don't Neglect This One, Saying". Unknown. P62
"The Dying Chief with Effort Tells His Son". Unknown. P62
"The Earth with Its Palasha Blossoms". Unknown. P62
"Even Though Everything Gets Burned up ". Unknown. P62
"The Fire Burns in the Sacrifice Enclosure". Unknown. P62
"The Flash of Lightning Gives a Glimpse of the Clouds". Unknown. P62
"The Flop-Eared Dog Is Gone". Unknown. P62
"For Those Who Know Their Own Hearts". Unknown. P62
"The Garland-Girl Giving Out Freshly Broken Blossoms". Unknown. P62
"The Godavari River, at Midnight". Unknown. P62
"A Good Man, Lacking Wealth. Unknown.

P62

"Good People Are Not Vexed in Misery".
Unknown. P62

"A Good Person Does Not Get Angry".
Unknown. P62

"Grabbing a Handful of Powder in Her
Hand". Unknown. P62

"Greetings to Thee, Oh Lord of the Day".
Unknown. P62

"Having Seen the Clouds Welling Up".
Unknown. P62

"Having Seen the Son of the Lord of the
House". Unknown. P62

"Having Seen the Tip of a Tooth".
Unknown. P62

"He Drinks in the Lovliness of the Young
Girl's...". Unknown. P62

"He Is Truly a Friend Who Does What Is To
Be Done". Unknown. P62

"The Hearts of Great Men". Unknown. P62

"Her Face in Separation from You".
Unknown. P62

"Her Face Is Like the Moon--.". Unknown.
P62

"Her Lips with Noisy Curses". Unknown.
P62

"Here and There in the Bamboo Grove".
Unknown. P62

"Hey, Slim-Wasted girl, Clean Off Your
Back". Unknown. P62

"His Beauty Remains in My Eyes". Unknown.
P62

"His Form Is in My Eyes". Unknown. P62

"The Housewife, Pursuing the Child".
Unknown. P62

"How Can the One Who Is Somehow the
Sweetheart". Unknown. P62

"How Can There be Unpleasantness from the
Mouth...". Unknown. P62

"How Like the Black-Spotted Antelope".
Unknown. P62

"However Much It Takes To Create
Friendship". Unknown. P62

"The Husband Laughs When His Face".
Unknown. P62

"I Have No Use for Either the Bad Man or
the Good". Unknown. P62

"I Heard That Person Say". Unknown. P62

"I Remember Her Mouth Screeching an
Oath". Unknown. P62

"I Remember My Beloved Stepping
Backwards". Unknown. P62

"I Remember the Joy". Unknown. P62

"If He Is Not Your Lover". Unknown. P62

"If He Is Not Your Lover, Oh Friend".
Unknown. P62

"If Her Eyes Are Not Half Shut". Unknown.
P62

"If People Get Angry, Let Them, If They

Carry On...". Unknown. P62

"If the Traveller Were to Go". Unknown.
P62

"If You Are Not His Beloved". Unknown.
P62

"In a Forest Region There Might Occur a
Crooked Tree". Unknown. P62

"In a Grove by the Godavari River, a
Monkey". Unknown. P62

"In Its Last Hours, the Mind of a Great
Man". Unknown. P62

"In Separation, an Unfaithful Woman Is
Like Poison". Unknown. P62

"In the Autumn, the Water of a Great
Lake". Unknown. P62

"In the Belly of the Weeping Cloud-Bull".
Unknown. P62

"In the Evening Give Homage". Unknown.
P62

"In the Town Are Many Youths". Unknown.
P62

"In This Whole Wide Earth". Unknown. P62

"In Youth, Oh Daughter, You Are Like a
Full River". Unknown. P62

"Just As the Full Moon, At the Moment of
Daybreak". Unknown. P62

"Just Today He Awoke and Left". Unknown.
P62

"The Kindly Speech of a Great Man".
Unknown. P62

"The Laughing Girl is 'liberated'...".
Unknown. P62

"Look! a Bow-Shaped Line". Unknown. P62

"Look! a Newly Dyed Flag Put on the
Roof". Unknown. P62

"Look! At the Gate of the Little Village
Temple". Unknown. P62

"Look! Coming Out of the Hollow Tree".
Unknown. P62

"Look! Coming Out of the Ripe Mango
Seed". Unknown. P62

"Look! In the Middle of the Cow-Pen".
Unknown. P62

"Look! Motionless and Still on a Lotus-
Leaf". Unknown. P62

"Look! Oh Slender One. The White Clouds
in the Fall". Unknown. P62

"Look! Suspended Upside-Down on His Web".
Unknown. P62

"Look! The Anger Held by This Strong-
Minded Girl". Unknown. P62

"Look! the Buffalo Cows, Being Led
Away...". Unknown. P62

"Look! The Cloud, Not Strong Enough".
Unknown. P62

"Look! the Forest Elephant Vainly Tries".
Unknown. P62

"Look! the Traveller Smells, Touches,
Kisses". Unknown. P62

"Look! There Descends from the Plane of the Heavens". Unknown. P62

"Look! There Is a Sobbing from the Laundry". Unknown. P62

"Look, Oh Traveller, Even That Shadow of Yours". Unknown. P62

"Love's Arrows Come in Dual Form". Unknown. P62

"Love's Qualities Are Very Frustrating". Unknown. P62

"A Man Is Not Angered by an Event". Unknown. P62

"A Man Whose Wife Is the Boss". Unknown. P62

"The Mate of the Bull Elephant Who Is Trampled...". Unknown. P62

"The Men of Ceylon, Oh Son". Unknown. P62

"The Mendicant Watches the Circle of Her Navel". Unknown. P62

Methinks the Divine Nectar. Unknown. P62

"The Monkey Pauses, Shakes the Branch". Unknown. P62

"The Moon-Beams, Set in Motion". Unknown. P62

"The Mother-in-Law, with singleness of Purpose". Unknown. P62

"'My Boy, Just As an Old Cow Pours Forth Milk'". Unknown. P62

"My Boy, She Takes Notice of Other Youths". Unknown. P62

"My Dear, Go Down Only the Most Likely Road". Unknown. P62

"My Friends, Why Do You Tell Me". Unknown. P62

"My Old Friends Are Gone". Unknown. P62

"The Necklace of a Young Women". Unknown. P62

"The Nectar of the Jasmine Bud". Unknown. P62

"The New-Moon Sliver in the Sky". Unknown. P62

"Oh Auntie, Just as Thirst Is Not Quenched". Unknown. P62

"Oh Bee Desirous of Drinking the Nectar". Unknown. P62

"Oh Beloved with Eyes Closed in Feigned Sleep--.". Unknown. P62

"Oh Child, My Own Life Is More Dear to Me". Unknown. P62

"Oh Clever Poverty, You Are Enamoured". Unknown. P62

"Oh Cupid, I Will Worship Your Feet". Unknown. P62

"Oh Daughter, If You Enter the House". Unknown. P62

"Oh Friend, Do Not Cry". Unknown. P62

"Oh Friend, Whoever Stretched and Dappled". Unknown. P62

"Oh God, Make an Affair with Another Woman...". Unknown. P62

"Oh Heart, at the End of the Third Day". Unknown. P62

"Oh Heart, If You Must Depart, Then Leave". Unknown. P62

"Oh Heart, Unafraid of Your Own Judgement". Unknown. P62

"Oh Madhuka Flower in the Great Glade". Unknown. P62

"Oh Mendicant, Go Your Way". Unknown. P62

"Oh Moon, Full of Nectar, Diadem of the Heavens". Unknown. P62

'Oh Mother, Today I am Pained". Unknown. P62

"Oh Slave-Girl Longing for the Sound...". Unknown. P62

"O Son of the Village-Headman". Unknown. P62

"Oh Thou Shameless and Ungrateful!.". Unknown. P62

"'On My Hands and Feet'". Unknown. P62

"On the Pretext of a Rough Descent to the River". Unknown. P62

"Once, Oh Ungrateful Bee". Unknown. P62

"One Nipple Drips, One Is Made Erect". Unknown. P62

"The Ones Who Know Not How". Unknown. P62

"Only When Women's Eyes". Unknown. P62

"Overcoming Untimely Anger". Unknown. P62

"The Peaks of the Vinhya Mountains". Unknown. P62

"People Who Do Not Even Know the Alphabet". Unknown. P62

"The Ploughman Drinks the Bitter-Herb Tea". Unknown. P62

"The Poor Man in the Wintertime". Unknown. P62

"Praise Pasupati's Evening Libation". Unknown. P62

"The Pulinda Tribesmen Standing on the Mountain Peak". Unknown. P62

"Quickly Embracing the Neck of Her Husband". Unknown. P62

"The Redness of Her Lower Lip". Unknown. P62

"Remembering the Angry Words in the Meeting with Her". Unknown. P62

"Remembering, with Full Throat Uplifted". Unknown. P62

"The Rooster Speaks to Thieves". Unknown. P62

"The Row of Bees, Delighted by the Nectar". Unknown. P62

"The Secrets of a Good Man". Unknown. P62

"Seeing Her Beloved with a Swollen Lip". Unknown. P62

"Separation from the One We Love". Unknown. P62

"She Is Sending Out Her Messenger".

Unknown. P62
"She Runs in Front of You". Unknown. P62
"She Who in Love-Making Gave Hundreds of
   Orders". Unknown. P62
"The Slender Girl". Unknown. P62
"Smiling Without Showing Her Teeth".
   Unknown. P62
"Son, Although She Is Shy". Unknown. P62
"Surely You Can See That Love Is Proper".
   Unknown. P62
"Surely You Dwell in My Heart". Unknown.
   P62
"'Take a Look at This!' says the wife".
   Unknown. P62
"Tell Me, Oh Subhaga, Which One Of Your
   Mistakes". Unknown. P62
"That Redness of Her Lip". Unknown. P62
"There Are Some Especially Who Stretch
   Their Mouths". Unknown. P62
"They Torment Us, Yet Give Us Happiness".
   Unknown. P62
"A Thing of True Value Is That Which Is
   Handy". Unknown. P62
"Thinking to Himself, 'I Will Make Love
   to Her'". Unknown. P62
"Those Who Know the Good and Bad".
   Unknown. P62
"Thoughtless!.". Unknown. P62
"Today with My Remembrance of Pleasures".
   Unknown. P62
"The Trap-Wary Crow Doesn't Want the Rice
   Ball". Unknown. P62
"The Traveller's Wife with Continually
   Flowing Tears". Unknown. P62
"Truly, Mother, Winter Has Made".
   Unknown. P62
"The Two Sit Sadly". Unknown. P62
"The Unfaithful Wife Gathers Together,
   Crying". Unknown. P62
"Virtuous Women, Still Undressed and
   Bashful". Unknown. P62
"We Think Less of Women When Out of Our
   Vision". Unknown. P62
"What Can Be Said in Words". Unknown. P62
"What Does the Beautiful One". Unknown.
   P62
"What Was Said by Him, His Eyes
   Blossoming...". Unknown. P62
"Whatever Part of My Body He Meditates
   On". Unknown. P62
"Whatever Tune My Lover Plays I Dance
   to". Unknown. P62
"When Her Husband's Brother Is of
   Improper Mind". Unknown. P62
"When Her Son Was Climbing on the Back".
   Unknown. P62
"When In His View, I Will Stand".
   Unknown. P62
"When the Noble Girl Looks at Her New

Nail Wounds". Unknown. P62
"When the Pair of Deer Face the Blow".
   Unknown. P62
"When the Solitary Deer, Erect and with
   Longing Ears". Unknown. P62
"Whenever the Traveller, with Fingers
   Spread". Unknown. P62
"Where Has the Disc of the Sun Gone".
   Unknown. P62
"Wherever I Look". Unknown. P62
"Wherever the Brother-in-Law Whirls".
   Unknown. P62
"While Her Husband Is Asleep". Unknown.
   P62
"Who Does Not Gain Wisdom". Unknown. P62
"Who Is Stronger Than a Couple Angered by
   Love". Unknown. P62
"Who Uses Goods Made by the Base?.".
   Unknown. P62
"Whoever Is Fat Was Born Like That".
   Unknown. P62
"Whom Do You Greet, Oh Son". Unknown. P62
"Why Do You Cry with Downcast Face".
   Unknown. P62
"'Why Don't You Keep Asking the Red
   Amarinth'". Unknown. P62
"Why Is It, Even as I Lie on My Half of
   the Bed". Unknown. P62
"With Bent Neck, the Traveller's Wife".
   Unknown. P62
"With Deep Regret for My Anger". Unknown.
   P62
"With Effort Is a Lover Got". Unknown.
   P62
"With Lamp Blown Out, Breath Held".
   Unknown. P62
"The Woman, with the Palm of Her Hand".
   Unknown. P62
"You Are Gone, Not Caring!.". Unknown.
   P62
"The Young Bees Pursue the Nail-Shredded
   Mango...". Unknown. P62
"Your Wife Is Faithful, but Mine Is
   Unfaithful". Unknown. P62
"Robin and Richard". Unknown. P51
Robin Hood. Rachel MacAndrew. P51
"Robin Hood, Robin Hood". Unknown. P51
"Robin Sang Sweetly". Unknown. P51
"Robin friend has gone to bed". Bed-Time.
   Laurence Alma-Tadema. P51
Robin's Song. Rodney Bennett. P51
The Robin's Song. Unknown. P51
The Robin. Laurence Alma-Tadema. P51
The Robin. O. M. Bent. P51
Robins
   Credo. William DeWitt Snodgrass. P63
"Robins sang in England". Robin's Song.
   Rodney Bennett. P51
Robinson. Weldon Kees P84

"Robinson at cards at the Algonquin; a
    thin". Aspects of Robinson. Weldon
    Kees. P84
Robinson, Edward Arlington
    Ben Johnson Entertains a Man from
        Stratford. P81
    Cassandra. P81
    The Clerks. P81
    Credo. P81
    Hillcrest. P81
    Isaac and Archibald. P81
    The Klondike. P81
    Luke Havergal. P81
    The Man Against the Sky. P81
    Miniver Cheevy. P81
    Mr. Flood's Party. P81
    On the Night of a Friend's Wedding. P81
    Reuben Bright. P81
    Richard Cory. P89,P81
    Three Quatrains. P81
Robinson, Mary K.
    The Brown Frog. P51
    The Dandelion Puff. P51
    The Queen Bee. P51
Rock Art Prayer. Ron Pickup. P77
Rock Me to Sleep. Elizabeth Akers. P89
"The rock that withstands man's arrogance".
    Divorce. Richard Eberhart. P79
The Rock-a-by Lady. Eugene Field. P51
"Rock-a-bye, Baby, thy Cradle Is Green".
    Unknown. P51
Rockbound Pass in January. Jon Olander. P77
Rockey, Tobin F.
    Muse. P68
Rocks
    "The Pale Stone Under My Rib". Simon
        Perchik. P64
    Pebbles. Edith King. P51
    Pebbles on a Lonely Beach. H. Olav Wang.
        P68
    Stone Quarries. Salvatore Quasimodo. P61
Rodas, Virginia
    When You Realize That... P72
Roeske, Paulette
    Dream of Trains. P88
    Going Under. P88
    A Little Drama. P88
    Snake in the Yard. P88
Roethke, Theodore
    The Auction. P84
    Big Wind. P84
    The Coming of the Cold. P84
    The Far Field. P84
    Fau Bauman, Frau Schmidt, and Frau
        Schwartze. P84
    Highway: Michigan. P84
    The Lost Son. P84
    Lull. P84
    Moss-Gathering. P84

My Papa's Waltz. P84
Orchids. P84
The Shape of the Fire. P84
Transplanting. P84
A Walk in Late Summer. P84
Where Knock Is Open Wide. P84
Rogers, F.
    Wishes. P51
Rogers, Samuel
    A Tear. P90
    A Wish. P51
Rojas, Waldo
    Chess. Steven F. White (tr.). P71
    The Circle Closes Here. Steven F. White
        (tr.). P71
    Hotel De La Gare. Steven F. White (tr.).
        P71
    Rotterdam. Steven F. White (tr.). P71
    Street. Steven F. White (tr.). P71
    We Will Not Hand Over the Night. Steven
        F. White (tr.). P71
Rojek, Amy
    What Sparks My Imagination. P74
"Roll on, thou ball, roll on!.". To the
    Terrestrial Globe. Sir William
    Schwenck Gilbert. P90
Rolle, Richard
    The Form of Living. P66
    'Love Is Life That Lasts Ay'. P66
Rollings, Alane
    Laws of Drifting. P88
Romains, Jules
    Light, Light, Somewhat Revolving...
        Charles Guenther (tr.). P61
"Roman ashes are all around us now". Voices
    from Pompeii. Chester A. Beck Jr. P68
Romance. Gabriel Setoun. P51
The Romance Language. James Merrill. P79
A Romance. Kandy Arnold. P58
Romantic Letter. Josephine Miles. P84
Rome, Italy
    All Roads Lead to Rome. Freddie P.
        Hanson. P72
    Love Song: Pincio, sels. Frederika
        Blankner. P65
Ronan, Richard
    Seated Nude. P57
Rondine of the Rare Device. Wesli Court. P63
Roner, C. J.
    Percussion Grenade Democracy. P72
Roney, Alice Mann
    Returning Home. P72
Ronsard, Pierre de
    The Rose. Andrew Lang (tr.). P90
Roofs
    Eaves. Ellis Jones. P87
Roofs. Lyubomir Levchev. P70
Rook, Pearl Newton
    Camp of the inds. P72

Decorators Incorporated. P68
If I Am Your Daughter. P68
Like Swallows. P68
"The **rooks** are alive". What the Weather
    Does. Unknown. P51
The **Room**. Nino Nikolov. P70
Rooms
    The Bedroom. Nino Nikolov. P70
    Father's Bedroom. Robert Lowell. P84
    Robinson. Weldon Kees. P84
    The Room. Nino Nikolov. P70
"The **Rooster** Speaks to Thieves". Unknown.
    P62
Roots and Branches. Robert Duncan. P84
Ropes, P. A.
    Before Spring. P51
    Bluebells. P51
    Daffodils. P51
    The Disappointed Shrimper. P51
    Dust. P51
    Glow-Worms. P51
    I Will Keep Christmas. P51
    If. P51
    In February. P51
    Poppies. P51
    Violets. P51
    A Watering Rhyme. P51
Rosanov, Vasily Vasilievich
    The Apocalypse of Our Times, sel. S. S.
        Koteliansky (tr.). P48
Rosberg, Rose
    Aztec Gods. P56
Rose. Mehdi Akhavan Sales. P91
The **Rose** and the Gauntlet. John Sterling.
    P90
The **Rose** and the Heather. Pedrog. P87
The **Rose** and the Worm. James Camp. P63
"A **rose** crushed by a passing hurricane!.".
    Love. Alice Boughtwood. P68
"A **rose** is not a rose". Rose of God. Hemant
    Kulkarni. P72
Rose of Sharon. Ann Griffiths. P87
Rose, M.
    Carp. P77
Rose, Margaret
    Autumn Song. P51
    The Butterfly. P51
    A Little Bird's Song. P51
    The Little Fir Tree. P51
    The Magic Whistle. P51
    November. P51
The **Rose**. Johann Wolfgang von Goethe. P89
The **Rose**. Pierre de Ronsard. P90
Roseliep, Raymond
    Man Holding Cat. P68
"**Rosemary** Blossoms". Jerald Ball. P72
Rosemary's French Garden Basket. Carolyn
    O'Harrow Pintye. P72
Rosenau, Anita H.

En Route. P68
Rosenberger, F. C.
    At Seventy. P63
    A Slender Book of Verse and It's
        Purchaser. P63
Roses. George (Mary Ann Cross) Eliot. P51
Roses
    Of a Rose, a Lovely Rose. Unknown. P66
    Rose. Mehdi Akhavan Sales. P91
    Rose of God. Hemant Kulkarni. P72
    The Rose. Pierre de Ronsard. P90
    A Sigh. Harriet Elizabeth Spofford. P81
"**Roses** are red". Blue Poem. Hubert E. Hix.
    P63
Rosetti, Christina
    Boats Sail on the Rivers. P51
Rosetti, Christina Georgina
    Minnie and Mattie. P51
Rosetti, Christine
    Love Me--I Love You. P51
Rossetti, Christina Georgina
    The Catepillar. P51
    A Chill. P51
    The City Mouse and the Garden Mouse. P51
    The Ferryman. P51
    A Frisky Lamb. P51
    Goblin Market, sel. P51
    The Green Cornfield. P51
    Is the Moon Tired?. P51
    Lambs at Play. P51
    Love Me -- I Love You. P51
    The Milking-Maid. P89
    O Sailor, Come Ashore. P51
    O Wind, Where Have You Been?. P51
    October. P51
    The Pancake. P51
    The Sound of the Wind. P51
    Spring Quiet. P51
    There's Snow on the Fields. P51
    Three Plum Buns. P51
    Up Hill. P89
    What Does the Bee Do?. P51
    Who Has Seen the Wind?. P51
    Winter. P51
Rossetti, Dante Gabriel
    The Nevermore. P89
    Sudden Light. P90
Rossetti, Dante Gabriel (tr.)
    Of England, and of Its Marvels. Fazio
        degli Uberti. P90
    Of Three Girls and of Their Talk.
        Giovanni Boccaccio. P90
"A **rosy** shield upon its back". The Dead
    Crab. Andrew Young. P89
Rot Below Adam's Peak (Sri Lanka). Earle
    Birney. P49
Rotella, Alexis
    Haiku. P63
Rothenberg Jerome (tr.)

Archaic Song of Dr. Tom the Shaman. Unknown. P78

Before They Made Things Be Alive They Spoke. Lucario Cuevish. P78

"Big Rabbit Goes To See His Baby". Unknown. P78

"Chipmunk Can't Drag it Along". Unknown. P78

"Chipmunk was standing". Unknown. P78

Five Flower World Variations. Unknown. P78

The Flowering War. Unknown. P78

For the God of Peyote. Unknown. P78

THe Great Farter. Nakasuk. P78

The Killer. Unknown. P78

"Mole Makes His Pole Redhot". Unknown. P78

Muu's Way or Pictures from the Uterine World. Unknown. P78

The Net of Moon: a Pawnee Hand Game Vision. Unknown. P78

"Pinionjay Shits Pebbles". Unknown. P78

Sixty-Six Poems for a Blackfoot Bundle. Unknown. P78

Song Picture No. 106. Unknown. P78

Song Picture No. 17. Unknown. P78

Song Picture No. 27. Unknown. P78

Song Picture No. 29. Unknown. P78

Song Picture No. 30. Unknown. P78

Song Picture No. 34. Unknown. P78

Song Picture No. 54. Unknown. P78

Song Picture No. 56. Unknown. P78

Song Picture No. 58. Unknown. P78

Song Picture No. 64. Unknown. P78

Song Picture No. 66. Unknown. P78

Song Picture No. 68. Unknown. P78

Song Picture No. 69. Unknown. P78

Song Picture No. 71. Unknown. P78

Song Picture No. 82. Unknown. P78

Song Picture No. 83. Unknown. P78

Song Picture No. 85. Unknown. P78

Song Picture No. 86. Unknown. P78

Song Picture No. 87. Unknown. P78

Song Picture No. 96. Unknown. P78

A Song, from Red Ant Way. Unknown. P78

Sweat-House Ritual No.1. Unknown. P78

The 13th Horse Song of Frank Mitchell (White). Unknown. P78

"A Turkey Is Dancing Near the Rocks". Unknown. P78

The 12th Horse Song of Frank Mitchell (Blue). Unknown. P78

"Wildcat Was Walking". Unknown. P78

"A rotten doll buried in a garden". I Play Childish Songs with a Grimace on My Lips. Gonzalo Millan. P71

Rotterdam. Waldo Rojas. P71

Rotterdam, Holland

Vision of Rotterdam. Gregory Corso. P85

"Roughly stated". My Rumi-Nation. Julia Older. P63

"Round About in a Fair Ring-a". Unknown. P51

Route Seven. Juan Cameron. P71

"Row after row with strict impunity". Ode to the Confederate Dead. Allen Tate. P67, P83

"The Row of Bees, Delighted by the Nectar". Unknown. P62

The Rowan Tree. Ruth G. Iodice. P68

"The royal feast was done...". The Fool's Prayer. Edward Rowland Sill. P90

Royalty

The King's Wood. C. S. Holder. P51

Roys, Ralph L. (tr.)

The Book of Chilam Balam: a Chapter..., sel. Unknown. P78

Ruac, Phillip Macar

White Girls. Terese Svoboda (tr.). P53

Rubio, Armando

Anonymous Biography. Steven F. White (tr.). P71

Rudolph the Headsman, from This Is It. Oliver Wendell Holmes. P90

Rufinus

Golden Eyes. Andrew Lang (tr.). P89

Rufty and Tufty. Isabell Hempseed. P51

The Ruin. Dafydd ab [or ab] Gwilym. P87

The Ruined Hearth of Rheged, fr. Poetry from Lost Sagas. Unknown. P87

Rukeyser, Muriel

Easter Eve, 1945. P52

Effort at Speech Between Two People. P84

Poem Out of Childhood. P84

The Speaking Tree. P84

Theory of Flight. P84

Rule Britannia, from Lost Youth: the Last War. Alfred Kreymborg. P82

"Rum-headed, footloose and rainfall fluent". Stormwatch: Fogo Island. Gregory Betts. P49

Runaway. Jerri DuBose. P74

A Rune of Riches. Florence Converse. P51

The Runner. Virginia Bagliore. P72

Running in Winter. William Carpenter. P48

"Rushes of sliver light. A little wind...". City. Roo Borson. P49

Russell, George William ("A.E.")

Frolic. P51

Russell, Hilary

The Day Willis Harder Didn't Kill His Beagle. P63

Earlene Spratt's Lot. P63

Russell, Norman H.

The Boy Wants to Leave. P68

"The russet leaves of the sycamore". The Last Days. George Sterling. P81

Rutherford McDowell, from Spoon River Anthology. Edgar Lee Masters. P82

Rutter, Dawn E.
    Jessie's Cat. P72
Ryan, Abram Joseph
    Sentinel Songs. P90
Ryder Jr., William H.
    The Angel. P86
Ryerson, Alice
    Woe One. P88
    Woe Three. P88
    Woe Two. P88

Sabina, Maria
    The Chants, sel. Henry Munn (tr.). P78
Sachara, Betty Jane
    Old Mother. P72
The Sacred Passion of St. Joseph. Jose
    Lacaba. P92
"The sad great gifts the austere muses bring-
    -.". Our Israfel. Edwin Markham. P81
Sadie and Maud, fr. A Street in Bronzeville.
    Gwendolyn Brooks. P84
Sadness
    My Sad Self. Allen Ginsberg. P85
    Sadness. T. A. Shulgin. P58
Sadness in Springtime. Unknown. P87
"Sadness is a dragon". Sadness. T. A.
    Shulgin. P58
Saffron Pig Pinata. Roger Weingarten. P63
Sag Harbor, the Tchekov Letters. Barbara
    Guest. P64
Sagas
    The Deluge, 1939. Saunders Lewis. P87
    Gwen ap Llywarch and his Father, fr.
        Poetry from Lost Sagas . Unknown. P87
    The Haldighat of New India. Kazi Nazrul
        Islam. P91
The Sage Lectured Brilliantly. Stephen
    Crane. P81
Sager, Jeffrey Adam
    The Illusion II. P72
"Said a Frog on a Log". Unknown. P51
Said I Not So?. George Herbert. P89
"Said the first little chicken". Wishes.
    Unknown. P51
"Said the lion to the lioness--...". Heart
    and Mind. Edith Sitwell. P90
"Said the matron to pretty Miss Whytal".
    Well Bed. Lola Strong Janes. P63
"Said the table to the chair". The Table and
    the Chair. Edward Lear. P90
Said, Fatthy
    A Dialogue. Ameen El Ayoty (tr.). P91
    Hymn of the Lyre Player. Ameen El Ayoty
        (tr.). P91
The Sail of Ulysses. Wallace Stevens. P83
"Sail, Monarchs, rising and falling". Roots

and Branches. Robert Duncan. P84
A Sail. Mikhail Lermontov. P90
"Sailing on the Gulf of Oman". Ribald River
    Rhyme. William Cole. P63
Sailing, Sailing. Lillian Morrison. P63
Saint Cecilia's Day, 1941. Paul Goodman. P84
Saint Flannery. David Ray. P57
St. George's Harbour. Bruce St. John. P68
"St. Jerome". Clerihews. Adrian Vonna. P63
St. John, Bruce
    St. George's Harbour. P68
    Waiting: November 30th. P68
"St. John:.". Letter from the Islands. Diana
    Kwiatkowski. P56
St. Malachy. Thomas Merton. P84
Saint Mark, from Animated Film... James
    Reaney. P49
The Saint Wears a Halo. Peter [pseud.]. P51
Saint-Pol-Roux
    Larks. Charles Guenther (tr.). P61
Saints
    St. Malachy. Thomas Merton. P84
Sais, Elidir
    It Must Someday be Answered. Tony Conran
        (tr.). P87
Salamon, Joanna
    Ballad for a Solonaut. Marianna
        Abrahamowicz (tr.). P92
Sales, Mehdi Akhavan
    Grafts and the Garden. Amin Banani and
        Jascha Kessler (tr.). P91
    A Parched Pitcher. Amin Banani and Jascha
        Kessler (tr.). P91
    Rose. Amin Banani and Jascha Kessler
        (tr.). P91
Salis-Seewis, Johann Gaudenz von
    Song of the Silent Land. Henry Wadsworth
        Longfellow (tr.). P89
Sallah, Tijan M.
    Freedom in the New Air. P72
Sally in Our Alley. Henry Carey. P89
"Sally sat". Tuning the Trumpet. Noa Spears.
    P63
"The salmon's no traitor--from his
    adventure". Going Home. LLawdden. P87
Sam, Kim Young
    My Love (Liliaceae). P72
Sambrook, Joyce
    Wild Thyme. P51
    The Woodpecker. P51
Samik
    Hunger. Edward Field (tr.). P78
Samson on His Blindness, from Samson
    Agonistes. John Milton. P89
"San Francisco airport--.". Coming Home. W.
    D. Ehrhart. P86
San Garde, Evelina
    A Giant's Cake. P51
Sand Castle. Constance Andrea Keremes. P76

Sand Scribblings, sel. Carl Sandburg. P76
"The sand, the wind, and the sea". Free.
        Esther Uhrman. P72
"The sandbacks the tinted trees". Peconic
        Autumn Day. R. B. Weber. P64
Sandbank, Jennie H.
        Stage Fright. P72
Sandburg, Carl
        Blue Island Intersection. P82
        Chicago. P82
        Cool Tombs. P82
        Crapshooters. P82
        Flash Crimson. P82
        Fog. P82
        Four Preludes on Playthings of the Wind.
            P82
        Gargoyle. P82
        Grass. P82
        Halsted Street Car. P82
        Languages. P82
        Love in Labrador. P82
        The People Will Live On. P82
        Prairie Waters by Night. P82
        Prayer After World War. P82
        River Roads. P82
        Sand Scribblings, sel. P76
        The Sins of Kalamazoo. P82
        Ten Definitions of Poetry. P82
Sanders, Mark
        Great Plains Lit. P63
        The Red-Handled Hatchet. P63
        The Turtle. P63
Sandford, Michael
        Clouds. P72
The Sandpiper. Charlotte Zolotow. P76
"Sandra and that boy that's going to get
        her...". Cora Punctuated with
        Strawberries. George Starbuck. P85
"Sandra built a castle out of sand". Sand
        Castle. Constance Andrea Keremes. P76
The Sands O' Dee. Charles Kingsley. P90
Sandstrom, Flora
        The Stately Lady. P51
Sandweiler and Hamm, the Military
        Cemeteries... Wayne Kvam. P68
Sanfield, Steve
        "All Day". P77
        "The Power of Snow". P77
        Preparing for Winter. P77
        The Quality of Life. P77
        Sierra Song. P77
Sangster, Margaret Elizabeth (Munson)
        Are the Children at Home? P89
        Awakening. P81
        Whittier. P81
Sanskrit Songs for Modern Dreamers'. Sheila
        Craft. P72
Sansom, Clive
        The Dustman. P51

The Milkman. P51
The Postman. P51
Santa Claus
        The Gifts. John N. Morris. P79
        Santa Claus. Unknown. P51
Santa Filomena (Florence Nightingale). Henry
        Wadsworth Longfellow. P89
Santayana, George
        As in the Midst of Battle There Is Room.
            P81
        Faith. P89,P81
        Odes. P81
        On a Piece of Tapestry. P81
        On the Death of a Metaphysician. P81
        Solipsism. P81
        These Strewn Thoughts by the Mountain
            Pathway Sprung. P81
        To W.P. P81
        We Needs Must be Divided in the Tomb. P81
"The saplings of the green-tipped birch".
        Never Tell. Unknown. P87
Sapphics on the Violet. John C. Anderson.
        P68
"Sarah told me: you have". Poesia 50 (The
        Quanta of Anguish). Helle Busacca. P72
Sarajevo, from Lost Youth: the Last War.
        Alfred Kreymborg. P82
Sargeant, Lowell E.
        Self Employment. P63
Sargent, Genevieve
        Stopping by Brook at 18. P72
Sargent, Michael T.
        Dying Is Forever. P86
Sarson, H. M.
        Lovely Things. P51
        The Road to Town. P51
Sarson, May
        I Must Away. P51
Sarton, May
        Prisoner at a Desk. P52
Sassafras. Susan Glickman. P49
Sassoon, Siegfried
        A Child's Prayer. P51
        Daybreak in a Garden. P51
        South Wind. P51
Satan
        Envious Satan, from Lost Youth: the Last
            War. Alfred Kreymborg. P82
        Lucifer Alone. Josephine Miles. P84
        The Sifting of Peter. Henry Wadsworth
            Longfellow. P89
"Satan/The envious". Envious Satan, from
        Lost Youth: the Last War. Alfred
        Kreymborg. P82
Satellite City. Mauricio Electorat. P71
Satire
        The Cheshire Cat. Juan Luis Martinez. P71
        Fox Terrier Disappears at the
            Intersection... Juan Luis Martinez.

P71
   Non-Missing Fox Terrier Does Not
      Reappear... Juan Luis Martinez. P71
   To the Noble Women of Llanarth Hall. Evan
      Thomas. P87
   Wynnere and Wastoure. Unknown. P66
Satire 3. John Donne. P59
Saturday Night. Langston Hughes. P83
Saturday Night in the Parthenon. Kenneth
      Patchen. P84
Saturn the Last Titan. Arthur Avergun. P68
Savitzsky, Isabel de
   The Christmas Tree. P51
Saw the Cloud Lynx. Samuel Makidemewabe. P78
Sawyer, Paul
   Quidiron Pro Quo. P63
   Sharper Than a Serpent's Tooth. P63
"The sawyers lie outside the shed". The
      Boathouse. Robert Minhinnick. P54
Saxe, John Godfrey
   The Blind Men and the Elephant. P90
   The Blind Men and the Elephant. P51
Saxton, Jerry
   View from Autumn. P72
"Say not of beauty she is good". Beauty.
      Elinor Wylie. P82
Scalloping Northwest. Allen Planz. P64
"A scarecrow stood in a field one day". The
      Scarecrow. Michael Franklin. P51
"Scared the living". Aurora. Peter Stevens.
      P49
The Scarf. Ivy O. Eastwick. P51
Scaring Crows. Unknown. P51
The Scarlet Woman. Fenton Johnson. P82
Scenes from the Life of the Peppertrees.
      Denise Levertov. P85
Schade, Richard
   The Silver Shadows. P72
Scharper, Diane
   Benedictus. P68
Schemm, Ripley
   9:00 a.m. at Broadway and Walnut on Your
      Birthday. P57
Schevill, James
   The Graffiti Fingers of the Theology
      Student. P48
Schizophrenic Kiss. James Tate. P85
Schleef, Helen
   The Fallen Star. P68
Schlosser, Robert
   Bangkok Sights. P86
   Fear of Sky Death. P86
   Support Troops/Our Brains Are Cooking
      Bugs. P86
Schmidt, Ashley
   Endless Thought. P73
Schneider, Claire
   Inspirations Unlimited. P72
Schneider, Vicki

   Our Parents. P72
Schoeberlein, Marion
   The Music of Spring. P68
The Scholar, from Edwin the Fair. Sir Henry
      Taylor. P90
"Scholars and ardent lovers...". Cat.
      Charles Baudelaire. P61
School
   The Free School-house, Llanrwst. Ieuan
      Glan Geirionydd. P87
   The Madness of a Headmistress. Gavin
      Ewart. P63
   Preposterous. Jim Hall. P63
   School Cheer (Progressive Style). Alma
      Denny. P63
   University. Karl Shapiro. P84
School Cheer (Progressive Style). Alma
      Denny. P63
School Creed. Unknown. P51
School Yard in Summer. T. A. Shulgin. P58
"The School of Beauty's a tavern now".
      Southeast Corner, fr. A Street in
      Bronzeville. Gwendolyn Brooks. P84
Schoonover, Amy Jo
   Divertissement. P72
Schott, Erika
   The Primal Rain. P72
Schulman, Grace
   Blessed Is the Light. P64
   Easy As Wind. P64
   Images of Gravity. P64
   The Island. P64
   'Let There Be Translators!'. P79
   The Marsh. P64
   Songs of Our Cells. P64
   The Swans. P64
Schulze, Axel
   Landscape. Frederic Will (tr.). P92
Schuster, David
   Concrete Green. P56
Schuyler, James
   Empathy and New Year. P64
   In January. P64
   Poem. P64
   The Sky Eats up the Trees. P64
Schwartz, Delmore
   Calmly We Walk Through This April's Day.
      P84
   A Dog Named Ego, the Snowflakes as
      Kisses. P84
   Dogs Are Shakespearean, Children Are
      Strangers. P84
   During December's Death. P84
   Father and Son. P84
   The Heavy Bear Who Goes with Me. P84
   I Am to My Own Heart Merely a Serf. P84
   In the Naked Bed, in Plato's Cave. P84
   Once and for All. P84
   Parlez-Vous Francais?. P84

Prothalamion. P84
The Sin of Hamlet. P84
Socrates' Ghost Must Haunt Me Now. P84
Schwerner, Armand
Tablet IX. P64
Tablet XXIII. P64
Tablet XXV. P64
Schwerner, Armand (tr.)
Coon Cons Coyote, Coyote Eats Coon...
Unknown. P78
Dream. Unknown. P78
Her Elegy. Unknown. P78
Insult Before Gift-Giving. Unknown. P78
The Little Random Creatures. Unknown. P78
A Man's Song About His Daughter. Unknown.
P78
Moon Eclipse Exorcism. Unknown. P78
The Old Man's Song, About His Wife.
Unknown. P78
Spring Fjord. Unknown. P78
Tsimshian Mourning Song. Unknown. P78
What the Informant Said to Franz Boas in
1920. Unknown. P78
A Woman's Song, About Men. Unknown. P78
The Science of the Night. Stanley Kunitz.
P83
The Scissor-Man. Madeleine Nightingale. P51
Scobie, Stephen
Lethbridge, Alberta; Thursday Evening,
November... P49
Scorpion Summer. Terry M. Paulsgrove. P77
Scotland
Up Fair Kilties!. Russ Traunstein. P63
"Scott Joplin". Gavin Ewart. P63
Scott, Robert N.
Barefoot. P68
Scott, Sir Walter
Breathes There the Man?. P90
Friday. P51
The Gallant Ship. P51
Hie Away!. P51
Hunting Song. P89
Lochinvar. P51
An Old Time Christmas, from Marmion. P90
Rebecca's Hymn, from Ivanhoe. P89
Scott-Gatty, Sir Alfred A.
The Three Little Pigs. P51
Scott-Hopper, Queenie
Amy Elizabeth Ermyntrude Annie. P51
My Party. P51
What the Thrush Says. P51
Scottsboro, too, Is Worth Its Song. Countee
Cullen. P83
Scrapbooks. Nikki Giovanni. P85
Scratch Farmer. John Tripp. P54
The Scream Is a Kind of Coffin. Paz Molina.
P71
The Scream. Majeed Amjad. P91
The Scrutiny. Richard Lovelace. P59

Scudder, Eliza
The Love of God. P89
Vesper Hymn. P89
Sculpture and Sculptors
The Hook. Theodore Weiss. P84
The Monument. Elizabeth Bishop. P84
Sea
Adriatc. Charles Tinkham. P56
At Melville's Tomb. Hart Crane. P83
The Autumn Sea. Tong-Choon Shin. P72
The Castle by the Sea. Johann Ludwig
Uhland. P90
Cauquil. Sergio Mansilla. P71
Come Unto These Yellow Sands. William
Shakespeare. P51
Concrete Green. David Schuster. P56
The Forsaken Merman, sel. Matthew Arnold.
P51
A Grave. Marianne Moore. P83
The Idea of Order at Key West. Wallace
Stevens. P83
Memo to a Far Descendant. Ann Shermer.
P65
O Sailor, Come Ashore. Christina Georgina
Rossetti. P51
The Ocean's Treasure. Todd Kusserow. P74
On the Watershed. Tibor Tollas. P61
On This Shore. Siv Cedering. P64
Oread. Hilda ("H.D.") Doolittle. P82
Partner of the Sea. Kevin Cline. P58
Sea. David Shreve. P73
Sea Embrace. Lakshmi Bai. P72
Sea Gods. Hilda ("H.D.") Doolittle. P82
Sea Song. Allan Cunningham. P51
The Sea. Bryan Waller ("Barry Cornwall")
Procter. P89
The Sea. Angie Chung. P73
Seascape. Eugenio Montale. P61
Sea. David Shreve. P73
Sitting in the Sand. Karla Kuskin. P76
There Are Big Waves. Eleanor Farjeon. P51
Until I Saw the Sea. Lilian Moore. P76
Wave, sel. Barbara Guest. P64
White Horses. Irene F. Pawsey. P51
Words or Spoors, fr. Omneros. Mohammed
Dib. P91
Sea Embrace. Lakshmi Bai. P72
Sea Fairies. Patricia Hubbell. P55
Sea Fairies. Eileen Mathias. P51
Sea Gods. Hilda ("H.D.") Doolittle. P82
Sea Gulls in the Rain. H. Wendy Jones. P72
The Sea Gypsy. Richard Hovey. P81
Sea Shell. Amy Lowell. P51
Sea Shore Shanty. Bobbi Katz. P76
Sea Song. Allan Cunningham. P51
A Sea Song from the Shore. James Whitcomb
Riley. P51
Sea Travel
The Image Repetition. Douglas Barbour.

P49
    Sailing, Sailing. Lillian Morrison. P63
"The sea at a distance glints now and
    again...". Burning Brambles. Roland
    Mathias. P54
"The sea flows in silently". For the Desert
    Island, from For the Desert Island.
    Tae-ch'ul Shin. P92
"Sea spray glistens the marble god". A
    Vision. Kolyo Sevov. P70
"Sea, oh sea". Sea. David Shreve. P73
Sea-Drift. Siv Cedering. P64
The Sea-Gull. Mary Howitt. P51
Sea-Weed. David Herbert Lawrence. P76
"The Sea-god, when he walked the beach,
    shared out". Foam. Roland Jones. P87
"Sea-weed sways and sways and swirls". Sea-
    Weed. David Herbert Lawrence. P76
"Sea/Alive, moving, shimmering, quivering".
    Sea Embrace. Lakshmi Bai. P72
The Sea. E. M. Adams. P51
The Sea. Angie Chung. P73
The Sea. Bryan Waller ("Barry Cornwall")
    Procter. P89
The Seafarer. Ezra Pound. P82
Seager, Millicent
    Bird's Nests. P51
"Seagull". Magic Words to Feel Better.
    Nakasuk. P78
"Seagull flying from the sea". A Feather for
    My Cap. Ivy O. Eastwick. P51
The Seagull. Dafydd ab [or ab] Gwilym. P87
The Seagull. Stanley Moss. P64
Seagulls
    The Seagull. Dafydd ab [or ab] Gwilym.
    P87
    The Seagull. Stanley Moss. P64
"The seagulls and the terns". Ocean Beach
    House. R. B. Weber. P64
"Seagulls' Crying". Sunset Blues. Maxine
    Kumin. P76
Seamen
    Columbus. Joaquin Miller. P81
    The Lighthouse. Marjorie Wilson. P51
    Ode for à Master Mariner Ashore. Louise
    Imogen Guiney. P81
    Phantoms All. Harriet Elizabeth Spofford.
    P81
    Relativity. Bozhidar Bozhilov. P70
    The Sea Gypsy. Richard Hovey. P81
    A Sea Song from the Shore. James Whitcomb
    Riley. P51
    The Seafarer. Ezra Pound. P82
Seascape. Eugenio Montale. P61
Seashell. Sandra Liatsos. P76
"A seashell is a castle". Shell Castles.
    Rowena Bennett. P76
"A seashell sits on a lonely shore". The
    Ocean's Treasure. Todd Kusserow. P74

Seashore
    Barefoot. Robert N. Scott. P68
    Castles in the Sand. Dorothy Baker. P51
    The Cliff-Top. Robert Bridges. P51
    Crossing a Shore. Gwyn Thomas. P87
    Down by the Beach. Dolores Guglielmo. P72
    Foam. Roland Jones. P87
    Freshwater West Revisited. Roland
    Mathias. P54
    Images on the Beach. Elsa Cross. P92
    A Letter from Gwyther Street. Roland
    Mathias. P54
Seashore. Ondra Lysohorsky. P72
    Portrait in Veiled Waters. Anselm
    Parlatore. P64
    The Sea. E. M. Adams. P51
    Seashore. Ondra Lysohorsky. P72
    Sker. Robert Minhinnick. P54
    The South Shore (Aberystwyth). Bobi
    Jones. P87
    The Stretches of Time and Delights.
    Morgan Hewitt. P68
    Walking Sag Beach. George Bradley. P64
    Whitened Sand. James Richard Hurst. P68
Season of Content. Edna Bacon Morrison. P68
The Season of Phantasmal Peace. Derek
    Walcott. P48
"Season of mists and mellow fruitfulness!.".
    To Autumn. John Keats. P51,P89
Seasons
    Affair D'Amour. Margaret Deland. P89
    All Seasons Shall Be Sweet. Samuel Taylor
    Coleridge. P51
    August. Eunice Fallon. P51
    Autumn Song. Margaret Rose. P51
    Black Beloved. Jamini K. Jagadev. P65
    Calendar Rhyme. Flora Willis Watson. P51
    Changing Times. Vivian M. Singerling. P72
    In February. P. A. Ropes. P51
    Llywarch the Old, fr. Poetry from Lost
    Sagas. Unknown. P87
    Now That the Winter's Gone. Thomas Carew.
    P51
    On the Way to Summer. John Hollander. P79
    Outside. Hugh Chesterman. P51
    Promise. Florence Lacey. P51
    Reckoning. Harry B. Sheftel. P72
    Slow Spring. Katharine (Hinkson) Tynan.
    P51
    Summer Is Nigh. Unknown. P51
    Wild Peaches. Elinor Wylie. P82
    Winter. W. D. Landor. P51
    Winter and Spring. Coventry Patmore. P51
    A Year. Angie You. P73
The Seasons. Yahya Kemal. P91
Seated Nude. Richard Ronan. P57
Seay, James
    Grabbling in Yokna Bottom. P67
    It All Comes Together Outside he

Restroom... P67
No Man's Good Bull. P67
Second Portrait. Sarmad Sehbai. P91
"' Second mistress of the robes--'.". IX--
    Royal Favor. Mary F. Lindsley. P72
Second-Hand Trousers. Taufiq Rafat. P91
The Secret of Death. Sir Edwin Arnold. P89
Secret Places. Irene Thompson. P51
The Secret. Elizabeth Fleming. P51
Secrets. Dorothy C. Dunlap. P72
Secrets
    The Elfin People Fill the Tubes. Winifred
        M. Letts. P51
    The Muse. Bhanushanker O. Vyas. P72
    Never Tell. Unknown. P87
    Secrets. Dorothy C. Dunlap. P72
    'Sheaves in Winter'. James A. Hanf. P65
    Without and Within. Pietro Metastasio.
        P90
"The Secrets of a Good Man". Unknown. P62
Sedley, Sir Charles
    Phillis Is My Only Joy. P89
The Seducer Steps Out, Just at Dusk. Janis
    Lull. P88
See Jane Run. Maryann Calendrille. P64
"See how each of them heaps its own wee
    pile". Riddle with Guesses. Tom Disch.
    P63
"See how the orient dew". On a Drop of Dew.
    Andrew Marvell. P59
"See the bunnies sitting there". Timid
    Bunnies. Jeannie Kirby. P51
"See the kitten on the wall". The Kitten at
    Play. William Wordsworth. P51
"See the yellow catkins cover". A Spring
    Song. Mary Howitt. P51
"See what a lovely shell". The Shell. Lord
    Tennyson. P51
"See with what simplicity". The Picture of
    Little T. C. in a Prospect of Flowers.
    Andrew Marvell. P59
"See! I give myself to you, beloved!.". A
    Gift. Amy Lowell. P82
"See, Mignonne, hath not the rose". The
    Rose. Pierre de Ronsard. P90
Seedam. Lily D. Angle. P63
"Seeding the azure". Spun to Life. Perry
    Brass. P65
Seeds
    Little Brown Seed. Rodney Bennett. P51
"Seeds in a dry pod, tick, tick, tick".
    Petit, the Poet, from Spoon River
    Anthology. Edgar Lee Masters. P82
"Seeing Her Beloved with a Swollen Lip".
    Unknown. P62
Seekers
    Cino. Ezra Pound. P82
    In the Field, Treasure. Anita Skeen. P88
    Three Quatrains. Edward Arlington

Robinson. P81
Seekers of Freedom. Walt Jones. P86
The Seekonk Woods. Galway Kinnell. P52
Seen in Wawa. Michael Joseph Phillips. P56
Seer. Josephine Miles. P84
Segovia, Tomas
    At the Sources. James Irby (tr.). P92
    Canciones sin Su Musica. Nathaniel Tarn
        (tr.). P92
    Dawn of Tomorrow. James Irby (tr.). P92
    Interludio Idilico: Coda. Nathaniel Tarn
        (tr.). P92
Sehbai, Sarmad
    First Portrait. Taufiq Rafat (tr.). P91
    Second Portrait. Taufiq Rafat (tr.). P91
Seidman, Hugh
    Alberts Landing. P64
    Eurydice. P64
    The Immortal. P64
    O Tree. P64
Seiler, Sheila
    Afterglow. P56
    Hard to Say. P56
Selden, Gary
    Deight in Order, Too. P63
    Red Raspberries. P63
"Seldom/I hear foot steps". Flickers.
    Dwarakanath H. Kabadi. P72
Self
    An Aging Canvas. Kandy Arnold. P58
    Anne Rutledge, from Spoon River
        Anthology. Edgar Lee Masters. P82
    Another Side of Me. Beth Hirschfeld. P74
    As You Leave the Room. Wallace Stevens.
        P83
    Belabored Blossom. M. Yvette Hamilton.
        P56
    Blank Spaces. Mary Ann Henn. P56
    Cancion. Denise Levertov. P85
    Cassandra. Louise Bogan. P83
    Cataract. Theodore Weiss. P84
    Coral Stanzas. Michael Heller. P64
    Covered Bridge. Robert Penn Warren. P67
    The Delight Song of Tsoai-Talee. N. Scott
        Momaday. P85
    A Dialogue Between the Soul and Body.
        Andrew Marvell. P59
    Diving into the Wreck. Adrienne Rich. P85
    A Dog Named Ego, the Snowflakes as
        Kisses. Delmore Schwartz. P84
    Ego at the Wheel. Ernest Kroll. P63
    Equations. Yaedi Ignatow. P64
    The Far Field. Theodore Roethke. P84
    For You. Orhan Veli Kanik. P91
    Fugitive. Lisel Mueller. P88
    Ghazal. Jonaid. P92
    The Gift. Lara Colton. P73
    The Good Things in Me. Patricia Lounds.
        P73

Hamilton Greene, from Spoon River
    Anthology. Edgar Lee Masters. P82
He Invents a Vertigo. Alain Bosquet. P61
The Heavy Bear Who Goes with Me. Delmore
    Schwartz. P84
Hello. Gregory Corso. P85
Her Seasons. David Wevill. P49
Histrion. Ezra Pound. P82
Hunting the Snow Owl. Frank Finale. P56
I Am. Jason Gelinas. P73
I Arrive at the Coliseum... Doris Eliz
    Einolf. P72
I Believe in Me. Anisa Dalal. P73
I Was as Full of Air as An Old Bullfrog.
    Pilual Juoc. P53
I Will Go into the Ghetto. Charles
    Reznikoff. P83
Into My Own. Robert Frost. P89
June @!21/84* a Poem with Mistakes
    Included. Eli Mandel. P49
Let No Charitable Hope. Elinor Wylie. P82
Let's Shield Your Light with Our Hand, My
    Heart. Jules Supervielle. P61
A Life's Love. Unknown. P90
Mhtis Outis. William DeWitt Snodgrass.
    P85
Minerals from Stone. Joy Kogawa. P49
Monkhood. John Berryman. P79
Monochrome. Louise Imogen Guiney. P81
My Whisper. Unknown. P61
Myself, from The Song of Myself. Walt
    Whitman. P90
Near the Screen Door. Kevin Cline. P58
No Answers. Mary Ann Henn. P56
Nobility. Tudur Aled. P87
Observe:. Geoff Fiorito. P58
Personification. Josephine Miles. P84
Piazza. John Crowe Ransom. P83
The Place. Robert Penn Warren. P67
Poorly Run Marionette. Kevin Cline. P58
Reflections. Miriam Waddington. P49
Revival. John Berryman. P79
Self-Inquiry. Isaac Watts. P89
Solipsism. George Santayana. P81
The Spirit of the Wood. Paul Baudin. P77
They Found Him Sitting in a Chair. Horace
    Gregory. P83
To Sing the Song. Robert M. Howell. P65
Turning. Lucille Clifton. P52
Untitled #1. Kevin Cline. P58
Untitled #3. Ian Brennan. P58
The Weather. John Newlove. P49
What Could I Be If I Couldn't Be Me?.
    Jaime Ellis. P74
World Breaking Apart. Louise Gluck. P85
The World in Us. Jules Supervielle. P61
XVIII, from Irradiations. John Gould
    Fletcher. P82
Self Employment. Lowell E. Sargeant. P63

Self Help. William Trowbridge. P63
Self, Daniel
    The Dreamer. P74
Self-Hate
    An Agony. As Now. Amiri (LeRoi Jones)
        Baraka. P85
    The Auction. Theodore Roethke. P84
    A Biblical Motif. Boris Kristov. P70
    I Am to My Own Heart Merely a Serf.
        Delmore Schwartz. P84
    The Poet Is a Hospital Clerk. David
        Ignatow. P84
Self-Inquiry. Isaac Watts. P89
Self-Love
    Sing with Your Body. Janice Mirikitani.
        P85
Self-Portrait. Abdul-Latif Akel. P92
Self-Reliance
    How Stump Stood in the Winter. David
        Wagoner. P57
Sellin, Eric (tr.)
    Ifriqiyad/Alternatives, sels. Majid El
        Houssi. P91
    Opening Figure. Mohammed Dib. P91
    The Palaces Under the Moon. Chems Nadir.
        P91
    Poem, fr. Iris Ifriqiya. Majid El Houssi.
        P91
    Sleep Work. Mohammed Dib. P91
    The Third Poem of Leave-Taking. Hamid
        Skif. P91
    Untuned Lute. Chems Nadir. P91
    Words or Spoors, fr. Omneros. Mohammed
        Dib. P91
"Selma, the Io moth that brushes the blue".
    The Io Moth. Betty Wallace. P68
Seltzer, Joanne
    Free Verse. P65
Semper Paratus: to the Graduating Class.
    Doug Rawlings. P86
"Send him off into the wrong". Act of
    Creation. Peter Stevens. P49
"Senora, it is true the Greeks are dead".
    Invocation to the Social Muse.
    Archibald MacLeish. P83
A Sense of Place. Judith Minty. P88
"The senseless sin of the sea is". Superego
    Dictatorship. Kenneth Lynn. P72
Senses and Sensations
    Dinosaur Hill. Robert Hahn. P58
    "From the Quiet Stream". Lorenzo. P77
    "The Full Moon Brimming". Jeff Jones. P77
    "The Sweet Smell of Cedar Sucked Out My
        Breath". Lorenzo. P77
Sentinel Songs. Abram Joseph Ryan. P90
"A sentinel angel, sitting high in glory". A
    Woman's Love. John Hay. P89
The Sentry of Portoferraio. Daniel Mark
    Epstein. P57

Sentry of the Silent. Rene Char. P61

Separation

"Alas! As the Ocean of Milk Was
    Stirred...". Unknown. P62
All in All. C. B. Oppenheimer. P68
Autumn. Georgi Djagarov. P70
"The Beautiful Women, in Separation...".
    Unknown. P62
"Because She Is Overcome at Seeing You".
    Unknown. P62
Black-Eyed Susan. John Gay. P89
"Blessed Are Those Women". Unknown. P62
The Boy Wants to Leave. Norman H.
    Russell. P68
Divorce. Richard Eberhart. P79
Farewell to His Wife. George Gordon, 6th
    Baron Byron. P89
A Farewell. Charles Kingsley. P89
"The Flop-Eared Dog Is Gone". Unknown.
    P62
A Good-by. Alain Bosquet. P61
"Having Seen the Clouds Welling Up".
    Unknown. P62
"Her Face in Separation from You".
    Unknown. P62
"His Beauty Remains in My Eyes". Unknown.
    P62
"How Like the Black-Spotted Antelope".
    Unknown. P62
"I Heard That Person Say". Unknown. P62
I Will Not Let Thee Go. Robert Bridges.
    P89
The Ice Cream Parlor Romance. David
    Ignatow. P84
The Little Girl with Bands on her Teeth.
    Genevieve Taggard. P83
Look Evening's Black Feet Are. Carol
    Pearce. P68
"Oh Heart, at the End of the Third Day".
    Unknown. P62
"Oh Moon, Full of Nectar, Diadem of the
    Heavens". Unknown. P62
"Oh Slave-Girl Longing for the Sound...".
    Unknown. P62
On Leaving. Atanas Dalchev. P70
"'On My Hands and Feet'". Unknown. P62
"The Peaks of the Vinhya Mountains".
    Unknown. P62
Relics of Love. Biswakesh. P72
There Came Whisperings. Stephen Crane.
    P81
"The Two Sit Sadly". Unknown. P62
The Walled Light. Elaine Dallman. P65
"What Can Be Said in Words". Unknown. P62
"With Bent Neck, the Traveller's Wife".
    Unknown. P62
"You Are Gone, Not Caring!.". Unknown.
    P62
"Separation from the One We Love". Unknown.
    P62
September. Mary Howitt. P51
September. Fairfield Porter. P64
"September 1957 summoned by my vision-
    agent". Vision of Rotterdam. Gregory
    Corso. P85
"September now". Six Poems for Nine Crows.
    Judith Minty. P88
"September twenty-second...". After the
    Surprising Conversions. Robert Lowell.
    P84
Sequence. Richard Armour. P63
Serenade, from The Spanish Student. Henry
    Wadsworth Longfellow. P89
"Serene, I fold my hands and wait". Waiting.
    John Burroughs. P89
"Serene, steadfast". The Oaks. Ivan McShane.
    P68
"A serious moment for the water...". The
    Boiling Water. Kenneth Koch. P64

Service

The Lovers of the Poor. Gwendolyn Brooks.
    P84
Sestina from the Home Gardener. Diane
    Wakoski. P85
Sestina: Altaforte. Ezra Pound. P82

Sestinas

Sestina from the Home Gardener. Diane
    Wakoski. P85
Seth Compton, from Spoon River Anthology.
    Edgar Lee Masters. P82

Setoun, Gabriel

Jack Frost. P51
Romance. P51
Setting for the Portrait. Margaret Avison.
    P49
The Setting Sun. Lawrence V. Jowers. P68
The Settler. Alfred Street. P90
"7 a.m. -- Late November". Ben L. Hiatt. P77
The Seven Ages of Elf-Hood. Rachel (Lyman)
    Field. P55
Seven Ages of Man, from As You Like It.
    William Shakespeare. P90
Seven Little Pigs. Unknown. P51
"Seven figures positioned at the Falls".
    Daguerreotypie Der Niagara Falls...
    Herbert Morris. P79
"Seven lovely poplars". Poplars. Helen
    Leuty. P51
"Seven/Were their number". Challenger Lost.
    Edwin A. Falkowski. P72
"'The seventeen of us left...'.". Weathers.
    R. B. Weber. P64
"Seventeen Sylla-.". Haiku. Edmund Conti.
    P63
Several Short Poems. George Swede. P49

Sevov, Kolyo

An Afternoon's Wandering. John Balaban
    (tr.). P70

Song Between the Sea and Sky. John
    Balaban (tr.). P70
A Vision. John Balaban (tr.). P70
Whirlpools. Josephine Jacobsen (tr.). P70
Sewing
    Cousin Shamsu, Durzi. Kaiser Haq. P91
Sexauer, Arwin G.
    Peace Is a Green Bough. P72
A **Shade** for My Scarred Soul. William Zeller.
    P72
The **Shade** of the Magnolia. Eugenio Montale.
    P61
The **Shadow** and the Cross. Salah Abdul-Sabur.
    P91
The **Shadow** of Faith. Michael A. Hemmingson.
    P56
Shadows. Robert Duncan. P84
Shadows
    My Shadow. Robert Louis Stevenson. P89
    Mystic Shadow, Bending Near Me. Stephen
        Crane. P81
    Shadows. Robert Duncan. P84
    Visible, Invisible. Salvatore Quasimodo.
        P61
"**Shadows** on the river crying". Black
    Migrants. Pearl Crayton. P68
Shady Woods. E. M. Adams. P51
"**Shaggy**, and lean, and shrewd...". The
    Woodman's Dog. William Cowper. P51
Shakepeare Sonnets Converted into Couplets.
    Gavin Ewart. P63
Shakespeare. Raymond McCarty. P72
Shakespeare, William
    Blow, Blow, Thou Winter Wind, from As You
        Like It. P89
    Come Unto These Yellow Sands. P51
    Dover Cliff, from King Lear. P89
    End of the Civil War, from Richard III.
        P90
    A Fairy Song. P51
    Fairy's Song, from A Midsummer Night's
        Dream. P90
    Hark! Hark! the Lark. P51
    Healthful Old Age, from As You Like It.
        P90
    Love Dissembled, from As You Like It. P89
    Love's Memory, from All's Well That Ends
        Well. P89
    Love, from The Merchant of Venice. P89
    Mark Antony, over the Body of Caesar. P90
    The Merry Heart. P51
    Seven Ages of Man, from As You Like It.
        P90
    The Shepherd's Life, from Henry VI. P89
    Sleep, from Henry IV. P90
    Spring. P51
    This England. P51
    Under the Greenwood Tree. P51
    Unrequited Love, from Twelfth Night. P89

When Icicles Hang by the Wall, from
    Love's Labor's... P89
When in the Chronicle of Wasted Time
    (Sonnet CVI). P89
Where the Bee Sucks. P51
You Spotted Snakes. P51
Shakespeare, William
    End of the Civil War, from Richard III.
        William Shakespeare. P90
    On the Portrait of Shakespeare. Ben
        Jonson. P90
    Shakepeare Sonnets Converted into
        Couplets. Gavin Ewart. P63
    Shakespeare. Raymond McCarty. P72
    Shakespeare, from Prologue. Samuel
        Johnson. P90
Shakespearean Sonnet. Leah Wroten. P73
"**Shaking** off its warm garments". Clothing.
    Jim Fields. P72
"**Shall** I have the girl I love". A Girls'
    Hair. Dafydd ab Edmwnd. P87
"**Shall** I leave some money...". The Offer.
    Yaedi Ignatow. P64
"**Shall** I mine affections slack". Answer to
    Master Wither's Song. Ben Jonson. P89
"**Shall** we win at love or shall we lose".
    Hotel Transylvanie. Frank O'Hara. P85
Shaman Song, from Wolf Songs and Others of
    the Tlingit. Unknown. P78
"**Shame** upon you, Robin". Song of the
    Milkmaid, from Queen Mary. Lord
    Tennyson. P89
Shammas, Anton
    Dedicatory Entry. Anton Shammas (tr.).
        P92
    Goodboy. Anton Shammas (tr.). P92
Shammas, Anton (tr.)
    Dedicatory Entry. Anton Shammas. P92
    Goodboy. Anton Shammas. P92
Shankar, T. G. Prabha
    TAJ. P72
"The **shape** alone let others prize". Song.
    Mark Akenside. P89
The **Shape** of the Fire. Theodore Roethke. P84
Shapiro, Harvey
    At the Shore. P64
    Battlements. P64
    The Bridge. P64
    July. P64
    Montauk Highway. P64
    Riding Westward. P64
Shapiro, Karl
    Auto Wreck. P84
    The Conscientious Objector. P84
    Elegy for a Dead Soldier. P84
    The Fly. P84
    The Gun. P84
    Jew. P84
    Lord, I Have Seen Too Much. P84

Lower the Standard. P84
My Father's Funeral. P84
Randall Jarrell. P84
The Synagogue. P84
Troop Train. P84
University. P84
V-Letter. P84
Shared Festivals. Wallace Winchell. P65
Sharfman, Bern
  Wine Coolers. P63
Sharks
  Mako. Allen Planz. P64
Sharma, Har Prasad
  Cause of My Distress. P72
Sharma, P. P.
  Advice Against Being Naive. P72
Sharp, William ("Fiona Macleod")
  The Bells of Youth. P51
  Invocation of Peace, sel. P51
  The Unknown Wind. P51
  The Wasp. P51
Sharper Than a Serpent's Tooth. Paul Sawyer.
  P63
Shaw, Anne
  My Temple. P73
Shaw, Janet Beeler
  The Divorce Poem. P88
  The Handless Maiden. P88
She Abandoned Her Body to the Color. Gonzalo
  Munoz. P71
She Don't Bop. Keith Casto. P63
She Is Not Fair to Outward View. Hartley
  Coleridge. P89
"She Is Sending Out Her Messenger". Unknown.
  P62
"She Runs in Front of You". Unknown. P62
"She Said She Don't Love Me Anymore...,"
  from Kiowa... Unknown. P78
"She Who in Love-Making Gave Hundreds of
  Orders". Unknown. P62
"She always stood upon the steps". Watching
  for Papa. Unknown. P89
"She asked me twice". Pity. William Mills.
  P67
"She bursts in on him". The Family in the
  Suburbs: A Situation Comedy. David
  Citino. P63
"She came, holy woman of Jerusalem...". On
  the Hazards of Writing Gloomy Verse.
  Edna Meudt. P68
"She comes from bed". For a Lady of
  Impressions. Richard Parks. P68
"She dances as she dies, as around a reed".
  Dancer. Edgar Degas. P61
"She drew back; he was calm". The Subverted
  Flower. Robert Frost. P82
"She even thinks that up in heaven". For a
  Lady I Know, fr. Four Epitaphs.
  Countee Cullen. P83

"She finally slept but even in sleep...".
  Vigil on a Bay. Julia Hartwig. P92
"She flashes platinum rings". Platinum Rings
  (11/8/76). Charles Cline. P72
"She gave us all her needles and her
  thread". Old Mother. Betty Jane
  Sachara. P72
"She grew up in bedeviled southern
  wilderness". The Ballad of Sue Ellen
  Westerfield. Robert Hayden. P84
"She had cornflowers in her ears". Gipsy
  Jane. William Brighty Rands. P51
"She had not planned it". Today, There Is
  Love. Faye Kicknosway. P88
"She had the children". The Outing. Lorene
  Erickson. P88
"She hangs about the bridge". Let Her Be
  Red. Nyakuoth Macar. P53
"She has a way of making hours sing". Mary's
  Melody (To Mary E. Cox). Grace Ridgway
  Rahamah. P72
"She has gone,--she has left us in
  passion...". Brother Jonathan's Lament
  for Sister Caroline. Oliver Wendell
  Holmes. P90
"She hath no beauty in her face". Patience.
  Paul Hamilton Hayne. P89
"She hides out in creative". Jessa's Late
  Assignment. Al Ortolani. P63
"She hiked; knew she had to". Seated Nude.
  Richard Ronan. P57
"She in whose lipservice". The Goddess.
  Denise Levertov. P85
"She is a rich and rare land". This Native
  Land. Thomas Davis. P51
"' She is dead!' they said to him...". The
  Secret of Death. Sir Edwin Arnold. P89
"She is new, yet in her veins flow". New Her
  Cherokee Face. Jerry Craven. P65
"She lay beside me". Annamese Hands. Richard
  A. Parque. P86
"She lied as much as she could, while she
  lived". Epitaph. Ellis Owen. P87
"She lifted up her head". Loreine: a Horse.
  Arthur Davison Ficke. P89
"She limps with halting painful grace".
  Portrait of an Old Woman. Arthur
  Davidson Ficke. P82
"She mixes blue and mauve and green". The
  Patchwork Quilt. Elizabeth Fleming.
  P51
"She never developed the talents". Epitaph.
  Lois Leurgans. P63
"She said 'Good morning' and he said". In a
  Station of the IRT. F. F. Burch. P63
"She sang beyond the genius of the sea". The
  Idea of Order at Key West. Wallace
  Stevens. P83
"She sits patiently like a nun". Waiting.

John J. Soldo. P65
"She slept, and he, impatient". Decorators
        Incorporated. Pearl Newton Rook. P68
"She stood". Bike Flight. Amy Hundley. P74
"She stood close to a tree and wrinkled".
        Tree Old Woman. Samuel Makidemewabe.
        P78
"She sweeps with many-coloured brooms".
        Evening. Emily Dickinson. P51
"She thinks about skeletons". Daughter.
        Robert Pinsky. P79
"She told the story, and the whole world
        wept". Harriet Beecher Stowe. Paul
        Laurence Dunbar. P90
"She turns and leaps, beautiful...". The
        Dreamer. Christina Leighty. P74
"She wanders in the April woods". Agatha.
        Alfred Austin. P89
"She wanted wine from foreign grapes".
        Applachian Courtship. Dorothy
        Williamson Worth. P65
"She was a lover of primary sources". In the
        Field, Treasure. Anita Skeen. P88
"She was his instrument, and oh". Viola
        D'Amore. Joan Van Poznak. P63
"She were thee Sainte-o-Cumber-Lee". Pitie
        Three Goode Dere Soules. Vivian
        Trollope-Cagle. P65
"She will define for you in the sunny
        morning". Personification. Josephine
        Miles. P84
"She's not addicted. Oh, no!". Bingoholic.
        Shirley Volger Meister. P63
"She's nothing more than the grassy
        waist...". Beverly Carneiro. Robert
        Hill Long. P63
Sheaffer, M. P. A.
        Last Laugh. P68
        Reading. P56
        Spinning Song. P68
' Sheaves in Winter'. James A. Hanf. P65
Sheep
        A Chill. Christina Georgina Rossetti. P51
        The Lamb. William Blake. P51
        The Sheep. Ann Taylor. P51
        The Wonderful Derby Ram. Unknown. P51
Sheep and Lambs. Katharine (Hinkson) Tynan.
        P51
Sheep That Pa in the Night. Irene Warsaw.
        P63
The Sheep. Ann Taylor. P51
Sheepdog. Thomas Richards. P87
Sheftel, Harry B.
        Reckoning. P72
A Shelf Is a Ledge. Gregory Orr. P85
Shell Castles. Rowena Bennett. P76
Shell Secrets. Unknown. P51
"A shell". Goodbye. Molly Johnson. P73
The Shell. James Stephens. P51

The Shell. Lord Tennyson. P51
Shelley, Percy Bysshe
        The Cloud. P89
        I Fear Thy Kisses, Gentle Maiden. P89
        A Lament. P89
        Lines to an Indian Air. P89
        To - ("Music, when soft voices"). P90
        To Ianthe, Sleeping, from Queen Mab. P90
        To Night. P89
        A Widow Bird. P51
Shells
        Goodbye. Molly Johnson. P73
        The Humble Shell. K. S. Venkataramu. P72
        Little Seashell. Celia Uhrman. P72
        On Some Shells Found Inland. Trumbull
                Stickney. P81
        Sea Shell. Amy Lowell. P51
        Seashell. Sandra Liatsos. P76
        Shell Castles. Rowena Bennett. P76
        Shell Secrets. Unknown. P51
        The Shell. James Stephens. P51
        The Shell. Lord Tennyson. P51
        You the Artifact. Alison Shepherd. P68
Shelton, Dave
        Winter. P74
Shepherd. Jeremy Hooker. P54
The Shepherd Boy's Song. J. Bunyan. P51
The Shepherd Boy. Heinrich Heine. P51
The Shepherd's Lament. Johann Wolfgang von
        Goethe. P89
The Shepherd's Life, from Henry VI. William
        Shakespeare. P89
Shepherd, Alison
        A Tale from the Arabian Nights. P68
        You the Artifact. P68
Shepherd, Barbara Kitterman
        Right Now and Here. P68
Shepherd, Hope
        Trains. P51
Shepherd, Jamie
        The Cry. P56
The Shepherd. William Blake. P51
Shepherds and Shepherdesses
        Shepherd. Jeremy Hooker. P54
        The Shepherd Boy. Heinrich Heine. P51
        The Shepherd's Life, from Henry VI.
                William Shakespeare. P89
Shepherds and shepherdesses
        The Shepherd. William Blake. P51
Shepherds and Shepherdesses
        Up, up! Ye Dames and Lasses Gay. Samuel
                Taylor Coleridge. P51
Sheridan; Lady Dufferin, Helen Selina
        Lament of the Irish Emigrant. P89
Sherman. Richard Watson Gilder. P81
Shermer, Ann
        Everyman's Walden. P65
        A Matter of Perspective. P65
        Memo to a Far Descendant. P65

Sherry, Kim
  My Fantasy. P73
Sherwood. Alfred Noyes. P51,P90,P51,P90
Shields, Bobi
  Memories. P74
"The shifting sands reach out to touch the
    sea". Requiem for Ralph. Sara Lewis
    Kline. P65
Shikatani, Gerry
  Postcards. P49
Shin, Tae-ch'ul
  For the Desert Island, from For the
    Desert Island. Marilyn Chin and Tae-
    ch'ul Shin (tr.). P92
  1974, Not Guilty?., from For the Desert
    Island. Marilyn Chin and Tae-ch'ul
    Shin (tr.). P92
  Waiting for Spring,..., from For the
    Desert Island. Marilyn Chin and Tae-
    ch'ul Shin (tr.). P92
Shin, Tong-Choon
  The Autumn Sea. P72
Shine, Perishing Republic. Robinson Jeffers.
    P83
Shining Things. Elizabeth Gould. P51
"Shining like a star--.". Song Picture No.
    69. Unknown. P78
Shinto Tombs. Carl Heinz Kurz. P72
The Shiny Little House. Nancy M. Hayes. P51
"A shiny arm from". Letting Him Go. James
    Tate. P85
A Ship Sails up to Bideford. Herbert
    Asquith. P51
Ship, Sea, and Star. Clifford Davidson. P68
Ships
  The Dream Ship. W. K. Holmes. P51
  The Gallant Ship. Sir Walter Scott. P51
  God Fashioned the Ship. Stephen Crane.
    P81
  The Lights. J. J. Bell. P51
  Old Ironsides. Oliver Wendell Holmes. P90
  Romance. Gabriel Setoun. P51
  A Ship Sails up to Bideford. Herbert
    Asquith. P51
  The Ships. J. J. Bell. P51
Shipwrecks
  Rotterdam. Waldo Rojas. P71
  Sea Gods. Hilda ("H.D.") Doolittle. P82
  The Wreck of the Hesperus. Henry
    Wadsworth Longfellow. P90
"Shirley Temple". Paul Curry Steele. P63
"A shirt is running on the meadow". Storm.
    Agnes Nemes Nagy. P92
Shirt of a Lad. Unknown. P87
Sho Chiku Bai. Howard O. Long. P72
"Shoals of Americans scout supper". Arles, 7
    p.m. Marge Piercy. P63
Shoemakers
  The Cobbler. Unknown. P51

Shooting
  The Mountain Passes, from Lost Youth: the
    Last War. Alfred Kreymborg. P82
  Sarajevo, from Lost Youth: the Last War.
    Alfred Kreymborg. P82
  Shooting Prairie Dogs. Linda M.
    Hasselstrom. P88
  Twenty Million, from Lost Youth: the Last
    War. Alfred Kreymborg. P82
Shooting Prairie Dogs. Linda M. Hasselstrom.
    P88
Shooting Rats at the Bibb County Dump. David
    Bottoms. P67
A Shooting Star. Robert Desnos. P48
Shops and Shopkeepers
  Drug Store. John V. A. Weaver. P82
  Marketing. E. J. Falconer. P51
Shore, Jane
  High Holy Days. P48
A Short Epic Poem in the English Language...
    James S. Koch. P63
A Short Poem. James S. Koch. P63
Short-Term Memory Loss. Tom Disch. P63
"Shot-off/Arms and legs". Vanishing Patriot,
    from Lost Youth: the Last War. Alfred
    Kreymborg. P82
"Should auld acquaintance be forgot". Auld
    Lang Syne. Robert Burns. P89
"Should I get married? Should I be good?.".
    Marriage. Gregory Corso. P85
Should the Wide World Roll Away. Stephen
    Crane. P81
"Should you ask me, whence these stories?.".
    The Song of Hiawatha Selections. Henry
    Wadsworth Longfellow. P90
Shower and Sunshine. Maud Morin. P51
"A shower, a sprinkle". Summer Rain. Eve
    Merriam. P75
Shreedharan, C. K.
  What a Fondness!. P72
Shreve, David
  Sea. P73
The Shrine. Hilda ("H.D.") Doolittle. P82
Shrines
  Shinto Tombs. Carl Heinz Kurz. P72
  The Shrine. Hilda ("H.D.") Doolittle. P82
"Shrivelled hearts, crippled limbs". Relics
    of Love. Biswakesh. P72
"Shrouds of lotus blossoms". Namaste.
    Katherine E. Landry. P72
Shulgin, T. A.
  For Lovers. P58
  Inner Eye. P58
  Landfall. P58
  Sadness. P58
  School Yard in Summer. P58
  Waiting. P58
  Waking. P58
  Water Color. P58

"Shun radiant love and bar him out". Love
        and Doubt. Harry Thurston. P81
"Shut fast again in beauty's sheath".
        Monochrome. Louise Imogen Guiney. P81
Sic Transit Vita. Louise Wilkerson Conn. P72
(SIC)Transcript Gloria, or The Body
        Politician. Irving Feldman. P63
"Sickles sound". Harvest Song. Ludwig Holty.
        P89
"The sickly leaf, still gree had fallen".
        Epitaph for Father and Son. John
        Phillips (Tegidon). P87
"The sickly spring has sadly driven away".
        Springtime. Stephane Mallarme. P61
"Side by side in harmony". Black and White.
        Carolyn Delaney. P74
Sidney, Sir Philip
        My True-Love Hath My Heart. P89
        Psalm 13. P59
Siege. Omar Lara. P71
Siegel, June
        To the Extent That I Haven't a Cat. P63
Siegfried. Randall Jarrell. P84
Siegfriedslage. Lincoln Kirstein. P79
Sierra Song. Steve Sanfield. P77
The Sifting of Peter. Henry Wadsworth
        Longfellow. P89
A Sigh. Harriet Elizabeth Spofford. P81
The Signalled Hour. Juan Cameron. P71
The Signature of Things. Raphael Vargas. P92
Signs of Rain. Edward Jenner. P89
Sigourney, Lydia Huntley
        The Coral Insect. P89
Silence. James Richard Hurst. P68
Silence
        Night Song at Amalfi. Sara Teasdale. P82
        Silence. James Richard Hurst. P68
        Silence, from Spoon River Anthology.
        Edgar Lee Masters. P82
"Silence brought by the dark night...".
        Nightfall. Gwallter Mechain. P87
Silence, from Spoon River Anthology. Edgar
        Lee Masters. P82
"Silence/The quiet before the storm". How
        Lovely. April Honeycutt. P74
"Silence/Walks". Summer Walks. Jaminikanta
        Jagdev. P72
"The silence". The Muse. Bhanushanker O.
        Vyas. P72
Silences. David Keller. P57
Silent Lover. Edward Watkins. P63
Silent Ship. Yahya Kemal. P91
The Silent Snake. Unknown. P51
The Silent Town. Richard Dehmel. P89
Silk Pyjamas. Michael Holstein. P63
Silko, Leslie MArmon
        The Invention of White People. P78
Sill, Edward Rowland
        The Fool's Prayer. P90

Silva, Eddie
        Night of Returning. P56
Silver. Walter De La Mare. P51
Silver Bells. Hamish Hendry. P51
The Silver House. John Lea. P51
The Silver Road. Hamish Hendry. P51
The Silver Shadows. Richard Schade. P72
"The silver birch is a dainty lady". Child's
        Song in Spring. E. Nesbit. P51
"A silver Lucifer". Lunar Baedecker. Mina
        Loy. P82
"The silver rain, the shining sun". The
        Harvest. Alice C. Henderson. P51
Silverman, Hirsch Lazaar
        Polarity. P72
Silverman, Maxine
        Meditations on the Body: Right Hand. P88
        Movements on a Theme. P88
Simmias
        The Grave of Sophocles. William M.
        Hardinge (tr.). P89
Simms, William Gilmore
        The Grape-Vine Swing. P89
Simone, Roberta
        Clerihew Couples. P63
        A Literary History of Cheese. P63
Simple Life
        Country Music. James Merrill. P79
        General Delivery. Ben L. Hiatt. P77
        Kwabenya. Okai. P92
        New England Village. Lou Orfanella. P72
A Simple Question. Joann Marie Everett. P72
"Simple Simon". Unknown. P51
Simplicity
        Once There Was a Man. Stephen Crane. P81
        Time in the Rock or Preludes to
        Definition Selections. Conrad Aiken.
        P82
Simpson, Betty Jane
        Grandma-in-Waiting. P72
Simpson, Louis
        American Poetry. P85
        Chocolates. P85
        Hot Night on Water Street. P85
        My Father in the Night Commanding No. P85
        Physical Universe. P85
        A Story About Chicken Soup. P85
        Stumpfoot on 42nd Street. P57
        Walt Whitman at Bear Mountain. P85
Simpson, Nancy
        Food Director's Testimony. P63
Sin
        "At the Round Earth's Imagined...," from
        Divine... John Donne. P59
        Black Riders. Stephen Crane. P81
        The Equilibrists. John Crowe Ransom. P83
        Flash Crimson. Carl Sandburg. P82
        A Hymn to God the Father. John Donne. P59
        I Stood Upon a High Place. Stephen Crane.

P81
Like a Dream. Raul Zurita. P71
Mary Magdalene. George Herbert. P59
"Oh My Black Soul!...," from Divine
    Meditations. John Donne. P59
On a Reformed Sinner. Laurence Perrine.
    P63
Piers Plowman, sels. Unknown. P66
Said I Not So?. George Herbert. P89
The Sin of Hamlet. Delmore Schwartz. P84
There Was One. Stephen Crane. P81
You Say You Are Holy. Stephen Crane. P81
The Sin of Hamlet. Delmore Schwartz. P84
Since Hanna Moved Away. Judith Viorst. P50
"Since Mercy Is of No Avail to Me...".
    Giacomo da Lentini. P69
"Since She Whom I Loved...," from Divine
    Meditations. John Donne. P59
Since That Time. Ellin E. Carter. P56
"Since few remember '24.". From an Athlete
    Living Old. James Camp. P63
"Since I am coming to that holy room". Hymn
    to God My God, in My Sickness. John
    Donne. P59
"Since I in storms used to be". The Wreath.
    Henry Vaughan. P59
"Since I invited the river". Wherever I Go.
    Al Mahmud. P91
"Since of no creature living the last
    breath". Fatal Interview, sel. Edna
    St. Vincent Millay. P82
"Since they were morose in August". The
    Branch. Stanley Moss. P64
"Sing a Song of People". Lois Lenski. P60
Sing Ivy. Unknown. P51
Sing Love, Small Frog. Lisa Grenelle. P65
"Sing a song of cobbler!.". Jeremy Hobbler.
    Unknown. P51
"Sing a song of hollow logs". Song of Summer
    Days. J. W. Foley. P51
"Sing a song of mincemeat". Mincemeat.
    Elizabeth Gould. P51
"Sing a song of scissor-men". The Scissor-
    Man. Madeleine Nightingale. P51
"Sing a song of washing-up". The Washing-up
    Song. Elizabeth Gould. P51
Sing with Your Body. Janice Mirikitani. P85
"Sing, magnarello, merrily". The Leaf-
    Picking. Frederic Mistral. P89
"Sing, oh, sing, sweet violin". Ode to
    Strings. Maia Linden. P65
Sing-Song Rhyme. Unknown. P51
Singerling, Vivian M.
    Changing Times. P72
The Singers in a Cloud. (Frederick) Ridgely
    Torrence. P81
Singh, R. K.
    3. P72
Singleton, Marti

From a Line by Cyril Dabydeen. P49
Northeast. P49
"Singling out a park ranger in Yosemite".
    Calvin. Bayla Winters. P56
Sinnah, Mohammed Ibrahim Abu
    The Betrayal of Violets. M.S. Farid
        (tr.). P91
    The Vision of a Martyr. M.S. Farid (tr.).
        P91
The Sins of Kalamazoo. Carl Sandburg. P82
"Sion, the companion of saints". Asking a
    Stallion. Gutun Owain. P87
Sioux Metamorphosis. Lucario Cuevish. P78
Sir Gawaine and the Green Knight. Yvor
    Winters. P83
Sir Gawayn and the Grene Knyght. Unknown.
    P66
Sir Lancelot and Queen Guinevere. Lord
    Tennyson. P89
Sir Launfal. Thomas Chestre. P66
Sir Nicketty Nox. Hugh Chesterman. P51
Sir Orfeo. Unknown. P66
"Sister, awake, close not your eyes".
    Madrigal. Unknown. P51
Sisters. See Brothers and Sisters
The Sisters. John Banister Tabb. P81
Sisyphus. Albert Tallman. P68
Sit Down, Sad Soul. Bryan Waller ("Barry
    Cornwall") Procter. P89
"Sit down beside me on the stadium stair".
    At Delphi. Abigail S. Bean. P68
"Sithen the sege and the assaut was sesed at
    Troye ". Sir Gawayn and the Grene
    Knyght. Unknown. P66
Sitting in the Sand. Karla Kuskin. P76
"Sitting on the porch I shuffle the cards".
    August. Dan Murray. P64
"Sitting, viewing the church". Summer Sun.
    Emily Welch. P74
Sitwell, Edith
    Heart and Mind. P90
    The King of China's Daughter. P51
"Six Little Mice Sat Down To Spin". Unknown.
    P51
Six O'Clock. Owen Dodson. P84
"Six day's labour". The Tree House. Kaleem
    Omar. P91
Six of One. George Bradley. P64
Six Poems for Nine Crows. Judith Minty. P88
"Six Years Have I Suffered". Mazzeo di
    Ricco. P69
"Six street-ends come together here". Blue
    Island Intersection. Carl Sandburg.
    P82
Sixty-Six Poems for a Blackfoot Bundle.
    Unknown. P78
Skating and Skaters
    Ice Skaters. John Gracen Brown. P68
Skeen, Anita

For Susan, Turning Thirty. P88
In the Field, Treasure. P88
Skeleton and Spirit. Unknown. P55
Skeletons
As You Leave the Room. Wallace Stevens. P83
The Palaces Under the Moon. Chems Nadir. P91
Skeleton and Spirit. Unknown. P55
The Witch of Coos. Robert Frost. P82
Sker. Robert Minhinnick. P54
Skif, Hamid
The Third Poem of Leave-Taking. Eric Sellin (tr.). P91
Skinner, Knute
Bailey. P63
The Girl Next Door. P63
The Obligation. P63
A Social Engagement. P63
Skippets, the Bad One. Christine E. Bradley. P51
Skunk. Will Staple. P77
Sky
Blue Magic. Roberta Goldstein. P72
Landscape. Omar Lara. P71
Old Manuscript. Alfred Kreymborg. P82
The Sky Is up Above the Roof. Paul Verlaine. P89
The Upper Skies. Robert Bridges. P51
The Sky Eats up the Trees. James Schuyler. P64
The Sky Is up Above the Roof. Paul Verlaine. P89
"The sky is dark, and the hills are white". Norse Lullaby. Eugene Field. P51
"The sky is only a white lens". Indian Summer. Nicolae Breban. P92
"A sky that has never known sun, moon or stars". Rear-Porches of an Apartment-Building. Maxwell Bodenheim. P82
"The sky was blue, so blue, that day". For the Candle Light. Angelina Weld Grimke. P89
"Sky-blue trees". In the Sense of Death. Salvatore Quasimodo. P61
"The sky". Old Manuscript. Alfred Kreymborg. P82
"The skylark's nest among the grass". Bird's Nests. Unknown. P51
A Slant of Sun. Stephen Crane. P81
Slappey, Mary McGowan
Translated to the Seven Astronauts. P72
"Slated to be a winner in the front runner". The Front Runner System. Wilma H. Clements. P68
Slater, Charles
Creation of the World According to Charles Slater. P78
The Slaughterhouse. Mauricio Electorat. P71

The Slave. James Oppenheim. P82
Slavery
Children of the Sun. Fenton Johnson. P82
Tired. Fenton Johnson. P82
"Slayer of winter, art thou here again?.". March. William Morris. P89
Sleep
After Apple Picking. Robert Frost. P82
The Court Rests. Robert N. Feinstein. P63
Night. Georgi Djagarov. P70
Nightfall in Dordrecht. Eugene Field. P81
Nod. Walter De La Mare. P51
A Pothersome Pair. John Ceiriog Hughes. P87
Serenade, from The Spanish Student. Henry Wadsworth Longfellow. P89
Sheep That Pa in the Night. Irene Warsaw. P63
A Tale. Georgi Borisov. P70
Taliesin, Selections. Richard Hovey. P81
3. R. K. Singh. P72
To Ianthe, Sleeping, from Queen Mab. Percy Bysshe Shelley. P90
To Sleep. Giovanni della Casa. P89
Willie Winkie. William Miller. P89
Wynken, Blynken and Nod. Eugene Field. P51
Sleep Baby Sleep. J. Pembroke Waller. P68
Sleep Work. Mohammed Dib. P91
"Sleep little one, and find sweet rest". Lullaby of Evening. James A. Hanf. P72
"Sleep softly...eagle forgotten...". The Eagle That Is Forgotten. Vachel Lindsay. P82
"Sleep, baby, sleep!.". A Cradle Song. Unknown. P51
Sleep, from Henry IV. William Shakespeare. P90
"Sleep, Sleep. My Little One!...". Unknown. P60
"Sleep, little pigeon...". Japanese Lullaby. Eugene Field. P89
Sleeping Beauty. Edward A. Gloeggler. P65
"The sleeves of fog's overcoat are dangling...". A Prayer. Boris Kristov. P70
A Slender Book of Verse and It's Purchaser. F. C. Rosenberger. P63
"The Slender Girl". Unknown. P62
"A slender young blackbird...". The Blackbird. D. M. Mulock. P51
"Sliced clear water--wedge--shape". Goal Far and Near. Margaret Avison. P49
"Sliding down the banisters". On the Banisters. Margaret E. Gibbs. P51
"Slight Drops in Ledge Pools". Jeff Jones. P77
The Slip. Wendell Bery. P67
Sloniker, Wendi

Changing. P74

Slow but Sure, from Lost Youth: the Last War. Alfred Kreymborg. P82

Slow Spring. Katharine (Hinkson) Tynan. P51

"Slow, horses, slow". Night of Spring. Thomas Westwood. P51

"Slowly walking along". The Loner. Thu-Phuong Do. P74

"Slowly, silently, now the moon". Silver. Walter De La Mare. P51

"Slowly, slowly, swinging low". Swinging. Irene Thompson. P51

Slumber in Spring. Elizabeth Gould. P51

Slumber Party. Carson McCullers. P50

Sly Thoughts. Coventry Patmore. P89

Slyman, Ernest
Olecranon. P63

Small Beginnings. Charles Mackay. P89

Small Wedding. Lisa Grenelle. P65

"Small fact and fingers...". A Poem for Emily. Miller Williams. P67

Smallness
Not Overlooked. James Oppenheim. P82

Smeeton, John P.
Jack Frost in the Garden. P51

"The smell of lemons". Night in Veracruz. Kathy Strange de Olguin. P72

"Smiling Without Showing Her Teeth". Unknown. P62

Smith's Garage. Robert Minhinnick. P54

Smith, Dave
The Colors of Our Age: Pink and Black. P67
The Tire Hangs in the Yard. P67

Smith, Delphia Frazier
Journey Back. P72

Smith, Dora K. T.
Time in Its Passing. P72

Smith, Douglas
On the 401 from Waterloo to Toronto. P49

Smith, Francis J.
Honeymoon in Rice. P63

Smith, Grace Haynes
Song of Love. P65

Smith, Gwen A.
Off We Go to Market. P51

Smith, H. Wendell
Molly Gaunt. P63

Smith, Horace
A Bit of Colour. P51

Smith, James Steel
Invitation. P63
Knitting-Sitting Song. P63
"Walter Savage Landor". P63

Smith, Richard Candida
Osiris' Song. P68

Smith, Samuel Francis
America. P90

Smith, Virginia E.

Edward Curtis Photographs the North American Indians. P68
To a Small Voyager Who Shares Her Room. P68

Smith, William Jay (tr.)
We Say This Prayer. Jozsef Tornai. P92

Smoker's Epitaph. John D. Engle Jr. P63

Smoking
An Old Fashioned Pipe. Kathryn G. Hansen. P72

"Smoking all that much has got her eyes". He Records a Little Song for a Smoking Girl. James Whitehead. P67

"A smoky rain riddles the ocean plains". My Father Paints the Summer. Richard Wilbur. P84

"Smooth steps that are easy to urge to the crags". Sheepdog. Thomas Richards. P87

Smullin, Sylvia
The Race. P74

"The snail says, 'Alas!'.". The Poor Snail. J. M. Westrup. P51

The Snail. William Cowper. P51

Snails
The Poor Snail. J. M. Westrup. P51
The Snail. William Cowper. P51

Snails in the Grass. Nyalual Pal. P53

Snake in the Yard. Paulette Roeske. P88

Snapshots of a Daughter-in-Law. Adrienne Rich. P85

The Snare. James Stephens. P51

Sneed, E. W.
Me Wants a Minks. P63

Sneezes
Sneezing. Leigh Hunt. P90

Snodgrass, William DeWitt
After Experience Taught Me. P85
April Inventory. P85
At the Park Dance. P85
The Campus on the Hill. P85
Coroner's Inquest. P63
Credo. P63
The Fuhrer Bunker, sels. P85
Inquest. P85
Mhtis Outis. P85
Monet: 'Les Nympheas'. P85
Old Apple Trees. P85
The Poet Ridiculed by Hysterical Academics. P63
W. D., Don't Fear That Animal. P63

"Snot goes down". Pieces of Snot, from String Games. Unknown. P78

Snow
And Then. Prince Redcloud. P80
Breathing in the Woods. Judith Minty. P88
Cynthia in the Snow. Gwendolyn Brooks. P80
A Dog Named Ego, the Snowflakes as Kisses. Delmore Schwartz. P84

A Finger Play for a Snowy Day. Unknown.
    P51
First Snow. Marie Louise Allen. P80
Gnomic Stanzas. Unknown. P87
Snow. Mary Ann Hoberman. P80
    Identified Flying Objects. Joseph
        Cherwinski. P68
    Jack Frost. Cecily E. Pike. P51
    Jack Frost. Gabriel Setoun. P51
    Jack Frost in the Garden. John P.
        Smeeton. P51
Snow. Barry Kaufman. P73
Snow. Karla Kuskin. P80
Snow. Henry Wadsworth Longfellow. P51
    A Lost Snowflake. Charlotte B. Deforest.
        P80
    "The Power of Snow". Steve Sanfield. P77
    Read This with Gestures. John Ciardi. P80
    Snow. Mary Ann Hoberman. P80
    Snow. Barry Kaufman. P73
    Snow. Karla Kuskin. P80
    Snow. Henry Wadsworth Longfellow. P51
    Snow 1929. Atanas Dalchev. P70
    Snow Country. David Wevill. P49
    Snow in Town. Rickman Mark. P51
    Snow Woman. Nancy Dingman Watson. P80
    Snow-Flakes. Mary Mapes Dodge. P89
    The Snow-Storm. Ralph Waldo Emerson. P89
    The Snow. F. Ann Elliot. P51
    Snowfall. Barry Callaghan. P49
    The Snowflake. Paul Holder. P73
    Snowflakes. Suk-Joong Yoon. P80
    Snowflakes. Ruth M. Arthur. P51
    The Snowman. E. M. Adams. P51
    Snowy Morning. Ai Qing. P92
    That Cheerful Snowman. Hannah Lyons
        Johnson. P80
    Velvet Shoes. Elinor Wylie. P89
    White Fields. James Stephens. P51
    Winter Is Tacked Down. Sister Noemi
        Weygant. P80
    Winter's Song. Unknown. P51
Snow 1929. Atanas Dalchev. P70
Snow Country. David Wevill. P49
"Snow falling and night falling fast...".
    Desert Places. Robert Frost. P82
Snow in Town. Rickman Mark. P51
Snow Scene. Louise Marsh Gabriel. P72
Snow Woman. Nancy Dingman Watson. P80
"Snow is falling, falling without sound".
    Snowy Morning. Ai Qing. P92
"Snow is on the roof". Snow. Barry Kaufman.
    P73
"Snow kept on sifting through the night".
    Moonwalk. X. J. Kennedy. P80
"Snow makes whiteness where it falls". First
    Snow. Marie Louise Allen. P80
"The Snow Queen comes out on dazzling feet".
    The North Wind. Dorothy Gradon. P51

"Snow rises on roses". Identified Flying
    Objects. Joseph Cherwinski. P68
"The snow, in bitter cold". The Snow. F. Ann
    Elliot. P51
Snow-Flakes. Mary Mapes Dodge. P89
The Snow-Storm. Ralph Waldo Emerson. P89
"Snow/Snow". Snow. Mary Ann Hoberman. P80
The Snow. F. Ann Elliot. P51
Snowball Wind. Aileen Fisher. P80
Snowdrop. Anna Bunston de Bary. P51
Snowdrops. Laurence Alma-Tadema. P51
Snowdrops. Nigel Jenkins. P54
Snowdrops. Mary Vivian. P51
Snowfall. Barry Callaghan. P49
Snowflake Souffle. X. J. Kennedy. P80
"A snowflake is white". The Snowflake. Paul
    Holder. P73
Snowflakes. Ruth M. Arthur. P51
Snowflakes. Suk-Joong Yoon. P80
"The snowflakes fell, the first this year".
    A Lost Snowflake. Charlotte B.
    Deforest. P80
Snowflower. Tamara Downing. P77
The Snowman. E. M. Adams. P51
"Snowmelt pond warm granite". Bedrock. Gary
    Snyder. P85
Snows of Aconcagua. Raul Zurita. P71
The Snowstorm. Kaye Starbird. P80
Snowy Benches. Aileen Fisher. P80
Snowy Morning. Lilian Moore. P80
Snowy Morning. Ai Qing. P92
Snyder, Gary
    Affluence. P85
    Bedrock. P85
    Four Poems for Robin. P85
    The .Late Snow and Lumber Strike of the
        Summer of Fifty-Four. P85
    Milton by Firelight. P85
    Myths and Texts (Burning). P85
    Myths and Texts (Hunting). P85
    Myths and Texts (Logging). P85
    Riprap. P85
    Things to Do Around a Lookout. P85
    Water. P85
Snyder, Virginia (Jacques).
    Not in Vain. P72
So It Was Done. Barry Callaghan. P49
So Many Moons Ago (Acrostic/Sonnet). Naomi
    Young Armstrong. P72
So Sweet Love Seemed. Robert Bridges. P89
"So clear! so glorious and so bright!.".
    October Morning. William Young Elliot.
    P72
"So dark, the nyte, like velvet spread". Non
    Omnis Moriar. Leilah Wendell. P68
"So delicate, so airy". Pink Almond.
    Katharine (Hinkson) Tynan. P51
"So frightened by your death". Non Omnis
    Moriar. Teresinka Pereira. P72

"So gentle and so gracious doth appear". My
        Lady. Dante. P89
"So much comes to mind". Greensleeves. Mark
        Jarman. P85
"So much depends". The Red Wheelbarrow.
        William Carlos Williams. P75,P82
"So much I have forgotten in ten years".
        Flame-Heart. Claude McKay. P82
"So slender". The Island. Grace Schulman.
        P64
"So still the". First Love. Anne Yannie
        Corrado. P65
"So that soldierly legend...". Kearny at
        Seven Pines. Edmund Clarence Stedman.
        P90
"So the stones are dead, and the soil...".
        Why Is Man Born? Georgi Djagarov. P70
"So then came his word here". The Popol Vuh:
        Beginnings, sel. Unknown. P78
"So there he was that earliest hour". Our
        First Journey. N.M. Rashed. P91
"... So these then are the deeds...". The
        Popol Vuh: Alligator's Struggles...,
        sel. Unknown. P78
"So what said the others and the sun went
        down". Mrs. Alfred Uruguay. Wallace
        Stevens. P83
"So you have swept me back". Eurydice. Hilda
        ("H.D.") Doolittle. P82
"So you're playing". Identities. Al Young.
        P85
A Social Engagement. Knute Skinner. P63
Social Problems
        The Chicken Coop. Diego Maquieira. P71
        Massasoit. Mary Jane Barnes. P68
        Terror to Unborn Children. Tonya
        McCulley. P74
        Trouble. Michele M. Helm. P74
Social Zoology: Prep for a Field Trip. Gary
        Pittenger. P63
Sociology, Urban
        Faces. Lola Ridge. P82
        The Sins of Kalamazoo. Carl Sandburg. P82
Socrates' Ghost Must Haunt Me Now. Delmore
        Schwartz. P84
"The soft dawn mist calls". A Day in
        Creation. Helena Parham. P72
"Soft falls the night". Evening Song. Edith
        King. P51
"Soft thud, startled screech". First Flight.
        Janet Carncross Chandler. P77
"The soft, breeze-swept meadow". Meadow's
        Song. Opie Houston. P65
"Softly along the road of evening". Nod.
        Walter De La Mare. P51
"Softly, softly, through the darkness".
        Christmas Night. B. E. Milner. P51
Soil. John Tripp. P54
Solace. Clarissa Scott Delany. P89

Solar Myth. Genevieve Taggard. P83
Soldato-Subkis, Heather D.
        The'Thing' in My House. P73
"Soldier boys". Martial Ditty, from Lost
        Youth: the Last War. Alfred Kreymborg.
        P82
Soldiers
        Elegy for a Dead Soldier. Karl Shapiro.
        P84
        Equals. James D. Hartman. P86
        Its Shells Pile Before Me. Ret Col and
        Stephen Ciec Lam. P53
        John Brown's Body. Henry Howard Brownell.
        P90
        Martial Ditty, from Lost Youth: the Last
        War. Alfred Kreymborg. P82
        "'Me, 20-Year-Old Sergeant, Ognyan
        Mihailov'". Luchesar Elenkov. P70
        Observation Post. R. L. Barth. P86
        Pacifist, from Lost Youth: the Last War.
        Alfred Kreymborg. P82
        Road to the Congo. Nyagak Pinien. P53
        Siegfried. Randall Jarrell. P84
        Transient Barracks. Randall Jarrell. P84
        Wise Guys. Ray Catina. P86
"Soldiers sleep because they must". Equals.
        James D. Hartman. P86
Soldo, John J.
        Memory. P65
        Puppet. P65
        Rare Stones. P65
        Waiting. P65
Solek-Fritsche, Patricia Anne
        Emotions Extinction. P72
"The solid sun". Silence. James Richard
        Hurst. P68
Solipsism. George Santayana. P81
Solitude
        The Garden. Andrew Marvell. P59
        Laughter. Olive Enoch. P51
Solitude. Iris Jean MacLeod. P72
Solitude. Harshdev Madhav. P72
        Solitude. Iris Jean MacLeod. P72
        Solitude. Harshdev Madhav. P72
        Things of the Blind. Paz Molina. P71
        Watching T.V. Oscar Hahn. P71
"Solomon, that generous judge". A Tale from
        the Arabian Nights. Alison Shepherd.
        P68
Solt, John (tr.)
        The Street. Sachiko Yoshihara. P92
        Woman. Sachiko Yoshihara. P92
Some Days Ago. Majeed Amjad. P91
Some Italian!. Linda Monacelli Johnson. P63
Some Trees. John Ashbery. P85
Some Words. John Ashbery. P52
"Some apples are bright shiny red". Apples
        and Leaves. James Richard Hurst. P68
"Some are & are going to my howinouse...".

The 12th Horse Song of Frank Mitchell (Blue). Unknown. P78
"Some folk like the Chaffinch". The Robin. O. M. Bent. P51
"Some men would gladly die". The Breasts of Women. David Kirby. P63
"Some murmur when their sky is clear". Different Minds. Richard Chenevix Trench. P89
"Some people in the sky". Song Picture No. 83. Unknown. P78
"Some people said the cabin". Ten Dreamers in a Motel. Josephine Miles. P84
"Some say the world will end in fire". Fire and Ice. Robert Frost. P82
"Some want to leave". Wishing. Omar Lara. P71
"Some young and saucy dandelions". The Dandelions. Unknown. P51
"Some're lovely N nawu nnnn but some're". The 13th Horse Song of Frank Mitchell (White). Unknown. P78
"Somebody loses whenever somebody wins". Crapshooters. Carl Sandburg. P82
"Somebody needs to look after the night". A Sort of Blues. D. G. Jones. P49
Somebody's Courting Somebody. Unknown. P89
"Someday I'll show you where I stood". Speaking in Tongues. Erin Moure. P49
"Someday, maybe--.". Maybe. Susan Headen Griffith. P72
Someone. Walter De La Mare. P51
"Someone has fallen to the earth". An Examination into Life and Death. Kenneth Patchen. P84
"Someone playing, Lord". My Son, the Tuba Player. Edmund Conti. P63
"Something has touched me". Dinosaur Hill. Robert Hahn. P58
"Something of the trouble of the mind". How Now, O, Brightener. Wallace Stevens. P79
"Something terrible happened". Strange Bird. Stefan Tsanev. P70
"Something that woke me out of sleep". End of Summer. William Everson. P84
"Something within her, always incomplete". Brownstone Revisited. Mary B. Finn. P68
The Sometime Sportsman Greets the Spring. John Updike. P63
"Sometimes I glimpse a rhythm". Hill Country Rhythms. Jeremy Hooker. P54
"Sometimes I panic". Let Me Go. Maria Berl Lee. P68
"Sometimes I've seen". A Little Bird's Song. Margaret Rose. P51
"Sometimes in summer when it gets so hot". Summer Sonnet. R. J. Larbes. P68

"Sometimes these days". Lonely for the Country. Bronwen Wallace. P49
"Sometimes things as they are". Things As They Are. Bonnie Jacobson. P63
"Sometimes when my eyes are red". My Sad Self. Allen Ginsberg. P85
Somewhere Near the Mekong River, 1966. Dennis Moore. P86
"Somewhere in my fortieth year". The Exclusion Principle. William Mills. P67
"Somewhere in this brick building...". In a Country Hospital. Anne Porter. P64
"Somewhere west of here". Dislocation. Mary Trimble. P88
"Somewhere, out on the blue seas sailing". When My Ship Comes in. Robert Jones Burdette. P89
Somlyo, Gyorgy
Fable of First Person. Donald Davie (tr.). P92
Wound and Knife. Maria Korosy and William Jay Smith (tr.). P92
"Son'ahchi/Ee--so". The Boy and the Deer. Andrew Peynetsa. P78
"Son, Although She Is Shy". Unknown. P62
Song. Mark Akenside. P89
Song. Laurence Binyon. P51
Song. Samuel Taylor Coleridge. P51
Song. Adelaide Crapsey. P81
Song. Robert Creeley. P85
Song. John Donne. P59
Song. Eugene Field. P51
Song. Richard Hovey. P81
Song. Robert M. Howell. P65
Song. Henry Neville Maughan. P51
Song. Nikola Vaptsarov. P70
A Song About Myself, sel. John Keats. P51
Song Between the Sea and Sky. Kolyo Sevov. P70
Song for a Ball-Game. Wilfred Thorley. P51
Song for a Little House. Christopher Morley. P51
Song for a Surf-Rider. Sarah Van Alstyne Allen. P76
A Song for T. S. Cristina Pina. P92
Song for the Richest Woman in Wrangell, from Wolf... Unknown. P78
A Song from Afar. Ahmad 'Abd Al-Muti Hijazi. P91
A Song in the Front Yard, fr. A Street in Bronzeville. Gwendolyn Brooks. P84
Song of a Dead Pilot. Ahmad 'Abd Al-Muti Hijazi. P91
The Song of a Traveller. Robert Louis Stevenson. P51
Song of Egla. Maria Gowen Brooks. P89
The Song of Hiawatha Selections. Henry Wadsworth Longfellow. P90

Song of Lawino, sel. Okot p' Bitek. P92
Song of Love. Grace Haynes Smith. P65
Song of Pasadena. Wen-Ying Hsu. P72
Song of Solomon, Old Testament. Unknown. P60
Song of Spring. John Keats. P51
Song of Summer Days. J. W. Foley. P51
Song of the Bald Eagle. Unknown. P78
The Song of the Bath. Margaret E. Gibbs. P51
The Song of the Bird. Henry Wadsworth
        Longfellow. P51
The Song of the Engine. H. Worsley-Benison.
        P51
Song of the Fleece. Louise Louis. P65
The Song of the Grass. Leigh Hunt. P51
Song of the Lonely. Kelly Morris. P73
Song of the Milkmaid, from Queen Mary. Lord
        Tennyson. P89
A Song of the Red & Green Buffalo. Unknown.
        P78
Song of the Silent Land. Johann Gaudenz von
        Salis-Seewis. P89
A Song of the Wave. George Cabot Lodge. P81
Song of Triumph. Lois Duncan. P50
Song on the Way to Jail, from Wolf Songs...
        Unknown. P78
Song Picture No. 106. Unknown. P78
Song Picture No. 17. Unknown. P78
Song Picture No. 27. Unknown. P78
Song Picture No. 29. Unknown. P78
Song Picture No. 30. Unknown. P78
Song Picture No. 34. Unknown. P78
Song Picture No. 54. Unknown. P78
Song Picture No. 56. Unknown. P78
Song Picture No. 58. Unknown. P78
Song Picture No. 64. Unknown. P78
Song Picture No. 66. Unknown. P78
Song Picture No. 68. Unknown. P78
Song Picture No. 69. Unknown. P78
Song Picture No. 71. Unknown. P78
Song Picture No. 82. Unknown. P78
Song Picture No. 83. Unknown. P78
Song Picture No. 85. Unknown. P78
Song Picture No. 86. Unknown. P78
Song Picture No. 87. Unknown. P78
Song Picture No. 96. Unknown. P78
"The song that was sung for Non and Sant's
        son". Awdl. Saunders Lewis. P87
Song to a Child. Unknown. P87
A Song to God. Salah Abdul-Sabur. P91
Song to the Nightingale. Alun. P87
"A song to the oak, the brave old oak". The
        Brave Old Oak. Henry Fothergill
        Chorley. P89
A Song, from Red Ant Way. Unknown. P78
Song, from The Marriage of Guenevere.
        Richard Hovey. P81
Song, sel. Elizabeth J. Coatsworth. P55
Songs and Singing
        "Before He Died," from Wolf Songs...

        Unknown. P78
Between the Anthill and the Heglig Tree.
        Unknown. P53
"Big Rabbit Goes To See His Baby".
        Unknown. P78
A Buried One in Me Sings. Salvatore
        Quasimodo. P61
The Carol Singers. Margaret G. Rhodes.
        P51
"Chipmunk Can't Drag it Along". Unknown.
        P78
"Chipmunk was standing". Unknown. P78
Cleaned the Crocodile's Teeth. Nyabuk
        Col. P53
"Cock Robin Got up Early". Unknown. P51
Cradle Songs, from Wolf Songs & Others of
        the Tlingit. Unknown. P78
Cradle Songs, from Wolf Songs & Others of
        the Tlingit. Unknown. P78
Cradle Songs, from Wolf Songs & Others of
        the Tlingit. Unknown. P78
Cradle Songs, from Wolf Songs & Others of
        the Tlingit. Unknown. P78
The Crocodile Scales. Moses Kuac Nyoat.
        P53
The Day Before April. May Carolyn Davies.
        P51
Death Song for Owain ab Urien. Taliesin.
        P87
Don't Be Discouraged. Phillip Macar. P53
Dream. Unknown. P78
Eat Nothing. Nyapal Kong. P53
Erthe Toc of Erthe. Unknown. P66
From a Line by Cyril Dabydeen. Martin
        Singleton. P49
Funeral Song, from Wolf Songs & Others of
        the Tlingit. Unknown. P78
Goldenhair. James Joyce. P51
"He Followed His Own Mind...," from Wolf
        Songs... Unknown. P78
He'd Die for Tobacco. Philip Macar. P53
The Holly. Unknown. P87
"How Is It All Gonna Turn Out," from Wolf
        Songs... Unknown. P78
How to Get Grizzly Spirit, from Wolf
        Songs... Unknown. P78
"I Don't Care If You're Married...," from
        Kiowa... Unknown. P78
"I Don't Know Why You Tell Me I'm Drunk,"
        from Wolf... Unknown. P78
"I Keep Dreaming I'm Dead," from Wolf
        Songs... Unknown. P78
"I Know How People Get Treated...," from
        Wolf Songs... Unknown. P78
I Syng of a Mayden. Unknown. P66
"I Think About You...," from Wolf Songs &
        Others... Unknown. P78
"I Thought You Were Good". Unknown. P78
"I Wonder What the Eagle Did to Him,"

from Wolf... Unknown. P78

"I'm Gonna Die & Won't See You...," from Wolf Songs... Unknown. P78

Idle Robin. Unknown. P87

"If You Really Love Me...," from Kiowa '49' Songs. Unknown. P78

If You'd Died, I Would've Cut Off My Hair, "from Wolf... Unknown. P78

"It Would Be Very Pleasant...," from Wolf Songs... Unknown. P78

"It's Only Whiskey...," from Wolf Songs... Unknown. P78

Just Anyone. Nyagak Pinien. P53

Kin to the Wolf. Unknown. P53

The Leaf-Picking. Frederic Mistral. P89

"Like a Warden at the Evening Meal". Simon Perchik. P64

Love's Songs. Vivian Trollope-Cagle. P65

Lucy Lavender. Ivy O. Eastwick. P51

A Man's Song About His Daughter. Unknown. P78

"Mole Makes His Pole Redhot". Unknown. P78

My Son, the Tuba Player. Edmund Conti. P63

"My Wife Went Away, Left Me," from Wolf Songs... Unknown. P78

Nou Goth Sonne Under Wod. Unknown. P66

Now Springs the Spray. Unknown. P66

"Now You Love Me". Unknown. P78

O Black and Unknown Bards. James Weldon Johnson. P83

The Old Man's Song, About His Wife. Unknown. P78

The One-Eyed. Nyalang Pinien Lual. P53

"Pinionjay Shits Pebbles". Unknown. P78

The Piper. William Blake. P51

Pippa's Song. Robert Browning. P51

A Psalm. Thomas Merton. P84

Saturday Night. Langston Hughes. P83

Sentinel Songs. Abram Joseph Ryan. P90

Shaman Song, from Wolf Songs and Others of the Tlingit. Unknown. P78

"She Said She Don't Love Me Anymore...," from Kiowa... Unknown. P78

Sing Love, Small Frog. Lisa Grenelle. P65

Snails in the Grass. Nyalual Pal. P53

Song. Eugene Field. P51

Song for the Richest Woman in Wrangell, from Wolf... Unknown. P78

Song of Love. Grace Haynes Smith. P65

Song on the Way to Jail, from Wolf Songs... Unknown. P78

A Song, from Red Ant Way. Unknown. P78

Spring Fjord. Unknown. P78

"That's a Rich Man Coming," from Wolf Songs... Unknown. P78

There's My Darling. Unknown. P87

"Throw Him Into the River," from Wolf

Songs... Unknown. P78

Tsimshian Mourning Song. Unknown. P78

"A Turkey Is Dancing Near the Rocks". Unknown. P78

The Unwritten Song. Ford Madox (Hueffer) Ford. P51

Vendor's Song. Adelaide Crapsey. P81

The Waits. John Freeman. P51

"We've All Been Invited up to Killisnoo," from Wolf... Unknown. P78

What the Informant Said to Franz Boas in 1920. Unknown. P78

Where Beth They Biforen Us Weren?. Unknown. P66

Who Will Bury Me? Tor Kej. P53

"Wildcat Was Walking". Unknown. P78

A Woman's Song, About Men. Unknown. P78

"You Know That I Love You...," from Kiowa '49' Songs. Unknown. P78

"You Surprise Me, Crow," from Wolf Songs... Unknown. P78

Songs of Apocalypse', sel. Nadya Aisenberg. P48

Songs of Autumn. Paul Verlaine. P89

The Songs of Maximus. Charles Olson. P85

Songs of Our Cells. Grace Schulman. P64

Songs to a Woman. Maxwell Bodenheim. P82

""Sonja Henie," the young girl". Preface. Theodore Weiss. P84

Sonnet. Louise Labe. P89

Sonnet. William Wordsworth. P90

Sonnet 016, fr. One person. Elinor Wylie. P82

Sonnet 1, fr. Three Sonnets From 'Deep Within the Heart'. Syed Shamsul Haque. P91

Sonnet 12, fr. Three Sonnets From 'Deep Within the Heart'. Syed Shamsul Haque. P91

Sonnet 25, fr. Three Sonnets From 'Deep Within the Heart'. Syed Shamsul Haque. P91

Sonnet to a Road Runner. Virginia Noble. P72

Sonnet to a Seagull. Patricia P. Kirby. P68

The Sonnet. Richard Watson Gilder. P90

Sonnets

    Not in Vain. Virginia (Jacques). Snyder. P72

    So Many Moons Ago (Acrostic/Sonnet). Naomi Young Armstrong. P72

    Sonnet to a Road Runner. Virginia Noble. P72

    Sonnet to a Seagull. Patricia P. Kirby. P68

    The Sonnet. Richard Watson Gilder. P90

Sonora Foothill Winter Rainstorm. David Kuehnert. P77

Sons of the King. John Agnew. P51

Sons of the Right Hand. Benjamin Hochman

P63
"Soo departed he from thens and
        commaunded...". Le Morte Darthur,
        sels. Sir Thomas Malory. P66
' Sooeep!'. Walter De La Mare. P51
"Soon I will be in her kitchen". In Her
        Kitchen. Mark Milotich. P56
"Soon will the lonesome cricket by the
        stone". The Sower. Edwin Markham. P81
"Sooner tears than sleep this midnight". The
        Wind's Lament. John Morris-Jones. P87
Soosai, G.
        Symbol of Courage. P72
"The soote season, that bud and bloom...".
        Summer Is Gone. Francesco Petrarch.
        P89
"Sorcerous half-light". Waking. T. A.
        Shulgin. P58
Sordid Love. Elaine Demakas. P58
Sorlie, Lynn
        Fear. P72
Sorrow
        Agatha. Alfred Austin. P89
        Bad Day. Marci Ridlon. P50
        Color the Day Blue. Helen Lair. P72
        Come, Fill the Cup. Mary V. Traeger. P72
        Do Not Weep, Maiden. Stephen Crane. P81
        Frozen with Time. Sherry Sue McCall. P56
        His Eyes Grew Old. Ethel Squires. P72
        "I Shall Never Find Solace". Rinaldo
          d'Aquino. P69
        Joseph Rodman Drake (Died in New York,
          September...). Fitz-Greene Halleck.
          P90
        Kings River Canyon, fr. Andree Rexroth.
          Kenneth Rexroth. P84
        Lament for Llywelyn ap Gruffudd, the Last
          Prince. Gruffudd ab yr Ynad Coch. P87
        Mourning. Andrew Marvell. P59
        Nelly Myers. Archie Randolph Ammons. P67
        Old Photograph of the Future. Robert Penn
          Warren. P67
        Passengers in a Time Beyond Orchards.
          Vesta P. Crawford. P65
        Reuben Bright. Edward Arlington Robinson.
          P81
        Running in Winter. William Carpenter. P48
        Sadness in Springtime. Unknown. P87
        Sit Down, Sad Soul. Bryan Waller ("Barry
          Cornwall") Procter. P89
        A Song to God. Salah Abdul-Sabur. P91
        Sorrow Is the Only Faithful One. Owen
          Dodson. P84
        The Star Obscure. Gueni Zaimof. P72
        To Joya, Despairing. Kent Clair
          Chamberlain. P72
        Voice in the Darkness. Richard Dehmel.
          P90
Sorrow Is the Only Faithful One. Owen

        Dodson. P84
"Sorrow is like a ceaseless rain". Ethiopia.
        Angel Clark. P73
"Sorrow is my own yard". The Widow's Lament
        in Springtime. William Carlos
        Williams. P82
"Sorry". Doc Dachtler. P77
A Sort of Blues. D. G. Jones. P49
Soul
        The Body Is Like Roots Stretching Down
          into the Earth. Charles Reznikoff. P83
        Flight. Yahya Kemal. P91
        On a Drop of Dew. Andrew Marvell. P59
Soul. Eleanor Otto. P72
        Soul-Search Ode. Dorsha Hayes. P65
"Soul brother". Soul. Eleanor Otto. P72
Soul-Search Ode. Dorsha Hayes. P65
"Soul/Cries in solitude". Broken Stanza.
        Jamini K. Jagadev. P65
Sound Effect. Edna Jones. P68
"Sound is fading out". Song Picture No. 106.
        Unknown. P78
Sound of Ripening. Alice Mackenzie Swaim.
        P65
"Sound of disquiet is in the great halls".
        Jerusalem Destroyed, sels. Eben Fardd.
        P87
The Sound of the Light. William Stanley
        Merwin. P52
The Sound of the Wind. Christina Georgina
        Rossetti. P51
"Sound the flute!.". Spring. William Blake.
        P51
Sound-Poem No. 1. Unknown. P78
Sound-Poem No. 2. Richard Johnny John. P78
Soundararaj, G.
        I, Poet. P72
Sounds
        Whistling in the Air. Jaime Quezada. P71
"Sounds that whip and lash...". One Solitary
        Voice. Marilyn Gordon. P72
The Soup Jar. Dabney Stuart. P67
"Sourdough mountian called a fire in:.".
        Myths and Texts (Burning). Gary
        Snyder. P85
Souster, Raymond
        At the Police Station. P49
        Blue Heron Near the Old Mill Bridge. P49
        Death of a Sunflower. P49
South (United States)
        Brother Jonathan's Lament for Sister
          Caroline. Oliver Wendell Holmes. P90
        Dixie. Albert Pike. P90
        Grandmother's Eyes. Linda McCormick. P56
        Southern Vortex. William Mills. P67
"South American peaks look at them then".
        Snows of Aconcagua. Raul Zurita. P71
South Dakota Scenery. Wayne Kvam. P68
The South Shore (Aberystwyt). Bobi Jones.

P87
South Wind. Siegfried Sassoon. P51
"The south-land boasts its teeming cane".
        Our State. John Greenleaf Whittier.
        P90
"The south-west wind is blowing". Autumn
        Morning. Adeline White. P51
"Southbound--/a couple in passage". Our
        Afterlife. Robert Lowell. P79
Southeast Corner, fr. A Street in
        Bronzeville. Gwendolyn Brooks. P84
Southern Gothic. Rodger Kamenetz. P63
Southern Vortex. William Mills. P67
Southey, Caroline Bowles
        The Cuckoo Clock, from The Birthday. P90
Southey, Robert
        The Cataract of Lodore. P90
        The Old Man's Comforts and How He Gained
        Them. P90
"Southey, Wordworth, Coleridge, I also
        live". Lake Poets. Menke Katz. P72
"Southrons, hear your country call you!.".
        Dixie. Albert Pike. P90
Southwell, Robert
        The Burning Babe. P59
Soviet Union (USSR)
        To Russia. Joaquin Miller. P81
The Sower and His Seed. William E. H. Lecky.
        P90
The Sower. Edwin Markham. P81
Sowing Seeds. Ursula Cornwall. P51
Space. Salvatore Quasimodo. P61
Space Exploration. Mildred B. Boydston. P72
Space and Space Travel
        Cosmic Resident. Eda Howink. P72
        Discovery II. Sara DeVaux. P68
        Distant Exploration. Allan R. Halcrow.
        P72
        Fancy. Mary Agnes White. P72
        This Humanity. Frances Adams Moore. P72
        Void. Krishna Srinivas. P72
"Space is too full. Did nothing happen
        here?.". American Farm, 1934.
        Genevieve Taggard. P83
"The spacious firmament on high". Ode, from
        The Spectator. Joseph Addison. P89
"Spades take up leaves". Gathering Leaves.
        Robert Frost. P82
Spain, Jane S.
        The Natural Way. P72
"A Spanish song crosses and recrosses". The
        Passing. James Deahl. P49
"A spark". Endless Thought. Ashley Schmidt.
        P73
"Sparks are sparkling". THe Metaphor's
        Shine. K. Sree Ramachandra Murthi. P72
The Sparrow--to My Father. William Carlos
        Williams. P82
"Spawn of fantasies". Love Songs. Mina Loy.

P82
Spaziani, Maria Luisa
        I Remember a Season. Charles Guenther
        (tr.). P61
        The Waters of Saturday, sel. Charles
        Guenther (tr.). P61
"Speak to me. Take my hand. What are you
        now?.". Effort at Speech Between Two
        People. Muriel Rukeyser. P84
Speaking in Tongues. Erin Moure. P49
The Speaking Tree. Muriel Rukeyser. P84
Spears, Noa
        Tuning the Trumpet. P63
The Special Language. Robert F. Allen. P65
"Special delivery, a gift muffled in
        tissue". My Hands in Purdah. Mary Di
        Michele. P49
"The speckled bird sings in the tree". The
        Nightingale. Katharine (Hinkson)
        Tynan. P51
Speech to a Crowd. Archibald MacLeish. P83
The Speed Track. Peter [pseud.]. P51
Spence, Michael
        Proofreader's Island. P63
Spencer, William Robert
        Wife, Children and Friends. P89
Spender, Stephen
        After Stefan George--Mein Kind Kam Heim.
        P79
        Auden Aetat XX, LX. P79
        Epilogue to a Human Drama. P48
Spending the Woodpile Well Into June. Jean
        Pape. P77
Spenser's Ireland. Marianne Moore. P83
Speracio, Mario
        Letter to a Census Taker. P65
Sphinx Echoes the Sound Left by the Dead.
        Osman Turkay. P72
Spices
        Wild Thyme. Joyce Sambrook. P51
The Spider and the Fly. Mary Howitt. P89
The Spider and the Ghost of the Fly. Vachel
        Lindsay. P82
Spiders
        The Spider and the Fly. Mary Howitt. P89
"A spill contained in the fissure of
        light...". Winter Central. Christopher
        Dewdney. P49
Spinden, Herbert J. (tr.)
        Three Songs of Mad Coyote. Unknown. P78
Spinning Song. M. P. A. Sheaffer. P68
The Spinning-Wheel Song. John Francis
        Waller. P89
"A spirit moves within my soul". The Gift.
        Lara Colton. P73
The Spirit of the Wood. Paul Baudin. P77
A Spirit Sped. Stephen Crane. P81
"--A spirit's gracing luster light". Elegy
        on a Spirit Luster's Polar Site of

Empyrean... Lee Ver Duft. P68
"The **spirits** are not fooled". Midnight.
Lisel Mueller. P88
Spiritual Healing
O Bird of Light. Sri Chinmoy. P68
Spiritualism
I Stood Musing in a Black World. Stephen
Crane. P81
Spirituality
Aldebaran. Miguel de Unamuno. P48
The Four Zoas: 'Night the Ninth, Being
the Last...'. William Blake. P48
Instructions to a Medium To Be
Transmitted... Daniel Hoffman. P79
Looking for th Innr Life in 100 Mile.
Bill Bissett. P49
The Morning-Watch. Henry Vaughan. P59
The Names. Gwendolyn Macewen. P49
Nightfall by the River. Brian Henderson.
P49
On Flower Wreath Hill. Kenneth Rexroth.
P52
Prisoner at a Desk. May Sarton. P52
Regeneration. Henry Vaughan. P59
The Retreat. Henry Vaughan. P59
Seer. Josephine Miles. P84
The World Is Not Conclusion. Emily
Dickinson. P48
"**Splitting** Cedar". Mike Dixon. P77
Spofford, Harriet Elizabeth
Evanescence. P81
Music in the Night. P81
Phantoms All. P81
A Sigh. P81
The **Spoils** of Annwn. Unknown. P87
Sponge. Maureen Cannon. P63
"**Spontaneous** is what I am". Who, Me?. Hallie
Hodgson. P63
The **Spooniad,** from Spoon River Anthology.
Edgar Lee Masters. P82
Spring
Aries Sideshow. Charles Ghigna. P63
Awakening. Ruth Newton Mattos. P72
Awakening. Margaret Elizabeth (Munson)
Sangster. P81
Awakenings (A Sedoka). Linda Hutton. P72
Spring. William Blake. P51
The Bride of Spring. I. H. Rizvi. P72
Cleaning the Garage. Edward Butscher. P64
A Cold Spring. Elizabeth Bishop. P84
Early May. Graham Everett. P64
The Early Primrose. Henry Kirke White.
P89
Fantasy Voyage. Marjorie Skonnord Martin.
P72
The First Blue-Bird. James Whitcomb
Riley. P89
First Spring Morning. Robert Bridges. P51
"Here We Come A-Piping". Unknown. P51

I Have Seen the Spring. Sara Teasdale.
P82
I Sing of Spring. Elaine Hardt. P72
Images. Pieter D. Williams. P68
In Springtime. Samuel Taylor Coleridge.
P51
"In the Month of February". Unknown. P51
In the Woods in Spring. Raymond
Kresensky. P68
The Magic Piper. E. L. Marsh. P51
Spring. Meleager. P89
Mother Lode Spring. Nan Townsend
Degelman. P77
The Music of Spring. Marion Schoeberlein.
P68
My Lady Spring. Unknown. P51
"On Monday We Dance". Unknown. P51
Outbreak of Spring. George Starbuck. P85
Primrose Hill. Rose Fyleman. P51
Sapphics on the Violet. John C. Anderson.
P68
Setting for the Portrait. Margaret
Avison. P49
Spring. William Shakespeare. P51
The Sometime Sportsman Greets the Spring.
John Updike. P63
Spring. Keri Walls. P73
Spring. Meleager. P89
Spring. William Blake. P51
Spring. William Shakespeare. P51
Spring and All. William Carlos Williams.
P82
Spring Goeth All in White. Robert
Bridges. P51
Spring Has Come. Unknown. P51
Spring in New Hampshire. Claude McKay.
P82
"Spring Is Coming, Spring Is Coming".
Unknown. P51
Spring Morning. Frances Cornford. P51
Spring Prayer. Ralph Waldo Emerson. P51
Spring Quiet. Christina Georgina
Rossetti. P51
A Spring Song. Mary Howitt. P51
Spring Steps. Chi Hsien. P72
Spring Work at the Farm. Thirza Wakley.
P51
Spring, the Travelling Man. Winifred M.
Letts. P51
Springtime. Stephane Mallarme. P61
This Year. Rebecca Caudill. P75
To Spring. William Blake. P51
The Toads of Spring. Mary B. Finn. P68
The Ugliest Person. Sheila Hogan. P68
Under a Keeping Spring. William Everson.
P84
A Walk in Spring. K. C. Lart. P51
Spring. Keri Walls. P73
Welcome to Spring. IreneThompson. P51

Spring and All. William Carlos Williams. P82
Spring Fjord. Unknown. P78
Spring Freshet. Crary Elwood. P72
Spring Goeth All in White. Robert Bridges.
     P51
Spring Has Come. Unknown. P51
Spring in New Hampshire. Claude McKay. P82
"Spring Is Coming, Spring Is Coming".
     Unknown. P51
Spring Is the Favorite Time for Suicide.
     Virginia M. Hahn. P58
Spring Morning. Frances Cornford. P51
Spring Night. Sara Teasdale. P82
Spring Prayer. Ralph Waldo Emerson. P51
Spring Quiet. Christina Georgina Rossetti.
     P51
A Spring Song. Mary Howitt. P51
Spring Steps. Chi Hsien. P72
Spring Work at the Farm. Thirza Wakley. P51
"Spring is dirty snow in unkempt patches".
     The Ugliest Person. Sheila Hogan. P68
"Spring it is cheery". What Can an Old Man
     Do But Die?. Thomas Hood. P89
"Spring's south winds pushing". Fantasy
     Voyage. Marjorie Skonnord Martin. P72
Spring, the Travelling Man. Winifred M.
     Letts. P51
Spring-Rice, Sir Cecil
     Day. P51
Springtime. Stephane Mallarme. P61
Spun to Life. Perry Brass. P65
Spurlock, Lu
     Last Rights. P56
Spyglass Conversations. Unknown. P78
Squire, Sir John Collings ("Solomon Eagle")
     The Discovery. P90
Squires, Bonnie
     Balloons. P68
     Beginning Writer. P72
     Hypothesis from the Wilderness. P68
Squires, Ethel
     His Eyes Grew Old. P72
Squirrel. K. V. S. Murti. P72
"The squirrel is the curliest thing". The
     Curliest Thing. Unknown. P51
The Squirrel. Mary Howitt. P51
The Squirrel. Unknown. P51
Squirrels
     Big Bang. Jay Meek. P63
     The Curliest Thing. Unknown. P51
     Joe. David McCord. P80
     Mr. Squirrel. V. M. Julian. P51
     Squirrel. K. V. S. Murti. P72
     The Squirrel. Unknown. P51
     The Squirrel. Mary Howitt. P51
     Whisky Frisky. Unknown. P51
Srilata, K.
     Change. P72
Srinivas, Krishna

Earth. P72
Fire. P72
Void. P72
Water. P72
Wind. P72
Stabat Mater Dolorosa. Jacopone da Todi
     (Jacobus de Benedictus). P89
Stafford, William
     Faux Pas. P63
Stage Fright. Jennie H. Sandbank. P72
The Stain. Pierre Jean Jouve. P61
The Stains Slid from Top to Bottom in
     Silence. Gonzalo Munoz. P71
Staley, E. O.
     Duo for Voice & Percussion. P63
Stalky Jack. William Brighty Rands. P51
"Stand from my shadow where it goes". Blind
     William's Song. William Stanley
     Merwin. P85
"Stand up straight and point your".
     Gymnastics. Tim Keegan. P73
"Standing by the River Ouse". Literary River
     Rhyme. William Cole. P63
"Standing just to the larboard of Europe".
     The Image Repetition. Douglas Barbour.
     P49
Standish, Celia
     New Year's Days. P51
Stanley, Thomas
     The Divorce. P59
Stanton, Frank Lebby
     The Mocking-Bird. P89
Stanzas for the Harp. Unknown. P87
Stanzas to the Lord Rhys ap Gruffudd, Prince
     of Deheubarth. Cynddelw Brydydd Mawr.
     P87
Staple, Will
     Skunk. P77
A Star Flowed. Yahya Kemal. P91
The Star Obscure. Gueni Zaimof. P72
Star of Bethlehem. Alun Llywelyn-Williams.
     P87
Star Picker. H. R. Felgenhauer. P68
Star Talk. Robert Graves. P90
The Star-Spangled Banner. Francis Scott Key.
     P90
Starbird, Kaye
     December Leaves. P80
     The Snowstorm. P80
Starbuck, George
     Bone Thoughts on a Dry Day. P85
     Communication to the City Fathers of
          Boston. P85
     Cora Punctuated with Strawberries. P85
     Of Late. P85
     On First Looking in on Blogett's Keats's
          'Chapman's Homer'. . P85
     Outbreak of Spring. P85
     Unfrienly Witness. P85

"A **stark** white streak ripples". Casino
      Royale. Estelle M. Zelner. P72
Starkey, James. See "O'Sullivan, Seumas"
Stars
      Constellation/Rorschach. Dan Murray. P64
      Counting. Fenton Johnson. P82
      Deeds in Orbit. Annie Laurie Leech. P72
      End of Summer. William Everson. P84
      The Fallen Star. Helen Schleef. P68
      The North Star. John Morris-Jones. P87
      Orion. William Everson. P84
      Out of the Starstream. Ruth C. Falk. P72
Stars. Marion Jane Richardson. P65
      Ship, Sea, and Star. Clifford Davidson.
         P68
      Star of Bethlehem. Alun Llywelyn-
         Williams. P87
      Star Picker. H. R. Felgenhauer. P68
      Star Talk. Robert Graves. P90
      Stars. Marion Jane Richardson. P65
      The Stars. Jane Augustine. P64
      Twinkle, Twinkle, Little Star. Jane
         Taylor. P51
      Twinkle, Twinkle, Little Star. Unknown.
         P89
The **Stars** Are Hidden, fr. Five Groups of
      Verse. Charles Reznikoff. P83
"**Stars** in the cosmos". The Prayer. Anna
      Marie Benado. P72
"The **stars** must make an awful noise". One
      Blackbird. Harold Monro. P51
"**Stars** of the summer night!.". Serenade,
      from The Spanish Student. Henry
      Wadsworth Longfellow. P89
The **Stars.** Jane Augustine. P64
"The **state** with the prettiest name".
      Florida. Elizabeth Bishop. P84
The **Stately** Lady. Flora Sandstrom. P51
Statue and Birds. Louise Bogan. P83
Statue of Liberty
      Lady with the Torch. Eddie-Lou Cole. P72
      Statue of Liberty. Becky Turner. P73
      To the Goddess of Liberty. George
         Sterling. P81
Statue of Liberty. Becky Turner. P73
Statues
      Aztec Gods. Rose Rosberg. P56
      Flood of Renaissance. Dorothy Mitchell
         Bechhold. P72
      The New Colossus. Emma Lazarus. P90
      Oh, Figures on the Portico... Antonio
         Machado. P61
      Statue and Birds. Louise Bogan. P83
Stay. LaNita Moses. P72
The **Steamboat** Bertrand. Gloria A. Martin.
      P68
Stearns, James
      How Does a Flower Know. P68
Stedman, Edmund Clarence

      The Dutch Patrol. P81
      Hymn of the West. P90
      John Brown of Osawatomie. P81
      Kearny at Seven Pines. P90
      Pan in Wall Street. P81
Steel, M.
      Little Lucy Lester. P51
Steele, Paul Curry
      "Shirley Temple". P63
Stefanile, Felix
      A Late Elegy for a Baseball Player. P57
Stefanova, Liliana
      And the Summer Still Persists. William
         Meredith (tr.). P70
      I See Again. William Meredith (tr.). P70
      The Ugly Man. Denise Levertov (tr.). P70
A **Stein** Song. Richard Hovey. P81
Stein, Alice P.
      Grounded. P63
Stein, Beverley W.
      Casey and the Vespula Diabolica. P72
Stein, Gertrude
      Gertrude and Alice. Joan Van Poznak. P63
"' **Stephen** Smith, University of Iowa...'.".
      Of Late. George Starbuck. P85
Stephens, James
      Danny Murphy. P51
      Day and Night. P51
      The Fifteen Acres. P51
      The Night. P51
      Reflections in the River. P68
      The Rivals. P51
      The Shell. P51
      The Snare. P51
      White Fields. P51
      The Wood of Flowers. P51
Stephens, Jan M.
      Partial to Marshall. P68
Stepping Out with My Big Cats. Naomi Lazard.
      P64
Steps. Frank O'Hara. P85
Sterling, George
      The Black Vulture. P81
      Kindred. P81
      The Last Days. P81
      Omnia Exeunt in Mysterium. P81
      To the Goddess of Liberty. P81
Sterling, John
      On a Beautiful Day. P89
      The Rose and the Gauntlet. P90
"**Sternly** my eyebrows meet as murmuring".
      Reading Adonais. Paul Goodman. P84
Stevens, Barbara
      Memories for Storage. P72
Stevens, Peter
      Act of Creation. P49
      Aurora. P49
Stevens, Wallace
      Anecdote of the Jar. P83

As You Leave the Room. P83
Disillusionment of Ten O'Clock. P83
Dutch Graves in Bucks County. P83
The Emperor of Ice-Cream. P83
Evening Without Angels. P83
A High-Toned Old Christian Woman. P83
How Now, O, Brightener. P79
The Idea of Order at Key West. P83
Metaphors of a Magnifico. P83
Mrs. Alfred Uruguay. P83
Note on Moonlight. P79
Of Mere Being. P83
Of Modern Poetry. P83
The Sail of Ulysses. P83
Sunday Morning. P83
Thirteen Ways of Looking at a Blackbird.
    P83
The Ultimate Poem is Abstract. P83
Stevenson, Anne
    Burnished. P54
    Green Mountain, Black Mountain. P54
    Himalayan Balsam. P54
    Walking Early by the Wye. P54
Stevenson, Robert Louis
    A Child's Thought. P51
    The Far-Farers. P51
    Farewell to the Farm. P51
    Foreign Children. P51
    Foreign Lands. P51,P89
    From a Railway Carriage. P51
    A Good Play. P89
    Happy Thought. P51
    The Land of Counterpane. P89
    The Land of Story-Books. P89
    Marching Song. P51
    My Shadow. P89
    The Song of a Traveller. P51
    The Unseen Playmate. P89
    The Wind. P51,P89
    Windy Nights. P51
Stewart, Jane G.
    June. P51
Stickney, Trumbull
    Age in Youth. P81
    At Sainte-Marguerite. P81
    An Athenian Garden. P81
    Be Still. The Hanging Gardens Were a
        Dream. P81
    Driftwood. P81
    Fidelity. P81
    In a City Garden. P81
    In Ampezzo. P81
    In Summer. P81
    Kalypso. P81
    Lakeward. P81
    Lodovico Martelli. P81
    Loneliness. P81
    Mnemosyne. P81
    Mt. Lykaion. P81

Near Helikon. P81
On Some Shells Found Inland. P81
On the Concert. P81
They Lived Enamoured of the Lovely Moon.
    P81
Still Life. William Carlos Williams. P79
Still Life Near Bangalore. Earle Birney. P49
Still Not Grown Up. Lisa May. P74
"Still as". Moon Shadows. Adelaide Crapsey.
    P81
"Still do the great mountains stay". What
    Passes and Endures. John Ceiriog
    Hughes. P87
"Still to be neat, still to be drest".
    Freedom in Dress, from Epicene or The
    Silent Woman. Ben Jonson. P90
Still, Citizen Sparrow. Richard Wilbur. P84
Still, Gloria
    Summer Storm, Highway 37. P88
"Stirring porchpots up...". Outbreak of
    Spring. George Starbuck. P85
Stocker, Mark
    Vita Longa, Cars Brevis. P63
Stoddard, Richard Henry
    The Flight of Youth. P89
    Men of the North and West. P90
Stone Quarries. Salvatore Quasimodo. P61
Stone Reality Meditation. Lawrence
    Ferlinghetti. P85
A Stone Tablet for Animal Ghosts, from My
    Hometown's... Wu Cheng. P92
Stone, Ken
    At the Used Book Sale. P56
    From Dusk to Dawn: Night Watch II. P86
    You Ask About Vietnam!. P86
Stone, Lloyd
    Windward Cycle. P72
Stone, P. M.
    Mr. Pennycomequick. P51
Stone, Phyllis M.
    Topsy-Turvy Land. P51
"The stones crowded together in the
    wall...". Sentry of the Silent. Rene
    Char. P61
The Stones of Florence. Bruce Bennett. P63
Stonestreet-See, Margielea
    Edge of Appalachia. P72
"Stood the afflicted mother weeping". Stabat
    Mater Dolorosa. Jacopone da Todi
    (Jacobus de Benedictus). P89
"Stop, mortal! Here thy brother lies,--.".
    Burns (A Poet's Epitaph). Ebenezer
    Elliot. P90
"Stop/A little". Epitaph on a Long Stone.
    Rudi Holzapfel. P72
Stopping by Brook at 18. Genevieve Sargent.
    P72
Stopping by Woods on a Snowy Evening. Robert
    Frost. P82

Stopple, Libby
  Papa Says. P75
Stories
    Blue Girls. John Crowe Ransom. P83
    Dickens in Camp. Bret Harte. P90
    The Story of Augustus Who Would Not Have
      Any Soup. Heinrich Hoffmann. P90
    The Story of Johnny Head-in-Air. Heinrich
      Hoffmann. P90
    Ten Dreamers in a Motel. Josephine Miles.
      P84
Storm. Agnes Nemes Nagy. P92
"The **storm** is out; the land is roused". Men
    and Boys. Karl Theodor Korner. P90
The **Storm,** sels. William Thomas (Islwyn).
    P87
The **Storm.** Heinrich Heine. P90
Storms
    Big Wind. Theodore Roethke. P84
    Electrical Storm. Robert Hayden. P84
    How Lovely. April Honeycutt. P74
    I, fr. Irradiations. John Gould Fletcher.
      P82
    A Midnight Storm To Turn to. Mary P.
      (Mary Dalles) Carey. P68
    Now and Again. Mary Trimble. P88
    The Storm. Heinrich Heine. P90
    Summer Storm. Rebecca Caudill. P75
    Thunderstorms. David Briggs. P73
Stormwatch: Fogo Island. Gregory Betts. P49
A **Story** About Chicken Soup. Louis Simpson.
    P85
The **Story** of Augustus Who Would Not Have Any
    Soup. Heinrich Hoffmann. P90
The **Story** of Fidgety Philip. Heinrich
    Hoffmann. P90
The **Story** of Johnny Head-in-Air. Heinrich
    Hoffmann. P90
Story of the Corn. K. Fisher. P51
A **Story** of the Eaters. Santiago Mendes
    Zapata. P78
Story, Robert
    The Whistle. P89
"**Storytellers** from around the world". O Holy
    Past. Mary Jude Kupper. P72
Stowe, Harriet Beecher
    The Other World. P89
Strahan, Jack
    Vietnam. P86
Strange Bird. Stefan Tsanev. P70
A **Strange** Man. Wazir Agha. P91
Strange Talk. L. E. Yates. P51
"**Strange** to be seeing waves of the sea". A
    Wish. Robert Williams Parry. P87
"**Strange** to reach paradise without crossing
    Jordan ". The Strangeness of Dawn.
    Robert Williams Parry. P87
"The **strange,** bright dancers". Poppies. P.
    A. Ropes. P51

The **Strangeness** of Dawn. Robert Williams
    Parry. P87
"A **stranger** came one night to Yussouf's
    tent". Yussouf. James Russell Lowell.
    P51
"The **stranger** in my gates--lo! that am I".
    Omnia Exeunt in Mysterium. George
    Sterling. P81
The **Stranger.** Adrienne Rich. P85
The **Strata:** To Llywelyn Sion. Robert
    Minhinnick. P54
Stratton, Christine
    Swish. P73
"The **straw** hat I left in a New York
    restaurant". Metropolitan LIfe. John
    Barton. P49
Strawberries
    Cora Punctuated with Strawberries. George
      Starbuck. P85
"The **strawberries** on the white
    porcelain...". The Strawberries.
    Tristan Dereme. P61
Stray Animals. James Tate. P85
Stray Dogs. Naomi Lazard. P64
"The **stray** was snake bit". Dog Adoption.
    Claudia Nabors. P72
Streams. See Brooks and Streams
Street. Waldo Rojas. P71
Street Lanterns. Mary E. Coleridge. P51
Street Scene. William Ernest Henley. P51
"A **street** in our town". The Watchmaker's
    Shop. Unknown. P51
Street, Alfred
    The Settler. P90
The **Street.** Sachiko Yoshihara. P92
Streetcar. Agnes Nemes Nagy. P92
Streets
    Blue Island Intersection. Carl Sandburg.
      P82
    Street Lanterns. Mary E. Coleridge. P51
"The **streets,** silent". No One. Gonzalo
    Millan. P71
"**Strength** in the iron draperies of her
    gown". Lady with the Torch. Eddie-Lou
    Cole. P72
"**Strengthened** to live, strengthened to die.
    for". In Distrust of Merits. Marianne
    Moore. P83
Stress (psychology)
    "Stress Crowds My Mind". Marla Swann. P74
The **Stretches** of Time and Delights. Morgan
    Hewitt. P68
The **Strife** Between the Poet and Ambition.
    Thomas Merton. P84
"**Strike** up the band". Exodus Unknown. James
    Marley. P68
"A **striped** blouse in a clearing by Bazille".
    Ceremony. Richard Wilbur. P84
Strode, William

Kisses. P89
The **Stroke**. Christopher Fahy. P57
Strokes (maladies)
Doves. Robert Duncan. P84
"**Strontium** 90 is slowly falling out". Cloud.
Josephine Miles. P84
Strutting with My Rifle. Daniel Cuol Lul
Wur. P53
Stuart, Dabney
Mining in Killdeer Alley. P67
No Yellow Jackets on the Mountian. P67
The Soup Jar. P67
Variable Service. P79
"**A student** who wanted an A". Office Hours.
Katharyn Machan Aal. P63
Students
The Hook. Theodore Weiss. P84
The Scholar, from Edwin the Fair. Sir
Henry Taylor. P90
To Delmore Schwartz. Robert Lowell. P84
"**Students** don't like Wright Morris". Great
Plains Lit. Mark Sanders. P63
"The **students**, lost in raucousness". The
Hook. Theodore Weiss. P84
Studer, Constance
Domain. P56
Stumpfoot on 42nd Street. Louis Simpson. P57
The **Stupas**, from Paradise. Montri Umavijani.
P72
"**Stupendous** universe!.". Alchemy. Alice M.
Boughtwood. P68
Stutterer. Alan Dugan. P57
Submarines
Precision. Lawrence Herman. P73
Suburbanitis. Grace D. Yerbury. P68
The **Subverted** Flower. Robert Frost. P82
Subway. Juan Cameron. P71
Subway Seasoning. Eve Merriam. P63
Subway Wind. Claude McKay. P82
Subways
Subway Seasoning. Eve Merriam. P63
Success
The First Draft. Kris Passantino. P74
Victor and Vanquished. Harry Thurston.
P81
Such a Blustery Day!. Elizabeth Gould. P51
"**Such** a wide, still landscape...". A
Greenland Winter. Lucy Diamond. P51
Suckling, Sir John
I Prithee Send Me Back My Heart. P89
Sudden Light. Dante Gabriel Rossetti. P90
"**Suddenly** the house had no doors". The
Handless Maiden. Janet Beeler Shaw.
P88
"**Suddenly** we fall from love". The Iron
Wheels of the Tricycle Without
Tires... Gonzalo Millan. P71
Suehiro, Chisachi
I Like Summer Rain. P75

"**Suelick** is the greatest Indian power". The
Origin of the Skagit Indians... Lucy
Williams. P78
Suffering
About Suffering They Were Never Wrong.
Lisel Mueller. P88
Apology for Bad Dreams. Robinson Jeffers.
P83
August. Elinor Wylie. P82
"Because of the Evil Husband I Have".
Compagnetto da Prato. P69
The Children. Abby Crone. P74
During the Eichmann Trial, sels. Denise
Levertov. P85
Ethiopia. Angel Clark. P73
A Shade for My Scarred Soul. William
Zeller. P72
"There Truly First Came to Me Deep
Sorrow". Giacomo da Lentini. P69
The Third World. Lawrence Ferlinghetti.
P85
Voices. Nesta Wyn Jones. P87
Suicide
About Suffering They Were Never Wrong.
Lisel Mueller. P88
After the Surprising Conversions. Robert
Lowell. P84
Black Mail. Maryann Calendrille. P64
Futile Death Wish. Simanchal Patnaik. P72
I Break the Sky. Owen Dodson. P84
Last Rights. Lu Spurlock. P56
Leaving the Door Open (1), sel. David
Ignatow. P64
The Lonely Death. Adelaide Crapsey. P81
Of Late. George Starbuck. P85
The Outing. Lorene Erickson. P88
P. S. Instead of a Beginning. Lyubomir
Levchev. P70
Richard Cory. Edward Arlington Robinson.
P89,P81
Sea-Drift. Siv Cedering. P64
Six O'Clock. Owen Dodson. P84
Song. Adelaide Crapsey. P81
Spring Is the Favorite Time for Suicide.
Virginia M. Hahn. P58
Streetcar. Agnes Nemes Nagy. P92
Suicide, from Lost Youth: the Last War.
Alfred Kreymborg. P82
The Widow's Lament in Springtime. William
Carlos Williams. P82
Suicide, from Lost Youth: the Last War.
Alfred Kreymborg. P82
Sullivan, Joanne Stevens
In the Midst. P72
Sumer Is Icumen In. Unknown. P66
Summer
Along the Roadside. Edna Jones. P68
And the Summer Still Persists. Liliana
Stefanova. P70

August. Dan Murray. P64
Battlements. Harvey Shapiro. P64
Bromeliad. Cathy Matyas. P49
Chokecherry Summers. Margot Kriel. P88
Curfew Summer. Maki Kureishi. P91
The First Day of Summer. Kathleen Norris.
    P88
"Full Early in the Morning". Unknown. P51
Hay-Time. C. M. Loew. P51
Haytime. Irene F. Pawsey. P51
I Like Summer Rain. Chisachi Suehiro. P75
In Fields of Summer. Galway Kinnell. P85
In the Fair Forest. Unknown. P51
Indian Summer. Nicolae Breban. P92
July. Dan Murray. P64
July. Harvey Shapiro. P64
Knoxville, Tennessee. Nikki Giovanni. P85
Summer. Michael Kreis. P74
Lanes in Summer. Malcolm Hemphrey. P51
My Father Paints the Summer. Richard
    Wilbur. P84
On the Way to Summer. John Hollander. P79
Song of Summer Days. J. W. Foley. P51
Sound of Ripening. Alice Mackenzie Swaim.
    P65
Sumer Is Icumen In. Unknown. P66
Summer. Michael Kreis. P74
A Summer Day. Florence Harrison. P51
Summer Evening. John Clare. P51
Summer Is Gone. Francesco Petrarch. P89
A Summer Noon. William Howitt. P89
Summer Rain. Eve Merriam. P75
Summer Rain. Georgi Djagarov. P70
Summer Sonnet. R. J. Larbes. P68
Summer Walks. Jaminikanta Jagdev. P72
Summertime and the Living... Robert
    Hayden. P84
'Tis the Last Rose of Summer, from Irish
    Melodies. Thomas Moore. P89
Unforgettable Summers. David Winwood. P92
A Walk in Late Summer. Theodore Roethke.
    P84
While Summer Stays. Margaret Longenecker
    Been. P68
Summer Breeze. Unknown. P51
Summer Concert. Reed Whittemore. P79
A Summer Day. Florence Harrison. P51
Summer Evening. John Clare. P51
Summer Is Gone. Francesco Petrarch. P89
Summer Is Nigh. Unknown. P51
A Summer Lullaby. Eudora S. Bumstead. P51
A Summer Noon. William Howitt. P89
Summer Rain. Georgi Djagarov. P70
Summer Rain. Eve Merriam. P75
A Summer Shower. Unknown. P51
Summer Snow. Charlotte Zolotow. P76
Summer Sonnet. R. J. Larbes. P68
Summer Storm. Rebecca Caudill. P75
Summer Storm, Highway 37. Gloria Still. P88

Summer Sun. Emily Welch. P74
Summer Vacation. Kathleen Iddings. P72
Summer Walks. Jaminikanta Jagdev. P72
"Summer clocks in at eight. By now". Curfew
    Summer. Maki Kureishi. P91
"Summer has doft his latest green". Winter.
    W. D. Landor. P51
"Summer is the time to swim in a pool".
    Summer. Michael Kreis. P74
"Summer joys are o'er". Winter Song. Ludwig
    Holty. P89
"Summer sandals, wilted welter". You Have No
    Lasting City Here. Mary Ann Henn. P65
"The summer sun is sinking low". Sunset.
    Henry Wadsworth Longfellow. P51
"The summer sun was sinking". The Fairy
    Child. John Anster. P90
"Summer. Sunset. Someone is playing".
    Transient Barracks. Randall Jarrell.
    P84
"Summers I come back to them". These Hills,
    Mother. Alice Derry. P88
"Summers in the south". Grandmother's Eyes.
    Linda McCormick. P56
Summers, Hollis
    Bleeder. P57
Summertime and the Living... Robert Hayden.
    P84
Sun
    Blackout into Sunlight. Yaedi Ignatow.
        P64
    "Early Morning Sun". Zana. P56
    The Street. Sachiko Yoshihara. P92
    Summer Sun. Emily Welch. P74
    Sun and Moon. Charlotte Druitt Cole. P51
    Sunlight Is Imagination. Richard Wilbur.
        P84
Sun and Moon. Charlotte Druitt Cole. P51
"The sun bends through the golden sea...".
    Maltepe. Yahya Kemal. P91
"The sun descending in the west". Night.
    William Blake. P51
"The sun doth arise". The Echoing Green.
    William Blake. P51
"The sun early rising, summer comes fast".
    Gwalchmai's Boat, sels. Meilir ap
    Gwalchmai. P87
"The sun exploded today". When Anger Came.
    Virginia M. Hahn. P58
"The sun goes down". Midsummer Night.
    Elizabeth Gould. P51
"The sun has gone from the shining skies". A
    Summer Lullaby. Eudora S. Bumstead.
    P51
"The sun has long been set". A Night in
    June. William Wordsworth. P51
The Sun is a Globe of Fire. Antonio Machado.
    P61
The Sun Rising. John Donne. P59

"The sun rises". In Fields of Summer. Galway
    Kinnell. P85
"The sun shines bright on our old...". My
    Old Kentucky Home. Stephen Foster. P89
"The sun sought thy dim bed and brought...".
    Africa. Claude McKay. P82
"The sun that shines all day so bright".
    Night. Unknown. P51
"The sun was shining on the sea". The Walrus
    and the Carpenter, from Alice in
    Wonderland. Charles Lutwidge ("Lewis
    Carroll") Dodgson. P89
"The sun woke me this morning loud". A True
    Account of Talking to the Sun at Fire
    Island. Frank O'Hara. P85
The Sun's Tongue. Rec Puk. P53
The Sun. Alexander Gerov. P70
Sunday Morning. Wallace Stevens. P83
Sundick, Sherry Small
    Dancing Waters. P72
Sunlight Is Imagination. Richard Wilbur. P84
"Sunlight and shallow water". Beidog. Jeremy
    Hooker. P54
"The sunlight trickles through". October
    Afternoon. Sarah Rigg. P74
"The sunlight was not our concern...". Notes
    from the Castle. Howard Moss. P64
"Sunlight/Played capriciously". Yosemite.
    Dick Hastings. P77
A Sunny Day, fr. Five Groups of Verse.
    Charles Reznikoff. P83
Sunny Eye. Maria Kukubaiska. P72
"A sunny shaft did I behold". Song. Samuel
    Taylor Coleridge. P51
Sunrise
    Passamaquoddy Sunrise. Dan Murray. P64
"Sunrise...& toward the sunrise stands...".
    Muu's Way or Pictures from the Uterine
    World. Unknown. P78
"Sunrse is just a prismatic mist away".
    Memories for Storage. Barbara Stevens.
    P72
Sunset
    An Autumn Evening. Chris Weideman. P74
    The Darkening Garden. Unknown. P51
    Day's Ending (Tucson). Sara Teasdale. P82
    Dusk in Changuitad. Sergio Mansilla. P71
Sunset. Henry Wadsworth Longfellow. P51
    The Setting Sun. Lawrence V. Jowers. P68
    Sunset. Henry Wadsworth Longfellow. P51
    Sunset Blues. Maxine Kumin. P76
Sunsets Be Dear. Richard Franklin. P65
"The sunshine is good". The Street. Sachiko
    Yoshihara. P92
Superego Dictatorship. Kenneth Lynn. P72
Supervielle, Jules
    The Face. Charles Guenther (tr.). P61
    Forest. Charles Guenther (tr.). P61
    Iguazu. Charles Guenther (tr.). P61

Let's Shield Your Light with Our Hand, My
    Heart. Charles Guenther (tr.). P61
Make Room. Charles Guenther (tr.). P61
Memory. Charles Guenther (tr.). P61
Posthumous. Charles Guenther (tr.). P61
Time's Horses. Charles Guenther (tr.).
    P61
The World in Us. Charles Guenther (tr.).
    P61
The World Is Full of Voices... Charles
    Guenther (tr.). P61
Support Troops/Our Brains Are Cooking Bugs.
    Robert Schlosser. P86
"Suppose Adam had corrupted Eve?.".
    Hypothesis from the Wilderness. Bonnie
    Squires. P68
"Suppose it is nothing but the hive". Davis
    Matlock, from Spoon River Anthology.
    Edgar Lee Masters. P82
Supposing That I Should. Stephen Crane. P81
"Sure thing". Song Picture No. 34. Unknown.
    P78
"Surely You Can See That Love Is Proper".
    Unknown. P62
"Surely You Dwell in My Heart". Unknown. P62
"Surely that moan is not the thing". Fog-
    Horn. William Stanley Merwin. P85
"Surely the godhead must be a goddess". The
    Great Marble Cake. Carl T. Endemann.
    P56
Surgery
    Going Under. Paulette Roeske. P88
    Hospital. Ardyth Bradley. P88
Surrealism
    All of Him, the Blue Filigree of the
        Gaze. Gonzalo Munoz. P71
    East, sel. Gonzalo Munoz. P71
    For Armando Rubio. Mauricio Electorat.
        P71
    Gargoyle. Carl Sandburg. P82
    Satellite City. Mauricio Electorat. P71
    She Abandoned Her Body to the Color.
        Gonzalo Munoz. P71
    Zelda. Geoff Fiorito. P58
Surrey, Henry Howard, Earl of (tr.)
    Summer Is Gone. Francesco Petrarch. P89
Survival
    About Thirty Jews Were Taken to Chelmno,
        fr. Mass Graves. Charles Reznikoff.
        P83
    After Experience Taught Me. William
        DeWitt Snodgrass. P85
    The Bear. Galway Kinnell. P85
    Chances Are. Lisel Mueller. P88
    Chaplinesque. Hart Crane. P83
    The Impossible Choices. William Everson.
        P84
    The Little Girl with Bands on her Teeth.
        Genevieve Taggad. P83

One More I'matation. Eleanore-Melissa.
    P68
Places Among the Stars. Stephen Crane.
    P81
Survivor's Manual. Doug Rawlings. P86
Waiting for Spring,..., from For the
    Desert Island. Tae-ch'ul Shin. P92
Survivor. Walter Hoefler. P71
Survivor's Manual. Doug Rawlings. P86
Susanna and the Elders. Adelaide Crapsey.
    P81
A Sussex Legend. Charles Dalmon. P51
Sutherland, Robert D.
    The Wonderful World. P63
"Sutures of shadows lace the grass". August
    Dusk: Sag Harbor. R. B. Weber. P64
Sutzkever, Abraham
    For a Comrade. Seymour Mayne (tr.). P48
    On the Subject of Roses. Seymour Mayne
        (tr.). P48
    Poem About a Herring. Seymour Mayne
        (tr.). P48
Svoboda, Terese (tr.)
    Always Praises You. Nyaruoth Atem. P53
    Ambush. Phillip Macar. P53
    As Helpless as a Dhow on a Still Day.
        Dhor Ding Cuol. P53
    Between the Anthill and the Heglig Tree.
        Unknown. P53
    The Big Knot. Nyalual Pal. P53
    Cleaned the Crocodile's Teeth. Nyabuk
        Col. P53
    The Crocodile Scales. Moses Kuac Nyoat.
        P53
    Don't Be Discouraged. Phillip Macar. P53
    Drink the Curse. Moses Kuac Nyoat. P53
    Eat Nothing. Nyapal Kong. P53
    Fishing for Girls with a Rod and Line.
        Kuek Taitai. P53
    Foreigners with Teeth. Peter Pal Kong.
        P53
    The Girl's Hearts Soften. Daniel Cuol
        Long. P53
    A Glutton. Nyagak Pinien. P53
    He Will Float in the River Like a
        Waterlily. Kong Tot. P53
    He'd Die for Tobacco. Philip Macar. P53
    He'd Eat Lizards. Buk Teny Women. P53
    I Was as Full of Air as An Old Bullfrog.
        Piluai Juoc. P53
    I Was Mistaken for a Red Dog. Nyakong
        Makui. P53
    I Won't Bow My Head for Anyone. Stephen
        Ciec Lam. P53
    I Would Give Him a Man. Dhor Ding Cuol.
        P53
    Its Eye Ran with Blood. Peter Pal Kong.
        P53
    Its Shells Pile Before Me. Ret Col and

        Stephen Ciec Lam. P53
    John Kennedy. Nyagak Pinien. P53
    Just Anyone. Nyagak Pinien. P53
    Kin to the Wolf. Unknown. P53
    Kual Is Left. Unknown. P53
    Leapt into the Dance. Nyanpandong. P53
    Let Her Be Red. Nyakuoth Macar. P53
    Magic That Comes at Dawn. Peter Pal Hoth
        Nyang. P53
    Moviestars. Daniel Cuol Long. P53
    The Old Fashioned Girls. Piluai Juoc. P53
    The One-Eyed. Nyalang Pinien Lual. P53
    Out of Step. Buk Teny Men. P53
    Paddlewheel Under a Boat. Peter Pal Hoth
        Nyang. P53
    The Radio, with its Breath Like a Trapped
        Bee. John Gatwec Lul. P53
    The Red Clouds at Sunset. Micen Atem. P53
    Road to the Congo. Nyagak Pinien. P53
    Snails in the Grass. Nyalual Pal. P53
    Strutting with My Rifle. Daniel Cuol Lul
        Wur. P53
    The Sun's Tongue. Rec Puk. P53
    The Tail of the Buffalo. Nyalual Pal. P53
    These Things Amaze Me. Nyagak Pinien. P53
    Wandering Off. Unknown. P53
    We Broke the Noose with a Snap. Majiok
        Wunyik. P53
    White Girls. Phillip Macar Ruac. P53
    Who Can Touch Me?. Micen Atem. P53
    Who Plays the Lyre?. Phillip Macar. P53
    Who Will Bury Me? Tor Kej. P53
    Women Beat the Life Out of Me. Piluai
        Juoc. P53
    You, a Red Man, and I, a Black Man. Moses
        Cot. P53
Swaim, Alice Mackenzie
    Double-Quick. P65
    For All the Violets. P65
Swaim, Alice MacKenzie
    Love Song for Today. P65
Swaim, Alice Mackenzie
    Mirage of Memory. P68
    Sound of Ripening. P65
Swan Song. R. J. Foster. P68
The Swan. Euros Bowen. P87
Swann, Marla
    "Stress Crowds My Mind". P74
Swans
    The Meeting. Stanley Moss. P64
    Mendocino Meadow. Arline Beryl Lawrence.
        P72
    No Swan So Fine. Marianne Moore. P83
    The Swan. Euros Bowen. P87
    The Swans. Grace Schulman. P64
    Two Swans in a Meadow by the Sea. Michael
        Heller. P64
"Swans mate for life and never sing". Bird
    Notes on a Beautifiul But Noisy April

Morning. Scott Bates. P63
The Swans. Grace Schulman. P64
Swarbrick, Fran
     Love's Blasphemy. P65
Sward, Robert
     Alpha the Dog. P49
     Name-Dropping. P49
"Swarte smekyd smethes smateryd wyth". The
     Blacksmiths. Unknown. P66
Sweat-House Ritual No.1. Unknown. P78
Swede, George
     Several Short Poems. P49
"Sweep the house, daughter of chatter". Eat
     Nothing. Nyapal Kong. P53
Sweet and Low. Lord Tennyson. P51
"Sweet Beginning:.". Giacomo da Lentini. P69
Sweet Sixteen Lines. Al Young. P85
"The Sweet Smell of Cedar Sucked Out My
     Breath". Lorenzo. P77
Sweet Surprises. S. Doudney. P51
"Sweet and low, sweet and low". Lullaby,
     from The Princess. Lord Tennyson. P89
"Sweet are the thoughts that savor of
     content". Content, from Farewell to
     Follie, 1617. Robert Greene. P90
"Sweet blackbird is silenced...". Winter.
     Christina Georgina Rossetti. P51
"Sweet day, so cool, so calm, so bright".
     Virtue. George Herbert. P59
"A sweet disorder in the dress". Delight in
     Disorder. Robert Herrick. P90
"Sweet little bird in russet coat". The
     Autumn Robin. John Clare. P51
"A sweet little kitten...". What a
     Fondness!. C. K. Shreedharan. P72
"Sweet Morfudd, Maytime's godchild". His
     Affliction. Dafydd ab [or ab] Gwilym.
     P87
"Sweet peace, where dost thou dwell?...".
     Peace. George Herbert. P89
"Sweet to the morning traveller". The
     Traveller's Return. Unknown. P51
"The Sweet, Pleasant face". Giacomino
     Pugliese. P69
"Sweetest love, I do not go". Song. John
     Donne. P59
Swenson, May
     Night Visits with the Family. P79
Swenson, May (tr.)
     My Mother in Paradise. Lyubomir Levchev.
     P70
     The Room. Nino Nikolov. P70
     Two Painters. Lyubomir Nikolov. P70
"Swift is stern". Witches' Sabbatical. G. N.
     Gabbard. P63
Swift, Jonathan
     AEIOU. P51
     Time (An Enigma). P90
     The Voels: an Enigma. P90

"Swiftly walk over the western wave". To
     Night. Percy Bysshe Shelley. P89
The Swimmers. Allen Tate. P67
Swimming. Elaine Emmons. P77
"Swimming against the coarse grain". Visit
     to the Institute for the Blind. Felix
     Pollak. P57
Swimming and Swimmers
     Families at the Shore. Graham Everett.
     P64
     Pizarro Teaches the Mentally Retarded To
     Swim. Lee Bassett. P57
"Swimming by me was a man". Backstage at the
     Fillmore. Elaine Demakas. P58
"Swimming just below the surface". Swimming.
     Elaine Emmons. P77
"Swinburne found thirty-nine rhymes...". One-
     Up. Bruce Berger. P63
Swinburne, Algernon Charles
     A Match. P89
"Swing low pregnant branch". Sing Love,
     Small Frog. Lisa Grenelle. P65
The Swing. Mary I. Osborn. P51
Swinging. Irene Thompson. P51
Swings and Swinging
     The Grape-Vine Swing. William Gilmore
     Simms. P89
     The Swing. Mary I. Osborn. P51
     Swinging. Irene Thompson. P51
Swish. Christine Stratton. P73
"Swishing tealeaves around". Reading. M. P.
     A. Sheaffer. P56
A Switched Career. X. J. Kennedy. P63
Switzerland. Edna Bacon Morrison. P68
A Sword in a Cloud of Light. Kenneth
     Rexroth. P84
"Syllables of shadows and leaves". Stone
     Quarries. Salvatore Quasimodo. P61
Symbol of Courage. G. Soosai. P72
Symonds, John Addington (tr.)
     To Sleep. Giovanni della Casa. P89
Symons, Arthur
     To a Portrait. P89
Symons, Arthur (tr.)
     On Living, from Life Is a Dream. Pedro
     Calderon de la Barca. P90
     Songs of Autumn. Paul Verlaine. P89
"The synagogue dispirits the deep street".
     The Synagogue. Karl Shapiro. P84
Syntax. Robert Canzoneri. P63
"Sythen that Bretayne was biggede, and
     Bruyttus... ". Wynnere and Wastoure.
     Unknown. P66
Sze, Arthur
     Black Lightning. P57

"T'other day, as I was twining". Cupid
      Swallowed. Unknown-Greek. P89
"T. S. Eliot". A Note Toward a Definition of
      Culture. James Camp. P63
Tabb, John Banister
      Anonymous. P81
      Brother Ass and St. Francis. P81
      Clover. P81
      Evolution. P81
      The Sisters. P81
      To Shelley. P81
      The Water-Lily. P89,P81
The Table and the Chair. Edward Lear. P90
The Tables Turned. William Wordsworth. P89
Tablet IX. Armand Schwerner. P64
Tablet XXIII. Armand Schwerner. P64
Tablet XXV. Armand Schwerner. P64
"Taddeo Gaddi built me. I am old.". The Old
      Bridge at Florence. Henry Wadsworth
      Longfellow. P90
Tadema, L. Alma. See Alma-Tadema, Laurence
The Tadpole. E. E. Gould. P51
Taggard, Genevieve
      American Farm, 1934. P83
      Dilemma of the Elm. P83
      The Little Girl with Bands on her Teeth.
      P83
      Solar Myth. P83
      Try Tropic. P83
      With Child. P83
Tahir, M. Athar
      Transition. P91
The Tail of the Buffalo. Nyalual Pal. P53
TAJ. T. G. Prabha Shankar. P72
"Taint my dreams". Muse. Tobin F. Rockey.
      P68
Taitai, Kuek
      Fishing for Girls with a Rod and Line.
      Terese Svoboda (tr.). P53
Takada, Sakuzo
      "Buddha's Disciples". P72
      "There's an Old Woman". P72
"'Take a Look at This!' says the wife".
      Unknown. P62
"Take a good look around". Siege. Omar Lara.
      P71
"Take care of your hands of gold". Hands of
      Gold. Margaret L. Fellinger. P72
"Take him away, he's as dead as they die".
      Obituary. Kenneth Fearing. P83
"'Take it from a consort of queens...'.".
      As I Was Dying at the Steak House...
      Scott Bates. P63
"Take your bucket, and take your spade". The
      Sea. E. M. Adams. P51
Taking a Step. Bernard Bell. P73
"Taking always a keen interest". Mssrs. Mice
      And Co. Mary J. McArthur. P63
Taking for Granted. Kim Unsong. P72

A Tale from the Arabian Nights. Alison
      Shepherd. P68
The Tale of a Dog and a Bee. Unknown. P51
A Tale. Georgi Borisov. P70
Tales from a Family Album. Donald Justice.
      P67
Taliesin
      Battle of Argoed Llwyfain. Tony Conran
      (tr.). P87
      Death Song for Owain ab Urien. Tony
      Conran (tr.). P87
Taliesin, Selections. Richard Hovey. P81
Talk
      All Which Isn't Singing Is Mere Talking.
      Edward Estlin Cummings. P83
Talk. Orhan Veli Kanik. P91
Tall Nettles. Edward Thomas. P51
Tall Tale Weather. Holly Hester. P74
Tall Trees. Eileen Mathias. P51
"Tall oaks". Primeval Method. Selma
      Youngdahl. P72
Tallman, Albert
      Sisyphus. P68
Tallow. Bruce Kingery. P68
Tallyho the Fox. Louis Hasley. P63
Tamborines
      "Tamborines!". Langston Hughes. P60
Tanka. Helen Fountain. P72
Tanka. Neal Henry Lawrence. P72
Tanker. Virginia M. Hahn. P58
Tanticlaiux, Leticia (tr.)
      The Signature of Things. Raphael Vargas.
      P92
"Taped to the wall of my cell...". The Idea
      of Ancestry. Etheridge Knight. P67
Tarn, Nathaniel (tr.)
      Canciones sin Su Musica. Tomas Segovia.
      P92
      Interludio Idilico: Coda. Tomas Segovia.
      P92
      Rabinal-Achi: Act IV. Unknown. P78
Tasting the Earth. James Oppenheim. P82
Tate, Allen
      The Cross. P83
      Mother and Son. P83
      Mr. Pope. P83
      The Oath. P67
      Ode to the Confederate Dead. P67,P83
      The Swimmers. P67
Tate, James
      The Eagle Exterminating Company. P85
      Letting Him Go. P85
      The Lost Pilot. P85
      Pity Ascending with the Fog. P85
      Read the Great Poets. P85
      Schizophrenic Kiss. P85
      Stray Animals. P85
Tatera, Agnes Wathall
      Counterpint. P65

Tavern Guitar Playing a Jota Today...
      Antonio Machado. P61
"Tawny are the leaves turned but they still
      hold". Antique Harvesters. John Crowe
      Ransom. P67,P83
Taxes
      What's All This Fuss About Tax Reform?.
      Ned Pastor. P63
Taxi Number One-Forty-Nine. F. Anthony
      Blankenship. P68
Taylor, Ann
      The Sheep. P51
Taylor, Ann and Jane
      Cow and the Ass. P51
      The Meadows. P51
Taylor, Bayard (tr.)
      The Shepherd's Lament. Johann Wolfgang
      von Goethe. P89
Taylor, Becky
      Poetry. P74
Taylor, D. Scott
      Living Alone. P63
Taylor, Eleanor Ross
      Rachel Plummer's Dream Winter 1836. P79
Taylor, J. E. (tr.)
      If It Be True That Any Beauteous Thing.
      Michelangelo Buonarroti. P89
Taylor, Jane
      The Field Daisy. P51
      Thank You, Pretty Cow. P51
      Twinkle, Twinkle, Little Star. P51
      Two Little Kittens. P51
Taylor, Jeffreys
      The Milkmaid. P90
Taylor, Peter
      The Hand of Emmagene. P79
Taylor, Sir Henry
      The Scholar, from Edwin the Fair. P90
Tea Time Remembered. Alma L. Wilson-Barry.
      P72
"Teach me the secret of thy loveliness". To
      a Wind-Flower. Madison Cawein. P81
"Teach me, Father, how to go". A Prayer.
      Edwin Markham. P51
"Teach me, my God and king". The Elixir.
      George Herbert. P51,P59
The Teacher. Leslie Pinckney Hill. P90
Teaching and Teachers
      Socrates' Ghost Must Haunt Me Now.
      Delmore Schwartz. P84
      The Teacher. Leslie Pinckney Hill. P90
      Theory. Dan Murray. P64
A Tear. Samuel Rogers. P90
Tears. Danielle Mann. P74
Tears. Lizette Woodworth Reese. P81
Tears, Good Little Fellows. William Walter
      De Bolt. P72
Teasdale, Sara
      Barter. P82

Blue Squills. P82
Buried Love. P82
Central Park at Dusk. P82
Day's Ending (Tucson). P82
Effigy of a Nun. P82
I Am Not Yours. P82
I Have Seen the Spring. P82
I Shall Not Care. P82
The Inn of Earth. P82
The Kiss. P82
The Long Hill. P82
Night Song at Amalfi. P82
Spring Night. P82
There Will Come Soft Rains. P82
The Voice. P82
Tedlock, Barbara (tr.)
      They Went to the Moon Mother. Unknown.
      P78
Tedlock, Dennis (tr.)
      The Boy and the Deer. Andrew Peynetsa.
      P78
Teigen, Maynard G.
      Divorce. P72
Tekk Me. Beryl Pierce. P72
The Telephone Call. Jack Prelutsky. P50
Television
      Television News. Judy Little. P88
Tell Brave Deeds of War. Stephen Crane. P81
Tell Me. Norma Lopez Garcia. P68
Tell Me a Lie. Vladimir Golev. P70
Tell Me If You Remember, Love. Antonio
      Machado. P61
"Tell Me, Oh Subhaga, Which One Of Your
      Mistakes". Unknown. P62
Tell Me, Tell Me, Sarah Jane. Charles
      Causley. P76
Tell Me, Ye Winged Winds. Charles Mackay.
      P89
"Tell her I love". Poems for My Daughter.
      Horace Gregory. P83
"Tell me". Venus Transiens. Amy Lowell. P82
"' Tell me a story'.". Bedtime Stories.
      Lilian Moore. P55
"Tell me not, in mournful numbers". A Psalm
      of Life. Henry Wadsworth Longfellow.
      P89
"Tell me where is fancy bred". Love, from
      The Merchant of Venice. William
      Shakespeare. P89
"Tell me your secrets pretty shell". Shell
      Secrets. Unknown. P51
"Tell me, my patient friends--...". Speech
      to a Crowd. Archibald MacLeish. P83
"Tell youth to play with wine and love".
      Compensation, from The House of a
      Hundred Lights. (Frederick) Ridgely
      Torrence. P81
Tellesbo Tom
      Dreams. P58

Last Dance. P58
Quiet Time. P58
Trails. P58
White Death. P58
Telling About Coyote. Simon Ortiz. P78
Temperature, Temperature. Tracy Campbell.
P74
Ten Definitions of Poetry. Carl Sandburg.
P82
Ten Dreamers in a Motel. Josephine Miles.
P84
"**Ten** Indians surround me". Forest. Jules
Supervielle. P61
Ten Little Christmas Trees. Rodney Bennett.
P51
Ten Little Dicky-Birds. A. W. I. Baldwin.
P51
Ten Little Indian Boys. M. M. Hutchinson.
P51
"Ten little children". Dancing on the Shore.
M. M. Hutchinson. P51
"**Tender,** semi-.". For My Mother: Genevieve
Jules Creeley. Robert Creeley. P85
"**Tenderly,** ivy, on Sophocles'...". The Grave
of Sophocles. Simmias. P89
Tending a Cookout in Pouring Rain... X. J.
Kennedy. P63
The **Tennis** Court Oath. John Ashbery. P85
The **Tennis** Player Waits for What Waits...
Philip Appleman. P64
Tennyson, Lord
The Beggar Maid. P51
The Brook. P51
Charge of the Light Brigade. P90
The City Child. P51
Come into the Garden, Maud. P89
Cradle Song. P51
The Death of the Old Year. P90
Doubt and Faith, from In Memoriam. P89
The Eagle. P51
Lullaby, from The Princess. P89
The Mermaid, sel. P51,P55
The Merman, sel. P51
The New Year, from In Memoriam. P89
The Owl. P51
Rizpah 17--. P90
The Shell. P51
Sir Lancelot and Queen Guinevere. P89
Song of the Milkmaid, from Queen Mary.
P89
Sweet and Low. P51
Terminal. Geoff Peterson. P86
"**Terrible** streets, the manichee hell of
twilight". The Peace of Cities.
Richard Wilbur. P84
"**Terrible** to see him, for no fault of his
own". Christ Before Pilate. Robert ab
Gwilym Ddu. P87
"**Terribly/Tough**". Cretaceous Period. A. J.

Kealoha Pendzik. P74
Terror to Unborn Children. Tonya McCulley.
P74
Testament of Love. Dorothea Neale. P65
"The **testimony** of Muffkin Puffkin unto the".
Religion Poem. Caroline Knox. P63
The **Tests** of Marriage (A Mason Sonnet
Sequence). Anne Marx. P65
Tewkesbury Road. John Masefield. P51
Texas
I'm a Texan Now. Gene Fehler. P63
Th Lovr Sighs if It All Revolvs Around Yu.
Bill Bissett. P49
"**Th** storee uv emil nelligan". Dew Yu Know.
Bill Bissett. P49
Thackeray, William Makepeace
The Age of Wisdom. P89
Little Billee. P90
A Tragic Story. P51
Thalman, Mark
The Ants. P63
The **Thames.** M. M. Hutchinson. P51
"**Thank** God for sleep in the Long Quiet
Night". John Drinkwater. P60
"**Thank** God for sleep in the long quiet
night". Morning Thanksgiving. John
Drinkwater. P51
A **Thank** You for Friends. Rodney Bennett. P51
Thank You, Pretty Cow. Jane Taylor. P51
Thank You: A Poem in Seventeen Parts.
Unknown. P78
"**Thank** heaven! the crisis,--.". For Annie.
Edgar Allan Poe. P89
"**Thank** you, God". Morning, Noon and Night in
Pacifica. Marrie Nunn. P72
"**Thanks** to a Perfect Love, I Feel So
Joyous". Rinaldo d'Aquino. P69
Thanks to Spring. Mary Anderson. P51
Thanksgiving
Attitudes of Thanksgiving. Jill
Breckenridge. P88
An Easter Chick. Thirza Wakley. P51
He Prayeth Well. Samuel Taylor Coleridge.
P51
Leavetaking. Anne Porter. P64
Morning Thanksgiving. John Drinkwater.
P51
Morning, Noon and Night in Pacifica.
Marrie Nunn. P72
Near Thanksgiving. Graham Everett. P64
Praise. Yaedi Ignatow. P64
Praise. Mary Anderson. P51
The Shepherd Boy's Song. J. Bunyan. P51
Thanks to Spring. Mary Anderson. P51
Thanksgiving Day
Journey Back. Delphia Frazier Smith. P72
Tharp, H. M.
Finger Folk. P51
That Cheerful Snowman. Hannah Lyons Johnson.

P80

"That Redness of Her Lip". Unknown. P62

"That center of attention-- an infantile face". Old Photograph of the Future. Robert Penn Warren. P67

"That day when among the sick". Meeting. Vassilis A. Papantoniou. P72

"That little grey-haired lady". The Little Old Lady. Rodney Bennett. P51

"That me alone you loved, you once did say". Carmina LXXII of Catullus. Richard Lovelace. P59

"That money talks". Money. Richard Armour. P63

"That profound cleft". June 9. William Carlos Williams. P79

"That shaman, owl man". The Deadly Dance. Unknown. P78

"That shell". You the Artifact. Alison Shepherd. P68

"That summer after high school". Only in a Poem. Mary B. Finn. P68

"That there's a bridegroom in the house". Loot. Taufiq Rafat. P91

"That voice cancels a host of voices as you leave". On a Mountain Road. Kaleem Omar. P91

"That was the second year...". Nightmare for Future Reference. Stephen Vincent Benet. P48

"That year the war went on...". The Colors of Our Age: Pink and Black. Dave Smith. P67

"That's a Rich Man Coming," from Wolf Songs... Unknown. P78

"That's/Your Son? the brother". A Man's Song About His Daughter. Unknown. P78

That...Who. Syed Ameeruddin. P72

Thayer, Ernest Lawrence
      Casey at the Bat. P90

Thee. Louise Louis. P65

"Their faces do not change at their mouths". Krasnopresnenskaya Station. N. Scott Momaday. P85

"Their housewarming present to themselves". Chinese Finches. Katha Pollit. P79

"Their time past, pulled down". Burning the Christmas Greens. William Carlos Williams. P82

"Theirs was a language within ours, a loge". The Parnassians. James Merrill. P85

Thelbitzer, William (tr.)
      "When I'm Out of the House in the Open, I Feel Joy". Unknown. P60

Theme for English B. Langston Hughes. P83

"Then all the nations of birds lifted...". The Season of Phantasmal Peace. Derek Walcott. P48

"Then Bedwyr carried the Lord of the land".

Arthur's Passing, sels. Thomas Gwynn Jones. P87

"Then sang Kalypso yet another song". Kalypso. Trumbull Stickney. P81

"Then the little Hiawatha". Hiawatha's Brothers. Henry Wadsworth Longfellow. P51

"Then, when I'd seen them leave the bay". And Back. Rodney Bennett. P51

Theory. Dan Murray. P64

Theory of Flight. Muriel Rukeyser. P84

There Are Big Waves. Eleanor Farjeon. P51

"There Are Some Especially Who Stretch Their Mouths". Unknown. P62

There Came Whisperings. Stephen Crane. P81

There Exists the Eternal Fact of Conflict. Stephen Crane. P81

There Has to be a Jail for Ladies. Thomas Merton. P84

There Is a Backyard. Haywood Jackson. P68

There Is a Garden in Her Face, from An Houre's... Unknown. P89

There Is a Love. Evelyn Evans. P72

"There Is a Time for Climbing and for Descending". Re Enzo. P69

"There Is a Wonder in the Sweep". Mary G. Faulconer. P72

There Is of Course a Legend. Al Purdy. P49

There Is Such Power Even in Smallest Things. Arlo Bates. P81

There Is Such Power, from Sonnets in Shadow. Arlo Bates. P90

There Isn't Time. Eleanor Farjeon. P51

There Must Be Something. Orhan Veli Kanik. P91

"There Truly First Came to Me Deep Sorrow". Giacomo da Lentini. P69

There Was a Crimson Clash of War. Stephen Crane. P81

"There Was a Crooked Man, and He Went a Crooked Mile". Unknown. P51

There Was a Great Cathedral. Stephen Crane. P81

"There Was a Little Dog, and He Had a Little Tail". Unknown. P51

"There Was a Little Rabbit Sprig". Unknown. P51

There Was a Man and a Woman. Stephen Crane. P81

There Was a Man Who Lived a Life of Fire. Stephen Crane. P81

"There Was a Young Lady of Wales". Edward Lear. P90

"There Was an Old Lady of France". Edward Lear. P90

"There Was an Old Man of Moldavia". Edward Lear. P90

"There Was an Old Man Who Supposed". Edward Lear. P90

"There Was an Old Man, Who When Little".
      Edward Lear. P90
"There Was an Old Person of Hurst". Edward
      Lear. P90
"There Was an Old Person Whose Habits".
      Edward Lear. P90
There Was One. Stephen Crane. P81
There Was Set Before Me. Stephen Crane. P81
There Was, Before Me. Stephen Crane. P81
There Were Many Who Went. Stephen Crane. P81
There Will Come Soft Rains. Sara Teasdale.
      P82
"There are all kinds of men". A Thank You
      for Friends. Rodney Bennett. P51
"There are always signs when the deer
      comes". The Deer. Noel M. Valis. P56
"There are bare places". On the 401 from
      Waterloo to Toronto. Douglas Smith.
      P49
"There are birds larger than us, I know
      that". The Eagle Exterminating
      Company. James Tate. P85
"There are gains for all our losses". The
      Flight of Youth. Richard Henry
      Stoddard. P89
"There are girls who should have been
      swans". After Whistler. Lisel Mueller.
      P88
"There are many monsters that a glassen
      surface". The Octopus. James Merrill.
      P85
"There are many ways of tenderness".
      Testament of Love. Dorothea Neale. P65
"There are miracles that happen". Breaking
      Silence. Janice Mirikitani. P85
"There are no bells". Solitude. Iris Jean
      MacLeod. P72
"There are no colors in the fairest sky".
      Walton's Book of Lives, from
      Ecclesiastical Sonnets. William
      Wordsworth. P90
"There are no dry bones". The Bones of My
      Father. Etheridge Knight. P52
"There are no handles upon a language".
      Languages. Carl Sandburg. P82
"There are no stars to-night". My
      Grandmother's Love Letters. Hart
      Crane. P83
"There are so many things to do to-day".
      Every Day. Mary I. Osborn. P51
"There are times when we men write". Three
      Poems on Death. Carlos Bousono. P61
"There are too many waterfalls here...".
      Questions of Travel. Elizabeth Bishop.
      P84
"There are twelve months throughout the
      year". September. Mary Howitt. P51
"There came to the beach a poor exile...".
      Exile of Erin. Thomas Campbell. P90

"There comes a day when the trees". Crossing
      over, from Your Tired, Your Poor.
      Lisel Mueller. P88
"There comes a time". Changing. Wendi
      Sloniker. P74
"There in his room, whene'er the moon". Ode
      for a Master Mariner Ashore. Louise
      Imogen Guiney. P81
"There is a bird bath on our grass". The
      Bird Bath. Florence Hoatson. P51
"There is a boy who waltzes by". Airport.
      Elaine Demakas. P58
"There is a flower, a little flower". The
      Daisy, sel. James Montgomery. P51
"There is a great amount of poetry in
      unconscious". Critics and
      Connoisseurs. Marianne Moore. P83
"There is a lure in the moonlit night!.".
      The Night. Nellie Parodi. P72
"There is a maker". Wizards. Alonzo Gonzales
      Mo. P78
"There is a painted bus". The Bus. Peter
      [pseud.]. P51
"There is a place that some men know". The
      Cross. Allen Tate. P83
"There is a singer everyone has heard". The
      Oven Bird. Robert Frost. P82
"There is a tide in the affairs of men".
      Poet's Reprieve, from August Presence.
      Ilango Kamalan. P72
"There is a time before snow". Interlude.
      Miriam Pederson. P56
"There is another who dwells in me". Another
      Side of Me. Beth Hirschfeld. P74
"There is but one May in the year". May-
      Time. Unknown. P51
"There is mud under the frizzling". Setting
      for the Portrait. Margaret Avison. P49
"There is no". Lament. Charles P. Martin.
      P58
"There is no chart of his movement...". Grey
      Owl's Poem. Gwendolyn Macewen. P49
"There is no evidence left". Crucifiction.
      Dan Valenti. P56
"There is no going back and re-aligning".
      Mirage of Memory. Alice Mackenzie
      Swaim. P68
"There is no impeding". Sailing, Sailing.
      Lillian Morrison. P63
"There is no longer". The Awakened Heart.
      Anne Yannie Corrado. P65
"There is no one". A Formal Appeal. Kaleem
      Omar. P91
"There is no place like home". Go Back.
      Nirupama Narasimham. P72
"There is one more mess in East Hampton".
      Inquiline. Allen Planz. P64
"There is some logic here to trace, and I".
      Three Darknesses. Robert Penn Warren.

P67
"There is something in the air". 3. R. K.
    Singh. P72
"There is the star bloom of the moss".
    Forest. Jean Garrigue. P84
"There is, all around us". Humpbacks. Mary
    Oliver. P52
"There isn't much that's left to tell".
    Smoker's Epitaph. John D. Engle Jr.
    P63
"There lay within a sandy tomb...". The
    Steamboat Bertrand. Gloria A. Martin.
    P68
"There lived a sage in days of yore". A
    Tragic Story. William Makepeace
    Thackeray. P51
"There lived in a laburnum tree". The Yellow
    Fairy. Charlotte Druitt Cole. P51
"There once was a boy named Peter".
    Limerick. Scott Bruno. P73
"There once was a cobbler". The Kind Mouse.
    Natalie Joan. P51
"There once was a man from Dandle".
    Limericks. Linda Galvao. P74
"There piped a piper in the wood". The Magic
    Piper. E. L. Marsh. P51
"There she swam in a pool". Flowerings. Jack
    Bernier. P56
"There wanders many a lighted star". The
    North Star. John Morris-Jones. P87
"There was a big bear". Honey Bear.
    Elizabeth Lang. P51
"There was a boy in a village who made". Saw
    the Cloud Lynx. Samuel Makidemewabe.
    P78
"There was a French writer named Sartre". A
    French Writer Named Sartre. Weldon
    Kees. P63
"There was a great battle Saturday morning".
    Battle of Argoed Llwyfain. Taliesin.
    P87
"There was a jovial beggar". The Jovial
    Beggar. Unknown. P51
"There was a knight of Bethlehem". Song.
    Henry Neville Maughan. P51
"There was a little baby once". A Child's
    Christmas Carol. Christine Chaundler.
    P51
"There was a naughty boy". A Song About
    Myself, sel. John Keats. P51
"There was a shout as dawn was breaking--.".
    The Hirlas of Owain, sels. Owain
    Cyfeiliog. P87
"There was a small boy of Quebec". Limerick.
    Rudyard Kipling. P90
"There was a time when she was so
    beautiful...". The Earth. Aric Chen.
    P74
"There was a witch who knitted things".

Knitted Things. Karla Kuskin. P55
"There was a young lady named Mitzi". Mitzi.
    Weldon Kees. P63
"There was a young lady of Niger".
    Limericks. Unknown. P90
"There was a young man from Kentucky".
    Limerick. Justin Petosa. P73
"There was an ape in the days...". Darwin.
    Mortimer Collins. P90
"There was an Indian, who had known no
    change". The Discovery. Sir John
    Collings ("Solomon Eagle") Squire. P90
"There was an infidel who". Water Walker.
    Richard Wilbur. P84
"There was an old party called
    Pennycomequick". Mr. Pennycomequick.
    P. M. Stone. P51
"There was an old wife and she lived...".
    The Old Wife and the Ghost. James
    Reeves. P55
"There was just a step to get into".
    Divorce. Judy Little. P88
"There was never a sound beside the
    wood...". Mowing. Robert Frost. P82
"There was snow curled in the lettuce...".
    Mother Lode Spring. Nan Townsend
    Degelman. P77
"There was such speed in her little body".
    Bells for John Whiteside's Daughter.
    John Crowe Ransom. P67,P83
"There were assembled, so the papers say".
    The Old Boatman. Robert Williams
    Parry. P87
"There were ninety and nine that safely
    lay". The Lost Sheep. Elizabeth
    Cecilia Clephane. P89
"There were saddened hearts in Mudville...".
    Casey's Revenge. James Wilson. P90
"There were things we". For Lovers. T. A.
    Shulgin. P58
"There were three gipsies a-come to my
    door". The Wraggle Taggle Gipsies.
    Unknown. P51
"There were three sailors of Bristol City".
    Little Billee. William Makepeace
    Thackeray. P90
"There will be rose and rhododendron". Elegy
    Before Death. Edna St. Vincent Millay.
    P82
"There'll be no need for poetry". Free
    Verse. Joanne Seltzer. P65
"There's a black fog hiding London".
    Promise. Florence Lacey. P51
"There's a merry brown thrush sitting...".
    The Brown Thrush. Lucy Larcom. P51
"There's a noise in my house". The 'Thing' in
    My House. Heather D. Soldato-Subkis.
    P73
"There's a ragged old man...". Mr.

Scarecrow. Sheila Braine. P51
"There's a silver house in the lovely sky".
    The Silver House. John Lea. P51
"There's a smile upon his face...". The TV
    Chef. Robert N. Feinstein. P63
"There's a story about a young quail".
    Quail. Katharyn Machan Aal. P63
"There's a tree out in our garden...". The
    Tree in the Garden. Christine
    Chaundler. P51
"There's an Old Woman". Sakuzo Takada. P72
There's My Darling. Unknown. P87
There's Snow on the Fields. Christina
    Georgina Rossetti. P51
"There's lots of things I'd like to be". The
    Hurdy-Gurdy Man. Elizabeth Fleming.
    P51
"There's moaning somewhere in the dark".
    Voice in the Darkness. Richard Dehmel.
    P90
"There's my war club". Song Picture No. 66.
    Unknown. P78
"There's no smoke in the chimney". The
    Deserted House. Mary E. Coleridge. P51
"There's so much trouble going on". Trouble.
    Michele M. Helm. P74
"There's something about the way". Evolution
    of Sand. Jean Pape. P77
"There's such a tiny little mouse". The
    Mouse. Thirza Wakley. P51
"There's that smell of the boats". Wharf.
    Myra Cohn Livingston. P76
"There, across the spread of hours and
    months". Re-cognition. Don Mager. P65
"There, truly they said in this house...".
    Ceremony of Sending: a Simultaneity...,
    sel. Unknown. P78
"There, where a French legionaire". In the
    Footsteps of Ghengis Khan. Jan Barry.
    P86
There--. Rodney Bennett. P51
Therefore I Must Tell the Truth. Torlino.
    P78
"Therefore all seasons shall be sweet to
    thee". All Seasons Shall Be Sweet.
    Samuel Taylor Coleridge. P51
Therese. Harold Leland Johnson. P65
Theriot, Jude
    Perception. P74
These Hills, Mother. Alice Derry. P88
These Perfect Years. Doanda Putnam Wheeler.
    P72
These Strewn Thoughts by the Mountain
    Pathway Sprung. George Santayana. P81
' These Students Couldn't Write Their
    Way...'. Ron Koertge. P63
These Things Amaze Me. Nyagak Pinien. P53
"These are amazing: each". Some Trees. John
    Ashbery. P85

"These are my murmur-laden shells that
    keep". On Some Shells Found Inland.
    Trumbull Stickney. P81
"These autumn gardens, russet, gray and
    brown". Loneliness. Trumbull Stickney.
    P81
"These dark colors I place against".
    Battlements. Harvey Shapiro. P64
"These dried-out paint brushes which
    fell...". Sestina from the Home
    Gardener. Diane Wakoski. P85
"These men were kings...". Black Majesty.
    Countee Cullen. P83
"These mornings when Matisse". Day/Night.
    Graham Everett. P64
"These patched mossy rocks by the shoreside--
    .". Back Country Feminist Landscape.
    Kay Murphy. P88
"These quick moments we". Fragments. Perry
    Walker. P68
"These transient years". These Perfect
    Years. Doanda Putnam Wheeler. P72
"These trees that fling their leafy
    boughs...". London Trees. Beryl
    Netherclift. P51
"These two are on collision course". Casey
    and the Vespula Diabolica. Beverley W.
    Stein. P72
"These/Few days we". Gambler's Wife (Right
    Diptych, an Extract). Pearl Crayton.
    P68
' They Are All Gone into the World of
    Light!'. Henry Vaughan. P59
They Clapped. Nikki Giovanni. P85
They Dragged Me Out by My Face. Diego
    Maquieira. P71
They Failed to Tell Me. James A. Rice. P86
They Found Him Sitting in a Chair. Horace
    Gregory. P83
They Have Not Survived. Roland Mathias. P54
They Lived Enamoured of the Lovely Moon.
    Trumbull Stickney. P81
"They Torment Us, Yet Give Us Happiness".
    Unknown. P62
They Went to the Moon Mother. Unknown. P78
"They are my Dresden, my Amritsar". Brood
    Queen (A Vision of Moths). Charles P.
    Martin. P58
"They are taking us beyond Miami". The
    Removal. Unknown. P78
"They are there from the beginning". Deer in
    the Open Field. Patricia Hooper. P88
"They are with us always...". The Ditances
    They Keep. Howard Nemerov. P79
"They brought me ambrotypes". Rutherford
    McDowell, from Spoon River Anthology.
    Edgar Lee Masters. P82
"They calld to me as Ezra". Reckoning.
    Harry B. Sheftel. P72

"They came down in spirals". Crash. Sandra
    Rasmussen. P72
"They came, the rangers of the other
    side...". The Inventors. Rene Char.
    P61
"They clapped when we landed". They Clapped.
    Nikki Giovanni. P85
"They could have told us that the
    particulars". About Suffering They
    Were Never Wrong. Lisel Mueller. P88
"They creep up from behind a corner". Tears.
    Danielle Mann. P74
"They eat toad-in-the-hole...". English
    Rats. X. J. Kennedy. P63
"They grow so comely, a quiet host, fine
    gems". Heather. Eifion Wyn. P87
"They have fenced in the dirt road". Burial.
    Alice Walker. P67
"They have gone. The silence resettles".
    Letter from a Far Country. Gillian
    Clarke. P54
"They have set up a committee". The
    Fifteenth Century. Kaleem Omar. P91
"They held everything together". At a
    Concert. R. P. Dickey. P63
"They lean over the path". Orchids. Theodore
    Roethke. P84
"They lie at anchor in an ice-locked bay".
    Northwest Passage. Charles P. Martin.
    P58
"They live 'neath the curtain". Puk-Wudjies.
    Patrick R. Chalmers. P51
"They looked as if". Job Action. Ray Catina.
    P86
"They photograph me in a large shed". Notes.
    Aristoteles Espana. P71
"They say there is no hope--.". Sea Gods.
    Hilda ("H.D.") Doolittle. P82
"They say you can only die once". Dying Is
    Forever. Michael T. Sargent. P86
"They sent me a letter, said greetings".
    They Failed to Tell Me. James A. Rice.
    P86
"They set the slave free...". The Slave.
    James Oppenheim. P82
"They sound like howling wolves from here".
    Song on the Way to Jail, from Wolf
    Songs... Unknown. P78
"They stained the great planes...". The
    Stains Slid from Top to Bottom in
    Silence. Gonzalo Munoz. P71
"They step in my cab the dudes and the
    drab". Taxi Number One-Forty-Nine. F.
    Anthony Blankenship. P68
"They take us to chop wood in the forests".
    Roads. Aristoteles Espana. P71
"They taught us backwards, father:.". The
    Chicken Coop. Diego Maquieira. P71
"They tell me I should pack my suitcase".

    Leaving. Aristoteles Espana. P71
"They told me not to keep a diary". P. S.
    Instead of a Beginning. Lyubomir
    Levchev. P70
"They told me, Heracleitus, they told
    me...". The Dead Poet-Friend.
    Callimachus. P89
"They went after him with a long stick". The
    Outlaw. David Ignatow. P84
"They went to sea in a sieve, they did". The
    Jumblies. Edward Lear. P89
"They were wise guys". Wise Guys. Ray
    Catina. P86
"They will never die on that battlefield".
    Uccello. Gregory Corso. P85
"They're always abusing the women". Women's
    Chorus. Aristophanes. P90
"They're at every firebase". Piss Tubes.
    Michael D. Clodfelter. P86
"They're hiding by the pebbles". Sea
    Fairies. Eileen Mathias. P51
They've Broken the Most Delicate Bone in My
    Ear. Manuel Silva Acevedo. P71
"Thia little bunny said, 'Let's play'.".
    Finger Play. Unknown. P51
Thibaudeau, Colleen
    The Tin Shop. P49
The Thief. Irene F. Pawsey. P51
"Thin lines". Waiting. T. A. Shulgin. P58
"Thin winter wind blows". Awakenings (A
    Sedoka). Linda Hutton. P72
"A Thing of True Value Is That Which Is
    Handy". Unknown. P62
The' Thing' in My House. Heather D. Soldato-
    Subkis. P73
Things As They Are. Bonnie Jacobson. P63
Things I Like. Marjorie H. Greenfield. P51
Things of the Blind. Paz Molina. P71
Things That Happen to You. Alonzo Gonzales
    Mo. P78
"The things that make a life to please".
    Martial's Epigrams, Book X, 47. Sir
    Richard Fanshawe. P59
Things to Do Around a Lookout. Gary Snyder.
    P85
Think as I Think. Stephen Crane. P81
"Think not I love him...". Love Dissembled,
    from As You Like It. William
    Shakespeare. P89
"Think of Galileo". Heresy. Gwendolyn
    Vincent. P58
"Think you I am not fiend and savage too?.".
    To the White Fiends. Claude McKay. P82
Thinking of Other Universes. Muneer Niazi.
    P91
"Thinking to Himself, 'I Will Make Love to
    Her'". Unknown. P62
The Third Poem of Leave-Taking. Hamid Skif.
    P91

The **Third** World. Lawrence Ferlinghetti. P85
"The **third** day of our honeymoon". Honeymoon
        in Rice. Francis J. Smith. P63
"13 Etznab was the day when the land...".
        The Book of Chilam Balam: a Chapter...,
        sel. Unknown. P78
The **13th** Horse Song of Frank Mitchell
        (White). Unknown. P78
Thirteen Ways of Looking at a Blackbird.
        Wallace Stevens. P83
"**30** Dreams Held in a Hand". Wolfgang D.
        Gugl. P72
This Day Is Not Like That Day. Jean
        Garrigue. P84
This England. William Shakespeare. P51
This Humanity. Frances Adams Moore. P72
This Is England. Laurence Binyon. P51
This Is How Memory Works. Patricia Hampl.
        P88
"**This** Is the Key of the Kingdom". Unknown.
        P51
This Native Land. Thomas Davis. P51
This Poor Man. William John Gruffydd. P87
This Very Hour. Lizette Woodworth Reese. P81
This Year. Rebecca Caudill. P75
"**This** blood will never dry up on the earth".
        Pledges. Pierre Emmanuel. P61
"**This** blue heron effortlessly managing".
        Blue Heron Near the Old Mill Bridge.
        Raymond Souster. P49
"**This** Bol is Bol Wor". The Big Knot. Nyalual
        Pal. P53
"**This** book is all that's left me now,--.".
        My Mother's Bible. George Pope Morris.
        P89
"**This** bronze doth keep the very form and
        mould". On the Life-Mask of Lincoln.
        Richard Watson Gilder. P81
"**This** day of all the destined days that
        are". Let Us Forego Life's Puppet
        Show. Helen Carter King. P72
"**This** day writhes with what? The lecturer".
        The Ultimate Poem is Abstract. Wallace
        Stevens. P83
"**This** ends: entering the show of silence".
        Night Has Been as Beautiful as
        Virginia. Kenneth Patchen. P84
"**This** figure, that thou here seest put". On
        the Portrait of Shakespeare. Ben
        Jonson. P90
"**This** hotel room suits me fine". The Girl of
        Rue Joli. Dennis Moore. P86
"**This** house uniquely built on its strange".
        Falling Water. James Russell Vaky. P68
"**This** is earth". The First Day of Summer.
        Kathleen Norris. P88
"**This** is how snowflakes play about". A
        Finger Play for a Snowy Day. Unknown.
        P51

"**This** is no haunt". Common Land Above
        Trefenter. Jeremy Hooker. P54
"**This** is our school". School Creed. Unknown.
        P51
"**This** is presented". Map of Vancouver
        Island. Neile Graham. P49
"**This** is the account...". The Popol Vuh:
        Beginnings, sel. Unknown. P78
"**This** is the age of boredom". The Shadow and
        the Cross. Salah Abdul-Sabur. P91
"**This** is the beauty of being alone". Stray
        Animals. James Tate. P85
"**This** is the black sea-brute bulling
        through...". Leviathan. William
        Stanley Merwin. P85
"**This** is the day when the fairy kind".
        Friday. Sir Walter Scott. P51
"**This** is the house that Jack built". The
        House That Jack Built. Unknown. P51
"**This** is the key to the playhouse". The
        Playhouse Key. Rachel (Lyman) Field.
        P51
"**This** is the life". Limbo. Yaedi Ignatow.
        P64
"**This** is the other season--.". Other Season.
        Bonnie McConnell. P68
"**This** is the song". Credo. William DeWitt
        Snodgrass. P63
"**This** is the song of the wave! The mighty".
        A Song of the Wave. George Cabot
        Lodge. P81
"**This** is the Strait of Messina". Fata
        Morgana. Siv Cedering. P64
"**This** is the way we make our hay".
        Haymaking. Alfred Perceval Graves. P51
"**This** is the way we wash our clothes". Wash-
        Day. Lilian McCrea. P51
"**This** is the weather the cuckoo likes".
        Weathers. Thomas Hardy. P51
"**This** is the world we wanted". Gretel in
        Darkness. Louise Gluck. P85
"**This** is where I stay". Somewhere Near the
        Mekong River, 1966. Dennis Moore. P86
"**This** is where the Plains Indians". Legend
        of Indian Summer. Edna Bacon Morrison.
        P68
"**This** knee-high nymph is three-year Johnny".
        Light and Shadow. Robert Francis. P63
"**This** letter, a cold wind in August...".
        Black Mail. Maryann Calendrille. P64
"**This** life, and all that it contains, to
        him". The Scholar, from Edwin the
        Fair. Sir Henry Taylor. P90
"**This** little flag to us so dear". The Union
        Jack. Jeannie Kirby. P51
"**This** loud morning". The Third World.
        Lawrence Ferlinghetti. P85
"**This** Louisiana sun". Southern Vortex.
        William Mills. P67

"This lovely flower fell to seed". For My
       Grandmother, fr. Four Epitaphs.
       Countee Cullen. P83
"This morning, the rain pucker over". A
       Letter from Gwyther Street. Roland
       Mathias. P54
"This music that can captivate my soul".
       Beethoven Pathetique. Mary B. Finn.
       P68
"This November, the brown leaves". For Susan,
       Turning Thirty. Anita Skeen. P88
"This old piano with a sweeter treble". For
       Sally, with a Piano. Paul Goodman. P84
"This past Saturday, while". At the Used
       Book Sale. Ken Stone. P56
"This photograph is a message". Beergarden
       Photo. Therese Becker. P88
"This poem". I. Marion Jane Richardson. P65
"This seashell is an ocean cove". Seashell.
       Sandra Liatsos. P76
"This sparrow". The Sparrow--to My Father.
       William Carlos Williams. P82
"This summer morning I walk down...".
       Origins of the Body. William
       Carpenter. P48
"This time I'll show up". Song Picture No.
       68. Unknown. P78
"This town, slung like a washline on the
       hill". Farther North. M. Travis Lane.
       P49
"This was a star stood still". Star of
       Bethlehem. Alun Llywelyn-Williams. P87
"This was no image that held me". Glint.
       Euros Bowen. P87
"This was the table. Its surface, its legs".
       The Ghost. Agnes Nemes Nagy. P92
"This Wednesday the sky ran out of
       batteries". Wire Meshes. Aristoteles
       Espana. P71
"This will be my last poem tonight". At the
       Poetry Reading: 'This Is a Poem About
       That'. Jim Daniels. P63
"This will be the last ditch to fall".
       Capital. John Tripp. P54
"This window". Window. P. D. Murphy. P56
"This world is not conclusion". The World Is
       Not Conclusion. Emily Dickinson. P48
"Thistle and darnel and dock grew there".
       Nicholas Nye. Walter De La Mare. P51
Thomas (Islwyn), William
       The Storm, sels. Tony Conran (tr.). P87
Thomas, Dylan
       A Refusal To Mourn the Death, by Fire, of
       a Child... P48
Thomas, Edward
       Tall Nettles. P51
Thomas, Evan
       To the Noble Women of Llanarth Hall. Tony
       Conran (tr.). P87

Thomas, Gwyn
       And For Your Children. Tony Conran (tr.).
       P87
       Crossing a Shore. Tony Conran (tr.). P87
       Goggy. Tony Conran (tr.). P87
       Leaf. Tony Conran (tr.). P87
Thomas, Joan Gale
       "God of All Our Cities". P60
Thompson, Francis
       Ex Ore Infantium. P51
Thompson, Irene
       Caravan. P51
       The Country Child. P51
       Feet. P51
       The Holiday Train. P51
       A Penny Wish. P51
       Rainy Nights. P51,P75
       Secret Places. P51
       Swinging. P51
       The Town Child. P51
       Welcome to Spring. P51
Thomson, James ("B.V.")
       In the Train. P51
"Thor hammered the Zildjians like fury".
       Turkish Thunder. Gwendolyn Vincent.
       P58
Thoreau, Henry
       Everyman's Walden. Ann Shermer. P65
Thoreau, Henry David
       Mist. P90
Thorley, Wilfred
       Fan, the Filly. P51
       Song for a Ball-Game. P51
Thorpe, Jennie
       The Young Indians. P74
Thorsen, Thor
       Why?. P72
"Those Who Know the Good and Bad". Unknown.
       P62
"Those living masters!.". The Living
       Masters. Gavin Ewart. P63
"Those rivers run from that land". Song.
       Robert Creeley. P85
"Those tunes don't recollect one memory". A
       Local Man Doesn't Like the Music.
       James Whitehead. P67
Thou Art Not Lovelier Than Lilacs,--No. Edna
       St. Vincent Millay. P82
"Thou Grace Divine, encircling all". The
       Love of God. Eliza Scudder. P89
"Though her vision fails". Tanka. Helen
       Fountain. P72
"Though I am little as all little things".
       Not Overlooked. James Oppenheim. P82
"Though it's true we were young girls...".
       For Jan, in Bar Maria. Carolyn Kizer.
       P79
"Though many a time we must weep...". Hope.
       Robert ab Gwilym Ddu. P87

"Though painters sat Italian light does well". Going to Italy. Donald Davie. P79

"Though the slate". The Mason's Law. Jeremy Hooker. P54

"Though the Turks hate us". As Helpless as a Dhow on a Still Day. Dhor Ding Cuol. P53

Thought

As in the Midst of Battle There Is Room. George Santayana. P81

Dreams. Thomas Traherne. P59

The Fountain. Donald Davie. P79

Once I Knew a Fine Song. Stephen Crane. P81

Poet's Reprieve, from August Presence. Ilango Kamalan. P72

Think as I Think. Stephen Crane. P81

"Thought was". Thought-Song Two, from Tepehua Thought-Songs. Unknown. P78

Thought-Song One, from Tepehua Thought-Songs. Unknown. P78

Thought-Song Three, from Tepehua Thought-Songs. Unknown. P78

Thought-Song Two, from Tepehua Thought-Songs. Unknown. P78

"Thoughtless!.". Unknown. P62

"... thoughts come and go wine". Great Chorus (For Gramps). Joseph S. Pecorella. P68

Thoughts for a Cold Day. Unknown. P51

"Thoughts soar along through time and space...". A Mountain Place. Ruby Phillipy. P72

"A thousand pardons". Proud Father with Buried Son. Judd Allen. P72

The Thousand-and-One Nights. Gwendolyn Vincent. P58

"Thousands of years of fine sand". The Art of Poetry. Pierre Emmanuel. P61

"3 A.M., the night is absolutely still". Night Below Zero. Kenneth Rexroth. P84

3. R. K. Singh. P72

Three. Charles West. P63

Three Darknesses. Robert Penn Warren. P67

Three Dogs. E. C. Brereton. P51

The Three Fishers. Charles Kingsley. P90

Three Ghost Songs. Unknown. P78

Three Hundred Thousand More. Unknown. P90

Three Little Birds. Stephen Crane. P81

Three Little Kittens a Cat's Tale with Additions. Eliza Lee Follen. P89

The Three Little Kittens. Unknown. P51

Three Little Men in a Boat. Rodney Bennett. P51

The Three Little Pigs. Sir Alfred A. Scott-Gatty. P51

Three Mice. Charlotte Druitt Cole. P51

Three Morning Scenes. Robert Hahn. P58

Three Plum Buns. Christina Georgina Rossetti. P51

Three Poems on Death. Carlos Bousono. P61

Three Quatrains. Edward Arlington Robinson. P81

Three Songs of Mad Coyote. Unknown. P78

Three Threnodies. Donald J. Kintner. P68

"Three hundred hours have gone by". Hell and Solitude. Aristoteles Espana. P71

"Three little chickens". A Tug-of-War. M. M. Hutchinson. P51

"Three little mice walked into town". Three Mice. Charlotte Druitt Cole. P51

"The three men coming down the winter hill". Winter Landscape. John Berryman. P79

"Three poets, in three distant ages born". Under the Portrait of John Milton. John Dryden. P90

"Three students were travelling...". The Landlady's Daughter. Johann Ludwig Uhland. P89

"Thro' the night Thy angels kept". A Child's Prayer. William Canton. P51

Through Night's Window. Mary Jane Barnes. P68

Through Nurseryland. Unknown. P51

"Through a grey day she searched". The Tilted Tombstone. Vivian Trollope-Cagle. P65

"Through an ice storm in Nashville...". False Youth: Two Seasons (Winter). James Dickey. P67

"Through dawn in February's wincing radiance". Walking Early by the Wye. Anne Stevenson. P54

"Through the Ages Man Has Sought HArd to Find". Eric-Frederic Wilson. P72

Through the Porthole. Marjorie Wilson. P51

"Through the crowded street return-.". Victor and Vanquished. Harry Thurston. P81

"Through the forest the boy wends all day". The Boy and the Flute. Bjornstjerne Bjornson. P89

"Through the sunny garden". Chillingham. Mary E. Coleridge. P51

"Throughout the day our sweet bells chime". Bluebells. P. A. Ropes. P51

"Throw Him Into the River," from Wolf Songs... Unknown. P78

"A thrush is tapping a stone". Dawn. Gordon Bottomley. P51

The Thrush's Nest. John Clare. P51

The Thrush. Dafydd ab [or ab] Gwilym. P87

Thunderbird Dynasty. Kevin Cline. P58

Thunderstorms. David Briggs. P73

"Thursday (you should understand) is the day...". Goggy. Gwyn Thomas. P87

Thurston, Hary

Love and Doubt. P81
Victor and Vanquished. P81
Tibbets, Laurene
Daybreak. P72
Tiger at the Bar. Chester G. Rider. P72
Tigers
The Tyger. William Blake. P51
"Tikeling, tikeling". Who Plays the Lyre?.
Phillip Macar. P53
The **Tilted** Tombstone. Vivian Trollope-Cagle.
P65
Time
An Afternoon's Wandering. Kolyo Sevov.
P70
Anti-Cycle for the New Year. Jane
Augustine. P64
Time. Rebecca Bailey. P73
Blind William's Song. William Stanley
Merwin. P85
Calmly We Walk Through This April's Day.
Delmore Schwartz. P84
The Chase. Mary Jane Barnes. P72
Time. Robert Creeley. P85
Cubes. Eleanore-Melissa. P68
Daily Joys. Barbara McCoy. P68
Day and Night. Eugenio Montale. P61
Day Into Night. Shane Iliff. P74
Time. Ted Fischer. P72
Time. George Herbert. P59
Time. Sergio Mansilla. P71
411 Days and Nights. Doug Rawlings. P86
Four Quartets, sels. Thomas Stearns
Eliot. P83
Fragments. Perry Walker. P68
Halley's Comet. Jaime Quezada. P71
I Count My Time by Times That I Meet
Thee. Richard Watson Gilder. P81
Imperfect Preterite. Juan Cameron. P71
Last Words. James Merrill. P85
Leisure. William Henry Davies. P51
Limping Boat. J. Bapu Reddy. P72
Little Boy Blue. Eugene Field. P81
Marking Time. T. Busch. P77
Mission of No Ends. P. K. Padhy. P72
New Season. Philip Levine. P52
On a Line from Sophocles. Carolyn Kizer.
P79
Poem ("What time"). Edward Estlin
Cummings. P79
Poem of the Forgotten Things. Jaime
Quezada. P71
The Rescue. Robert Creeley. P85
The Residual Years. William Everson. P84
Sonnet 25, fr. Three Sonnets From 'Deep
Within the Heart'. Syed Shamsul Haque.
P91
The Sound of the Light. William Stanley
Merwin. P52
"There Is a Time for Climbing and for
Descending". Re Enzo. P69
There Isn't Time. Eleanor Farjeon. P51
Time. Sergio Mansilla. P71
Time. Rebecca Bailey. P73
Time. Robert Creeley. P85
Time. Ted Fischer. P72
Time (An Enigma). Jonathan Swift. P90
Time in Its Passing. Dora K. T. Smith.
P72
Time Is. Bohumila Falkowski. P72
Time Is Leaving. James Richard Hurst. P68
Time Passes. Richard Eberhart. P72
The Time That Destroys Everything. Teresa
Calderon. P71
Time's Horses. Jules Supervielle. P61
Time, You Old Gipsy Man. Ralph Hodgson.
P51
The Ultimate Poem is Abstract. Wallace
Stevens. P83
A Year. Angie You. P73
Yesterday. Hugh Chesterman. P51
Time (An Enigma). Jonathan Swift. P90
"**Time** does not stand still". Cubes. Eleanore-
Melissa. P68
"The **time** has come--.". Returning Home.
Alice Mann Roney. P72
"**Time** has simply got to shut up. Or else".
Bones and Jewels. Paul Monette. P79
Time in Its Passing. Dora K. T. Smith. P72
Time in the Rock or Preludes to Definition
Selections. Conrad Aiken. P82
Time Is. Bohumila Falkowski. P72
Time Is Leaving. James Richard Hurst. P68
Time Passes. Richard Eberhart. P72
The **Time** That Destroys Everything. Teresa
Calderon. P71
"**Time** is". Meditation. Elizabeth M. Gilliam.
P72
"**Time** like the repetitions of a child's
piano". The Reconciliation. Archibald
MacLeish. P83
"**Time** present and time past". Four Quartets,
sels. Thomas Stearns Eliot. P83
"**Time** was created by man". Time. Ted
Fischer. P72
"The **time** will come when my mission is
over". L'Envoi. Caroline Kotowicz. P72
Time's Horses. Jules Supervielle. P61
Time, You Old Gipsy Man. Ralph Hodgson. P51
"**Time,** thieving herdsboy, has consumed...".
Sonnet 25, fr. Three Sonnets From
'Deep Within the Heart'. Syed Shamsul
Haque. P91
"**Time/Is** leaving". Time Is Leaving. James
Richard Hurst. P68
"The **times** come round again". To a Military
Rifle. Yvor Winters. P83
Timid Bunnies. Jeannie Kirby. P51
The **Tin** Shop. Colleen Thibaudeau. P49

Tinkham, Charles
    Adriatc. P56
"' Tinkle, tinkle, tinkle': 'tis the...".
    The Muffin-Man's Bell. Ann ("Aunt
    Effie") Hawkshawe. P51
Tiny Grandchild at the Beach. Alice M.
    Boughtwood. P68
"Tiny green birds skate over the
    surface...". Saturday Night in the
    Parthenon. Kenneth Patchen. P84
"Tiny shoes so trim and neat". The Fairy
    Shoemaker. Phyllis L. Garlick. P51
"Tipperty-toes, the smallest elf". Red in
    Autumn. Elizabeth Gould. P51
Tippett, James S.
    Familiar Friends. P51
Tippy-Tap. Virginia Junemann. P72
Tipton, Paul W.
    War. P86
    Webs. P86
The Tire Hangs in the Yard. Dave Smith. P67
Tired. Fenton Johnson. P82
Tired Tim. Walter De La Mare. P51
"The tires on my bike are flat". Since Hanna
    Moved Away. Judith Viorst. P50
"' Tis a lesson you should heed". Try Again.
    Unknown. P89
' Tis but a Little Faded Flower. Ellen
    Clementine Howarth. P90
"' Tis strange! I saw the skies". Dreams.
    Thomas Traherne. P59
' Tis the Last Rose of Summer, from Irish
    Melodies. Thomas Moore. P89
"Tit-tat-toe". A Baby Verse. Unknown. P51
The Tit. Llywelyn Goch ap Meurig Hen. P87
"Tithing/every Sunday". Worshiper. Gloria A.
    Maxson. P63
To - ("Music, when soft voices"). Percy
    Bysshe Shelley. P90
To a Cricket. William Cox Bennett. P51
To a Dog's Memory. Louise Imogen Guiney. P81
To a Fringed Genital. G. N. Gabbard. P63
To a Lady Who Reads Too Much. Alfred Dorn.
    P65
To a Mantled Prophet. Belle Adams. P68
To a Military Rifle. Yvor Winters. P83
To a Portrait. Arthur Symons. P89
To a Small Voyager Who Shares Her Room.
    Virginia E. Smith. P68
To a Walker of Ridges. Kaye Bache. P68
To a Wind-Flower. Madison Cawein. P81
To a Young Man. Edwin Markham. P81
To a Young Woman. Louis Dudek. P49
To Althea from Prison. Richard Lovelace. P90
To Amoret, of the Difference 'Twixt Him...
    Henry Vaughan. P59
To Amoret, Walking in a Starry Evening.
    Henry Vaughan. P59
To Amy from Her Father at Graduation. Carl

Moorefield. P65
"To all the humble beasts there be". Prayer
    for Gentleness to All Creatures. John
    Galsworthy. P51
"To Answer". A Reply. Jay Dougherty. P63
To an Optimist. Bessie Wherry Noe. P65
To Auden. Fahmida Riyaz. P91
To Autumn. John Keats. P51,P89
To Blossoms. Robert Herrick. P89
To Castara: the Reward of Innocent Love.
    William Habington. P59
To Celia. Ben Jonson. P59
To Delmore Schwartz. Robert Lowell. P84
To Diana. Evelyn Sewell Rineer. P65
To Discover. Janina Zydanowicz. P72
To Elsie. William Carlos Williams. P82
To George C. Wallace. Frances Clarkhandler.
    P72
"To Give Joy to My Heart". Stefano
    Protonotaro. P69
"To Grandfather". Lorenzo. P77
"To Guide You, He Is". David Kuehnert. P77
To Have and Too Old. Richard Armour. P63
To Have You Near. Terri L. Parent. P65
To His Coy Mistress. Andrew Marvell. P59
To His Importunate Mistress. Peter De Vries.
    P63
To Hywel ab Ifan Fychan. Guto'r Glyn. P87
To Ianthe, Sleeping, from Queen Mab. Percy
    Bysshe Shelley. P90
To John Ashbery. Frank O'Hara. P85
To Joya, Despairing. Kent Clair Chamberlain.
    P72
To Let. D. Newey-Johnson. P51
To Lucasta, Going Beyond the Seas. Richard
    Lovelace. P59
To Madame De Sevigne. Mathieu de Montreuil.
    P90
"To Market, to Market, To Buy a Fat Pig".
    Unknown. P51
To My Craft. Agnes Nemes Nagy. P92
To My Mother. Heinrich Heine. P89
To My Son. Muriel Ringstad. P72
To Night. Percy Bysshe Shelley. P89
To One Deaf. Sister Mary Lucina. P57
To Owain Gwynedd. Meilir ap Gwalchmai. P87
To Russia. Joaquin Miller. P81
To Seneca Lake. J. G. Percival. P51
To Shelley. John Banister Tabb. P81
To Sing the Song. Robert M. Howell. P65
To Sleep. Giovanni della Casa. P89
To Spring. William Blake. P51
"... To be a man and a woman as sun was...".
    A Myth of the Human Universe. Unknown.
    P78
"To be able to see every side...". Editor
    Whedon, from Spoon River Anthology.
    Edgar Lee Masters. P82
"To be an artist you need talent...". No

Muse Is Good Muse. Rochelle
Distelheim. P63

"To decapitate is to separate...". The
Cheshire Cat. Juan Luis Martinez. P71

"To every hearth a little fire". A Christmas
Wish. Rose Fyleman. P51

"To fall away finally". Last Gift. Lu
Cicada. P77

"To grass, or leaf, or fruit, or wall". The
Snail. William Cowper. P51

"To green nature, not the world, the poet
belongs". The Propaganda of the Poet.
Robert Williams Parry. P87

"To have been in Lotusland". My Everlasting
Vision. William Zeller. P65

"To hurt the Negro and avoid the Jew".
University. Karl Shapiro. P84

"To live at Kwabenya". Kwabenya. Okai. P92

"To live the mint and weeds with full
lungs". Dream. Georges Friedenkraft.
P72

"To loosen with all ten fingers held
wide...". Moss-Gathering. Theodore
Roethke. P84

"To me, one silly task is like another".
Cassandra. Louise Bogan. P83

"To mercy, pity, peace, and love". The
Divine Image. William Blake. P51

"To persist in what we do". To Write. Walter
Hoefler. P71

"To stand out in relief against the
visible". Movements on a Theme. Maxine
Silverman. P88

To the Bat. Edith King. P51

To the Beloved. Harry Maizel. P72

To the Cuckoo. William Wordsworth. P51,P89

To the Extent That I Haven't a Cat. June
Siegel. P63

To the Goddess of Liberty. George Sterling.
P81

To the Greyrock Woods. Llywelyn ap y Moel.
P87

To the Holy Spirit. Yvor Winters. P83

To the Immaculate Plains. Raul Zurita. P71

To the Memory of Ben Jonson. John Cleveland.
P90

To the Morning. Dawn R. Goodwin. P72

To the Noble Women of Llanarth Hall. Evan
Thomas. P87

To the Poetry Clubs of Wales. Bobi Jones.
P87

To the Supreme Being. Michelangelo
Buonarroti. P89

To the Terrestrial Globe. Sir William
Schwenck Gilbert. P90

To the White Fiends. Claude McKay. P82

To Thomas Moore. George Gordon, 6th Baron
Byron. P90

To Thy Will, O Lord. Bee Bacherig Long. P72

To W.P. George Santayana. P81

To Waken an Old Lady. William Carlos
Williams. P82

To Whistler, American. Ezra Pound. P82

To Write. Walter Hoefler. P71

To Wystan Auden in His Birthday. and Louise
Bogan, Edmund Wilson. P79

"To the music of the guzla". Attic Dance.
Joan Drew Ritchings. P63

"To think that always while for my sake".
Canciones sin Su Musica. Tomas
Segovia. P92

"To think when Diet made my lover less".
Triolet, After Titian. Sylvester
Pollet. P63

"To what new fates, my country, far".
Unmanifest Destiny. Richard Hovey. P81

"To-day as I went out to play". The Brown
Frog. Mary K. Robinson. P51

"To-day, I saw the catkins blow". February.
Dorothy Una Ratcliffe. P51

Toad the Tailor. N. E. Hussey. P51

The Toads of Spring. Mary B. Finn. P68

Toadstools. Elizabeth Fleming. P51

Toasts
Revelry of the Dying. Bartholomew
Dowling. P90
A Stein Song. Richard Hovey. P81

Tobacco Men. James Applewhite. P67

"Today a feast was given for my eleventh
year". Hieroglyphics. Bernice
Fleisher. P65

"Today her people starve". India. Dhiru
Desai. P72

"Today I will share adventure only".
Windward Cycle. Lloyd Stone. P72

"Today the art of our retreat". The Swan.
Euros Bowen. P87

"Today the child in me has triumphed". The
Child in Me. LaGrassa Nina. P56

"Today the house sighs, cottonwoods sway".
Stay. LaNita Moses. P72

"Today with My Remembrance of Pleasures".
Unknown. P62

Today, There Is Love. Faye Kicknosway. P88

Todd, Alice
If. P51
The Postman. P51

Todd, Elizabeth Simpson
Light. P72

Todde, Maria Celeste Achille
Night. Charles Guenther (tr.). P61

Toensmann, Wayne R.
Pine Night. P56

Together. Mary Magog Goggins. P72

"Together again at the same season...".
Pilgrimage. Yahya Kemal. P91

"Toil on! toil on!...". The Coral Insect.
Lydia Huntley Sigourney. P89

Tolkien, John Ronald Renel
For W. H. A. P79
Tollas, Tibor
Finale. Charles Guenther (tr.). P61
On the Site of the Convent. Charles
Guenther (tr.). P61
On the Watershed. Charles Guenther (tr.).
P61
Tomlinson, Charles
Van Gogh. P48
Tomorrow. Thelma L. Howard. P72
"Tomorrow I will take the train". Good-bye
California. Charles P. Martin. P58
Tomorrow in a Bubble. Maryann Calendrille.
P64
Tomorrow's Forecasts Are All Done. Alamgir
Hashmi. P91
Tongue Twisters
These Things Amaze Me. Nyagak Pinien. P53
"Tonight an old man, around seven o'clock".
Death in the Channel, fr. From a
Travel Diary. T.H. Parry-Williams. P87
"Too green the springing April grass".
Spring in New Hampshire. Claude McKay.
P82
"Too hard to go on any more". Terminal.
Geoff Peterson. P86
"Toothpaste/Toilet paper". Short-Term Memory
Loss. Tom Disch. P63
Topsy-Turvy Land. Phyllis M. Stone. P51
Topsy-Turvy Land. H. E. Wilkinson. P51
Topsyturvey-World. William Brighty Rands.
P90
Torlino
Therefore I Must Tell the Truth.
Washington Matthews (tr.). P78
Tornai and Daniel Weissbort, Jozsef (tr.)
Without Voice, Without Hope. Jozsef
Tornai. P92
Tornai, Jozsef
We Say This Prayer. William Jay Smith
(tr.). P92
Without Voice, Without Hope. Jozsef
Tornai and Daniel Weissbort (tr.). P92
Torrence, (Frederick) Ridgely
Carpe Diem, from The House of a Hundred
Lights. P81
Compensation, from The House of a Hundred
Lights. P81
The Conclusion of the Whole Matter, from
The House... P81
Evensong. P81
The Singers in a Cloud. P81
The Young Lovers, from The House of a
Hundred Lights. P81
Youth and Age, from The House of a
Hundred Lights. P81
"A torrential rain falls". Poem 20, from The
City. Gonzalo Millan. P71

Torture
(No Greater Pain Beneath the Trees).
Aristoteles Espana. P71
The Blindfold. Aristoteles Espana. P71
The Catholic Martyrs. Waldo Williams. P87
Notes. Aristoteles Espana. P71
Tot, Kong
He Will Float in the River Like a
Waterlily. Terese Svoboda (tr.). P53
Toth, Eva
The Creation of the World. Marianna
Abrahamowicz (tr.). P92
Tourist Death. Archibald MacLeish. P83
Tourists. Josephine Miles. P84
"The tourists were appalled...". Aztec Gods.
Rose Rosberg. P56
"Towards the Noel that morte saison".
Villonaud for This Yule. Ezra Pound.
P82
Tower of Babel. Thomas Merton. P84
The Tower. Gloria H. Procsal. P72
The Town Child. Irene Thompson. P51
The Town Tree. Alexander Gerov. P70
A Town Window. John Drinkwater. P51
"A town lies in the valley". The Silent
Town. Richard Dehmel. P89
Towns
Eglwys Newydd. John Tripp. P54
The Passing. James Deahl. P49
Rhigos. Robert Minhinnick. P54
The Silent Town. Richard Dehmel. P89
The Sins of Kalamazoo. Carl Sandburg. P82
The Town Child. Irene Thompson. P51
The Toy Band. Henry Newbolt. P51
Toys
His Toys. Michael Dennis Browne. P63
The Trace of God's Hand. Francis O.
Raniville. P72
Tract. William Carlos Williams. P82
Tradition. Helen Winter. P88
Tradition, Thou Art for Suckling Children.
Stephen Crane. P81
Traeger, Mary V.
Come, Fill the Cup. P72
Traffic Signals
In Traffic. Howard Moss. P64
A Tragic Story. William Makepeace Thackeray.
P51
Traherne, Thomas
Dreams. P59
On News. P59
Trails. Tom Tellesbo. P58
The Train. Mary E. Coleridge. P51
The Train. Dennis Moore. P86
Trains. Hope Shepherd. P51
The Trains. Seumas (James Starkey)
O'Sullivan. P51
Tramp, Tramp, Tramp. Unknown. P90
Tramps

Bowery. David Ignatow. P84
Tranquility
    All's Well, from The British Fleet.
        Thomas Dibdin. P89
    Carmel by the Sea. Alessandra A. Poles.
        P72
    Central Park at Dusk. Sara Teasdale. P82
    Hillcrest. Edward Arlington Robinson. P81
    The Lake Isle of Innisfree. William
        Butler Yeats. P89
    Medusa. Louise Bogan. P83
    Near Helikon. Trumbull Stickney. P81
    Of a Contented Spirit. Thomas, 2nd Baron
        Vaux. P90
    "To Grandfather". Lorenzo. P77
    Waiting. John Burroughs. P89
"The **transcript** records that day's dark...".
    (SIC)Transcript Gloria, or The Body
    Politician. Irving Feldman. P63
A **Transformation,** from The Metamorphoses.
    Ovid. P90
Transience
    As by the Shore At Break of Day. Thomas
        Moore. P90
    Erosion. Miriam Pederson. P88
    The Exclusion Principle. William Mills.
        P67
    The Flame. Isaac Daniel Hooson. P87
    Gathering Leaves. William Crwys Williams.
        P87
    The Island. Grace Schulman. P64
    It Must Someday be Answered. Elidir Sais.
        P87
    The Man Against the Sky. Edward Arlington
        Robinson. P81
    Meeting. Vassilis A. Papantoniou. P72
    Mysterious Evening. Verona Bratesch. P72
    Nothing Gold Can Stay. Robert Frost. P82
    "One Arc Ends Where the Next Begins".
        Judy Palen. P72
    The Slip. Wendell Berry. P67
    A Star Flowed. Yahya Kemal. P91
    To Blossoms. Robert Herrick. P89
    The Wood-Pile. Robert Frost. P82
Transient Barracks. Randall Jarrell. P84
Transition. M. Athar Tahir. P91
Translated to the Seven Astronauts. Mary
    McGowan Slappey. P72
Transplanting. Theodore Roethke. P84
"The **Trap-Wary** Crow Doesn't Want the Rice
    Ball". Unknown. P62
Traunstein, Russ
    Up Fair Kilties!. P63
Travel
    And Back. Rodney Bennett. P51
    Arrival. Vernon Edgar. P72
    "At Daybreak, with Snow Coming". Unknown.
        P62
    Beverly Carneiro. Robert Hill Long. P63

The Caravan. Madeleine Nightingale. P51
En Route. Anita H. Rosenau. P68
Envoy. Richard Hovey. P81
The Far-Farers. Robert Louis Stevenson.
    P51
Farewell to the Farm. Robert Louis
    Stevenson. P51
Follow Your Heart to the Land of
    Enchantment. Tom Hawkins. P63
Foreign Lands. Robert Louis Stevenson.
    P51,P89
From a Walking Song. Charles Williams.
    P51
Iguazu. Jules Supervielle. P61
An Invitation. Goronwy Owen. P87
Journey. Deb Plummer. P56
The Journey. Aidan Clarke. P51
The Jumblies. Edward Lear. P89
The Land of Cokaygne. Unknown. P66
Leaving. Sergio Mansilla. P71
"Look! the Traveller Smells, Touches,
    Kisses". Unknown. P62
Mandeville's Travels, sels. Unknown. P66
"The Mendicant Watches the Circle of Her
    Navel". Unknown. P62
Night of Returning. Eddie Silva. P56
"Oh Mendicant, Go Your Way". Unknown. P62
The Official Frisbee-Chasing Champion of
    Colorado. Robert Hill Long. P63
On the Northwest Hiawatha. Kathleen
    Norris. P88
Our First Journey. N.M. Rashed. P91
Over the Fields. Adeline White. P51
The Pedlar's Caravan. William Brighty
    Rands. P51
Questions of Travel. Elizabeth Bishop.
    P84
Recuerdo. Edna St. Vincent Millay. P82
Report 'Present'. Eleftheria Kounrouri.
    P72
A Rhyme Sheet of Other Lands. Hugh
    Chesterman. P51
A Sense of Place. Judith Minty. P88
The Song of a Traveller. Robert Louis
    Stevenson. P51
There--. Rodney Bennett. P51
Travel Journal, sel. Omar Lara. P71
Traveller's Rest. Bernard Hewitt. P72
The Traveller's Return. Unknown. P51
Travellers. Arthur St. John Adcock. P51
Travelling. Dorothy Gradon. P51
Travelling Alone. Blaga Dimitrova. P70
Voyages. Hart Crane. P83
The Wander-Lovers. Richard Hovey. P81
We Thank You!. L. E. Cox. P51
"Whenever the Traveller, with Fingers
    Spread". Unknown. P62
Where Lies the Land?. Arthur Hugh Clough.
    P51

Travel Journal, sel. Omar Lara. P71
Travel. See also Air Travel; Space...
"A traveller through a dusty road...". Small
    Beginnings. Charles Mackay. P89
Traveller's Rest. Bernard Hewitt. P72
The Traveller's Return. Unknown. P51
"The Traveller's Wife with Continually
    Flowing Tears". Unknown. P62
Travellers. Arthur St. John Adcock. P51
Travelling. Dorothy Gradon. P51
Travelling Alone. Blaga Dimitrova. P70
The Tree House. Kaleem Omar. P91
The Tree in the Garden. Christine Chaundler.
    P51
The Tree of the Sound of Silence. Greer
    Newcomb. P72
The Tree of the World. Clemente Riedemann.
    P71
Tree Old Woman. Samuel Makidemewabe. P78
Tree on the Hill. Ivan Tsanev. P70
The Tree. John Freeman. P51
Trees
    Behind His Eyes. David Ignatow. P64
    The Branch. Stanley Moss. P64
    The Brave Old Oak. Henry Fothergill
        Chorley. P89
    Cherry Tree. Ivy O. Eastwick. P51
    Child's Song in Spring. E. Nesbit. P51
    A Christmas-Tree Song. Rodney Bennett.
        P51
Trees. Samuel Taylor Coleridge. P51
    Dilemma of the Elm. Genevieve Taggard.
        P83
    Dutch Elm Disease. George E. Morrissey.
        P68
    The Five-Fingered Maple. Kate Louise
        Brown. P51
    "Here's to Thee". Unknown. P60
    Hill-Side Tree. Maxwell Bodenheim. P82
    If. Alice Todd. P51
    The Jungle Trees. Marjorie Wilson. P51
    "Juniper, Juniper". Unknown. P51
Trees. Donald J. Kintner. P68
    Larch Wood Secrets. Ivy O. Eastwick. P51
    London Trees. Beryl Netherclift. P51
    Loveliest of Trees. Alfred Edward
        Housman. P89
    No Anger in a Fallen Tree. Allan Maunula.
        P72
    O Tree. Hugh Seidman. P64
    The Oaks. Ivan McShane. P68
    Pine Music. Kate Louise Brown. P51
    Plain Chant for a Tree. Edna Meudt. P68
    Poplars. Helen Leuty. P51
    Primeval Method. Selma Youngdahl. P72
    Proud Little Spruce Fir. Jeannie Kirby.
        P51
    Pulling the Days Together. Graham
        Everett. P64

    Sho Chiku Bai. Howard O. Long. P72
    The Speaking Tree. Muriel Rukeyser. P84
    Tall Trees. Eileen Mathias. P51
    The Tree in the Garden. Christine
        Chaundler. P51
    The Tree of the Sound of Silence. Greer
        Newcomb. P72
    Tree on the Hill. Ivan Tsanev. P70
    The Tree. John Freeman. P51
    Trees. Donald J. Kintner. P68
    Trees. Samuel Taylor Coleridge. P51
    The War Against the Trees. Stanley
        Kunitz. P83
    When My Father Waters His Trees. Linda M.
        Hasselstrom. P88
    Willow Bend and Weep. Herbert Clark
        Johnson. P90
    Woodman, Spare That Tree. George Pope
        Morris. P89
    The Yewtree. Gruffudd Gryg. P87
"The Trees are waving to and fro". Just Like
    This. D. A. Olney. P51
The Trees in the Garden. Stephen Crane. P81
"The trees on the November hillsides".
    Scorpion Summer. Terry M. Paulsgrove.
    P77
"The trees rise from the darkness of the
    world". In the Ward: the Sacred Wood.
    Randall Jarrell. P84
Tregebov, Rhea
    Foot Soldier. P49
Trench, Richard Chenevix
    Different Minds. P89
    Harmosan. P90
Triads II. James Reaney. P49
"Tribunal, seed of virtue". Easter Hills of
    Peace. Emma Crobaugh. P68
Tricia's Fish. Lee Bennett Hopkins. P50
Trimble, Mary
    Dislocation. P88
    Now and Again. P88
    Port Letter. P88
Trinity. John Knoll. P86
Triolet, After Titian. Sylvester Pollet. P63
The Triple Fool. John Donne. P59
Tripp, John
    At Bosherston Ponds. P54
    Capital. P54
    Eglwys Newydd. P54
    Epitaph at Gilfach Goch. P54
    In the National Museum. P54
    A Note from Plwmp. P54
    Penarth. P54
    Scratch Farmer. P54
    Soil. P54
The Triumph of Life: Mary Shelley. Lisel
    Mueller. P88
Troll Trick. B. J. Lee. P55
Trollope-Cagle, Vivian

Love's Songs. P65
Pitie Three Goode Dere Soules. P65
The Tilted Tombstone. P65
Trolls
The Gnome. Harry Behn. P55
Troll Trick. B. J. Lee. P55
Troop Train. Karl Shapiro. P84
Tropical Night. John Tworoger. P72
Troubetzkoy, Ulrich
Reunion. P65
Trouble. Michele M. Helm. P74
Trouble at a Tavern. Dafydd ab [or ab]
Gwilym. P87
Trouble at the Farm. Ivy O. Eastwick. P51
Troubles. John Hildebidle. P56
Trowbridge, William
Self Help. P63
Viet Kong. P63
Trucks
Goggy. Gwyn Thomas. P87
I-35, South of Waco. William Virgil
Davis. P63
A True Account of Talking to the Sun at Fire
Island. Frank O'Hara. P85
True Love. Wade Newman. P63
"Truly, Mother, Winter Has Made". Unknown.
P62
Trust. Lizette Woodworth Reese. P81
The Trust. Gavin Burgess. P72
Trustworthiness
In Distrust of Merits. Marianne Moore.
P83
Truth
I Met a Seer. Stephen Crane. P81
Let Us Forego Life's Puppet Show. Helen
Carter King. P72
Mystic Shadow, Bending Near Me. Stephen
Crane. P81
Once There Was a Man. Stephen Crane. P81
The Sage Lectured Brilliantly. Stephen
Crane. P81
Sunny Eye. Maria Kukubaiska. P72
Therefore I Must Tell the Truth. Torlino.
P78
Truth, Said a Traveller. Stephen Crane.
P81
The Wayfarer. Stephen Crane. P81
Truth, Said a Traveller. Stephen Crane. P81
Try Again. Eliza Cook. P51
Try Again. Unknown. P89
Try Tropic. Genevieve Taggard. P83
Trying to Remember. Judith Minty. P88
Trysts
"'My Boy, Just As an Old Cow Pours Forth
Milk'". Unknown. P62
"She Is Sending Out Her Messenger".
Unknown. P62
"Son, Although She Is Shy". Unknown. P62
Tsanev, Ivan

Tree on the Hill. John Balaban (tr.). P70
Tsanev, Stefan
Hamlet XX. Roland Flint (tr.). P70
Strange Bird. Roland Flint (tr.). P70
Tsimshian Mourning Song. Unknown. P78
"' Tu-whitt, tu-whitt, tu-whoo, tu-whoo'.".
'Good Night', Says the Owl. Lady
Erskine Crum. P51
Tubal Cain. Charles Mackay. P90
Tucker, Memye Curtis
Airport Phone Booth. P63
Tudur, Sion
Two-faced. Tony Conran (tr.). P87
Warning to the Poets. Tony Conran (tr.).
P87
Tuesday. Alma Denny. P63
The Tuft of Flowers. Robert Frost. P82
A Tug-of-War. M. M. Hutchinson. P51
"Tumid ripe September morn on Beacon Hill--
.". Lipstick Graffito. Aletha
Humphreys. P68
Tuning the Trumpet. Noa Spears. P63
Tunnel Vision. David Cram. P63
Turco, Lewis
Amherst Neighbors. P63
The Gift. P63
Just God. P63
The Naked Eye. P63
Turkay, Osman
Sphinx Echoes the Sound Left by the Dead.
P72
"A Turkey Is Dancing Near the Rocks".
Unknown. P78
Turkish Thunder. Gwendolyn Vincent. P58
Turn To Go. William Howarth. P77
Turnbull, Eleanor (tr.)
Aldebaran. Miguel de Unamuno. P48
Turner, Becky
Statue of Liberty. P73
Turner, Nancy Byrd
London Rain. P75
Turning. Lucille Clifton. P52
Turning Once To Look Back. Ross Leckie. P49
"Turning into my own". Turning. Lucille
Clifton. P52
The Turtle. Mark Sanders. P63
The TV Chef. Robert N. Feinstein. P63
Turtles
The Turtle. Mark Sanders. P63
"Twa lyves thar er that cristen men
lyfes...". The Form of Living. Richard
Rolle. P66
Twain's Comet. Ted Plantos. P49
"' Twas brillig, and the slithy toves".
Jabberwocky, from Through the Looking-
Glass. Charles Lutwidge ("Lewis
Carroll") Dodgson. P90
' Twas but a Dream. Marjan Lindemans. P73
"' Twas in heaven pronounced...". A Riddle.

Catharine Fanshawe. P90

"' Twas the night before Christmas...". A
Visit from St. Nicholas. Clement Clark
Moore. P89

The 12th Horse Song of Frank Mitchell
(Blue). Unknown. P78

"Twelve moons ago". Sunsets Be Dear. Richard
Franklin. P65

"Twelve o' clock". Rhapsody on a Windy
Night. Thomas Stearns Eliot. P83

Twenty Million, from Lost Youth: the Last
War. Alfred Kreymborg. P82

"Twenty busy years ago". Double-Quick. Alice
Mackenzie Swaim. P65

"Twenty men crossing a bridge". Metaphors of
a Magnifico. Wallace Stevens. P83

Twice. M. M. Hutchinson. P51

"Twice I have promised you this". The Court
of Owain Glyndwr at Sycharth. Iolo
Goch. P87

Twice a Child. Naomi Long Madgett. P88

"Twice one are two". Twice. M. M.
Hutchinson. P51

"Twice or thrice had I loved thee". Air and
Angels. John Donne. P59

Twicknam Garden. John Donne. P59

Twilight. Heinrich Heine. P90

Twilight at Sea. Amelia B. Welby. P89

"' Twill soon be sunrise. Down the valley
waiting". Lakeward. Trumbull Stickney.
P81

"Twinkle! twinkle! little star!.". Deeds in
Orbit. Annie Laurie Leech. P72

Twinkle, Twinkle, Little Star. Jane Taylor.
P51

Twinkle, Twinkle, Little Star. Unknown. P89

"Twirling your blue skirts, traveling the
sward". Blue Girls. John Crowe Ransom.
P83

"2.30 a.m. These city streets are asleep".
At the Police Station. Raymond
Souster. P49

The Two Angels. John Greenleaf Whittier. P89

Two British Airmen. Thomas Merton. P84

Two Daughters Sing an Anniversary Ditty.
Wilma H. Clements. P68

Two Dicta of William Blake. Robert Duncan.
P52

Two Epitaphs. Louise Imogen Guiney. P81

The Two Families. Joyce L. Brisley. P51

Two Fool's Songs. Emile Verhaeren. P61

Two Hoorays for Holidays. Ned Pastor. P63

"Two dolphins paced me twenty feet from
shore". The Dolphin-Walk. Milton
Acorn. P49

"' Two hands upon the breast'.". Now and
Afterwards. Dinah Maria Mulock Craik.
P89

295. i. Sindhu Ratna Kul Bhaskar. P72

Two in August. John Crowe Ransom. P67,P83,
P83

Two Little Blackbirds. Unknown. P51

Two Little Kittens. Jane Taylor. P51

Two Masks Unearthed in Bulgaria. William
Meredith. P70

The Two Mysteries. Mary Mapes Dodge. P89

"Two little beaks went tap! tap! tap!.". To
Let. D. Newey-Johnson. P51

"Two little birdies, one wintry day". The
Birdie's Breakfast. Unknown. P51

"Two little clouds, one summer's day". The
Rainbow Fairies. Unknown. P51

"Two little dicky-birds". Dickey-Birds.
Natalie Joan. P51

"Two little elves". A Fairy Dream. Dorothy
Gradon. P51

"Two marks impressed gently, but firmly".
Unlikely Path. Mark L. Cannaday. P68

"Two old ghosts". Retired. Mary-Elizabeth
Epstein. P72

Two or Three Angels. Stephen Crane. P81

Two Painters. Lyubomir Nikolov. P70

The Two Parents. Christopher M. ("Hugh
MacDiarmid") Grieve. P89

"The Two Sit Sadly". Unknown. P62

Two Steps Forward. Jeanine Hathaway. P88

Two Swans in a Meadow by the Sea. Michael
Heller. P64

Two Tramps in Mud Time. Robert Frost. P82

Two Views of a Philosopher. Howard Nemerov.
P79

Two Ways. John V. A. Weaver. P82

The Two Wives. William Dean Howells. P90

Two Women. Barbara Goldberg. P63

"Two roads diverged in a yellow wood". The
Road Not Taken. Robert Frost. P82

"Two strides forward, two across". After
Interrogation. Georgi Djagarov. P70

"Two that could not have lived their single
lives". Two in August. John Crowe
Ransom. P67,P83,P83

"Two trees hold". Johnny's Woodpile. T. M.
Baker. P68

"Two trees in full leaf, one". Child Sketch
in Crayon. David Wevill. P49

"Two white heads the grasses cover". Two
Epitaphs. Louise Imogen Guiney. P81

Two-faced. Sion Tudur. P87

"Two-stepping Cindy versus". Cinderella
Spin. Gwendolyn Vincent. P58

Tworoger, John
Love for Poetry, from Wake up, My Heart
and Other Poems. P65
Tropical Night. P72

"' Twould ring the bells of heaven". The
Bells of Heaven. Ralph Hodgson. P51

The Tyger. William Blake. P51

Tynan, Katharine (Hinkson)

Leaves. P51
The Nightingale. P51
Pink Almond. P51
Sheep and Lambs. P51
Slow Spring. P51
Tyrant, fr. Three Voices. Faiz Ahmad Faiz.
P91

Uberti, Fazio degli
Of England, and of Its Marvels. Dante
Gabriel Rossetti (tr.). P90
Uccello. Gregory Corso. P85
The Ugliest Person. Sheila Hogan. P68
The Ugly Man. Liliana Stefanova. P70
Uhland, Johann Ludwig
The Castle by the Sea. Henry Wadsworth
Longfellow (tr.). P90
In a Lovely Garden Walking. G. MacDonald
(tr.). P89
The Landlady's Daughter. J. S. Dwight
(tr.). P89
A Leaf. J. S. Dwight (tr.). P89
Uhrman, Celia
Little Seashell. P72
Uhrman, Esther
Free. P72
"Ukranian fisherman". Carp. M. Rose. P77
Ultima Veritas. Washington Gladden. P89
The Ultimate Poem is Abstract. Wallace
Stevens. P83
Ulysses
The Sail of Ulysses. Wallace Stevens. P83
Umavijani, Montri
Heaven, from A Thai Divine Comedy. P92
Heaven, from Paradise. P72
Love, from A Thai Divine Comedy. P92
Mahayana, from Paradise. P72
A Poet, from A Thai Divine Comedy. P92
The Stupas, from Paradise. P72
Writing, from A Thai Divine Comedy. P92
Writing, from A Thai Divine Comedy. P92
Writing, from A Thai Divine Comedy. P92
A Young Poet, from A Thai Divine Comedy.
P92
Umbrella. Kandy Arnold. P58
Unamuno, Miguel de
Aldebaran. Eleanor Turnbull (tr.). P48
The Unappeasable. Cy Patteson. P72
Unchanging. Friedrich Martin von Bodenstedt.
P89
"Undaunted courser, your great valor stems".
Sonnet to a Road Runner. Virginia
Noble. P72
Under a Keeping Spring. William Everson. P84
Under Certain Circumstances. Walter Hoefler.
P71

"Under a spreading chestnut-tree". The
Village Blacksmith. Henry Wadsworth
Longfellow. P89
"Under a toadstool". The Elf and the
Dormouse. Oliver Herford. P89
"Under damp layers of pine needle".
Affluence. Gary Snyder. P85
"Under palm roofs". Images on the Beach.
Elsa Cross. P92
Under the Boathouse. David Bottoms. P67
Under the Green Ledge. Kenneth Patchen. P84
Under the Greenwood Tree. William
Shakespeare. P51
Under the Portrait of John Milton. John
Dryden. P90
"Under the Soursop Silver-Leaf Tree". Ian
McDonald. P60
Under the Vulture-Tree. David Bottoms. P67
"Under the green hedges, after the snow".
Violets. John Moultrie. P51
"Under the lamp your hands do not seem red".
Inquest. William DeWitt Snodgrass. P85
"Under the same sun I see nature so clear".
Your Face, a Better Indian Rose!. S.
Yesupatham. P72
"Under the shape of his sail, Ulysses". The
Sail of Ulysses. Wallace Stevens. P83
"Underneath the water-weeds". The Tadpole.
E. E. Gould. P51
"The underpaid young teacher". English as a
Second Language, from Your Tired...
Lisel Mueller. P88
Unemployment
The Depression. David Gwenallt Jones. P87
Necessities. Heather Miller. P73
"The Unfaithful Wife Gathers Together,
Crying". Unknown. P62
Unfired Pistol. Clive Matson. P65
Unforgettable Summers. David Winwood. P92
Unfriendly Witness. George Starbuck. P85
"Unhappy dreamer, who outwinged in flight".
On the Death of a Metaphysician.
George Santayana. P81
Unicorn. Sharon Goodier. P49
The Union Jack. Jeannie Kirby. P51
United States
Walt Whitman at Bear Mountain. Louis
Simpson. P85
With Fifty Stars. Francis Brown Price.
P68
Universe
Narcissus. Paul Little. P72
University. Karl Shapiro. P84
The Unknown Wind. William ("Fiona Macleod")
Sharp. P51
Unlikely Path. Mark L. Cannaday. P68
Unmanifest Destiny. Richard Hovey. P81
Unpleasant Surprise. Jay Dougherty. P63
Unprofitableness. Henry Vaughan. P59

Unrequited Love, from Twelfth Night. William
       Shakespeare. P89
The Unseen Playmate. Robert Louis Stevenson.
       P89
Unsong, Kim
       Taking for Granted. P72
Untermeyer, L. (tr.)
       The Storm. Heinrich Heine. P90
       Twilight. Heinrich Heine. P90
Untermeyer, Louis
       Against Time. P82
       Caliban in the Coal Mines. P82
       Food and Drink. P82
       Prayer. P82
Until I Saw the Sea. Lilian Moore. P76
"Until I fled the sound-fouled city
       streets". Deer Park. William A.
       Anderson. P68
"Until I reach the future". Travelling
       Alone. Blaga Dimitrova. P70
Untitled. T. M. Raghuram. P72
Untitled #1. Kevin Cline. P58
Untitled #1. Ian Brennan. P58
Untitled #2. Ian Brennan. P58
Untitled #3. Ian Brennan. P58
Untitled #4. Ian Brennan. P58
Untuned Lute. Chems Nadir. P91
Unwind My Riddle. Stephen Crane. P81
The Unwritten Song. Ford Madox (Hueffer)
       Ford. P51
Up Fair Kilties!. Russ Traunstein. P63
Up Hill. Christina Georgina Rossetti. P89
Up North. Lisel Mueller. P88
"Up and down he goes". America. Alfred
       Kreymborg. P82
"Up cross streets". Late. Elaine Dallman.
       P65
"Up from the meadows rich with corn".
       Barbara Frietchie. John Greenleaf
       Whittier. P51
"Up into the cherry tree". Foreign Lands.
       Robert Louis Stevenson. P51,P89
"Up on the north fork". Mining the American.
       Jon Olander. P77
"Up the coast from Seattle...". On the
       Northwest Hiawatha. Kathleen Norris.
       P88
"Up the reputable wlaks of old established
       trees". The Campus on the Hill.
       William DeWitt Snodgrass. P85
"Up through the rain I'd driven her, taut".
       First Calving. Nigel Jenkins. P54
"Up winding stair". Logic and 'the Magic
       Flute'. Marianne Moore. P79
"Up yonder on the mountain". The Shepherd's
       Lament. Johann Wolfgang von Goethe.
       P89
"Up! up, my friend! and quit your books".
       The Tables Turned. William Wordsworth.
       P89
"Up, boy! arise, and saddle quick". The
       Message. Heinrich Heine. P89
Up, up! Ye Dames and Lasses Gay. Samuel
       Taylor Coleridge. P51
Updike, John
       The Sometime Sportsman Greets the Spring.
       P63
Updike, John (tr.)
       Pain. Blaga Dimitrova. P70
       The Road (Version 1). Blaga Dimitrova.
       P70
       The Road (Version 2, with echoes of Emily
       Dickinson). Blaga Dimitrova. P70
       Travelling Alone. Blaga Dimitrova. P70
       Winter. Peter Karaangov. P70
"Upon a tree there mounted guard". The Cock
       and the Fox. Jean de La Fontaine. P90
Upon the Road of My Life. Stephen Crane. P81
"Upon the gale she stooped her side". The
       Gallant Ship. Sir Walter Scott. P51
"Upon the slanted iron eaves". Snow 1929.
       Atanas Dalchev. P70
The Upper Skies. Robert Bridges. P51
The Upside-Down World. Hamish Hendry. P51
"Upward a gull". Wild Day at the Shore.
       Felice Holman. P76
Upwardly Mobile Bean Curd. Bonnie Jacobson.
       P63
An Urban Convalescence. James Merrill. P85
The Urchin's Dance. John Lyly. P51
The Utopias. Raul Zurita. P71

V. Bogumil Wtorkiewicz. P72
V-Letter. Karl Shapiro. P84
The Vacant Lot, fr. A Street in Bronzeville.
       Gwendolyn Brooks. P84
Vacation Time. Frank Hutt. P51
Vacations
       Northeast. Martin Singleton. P49
       Vacation Time. Frank Hutt. P51
"Vacuum bursting life". Alpha/Omega Cycle of
       Peace. Josette Liliane Villias. P72
Vagabonds
       Anonymous Biography. Armando Rubio. P71
       No Thoroughfare. Ruth Holmes. P51
       The Old Woman of the Roads. Padraic
       Column. P51
       Pedlar Jim. Florence Hoare. P51
       Pensioners. Winifred M. Letts. P51
Vagrants
       Bowery. David Ignatow. P84
Vaky, James Russell
       Falling Water. P68
       Penthouse Enigma. P68
A Valediction: Forbidding Mourning. John

Donne. P59

Valenti, Dan
Crucifiction. P56
Valentine's Day. Charles Kingsley. P51
Valis, Noel M.
The Deer. P56
Values
Indirection. Richard Realf. P90
Taking for Granted. Kim Unsong. P72
The **Vampire** Came. Craig Lawler. P73
Van Doren, Mark
And Did the Animals?. P83
The Distant Runners. P83
The Escape. P83
Family Prime. P83
Van Dyke, Henry
A Wayfaring Song. P89
Work. P90
Van Gogh. Charles Tomlinson. P48
Van Poznak, Joan
Gertrude and Alice. P63
Love Portions. P63
On Seeing Gavin Ewart in Sainsbury's. P63
Viola D'Amore. P63
Van Til, Desiree
If I Could Control the Weather. P73
Vanishing Patriot, from Lost Youth: the Last
War. Alfred Kreymborg. P82
Vanity (1). George Herbert. P59
"The **vanity** of imposing reason".
Constellation/Rorschach. Dan Murray.
P64
Vanity. See Pride and Vanity
Vapor Trail Reflected in the Frog Pond.
Galway Kinnell. P85
Vaptsarov, Nikola
Epoch. William Meredith (tr.). P70
Song. William Meredith (tr.). P70
Vargas, Raphael
The Signature of Things. Leticia
Tanticlaiux (tr.). P92
Variable Service. Dabney Stuart. P79
"**Varnish** a moment...". Make Room. Jules
Supervielle. P61
"The **varnished** dashboard long ago was
chipped". Vita Longa, Cars Brevis.
Mark Stocker. P63
"A **vast** space of dry land". Satellite City.
Mauricio Electorat. P71
Vaughan, Henry
Anguish. P59
The Evening Watch. P59
'Joy of My Life! While Left Me Here'. P59
Man. P59
The Morning-Watch. P59
Peace. P59
Quickness. P59
Regeneration. P59
The Retreat. P59

'They Are All Gone into the World of
Light!'. P59
To Amoret, of the Difference 'Twixt
Him... P59
To Amoret, Walking in a Starry Evening.
P59
Unprofitableness. P59
The Water-Fall. P59
The World (1). P59
The Wreath. P59
The **Vaunting** Song of Louis L'Amour. Ernest
Kroll. P63
Vaux, Thomas, 2nd Baron
Of a Contented Spirit. P90
Veazey, Mary
For a Good Ole Boy. P63
Vegetables
The Beanfield. John Clare. P51
The Beet's Poem. Katharyn Machan Aal. P63
"**Velazquez de Maria**". Your Little Friends
Were a Bunch of Dogs. Diego Maquieira.
P71
Velvet Shoes. Elinor Wylie. P89
"**Velvet** thimbles". Red Raspberries. Gary
Selden. P63
Vendor's Song. Adelaide Crapsey. P81
"**Venerable** saguaros". Meditation. Mary K.
Mazotti. P72
The **Venetian** Blind. Randall Jarrell. P84
Veni Creator Spiritus. Saint Gregory the
Great. P89
Venice, Italy
From Venice Was That Afternoon. Jean
Garrigue. P84
Venkataramana, K. V.
Memories. P72
Venkataramu, K. S.
The Humble Shell. P72
Venus Transiens. Amy Lowell. P82
Ver Duft, Lee
Elegy on a Spirit Luster's Polar Site of
Empyrean... P68
Verger, Colette
Will-O-the-Wisp. P72
Verhaeren, Emile
Two Fool's Songs. Charles Guenther (tr.).
P61
Verhagen, Hans
Euthanasia. Peter Nijmeijer (tr.). P92
Verlaine, Paul
The Sky Is up Above the Roof. Ernest
Dowson (tr.). P89
Songs of Autumn. Arthur Symons (tr.). P89
"**Vermilion/The** road-cuts hold eyes...". At
Sunrise Along the American River...
William Howarth. P77
Verrocchio. Richard Harrison. P49
Verses Why Burnt. Walter Savage Landor. P90
"**Very** funny to see". Why?. Tho Thorsen. P72

Vesper Hymn. Eliza Scudder. P89
Vespers. T. E. Brown. P51
Vespers. Hugh McKinley. P68
The Vestal Lady on Brattle. Gregory Corso.
    P85
Veteran's Hospital. Ben Belitt. P57
VI. Raul Zurita. P71
Veterans
    Being a Vietnam Veteran. Michael E.
        Merrill. P86
    Coming Home. W. D. Ehrhart. P86
    Foot Soldier. Rhea Tregebov. P49
    VNV Rap Group. Joseph W. Nugent. P86
Victim, fr. Three Voices. Faiz Ahmad Faiz.
    P91
Victor and Vanquished. Harry Thurston. P81
"Victoria-- choosing, willy nilly". I Wish I
    Were Living in Your Century. A. L.
    Lazarus. P63
Victory
    Amazon. Elisaveta Bagriana. P70
    Nike. James Merrill. P79
Viet Kong. William Trowbridge. P63
Vietnam. James P. Bergman. P86
Vietnam. Jack Strahan. P86
Vietnam P.O.W. Camp. Theodore W. Gostas. P86
Vietnam War
    Body Bags, sel. Michael Andrews. P86
    "In the Morning He Came For Me". Jack
        Hill. P86
    "Just Nothingness, Just a Recruiter".
        Unknown. P86
    Vietnam. James P. Bergman. P86
    Vietnam. Jack Strahan. P86
    The Water Buffalo (Hanoi, 1972). Blaga
        Dimitrova. P70
    You Ask About Vietnam!. Ken Stone. P86
A View Across the Roman Campagna. Elizabeth
        Barrett Browning. P90
View from Autumn. Jerry Saxton. P72
"The view from the guest room". Visitors.
    Kathleen Norris. P88
View of a Comet. Robert Hahn. P58
Views to See Clayton From. Josephine Miles.
    P84
Vigil on a Bay. Julia Hartwig. P92
Vigils. Josephine Miles. P79
Vigna, Pier della
    "Because Love Is Not Invisible". Frede
        Jensen (tr.). P69
    "Love, in Which I Have Placed My Desire
        and My Hope". Frede Jensen (tr.). P69
    "Loving With a Loyal Heart and With
        Hope". Frede Jensen (tr.). P69
Vignette from the Past. Mary Frances
        Langford. P65
The Village Atheist, from Spoon River
        Anthology. Edgar Lee Masters. P82
The Village Blacksmith. Henry Wadsworth
        Longfellow. P89
Village Life
    A Certain Village. Theodore Weiss. P84
    My Village and I. Kaiser Haq. P91
"The village is straddled on both sides".
    Eglwys Newydd. John Tripp. P54
Villanelle: the Psychological Hour. Ezra
        Pound. P82
Villias, Josette Liliane
    Alpha/Omega Cycle of Peace. P72
Villonaud for This Yule. Ezra Pound. P82
Vincent, Gwendolyn
    Cinderella Spin. P58
    Dreams-in-Progress. P58
    The Final Gesture. P58
    Heresy. P58
    Letting the Cat Die. P58
    The Thousand-and-One Nights. P58
    Turkish Thunder. P58
Vio, Eric
    My Music Teacher. P72
Viola D'Amore. Joan Van Poznak. P63
"Viola:--Ay, but I know,--.". Unrequited
        Love, from Twelfth Night. William
        Shakespeare. P89
Violence
    Besides. Mark Irwin. P63
    Captain Carpenter. John Crowe Ransom. P83
    Darlene Friendship's Boyfriend. Ron Ikan.
        P63
    The Handless Maiden. Janet Beeler Shaw.
        P88
    Ifriqiyad/Alternatives, sels. Majid El
        Houssi. P91
    Percussion Grenade Democracy. C. J.
        Roner. P72
    The Position. Julio Monteiro Martins. P92
    Semper Paratus: to the Graduating Class.
        Doug Rawlings. P86
    Shooting Prairie Dogs. Linda M.
        Hasselstrom. P88
    Two in August. John Crowe Ransom. P67,P83
    Vietnam. Jack Strahan. P86
    Voice from the Unknown, fr. Three Voices.
        Faiz Ahmad Faiz. P91
    Within You. Jean-Jacques Wilson. P72
    Your Great Love. Diego Maquieira. P71
    Your Little Friends Were a Bunch of Dogs.
        Diego Maquieira. P71
"Violence strikes us everywhere".
        Ifriqiyad/Alternatives, sels. Majid El
        Houssi. P91
Violets. John Moultrie. P51
Violets. P. A. Ropes. P51
Violets. Unknown. P51
Viorst, Judith
    Since Hanna Moved Away. P50
Viosca, Renee Anne
    Eskimo Sleigh-Ride. P72

Virgidemiarum Book I, Satire 7. Joseph Hall. P59

Virgilia. Edwin Markham. P81

Virginia. Lorene Erickson. P88

Virtue. George Herbert. P59

Virtue
Supposing That I Should. Stephen Crane. P81
William Lloyd Garrison. James Russell Lowell. P90

"**Virtuous** Women, Still Undressed and Bashful". Unknown. P62

Virus. Roberta Mendel. P56

Visible, Invisible. Salvatore Quasimodo. P61

Vision. Gonzalo Millan. P71

Vision by Sweetwater. John Crowe Ransom. P67

The **Vision** Clear. J. M. Westrup. P51

The **Vision** of a Martyr. Mohammed Ibrahim Abu Sinnah. P91

Vision of Hiroshima. Oscar Hahn. P71

Vision of Rotterdam. Gregory Corso. P85

A **Vision.** Kolyo Sevov. P70

Visions
Abou Ben Adhem. Leigh Hunt. P89
My Everlasting Vision. William Zeller. P65
The Octopus. James Merrill. P85
A Vision. Kolyo Sevov. P70

A **Visit** from St. Nicholas. Clement Clark Moore. P89

Visit to the Institute for the Blind. Felix Pollak. P57

Visitors. Kathleen Norris. P88

Visitors. David Wevill. P49

Vita Longa, Cars Brevis. Mark Stocker. P63

The **Vital** Brine. Lois Wilson Parker. P68

VNV Rap Group. Joseph W. Nugent. P86

Vivian, Mary
Four Scarlet Berries. P51
Snowdrops. P51

Vizy, Antal
Winter. Charles Guenther (tr.). P61

"**Vodka.** Grapefruit juice. In paper cups". For a Good Ole Boy. Mary Veazey. P63

Voice
The World Is Full of Voices... Jules Supervielle. P61

Voice from the Unknown, fr. Three Voices. Faiz Ahmad Faiz. P91

Voice in the Darkness. Richard Dehmel. P90

"**Voice** of summer, keen and shrill". To a Cricket. William Cox Bennett. P51

The **Voice.** Sara Teasdale. P82

Voices. Nesta Wyn Jones. P87

Voices from Pompeii. Chester A. Beck Jr. P68

Void. Krishna Srinivas. P72

"**Volcanic** steepness". Ancient Convolutions. Elaine Emmons. P77

Vonna, Adrian

Clerihews. P63

Vote. Randy S. Atwood. P72

The **Vote.** Ralph Knevet. P59

The **Vowels:** an Enigma. Jonathan Swift. P90

The **Voyage.** Caroline Atherton Mason. P89

Voyager. Lisel Mueller. P88

Voyages. Hart Crane. P83

The **Voyages.** Gregory Orr. P85

"The **vultures** hover wheel and hover". Day of the Dead. Robert Hayden. P84

Vyas, Bhanushanker O.
The Muse. P72

W. D., Don't Fear That Animal. William DeWitt Snodgrass. P63

Waddington, Miriam
Reflections. P49

Wade, John Stevens
The Nomad. P68

"**Wade/Through** black jade". The Fish. Marianne Moore. P83

Wagoner, David
How Stump Stood in the Winter. P57

Wahlstrand, Myron
Autumn. P72

"**Wailing,** wailing, wailing...". Rizpah 17--. Lord Tennyson. P90

Waiting
Bangkok Sights. Robert Schlosser. P86

Waiting. John Burroughs. P89
In Expectation (To John Paul). Marie G. Kent. P72

Waiting. T. A. Shulgin. P58

Waiting. John J. Soldo. P65

Waiting for Spring,..., from For the Desert Island. Tae-ch'ul Shin. P92

"**Waiting** for an arrival". Frozen with Time. Sherry Sue McCall. P56

Waiting for the Detective. Michael Cadnum. P63

"**Waiting** in the front row". A Young Poet, from A Thai Divine Comedy. Montri Umavijani. P92

"**Waiting** seems to be best. Your remark might". Faux Pas. William Stafford. P63

Waiting: November 30th. Bruce St. John. P68

The **Waits.** John Freeman. P51

"**Wake/Gently** this morning". Snowy Morning. Lilian Moore. P80

"**Waken,** lords and ladies gay". Hunting Song. Sir Walter Scott. P89

Wakening
Getting Up. Lilian McCrea. P51
Madrigal. Unknown. P51
Morning. Ivy O. Eastwick. P51

Waking. T. A. Shulgin. P58
Waking Up. Jaime Quezada. P71
Waking up. Unknown. P51
Wakley, Thirza
    An Easter Chick. P51
    The Mouse. P51
    Spring Work at the Farm. P51
Wakoski, Diane
    An Apology. P85
    Belly Dancer. P85
    From a Girl in a Mental Institution. P85
    Patriotic Poem. P85
    Picture of a Girl Drawn in Black and
        White. P85
    Sestina from the Home Gardener. P85
Walcott, Derek
    The Fortunate Traveller. P48
    The Season of Phantasmal Peace. P48
Wales
    Capital. John Tripp. P54
    A Note from Plwmp. John Tripp. P54
    Wales Visitation. Allen Ginsberg. P85
A Walk in Late Summer. Theodore Roethke. P84
A Walk in Spring. K. C. Lart. P51
"Walk in the". Rain-Walking. Myra Cohn
    Livingston. P75
Walke, Julia Nelson
    Jewels of Freedom. P68
    My Clock. P68
Walker and Abby Wolf, Eric (tr.)
    Images on the Beach. Elsa Cross. P92
Walker, Alice
    Burial. P67
    Facing the Way. P85
    'Good Night, Willie Lee, I'll See You in
        the Morning'. P85
    Janie Crawford. P85
    Now That the Book Is Finished. P85
Walker, Jauvanta
    Block of Wood. P68
Walker, Jeanne Murray
    Writing to Get Through the Night While
        the Baby Cries. P63
Walker, Perry
    Fragments. P68
Walking
    Micro/Macro. Steve LaVine. P77
Walking. Judith Minty. P88
    Rain-Walking. Myra Cohn Livingston. P75
    Walking. Judith Minty. P88
Walking Early by the Wye. Anne Stevenson.
    P54
Walking in the Sky. Stephen Crane. P81
Walking Naked Around the House. R. P.
    Dickey. P63
Walking Sag Beach. George Bradley. P64
"Walking in the crowds". What Face?. Ricelda
    Payne. P72
"Walking into the shadows, walking alone".

Lee in the Mountains 1865-1870. Donald
    Davidson. P67
"Walking just after sunset". Stopping by
    Brook at 18. Genevieve Sargent. P72
"Walking out of Hay in the rain...".
    Burnished. Anne Stevenson. P54
"Walking slowly". Day Into Night. Shane
    Iliff. P74
"Walking the shores of the Ernestine". The
    Message. Marie Blood. P72
"Walking to the museum". Bone Thoughts on a
    Dry Day. George Starbuck. P85
Walking with Lulu in the Wood. Naomi Lazard.
    P64
"Walking, shoving my chin deep...". Walking.
    Judith Minty. P88
Walla, Edna Kingsley
    Christmas Eve. P51
Wallace, Betty
    The Io Moth. P68
Wallace, Bronwen
    Lonely for the Country. P49
Wallace, Kathleen Chan
    Life. P72
Wallace, Ronald
    After Being Paralyzed from the Neck
        Down... P57
The Walled Light. Elaine Dallman. P65
Wallenstein, Barry
    Recovery Song. P57
Waller, J. Pembroke
    Sleep Baby Sleep. P68
Waller, John Francis
    The Spinning-Wheel Song. P89
"Wallowing in this bloody sty". The Drunken
    Fisherman. Robert Lowell. P84
"Walls of my heart have crumbled". Crippled
    Walls. Phillip Britain. P72
Walls, Keri
    Spring. P73
The Walrus and the Carpenter, from Alice in
    Wonderland. Charles Lutwidge ("Lewis
    Carroll") Dodgson. P89
Walsh, William
    Rivalry in Love. P89
Walt Whitman. Edwin Markham. P81
Walt Whitman at Bear Mountain. Louis
    Simpson. P85
"Walt Whitman's postmortem brain...". The
    Broken Pianola. Ralph Gustafson. P49
"Walter Savage Landor". James Steel Smith.
    P63
Walton's Book of Lives, from Ecclesiastical
    Sonnets. William Wordsworth. P90
The Wander-Lovers. Richard Hovey. P81
Wandering Jack. Emile Jacot. P51
Wandering Off. Unknown. P53
Wandering Souls. Sergio Mansilla. P71
Wandering Was Always an Important Theme in

My Lyric. Tetsuo Nakagami. P92
"Wandering all alone in the night". A
    Dialogue. Fatthy Said. P91
"Wandering oversea dreamer". Prayer After
    World War. Carl Sandburg. P82
"Wandering up and down one day". The
    Cobbler. Unknown. P51
Wang, H. Olav
    Pebbles on a Lonely Beach. P68
Wang, Harold O.
    The Words That Never Came. P68
War
    After a Hypothetical War. Edwin Muir. P48
    The Blue and the Gray. Francis Miles
        Finch. P90
    Bugs. Carole Oles. P48
    Castell Carreg Cennen. Nigel Jenkins. P54
    The Death of the Ball Turret Gunner.
        Randall Jarrell. P84
    Do Not Weep, Maiden. Stephen Crane. P81
    Eastward the Armies. William Everson. P84
    IV, fr. Irradiations. John Gould
        Fletcher. P82
    Johnny Doe. Rick Allen House. P73
    Losses. Randall Jarrell. P84
    The Moon and the Night and the Men. John
        Berryman. P84
    A Night in the War. Wazir Agha. P91
    Night Operations, Coastal Command RAF.
        Howard Nemerov. P63
    Nightmare for Future Reference. Stephen
        Vincent Benet. P48
    Notes for an Unpublished Canto. Ezra
        Pound. P79
    Pilots, Man Your Planes. Randall Jarrell.
        P84
    Sestina: Altaforte. Ezra Pound. P82
    A Simple Question. Joann Marie Everett.
        P72
    Song. Nikola Vaptsarov. P70
    A Story About Chicken Soup. Louis
        Simpson. P85
    Tell Brave Deeds of War. Stephen Crane.
        P81
    There Was a Crimson Clash of War. Stephen
        Crane. P81
    There Will Come Soft Rains. Sara
        Teasdale. P82
    To a Military Rifle. Yvor Winters. P83
    Vanishing Patriot, from Lost Youth: the
        Last War. Alfred Kreymborg. P82
    Veteran's Hospital. Ben Belitt. P57
    War. Jason Parker. P74
    War. Paul W. Tipton. P86
    "War Is as Natural as the Rain". James
        Webb. P86
    The War. James Magorian. P68
    We Broke the Noose with a Snap. Majiok
        Wunyik. P53

Webs. Paul W. Tipton. P86
    You, a Red Man, and I, a Black Man. Moses
        Cot. P53
War. Jason Parker. P74
War. Paul W. Tipton. P86
The War Against the Trees. Stanley Kunitz.
    P83
"War Is as Natural as the Rain". James Webb.
    P86
War Poetry
    Siegfriedslage. Lincoln Kirstein. P79
"War is such a terrible thing". War. Jason
    Parker. P74
War or Peace. Margaret Baucom. P72
"War, war! This cry will infuriate". The Red
    Clouds at Sunset. Micen Atem. P53
"War, war, Wen shouts". Who Can Touch Me?.
    Micen Atem. P53
War-Nuclear
    Dream. Salvadore J. Coppola. P72
The War. James Magorian. P68
"A ward, and still in bonds, one day".
    Regeneration. Henry Vaughan. P59
Warden, Bette
    Earthbound. P72
"The wares are bright and cheap...".
    Discount Store. G. N. Gabbard. P63
"Warm blue ocean". Thinking of Other
    Universes. Muneer Niazi. P91
"A warm wind". September. Fairfield Porter.
    P64
"Warn all in authority". Voice from the
    Unknown, fr. Three Voices. Faiz Ahmad
    Faiz. P91
Warning to the Poets. Sion Tudur. P87
The Warning. Adelaide Crapsey. P81
Warren, Robert Penn
    Bearded Oaks. P83
    The Corner of the Eye. P67
    Covered Bridge. P67
    Debate: Question, Quarry, Dream. P83
    English Cocker: Old and Blind. P67
    Evening Hawk. P67
    I Am Dreaming of a White Christmas: The
        Natural... P47
    Mortal Limit. P67
    Muted Music. P67
    Old Photograph of the Future. P67
    Old-Time Childhood in Kentucky. P67
    The Place. P67
    Pondy Woods. P83
    Three Darknesses. P67
Warsaw, Irene
    Sheep That Pa in the Night. P63
"Wary of time O it seizes the soul tonight".
    Easter Eve, 1945. Muriel Rukeyser. P52
"A was once an apple pie". An Alphabet.
    Edward Lear. P90
"Wash, hands, wash". A Rhyme for Washing

Hands. Unknown. P51
Wash-Day. Lilian McCrea. P51
The **Washing-up** Song. Elizabeth Gould. P51
Washington, George
      General Washington. Paul Goodman. P84
      His Excellency General Washington.
         Phillis Wheatley. P90
      Patriotic Poem. Diane Wakoski. P85
The **Wasp.** William ("Fiona Macleod") Sharp.
      P51
"**Watch** the dullish political asses". The
      Political Asses. P. M. Mammen. P72
"**Watch** the sun sail". Nature Rhymes.
      Unknown. P89
"A **watch** will tell the time of day". Mr.
      Coggs. E. V. Lucas. P51
"The **watchers** wade and wait in the water".
      Field Guide to North American Birds.
      Barbara Crooker. P63
Watching for Papa. Unknown. P89
Watching T.V. Oscar Hahn. P71
Watching Whales Watching Us. Raymond Filip.
      P49
"**Watching** hands transplanting".
      Transplanting. Theodore Roethke. P84
The **Watchmaker's** Shop. Unknown. P51
Water
      Big Basin Waterfall. Ellis Ovesen. P72
      The Boiling Water. Kenneth Koch. P64
Water. John R. Crossland. P51
      Dancing Waters. Sherry Small Sundick. P72
      Puddles. Jennifer Gilgan. P73
Water. Gary Snyder. P85
Water. Krishna Srinivas. P72
      Water. John R. Crossland. P51
      Water. Gary Snyder. P85
      Water. Krishna Srinivas. P72
      The Water and your Eyes. Lee Pennington.
      P72
      When I Went Out. Karla Kuskin. P75
The **Water** and your Eyes. Lee Pennington. P72
The **Water** Buffalo (Hanoi, 1972). Blaga
      Dimitrova. P70
"**Water** Buffalo". James P. Bergman. P86
Water Color. T. A. Shulgin. P58
The **Water** Diviner. Gillian Clarke. P54
Water Walker. Richard Wilbur. P84
"**Water** has no taste at all". Water. John R.
      Crossland. P51
"The **water** is the color of your eyes". The
      Water and your Eyes. Lee Pennington.
      P72
"**Water** splashes from the tap". Dedication
      (To Tamara). Luchesar Elenkov. P70
"**Water's** flowing". Song Picture No. 29.
      Unknown. P78
The **Water-Fall.** Henry Vaughan. P59
The **Water-Lily.** John Banister Tabb. P89,P81
Waterchew!. Gregory Corso. P85

Waterfalls
      Wimmera Child's First Waterfall. Joyce
      Lee. P72
A **Watering** Rhyme. P. A. Ropes. P51
Waterman, Cary
      A Light in the Doorway. P88
The **Waters** of Saturday, sel. Maria Luisa
      Spaziani. P61
"The **waters** purled, the waters swelled,--.".
      The Fisher. Johann Wolfgang von
      Goethe. P90
Watkins, Edward
      The Daily Planet. P63
      Silent Lover. P63
Watkins, Vernon
      The Collier. P89
Watson, Flora Willis
      Calendar Rhyme. P51
Watson, Nancy Dingman
      Snow Woman. P80
Watson, Sir William
      April. P51
Watson, Wilfred
      Re Ezra Pound. P49
Watt, F. W.
      Letter to My Parents. P49
      On a Gestapo Photograph Purported To
      Be... P49
Watts, Isaac
      Kind Deeds. P51
      Our God, Our Help in Ages Past. P89
      Self-Inquiry. P89
"A **wave** white with foam washes a grave".
      Hywel's Boast of His Country. Hywel ab
      Owain Gwynedd. P87
Wave, sel. Barbara Guest. P64
Waves
      Movement, Their Way. Charlotte L.
      Babicky. P72
      Song for a Surf-Rider. Sarah Van Alstyne
      Allen. P76
      A Song of the Wave. George Cabot Lodge.
      P81
      Waves of the Sea. Aileen Fisher. P76
"The **waves** all come ashore, the birds".
      Closing of a Day on Earth. B. R. De.
      P72
"The **waves** forever move". The Sisters. John
      Banister Tabb. P81
Waves of the Sea. Aileen Fisher. P76
The **Way** It All Was. Constance Pultz. P65
The **Way** Things Are Above and Below. Jaime
      Quezada. P71
"**Way** down upon de Swanee Ribber". Old Folks
      at Home. Stephen Foster. P89
The **Way** to Fairyland. Eunice Close. P51
The **Wayfarer.** Stephen Crane. P81
A **Wayfaring** Song. Henry Van Dyke. P89
"**We** all know about the edge they walked".

The Edge. Ken Norris. P49
"We all live within a glass wall". Glass
    Walls. Karen Birch. P73
"We all say th rain is terribul...". Looking
    for th Innr Life in 100 Mile. Bill
    Bissett. P49
"We all slave". Mondays. Miriana Basheva.
    P70
We and the Weekend. Alma Denny. P63
"We Are Little Mice," from Mother Goose...
    Unknown. P90
We Broke the Noose with a Snap. Majiok
    Wunyik. P53
We Have Been Friends Together. Caroline
    Elizabeth Sarah Norton. P89
We Love But Few. Unknown. P89
We Needs Must be Divided in the Tomb. George
    Santayana. P81
We Parted in Silence. Julia Crawford. P89
We Say This Prayer. Jozsef Tornai. P92
We Thank You!. L. E. Cox. P51
"We Think Less of Women When Out of Our
    Vision". Unknown. P62
We Will Not Hand Over the Night. Waldo
    Rojas. P71
"We are born; we laugh; we weep". Life.
    Bryan Waller ("Barry Cornwall")
    Procter. P89
"We are children of the sun". Children of
    the Sun. Fenton Johnson. P82
"We are coming, Father Abraham...". Three
    Hundred Thousand More. Unknown. P90
"We are going on a journey". The Journey.
    Aidan Clarke. P51
"We are here, in another provisional city".
    Lullaby for Amy. Mark Jarman. P85
"We are large with pity, slow and awkward".
    False Country of the Zoo. Jean
    Garrigue. P84
"We are little airy creatures". The Vowels:
    an Enigma. Jonathan Swift. P90
"We are not characters of fiction drawn". To
    a Lady Who Reads Too Much. Alfred
    Dorn. P65
"We are talking about metaphor". Vigils.
    Josephine Miles. P79
"We are the hollow men". The Hollow Men.
    Thomas Stearns Eliot. P83
"We are the ruthless young". Lovers in Wild
    Grass. Lisa Grenelle. P65
"We are things of dry hours...". Kitchenette
    Building, fr. A Street in Bronzeville.
    Gwendolyn Brooks. P84
"We are very little creatures". AEIOU.
    Jonathan Swift. P51
"We are waiting in separate rooms".
    Marriage. David Ignatow. P84
"We argued. Running poor land had to be".
    Scratch Farmer. John Tripp. P54

"We brought him home, I was so pleased". My
    New Rabbit. Elizabeth Gould. P51
"We built a ship upon the stairs". A Good
    Play. Robert Louis Stevenson. P89
"We chance upon it, unaware". Found--A
    Poem!. Clarence L. Weaver. P72
"We could get the whole town out...". Summer
    Concert. Reed Whittemore. P79
"We couldn't even keep the furnace lit". To
    Delmore Schwartz. Robert Lowell. P84
"We drink the rain". Polonaise. David
    Wevill. P49
"We fear to try, for we may fail". Fear.
    Lynn Sorlie. P72
"We feed the birds in winter". Joe. David
    McCord. P80
"We feed the chickens every day". Off We Go
    to Market. Gwen A. Smith. P51
"We have all seen them circling pastures".
    Under the Vulture-Tree. David Bottoms.
    P67
"We have no word for female warlord". Our
    Mother the General. Jessie Kachmar.
    P88
"We know not what it is, dear, this
    sleep...". The Two Mysteries. Mary
    Mapes Dodge. P89
"We know that death and taxes". What's All
    This Fuss About Tax Reform?. Ned
    Pastor. P63
"We lie together". Afterglow. Sheila Seiler.
    P56
"We line up in the village". Just Anyone.
    Nyagak Pinien. P53
"We live, while we see the sun". On Living,
    from Life Is a Dream. Pedro Calderon
    de la Barca. P90
"We love with great difficulty". Sing with
    Your Body. Janice Mirikitani. P85
"We made them with shut eyes...". In Class
    We Create Ourselves-Having Been
    Told... P. K. Page. P49
"We make both mead and garden gay".
    Daffodils. P. A. Ropes. P51
"We make our meek adjustments".
    Chaplinesque. Hart Crane. P83
"We may shut our eyes". Joys. James Russell
    Lowell. P51
"We meet 'neath the sounding rafter".
    Revelry of the Dying. Bartholomew
    Dowling. P90
"We must give the dead everyday speech".
    Posthumous. Jules Supervielle. P61
"' We never thought this maple would
    twin'.". Plain Chant for a Tree. Edna
    Meudt. P68
"We planned to keep your first toys". His
    Toys. Michael Dennis Browne. P63
"We play that we are soldiers". Noises.

Aileen Fisher. P50

"We put more coal on the big red fire".
Father's Story. Elizabeth Madox
Roberts. P89

"We quarry stones". Flood of Renaissance.
Dorothy Mitchell Bechhold. P72

"We quipped, we scoffed, we argued...".
Counterpoint. Agnes Wathall Tatera.
P65

"We sat at the hut of the fisher". Twilight.
Heinrich Heine. P90

"We saw and wooed each others' eyes". To
Castara: the Reward of Innocent Love.
William Habington. P59

"We saw the tulip tree". Like Swallows.
Pearl Newton Rook. P68

"We set out looking for light--.". The Boy's
Song. Zahid Dar. P91

"We shall not hear the mockingbird".
Consolation. Winifred Hamric Farrar.
P72

"We sit at the table. On a white cloth".
Mysterious Evening. Verona Bratesch.
P72

"We somehow fill the time". Time. Rebecca
Bailey. P73

"We spend our morning". The Memory of Elena.
Carolyn Forche. P52

"We stacked each other". Firewood (for Steve
Sanfield). Doc Dachtler. P77

"We stare at eachother". At Each Other.
Shaheed Quadri. P91

"We start talking, we start talking this
way". Between the Anthill and the
Heglig Tree. Unknown. P53

"We step from the barge, hands in the air".
Arrival. Aristoteles Espana. P71

"We still can't announce when we'll leave".
When It's Over. Juan Cameron. P71

"We stood up before day". In the Dordogne.
John Peale Bishop. P83

"We stretched a rope between two trees". The
Funny House. Margaret Hillert. P50

"We thank Thee, Heavenly Father". Thanks to
Spring. Mary Anderson. P51

"We thank Thee, Lord, for quiet upland
lawns". Grace and Thanksgiving.
Elizabeth Gould. P51

"We the fairies blithe and antic". Fairies'
Song. Thomas Randolph. P90

"We waded silt waters, submerging...". Fire
Dream. Jerry Craven. P65

"We wait for our dead countless years".
Life. Sergio Mansilla. P71

"We want to pretend...". The Names.
Gwendolyn Macewen. P49

"We want what is real". Song of the Bald
Eagle. Unknown. P78

"We wasted time designing boats". Face to

Face in Another Time. Teresa Calderon.
P71

"We were discussing Alfred Noyes". Duo for
Voice & Percussion. E. O. Staley. P63

"We were friends". The Words That Never
Came. Harold O. Wang. P68

"We were islands". Song of the Fleece.
Louise Louis. P65

"We were not many,--we who stood". Monterey.
Charles Fenno Hoffman. P90

"We were rounding up cattle, riding
trees...". Night Visits with the
Family. May Swenson. P79

"We were very tired, we were very merry--.".
Recuerdo. Edna St. Vincent Millay. P82

"We who roam the skyways". From Here to
Eternity. Pearl Crayton. P68

"We will probably be angry for over a year".
A Glutton. Nyagak Pinien. P53

"We worked for William". Moviestars. Daniel
Cuol Long. P53

"We wreathed about our darling's head". The
Morning-Glory. Maria White Lowell. P89

"We'd ever so many kinds of cake". The
Pirate's Tea-Party. Dorothy Una
Ratcliffe. P51

"we'd rather have the iceberg than the
ship". The Imaginary Iceberg.
Elizabeth Bishop. P84

"We'll go to the meadows, where
cowslips...". The Meadows. Ann and
Jane Taylor. P51

"We'll play in the snow". Snow. Karla
Kuskin. P80

"We're downstream from Esna". Nile (1).
Cathy Matyas. P49

"We're going to have a party". The Christmas
Party. Adeline White. P51

"We're inside a truck". (No Greater Pain
Beneath the Trees). Aristoteles
Espana. P71

"We've All Been Invited up to Killisnoo,"
from Wolf... Unknown. P78

We've Heard the Sea Again. Salvatore
Quasimodo. P61

"We've all learned about that geezer". Pisa
Visa. Felicia Lamport. P63

"We've laughed until my cheeks are tight".
Bursting. Dorothy Aldis. P51

"We've our business to attend Day's duties".
Bending the Bow. Robert Duncan. P84

"We've rented a modern house...". Postcard
from Civilization. Charles W. Pratt
P63

"We, the red and white oxen, wash our
hands". The Radio, with its Breath
Like a Trapped Bee. John Gatwec Lul.
P53

"We/Rush every moment". Mission of No Ends.

P. K. Padhy. P72
"We/Were the kids of the fifties".
        Heartbreak Hotel. Oscar Hahn. P71
Weakley, Sherry
        The Real World. P74
Weakness. Unknown. P87
The Weary Blues. Langston Hughes. P83
"Weary and travel-worn,--her lips unwet". A
        Transformation, from The
        Metamorphoses. Ovid. P90
"A weary weed, tossed to and fro". Gulf-
        Weed. Cornelius George Fenner. P89
Weather
        Chimney-Tops. Unknown. P51
        The Daily Planet. Edward Watkins. P63
        Decorators Incorporated. Pearl Newton
        Rook. P68
        A Fine Day. Michael Drayton. P51
        Go Out. Eileen Mathias. P51
        If I Could Control the Weather. Desiree
        Van Til. P73
Weather. Eve Merriam. P75
        The Snowstorm. Kaye Starbird. P80
        Turkish Thunder. Gwendolyn Vincent. P58
        Weathering. Wilma H. Clements. P68
        Weathers. Thomas Hardy. P51
        When the Day Is Cloudy. Unknown. P75
The Weather. John Newlove. P49
Weathercock
        The Weathercock. Rose Fyleman. P51
Weathering. Wilma H. Clements. P68
Weathers. Thomas Hardy. P51
Weathers. R. B. Weber. P64
Weaver, Clarence L.
        Found--A Poem!. P72
Weaver, John V. A.
        Drug Store. P82
        Nocturne. P82
        Two Ways. P82
Weaving
        Claire's Braids. Nancy McCleery. P88
Webb, James
        "War Is as Natural as the Rain". P86
Webb, Mary
        Foxgloves. P51
Webb, Phyllis
        Performance. P49
Weber, R. B.
        August Dusk: Sag Harbor. P64
        Behind These Lids. P64
        Late Autumn Afternoons. P64
        November. Over the Hills. P64
        Ocean Beach House. P64
        Peconic Autumn Day. P64
        Weathers. P64
Webs. Paul W. Tipton. P86
Webster, Daniel
        The Memory of the Heart. P89
Webster, Daniel

Daniel Webster. Oliver Wendell Holmes.
        P90
Wedding-Ring. Denise Levertov. P85
Wednesday's Child. Peggy Kahn. P56
"Wee kilties in the bonnie breese". Up Fair
        Kilties!. Russ Traunstein. P63
"A wee little nut lay deep in its nest".
        Among the Nuts. Unknown. P51
"Wee Willie Winkie". Willie Winkie. William
        Miller. P89
"Weep not, weep not". Go Down Death. James
        Weldon Johnson. P83
Weideman, Chris
        An Autumn Evening. P74
"Weighing the steadfastness and state". Man.
        Henry Vaughan. P59
Weingarten, Roger
        Saffron Pig Pinata. P63
Weiss, Theodore
        Cataract. P84
        A Certain Village. P84
        The Hook. P84
        Preface. P84
Weiss, Theodore (tr.)
        After Interrogation. Georgi Djagarov. P70
        Autumn. Georgi Djagarov. P70
Weissbort, Daniel (tr.)
        Life. Georgi Belev. P70
"Wekufe is sleeping". Wekufe's Dream.
        Clemente Riedemann. P71
Welby, Amelia B.
        Twilight at Sea. P89
Welch, Emily
        Summer Sun. P74
"Welcome me, if you will". For James Dean.
        Frank O'Hara. P85
Welcome to Spring. Irene Thompson. P51
"Welcome to you, rich Autumn days". Rich
        Days. William Henry Davies. P51
"Welcome, Little Robin". Unknown. P51
"Welcome, happy Easter day!.". Easter
        Praise. Rodney Bennett. P51
The Welcome. Thomas Davis. P89
Well Bed. Lola Strong Janes. P63
"Well, as you say, we live...". Palimpsest:
        a Deceitful Portrait. Conrad Aiken.
        P82
"Well, he stuck his what cannot be
        mentioned". Mrs. Whitehouse's View of
        Sexual Intercourse. Gavin Ewart. P63
"Well, I've been crying, crying". The Broken
        Sun. Anthony (Tony). Kellman. P68
"-- Well, my face is a vast skyblue". Sphinx
        Echoes the Sound Left by the Dead.
        Osman Turkay. P72
"Well, why should I be sad to go?.". On
        Leaving. Atanas Dalchev. P70
Wendell, Leilah
        Non Omnis Moriar. P68

"Went to the garden to pick a posy". Stanzas
      for the Harp. Unknown. P87
Wesley, Charles
      Wrestling Jacob. P89
West (United States)
      Hymn of the West. Edmund Clarence
          Stedman. P90
West, Charles
      Three. P63
Westhampton Cemetery. Philip Appleman. P64
Westport. Galway Kinnell. P85
Westrup, J. M.
      Best of All. P51
      Flying. P51
      The Furry Home. P51
      A Growing Rhyme. P51
      My Little House. P51
      The Poor Snail. P51
      The Vision Clear. P51
Westward Ho!. Joaquin Miller. P81
Westwood, Thomas
      Night of Spring. P51
"A wet sheet and a flowing sea". Sea Song.
      Allan Cunningham. P51
Wevill, David
      Animula. P49
      Child Sketch in Crayon. P49
      Her Seasons. P49
      Polonaise. P49
      Snow Country. P49
      Visitors. P49
Weygant, Sister Noemi
      Winter Is Tacked Down. P80
Whale. Geoffrey Dearmer. P51
Whales and Whaling
      Encounter. Addison Merrick. P56
      Humpbacks. Mary Oliver. P52
      Leviathan. William Stanley Merwin. P85
      Watching Whales Watching Us. Raymond
          Filip. P49
      Whale. Geoffrey Dearmer. P51
Wharf. Myra Cohn Livingston. P76
What a Fondness!. C. K. Shreedharan. P72
What a Friend We Have in Cheeses! William
      Cole. P63
What Are Years?. Marianne Moore. P83
What Became of Them?. Unknown. P51
What Can an Old Man Do But Die?. Thomas
      Hood. P89
"What Can Be Said in Words". Unknown. P62
What Could I Be If I Couldn't Be Me?. Jaime
      Ellis. P74
"What Day Is Tomorrow?," from Mother
      Goose... Unknown. P90
What Days, Indeed. Majeed Amjad. P91
What Did the Midge Say to the Mildew?.
      Bonnie Jacobson. P63
What Do I Know of the Old Lore?. Robert
      Duncan. P84

What Do You Want, Shepherd of Wind?.
      Salvatore Quasimodo. P61
"What Does the Beautiful One". Unknown. P62
What Does the Bee Do?. Christina Georgina
      Rossetti. P51
What Face?. Ricelda Payne. P72
What Happened to a Young Man... Unknown. P78
What Happened?. Mary Ann Lowry. P72
What I Live For. George Linnaeus Banks. P89
What Is It?. H. E. Wilkinson. P51
What Is Prayer?. James Montgomery. P89
What Lips My Lips Have Kissed, and Where,
      and Why. Edna St. Vincent Millay. P82
What Passes and Endures. John Ceiriog
      Hughes. P87
What Piggy-Wig Found. Enid Blyton. P51
What Should I Do Now?. Aristoteles Espana.
      P71
What Sparks My Imagination. Kelli Jensen.
      P73
What Sparks My Imagination. Amy Rojek. P74
"' What a lovely world,' said the baby
      chick". An Easter Chick. Thirza
      Wakley. P51
"What a moment, what a doubt!.". Sneezing.
      Leigh Hunt. P90
"What can a herring do?.". The Achievements
      of Herrings. Gavin Ewart. P63
"What can be the matter". The Wind. Dorothy
      Gradon. P51
"What can lambkins do". A Chill. Christina
      Georgina Rossetti. P51
"What could be nicer than the spring". A
      Walk in Spring. K. C. Lart. P51
"What dew i dew whn yr not heer cascading".
      Th Lovr Sighs if It All Revolvs Around
      Yu. Bill Bissett. P49
"What did my old song say?.". Joe Clisby's
      Song. Donald Davidson. P67
"What divides me from the unknown--...". In
      the Thickness. Phillipe Denis. P92
"What do you think I saw to-day". The Fairy
      Cobbler. A. Neil Lyons. P51
"What do you think? Last night I saw". The
      Dragon. Mary Mullineaux. P51
"What does a man leave". The Closet. Nino
      Nikolov. P70
"What does little birdie say". Cradle Song.
      Lord Tennyson. P51
"What does not change is the will to
      change". The Kingfishers. Charles
      Olson. P85
"What does one need?". The Room. Nino
      Nikolov. P70
"What does the farmer in the spring?.".
      Spring Work at the Farm. Thirza
      Wakley. P51
"What does the horse give you". Horse.
      Louise Gluck. P52

"What god will chose me from this
        labouring". Odes. George Santayana.
        P81

"What good is life without music". Read the
        Great Poets. James Tate. P85

"What great yoked brutes with briskets low".
        Crossing the Plains. Joaquin Miller.
        P81

"What had you been thinking about". The
        Tennis Court Oath. John Ashbery. P85

"What happened, I'm lost in my home!.". The
        Distance. Khalilur Rahman Azmi. P91

"What happy reciprocity". Quidiron Pro Quo.
        Paul Sawyer. P63

"What has been said of love ten
        thousand...". What's Said of Love.
        Darrell H. Bartee. P65

"What I am trying to say is this". The Poet
        Is a Hospital Clerk. David Ignatow.
        P84

"What I didn't know in that photograph".
        Chokecherry Summers. Margot Kriel. P88

"What I saw was just one eye". The Bird at
        Dawn. Harold Monro. P51

"What is a sonnet? 'Tis the pearly shell".
        The Sonnet. Richard Watson Gilder. P90

"What is Africa to me:.". Heritage. Countee
        Cullen. P83

"What is it now with me". Fear of Death.
        John Ashbery. P85

"What is our innocence". What Are Years?.
        Marianne Moore. P83

"What is the boy now, who has lost his
        ball". The Ball Poem. John Berryman.
        P79

"What is there about a blue, blue sky". Blue
        Magic. Roberta Goldstein. P72

"What is this life if, full of care".
        Leisure. William Henry Davies. P51,P90

"What is this, behind this veil, is it
        ugly...". A Birthday Present. Sylvia
        Plath. P85

"What is your sorrow?.". To Joya,
        Despairing. Kent Clair Chamberlain.
        P72

"What keeps me awake at night?.". Insomnia.
        Ardele L. Jessen. P72

"What Merida looked like the first time...".
        Things That Happen to You. Alonzo
        Gonzales Mo. P78

"What new element before us unborn...".
        Plutonian Ode. Allen Ginsberg. P52

"What price peace bought...". War or Peace.
        Margaret Baucom. P72

"What prompts me to flash back". Day in May.
        Dominick J. Lepore. P56

"What rotten luck has dumped me here". 44,
        Avenue de Maine. Atanas Dalchev. P70

"What shall her silence keep". Dirge.

        Madison Cawein. P81

"What shall I do this afternoon?.". Half
        Holiday. Olive Enoch. P51

"What she wanted was something untouched".
        Northeast. Martin Singleton. P49

"What slender maiden waits upon you now".
        From Milton's Translation of Horace's
        Fifth Ode. Terri B. Joseph. P68

"What strength! what strife! what rude
        unrest!.". Westward Ho!. Joaquin
        Miller. P81

What the Informant Said to Franz Boas in
        1920. Unknown. P78

What the Thrush Says. Queenie Scott-Hopper.
        P51

What the Thunder Said. Thomas Stearns Eliot.
        P83

What the Weather Does. Unknown. P51

What Trial?. Frank Finale. P56

"What Was Said by Him, His Eyes
        Blossoming...". Unknown. P62

"What the blind lost when radio". After the
        Revolution for Jesus... Miller
        Williams. P67

"What the neighbors bring to her kitchen".
        Widow. Lisel Mueller. P88

"What then? Am I to say". Divertissement.
        Amy Jo Schoonover. P72

"What time is is? it is every star". Poem
        ("What time"). Edward Estlin Cummings.
        P79

"What treasures lie beneath". Ocean
        Treasures. Constance Andrea Keremes.
        P76

"What was he doing, the great god Pan". A
        Musical Instrument. Elizabeth Barrett
        Browning. P90

"What was it? was Ruskin's foreskin
        stuck?.". To a Fringed Genital. G. N.
        Gabbard. P63

"What way does the wind come...". The Wind.
        Dorothy Wordsworth. P51

"' What we'd like to do', he said". The
        Latin American Solidarity Committee
        Fundraising... Ed Ochester. P63

"What wholly blameless fun". A Dutch
        Courtyard. Richard Wilbur. P84

What's All This Fuss About Tax Reform?. Ned
        Pastor. P63

"What's all this". The Return. Mauricio
        Electorat. P71

"What's going on in the hills, this May
        morning?.". Ascension Thursday.
        Saunders Lewis. P87

"What's here?.". Self-Portrait. Abdul-Latif
        Akel. P92

What's in a Name. Ed Orr. P63

What's Said of Love. Drrell H. Bartee. P65

What's That?. Florence Parry Heide. P55

"What's that you're telling me?.". Song
          Picture No. 71. Unknown. P78
"' What's the Matter,' He Says, Tying on
          the". Jon Olander. P77
"What's the brightness of a brow?.".
          Evanescence. Harriet Elizabeth
          Spofford. P81
"What's this? A dish for fat lips". The
          Shape of the Fire. Theodore Roethke.
          P84
"Whatever Part of My Body He Meditates On".
          Unknown. P62
"Whatever Tune My Lover Plays I Dance to".
          Unknown. P62
"Whatever it is, it must have". American
          Poetry. Louis Simpson. P85
"Whatever it was". On First Looking into
          Chapman's Refrigerator. Edmund Conti.
          P63
"Whatever opens also". On the Passing of
          Heidegger. Marshall Hryciuk. P49
Whatley, Wallace
          Eighth and Broad. P63
Wheatley, Phillis
          His Excellency General Washington. P90
Wheeler, Doanda Putnam
          These Perfect Years. P72
When. Sarah Wollsey. P89
When All the World Is Young. Charles
          Kingsley. P51
When Anger Came. Virginia M. Hahn. P58
When Gods Grow Weary. Steve Kline. P68
"When Good King Arthur Ruled This Land".
          Unknown. P51
"When Her Husband's Brother Is of Improper
          Mind". Unknown. P62
"When Her Son Was Climbing on the Back".
          Unknown. P62
"When I See". Giacomino Pugliese. P69
"When I Was a Little Boy". Unknown. P51
When I Went Out. Karla Kuskin. P75
"When I'm Out of the House in the Open, I
          Feel Joy". Unknown. P60
When Icicles Hang by the Wall, from Love's
          Labor's... William Shakespeare. P89
"When In His View, I Will Stand". Unknown.
          P62
"When a mere". Sarajevo, from Lost Youth:
          the Last War. Alfred Kreymborg. P82
"When a sighing begins". Songs of Autumn.
          Paul Verlaine. P89
"When a storm grows final on an ash". No
          Anger in a Fallen Tree. Allan Maunula.
          P72
"When Abraham Lincoln...". Cool Tombs. Carl
          Sandburg. P82
"When Achilles, the great Greek hero...".
          Achilles' Fatal Flaw. Debbie Dristle.
          P74

"When Alexander Pope strolled in the city".
          Mr. Pope. Allen Tate. P83
"When all is done and said...". Of a
          Contented Spirit. Thomas, 2nd Baron
          Vaux. P90
"When all the world is young, lad". The 'Old,
          Old Song'. Charles Kingsley. P89
"When an elf is as old as a year and a
          minute". The Seven Ages of Elf-Hood.
          Rachel (Lyman) Field. P55
"When autumn leaves were scattered". I Meet
          Lee San in the Nether World and Talk
          of Home. Ahmed Ali. P91
"When azure sky shadows". Carmel by the Sea.
          Alessandra A. Poles. P72
"When blessed Mary wiped her Savior's feet".
          Mary Magdalene. George Herbert. P59
"When bronze lay dreaming, and the ice".
          Goat's Hole, Paviland. Nigel Jenkins.
          P54
"When cats run home and light is come". The
          Owl. Lord Tennyson. P51
"When children are playing alone on the
          green". The Unseen Playmate. Robert
          Louis Stevenson. P89
"When Christmas-Eve is ended". The Dutch
          Patrol. Edmund Clarence Stedman. P81
"When darkest winter comes to siege my
          brow". Through Night's Window. Mary
          Jane Barnes. P68
"When death comes over me". Last Will &
          Testament No. 1. Robyn Martin. P77
"When do we say we'll do it". We and the
          Weekend. Alma Denny. P63
"When downward dips the roadway". The Road
          (Version 2, with echoes of Emily
          Dickinson). Blaga Dimitrova. P70
"When dreams of a live wife". Father. Martha
          Friedberg. P88
"When falls the soldier brave". Sentinel
          Songs. Abram Joseph Ryan. P90
"When father goes to town...". When Polly
          Buys a Hat. E. Hill. P51
"When father takes his spade to dig". The
          Robin. Laurence Alma-Tadema. P51
"When first I walked here I hobbled". The
          Seekonk Woods. Galway Kinnell. P52
"When first in love I breakfasted by water".
          The Romance Language. James Merrill.
          P79
"When first my lines of heavenly joys...".
          Jordan (2). George Herbert. P59
"When first this canvas felt Giorgione's
          hand". On the Concert. Trumbull
          Stickney. P81
"When first thou didst entice to thee my
          heart". Affliction. George Herbert.
          P59
"When for the thorns with which I long...".

The Coronet. Andrew Marvell. P59

"When God at first made man". The Pulley. George Herbert. P59

"When God confused our languages...". 'Let There Be Translators!'. Grace Schulman. P79

"When God was learning to draw the human face". Two Masks Unearthed in Bulgaria. William Meredith. P70

"When Gutenberg met Eula Snopes". Gutes and Eulas. Roy Blount Jr. P63

"When he ambushed you in Lit Nhial's camp". Ambush. Phillip Macar. P53

"When he came out, into the world". Born Tying Knots. Samuel Makidemewabe. P78

"When Henry kissed Heather". Hat Trick. Paul Humphrey. P63

"When I am dead and over me bright April". I Shall Not Care. Sara Teasdale. P82

"When I am feeling depressed and anxious sullen". Poem ("When I am feeling"). Frank O'Hara. P85

"When I am the sky". Cancion. Denise Levertov. P85

"When I consider how much time is spent". The Editor Regrets. David Cram. P63

"When I consider life and its few years--.". Tears. Lizette Woodworth Reese. P81

"When I died last (and, dear, I die...).". The Legacy. John Donne. P59

"When I died, the circulating library". Seth Compton, from Spoon River Anthology. Edgar Lee Masters. P82

"When I first asked Mother". Song of Triumph. Lois Duncan. P50

"When I first put this suit on". Metamorphosis, sel. Argyris Hionis. P92

"When I get up in the morning". Getting Up. Lilian McCrea. P51

"When I go to". Alfred Hitchcock U. Geoff Fiorito. P58

"When I have come". To a Walker of Ridges. Kaye Bache. P68

"When I put my head". The Xenoplile. Geoff Fiorito. P58

"When I saw the squirrel". Big Bang. Jay Meek. P63

"When I show up". Song Picture No. 30. Unknown. P78

"When I sit up to bread and milk". At Breakfast. Ida M. Mills. P51

"When I was a boy I saw the world I was in". Old-Time Childhood in Kentucky. Robert Penn Warren. P67

"When I was a boy the lamp lighter used fire". Light Talk (I). Adjutor. P72

"When I was a boy the rain was a gentle ally". Monsoon. Michael D. Clodfelter. P86

"When I was a child". Is the Pathetic Fallacy True?. Elizabeth Brewster. P49

"When I was a child, before I knew the word". The Seagull. Stanley Moss. P64

"When I was a runt, dragged". Penarth. John Tripp. P54

"When I was a young lad, no pleasure was higher". A Bushel of Chaff. John Ceiriog Hughes. P87

"When I was about ten". Making Beasts. Gregory Orr. P85

"When I was at Costa Del Sol". Costa Del Sol, at Night. Vita Andersen. P92

"' When I was at the party'.". Betty at the Party. Unknown. P51

"When I was born on Amman hill". The Collier. Vernon Watkins. P89

"When I was down with frogs and toads...". Because of You. Cecilia N. Rahl. P72

"When I was in the garden". The Queen Bee. Mary K. Robinson. P51

"When I was one, in a single year". Older Is Safer. Robert N. Feinstein. P63

"When I was sick and lay a-bed". The Land of Counterpane. Robert Louis Stevenson. P89

"When I was young I chased fleet time". The Chase. Mary Jane Barnes. P72

"When I was young my mother flung". Reflections of a Sometime Child. Gaston Pelletier. P68

"When I was young, I had no sense". The Fiddle. Neil Munro. P51

"When I went to bed at night". Through the Porthole. Marjorie Wilson. P51

"When I'm feeling lonely". Journey Back. Delphia Frazier Smith. P72

"When I'm in bed at night". Noises in the Night. Lilian McCrea. P51

"When I'm in health and asked to choose". Carpe Diem, from The House of a Hundred Lights. (Frederick) Ridgely Torrence. P81

"When I'm upstairs playing with my toys". The Horrible Noise. Samantha Adams. P74

"When Israel, of the Lord beloved". Rebecca's Hymn, from Ivanhoe. Sir Walter Scott. P89

When in the Chronicle of Wasted Time (Sonnet CVI). William Shakespeare. P89

When It's Over. Juan Cameron. P71

When Mary Goes Walking. Patrick R. Chalmers. P51

When Mary Thro' the Garden Went. Mary E. Coleridge. P51

When My Father Waters His Trees. Linda M. Hasselstrom. P88

When My Ship Comes in. Robert Jones
       Burdette. P89
"When it rained in Devon". London Rain.
       Nancy Byrd Turner. P75
"When learning's triumph...". Shakespeare,
       from Prologue. Samuel Johnson. P90
"When love with unconfined wings". To Althea
       from Prison. Richard Lovelace. P90
"When Maritess was kidnapped". Force of
       Circumstance. Jose Lacaba. P92
"When meeting a sidehill dodger, a prock".
       Fearsome Critters. Walter H. Kerr. P68
"When my devotions could not pierce".
       Denial. George Herbert. P59
"When my grave is broke up again". The
       Relic. John Donne. P59
"When nature had made all her birds". The
       Bobolinks. Christopher Pearse Cranch.
       P89
"When night believes itself alone". Five
       Women Bathing in Moonlight. Richard
       Wilbur. P84
"When night comes down on the children's
       eyes". At Night in the Wood. Nancy M.
       Hayes. P51
"When night declines, the moon". A Night in
       the War. Wazir Agha. P91
When on the Marge of Evening. Louise Imogen
       Guiney. P81
When Polly Buys a Hat. E. Hill. P51
"When our dear earth is hid by night". Song
       to the Nightingale. Alun. P87
"When pavements were blown up...". Epilogue
       to a Human Drama. Stephen Spender. P48
"When people call this beast to mind". The
       Elephant. Hilaire Belloc. P51
"When psalms surprise me with their music".
       A Psalm. Thomas Merton. P84
"When reading a slam". Emphasis Mine. Edmund
       Conti. P63
"When somebody loves you". Love's Not Words.
       LeRoy Coffie. P72
"When someone dies, and he is a VIP".
       Funeral Song. Patricio Esteve. P92
"When stars pursue their solemn flight".
       Music in the Night. Harriet Elizabeth
       Spofford. P81
"When sun, light handed, sows this Indian
       water". Aubade: Lake Erie. Thomas
       Merton. P84
When the Autumn. Ioan Maier. P72
When the Day Is Cloudy. Unknown. P75
When the Frost Is on the Punkin. James
       Whitcomb Riley. P89
When the Green Lies over the Earth. Angelina
       Weld Grimke. P89
When the Mocking Bird Sings. Harriet G.
       Hunt. P72
"When the Noble Girl Looks at Her New Nail

Wounds". Unknown. P62
"When the Pair of Deer Face the Blow".
       Unknown. P62
"When the Solitary Deer, Erect and with
       Longing Ears". Unknown. P62
"When the Wind Is in the East". Unknown. P51
When We Are Men. E. Stella Mead. P51
"' When Windham Lewis'". Bonnie Jacobson.
       P63
When You Are Old. William Butler Yeats. P90
When You Realize That... Virginia Rodas. P72
"When the autumn comes, and the leaves
       fall". The Autumn. Jeremy Yuenger. P74
"When the black-lettered list to the
       gods...". Wife, Children and Friends.
       William Robert Spencer. P89
"When the bright eyes of the day". Day and
       Night. James Stephens. P51
"When the Clements married...". Two
       Daughters Sing an Anniversary Ditty.
       Wilma H. Clements. P68
"When the day darkens". The Unknown Wind.
       William ("Fiona Macleod") Sharp. P51
"When the feud of hot and cold". December.
       Joel Benton. P89
"When the flowers turn to husks". Cells
       Breathe in the Emptiness. Galway
       Kinnell. P85
"When the forests have been destroyed...".
       The Asians Dying. William Stanley
       Merwin. P85
"When the green woods laugh...". Laughing
       Song. William Blake. P51
"When the herd were watching". Bethlehem.
       William Canton. P51
"When the moon". Ghost Sounds. Unknown. P55
"When the morning train blows...". The
       Morning Train. Fairfield Porter. P64
"When the norn mother saw the whirlwind
       hour". Lincoln, the Man of the People.
       Edwin Markham. P81
"When the one-legged sailors". Leaving.
       Sergio Mansilla. P71
"When the ripe pears droop heavily". The
       Wasp. William ("Fiona Macleod") Sharp.
       P51
"When the road dips down". The Road (Version
       1). Blaga Dimitrova. P70
"When the seven-thousand-year-old skulls".
       Peering at the Past. Mark Lawson
       Cannaday. P68
"When the shades of night are falling...".
       The Dustman. Unknown. P51
"When the starry moon". Tomorrow. Thelma L.
       Howard. P72
"When the sun goes down and the world is
       still". Jock O' Dreams. Rose Fyleman.
       P51
"hen the sun has left the hill top". A

Blessing for the Blessed, sel.
Laurence Alma-Tadema. P51

"When the sun is shining overhead". Shady
Woods. E. M. Adams. P51

"When the tea is brought at five o'clock".
Milk for the Cat. Harold Monro. P51

"When the tears stop". Change. K. Srilata.
P72

"When the water's calm". Song Picture No.
27. Unknown. P78

"When the woods are green again". Midsummer
Moon. E.M.G. R. P51

"When the world turns completely upside
down". Wild Peaches. Elinor Wylie. P82

"When they play like that where everyone
is". Thought-Song Three, from Tepehua
Thought-Songs. Unknown. P78

"When time has passed for speculation".
Reality. Robert B. Bradley. P72

"When to the flowers so beautiful". The
Forget-Me-Not. Unknown. P51

"When we return from the north...". We Broke
the Noose with a Snap. Majiok Wunyik.
P53

"When we sailed". Port Letter. Mary Trimble.
P88

"When we shall hold our head between our
hands". Memory. Jules Supervielle. P61

"When we were young we rode this carrousel".
Playland at the Beach. Gertrude May
Lutz. P72

"When winter's glaze is lifted from the
greens". The Sometime Sportsman Greets
the Spring. John Updike. P63

"When you have reached". Foot Hills. Carl T.
Endemann. P56

"When you're fall". Spring Is the Favorite
Time for Suicide. Virginia M. Hahn.
P58

"When your pre-schooler brings you". Oh, Now
I See... Keith Casto. P63

"When, stricken by the freezing blast".
Daniel Webster. Oliver Wendell Holmes.
P90

"Whence, O fragrant form of light". The
Water-Lily. John Banister Tabb. P89,
P81

"Whene'er a noble deed is wrought". Santa
Filomena (Florence Nightingale). Henry
Wadsworth Longfellow. P89

"Whenever a snow-flake leaves the sky". Snow-
Flakes. Mary Mapes Dodge. P89

"Whenever I go fishing". Tricia's Fish. Lee
Bennett Hopkins. P50

"Whenever one of the family...". The Ants.
Mark Thalman. P63

"Whenever Richard Cory went down town".
Richard Cory. Edward Arlington
Robinson. P89,P81

"Whenever the Traveller, with Fingers
Spread". Unknown. P62

"Whenever the horses of time stop...".
Time's Horses. Jules Supervielle. P61

"Whenever the moon and stars are set". Windy
Nights. Robert Louis Stevenson. P51

Where. Wendell Berry. P67

"Where Are You Going". Unknown. P51

Where Are You Going, My Pretty Maid?.
Unknown. P89

Where Beth They Biforen Us Weren?. Unknown.
P66

Where God Rested His Head. Jerry F. Borba.
P72

"Where Has the Disc of the Sun Gone".
Unknown. P62

Where Knock Is Open Wide. Theodore Roethke.
P84

Where Lies the Land?. Arthur Hugh Clough.
P51

"Where are Elmer, Herman, Bert, Tom...". The
Hill, from Spoon River Anthology.
Edgar Lee Masters. P82

"Where are the old men? Dead, at last?.". In
His Old Age and Blindness. Guto'r
Glyn. P87

"Where are the poems I have lost, the
lines". Lost Poems. Mary B. Finn. P68

"Where are you going, you little pig?.". The
Little Piggies. Thomas Hood. P51

"Where are you, Alaknanda!...". Solitude.
Harshdev Madhav. P72

"Where are your oranges?.". The Children's
Bells. Eleanor Farjeon. P51

"' Where art thou wandering, little
child?'.". Little Maid and Cowslips.
John Clare. P51

"Where comes a call,'Is Duffy a
kinsman...'.". Death Comes Calling.
David Mahr. P72

"Where did the sea of light roll from". In
Two Fields. Waldo Williams. P87

"Where do you call from? This mist
resounds". The Crossing. Salvatore
Quasimodo. P61

"Where do you think I've been to-day?.". The
Pigeon's Story. Jeannie Kirby. P51

"Where have all the colours gone?.". The
Darkening Garden. Unknown. P51

"' Where have you been'.". 'Banbury Fair'.
Edith G. Millard. P51

"Where Have you been, south wind...". South
Wind. Siegfried Sassoon. P51

"Where have you gone to, Yesterday".
Yesterday. Hugh Chesterman. P51

"Where is". And the Physician?., from Lost
Youth: the Last War. Alfred Kreymborg.
P82

Where the Bee Sucks. William Shakespeare.

P51

Where the Rainbow Ends. Robert Lowell. P84

"Where the buttercups so sweet". The Little
        Herd-Boy's Song. Robert Buchanan. P51

"Where the pools are bright and deep". The
        Boy's Song. James Hogg. P51

"Where the remote Bermudas ride". Bermudas.
        Andrew Marvell. P59

"Where the wind". Footprints on the Glacier.
        William Stanley Merwin. P85

"Where the wind whips through clothelines".
        Down by the Beach. Dolores Guglielmo.
        P72

"Where there were houses there is grass".
        Visitors. David Wevill. P49

Where to Spend the Winter. Robert Francis.
        P63

"Where were the greenhouses going". Big
        Wind. Theodore Roethke. P84

"Where were they when you lay in". For
        Kenneth Patchen. A. D. Williams. P56

"Where you going?.". Getting Berries, from
        String Games. Unknown. P78

"Where, like a pillow on a bed". The
        Ecstasy. John Donne. P59

"Whereas, the time for heroes is past".
        King's Orders. Jose Lacaba. P92

"Wheres the fire he said and I said
        Officer". My Luck. Bonnie Jacobson.
        P63

Wherever I Go. Al Mahmud. P91

"Wherever I Look". Unknown. P62

"Wherever he looks, standing still...".
        Leaving the Door Open (31), sel. David
        Ignatow. P64

"Wherever the Brother-in-Law Whirls".
        Unknown. P62

"Whether it's". The Encyclopedist's
        Conundrum. Kirby Olson. P63

"Whether the Weather Be Fine...". Unknown.
        P51

"' Which Is the Way to London Town'".
        Unknown. P51

"Which Is the Way to London Town?". Unknown.
        P51

"Which cow had Biel brought--the red...".
        Always Praises You. Nyaruoth Atem. P53

"' Which is the way to Baby-land?'.". Baby-
        Land. George Cooper. P51

"Which is the way to Fairyland". The Way to
        Fairyland. Eunice Close. P51

"Which of you". Song Picture No. 87.
        Unknown. P78

"Whichever way the wind doth blow". The
        Voyage. Caroline Atherton Mason. P89

"While Her Husband Is Asleep". Unknown. P62

While Summer Stays. Margaret Longenecker
        Been. P68

"While a witness is deposing...". The Court

Rests. Robert N. Feinstein. P63

"While everyone". Waking Up. Jaime Quezada.
        P71

"While my hair was still cut straight...".
        The River-Merchant's Wife: a Letter.
        Ezra Pound. P82

"While this America settles in the mold...".
        Shine, Perishing Republic. Robinson
        Jeffers. P83

"While trees and wings". Winds Curled
        Incense. Emma Crobaugh. P68

"While we were seven men alive, not three
        sevens". The Killing of Hywel. Peryf
        ap Cedifor. P87

"While yet these tears have power to flow".
        Sonnet. Louise Labe. P89

"The whippoorwill is". Night Music. Grace
        Shattuck Bail. P72

"Whirl up, sea--.". Oread. Hilda ("H.D.")
        Doolittle. P82

Whirlpools. Kolyo Sevov. P70

"The whiskey on your breath". My Papa's
        Waltz. Theodore Roethke. P84

Whisky Frisky. Unknown. P51

The Whistle. Robert Story. P89

Whistles and Whistling
        The Magic Whistle. Margaret Rose. P51

Whistling in the Air. Jaime Quezada. P71

Whitacre, Agnes Finch
        Loveliness Destroyed. P72

White. Tsutomu Fukuda. P72

White Death. Tom Tellesbo. P58

White Fields. James Stephens. P51

White Girls. Phillip Macar Ruac. P53

White Horses. Irene F. Pawsey. P51

White Ink on Sky Parchment. Francis Brown
        Price. P68

White Lie. Deanna Fleysher. P73

White Morning. L. Stanley Cheney. P68

White Sheep. William Henry Davies. P51

White Symphony. John Gould Fletcher. P82

White and Jonaid, Mary Jane (tr.)
        Ghazal. Jonaid. P92

"White darkness". Woman. Sachiko Yoshihara.
        P92

"White fog lifting and falling on mountain-
        brow". Wales Visitation. Allen
        Ginsberg. P85

"A white head-band waving". November 25,
        1970. Brian O'Riordan. P49

"White is the sail and lonely". A Sail.
        Mikhail Lermontov. P90

"White jackets". White Death. Tom Tellesbo.
        P58

"White pine, sifter of sunlight". Green
        Mountain, Black Mountain. Anne
        Stevenson. P54

"The white seashell on the beach". Poem of
        the Forgotten Things. Jaime Quezada.

P71
"A white sheet on the tail-gate of a truck".
    Elegy for a Dead Soldier. Karl
    Shapiro. P84
"White stars falling gently". Winter Joys.
    Dorothy Gradon. P51
"A white street". Winter. Peter Karaangov.
    P70
"White white angel-white". A Child Lost.
    Sigurdur A. Magnusson. P92
White, Adeline
    Autumn Morning. P51
    The Christmas Party. P51
    Colour. P51
    Over the Fields. P51
White, Henry Kirke
    The Early Primrose. P89
White, Mary Agnes
    Fancy. P72
White, Molly
    An Indian Grandaughter's Wish. P73
White, Steven F. (tr.)
    (No Greater Pain Beneath the Trees).
        Aristoteles Espana. P71
    All Night Long by Train, All Night Long.
        Mauricio Electorat. P71
    All of Him, the Blue Filigree of the
        Gaze. Gonzalo Munoz. P71
    Anonymous Biography. Armando Rubio. P71
    Arrival. Aristoteles Espana. P71
    Ars Poetique. Rodrigo Lira. P71
    Beach. Juan Cameron. P71
    The Beaches of Chile X. Raul Zurita. P71
    Beneath Each Stone. Walter Hoefler. P71
    Beyond Torture. Aristoteles Espana. P71
    The Birds Have Gone. Omar Lara. P71
    The Blindfold. Aristoteles Espana. P71
    Blue Danube. Manuel Silva Acevedo. P71
    Captured City. Omar Lara. P71
    Cauquil. Sergio Mansilla. P71
    Chain Reaction. Manuel Silva Acevedo. P71
    The Cheshire Cat. Juan Luis Martinez. P71
    Chess. Waldo Rojas. P71
    The Chicken Coop. Diego Maquieira. P71
    CIII. Raul Zurita. P71
    The Circle Closes Here. Waldo Rojas. P71
    City on Fire. Oscar Hahn. P71
    Code of Waters. Teresa Calderon. P71
    The Cordilleras of Il Duce. Raul Zurita.
        P71
    Corner. Gonzalo Millan. P71
    Death Is Sitting at the Foot of My Bed.
        Oscar Hahn. P71
    Deductions. Teresa Calderon. P71
    Dusk in Changuitad. Sergio Mansilla. P71
    East, sel. Gonzalo Munoz. P71
    Events Like Palaces. Paz Molina. P71
    Face to Face in Another Time. Teresa
        Calderon. P71

    For Armando Rubio. Mauricio Electorat.
        P71
    Fox Terrier Disappears at the
        Intersection... Juan Luis Martinez.
        P71
    "Go Slowly Over the Stones". Paz Molina.
        P71
    Halley's Comet. Jaime Quezada. P71
    Heartbreak Hotel. Oscar Hahn. P71
    Hell and Solitude. Aristoteles Espana.
        P71
    Heraclitus. Juan Cameron. P71
    Hotel De La Gare. Waldo Rojas. P71
    I Blew up the Virgin of My Legs. Diego
        Maquieira. P71
    I Never Realized. Teresa Calderon. P71
    I Play Childish Songs with a Grimace on
        My Lips. Gonzalo Millan. P71
    'I Wouldn't Be Able To Tell the
        Story...'. Walter Hoefler. P71
    Imperfect Preterite. Juan Cameron. P71
    In the Center of the Bedroom. Oscar Hahn.
        P71
    Intimate. Aristoteles Espana. P71
    The Iron Wheels of the Tricycle Without
        Tires... Gonzalo Millan. P71
    Is There Anyone. Walter Hoefler. P71
    A Kind of Song. Aristoteles Espana. P71
    A La Apollinaire. Manuel Silva Acevedo.
        P71
    Landscape. Omar Lara. P71
    Leaving. Aristoteles Espana. P71
    Leaving. Sergio Mansilla. P71
    Life. Sergio Mansilla. P71
    Like a Dream. Raul Zurita. P71
    Little Ghosts. Oscar Hahn. P71
    Love. Sergio Mansilla. P71
    The Man from Leipzig. Clemente Riedemann.
        P71
    "My Apparition There Is No". Gonzalo
        Munoz. P71
    The New Life. Raul Zurita. P71
    No One. Gonzalo Millan. P71
    No One Knows What I'm Talking About.
        Diego Maquieira. P71
    Non-Missing Fox Terrier Does Not
        Reappear... Juan Luis Martinez. P71
    Notes. Aristoteles Espana. P71
    Of the Nameless Birds. Teresa Calderon.
        P71
    Photograph. Oscar Hahn. P71
    Photograph. Omar Lara. P71
    The Place You Inhabit. Walter Hoefler.
        P71
    Poem 13, from The City. Gonzalo Millan.
        P71
    Poem 20, from The City. Gonzalo Millan.
        P71
    Poem 48, from The City. Gonzalo Millan.

P71
Poem 60, from The City. Gonzalo Millan.
    P71
Poem of the Forgotten Things. Jaime
    Quezada. P71
The Poet's Days. Omar Lara. P71
The Probable and Improbable Disappearance
    of a Cat... Juan Luis Martinez. P71
The Radiant Beaches. Raul Zurita. P71
Reincarnation of the Butchers. Oscar
    Hahn. P71
The Return. Mauricio Electorat. P71
Roads. Aristoteles Espana. P71
Rotterdam. Waldo Rojas. P71
Route Seven. Juan Cameron. P71
Satellite City. Mauricio Electorat. P71
The Scream Is a Kind of Coffin. Paz
    Molina. P71
She Abandoned Her Body to the Color.
    Gonzalo Munoz. P71
Siege. Omar Lara. P71
The Signalled Hour. Juan Cameron. P71
The Slaughterhouse. Mauricio Electorat.
    P71
Snows of Aconcagua. Raul Zurita. P71
The Stains Slid from Top to Bottom in
    Silence. Gonzalo Munoz. P71
Street. Waldo Rojas. P71
Subway. Juan Cameron. P71
Survivor. Walter Hoefler. P71
They Dragged Me Out by My Face. Diego
    Maquieira. P71
They've Broken the Most Delicate Bone in
    My Ear. Manuel Silva Acevedo. P71
Things of the Blind. Paz Molina. P71
Time. Sergio Mansilla. P71
The Time That Destroys Everything. Teresa
    Calderon. P71
To the Immaculate Plains. Raul Zurita.
    P71
To Write. Walter Hoefler. P71
Travel Journal, sel. Omar Lara. P71
The Tree of the World. Clemente
    Riedemann. P71
Under Certain Circumstances. Walter
    Hoefler. P71
The Utopias. Raul Zurita. P71
VI. Raul Zurita. P71
Vision. Gonzalo Millan. P71
Vision of Hiroshima. Oscar Hahn. P71
Waking Up. Jaime Quezada. P71
Wandering Souls. Sergio Mansilla. P71
Watching T.V. Oscar Hahn. P71
The Way Things Are Above and Below. Jaime
    Quezada. P71
We Will Not Hand Over the Night. Waldo
    Rojas. P71
Wekufe's Dream. Clemente Riedemann. P71
What Should I Do Now?. Aristoteles

Espana. P71
When It's Over. Juan Cameron. P71
Whistling in the Air. Jaime Quezada. P71
Wire Meshes. Aristoteles Espana. P71
Wishing. Omar Lara. P71
Wolves and Sheep, sels. Manuel Silva
    Acevedo. P71
Your Anger. Paz Molina. P71
Your Great Love. Diego Maquieira. P71
Your Little Friends Were a Bunch of Dogs.
    Diego Maquieira. P71
White-arm
    "I Am Making," from Crow Versions.
        William Stanley Merwin (tr.). P78
Whitehead, James
    About a Year After He Got Married He
        Would Sit Alone... P67
    He Records a Little Song for a Smoking
        Girl. P67
    A Local Man Doesn't Like the Music. P67
Whitened Sand. James Richard Hurst. P68
Whitetail, 2:30 a.m. Diane P. Lando. P77
"Whitman took the cars". Empathy and New
    Year. James Schuyler. P64
Whitman, S. W.
    October. P51
Whitman, Walt
    Myself, from The Song of Myself. P90
    O Captain! My Captain!. P90
    Out from Behind This Mask, from Leaves of
        Grass. P90
Whitman, Walt
    Walt Whitman. Edwin Markham. P81
Whitman, William (tr.)
    A Song of the Red & Green Buffalo.
        Unknown. P78
Whitmore, Alice E. W.
    Dance. P72
Whittemore, Reed
    The Boy and the Wolf. P63
    The City Mouse and the Country Mouse. P63
    In Memory of an English Professor. P63
    The Mocking Bird and the Owl. P63
    Summer Concert. P79
Whittemore, Reed (tr.)
    Why Is Man Born? Georgi Djagarov. P70
Whittier. Margaret Elizabeth (Munson)
    Sangster. P81
Whittier, John Greenleaf
    Barbara Frietchie. P51
    Maud Muller. P89
    Our State. P90
    The Two Angels. P89
Who Can Touch Me?. Micen Atem. P53
"Who Does Not Gain Wisdom". Unknown. P62
Who Has Seen the Wind?. Christina Georgina
    Rossetti. P51
"Who Is Stronger Than a Couple Angered by
    Love". Unknown. P62

Who Is That a-Walking in the Corn?. Fenton
        Johnson. P82
Who Likes the Rain?. Unknown. P51
Who Plays the Lyre?. Phillip Macar. P53
Who Takes Care of the Blind Stork?. Blaga
        Dimitrova. P70
"Who Uses Goods Made by the Base?.".
        Unknown. P62
Who Will Bury Me? Tor Kej. P53
"Who are these people at the bridge to meet
        me?... ". The Bee Meeting. Sylvia
        Plath. P85
"Who but x". Benedictus. Diane Scharper. P68
"Who can keep the northwind...". The
        Elements. Elisaveta Bagriana. P70
"Who can make a delicate adventure". Advice
        to a Blue-Bird. Maxwell Bodenheim. P82
"Who has ever stopped to think...". In
        Memory of Radio. Amiri (LeRoi Jones)
        Baraka. P85
"Who has not dreamed a world of bliss". A
        Summer Noon. William Howitt. P89
"Who is this I infesting my poems? Is
        it...". Performance. Phyllis Webb. P49
"Who killed Cock Robin?.". Coroner's
        Inquest. William DeWitt Snodgrass. P63
"Who rides so late through the midnight...".
        The Erl-King. Johann Wolfgang von
        Goethe. P90
"Who shall be the sign of". Statue of
        Liberty. Becky Turner. P73
"Who smiles". That...Who. Syed Ameeruddin.
        P72
"Who tamed your lawless Tartar blood?.". To
        Russia. Joaquin Miller. P81
"Who under my ribs but pain". Invitation to
        Morfudd. Robin Ddu. P87
"Who will believe". I, Golden Strings. Alice
        M. Boughtwood. P68
"Who will feed the dicky-birds...". Who?.
        Florence Hoatson. P51
"Who would be". The Mermaid, sel. Lord
        Tennyson. P51,P55
"Who would true valaour see". The Pilgrim.
        John Bunyan. P51
"Who writes these funny accidents". Just
        God. Lewis Turco. P63
"Who you are not". Her Seasons. David
        Wevill. P49
Who'll Help a Fairy? Unknown. P51
"Who'll buy my laces? I've laces to sell!.".
        The Lace Peddler. Catherine A. Morin.
        P51
Who's In?. Elizabeth Fleming. P51
Who's That a-Knocking?. Emile Jacot. P51
"' Who's That Ringing at the Front Door
        Bell?'". Unknown. P51
Who, Me?. Hallie Hodgson. P63
Who?. Florence Hoatso. P51

"Whoever Is Fat Was Born Like That".
        Unknown. P62
"Whoever unweaves love". At the Sources.
        Tomas Segovia. P92
"The whole desert could be Notre Dame...".
        The Utopias. Raul Zurita. P71
"Whole towns shut down". The .Late Snow and
        Lumber Strike of the Summer of Fifty-
        Four. Gary Snyder. P85
"The whole village was burning". The Divorce
        Poem. Janet Beeler Shaw. P88
"Whom Do You Greet, Oh Son". Unknown. P62
"Whose furthest footsteps never strayed".
        Envoy. Richard Hovey. P81
"Whose woods these are I think I know".
        Stopping by Woods on a Snowy Evening.
        Robert Frost. P82
Why Comtemporary American Poets Rarely
        Write... Louis Phillips. P63
"Why Do You Cry with Downcast Face".
        Unknown. P62
Why Do You Strive for Greatness, Fool?
        Stephen Crane. P81
"' Why Don't You Keep Asking the Red
        Amarinth'". Unknown. P62
Why I Am Not a Painter. Frank O'Hara. P85
"Why Is It, Even as I Lie on My Half of the
        Bed". Unknown. P62
Why Is Man Born? Georgi Djagarov. P70
"Why aren't you sleeping, little one".
        Night. Georgi Djagarov. P70
"Why do the bells of Christmas ring?.".
        Song. Eugene Field. P51
"Why do you". Ironica, from Lost Youth: the
        Last War. Alfred Kreymborg. P82
"Why do you talk so much". For Robert Frost.
        Galway Kinnell. P85
""Why do".". Susanna and the Elders.
        Adelaide Crapsey. P81
"Why does the wind so want to be". The Wind.
        Elizabeth Rendall. P51
"Why has our poetry eschewed". Food and
        Drink. Louis Untermeyer. P82
"Why have you come back?.". For You, in the
        Darkness, Returning. Karen Kania. P88
"Why if it is possible to pass the". 'The
        Ninth Elegy', from The Duinesian
        Elegies. Rainer Maria Rilke. P48
"Why make your lodging here in this spent
        lane". Wild Cherry. Lizette Woodworth
        Reese. P81
"' Why question death?' he asked at Anzio".
        Incident at Bien Hoa. Herbert M.
        Kirkham. P68
"Why seraphim like lutanists arranged".
        Evening Without Angels. Wallace
        Stevens. P83
"Why should this Negro insolently stride".
        August. Elinor Wylie. P82

"**Why** should you swear I am forsworn". The
        Scrutiny. Richard Lovelace. P59
"**Why** shun a nude tag?.". Wystan Hugh Auden:
        a Villanelle. David Lehman. P63
"**Why** sit at home mulling words". Why? Verna
        Lee O'Brien Clark. P56
"**Why** then should we try for immortality?.".
        The Mind Machines. Haywood Jackson.
        P68
"**Why** will they never sleep". The
        Grandfathers. Donald Justice. P67
Why? Verna Lee O'Brien Clark. P56
Why?. Thor Thorsen. P72
Widow. Lisel Mueller. P88
A **Widow** Bird. Percy Bysshe Shelley. P51
The **Widow's** Lament in Springtime. William
        Carlos Williams. P82
The **Widow's** Mite. Frederick Locker-Lampson.
        P89
Widows and Widowers
        Burning the Letters. Randall Jarrell. P84
        Widow. Lisel Mueller. P88
        Widows, from Spoon River Anthology. Edgar
        Lee Masters. P82
A **Wife's** Epitaph. R. Williams Parry. P87
Wife, Children and Friends. William Robert
        Spencer. P89
Wilbur, Richard
        The Beautiful Changes. P84
        Beowulf. P84
        Ceremony. P84
        A Dutch Courtyard. P84
        The Eye (Part II). P57
        Five Women Bathing in Moonlight. P84
        In a Bird Sanctuary. P84
        My Father Paints the Summer. P84
        On the Eyes of an SS Officer. P84
        Pangloss's Song. P84
        The Pardon. P84
        The Peace of Cities. P84
        Still, Citizen Sparrow. P84
        Sunlight Is Imagination. P84
        Water Walker. P84
Wilbur, Richard (tr.)
        Elegy. Georgi Djagarov. P70
Wilcox, Ella Wheeler
        Five Little Brothers. P51
Wilcox, Violet
        Morning Stillness. P72
"**Wild** Carthage held her, Rome". A Puritan
        Lady. Lizette Woodworth Reese. P81
Wild Cherry. Lizette Woodworth Reese. P81
Wild Day at the Shore. Felice Holman. P76
Wild Duck. Euros Bowen. P87
Wild Flower's Song. William Blake. P51
Wild May. Claude McKay. P82
Wild Peaches. Elinor Wylie. P82
The **Wild** Ride. Louise Imogen Guiney. P81
Wild Thyme. Joyce Sambrook. P51

"**Wildcat** Was Walking". Unknown. P78
Wilde, Richard Henry
        Life. P90
Wilkinson, H. E.
        Bread. P51
        Topsy-Turvy Land. P51
        What Is It?. P51
Wilkinson, Rosemary Challoner
        With Voices Strong. P72
Will You Be There?. Shelly Repine. P74
"**Will** you come to Turvy Land". Topsy-Turvy
        Land. Phyllis M. Stone. P51
"' **Will** you take a walk with me'.". The
        Clucking Hen. Unknown. P51
"' **Will** you walk a little faster?'...". The
        Lobster Quadrille. Charles Lutwidge
        ("Lewis Carroll") Dodgson. P51
"' **Will** you walk into my parlor?'...". The
        Spider and the Fly. Mary Howitt. P89
"' **Will** you walk with me'.". Invitation.
        James Steel Smith. P63
Will, Frederic (tr.)
        Landscape. Axel Schulze. P92
Will-O-the-Wisp. Colette Verger. P72
Willey, Edward
        At Home. P63
William Lloyd Garrison. James Russell
        Lowell. P90
"**William**, the sea's partner". Partner of the
        Sea. Kevin Cline. P58
Williams, A. D.
        For Kenneth Patchen. P56
Williams, Charles
        From a Walking Song. P51
Williams, Lucy
        The Origin of the Skagit Indians... Carl
        Cary (tr.). P78
Williams, Miller
        After the Revolution for Jesus... P67
        My Wife Reads the Paper at Breakfast on
        the Birthday... P63
        The Ones That Are Thrown Out. P57
        A Poem for Emily. P67
Williams, Pieter D.
        Africa. P68
        Images. P68
Williams, Waldo
        The Catholic Martyrs. Tony Conran (tr.).
        P87
        In Two Fields. Tony Conran (tr.). P87
        The Moment. Tony Conran (tr.). P87
Williams, William Carlos
        Burning the Christmas Greens. P82
        Danse Russe. P82
        Death. P82
        Gulls. P82
        June 9. P79
        Overture to a Dance of Locomotives. P82
        Poem. P82

Portrait of Lady. P82
Queen-Ann's-Lace. P82
The Red Wheelbarrow. P75,P82
The Sparrow--to My Father. P82
Spring and All. P82
Still Life. P79
To Elsie. P82
To Waken an Old Lady. P82
Tract. P82
The Widow's Lament in Springtime. P82
The Young Housewife. P82
Williams, William Crwys
Gathering Leaves. Tony Conran (tr.). P87
"Willie Blake blasted the rose". The Rose
and the Worm. James Camp. P63
"Willie Boy, Willie Boy, Where Are You
Going?". Unknown. P51
Willie Winkie. William Miller. P89
Willis, Marjorie Burney
Consider the Flowers. P72
Willis, Nathaniel Parker
The Annoyer. P89
Willow Bend and Weep. Herbert Clark Johnson.
P90
"The **willow**, still green". Country Road in
October. Judith Minty. P88
The **Willow-boughs**. Alexander Block. P51
Wills and Testaments
Last Will & Testament No. 1. Robyn
Martin. P77
Legacy. Gladys Pearl Allen. P72
Wilson, and Louise Bogan, Edmund
To Wystan Auden in His Birthday. P79
Wilson, Eric-Frederic
"Through the Ages Man Has Sought HArd to
Find". P72
Wilson, Irene K.
The Interior Castle. P72
Wilson, James
Casey's Revenge. P90
Wilson, Jean-Jacques
Within You. P72
Wilson, John
The Evening Cloud. P90
Wilson, Katharine
Bermuda Dream. P72
Wilson, Marjorie
From the Train. P51
The Gates to England. P51
The Jungle Trees. P51
The Lighthouse. P51
The Little Things That Happen. P51
Through the Porthole. P51
Wilson-Barry, Alma L.
Tea Time Remembered. P72
"**Wilt** thou forgive that sin where I begun".
A Hymn to God the Father. John Donne.
P59
Wimmera Child's First Waterfall. JoyceLee.

P72
Winans, A. D.
High on a Hill. P56
Winchell, Wallace
October Among the Hills. P65
Shared Festivals. P65
Winchell, Wallace William
Out of These, the First Love. P72
Wind
Behind These Lids. R. B. Weber. P64
Camp of the Winds. Pearl Newton Rook. P72
The East Wind. T.H. Parry-Williams. P87
Easy As Wind. Grace Schulman. P64
The March Wind. E. H. Henderson. P51
The North Wind. Dorothy Gradon. P51
The North Wind. Unknown. P51
Snowball Wind. Aileen Fisher. P80
The Sound of the Wind. Christina Georgina
Rossetti. P51
South Wind. Siegfried Sassoon. P51
Wind. Krishna Srinivas. P72
Subway Wind. Claude McKay. P82
Such a Blustery Day!. Elizabeth Gould.
P51
The Thief. Irene F. Pawsey. P51
The Unknown Wind. William ("Fiona
Macleod") Sharp. P51
What Do You Want, Shepherd of Wind?.
Salvatore Quasimodo. P61
Who Has Seen the Wind?. Christina
Georgina Rossetti. P51
Wind. Krishna Srinivas. P72
Wind and the Leaves. Unknown. P51
The Wind in the Grass. Ralph Waldo
Emerson. P51
The Wind's Lament. John Morris-Jones. P87
The Wind. Dorothy Wordsworth. P51
The Wind. Elizabeth Rendall. P51
The Wind. Robert Louis Stevenson. P51,P89
The Wind. Dorothy Gradon. P51
The Wind. Dafydd ab [or ab] Gwilym. P87
Winds Curled Incense. Emma Crobaugh. P68
Windsong. Leonorv (I am Cree). McDowell.
P72
Windward Cycle. Lloyd Stone. P72
Wind and the Leaves. Unknown. P51
Wind Blew Once. Jeremy Hooker. P54
"A **wind** came up out of the sea". Daybreak.
Henry Wadsworth Longfellow. P51,P89
"The **wind** has such a rainy sound". The Sound
of the Wind. Christina Georgina
Rossetti. P51
The **Wind** in the Grass. Ralph Waldo Emerson.
P51
"The **wind** is silent; but the moon is full".
Morning Stillness. Violet Wilcox. P72
"A **wind** passed over my mind". The Image-
Maker. Stanley Kunitz. P52
"The **wind** rises, the dark is torn to

shreds". Seascape. Eugenio Montale. P61

"The **wind** sang to the cornfields". August. Eunice Fallon. P51

"The **wind** shakes the mists". Mutability. John Gould Fletcher. P82

"**Wind** sharp, hillside bleak, hard to win shelter". Winter. Unknown. P87

"The **wind** tears up the sun". Poem. James Schuyler. P64

"The **wind** was gently blowing". The Young Indians. Jennie Thorpe. P74

"The **wind** was throwing snowballs". Snowball Wind. Aileen Fisher. P80

"**wind** whistled loud at the window pane--.". Lullaby. William Brighty Rands. P51

The **Wind's** Lament. John Morris-Jones. P87

The **Wind**. Dafydd ab [or ab] Gwilym. P87

The **Wind**. Dorothy Gradon. P51

The **Wind**. Elizabeth Rendall. P51

The **Wind**. Robert Louis Stevenson. P51,P89

The **Wind**. Dorothy Wordsworth. P51

The **Windmill**. E. V. Lucas. P51

Windmills

    Clouds Near the Windmill. Barbara Guest. P64

Window. P. D. Murphy. P56

The **Window** Cleaner. Elizabeth Fleming. P51

Window Seat. Ruth O. Maunders. P72

"The **window** of the florist shop". 'The Knight-a Lady's Hero'. Eleanor Otto. P65

"The **window**, the best is the window". Inside. Orhan Veli Kanik. P91

The **Window**. Patricia Hooper. P88

The **Window**. Boris Khristov. P92

Windows

    Four Squares. Agnes Nemes Nagy. P92
    Inside. Orhan Veli Kanik. P91
    A Town Window. John Drinkwater. P51
    Window. P. D. Murphy. P56

The **Windows**. George Herbert. P59

Winds Curled Incense. Emma Crobaugh. P68

"**Winds** are necessary. Times wouldn't be there". The East Wind. T.H. Parry-Williams. P87

"The **winds** of hatred blow". Lull. Theodore Roethke. P84

"The **winds** they did blow". The Squirrel. Unknown. P51

"**Winds** through the olive trees softly...". A Christmas Song. Unknown. P51

"The **winds** transferred into the friendly sky". The Camp at Night, from The Iliad. Homer. P89

Windsong. Leonorv (I am Cree). McDowell. P72

Windward Cycle. Lloyd Stone. P72

Windy Nights. Robert Louis Stevenson. P51

Wine Coolers. Bern Sharfman. P63

"The **wing** gripped the stiff mist tightly". Winter. Antal Vizy. P61

"**Wings** its way into the distance". The Time That Destroys Everything. Teresa Calderon. P71

"**Winked** too much and were afraid of snakes...". The Monkeys. Marianne Moore. P83

Winter

    As You Wish. Mario Luzi. P61

Winter. Enid Blyton. P51

Winter. Mathias Claudius. P89

    Clothing. Jim Fields. P72
    Cold Hangs the Quarter Moon. Frank P. Zeidler. P68
    The Coming of the Cold. Theodore Roethke. P84
    The Crystal Flow. James Richard Hurst. P68
    "Dame Trot and Her Cat". Unknown. P51
    Empathy and New Year. James Schuyler. P64

Winter. Gary Erb. P56

    First Snowfall. Barbara Juster Esbensen. P80
    A Greenland Winter. Lucy Diamond. P51
    In the Wood. Eileen Mathias. P51
    Johnny's Woodpile. T. M. Baker. P68

Winter. Peter Karaangov. P70

Winter. W. D. Landor. P51

    Lethbridge, Alberta; Thursday Evening, November... Stephen Scobie. P49

Winter. Myra Cohn Livingston. P80

    Musica Ficta. D. G. Jones. P49
    Old Man Winter. Tilda S. Akers. P72
    The Playhouse Key. Rachel (Lyman) Field. P51
    Poem. James Schuyler. P64
    Poem of the Frost and Snow. Lewis Morris. P87
    Preparing for Winter. Steve Sanfield. P77

Winter. Christina Georgina Rossetti. P51

    The Shade of the Magnolia. Eugenio Montale. P61

Winter. Dave Shelton. P74

    Snow Scene. Louise Marsh Gabriel. P72
    There's Snow on the Fields. Christina Georgina Rossetti. P51
    Thoughts for a Cold Day. Unknown. P51
    Trails. Tom Tellesbo. P58

Winter. Unknown. P87

Winter. Antal Vizy. P61

    The Waters of Saturday, sel. Maria Luisa Spaziani. P61
    When Icicles Hang by the Wall, from Love's Labor's... William Shakespeare. P89
    Where to Spend the Winter. Robert Francis. P63
    Winter. Unknown. P87

Winter. Antal Vizy. P61
Winter. Myra Cohn Livingston. P80
Winter. Enid Blyton. P51
Winter. Christina Georgina Rossetti. P51
Winter. Mathias Claudius. P89
Winter. Dave Shelton. P74
Winter. Gary Erb. P56
Winter Joys. Dorothy Gradon. P51
Winter Morning. Ogden Nash. P80
Winter Song. Ludwig Holty. P89
Winter and Spring. Coventry Patmore. P51
Winter Central. Christopher Dewdney. P49
Winter Frost. Alison Hoelz. P73
Winter Is Tacked Down. Sister Noemi Weygant.
   P80
Winter Joys. Dorothy Gradon. P51
Winter Landscape. John Berryman. P79
Winter Morning. Ogden Nash. P80
Winter Song. Ludwig Holty. P89
"Winter etches windowpanes...". Winter. Myra
   Cohn Livingston. P80
"Winter is frost". Winter Frost. Alison
   Hoelz. P73
"Winter is the king of showmen". Winter
   Morning. Ogden Nash. P80
"Winter whistles around the steeple". The
   Waters of Saturday, sel. Maria Luisa
   Spaziani. P61
Winter's Song. Unknown. P51
Winter, Brian
   Rain. P73
Winter, Helen
   Tradition. P88
"The winters close, springs open, no child
   stirs". Homage to Mistress Bradstreet,
   sels. John Berryman. P84
Winters, Bayla
   Calvin. P56
Winters, Yvor
   Orpheus. P83
   Sir Gawaine and the Green Knight. P83
   To a Military Rifle. P83
   To the Holy Spirit. P83
Winwood, David
   Unforgettable Summers. David Winwood
   (tr.). P92
Wire Meshes. Aristoteles Espana. P71
Wireless. Rodney Bennett. P51
"Wirikota wirikota/Where the roses are
   born". For the God of Peyote. Unknown.
   P78
A Wisconsin Dawn. Abby Arthur Johnson. P68
Wise Guys. Ray Catina. P86
Wish... Oceana Feldman. P74
A Wish. Elizabeth Gould. P51
A Wish. Robert Williams Parry. P87
A Wish. Samuel Rogers. P51
The Wish. Goronwy Owen. P87
Wishes

A Christmas Wish. Rose Fyleman. P51
An Indian Grandaughter's Wish. Molly
   White. P73
Me Wants a Minks. E. W. Sneed. P63
An Orphan's Wish. Lee Ann Braunecker. P74
A Penny Wish. Irene Thompson. P51
Wishes. F. Rogers. P51
Wishes. Unknown. P51
   Wish... Oceana Feldman. P74
   A Wish. Robert Williams Parry. P87
   A Wish. Samuel Rogers. P51
   A Wish. Elizabeth Gould. P51
   The Wish. Goronwy Owen. P87
   Wishes. F. Rogers. P51
   Wishing. Omar Lara. P71
   Wishing. William Allingham. P51
   The Wishing Bone Cycle, sel. Jacob
      Nibenegenesabe. P78
Wishing. William Allingham. P51
Wishing. Omar Lara. P71
The Wishing Bone Cycle, sel. Jacob
   Nibenegenesabe. P78
Wishing for Water in February. Elisavietta
   Ritchie. P56
The Witch of Coos. Robert Frost. P82
The Witch. Percy H. Ilott. P51
Witches and Witchcraft
   Knitted Things. Karla Kuskin. P55
   The Witch. Percy H. Ilott. P51
   Witches' Sabbatical. G. N. Gabbard. P63
   Witches' Song. Elizabeth J. Coatsworth.
      P55
   Wizards. Alonzo Gonzales Mo. P78
Witches' Sabbatical. G. N. Gabbard. P63
Witches' Song. Elizabeth J. Coatsworth. P55
"With a Sieve". Tilly Boesche Zacharow. P72
"With Bent Neck, the Traveller's Wife".
   Unknown. P62
With Child. Genevieve Taggard. P83
"With Deep Regret for My Anger". Unknown.
   P62
"With Effort Is a Lover Got". Unknown. P62
With Eye and with Gesture. Stephen Crane.
   P81
With Fifty Stars. Francis Brown Price. P68
"With Lamp Blown Out, Breath Held". Unknown.
   P62
"With a name like that". A Note from Plwmp.
   John Tripp. P54
"With a very big yawn". Mr. Beetle. Emily
   Hover. P51
"With a yellow lantern". Glow-Worms. P. A.
   Ropes. P51
"With dawn". Window Seat. Ruth O. Maunders.
   P72
"With ears like petals or wings".
   Grandmother God. Jeanine Hathaway. P88
"With eyes hand-arched he looks into".
   Comradery. Madison Cawein. P81

"With grass like a bull's eye". Mrs.
        MacQueen (or The Lollie-Shop). Walter
        De La Mare. P51
"With his fiftieth birthday behind him...".
        The Dead. David Gwenallt Jones. P87
"With its baby rivers and little towns...".
        England. Marianne Moore. P83
"With many a scowl". Troll Trick. B. J. Lee.
        P55
"With shining certainty...". New Moon or
        No?. Maryann Calendrille. P64
"With snort and pant the engine dragged".
        The Song of the Engine. H. Worsley-
        Benison. P51
"With spangles gay and candle light". The
        Christmas Tree. Isabel de Savitzsky.
        P51
"With sunburn on my everything". It's Such a
        Wonderful Day at Camp. Rana L.
        Landseadel. P73
"With sweetest milk and sugar first". The
        Girl and Her Fawn. Andrew Marvell. P51
With the Dawn. Sally T. McCullough. P68
With the Flashes of the Night. Phoebus
        Delphis. P61
With Trembling Hands. Rex Quartey. P72
With Voices Strong. Rosemary Challoner
        Wilkinson. P72
"With their feet in the earth". Tall Trees.
        Eileen Mathias. P51
"With what deep murmurs...". The Water-Fall.
        Henry Vaughan. P59
"With what painful deliberation...". English
        Cocker: Old and Blind. Robert Penn
        Warren. P67
"With wild pears and a piece of bread...". A
        Woman Called Maria. Boris Kristov. P70
Within You. Jean-Jacques Wilson. P72
"Within a delicate grey ruin". The Vestal
        Lady on Brattle. Gregory Corso. P85
"Within a thick and spreading hawthorn
        bush". The Thrush's Nest. John Clare.
        P51
"Within that town of David where you
        stayed". Letter to a Census Taker.
        Mario Speracio. P65
"Within the secret garden of my soul". The
        Exotic Plant. Mauricia Price. P68
""The withness of the body".". The Heavy
        Bear Who Goes with Me. Delmore
        Schwartz. P84
Without a Prop. Bella Cameron. P72
Without a Tear. Lillian Hammer. P72
Without and Within. Pietro Metastasio. P90
Without Voice, Without Hope. Jozsef Tornai.
        P92
"Without haste! without rest!.". Haste Not!
        Rest Not!. Johann Wolfgang von Goethe.
        P90

"Without hope the knight...". The Conqueror.
        Jan Anker Froydarland. P72
"Without wind, the leaves and lake". Camp of
        the Winds. Pearl Newton Rook. P72
"Without you". TAJ. T. G. Prabha Shankar.
        P72
"Witness now this trust! the rain".
        Possessions. Hart Crane. P83
Wittner, Mary Margaret
        Inamorata. P72
Witty, Rosemary
        Mysterious. P72
Wizards. Alonzo Gonzales Mo. P78
"Wodland's Broadway raised a curtain".
        Dramatic Compensation. Francis Brown
        Price. P68
Woe One. Alice Ryerson. P88
Woe Three. Alice Ryerson. P88
Woe Two. Alice Ryerson. P88
Wolcott, John
        The Razor-Seller. P90
The Wolf and the Lambs. Ivy O. Eastwick. P51
Wolfe, Charles
        Burial of Sir John Moore. P90
Wolfe, Ffrida
        Four and Eight. P51
        The Poppies in the Garden. P51
Wolfe, Humbert
        The Blackbird. P51
Wollsey, Sarah
        When. P89
Wolves
        The Dead Wolf. Roger A. Chrastil. P56
Wolves and Sheep, sels. Manuel Silva
        Acevedo. P71
Woman. Sachiko Yoshihara. P92
A Woman Alone on the Road. Blaga Dimitrova.
        P70
A Woman Brought Naked Face to Face with the
        Sky. Pierre Emmanuel. P61
A Woman Called Maria. Boris Kristov. P70
"The woman attendant peels her lunch".
        Laundromat Eulogies. James D. Hartman.
        P86
"Woman greater the patience". Opening
        Figure. Mohammed Dib. P91
"A woman in the shape of a monster".
        Planetarium. Adrienne Rich. P85
"The woman knows how it's done". Claire's
        Braids. Nancy McCleery. P88
"The woman named Tomorrow". Four Preludes on
        Playthings of the Wind. Carl Sandburg.
        P82
A Woman of Style. Edith Freund. P88
Woman of the Late Fall Run. Anselm
        Parlatore. P64
"A woman was made chief not long ago". Women
        Beat the Life Out of Me. Pilual Juoc.
        P53

"The **woman** who used to be my age". After the
	Face Lift. Lisel Mueller. P88
A **Woman's** Answer. Adelaide Anne Procter. P89
Woman's College. John Frank. P72
Woman's Constancy. John Donne. P59
A **Woman's** Love. John Hay. P89
A **Woman's** Question. Adelaide Anne Procter.
	P89
A **Woman's** Song, About Men. Unknown. P78
"The **Woman,** with the Palm of Her Hand".
	Unknown. P62
"**Womb** dried of love and birth". Woods Are
	Sleeping. Salvatore Quasimodo. P61
Women
	American Body Binding. Elaine Demakas.
		P58
Women. Louise Bogan. P83
	Bramble Jam. Irene F. Pawsey. P51
	"The Delicate Girl Is Washed". Unknown.
		P62
	Fau Bauman, Frau Schmidt, and Frau
		Schwartze. Theodore Roethke. P84
	"The Garland-Girl Giving Out Freshly
		Broken Blossoms". Unknown. P62
	Gipsy Jane. William Brighty Rands. P51
	"Her Face Is Like the Moon--.". Unknown.
		P62
	I Was Mistaken for a Red Dog. Nyakong
		Makui. P53
	"In Separation, an Unfaithful Woman Is
		Like Poison". Unknown. P62
	"In This Whole Wide Earth". Unknown. P62
	Iqleema. Fahmida Riyaz. P91
	Janie Crawford. Alice Walker. P85
	Letter from a Far Country. Gillian
		Clarke. P54
	The Little Old Lady. Rodney Bennett. P51
	"The Moon-Beams, Set in Motion". Unknown.
		P62
	The Old Fashioned Girls. Pilual Juoc. P53
	Old Mrs. Jarvis. Elizabeth Fleming. P51
	Old Women Are Taking Over the World. Jay
		Dougherty. P63
	"Only When Women's Eyes". Unknown. P62
	Opening Figure. Mohammed Dib. P91
	Orion. Adrienne Rich. P85
	Our Mother the General. Jessie Kachmar.
		P88
	Poem. Nadia Bishai. P92
	Portrait d'une Femme. Ezra Pound. P82
	Portrait of Lady. William Carlos
		Williams. P82
	Pretty Lady. Rose Fyleman. P51
	Snapshots of a Daughter-in-Law. Adrienne
		Rich. P85
	Tanka. Helen Fountain. P72
	Tradition. Helen Winter. P88
	Two Women. Barbara Goldberg. P63
	The Vestal Lady on Brattle. Gregory

	Corso. P85
	When Mary Goes Walking. Patrick R.
		Chalmers. P51
	Will-O-the-Wisp. Colette Verger. P72
	A Woman Alone on the Road. Blaga
		Dimitrova. P70
	Woman of the Late Fall Run. Anselm
		Parlatore. P64
	A Woman's Question. Adelaide Anne
		Procter. P89
	Women. Louise Bogan. P83
	Women Beat the Life Out of Me. Pilual
		Juoc. P53
	Women in Love. Donald Justice. P67
	Women's Chorus. Aristophanes. P90
Women Beat the Life Out of Me. Pilual Juoc.
	P53
"**Women** have no wilderness in them". Women.
	Louise Bogan. P83
Women in Love. Donald Justice. P67
Women's Chorus. Aristophanes. P90
Women-Black
	Beautiful Black Women. Amiri (LeRoi
		Jones) Baraka. P85
	The Help. James Merrill. P79
Women-Housewives
	The Young Housewife. William Carlos
		Williams. P82
Wonder
	I Am Waiting. Lawrence Ferlinghetti. P85
The **Wonderful** Derby Ram. Unknown. P51
The **Wonderful** World. Robert D. Sutherland.
	P63
"**Wonderfully**". Giacomo da Lentini. P69
"**Wood** duck". Conversation in June. Barbara
	S. Berstein. P68
"The **wood** is a good place to find". Walking
	with Lulu in the Wood. Naomi Lazard.
	P64
The **Wood** of Flowers. James Stephens. P51
The **Wood-Pile**. Robert Frost. P82
Woodknot. Allen Planz. P64
The **Woodman's** Dog. William Cowper. P51
Woodman, Spare That Tree. George Pope
	Morris. P89
The **Woodpecker**. Joyce Sambrook. P51
Woods Are Sleeping. Salvatore Quasimodo. P61
"The **woods** and fields are silent now".
	Evening Prayer. Brierly Ashour. P68
"The **woods** stretch wild to the mountain
	side". The Man Hunt. Madison Cawein.
	P81
Woolfolk, Miriam L.
	World Poets Everywhere. P72
Woomer, Matthew
	Haiku. P74
"A **word** is like a silver thread". Sound
	Effect. Edna Jones. P68
Words

Doves. Robert Duncan. P84
Words. Sylvia Plath. P85
411 Days and Nights. Doug Rawlings. P86
Four Letter Words. Stella Moss. P63
Garza. Bruce Bennett. P63
A Gift. Amy Lowell. P82
In the Garden of Your Words. Margaret
   Flanagan Eicher. P65
The Language. Robert Creeley. P85
Mutiny. Goldie Morales. P72
One Solitary Voice. Marilyn Gordon. P72
The Parnassians. James Merrill. P85
Poem, fr. Iris Ifriqiya. Majid El Houssi.
   P91
Pretty Words. Elinor Wylie. P82
The Quarrel. Viola K. Hunt. P68
Riprap. Gary Snyder. P85
A Song for T. S. Cristina Pina. P92
Sound Effect. Edna Jones. P68
Tower of Babel. Thomas Merton. P84
Verses Why Burnt. Walter Savage Landor.
   P90
Without a Tear. Lillian Hammer. P72
Words. Sylvia Plath. P85
The Words That Never Came. Harold O.
   Wang. P68
Words or Spoors, fr. Omneros. Mohammed Dib.
   P91
The **Words** That Never Came. Harold O. Wang.
   P68
"**Words/Dripping** venom". The Quarrel. Viola
   K. Hunt. P68
Wordsworth, Dorothy
The Wind. P51
Wordsworth, William
A Change in the Year. P51
Daffodils. P89
I Wandered Lonely. P51
The Kitten at Play. P51
My Heart Leaps Up. P89
A Night in June. P51
"On poetry and geometric truth", fr. The
   prelude. P48
Sonnet. P90
The Tables Turned. P89
To the Cuckoo. P51,P89
Walton's Book of Lives, from
   Ecclesiastical Sonnets. P90
Written in March. P51
Wordsworth, William (tr.)
To the Supreme Being. Michelangelo
   Buonarroti. P89
Work
A Bit of Enlightenment. Tom Riley. P63
Every Day. Mary I. Osborn. P51
Good Night and Good Morning. Richard
   Monckton Milnes; 1st Baron Houghton.
   P51
The Mouse, the Frog and the Little Red

Hen. Unknown. P51
Number 7. Doug Rawlings. P86
Work. Aleksandr Pushkin. P90
Self Employment. Lowell E. Sargeant. P63
"Splitting Cedar". Mike Dixon. P77
To My Craft. Agnes Nemes Nagy. P92
The Tuft of Flowers. Robert Frost. P82
Two Tramps in Mud Time. Robert Frost. P82
Work. Henry Van Dyke. P90
Work. Aleksandr Pushkin. P90
Work Song. Wendell Berry. P67
"The **work** of the saws separating the
   vertebrae". The Slaughterhouse.
   Mauricio Electorat. P71
"A **workday** is from sun to sun". Home Owner's
   Lament. Pier Munn. P63
"**Working** class clouds are living together".
   Clouds. Stanley Moss. P64
The **World** (1). Henry Vaughan. P59
World Breaking Apart. Louise Gluck. P85
World War, Second
Pleiku. David Biles. P86
"The **world** goes up and the world goes down".
   Dolcino to Margaret. Charles Kingsley.
   P89
The **World** in Us. Jules Supervielle. P61
The **World** Is a Mighty Ogre. Fenton Johnson.
   P82
The **World** Is Full of Voices... Jules
   Supervielle. P61
The **World** Is Not a Pleasant Place To Be.
   Nikki Giovanni. P85
The **World** Is Not Conclusion. Emily
   Dickinson. P48
World Poets Everywhere. Miriam L. Woolfolk.
   P72
The **World** Was No Temptation. Margaret
   Longenecker Been. P68
"The **world** is full of colour!.". Colour.
   Adeline White. P51
"The **world** is so full of a number of
   things". Happy Thought. Robert Louis
   Stevenson. P51
"The **world** is winter". Musica Ficta. D. G.
   Jones. P49
"The **world** is wise, for the world is old".
   The World. Frederick William Faber.
   P89
"**World** of my morning's playground". The Free
   School-house, Llanrwst. Ieuan Glan
   Geirionydd. P87
The **World**. Robert Creeley. P85
The **World**. Frederick William Faber. P89
The **World**. William Brighty Rands. P51,P90
"The **worm** in Newton's apple said".
   E=MCround. Ann Deagon. P63
Worship
At Mass. Vachel Lindsay. P82
Sonnet 016, fr. One person.Elinor Wylie.

P82
Worshiper. Gloria A. Maxson. P63
Worsley-Benison, H.
    The Song of the Engine. P51
"The worst of husbands...". From a Marriage
    Counselor's Notebook. Alfred Dorn. P65
Worth, Dorothy Williamson
    Applachian Courtship. P65
Wotton, Sir Henry
    The Character of a Happy Life. P90
"Would you see the little men". The Little
    Men. Flora Fearne. P51
"Wouldn't you like to be a whale". Whale.
    Geoffrey Dearmer. P51
Wound and Knife. Gyorgy Somlyo. P92
The Wraggle Taggle Gipsies. Unknown. P51
"Wrap me in night". The Darkness Before.
    Eleanore-Melissa. P68
"Wrap up in a blanket in cold weather...".
    Things to Do Around a Lookout. Gary
    Snyder. P85
A Wreath. George Herbert. P59
The Wreath. Meleager. P89
The Wreath. Henry Vaughan. P59
"A wreathed garland of deserved praise". A
    Wreath. George Herbert. P59
The Wreck of the Hesperus. Henry Wadsworth
    Longfellow. P90
"The wren house sways on its long pole". A
    Little Drama. Paulette Roeske. P88
Wrestling. Kathleen Fraser. P50
Wrestling Jacob. Charles Wesley. P89
Wrestling with Angels. Walter McDonald. P57
Wright, A. J.
    Maps in the Brain. P56
Wright, Charles
    Dead Color. P67
    Northhanger Ridge. P67
    The Other Side of the River. P52
    Portrait of Mary. P79
Wright, E. (tr.)
    The Cock and the Fox. Jean de La
    Fontaine. P90
Wright, James
    Mutterings Over the Crib of a Deaf Child.
    P57
Wright, Richard
    I Have Seen Black Hands. P90
Writing and Writers
    Act of Creation. Peter Stevens. P49
    Beginning Writer. Bonnie Squires. P72
    Bones and Jewels. Paul Monette. P79
    David Hume. Donald Hall. P79
    Duo for Voice & Percussion. E. O. Staley.
    P63
    Dusk. Mary Alice Lipes. P74
    'Fool!' Said My Muse to Me:. G. N.
    Gabbard. P63
    For My Birthday, 1939. Paul oodman. P84

Ford Maddox Ford. Robert Lowell. P79
"I Should Wear Gloves, These White
    Pages". Simon Perchik. P64
Instead. David Lunde. P63
The Instruction Manual. John Ashbery. P85
IX--Royal Favor. Mary F. Lindsley. P72
Jack O' the Inkpot. Algernon Blackwood.
    P51
Jessa's Late Assignment. Al Ortolani. P63
The Lament of the Poet, from Animated
    Film... James Reaney. P49
Letter to Shadow. Daryl Hine. P79
The Man Who Made up Roses, from Animated
    Film... James Reaney. P49
Many Red Devils Ran from My Heart.
    Stephen Crane. P81
Muses. Kandy Arnold. P58
My Luck. Bonnie Jacobson. P63
My Poetic Nature. Blythe Gillespie. P73
Name-Dropping. Robert Sward. P49
November 25, 1970. Brian O'Riordan. P49
Now That the Book Is Finished. Alice
    Walker. P85
On the Hazards of Writing Gloomy Verse.
    Edna Meudt. P68
Parlez-Vous Francais?. Delmore Schwartz.
    P84
Poem 60, from The City. Gonzalo Millan.
    P71
The Poet of the Mountains. Tom McCarthy.
    P92
Romantic Letter. Josephine Miles. P84
Sag Harbor, the Tchekov Letters. Barbara
    Guest. P64
Saint Mark, from Animated Film... James
    Reaney. P49
Syntax. Robert Canzoneri. P63
'These Students Couldn't Write Their
    Way...'. Ron Koertge. P63
To Write. Walter Hoefler. P71
Twain's Comet. Ted Plantos. P49
Writing in the Dark. Denise Levertov. P85
Writing and writers
    Writing Letters. Rodney Bennett. P51
Writing and Writers
    Writing to Get Through the Night While
    the Baby Cries. Jeanne Murray Walker.
    P63
    Writing, from A Thai Divine Comedy.
    Montri Umavijani. P92
    Writing, from A Thai Divine Comedy.
    Montri Umavijani. P92
Writing for Nora. Mark Jarman. P85
Writing in the Dark. Denise Levertov. P85
Writing Letters. Rodney Bennett. P51
Writing to Get Through the Night While the
    Baby Cries. Jeanne Murray Walker. P63
Writing, from A Thai Divine Comedy. Montri
    Umavijani. P92

Writing, from A Thai Divine Comedy. Montri
    Umavijani. P92
Writing, from A Thai Divine Comedy. Montri
    Umavijani. P92
Written in March. William Wordsworth. P51
Wroten, Leah
    Shakespearean Sonnet. P73
Wtorkiewicz, Bogumil
    V. P72
Wu Cheng
    Dog, from My Hometown's Base Creatures.
        Marilyn Chin and Jesse Wang (tr.). P92
    The Morning Reading. Eunice Chen and
        Marilyn Chin (tr.). P92
    A Stone Tablet for Animal Ghosts, from My
        Hometown's... Marilyn Chin and Jesse
        Wang (tr.). P92
Wunyik, Majiok
    We Broke the Noose with a Snap. Terese
        Svoboda (tr.). P53
Wur, Daniel Cuol Lul
    Strutting with My Rifle. Terese Svoboda
        (tr.). P53
Wylie, Elinor
    August. P82
    Beauty. P82
    Bronze Trumpets and Sea Water--on Turning
        Latin... P82
    Full Moon. P82
    Let No Charitable Hope. P82
    The Pebble. P82
    Pretty Words. P82
    Sonnet 016, fr. One person. P82
    Velvet Shoes. P89
    Wild Peaches. P82
Wyn, Eifion
    Heather. Tony Conran (tr.). P87
Wynken, Blynken and Nod. Eugene Field. P51
"Wynken, Blynken and Nod one night". A Dutch
    Lullaby. Eugene Field. P89,P81
Wynnere and Wastoure. Unknown. P66
Wystan Hugh Auden: a Villanelle. David
    Lehman. P63

The Xenoplile. Geoff Fiorito. P58
Xerxes and Xanthippe. Caroline Knox. P63
XVIII, from Irradiations. John Gould
    Fletcher. P82

Yair, Ish
    Lullalye-Acidby. P72
Yang, Bo
    A Feeling. P72

Yang, Hsiang
    My Cares. John J. S. Balcom (tr.). P72
Yang-Shik, Kim
    L'Echo. P72
"The yard has sopped...". In January. James
    Schuyler. P64
Yarrow. Margaret Drake Elliot. P72
Yates, L. E.
    Strange Talk. P51
Yates, Michael J.
    The Queen Charlotte Islands Meditations.
        P49
"Ye living lamps, by whose dear light". The
    Mower to the Glow-Worms. Andrew
    Marvell. P59
"Ye young debaters over the doctrine". The
    Village Atheist, from Spoon River
    Anthology. Edgar Lee Masters. P82
Yeager, Kitty
    Night Brushes. P72
"The year stood at its equinox". The Milking-
    Maid. Christina Georgina Rossetti. P89
"The year's at the spring". Pippa's Song.
    Robert Browning. P51
A Year. Angie You. P73
"The years have gone. It is spring". Mt.
    Tamalpais, fr. Andree Rexroth. Kenneth
    Rexroth. P84
Yeats, William Butler
    The Lake Isle of Innisfree. P89
    When You Are Old. P90
The Yellow Fairy. Charlotte Druitt Cole. P51
"The yellow bird darted out of the bush".
    Apprehension. Wazir Agha. P91
"The yellow martian sky". Distant
    Exploration. Allan R. Halcrow. P72
"Yellow the bracken". Autumn. Florence
    Hoatson. P51
Yeo, Robert
    A Dragon for the Family. P92
Yerbury, Grace D.
    Etchings in Meaning. P72
    River Boats. P68
    Suburbanitis. P68
Yes, I Have a Thousand Tongues. Stephen
    Crane. P81
Yes, Lord. Julia N. Aue. P72
"Yes, ducks are valiant things". Ducks, sel.
    F. W. Harvey. P51
"Yes, I agree. We'll pull ourselves
    together". The New Regime. Wendy Cope.
    P63
"Yes, it is bad to be too few". I Would Give
    Him a Man. Dhor Ding Cuol. P53
"Yes, Jules sleeps but trouble". Road to the
    Congo. Nyagak Pinien. P53
"Yes, there is yet one way to where she is".
    Three Quatrains. Edward Arlington
    Robinson. P1

"Yes, this is my voice--.". Voices. Nesta Wyn Jones. P87

Yesterday. Hugh Chesterman. P51

"Yesterday I saw a jointed stick of horn". Deer. Dafydd ab [or ab] Gwilym. P87

Yesupatham, S.
Your Face, a Better Indian Rose!. P72

The Yewtree. Gruffudd Gryg. P87

Yoon, Suk-Joong
Snowflakes. P80

Yosemite. Dick Hastings. P77

Yoshihara, Sachiko
The Street. John Solt (tr.). P92
Woman. John Solt (tr.). P92

"You Are Gone, Not Caring!.". Unknown. P62

You Are Old, Father William. Charles Lutwidge ("Lewis Carroll") Dodgson. P90

You Ask About Vietnam!. Ken Stone. P86

"You Do Know That the Stars". Jean Paul Mestas. P72

You Have No Lasting City Here. Mary Ann Henn. P65

"You Know That I Love You...," from Kiowa '49' Songs. Unknown. P78

You Look. Lorene Erickson. P88

You Say You Are Holy. Stephen Crane. P81

You Spotted Snakes. William Shakespeare. P51

"You Stand Like Good Ivory". Antonio Giraudier. P72

"You Surprise Me, Crow," from Wolf Songs... Unknown. P78

"You also, our first great". To Whistler, American. Ezra Pound. P82

"' You always kill the thing you love'.". The Dangerous Cliffs. Bruce Bennett. P63

"You are a blossom". My Love (Liliaceae). Kim Young Sam. P72

"You are a friend then, as I make it out". Ben Johnson Entertains a Man from Stratford. Edward Arlington Robinson. P81

"You are beautiful! When I'm near". Unfired Pistol. Clive Matson. P65

"You are leaving". Pain. Blaga Dimitrova. P70

"You are like startled song-wings...". Songs to a Woman. Maxwell Bodenheim. P82

"You are my feverish child". Convalescence. Barbara Dirlam. P68

"You are my friends. You do things". The Game. Harold Bond. P57

"' You are old, Father William,'...". The Old Man's Comforts and How He Gained Them. Robert Southey. P90

"You are stepping off a train". This Is How Memory Works. Patricia Hampl. P88

"¢ou asked me whether you are beautiful". To a Young Woman. Louis Dudek. P49

"You bet it would've made a tender movie!.". Sweet Sixteen Lines. Al Young. P85

"You bring a vague dream". Second Portrait. Sarmad Sehbai. P91

"You bring me red roses and sorrow". A Romance. Kandy Arnold. P58

"You can go a long way back in the mind". The Cave. Joseph Awad. P56

"You can never hold". Lesson One. Guanetta Gordon. P72

"You cannot see mountians...". Spyglass Conversations. Unknown. P78

"You charm when you talk, walk, or move". To Madame De Sevigne. Mathieu de Montreuil. P90

"' You correct. I scheme'.". The Man Who Made up Roses, from Animated Film... James Reaney. P49

"You do not do, you do not do". Daddy. Sylvia Plath. P85

"You flocked from campuses around the globe". White Ink on Sky Parchment. Francis Brown Price. P68

"You had no need to ask me to recall". Covenant. Merle Price. P65

"You have driven out the Lion". Unicorn. Sharon Goodier. P49

"' You have heard,' said a youth...". The Whistle. Robert Story. P89

"You have told me for my own good". My Own Good. Pamela Painter. P88

"You hold in your embrace". And the Summer Still Persists. Liliana Stefanova. P70

"You know they're coming when sharp cries". Captured City. Omar Lara. P71

"You know we French stormed Ratisbon". Incident of the French Camp. Robert Browning. P90

"You look". General Self-Satisfied, from Lost Youth: the Last War. Alfred Kreymborg. P82

"You look beautiful one way in the mirror". Talk. Orhan Veli Kanik. P91

"You love the roses--so do I. I wish". Roses. George (Mary Ann Cross) Eliot. P51

"You mold the rose". What Did the Midge Say to the Mildew?. Bonnie Jacobson. P63

"You never knew the warm night of the womb". Athena. Alfred Dorn. P65

"You never say anything in your letters...". Driving. John Newlove. P49

"You never shut your eyes". Rachel Plummer's Dream Winter 1836. Eleanor Ross Taylor. P79

"You open your eyes one morning". A Bit of Enlightenment. Tom Riley. P63

"You opened up like a plum". We Say This

Prayer. Jozsef Tornai. P92

"You opened your heart, my heart flew in".
        Soul-Search Ode. Dorsha Hayes. P65

"You poets of the Late T'ang send me...".
        July. Harvey Shapiro. P64

"You rode in on a comet". Twain's Comet. Ted
        Plantos. P49

"You said I was perceptive, had a mind...".
        On a Compliment. R. P. Dickey. P63

"You sashay in in summer whites". Tomorrow
        in a Bubble. Maryann Calendrille. P64

"You say two alien muses". Answer to Sion
        Cent, sels. Rhys Goch Eryri. P87

"You say you love me...". If This Be Love.
        Alice Morrey Bailey. P65

"You say, but with no touch of scorn". Doubt
        and Faith, from In Memoriam. Lord
        Tennyson. P89

"You speak. You say: Today's character is
        not". As You Leave the Room. Wallace
        Stevens. P83

"You spell rebellion in my ordered life".
        Love Song for Today. Alice MacKenzie
        Swaim. P65

"You stretch a hundred boneless hands". For
        a Flower Whose Name I Don't Know. Pat
        Bridges. P56

"You that know the way". Lemuel's Blessing.
        William Stanley Merwin. P85

You the Artifact. Alison Shepherd. P68

You Were Wearing. Kenneth Koch. P85

"You think". Misconception. Mildred Offerle.
        P72

"You throw yourself in--.". Pond & Stream.
        Angela Karszo. P77

"You took the sleeve of a passing woman".
        Mother and Son. Barry Callaghan. P49

"You walk with me in the moonlight".
        Miscalculation. Kathleen W. Vander
        Meide. P68

"You were angry and manly to shatter the
        sleep...". The Gun. Karl Shapiro. P84

"' You were in my dream...'.". The Big Bang.
        Howard Nemerov. P63

"You were the sun and you burned me". I
        Remember. Gigi Lord. P65

"You were wrong about the way it happens".
        Instructions to a Medium To Be
        Transmitted... Daniel Hoffman. P79

"You who read beautifully". The Reader.
        Fairfield Porter. P64

"You will reach tomorrow". To an Optimist.
        Bessie Wherry Noe. P65

"You would think the fury of aerial
        bombardment". The Fury of Aerial
        Bombardment. Richard Eberhart. P83

"You'd say when we ate a late breakfast".
        Old Foss, (The Cat) Recalls His
        Life... J. Patrick Lewis. P63

"You're like a drifting log...". Funeral
        Song, from Wolf Songs & Others of the
        Tlingit. Unknown. P78

"You're overdue. I watch the garden shrink".
        Spring Freshet. Crary Elwood. P72

"You're/An obscure". The Laxness Monster; or,
        I Be Singer... William Harmon. P63

"You've seen those pictures". Hearth.
        Patricia Hampl. P88

You, Angie
        A Year. P73

You, a Red Man, and I, a Black Man. Moses
        Cot. P53

You, Andrew Marvell. Archibald MacLeish. P83

"You, once a belle in Shreveport". Snapshots
        of a Daughter-in-Law. Adrienne Rich.
        P85

"You, stranger, who only see us happy...".
        Hunger. Samik. P78

"You, that decipher out the fate". Mourning.
        Andrew Marvell. P59

"You, you caribou". Magic Words for Hunting
        Caribou. Unknown. P78

"You--the young bow-tyed near albino...".
        Auden Aetat XX, LX. Stephen Spender.
        P79

Young Bear, Ray
        Dance of the Rain Gods. Anselm Hollo
        (tr.). P78
        Four Poems. P78

"The Young Bees Pursue the Nail-Shredded
        Mango...". Unknown. P62

The Young Housewife. William Carlos
        Williams. P82

The Young Indians. Jennie Thorpe. P74

The Young Lovers, from The House of a
        Hundred Lights. (Frederick) Ridgely
        Torrence. P81

A Young Poet, from A Thai Divine Comedy.
        Montri Umavijani. P92

"A young editor wants me to write...". What
        Do I Know of the Old Lore?. Robert
        Duncan. P84

Young, Al
        Birthday Poem. P85
        Identities. P85
        One West Coast. P85
        Sweet Sixteen Lines. P85

Young, Andrew
        The Dead Crab. P89

Youngdahl, Selma
        Primeval Method. P72

"Your 'L'Eggs' make (or makes) not a
        particle". E Pluribus Ovum. Bob
        McKenty. P63

Your Anger. Paz Molina. P71

Your Face, a Better Indian Rose!. S.
        Yesupatham. P72

Your Great Love. Diego Maquieira. P71

Your Leaving Me. Manjushree. P72
Your Little Friends Were a Bunch of Dogs.
      Diego Maquieira. P71
"Your Way," from Crow Versions. Plenty-Hawk.
      P78
"Your Wife Is Faithful, but Mine Is
      Unfaithful". Unknown. P62
"Your air, nice and legal". The Seducer
      Steps Out, Just at Dusk. Janis Lull.
      P88
"Your ample house has amplified your
      plight". Affluence. Richard Moore. P63
"Your beauty is the cause of my distress".
      Cause of My Distress. Har Prasad
      Sharma. P72
"Your face did not rot". The Lost Pilot.
      James Tate. P85
"Your face shakes like a torn kite...". The
      Fortunate Fall. William Harrold. P68
"Your hand in mine, we walk out". A Sword in
      a Cloud of Light. Kenneth Rexroth. P84
"Your home still steeps in mid-July sun".
      Three Threnodies. Donald J. Kintner.
      P68
"' Your horse is faint, my King...'.". The
      Lord of Butrago. John Gibson Lockhart.
      P90
"Your lilting voices ring...". Dance of
      Words. Beth Martin Haas. P72
"Your long hair flows". Mr. Computer
      Science. Elaine Demakas. P58
"Your mind and you are our Sargasso Sea".
      Portrait d'une Femme. Ezra Pound. P82
"Your name". Last Dance. Tom Tellesbo. P58
"Your neighbor's telephone". July. Dan
      Murray. P64
"your single avocado hangs, waiting".
      Waiting: November 30th. Bruce St.
      John. P68
"Your song of love stills temple bells--.".
      Song of Love. Grace Haynes Smith. P65
"Your thighs are appletrees". Portrait of
      Lady. William Carlos Williams. P82
"Your wife was foremost on your mind those".
      For Frank (5-70). Bruce Langbien. P86
Yousof, Ghulam-Sarwar
      God's Rain. P91
Youth
      After Whistler. Lisel Mueller. P88
      Age in Prospect. Robinson Jeffers. P83
      America. Alfred Kreymborg. P82
      Anne. Lizette Woodworth Reese. P81
      An Apology. Diane Wakoski. P85
      The Bells of Youth. William ("Fiona
            Macleod") Sharp. P51
      Youth. Robert Browning. P51
      Compensation, from The House of a Hundred
            Lights. (Frederick) Ridgely Torrence.
            P81

First Time. Edwin M. Goldman. P65
      A Girl in a Library. Randall Jarrell. P67
      Godfrey Gordon Gustavus Gore. Unknown.
            P51
      Lightly Like Music Running. Jean
            Garrigue. P84
Youth. George Cabot Lodge. P81
      Love Dissembled, from As You Like It.
            William Shakespeare. P89
      Maggie and Milly and Molly and May.
            Edward Estlin Cummings. P76
      O, Fairest of Rural Maids! William Cullen
            Bryant. P89
      Of Three Girls and of Their Talk.
            Giovanni Boccaccio. P90
      On News. Thomas Traherne. P59
      The Picture of Little T. C. in a Prospect
            of Flowers. Andrew Marvell. P59
      Polly. William Brighty Rands. P89
      Preface to a Twenty Volume Suicide Note.
            Amiri (LeRoi Jones) Baraka. P85
      Sally in Our Alley. Henry Carey. P89
      Vision by Sweetwater. John Crowe Ransom.
            P67
      White Ink on Sky Parchment. Francis Brown
            Price. P68
      Youth. George Cabot Lodge. P81
      Youth. Robert Browning. P51
      Youth and Age, from The House of a
            Hundred Lights. (Frederick) Ridgely
            Torrence. P81
Youth and Age
      Casual Encounter. Edna Bacon Morrison.
            P68
      False Youth: Two Seasons (Winter). James
            Dickey. P67
      Idyll. Frederika Blankner. P65
      Night Thoughts, Sierra. William Howarth.
            P77
Youth and Age, from The House of a Hundred
            Lights. (Frederick) Ridgely Torrence.
            P81
The Youth Dreams. Rainer Maria Rilke. P90
A Youth in Apparel That Glittered. Stephen
      Crane. P81
The Yucca Moth. Archie Randolph Ammons. P79
Yuenger, Jeremy
      The Autumn. P74
Yuppies vs. Nopies. Ned Pastor. P63
Yussouf. James Russell Lowell. P51

Zacharow, Tilly Boesche
      "With a Sieve". Werner Manheim (tr.). P72
Zaimof, Gueni
      The Star Obscure. P72
Zana

"Early Morning Sun". P56

"Hermit's Cabin". P56

"Zane is in heaven". The Vaunting Song of
   Louis L'Amour. Ernest Kroll. P63

"Zany--from Giovanni (John).". The
   Consolations of Etymology, with
   Fanfare. John Frederick Nims. P63

Zapata, Santiago Mendes

   A Story of the Eaters. William Stanley
      Merwin (tr.). P78

The **Zebra**. Bob McKenty. P63

Zebras. Terry P. Beh. P63

Zeidler, Frank P.

   Cold Hangs the Quarter Moon. P68

Zeiger, L. L.

   Food Processor. P63

   Misfortune's Darlings. P63

Zelda. Geoff Fiorito. P58

Zeller, William

   My Everlasting Vision. P65

   A Shade for My Scarred Soul. P72

Zelner, Estelle M.

   Casino Royale. P72

Zeppieri, Carla

   Lonely Boat. P74

Zieger, L. L.

   Envoi. P63

Zizi's Lament. Gregory Corso. P85

Zolotow, Charlotte

   Missing You. P50

   The Sandpiper. P76

   Summer Snow. P76

Zoo Manners. Eileen Mathias. P51

The **Zookeeper**. Jason Goode. P74

Zoos

   Zoo Manners. Eileen Mathias. P51

Zuni Derivations. Unknown. P78

Zurita, Raul

   The Beaches of Chile X. Steven F. White
      (tr.). P71

   CIII. Steven F. White (tr.). P71

   The Cordilleras of Il Duce. Steven F.
      White (tr.). P71

   Like a Dream. Steven F. White (tr.). P71

   The New Life. Steven F. White (tr.). P71

   The Radiant Beaches. Steven F. White
      (tr.). P71

   Snows of Aconcagua. Steven F. White
      (tr.). P71

   To the Immaculate Plains. Steven F. White
      (tr.). P71

   The Utopias. Steven F. White (tr.). P71

   VI. Steven F. White (tr.). P71

Zurlo, John

   Echoes. P56

Zydanowicz (tr.)

   To Discover. Janina Zydanowicz. P72